Baseball's First Inning

ALSO BY WILLIAM J. RYCZEK
AND FROM MCFARLAND

*Crash of the Titans: The Early Years
of the New York Jets and the AFL*, rev. ed. (2009)

The Amazin' Mets, 1962–1969 (2008)

The Yankees in the Early 1960s (2008)

*When Johnny Came Sliding Home: The Post–Civil War
Baseball Boom, 1865–1870* (1998; paperback 2006)

*Blackguards and Red Stockings: A History of Baseball's
National Association, 1871–1875* (1992; paperback 1999)

BASEBALL'S FIRST INNING

*A History of
the National Pastime
Through the Civil War*

William J. Ryczek

McFarland & Company, Inc., Publishers
Jefferson, North Carolina, and London

LIBRARY OF CONGRESS CATALOGUING-IN-PUBLICATION DATA

Ryczek, William J., 1953–
Baseball's first inning : a history of the national pastime through the Civil War / William J. Ryczek.
p.   cm.
Includes bibliographical references and index.

ISBN 978-0-7864-4194-5
softcover : 50# alkaline paper ∞

1. Baseball — United States — History — 19th century. 2. Baseball — New York (State) — History. 3. United States — History — Civil War, 1861–1865 — Social aspects. I. Title.
GV863.A1R928   2009   796.3570973 — dc22   2009009466

British Library cataloguing data are available

©2009 William J. Ryczek. All rights reserved

No part of this book may be reproduced or transmitted in any form or by any means, electronic or mechanical, including photocopying or recording, or by any information storage and retrieval system, without permission in writing from the publisher.

On the cover: Atwater Club of Westfield, Massachusetts, 1858, one of the first in Massachusetts to play the New York version of base ball.

Manufactured in the United States of America

McFarland & Company, Inc., Publishers
Box 611, Jefferson, North Carolina 28640
www.mcfarlandpub.com

Acknowledgments

Many people are deserving of thanks for assisting me during the writing of this book, but first among them is Fred Ivor-Campbell, one of America's foremost authorities on nineteenth century baseball. As he did with my first two books, Fred painstakingly reviewed a draft manuscript, line by line and word by word. He made many substantive suggestions on the content, factual and analytical, and gave the work a thorough edit. Fred is a stern taskmaster, and I followed most of his suggestions obediently. As a result, the final product is much improved over the draft. I also appreciate Fred's unflagging encouragement throughout the lengthy period it took me to produce a manuscript. Despite the best efforts of others, errors must surely remain, for which I am solely responsible.

Research on nineteenth century baseball has blossomed over the past decade, and I thank several seasoned scholars for pointing me in the direction of some gems. John Shiffert, author of *Baseball in Philadelphia: A History of the Early Game, 1831–1900*, was kind enough to review my chapter on Philadelphia and generous enough to send me copies of many of his source materials. Larry McCray provided me with the materials assembled by the Protoball project, and Gary Mitchem sent me a number of relevant articles.

Tom Shieber, a curator at the Hall of Fame, hosted me during my stay in Cooperstown and loaned me copies of his clippings from the *Atlas* and the *Brooklyn Daily Times* as well as his microfilm reel containing the *Rankin Scrapbooks*. He also proved an invaluable source regarding the resources of the Giamatti Research Center at the Hall, reviewed a draft of the manuscript, and set me straight regarding his definition of a pace. Freddy Berowski of the Research Center staff was most attentive and helpful during my visit, producing a vast assemblage of materials without a hitch.

My friend Fred Dauch reviewed the draft manuscript and offered a number of cogent suggestions that helped craft the direction of the work and clarify some points in the text.

My research took me to a number of libraries, including the Performing Arts Research Center at Lincoln Center in New York City, the main branch of the New York Public Library, the hometown Wallingford Public Library, and the New Orleans Public Library. At each stop, reference librarians were most helpful in providing material from old newspapers and periodicals.

I give my sincere appreciation to all those mentioned, and to anyone I may have inadvertently omitted. Thank you one and all.

Contents

Acknowledgments v
Preface 1
Prologue: Reliving the Past 7

1. No Rounders! 15
2. If Not Doubleday, What About Cartwright? If Not Cartwright, What About Adams? Or Wheaton? 28
3. What About Rounders? What About Old Cat? 37
4. The Jolly Old Knickerbockers, 1845–1856 43
5. The Base Ball Club 53
6. The Transition Years, 1857–1859 67
7. Mad Dogs and Englishmen: Other Antebellum Sports 83
8. Why Not Cricket? 101
9. The Southern Front: Sporting Life in Antebellum New Orleans 109
10. Baseball in Philadelphia 114
11. The Massachusetts Game 127
12. Year of the Excelsiors, 1860 134
13. Abner Doubleday Invents the Civil War, 1861 151
14. The Sporting and Not So Sporting Press 163
15. The Manly Fly Game vs. the Boyish Bound Rule and the Fair Pitch vs. the Jerk 174
16. The Eckfords Take the Championship, 1862–1863 185
17. The Evils of Championship Play, 1864 199
18. The Road to Professionalism 208

Appendix A: Letter from Frank Pidgeon of Eckfords re: Professionalism . . 213
Appendix B: Rules and Regulations of Base Ball as Adopted by the Convention of Base Ball Clubs Held February 25, 1857 215

Appendix C: Location of Grounds 218
Appendix D: Extended Box Score, Brooklyn–Philadelphia, 1862 221
Appendix E: Records of Top Teams, 1857–1864 223
Appendix F: Knickerbocker Rules, September 23, 1845 224
Appendix G: Knickerbocker Matches with Other Clubs 226
Chapter Notes 235
Bibliography 253
Index 257

Preface

When I began researching my first book on nineteenth century baseball almost three decades ago, little was known about anything that preceded the formation of the National League in 1876. Pre–National League history was mostly unauthenticated, secondhand accounts, and statistics for the professional National Association were virtually non-existent, consisting principally of the number of games for each player during a season and the won-and-lost records of the pitchers. Of the days before the National Association, there was nothing but a great void. By the time my first volume, *Blackguards and Red Stockings,* which covered the years 1871–1875, was published in 1992, *The Baseball Encyclopedia* had compiled batting averages and more statistical detail for Association players, and the members of the Society for American Baseball Research had embarked upon a project to re-construct complete NA averages.

My second volume, *When Johnny Came Sliding Home,* covered the years 1865–1870. By the time *Johnny* was published in 1998, knowledge of the nineteenth century had expanded, and more books were beginning to appear in print. Vintage baseball, played under the rules of the mid-nineteenth century, was becoming popular and generated more interest in the old game. Still, the amount of information was limited and quantitative pre–1871 player data were almost non-existent. Since there were no statistics for the players who took part in games of the late '60s, I compiled team rosters from box scores and presented the rudimentary findings in an appendix.

Since the appearance of *Johnny,* a plethora of new information has become available. When men began playing baseball in the 1840s, they were frequently ridiculed for playing a child's game. Serious historians writing about the sport a century later were subjected to the same lack of respect. Many of the early histories of the game were written by newspaper reporters whose work was often lightly researched and contained many oft-repeated apocryphal tales. Gradually, however, top flight scholars undertook the task of delving into baseball's cloudy past. For many years, the definitive work on early baseball and its antecedents was the ground-breaking *Bat, Ball and Bishop* by Robert Henderson, published in 1947. After Professor Harold Seymour wrote an excellent history of early baseball in 1960, attitudes began to change, and the study of baseball eventually became academically respectable.

A number of talented historians put their hands and minds to work on the world of pre-twentieth century baseball, and each effort fed the others. In 2004, David Block produced *Baseball Before We Knew It,* which, in addition to its exhaustive, extensively documented research on pre-modern sports, disclosed information about the relationship between Abner

Doubleday and Albert Spalding that had never before been made public. No serious historian believed that Doubleday invented baseball, but the revelations of Block's brother, Phillip, about Doubleday and Spalding's involvement with the Theosophical Society, in combination with correspondence preserved in the Doyle Scrapbooks now at the Hall of Fame, add spice to the story of the Mills Commission. Block's research into the history of bat-and-ball games built upon and surpassed that of Henderson, and his theories about which games were true antecedents to baseball provide much food for thought.

Other important works appeared during the last decade of the twentieth century and the first years of the new millennium. Thomas Melville's history of American cricket is a serious, scholarly study that explores the evolution of the sport in the United States and examines the reasons it was exceeded in popularity by baseball. George Kirsch and Patricia Millen wrote the story of baseball during the Civil War, Tom Shieber traced the evolution of the baseball diamond, and Peter Morris wrote about everything. When my book was in its latter stages, I learned that Peter's history of the 1843–1870 era was due out shortly, which is like hearing that Jude Law has an interest in a woman you've been planning to ask for a date.

Marshall Wright, in *The National Association of Base Ball Players, 1857–1870*, listed for the first time the records and individual statistics for virtually every team of any significance that played before the professional National Association era. His work saves researchers the hundreds of hours of laboring through fuzzy microfilm images that was necessary to re-construct these statistics.

The Protoball Chronology of Early Ball Play (2000 B.C. to 1860 A.D.) is a remarkably ambitious effort spearheaded by Larry McCray, John Thorn and Tom Heitz that presents references to "safe haven" games — those in which the object is to reach a base safely — in newspapers, novels, songs, plays and other reference documents. Covering nearly four millennia is a formidable task even for such intrepid researchers as McCray, Thorn and Heitz, but they have done a marvelous job of locating and cataloguing over 100 pages of references. *Protoball* remains a work in progress, and may be ever so, for new information is being discovered almost continuously.

The years since the genesis of *Blackguards and Red Stockings* have also witnessed the advent of the internet, which contains an immeasurable amount of information on nineteenth century baseball. Other than primary sources such as newspapers and periodicals, however, a large portion of it consists of inaccurate but often repeated tales, and the data require a great deal of verification before they can be used.

I covered the 1865–1875 period in my first two books, and it had long been my intention to continue to work backward to baseball's beginnings. After reading all of the recent, remarkable works on nineteenth century baseball, one large question formed itself. Had these writers stolen my thunder, or had they added to the potential quality of what I might produce? If the latter was true, what direction should the work assume? Was I to be a one-man, unbiased Mills Commission, attempting to find the origin of baseball, or should I take a different approach?

Each of the authors mentioned covered one aspect of early baseball in terrific detail. Block wrote of baseball's ancient antecedents. Melville wrote about cricket. Wright gave us statistics. Kirsch and Millen covered the Civil War. No one, however, had pieced together the entire era that began with ancient games and concluded with the end of the Civil War. No one had traced the story from its beginnings to the point where baseball was poised for the great boom that followed the war. Several of the authors noted are historians, whose scholarly work, in conjunction with numerous primary sources, could be used to tell the story in narrative form. I've provided citations that will enable curious readers to delve deeper into areas of particular interest, but the tone of the work is decidedly light and, I hope, of interest to baseball fans as well as historians. Scholarly works generally focus on "why?" and often ignore "what?" What actually happened? Who won the games? What were they like? Which were the top teams and who were the best players on those teams? What aspects of baseball as played prior to the end of the Civil War led to the changes that made the game what it is today, and why were some elements, such as the bound game, destined to fade away? Reading the source documents, I tried to obtain a sense of what was important at the time and what it was like to be a mid-nineteenth century baseball player and to convey that sense to the reader. "The historian is a reporter," wrote J. H. Powell, chronicler of the 1793 yellow fever outbreak in Philadelphia, "not a referee. The historian's business is to understand, and relate."[1]

In most histories of early baseball, Abner Doubleday is quickly dismissed, as many believe he should be. Doubleday, however, was an interesting, noteworthy individual, and the complex manner in which he became anointed as the inventor of the game is a story worth telling. Alexander Cartwright, whose cause was taken up intermittently, most recently in the 1960s, and minimized thereafter, was also a man of many accomplishments beyond his involvement with baseball. They are both part of the history of the game, even if they didn't invent it, and the evolution of the theories of baseball's beginnings is almost as interesting as the evolution of the game itself.

This book examines various theories of how baseball originated, the context in which it grew, and the early years of its popularity. In the mid–1840s, a number of bat-and-ball games somehow merged into the sport played by the Knickerbockers, a version of baseball that became known as the New York Game. Other clubs sprung up in imitation of the Knicks, and by the 1860s, organizations were competing for the honor of being called the champion club of the United States. The leisurely play which characterized the 1850s had, among a select group of top clubs, yielded to the serious pursuit of victory. Still, professionalism was rare and secretive, and, as the Civil War ended, the overwhelming majority of players were relatively unskilled amateurs.

Writing the third volume of a trilogy presents some unique problems. I re-read the introduction to *When Johnny Came Sliding Home* and noted that I'd called the period 1865 through 1870 the most pivotal in the history of baseball. Clearly, I couldn't now call the pre–1865 era the most pivotal. And if it wasn't all that critical, why write about it?

What makes the years prior to 1865 interesting? First, the Abner Doubleday, Alexander Cartwright, Doc Adams, William Wheaton or someone-else theory of baseball's genesis can be a story in itself. While no one individual "invented" baseball, a number of very interesting people contributed to its growth and popularity. In addition to Cartwright, Adams and Wheaton, there were Jim Creighton, baseball's first superstar and the man who changed the art of pitching forever, and Frank Pidgeon of the Eckfords, who personified the old, gentlemanly style. Other players, such as Dickie Pearce and Joe Start of the Atlantics, were superior performers who would continue to play into the 1870s and 1880s.

In *Johnny*, I traced the development of baseball from a relatively localized activity to a nationwide phenomenon. The thread flowing through this work is the manner in which the sport got to the launching pad, the way in which shallow roots were planted throughout the Northeast and Midwest and how baseball became a contender for the title of America's National Game. In order to place baseball in context, I've devoted a chapter to other sports played prior to 1865. Ice skating experienced a boom in the 1860s, then faded. Other sports that were popular in antebellum times, such as boxing, cock-fighting, and the repugnant canine sports, have a tabloid-like fascination. I became enthralled with boxing and American champion John C. Heenan, probably the most famous athlete of his time, and spent far more time than necessary reading about Heenan and his exploits in the United States and abroad.

One of the themes of early baseball's development was the central role of New York City in nurturing and spreading the infant game. Virtually all the best ball was played in and around New York, and the sport generally appeared in other regions as the result of a New York ballplayer relocating and bringing the game with him. The battle that took place in New York and Brooklyn among the Excelsiors, Atlantics and Eckfords for the supremacy of the baseball world is a story ignored in most histories of early baseball where the focus is on theory rather than action. The passing of the baton from the gentlemanly Knickerbockers, Gothams and Excelsiors to the rougher-hewn Atlantics, Eckfords and Mutuals signaled a change in the direction of baseball, one that came much sooner than the post-war boom.

With so much fresh information available, the task of telling the story of baseball as it was played prior to 1865 became much easier. I discovered facts I hadn't known previously and in some cases corrected errors I committed in one of the earlier books.

In this third work on the nineteenth century, I've taken a slightly different approach from that used in the others. In my first two volumes, I'd utilized a season-by-season chronology, a formula that wasn't applicable to the years before 1865. The earlier era falls more easily into periods, each of which represented a change in the way the game was played, accepted and perceived.

I didn't want to repeat topics I'd covered in the previous two books, but in some instances it was necessary in order to provide sufficient background. If I'd dealt with a subject thoroughly in a prior volume, I spent only enough time here to give the reader the necessary context. In that vein, since I'd previously written quite a bit about trail-blazing sportswriter Henry Chadwick, I intended to go light on Chadwick this time. The writer, who turned 40 in 1864, the end of the period covered by this book, is such an influential figure, however, and such an opinionated and insightful commentator, whose scope covered every important issue that faced the game of baseball, that I found it impossible to leave him out. His opinions will be found frequently throughout these pages, sometimes priggish, usually one-sided, frequently out-of-date, but always in what he believed to be the best interests of the game he loved.

A native of Great Britain, Chadwick reminded me of another great Englishman, Winston Churchill. Like Churchill, Chadwick was never hesitant to voice his opinion, for better or worse, even when it was sadly out of fashion. One of Churchill's friends, F.E. Smith, once said, "Winston was often right, but when he was wrong, well, my God."[2] Chadwick was absolutely correct in urging the elimination of the bound game, in advocating upright behavior and in his insistence that gambling was an evil influence that must be curbed. He was dead wrong in his contention that swift pitching would ruin the game and that a return to the soft tosses of the 1850s was necessary to save baseball. His abhorrence of the quest for championships and his desire to return to the truly amateur days of the 1850s was chimerical, and his support of the rounders theory of baseball's evolution was without evidence. Likewise, Chadwick's steadfast aversion to Sunday baseball was doomed to failure, as was his proposal to change to a 10-man, 10-inning game in 1874. Right or wrong, however, his influence on the game in its formative stages is undeniable, and Chadwick in high dudgeon is always a treat.

With new sources in hand, and Chadwick available for editorial comment, I enthusiastically commenced upon the task at hand. With grateful thanks to the many who have done trail-blazing research, I present the story of baseball from its origins through 1864.

Prologue: Reliving the Past

Darryl Brock, author of the fabulous baseball time travel novel, *If I Never Get Back,* was the keynote speaker at the 1999 Vintage Base Ball Convention. For three days, Darryl, writers Greg Rhodes, Tom Shieber, John Husman and I roamed the streets of Cincinnati, went to ball games, shared our ideas on nineteenth century ball, drank a few beers, and held animated discussions on subjects of scant interest to anyone in the United States other than the five of us. On Sunday, many of us (although not Darryl) played two innings under nineteenth century rules in Cinergy Field as a preliminary to the game between the Reds and Pirates.

Shortly thereafter, Darryl published the sequel to *If I Never Get Back*, called *Two in the Field*. In the first pages, he described the activity of his hero, Sam Fowler, in modern-day Cincinnati. Sam followed the footsteps we had taken in 1999, visiting Arnold's, the famous old saloon, and walking the streets as we had during that wonderful April weekend. I was enjoying the section immensely until I came to a description of Sam watching a display of vintage baseball prior to a Reds-Pirates game. Although the work was fictional, I clearly recognized myself and my teammates in what Darryl described as a "laughable exhibition."

Laughable exhibition? The splendid display of historical athletics we had performed? Could they be one and the same? Only one person could answer that question. In response to my emailed query, Darryl provided a plausible explanation. The "damnable copy editor," he wrote, had inexplicably changed his "magnificent" to "laughable," and by the time Darryl noted the egregious blunder, the book had already gone to print.

While our exhibition was somewhere between magnificent and laughable, no one can seriously claim that the level of skill seen in vintage games is comparable to that of current day major leaguers. How does it compare, one might speculate, to the level of play in the 1850s and 1860s? Greg Rhodes, author of *The First Boys of Summer,* the story of the 1869 Cincinnati Red Stockings, was a participant in the laughable exhibition in Cincinnati. One day, between games of a tournament in Bethpage, New York, the birthplace of modern day vintage baseball, Greg and I discussed the caliber of vintage ball players. Perhaps, he surmised, our playing ability was equal to that of the professionals of the 1860s and 1870s. After all, in any athletic endeavor that can be measured objectively, such as track and field or swimming, the world records of the early twentieth century can be matched today by good high school athletes. At the 1896 Olympics, the high jump was won with a leap of 5'11", which today would not take first place in most scholastic competitions. The bronze medal winner cleared 5'5". The gold medal in the pole vault was captured with a vault of 10'10" and the bronze with 8'6¼".

Athletes of the nineteenth century were small men by today's standards. Few were more than six feet tall, and most weighed 150 to 175 pounds. In the 1860s, when Brooklyn and New York ball players wanted to stage a "heavyweight" match, including only the largest players in the area, the original plan was to limit the contestants to those who weighed more than 200 pounds. When they couldn't find 18 of them, they had to reduce the lower limit to 180 pounds, so long as each nine averaged at least 200.[1] Would present-day, 180-pound ball players qualify as "heavyweights"? In addition to the fact that the players were much smaller, little was known of training and nutrition, so that, pound for pound, they were not as strong as today's ballplayers.

How skilled were these smaller, weaker men? Few of those who played in the mid-nineteenth century had been playing and watching baseball since childhood as have most of today's adults. In a number of games in the early 1860s, players who had not taken part in a match all season, or perhaps several seasons, played for relatively prominent teams, and often acquitted themselves reasonably well.

Both experienced hands and novices made a lot of fielding errors, often dozens in a single game. The nineteenth century players weren't coached in Little League, nor were they able to study the techniques of professional players. On the other hand, many of today's vintage players were high school and college ballplayers, and in addition to decades of experience, have the advantage of greater size, better nutrition and more than a century of refinement of playing techniques.

While comparing times, heights and distances of track and field performers or swimmers is relatively easy, judging the relative skills of current and former baseball players is much more difficult. Baseball matches the skill of the batter against that of the pitcher and fielders, and as hitters got better, so did those trying to prevent them from hitting. Baseball historians stage endless debates over whether a young Ty Cobb could hit Roger Clemens, or if Babe Ruth could deposit Nolan Ryan's best fastball in Yankee Stadium's right field bleachers. There is no answer, for baseball is measured in relative rather than objective terms. Has the progress of baseball skill been similar to that of track and swimming? Are we as good as George and Harry Wright and the other early professionals? As skilled as Peter O'Brien and Jim Creighton, stars of the pre-professional era?

The quality of early baseball games was frequently measured by the number of runs scored, for good defense was rare. A team that could field well enough to hold its opponents to a relatively small number of runs was considered superior to one that allowed a high scoring total, even if the latter nine was able to score a lot of runs themselves. Games among "muffins" (the least skilled players) often featured scores such as 50–30, or 75–42. Games between two talented, evenly matched nines might result in a score of 9–7 or 13–10. While some modern day vintage games produce very high scores, the majority yield run totals roughly equivalent to the better-played games of the mid-nineteenth century, a hopeful sign that we might be major leaguers born a hundred years too late.

In order to describe something accurately in print, one must first visualize the event as it occurred, complete with sights, sounds and smells, rather than as portrayed in a black and white, two dimensional image. The process is a blend of the present and the past, relating current sensations to prior events. Sometimes this can be done through a vivid written description, or a photograph, but, in the case of nineteenth century baseball, the vintage game as played today is a much better method of bringing the past to the present.

The first modern players to conduct games under nineteenth century rules on a regular basis were from Old Bethpage Village, a restored Long Island hamlet a short drive from Manhattan. The vintage ballists began playing in 1980 as a demonstration activity for the village, and the program grew very slowly with only about four games per summer taking place each year through 1991. In 1992, two Bethpage teams began playing under 1887 rules, and two years later, 22 games took place in a single season. Due in part to the interest created by the old time games, tour flow at the village increased by twenty-five percent.

During the late 1990s, the number of teams on Long Island multiplied, and the frequency of games taking place at Bethpage increased dramatically. The program's publicity engine was fueled by a cover story in *Smithsonian* magazine, a feature article in the *Boston Globe* and, more recently, a visit by late night talk show host Conan O'Brien. The village became the hub of vintage baseball activity. For many years, the players of Bethpage have hosted an annual tournament which draws teams from all along the East Coast and the Midwest. The Bethpage diamonds are fabulous sites on which to play the old game, open fields nestled among nineteenth century buildings filled with period artisans, shopkeepers, and homemakers.

Vintage baseball has long since expanded beyond re-created villages and now encompasses more than 250 teams located in 28 states. The young and the old, the fit and the halt, often come together on the same team, and the level of competition varies greatly. The vintage game has wide appeal, providing exercise and entertainment for athletes, former athletes, historians, the curious, and any combination thereof.[2]

One can read about the rules of baseball as they were in the nineteenth century, but the best way to gain an appreciation of the nuances of the old game is to play it. One of the first things that becomes apparent is the great variation among the hand-stitched balls. Some are mushy while others have the consistency of today's baseball. No matter what its original state, the ball changes its shape and form after being batted around for a few innings. Catching a softened ball bare-handed, particularly when one is stationary, is not that hard. Catching a line drive of a hard, tightly wound ball is nearly impossible. Harder balls, of course, tend to be hit with greater velocity, and anyone who has attempted to catch a line drive or sharp grounder with a new, rock-hard 1860s vintage baseball will understand perfectly the heated disputes that took place over which balls were to be used during a game. The good fielding teams invariably wanted to use a softer ball, while the hard-hitting, less sure-handed nines preferred the harder variety.

Familiarity with the modern game is sometimes a great hindrance to playing the old in instances where the rules conflict. For example, when a runner is at first base with none out or one out, his instinctive reaction when a one hop ground ball is hit to the pitcher or an infielder is to run toward second base. Under the bound rule, however, which was in existence until 1865, the batter is out as soon as the ball is caught on the first bound, as if it were caught on the fly, and the force is removed. The runner can return safely to first and advances at his own risk. Anyone unaccustomed to playing under the bound rule is virtually certain to break for second and run into a double play rather than ducking safely back to first. A second rule which creates difficulty is the one in force until 1871 under which runners were not permitted to overrun first base. This nuance is frequently forgotten by novice vintage players, who, heeding the screams of their teammates, attempt to scramble back to the bag.

In many circumstances, the ball must be returned to the pitcher before a play can be made. For example, players must return to their bases after a foul ball, whether it is caught or not, or they can be put out. They can only be retired, however, if the ball is first thrown to the pitcher and then to the base to which the runner is returning. Invariably, a new player will follow the rule of modern ball and throw directly to the base. The dodgy, veteran pitcher will run near the base to take the throw and then put the player out. Likewise, in certain situations, no advance can be made before the ball is in the hands of the pitcher. If it is thrown to the pitcher and he misses it, the ball is not in the hands of the pitcher and no one can run. The clever pitcher can miss the ball intentionally, tricking the runner into trying to advance.

Another rule that frequently confuses novice vintage players is the one, employed until 1878, that decrees that the first batter in an inning is the one following the player who made the final out in the preceding inning. When a batter grounds out or flies out to retire the side, the rule follows modern custom. When a player is put out on the bases, however, the confusion begins. If a batter forces the man in front of him in the order, he leads off the next inning, batting twice in succession. If there are runners on first and second, and the man is forced out running to third, the man running to second leads off.

The rule requiring the home team to bat last was not enacted until 1950 although custom had decreed it so since the end of the nineteenth century.[3] The order of batting in the vintage game is determined by the toss of a coin or some similar method with the winning captain given his choice of batting first or last. Teams also bat in the last half of the ninth inning, even if they are leading.

Other differences are equally baffling. The first time one has a foul tip caught on the bound, the feeling is akin to robbery. How could the turn at bat end so quickly? Only then does one realize how frustrating it must have been to hit against slow pitchers like Phonney Martin who imparted a tantalizing twist to the ball.

During most vintage games, if the old rules are employed literally, it is ridiculously easy to steal second base. The pitch is delivered underhanded and slowly to the plate, affording the runner a good jump. The catcher must receive the ball bare-handed and throw it to second where the second baseman or shortstop must catch it bare-handed and tag the runner coming in. In many vintage games, the stealing rule is modified, restricting the runner to leaving only after the ball crosses the plate. Otherwise, the game becomes a ritual of every runner stealing second each time he gets to first. This gives one added appreciation for the great early catchers such as Joe Leggett and Waddy Beach. It also explains why it was so important for pitchers to "keep a close eye on the bases." When discussing a pitcher's performance in the early days of the game, one of the aspects reporters nearly always noted was whether the pitcher held the runners close.

Yet another disconcerting facet of the vintage game for first time players is the provision that everything is in play. Vintage ball is most enjoyable when played on the same types of fields that were used in the mid-nineteenth century. That means that trees may overhang fair territory or that a building might encroach dangerously close to the field. Teams can establish their own grounds rules, and most have chosen to leave obstacles in play. If a fly ball gets into a tree, it remains live and, if the offending tree is in fair territory, the batter is entitled to as many bases as he can get. If the fielder, on the other hand, can catch the ball after it caroms off the trunk or rattles around the branches, the batter is out. If a ball bounces off the roof of a building, it can be caught on the fly or first bound for an out. If a ball gets tangled in underbrush deep in the outfield, it is the fielder's responsibility to dig it out as the runners streak (or lumber) around the bases.

Some vintage players have become masters of the "fair-foul" hit in which the batter chops down on the ball, attempting to get it to bounce in fair territory and then spin off into foul ground. Until 1877, any ball that hit first in fair territory, even if it rolled foul before reaching first or third base, was a fair ball. If the fair-foul is executed properly, it is almost impossible to throw the batter out. The threat of the fair-foul also causes the defense to leave the middle of the infield open and vulnerable. The batter can attempt the maneuver almost indefinitely since foul balls do not count as strikes.[4]

At bats can last a long time, for under the rules of the early 1860s, there are no called balls or strikes. Games move along quickly, however. With no television timeouts and no signals given by the catcher or the base coaches, one pitch follows the next, and well-played games can be completed in a hour and a half or less.

When playing the bound game, where any ball caught on the first bounce is an out, the key is to hit the ball on the ground. "Hard and low! Hard and low!" is the cry from the bench. Long fly balls are usually caught on one bounce, while bare-handed infielders have a difficult time picking up ground balls and throwing them so that the bare-handed first baseman can catch them. Since the bound rule was used in baseball's early days, when fielders were usually not very skilled, driving the ball hard on the ground was the best way to hit safely, as it is today. "[O]ld fashioned sky rocket batting is completely played out," said the *New York Atlas* in 1859.[5]

Taking chances on the basepaths is more often than not a rewarding exercise when practiced in the vintage game. As in base stealing, it is difficult for fielders to successfully complete several elements of a play in sequence. Singles can be stretched into doubles, and runners can go from first to third on singles, for it is rare that a good bare-handed fielding play is succeeded by an accurate throw and a catch and tag on the runner sliding into the base. More often the outcome is a throw that eludes the fielder and results in yet another base.

"That's a stupid rule!" is a lament often heard from a novice vintage player when he is victimized by an unfamiliar nineteenth century standard. "Well," is the typical reply, "that's why they changed it." In the 1860s, for example, catchers could intentionally drop a third strike and start a double or even triple play. Eventually, the rule was changed to render a hitter automatically out when there is a runner on first and less than two out. Infielders could use the same gambit before the advent of the infield fly rule. In baseball's early days, rule makers were constantly revising the code as smart players found ways to circumvent the old standards.

One of the most interesting things I discovered while playing vintage baseball is the way in which it unintentionally followed the path forged in the nineteenth century. The game has emulated the early days of baseball in more than just the rules.

My experience with the vintage game was as a member of the Middletown (Connecticut) Mansfields, named after the National Association team of 1872. The Mansfields' first game was with the Swamp Frogs of Sylvania, Ohio, a touring entourage that visited Middletown in 1996. The Swamp Frogs arrived in Middletown in their period uniforms, accompanied by their wives, who were dressed in nineteenth century feminine attire. The Frogs were showmen, playing up the era's idiosyncrasies, using antiquated language, and acting the part of nineteenth century gentlemen. The Mansfields who assembled for the game had never played under nineteenth century rules, and consisted of local attorneys, teachers, professors, members of the historical society and the like. The game, in which the Mansfields were soundly beaten, was played in a most sportsmanlike and gentlemanly fashion. We took our overwhelming defeat with grace, applauded the good plays of our opponents and socialized with them after the game. Everything was as it was in the 1850s or 1860 when the Excelsiors of Brooklyn went on tour to show country bumpkins like the Mansfields a taste of top flight baseball.

The next year, the Brooklyn Atlantics from the vintage baseball Mecca of Bethpage came to Middletown. The Atlantics were younger and more athletic than the Swamp Frogs, who were more historian than athlete, and administered a second drubbing to the local nine. The Atlantics took the game a little more seriously than the Frogs, and had some fine ballplayers among their nine. Clearly, a number of them had played high school or college ball, and they knew several tricks unique to the nineteenth century game. The Mansfields were made up essentially of the same players who had opposed the Frogs, and while some also had a fair amount of baseball experience, they were no match for the Atlantics, who played and practiced regularly. We were still in the 1850s or early 1860s. The Mansfields were delighted with the entire affair, fully expecting to be beaten and grateful that the Atlantics had shown Middletown fans the beauties of nineteenth century ball. Later that summer, for the first time, the Mansfields took to the road, traveling to Bethpage to absorb a second defeat at the hands of the Atlantics.

The following year (1998), the Mansfields decided to play a few more games and take the sport a bit more seriously. We actually held some practices and were no longer content to be the hapless victims of our opponents. In one game, our pitcher, enraged by the call of the umpire, slammed the ball to the ground in disgust and shouted an obscenity. This was clearly not the game of the 1850s when players never, ever, disputed the call of the umpire, no matter how erroneous or ill-informed it might be. The rest of the team apologized profusely, but a sea change had taken place. The 1850s were over. We wanted to win. It was 1860.

Over the next two years, the membership of the Mansfields began to change. The older, respectable, but less talented members of the team, the lawyers, historical society members and professors, began to yield to younger players who didn't know much about vintage baseball or the history of the game but had a little bit of playing experience and the springy legs and strong arms that enabled them to make a better showing. Misplays on the field led to grumbling on the bench, and the respectable gentlemen who remained were sometimes the object of resentment when their muffs led to a series of runs. They were nice fellows, but, gosh, they just couldn't play ball like the youngsters. We were in the early 1860s when the Knickerbockers, Excelsiors and Gothams yielded to the Atlantics, Mutuals and Eckfords.

On a few occasions, we received money for appearing at historical festivals. It was used for the purchase of equipment, not for the compensation of players, but we had taken a baby step toward professionalism. It was 1862 when the Union Grounds opened to the public and gate money became an accepted feature of the game.

As the years went on, the Mansfields played more games, traveling to Massachusetts, New York, Rhode Island and Michigan. Playing for the nine required a greater commitment of time, and many of the professionals with busy schedules left the club. We were in 1865 and 1866 when lengthy tours required an extended absence from daily business and limited top flight competition to those who were willing to make a substantial commitment to the game and forego other professions.

By the twenty-first century, there were vintage tournaments with corporate sponsors at which clubs vied for trophies. In 2003, the Mansfields won the Capital City Cup at a tournament in Hartford and finished atop the New England Vintage Base Ball Association. Prior to the formation of the league, substitution rules had been very loose, and players shuttled in and out of games. Everyone got to play, and the older men got to rest an inning or two and then return to action. In the new league, any player who left the game could not re-enter. The rules could no longer be ignored or amended to suit the whims of the participants. We were in 1871, when the first league, the National Association, was formed and a set of championship rules was developed.

At the Capital City tourney, there was a near-brawl after which some players threatened to call the police. In 1996, this would have been unheard of, but by 2003, vintage baseball had become serious business. A string of emotional emails followed the altercation, reminiscent of the flurry of letters to the sporting press in the wake of the 1860 Atlantic-Excelsior imbroglio. Some of the emailers advocated banning the Mansfields from future play and called for a return to the pristine, gentlemanly play of the mid–1990s. More than a century earlier, in the mid–1860s, early ballplayers were longing for the halcyon days of the 1850s, when gentlemen played the game for enjoyment, and the idea of disputing an umpire's decision or using foul language was reprehensible.

In 2006, former major league pitcher Jim Bouton organized the Vintage Base Ball Federation, leading to some bad feelings between the new organization and the older Vintage Base Ball Association. The VBBF is composed of clubs that contain players much more athletic than those on most of the VBBA teams and is much more conscious of the profit potential of the sport as were the founders of the National League in 1876. VBBF clubs play the 1880s version of baseball, which includes fast pitching and requires much more skill than the slow pitch 1860s game played by most VBBA clubs. They hold a World Series, with playoffs, and require a five hundred dollar membership fee, reminiscent of when the National League increased the fee from ten dollars to one hundred to keep out the marginal clubs. VBBF clubs have lined up corporate sponsors who subsidize the estimated $6500 cost of organizing a team. Bouton's organization has again left the old vintage players longing for the good old days of the 1980s and 1990s when gentleman ran the game and the spirit of competition was secondary to good fellowship and fair play.[6]

Unknowingly, the practitioners of vintage baseball in the twenty-first century have emulated their nineteenth century predecessors, not just in the playing of the game, but in the evolution of the sport, shedding light upon the reasons baseball developed as it did. Perhaps it is the American spirit of accomplishment and achievement so celebrated by the jingoistic xenophobes of the post–Civil War era, or maybe it's just a universal trait of human nature. An activity becomes enjoyable, and yet it must become better; it must achieve a higher quality. So it was with baseball in the nineteenth century, and so it has become with vintage baseball in the twenty-first century. I began playing vintage ball with the idea of learning how the game was played. I wound up learning how it evolved.

Chapter 1

No Rounders!

What better way to start a history of the origins of baseball than with Abner Doubleday and the charming New York village of Cooperstown? After all, a visit to Cooperstown can leave one with the impression that General Doubleday had something very important to do with the game of baseball. Mystical figures are harder to destroy than those of flesh and bone, and Cooperstown is in no hurry to obliterate the memory of the man who provided the town with its principal identity. Although the hamlet got its name from the family of novelist James Fenimore Cooper, Nattie Bumpo and Alice Munro never acquired the panache of Babe Ruth, Hank Aaron and the other immortals enshrined in the quaint brick building at 25 Main Street. Nor does the number of tourists who come to Lake Glimmerglass each year in memory of Cooper approach the estimated 350,000 annual visitors to the Hall of Fame.[1]

Leaving the Hall of Fame and taking a short stroll down Main Street, one finds a plaque at the entrance to Doubleday Field that reads, "Dedicated to Major General Abner Doubleday, Inventor of Baseball. Chosen by Radio Listeners to 'People's Rally' as the Outstanding Figure in Baseball's First One Hundred Years." Just a few yards away, one can get ice cream and hot dogs at Doubleday Dip or souvenirs at the Doubleday Clubhouse Shop, and around the corner on Main Street, one can get a full meal (and cocktails) at the Doubleday Café where the wait staff wears T-shirts that say "Cooperstown — a drinking town with a baseball problem."

Other references are subtle, such as the Where It All Began Bat Company, and in the years since 1939, when the Hall opened, there has been some backtracking. A plaque within the Doubleday Field complex admits, "Although most scholars and fans agree that Abner Doubleday was not baseball's *sole* [author's italics] inventor, over 300,000 visitors a year confirm that Cooperstown is the spiritual home of baseball."

"Abner Doubleday didn't invent baseball," said Hall of Fame curator and baseball historian Tom Shieber, "and we're OK with that. But that doesn't mean we should forget about Doubleday because myth is important to history ... and we're not moving."

In the process of being endowed with a fame not of his making and subsequently being stripped of the honor he had not sought, the real Doubleday has eluded most Americans. Who was Abner Doubleday, and how did he attain such a prominent place in our folklore? The answer to the first part of the question is relatively easy to find since much of Doubleday's life took place on the public record. He was born in Ballston Spa, New York, near Saratoga, in 1819, attended Green's Select School in Cooperstown and was appointed to the U.S. Military Academy at West Point where he began his studies in the fall of 1838. Doubleday was a mediocre student, graduating 24th in a class of 56 in 1842.[2] "He enjoyed a good anecdote," recalled one of his classmates. "He was rather averse to outdoor sports and retiring in his manner."[3]

Doubleday fought in the Mexican War and played a major role at the siege of Fort Sumter in April 1861. A captain on the staff of Major Robert Anderson, Doubleday sighted the gun that sent the first reply to the garrison of Charleston, thus marking the beginning of the Civil War. Anderson was a sensitive man who had been deeply affected by the bloodshed he'd seen during his service in Mexico. He hoped to avoid war at all costs. Doubleday, on the other hand, wanted to give the southerners no quarter and expressed his frustration in his diary as Anderson followed his cautious strategy of making certain the rebels fired the first shot.

Doubleday served well and bravely for the duration of the conflict, fighting at Second Manassas, Antietam, Fredericksburg, Chancellorsville and Gettysburg and eventually attaining the rank of Major General. At Gettysburg, he took over the First Corps after General John Reynolds was killed on the initial day of the fighting and repulsed Pickett's futile charge in the final stages of the battle. After Appomattox, Doubleday remained in the peacetime army, serving in Texas and California, before retiring in 1873. He died at Menden, New Jersey, in 1893.

Throughout his long life, Doubleday acquired numerous friends and acquaintances, but none recall him saying anything about baseball. The General also wrote frequently, but his only correspondence connected with baseball was an 1871 request to send bats and balls to his troops.[4] By the time of Doubleday's death, baseball had become the unchallenged national sport with the first World Series having been played nearly ten years earlier. If he had been the "inventor" of the sport, one would think that, given the game's popularity, he might occasionally have interjected a comment such as "By the way, I invented that game" into a baseball conversation. Yet, there is no surviving record of Doubleday speaking of baseball or, prior to his death, of anyone else mentioning the General in connection with the game. He passed to the great beyond in total ignorance of the fame that would eventually be associated with his name.

How, then, was it determined in 1908, fifteen years after his death, that General Abner Doubleday was the inventor of the game of baseball? To answer this question, one must introduce a smart, patriotic and strong-willed man named Albert G. Spalding.

Spalding was born in Byron, Illinois, in 1850, and by the age of 17 had achieved national renown as the pitcher of the Forest City Club of Rockford, Illinois. In 1867, baseball in the West was in its infancy, and in July of that year, the National Club of Washington, D.C., brought a top-flight version of the sport to the region for the first time, playing in Ohio, Missouri, Kentucky, Indiana and, as the culmination of the trip, Chicago where the Nationals played the final three games of their tour.

Prior to reaching the shores of Lake Michigan, the Nationals, as expected, ran roughshod over all competition, victorious by scores such as 90–10, 113–26, and 78–17. In the final game of the tour, the Excelsiors, Chicago's best nine, received an unexpected 49–4 thumping, which shocked the local fans. The previous day, however, the spectators had received an even greater jolt when the Nationals were upset by the Forest City Club of little Rockford and their teen-aged pitcher, Albert Spalding. It was the Washington club's only defeat of the tour.

After three more seasons in Rockford, Spalding was recruited by Harry Wright for his new Boston Red Stocking Club, about to begin play in the National Association, baseball's first professional league. From 1871 through 1875, Spalding was the finest pitcher in baseball, leading Boston to four consecutive championships, pitching in nearly every game and compiling a phenomenal 204–53 record.

In 1875, in the midst of a 54–5 season, the young pitcher made a very practical decision, one of a series of wise choices that would eventually make him a wealthy man. Spalding decided to leave Boston and sign with the Chicago White Stockings for the astronomical salary of $4,000 per year. Although the contract was for 1876, the signing became public knowledge in July 1875. The news was stunning for not only was Spalding to join the White Stockings, he was also bringing three other Boston stars with him.

The early signings were in clear violation of National Association rules, which prohibited any player from entering into a contract for the next season until the current campaign had ended. Although the NA was a loosely-run organization whose rules were generally ignored, Chicago president William Hulbert feared his club might be expelled. He therefore took pro-active measures. Hulbert enlisted the other strong NA clubs, including the cuckolded Boston nine, and formed the National League, leaving the carcass of the old Association in his wake.

In 1876, Spalding pitched the White Stockings to the first NL pennant with a 47–12 mark. After playing first base in 1877, he retired from active play. Spalding could neither hit nor throw a curve ball, which was becoming a bigger part of the game, and decided to leave the playing field at the relatively young age of 27. For the remainder of his life, Spalding pursued two vocations. One was the management of the White Stockings. He assumed the presidency of the club following Hulbert's unexpected death in 1883, and, in addition to operating his own team, gained significant influence in National League councils.

Spalding's second interest was the sporting goods business he founded with his brother, a company that continues in existence to the present day. Spalding utilized his association with baseball to obtain an exclusive concession for the production of the League ball in 1880, and he published annual guides, edited by legendary journalist Henry Chadwick, which set forth detailed statistical records of the prior season.

Spalding's success in the business world was due to his intelligence, his opportunism and the maturity and judgment he displayed at a very young age. It was those qualities that led Harry Wright to select the 23-year-old pitcher as the Boston Club's emissary to Europe in the winter of 1873-74. In 1859, and again in 1868, the English had sent an all-star team of cricketers to the United States to play a series of games, which were rousing successes. By the middle 1870s, with baseball firmly established as America's national game, Wright, a former cricketer, was eager to show the British the fast-moving, dynamic sport that had arisen in their former colonies. There had been talk of such a journey since the mid-'60s, and, late in 1873, after the NA's third season, it appeared that the European junket was about to become reality.

Spalding sailed to England in January 1874 and met with the cream of the British sporting world. He dined with the officers of the Marylebone Cricket Club, which for nearly a century had been the most revered athletic club in Britain. A number of playing dates were arranged, and Spalding contracted with Charles Allcock, a well-known sportsman, to complete the schedule during the spring.

Although Spalding succeeded in arranging the tour, there had been a disquieting note to his conversations. The Americans' principal goal was to show Europeans their new sport of baseball. The main interest of the English, however, was in seeing the Americans play cricket against their top clubs. Spalding, always adaptable to a fluid situation, stated that the ballplayers who would visit the island were the finest cricketers in America, which they clearly were not.

With an understanding in place, Spalding returned to America and informed Wright that the British were eager to see the Americans play baseball. Communication across the vast ocean was limited, and the young pitcher was able to keep both sides ignorant of the other's expectations. Wright's correspondence anticipated a great success but he was aware of the British predispositions. "Although they will be impressed by baseball," he wrote to Allcock in March, "it will never replace cricket."[5]

On July 16, 1874, the American tourists, who consisted of the Red Stockings and the Philadelphia Athletics, departed from Philadelphia in a festive atmosphere. As the *Abbottsford* sailed toward Delaware Bay with its unsuspecting cargo of ballplayers, cheering fans lined the riverbanks, crowded onto bridges and hung banners celebrating the journey of their heroes.

After eleven days on the water, the players arrived in Liverpool anticipating a similarly enthusiastic welcome. Bounding down the gangplank, they were greeted by a pair of transplanted Philadelphians who had somehow, despite an almost complete lack of publicity, learned of their arrival. Two games in Liverpool drew meager crowds, and attendance improved only slightly when the Americans moved to London and other cities. It turned out that Allcock, injured in a soccer match during the spring, had been less than diligent in promoting the tour, and the British were less than interested in watching baseball.

As the exhibitions continued and the Britons' lack of enthusiasm for baseball became annoyingly obvious, the Americans began to find fault with their hosts. The English were too slow-witted, they declared, to appreciate this modern, fast-moving American game. They were hopelessly mired in the past, their anachronistic royalty and hide-bound traditions.[6] Spalding, who should have anticipated the underwhelming reception, became particularly and permanently ill-disposed toward the English people. In 1911, he wrote a history of baseball called *America's National Game*. The opening chapter bristles with Anglophobic quotes, such as:

"Cricket is a splendid game, for Britons. It is a genteel game, a conventional game — and our cousins across the Atlantic are nothing if not conventional. They play Cricket because it accords with the traditions of their country so to do; because it is easy and does not overtax their energy or their thought."[7] "Cricket is a gentle pastime," Spalding added. "Base Ball is War!"[8]

"It would be impossible for a Briton," Spalding continued, "who had not breathed the air of this free land as a naturalized American citizen; for one who had no part or heritage in the hopes and achievements of our country, to play Base Ball."[9]

Racial and ethnic stereotyping were quite popular in the nineteenth century as evidenced by an 1858 article in the *New York Clipper*, one of the best American sporting papers. The *Clipper* quoted a British journalist who had asserted the superiority of the English in intelligence, character and physical strength, and contrasted residents of the Isles with Americans. "The American branch of the Anglo-Saxon race," he stated, "has lost nothing in courage, and gained in intelligence and activity; but partly by climate, and more by sanatory [sic — apparently the British had lost something in spelling] neglects and mismanagement, of which they have to be admonished, they have deteriorated in bodily strength." His American counterpart at the *Clipper* agreed that the climate caused an accumulation of fat and an inability to hold liquor in the same quantities as an Englishman, but questioned the claim of the Americans' muscular weakness. The battle continued over the years with British and Americans each claiming superior physical characteristics for their race.[10]

Spalding was a pragmatic man and, despite his outspoken antipathy toward the British game, eventually became a member of Chicago Cricket Club, whose members included the elite of the city's society. Spalding was in business, that of both baseball and sporting goods, and wanted access to Chicago's wealthy citizens. If they could be found at the cricket club, playing and watching that slow, genteel, tedious game, Spalding would join the club. He played on occasion (as he had in England in 1874) and coached his touring baseball players in the sport in 1888 (see below).[11] Spalding even donated a cup to be awarded to the winner of the cricket league championship.

Although the 1874 journey to England was memorable for its ambition and its groundbreaking nature, it was disappointing both financially and to those who expected a better reception for the new sport. With American sportsmen chastened by the Europeans' lack of enthusiasm for baseball, there were no more tours until the winter of 1888–89. That journey, planned in large part by Spalding, was a virtual trip around the world. Spalding's White Stockings and a team of all-stars known as the All-American nine visited Australia, the Middle East, and Europe. Upon reaching England, the tourists found the British much more accepting of baseball than they had been fourteen years earlier. "I like baseball," said the Duke of Buccleuch, "and I am sure that all Englishmen will like it, too, when they come to understand it better."[12] Quite innocently, however, the English struck a raw nerve in Spalding. In addition to baseball, the two teams were invited to participate in a game of rounders, an old English pastime many considered the inspiration for the American national game. The English described baseball as "scientific rounders."[13]

Henry Chadwick, the venerable baseball writer known as the "Father of the Game," was born in England and had played rounders many times as a young boy. He was the foremost proponent of the rounders theory, which to some extent relied upon Chadwick's linkage of the game to the American game of town ball. Although he was certain the old British game had been the forerunner of the American, Chadwick admitted that baseball had risen to such a level of perfection that the original sport could scarcely be recognized. "[T]his little acorn of rounders," Chadwick wrote, "has grown to be the giant oak of our national game; and just as much difference exists between the two games as between the seedling acorn and the full-grown king of the forest. The Americanized rounders played in this country over fifty years ago was 'Town Ball' and this game, an improved form of rounders, was played as early as 1833 by the old Olympic Club of Philadelphia."[14] Town ball, supposedly named because games often took place on the occasion of town meetings, had been played frequently in the United States, but rounders had not. There were similarities between the two games, but town ball was not called rounders, and the distinction weakened Chadwick's case. For many years, Chadwick stated his rounders theory without offending anyone. Eventually, however, Spalding, with his pithy attitude toward the English, became aroused by the writer's insistence that baseball evolved from rounders.

The rounders controversy notwithstanding, Chadwick and Spalding shared a healthy mutual respect for each other. They first met in 1867 when Spalding was the 17-year-old pitcher of the Rockford Club and Chadwick was traveling with the Nationals.[15] Spalding recognized Chadwick's value in promoting baseball, and the old journalist admired Spalding as an example of the manly, honorable ballplayer he praised in his writings. In the early years of the twentieth century, as Spalding took a greater interest in the origins of baseball, the issue of rounders placed a strain on the relationship. In 1905, Chadwick wrote an article in which he good-naturedly jabbed at his friend. He recounted a visit the younger man made to his office when old ballplayer Andrew Peck happened to stop by. Spalding asked Peck when he began playing ball. It was 1848 or so, Peck recalled. "What was the game called?" Spalding asked. "Why, rounders," Peck answered. As Chadwick and Peck dissolved into laughter, Spalding said, "Why did you come in just now for? I was getting the best of the old man on his rounders theory."[16]

The American-born Spalding had not seen rounders as a child and was not about to admit that his beloved sport had origins in the despised country of England, even if the distance were as great as that between a seedling acorn and the king of the forest. A further irritant to Spalding was the fact that rounders had few adult adherents by the 1880s; it was primarily a child's game, played more often by girls than by boys. Albert Spalding, a patriotic American, could not stomach the idea that the noble American sport of baseball was an evolved version of a game played by English girls.

Spalding compared his own fury with that of an Englishman who might be told that cricket originated from rounders or a Scot informed that golf was derived from rounders. "My investigation and research so far," he wrote, "inclines me to the opinion that Base Ball did have its origin in the old colonial game of 'One Old Cat.'"[17] "The tea episode in Boston harbor," he wrote on another occasion, "and our later fracas with England in 1812, had not been sufficiently forgotten in 1840 for anyone to be deluded into the idea that our national prejudices would permit us to look with favor, much less adopt any sport or game of an English flavor."[18]

Hiram Waldo, a pioneer of Rockford baseball, whom Spalding had known as a teenager, shared Spalding's antipathy. "We had too much national pride in those days," he wrote to Spalding in 1905, "to adopt anything that was English in our sporting life!!"[19]

The experience of playing rounders during the 1888-89 tour rekindled the debate concerning baseball's origins. It firmly convinced Spalding, who claimed he had until then believed the rounders gospel (which is doubtful) that the old game had nothing to do with the birth of baseball.[20] He compared it to Drop the Handkerchief.[21]

Upon their return to New York, the two touring teams were welcomed at an elaborate dinner at Delmonico's, one of New York's finest restaurants, located near Madison Square. Even with an admission fee of ten dollars, nearly 300 were in attendance, including Mark Twain and Theodore Roosevelt. The menu was divided into nine innings, and American flags were hung around the room. During one of the many speeches, the issue of baseball's development was raised. The suggestion of an English origin provoked a deafening chant of "No rounders! No rounders!"[22]

Nearly twenty years later, the debate had not resulted in a definitive conclusion. Chadwick and Spalding each published articles supporting their claims, and the two agreed that an investigation should take place to settle the question. Spalding first made the suggestion in his 1905 *Guide*, and later that year empanelled a commission to reach a final conclusion on the origins of baseball. The committee would study the available evidence and lay to rest forever the question of baseball's genesis although Spalding limited the choices to Chadwick's rounders theory and his own "Old Cat" idea, which would render the game American in origin. The commission consisted of the following persons:

Abraham G. Mills, former president of the National League

George Wright, star shortstop of the 1860s and 1870s and later, like Spalding, a sporting goods magnate

Arthur P. Gorman, former U.S. Senator and an early player

Morgan G. Bulkeley, first National League president, U.S. Senator and former Governor of Connecticut

Nicholas E. Young, early player and former National League president and secretary

Alfred J. Reach, early player, owner of the Philadelphia Phillies and yet another sporting goods proprietor

James E. Sullivan, President of the Amateur Athletic Union and publisher of Spalding's Official Baseball Guides

Why wasn't Chadwick, probably the most knowledgeable student of baseball in America, a member of the commission? Was it due to his bias? Spalding did some pre-screening prior to selecting the participants, asking a number of prominent baseball men what they thought of his Old Cat theory and his quest to prove that baseball was solely of American origin. Al Reach wrote back and wished him luck and became a member of the commission. Reach was almost as jingoistic as Spalding, declaring that as Wellington had said the Battle of Waterloo was won on the playing fields of Eton, the recent Spanish-American War had been won through American training at baseball.[23] "Rounders and town ball," he said, "which suggested baseball, were nothing more than schoolboy games, which of themselves never could have held attention long."[24] Young established his qualifications for service with the statement that he would be glad to serve on the commission to "investigate the origin of the great *American* [author's italics] game."[25]

Mills, prior to his appointment, had also expressed the opinion that "On the whole, I am inclined to accept your version of the inception of the National game."[26] Later he wrote, "The game of rounders I never heard of until Chadwick claimed it was the origin of the American game of baseball.... I never heard any person but Chadwick claiming that baseball had its origin in the game of rounders."[27] After reading the letters, Spalding decided Mills would be an excellent candidate for his commission. The final member, Sullivan, was Spalding's employee, and could be counted upon to back the Old Cat theory unless he desired other employment.

In addition to Chadwick, there were other surviving pioneers who were not included in the august body. John Lowell, a fixture of early Massachusetts baseball, responded to Spalding's inquiry with the opinion that he thought Chadwick might be correct. Lowell was not a member of the commission.[28]

Spalding, of course, made no pretense of being a disinterested observer. In the 1905 *Guide*, he referred to rounders as "juvenile" and "asinine."[29] When forming his commission, after paying the customary homage to the legendary Chadwick, he stated, "I am unwilling longer to accept his Rounders theory without something more convincing than his oft-repeated assertion that 'Base Ball did originate from Rounders.' For the purpose of settling this question, I hereby challenge the Grand Old Man of Base Ball to produce his proofs.... I have been fed on this kind of 'Rounder pap' for upward of forty years, and I refuse to swallow any more of it without some substantial proof sauce with it."[30] He indicated that Chadwick was biased due to his English origin.[31] "The more I investigate," he wrote sportswriter and former player Tim Murnane, "the more certain I am that Rounders had nothing whatever to do with it."[32]

Mills counseled ignoring Chadwick, writing to Spalding in words that never saw publication, for obvious reasons, "Chadwick is a feeble old man now, and I am inclined to advise you not to be too hard on him. In the course of nature, he will pass away soon, and then it will be time enough to wipe up the floor with his peculiar theories."[33]

William Rankin of *The Sporting News* was also determined to refute the rounders claim. He queried old ballplayers Thomas Tassie, John Price, Duncan Curry, John Chapman and others, all of whom said they had never heard of rounders, which indicated that Thomas Tassie, John Price, Duncan Curry, John Chapman and others had never heard of rounders, and very little else.[34] Rankin, like Spalding, believed that baseball was a game of American origin but, unlike Spalding, thought it evolved from Native American bat-and-ball games.[35]

John Montgomery Ward, a star player of the 1880s, and a leader of the players' revolt of 1890, agreed with Spalding that baseball's origins were rooted in America. He had no proof, he said, since the history of older games was generally not written down, but debunked the rounders claim based upon the fact that in rounders, when one batter was out, the entire side was out in contrast to baseball's three outs per inning.[36] In his book, *Baseball: How to Become a Player with the Origin, History and Explanation of the Game,* Ward castigated "persons who believed that everything good and beautiful in the world must be of English origin."[37]

With Ward and Spalding, two of the most influential men in baseball, having weighed in against rounders, the commission, Chadwick notwithstanding, would have a difficult battle on its hands if it backed the rounders claim for there was no question that the entire matter was a contest between Chadwick and Spalding. Given the prior bias of the members, it was unlikely, however, that Chadwick would have much support.

The members of the panel were elderly; Gorman passed away before the final report was issued. Mills, whose name ended up being attached to the commission, was 63 at the time the committee completed its task. He had enlisted as a private in the Union Army at the age of 18 in 1862 and earned a second lieutenant's rank within two years. Mills had been an enthusiastic ballplayer prior to becoming a soldier and took ball and bat along on campaign. He played in a legendary game between two Union Army teams at Hilton Head on Christmas Day in 1862, a match reportedly witnessed by 40,000 spectators.[38]

After the war, Mills moved to Washington, D.C., and established a law practice. He maintained his interest in baseball, occasionally playing with the local Olympics and eventually became president of the club. After moving to Chicago, Mills wrote a newspaper article condemning the practice of contract-breaking that was in vogue in baseball in the mid–1870s. National League President Hulbert saw the piece and asked Mills to become more active in the management of the sport. Mills eventually became an advisor to Hulbert and, when the latter passed away unexpectedly in 1882, succeeded him as League President.

Mills' tenure as president was brief (two years) and tumultuous for it included a hectic 1884 season during which the National League and American Association were challenged by the upstart Union Association, which did not recognize the reserve rule observed by the two other leagues. When National League owners insisted on making peace with Union Association at the end of the season, Mills, who favored a hard line, stepped down.

Although he was no longer league president, Mills continued to play an active role as an advisor. He had a good relationship with Spalding and campaigned for him in 1910 when Spalding ran unsuccessfully for the U.S. Senate. Mills had also served as chairman of the committee and master of ceremonies at the Delmonico's dinner where the outburst against rounders took place.[39]

The principal goal of the commission, it seemed, was to put the rounders theory to rest, a point Spalding made abundantly clear in his letters soliciting participation. Duncan Curry, the first president of the Knickerbockers, was asked about rounders. "That is one of Henry Chadwick's theories," he replied, "and it seems strange to me that none of the writers on baseball will correct it, but are willing to let it go as the truth. He makes many other statements that are not strictly according to facts."[40]

It is not certain that any of the commission members were very active or how much evidence they actually examined. The "evidence" consisted principally of reminiscences and unsubstantiated opinions from old men who had some involvement with the early days of baseball. A letter from an elderly New Hampshire resident that leaned toward the rounders theory was not passed along.[41] Hiram Waldo of Rockford sent a long, rambling letter regarding town ball and other subjects, and then admitted, "I must confess I am absolutely ignorant as to what the American game of Base Ball 'evoluted' from." Still, he ended on a patriotic note, surmising that baseball must have 'evoluted' from town ball, and stated, "Yankee Doodle with variations is still the regular old Doodle."[42]

Henry Sargent of Massachusetts wrote of his youthful memories of roundball, which was another name for the Massachusetts version of baseball. "So if round ball is the English rounders," he concluded, "and the difference between Mr. Chadwick and Mr. Spalding is whether base-ball sprung from rounders or from four old cat, there is no difference between them. They are talking about the same thing, only they don't know it."[43]

William Cauldwell, a well-known reporter for the *New York Mercury,* wrote a letter indicating he had covered baseball nearly since its inception and had never heard of it evolving from rounders.[44] Thomas Tassie, after stating *he* had never heard of rounders, concluded, "Baseball is purely an American game."[45]

Eventually, in the late summer of 1907, Sullivan circulated sixty-seven-and-one-half pages of evidence, of which sixty-six supported the cherished Old Cat theory.[46] Chadwick contributed his argument in support of the rounders theory, which he whimsically signed, "Henry Chadwick, Counsel for the Defence."[47]

No response to Sullivan's communication was received from five of the other six members of the commission. Mills answered with a letter dated December 30, 1907, which read, in part, "the first known diagram, indicating positions for the players, was drawn by Abner Doubleday in Cooperstown, N.Y., in 1839."[48] Mills' proclamation gave a brief sketch of Doubleday and made a weak, unsubstantiated attempt to tie Doubleday's famous diagram to the Knickerbocker Club of New York. The Knickerbockers had been furnished with a diagram on which they based their early rules. Perhaps, Mills said, the diagram was the one drawn six years earlier by Doubleday.

Mills' letter was circulated to the other members of the commission, who dutifully signed it. Since he had been the only one to respond to Sullivan's presentation of the "evidence," Mills took first position among the members. The body would henceforth be known to history as the Mills Commission.

When the commission's conclusion was announced, Spalding was exultant. "The founder of our National Game became a Major General in the United States Army!" he declared in *America's National Game*.⁴⁹ Could baseball be more American? More patriotic? Bah to the British and rounders, which went completely unmentioned in Mills' statement.

The Knickerbocker origin, mentioned in Mills' letter, was a difficult one to dismiss. Unlike Doubleday's miraculous revelation in a field in Cooperstown, the Knickerbocker story took place in metropolitan New York and was well documented. Mills admitted that, before starting the work of the commission, he had believed that the Knickerbockers had originated the game but said his mind was changed by "interesting and pertinent testimony for which we are indebted to Mr. A. G. Spalding."⁵⁰

What was the convincing evidence with which Spalding had enlightened the commission and upon which they made their judgment? It was principally two letters received from Abner Graves, a 73-year-old former acquaintance of Doubleday, who claimed he had been present on that fateful day in 1839 when the future general had drawn his diagram and laid out the first baseball field. One of the letters closed with the assertion, "'Baseball is undoubtedly a pure American game, and its birthplace Cooperstown, New York, and Abner Doubleday entitled to first honor of its invention."⁵¹

There were unsettling aspects to Graves and his assertions. First, as stated earlier, Doubleday had matriculated to West Point in 1838, a year prior to his supposed invention of the game in Cooperstown. In 1908, journalist William Rankin, championing the cause of the Knickerbockers as the inventors of baseball, obtained a letter from West Point indicating that leave for first year cadets was granted only in exceptional circumstances, and it was doubtful Doubleday would have been allowed to go to Cooperstown.⁵²

Further, at the time Graves claimed that Doubleday invented baseball, the former was but six or seven years old. When he wrote his letter in 1905, he was 71, a distance of 65 years. The memories of a young child are a precarious foundation upon which to base history in any case, but after the passage of 65 years and the lack of any corroborating statements, it is absolute folly. Further, when Graves wrote his first letter, to the *Beacon Journal* of Akron, Ohio in April 1905, he didn't say he'd been present at the game, only that he had been in Cooperstown and heard about it.

Spalding was delighted with Graves' appearance on the scene and requested more specifics. If they were forthcoming, Spalding hinted, the committee would be very likely to accept Graves' claim.⁵³ In November, in reply to Spalding's request, Graves wrote that he had actually played in the game, a curious occurrence for a six-year-old in a crowd of much older boys. That problem was disposed of when Graves said in his second telling that he was in college at the time. He and his friends were playing marbles, he related, when Doubleday appeared and showed them how to play baseball.⁵⁴ "Yes, sir," he wrote, "I played in the first baseball game ever played in the United States. I am proud of it." Graves admitted in his letter that it would be very difficult to verify his claim but hoped the added detail would suffice.⁵⁵

Graves was hazy, as can be expected after such a great passage of time, about the year in which the momentous event took place. He said it was either the spring before or the one after William Henry Harrison's "Log Cabin and Hard Cider" campaign, which would place it in either 1839 or 1841. As the years went on, however, Graves' memory became sharper. He recalled many details of the game and embellished his original tale in the manner that might be expected of a man of his many eccentricities.

Graves left Cooperstown long before he wrote his momentous letters, having settled in

Colorado and pursued a career as a mining engineer. He told reporters he had been a Pony Express rider in 1852 although the mail service did not begin operations until 1860. Even in his eighties, he claimed he was still playing baseball although no one actually saw him play.[56]

In 1924, at the age of 90, Graves became convinced that his second wife, who at 48 was little more than half his age, was trying to poison him and shot her four times, killing her. Graves was found not guilty by reason of insanity and committed to an institution. He died two years later.[57]

All in all, it was an unsubstantiated, sketchy, inconsistent account from a wildly eccentric old man. After examining it closely, Spalding wrote, "Personally, I confess that I am very much impressed with the straightforward, positive and apparently accurate manner in which Mr. Graves writes his narrative."[58] While Spalding pointed out a number of Graves' attributes, he failed to note one of his most prominent traits — his very vivid imagination. Still, with all its shortcomings, the Graves testimony gave Spalding the heroic inventor he craved, and set aside, at least in his mind, the possibility of any un–American origin of this uniquely American game.

By the mid-twentieth century, the notion that Abner Doubleday was the "inventor" of baseball was almost universally doubted. Before the commission had even issued its statement, Rankin expressed his skepticism concerning the Doubleday assertion.[59] A few years later, he noted the documentary evidence of baseball's beginnings and stated, "[I]t is not necessary to wait some 50 or 60 years afterwards to depend upon the unsupported word of some fellow who is seeking cheap notoriety."[60]

By the 1930s, however, baseball had a serious investment in the Cooperstown legend. In 1935, a relative of Abner Graves discovered an old, moldy baseball in his attic. He sold it for five dollars to Cooperstown's National Baseball Museum where it was christened the "Abner Doubleday Baseball."[61] Stephen Clark, heir to the Singer sewing machine fortune, had a sizable economic stake in Cooperstown and saw an opportunity to increase tourism in the isolated village. He donated $43,000 and a parcel of land to build the museum we know as The Baseball Hall of Fame.[62]

The Hall of Fame was dedicated in 1939, and although the Doubleday legend was exceedingly fragile, no one was ready to tear the museum down or move it to New York City. Cooperstown, an idyllic little village, bursts with all that we ache to believe represents the virtue of small town America, the ideal spot to celebrate this American game. Thus, the Doubleday legend has been perpetuated, much as the story of Santa Claus. It is a pleasing tale, and, unless one is a fussy historian, no harm is done by its telling.

While there is no evidence linking General Abner Doubleday with the creation of baseball, there has in recent years arisen a "second Doubleday" theory, similar to the "second gunman" speculation developed to explain the assassination of John Kennedy. There *was* an Abner Doubleday who lived in Cooperstown in 1839, Abner Demas Doubleday, a cousin of the General.[63] Is it possible that Abner Graves saw *that* Abner Doubleday playing some form of baseball and confused him with the general? Abner Demas, however, was just ten years old in 1839 and an unlikely inventor of the national game.

In fairness to Graves, it is possible that, as a young boy in Cooperstown, he saw someone, maybe one of the Doubledays, playing baseball and, since the game was unfamiliar to him, imagined that he was seeing the invention of a new sport.

Prior to the receipt of Graves' letter, Abraham Mills had not been unaware of Abner

Doubleday. Both had served in the Civil War, and both were members of the same veterans' organization. When Doubleday died, Mills organized the military honor guard at the funeral.[64]

Doubleday's connection with Mills was well-known. Phillip Block, in his brother David's monumental work, *Baseball Before We Knew It,* discovered a relationship between Doubleday and Spalding, a connection Spalding never publicly acknowledged. In his letter to Graves, he had posed a number of questions, one of which was "Who was Abner Doubleday?"[65]

According to Phillip Block, the question was disingenuous, for Spalding knew very well who Abner Doubleday was. Apparently, Spalding had not been quite the paragon of the American virtue he championed. While still married to his first wife, Josie, he had an extramarital affair and conceived a son with Elizabeth Mayer, an old friend from Rockford. After Josie died in 1899, Spalding and Mayer married and adopted the young boy.[66]

Elizabeth Mayer Spalding was a dedicated member of the Theosophical Society, an organization that supports "a vision of wholeness that inspires a fellowship united in study, meditation and service, which encourages open-minded inquiry into world religions, philosophy, science and the arts, in order to understand the wisdom of the ages, respect the unity of all life, and help people explore spiritual self-transformation, and holds that every action, feeling and thought affects all other beings and that each of us is capable of and responsible for contributing to the benefit of the whole."[67] Although Spalding did not employ the society's inquisitive philosophy in his study of the origins of baseball, he was a generous benefactor. Following his marriage to Elizabeth, the couple lived at the Society's retreat in Point Loma, California.

For an outwardly conventional, conservative, military man, Abner Doubleday had been an uncommonly free thinker who at one time subscribed to the transcendentalist publication, *The Dial.* During the 1870s, following his retirement from the Army, Doubleday met Helena Petrovna Blavatsky, a Russian émigré who was considered one of the world's most knowledgeable teachers of the occult. In 1878, Doubleday joined the Theosophical Society, which Madame Blavatsky had founded a few years earlier.

Doubleday was far more than a nominal dues-paying member, assuming the position of president ad-interim in 1879. For the next five years, he played a leading role in the Society, including a term as vice president of the New York chapter. In 1884, when his health began to fade, his role diminished. Doubleday continued his interest in the Society and the occult, however, until his death, and in an obituary in the Society's journal, *The Path*, the general was lauded for his contributions and for his own psychic experiences. Perhaps his most remarkable psychic experience was inventing baseball in one place while actually being in another, and then forgetting about it so completely that he never mentioned it again.[68]

Not surprisingly, in light of the questionable process and sketchy evidence, Spalding's victory was hollow. Chadwick wrote to Mills in March 1908, "I read your decision in the case of Chadwick Vs. Spalding ... and I want to say to you that it is a masterpiece of special pleading, which lets my dear friend Albert escape a bad defeat.... I was so sure of my case that I failed to present more detailed evidence. The fact is the whole matter was a Joke, between Albert and myself, for the fun of the thing."[69]

Just a year after the Mills Commission made its announcement, journalist Will Irwin pointed out the glaring inconsistencies in the Doubleday fable although he provided no documentary evidence for an alternative birth. In 1947, Robert Henderson, in his classic work, *Bat, Ball and Bishop,* made the first scholarly inquiry into the roots of ancient sport and put the Doubleday claim to rest for good. Henderson traced ball games back to ancient religious rites involving the sun, human skulls, and religious orders, and paid particular attention to games such as Chadwick's beloved rounders, stool ball, one old cat, and the like. He gave short shrift to Doubleday and asserted that no one person had "invented" baseball. It had simply evolved.

If no one "invented" the game, was there one individual who played the most prominent role in its evolution from ancient games? With Doubleday discredited, attention shifted to Alexander Cartwright, a husky young bookseller who had been instrumental in the activities of the first organized baseball club.

CHAPTER 2

If Not Doubleday, What About Cartwright? If Not Cartwright, What About Adams? Or Wheaton?

Although the Doubleday theory was discredited shortly after its emergence, there was no immediate rush to place the mantle on the shoulders of another. Chadwick, the foremost advocate of the rounders theory, died in 1908, and his cause essentially died with him. William Rankin of *The Sporting News* wrote of the Knickerbockers but was unable to gain significant traction for his theory, which was more anti–Doubleday than pro-anything else. Further, some of Rankin's facts were inconsistent as he was working with second hand material sixty years after the events.

Some espoused the notion of gradual evolution although they weren't sure from what, while others, like the befuddled Hiram Waldo, had no idea whatsoever of how baseball began. Eventually, the story of the Knickerbockers, who virtually everyone acknowledged to be the first organized baseball club, became commonly known, and the name of Alexander Joy Cartwright, Jr. was put forth as the "inventor" of baseball.

Albert Spalding met Cartwright in 1888, twenty years before the Mills Commission announced its findings, when Spalding brought his entourage to Hawaii on their world tour. He later referred to Cartwright as "one of the devotees of baseball," but beyond that seemed to take little notice of any part the old man might have played in the genesis of the game.[1] When Spalding searched for baseball's origins, there is no evidence that he considered Cartwright's role.

Hundred year anniversaries seemed to bring Cartwright out of the wilderness and into the public eye. In 1939, as the centennial of the Doubleday alleged creation event was marked in Cooperstown, Cartwright was honored in his adopted land of Hawaii and in some major league parks. In 1969, as baseball celebrated the centennial of the Cincinnati Red Stockings' famous campaign, the point agreed upon as the beginning of professional baseball, Harold Peterson published a lengthy article about Cartwright in *Sports Illustrated*, titled "Baseball's Johnny Appleseed." Peterson eventually expanded his article into a book called *The Man Who Invented Baseball*.

According to Peterson, Cartwright, like Doubleday, created the sport in one dramatic moment. The future general, on that momentous spring afternoon in Cooperstown, supposedly arrived at Elihu Phinney's cow pasture with the rules of baseball completely formulated in his mind. Peterson credited Cartwright with a similar epiphany. One day, Peterson related, in the spring of 1845, Cartwright came to an open field in the Murray Hill section of lower Manhattan and presented his friends with a fully-conceived plan for a new game, one that differed dramatically from the brand of ball they had been playing for the past few years.[2]

Was it Cartwright, and Cartwright alone, who set the game upon a different course? On one occasion, Duncan Curry, the first president of the Knickerbockers, said Cartwright was the architect of the rules, and on another that he (Curry) and William Tucker had crafted them.[3] In 1886, Rankin wrote that Tucker and William Wheaton had drafted the first Knickerbocker rules.[4]

There was a mystery surrounding the plan supposedly presented by Cartwright on that spring day, a question that revolved around a diagram shown by Cartwright to the other players. The diagram had supposedly been given to him by a Mr. Wadsworth. Who was Mr. Wadsworth? Was *he* the Father of Baseball?

Louis Wadsworth was later a well-known member of the Knickerbockers, but apparently Louis was not the Wadsworth in question. Veteran sportswriter William Cauldwell later declared that Louis was the only Wadsworth he knew of with any connections to baseball and that he had nothing to do with any diagram. The initial rules, Cauldwell said, were entirely Cartwright's creation. Others, including Thomas Tassie, longtime president of the Atlantics, said there was another Wadsworth, a brilliant after-dinner speaker employed by the Custom House. That Wadsworth, Tassie intimated, was the one who might have contributed the diagram.[5] If so, he, like Doubleday, invented baseball and then severed all connection with it for he was never heard from again.

Cartwright was the descendant of Nantucket sea captains, many of whom served in the Revolutionary Navy.[6] Some

Husky young bookseller Alexander Cartwright was one of the original members of the Knickerbockers and thought by some to be the creator of baseball's first written code of rules. Cartwright left New York for Hawaii in early 1849 and never returned, becoming a business leader in the Islands. He was elected to baseball's Hall of Fame in 1938.

Cartwrights worked their way down through New England; one of them, Alexander's father, arrived in New York in 1816 after being imprisoned for eight months by the British during the War of 1812.[7] The senior Cartwright established a prosperous shipping business on the New York waterfront, married into one of the city's most respectable families and fathered seven children.[8] The oldest, Alexander Cartwright, Jr., was born in 1820.

When Alexander Jr. came of age, he found work first in a brokerage office, then as a bank teller, which was, in the nineteenth century, a prestigious position. His supervisor at Union Bank, Daniel Ebbets, was the father of Charles Ebbets, who would later become the owner of Brooklyn's National League franchise. In 1842, Alex married Eliza Ann Gerrits van Wie, a well-bred young lady from an old-line Dutch family. The younger Cartwrights began to build their own family, and Alex joined a group of young professionals who played ball games at Murray Hill for recreation. Cartwright was a big man, 6'2" and 210 pounds, and a decent athlete who played well enough to enjoy the games.

By 1845, Cartwright's family fortunes had declined. His father's shipping business fell on hard times, and Alex Sr. was forced to take a job as an inspector for an insurance company. Alex Jr. had his life dramatically altered by a fire that destroyed Union Bank's single office and put an end to his banking career. In partnership with his brother, Alex opened a stationary and book store on Wall Street.[9]

Something good also happened to Cartwright in 1845 for that was the year he suggested that the men who played ball on Murray Hill take steps to formalize their organization. For the next few years, nearly every Monday and Thursday, the regular meeting days of the Knickerbockers, Alex played baseball. He was usually the pitcher for one of the sides, and a perusal of the club's scorebook indicates that he often did well, scoring many runs while making a minimal number of outs. He played in most of the games through 1848, including the final match of that season. It was the last game of baseball Cartwright would play in New York.[10]

Like Doubleday, Cartwright's best years occurred long after his brush with baseball immortality. Doubleday, a teenager in 1839, went on to a distinguished military career; his alleged involvement with the sporting world consisted only of that mystical day in the spring of 1839. Cartwright, who became an accomplished entrepreneur and pioneer, severed his connection with New York baseball in 1849 but continued to support the game until the end of his life.

On the final 1848 play day of the Knickerbockers, Alex was in the pitcher's box. By the time the next season came to a close, Cartwright was far from New York and his teammates. One day in 1848, Jim Marshall, a foreman at Sutter's Mill on the *Rio Americano* in northern California, happened to notice a few flakes of gold in the water. Marshall's discovery would change the face of the American continent in a way that neither he, Alexander Cartwright, nor anyone else could foresee. Over the next few years, thousands of covered wagons pointed westward toward a land they knew nothing of, other than it might contain so much gold that they would become wealthy beyond their wildest dreams.

The pioneers didn't know how much gold was in California, and most of them hadn't the slightest idea how to get there. There were no global positioning satellites and, for the most part, no roads. Few had crossed the country by land for most who journeyed to California took the ocean route around Cape Horn. The overland passage was uncertain and treacherous, and many died along the trail.

On March 1, 1849, Alexander Cartwright left his home, his family, his business and the Knickerbockers behind and set out for California. He traveled by rail to St. Louis and by land to Independence, Missouri, where he joined a group of 110 men in 32 wagons, led by noted pioneer William "Owl" Russell.[11] Among the possessions Cartwright took with him were a baseball and a rule book.

Many Americans went west in the 1840s, most cloaked in anonymity. Fortunately, Cartwright would not be part of the nameless horde, for he kept a voluminous, detailed record of his travels. He proved a fascinating journalist, describing brushes with danger, immense buffalo herds, meetings with the Pottawatomie Indians and the interpersonal difficulties that were bound to arise with protracted association at close quarters. He also recorded his recreational activities, which included playing a little baseball during rest breaks along the trail.

Cartwright's group followed the Santa Fe Trail to the Oregon Trail and crossed the Sierra Nevada Range to California. In August, Cartwright arrived in Sacramento and took a steamer to San Francisco where he met his brother Alfred, who had arrived via the Cape. In addition, he encountered former Knickerbocker Frank Turk.[12] The wagons and much of the travelers' luggage had been abandoned along the route, and according to Alfred, all Alex had left after his arduous journey were a cup and spoon, his journal, his rifle and ammunition and his copy of the Knickerbocker rules.[13]

The two Cartwrights purchased an interest in a mining company, a venture that apparently was not successful for it was abandoned in short order. Cartwright contracted dysentery and was advised to go to the Hawaiian Islands to recuperate. Once he had recovered, Alex intended to continue on to China and then return to New York.[14]

Cartwright departed for Hawaii on the Peruvian ship *Pacifico*, and, after a two-week voyage, reached Oahu on August 28, 1849.[15] He was still sick and decided to forego the China leg of the journey. A businessman named Aaron Howe, whom Cartwright had known in New York, hired him as a bookkeeper, and Alex made two trips to California on his behalf. On each occasion, he returned to the Islands and, after 1852, never left them again.

Ever enterprising, Cartwright established a number of business ventures in Hawaii, including a whaling agency, a commission merchant company, a hotel, and banking, insurance and real estate concerns. He befriended the royal family of the islands and became their financial advisor. Some of Cartwright's ventures survived his own demise and, more than a century later, Cartwright and Company was still managing the former royal properties.[16] By 1851, Cartwright had achieved sufficient success to send for his family to join him. Unfortunately, all three of the children who came from New York died, but Alex and his wife had two more offspring after she arrived.

Cartwright served on a number of corporate boards and became one of the leading businessmen in the islands. He was interested in many things, including history, religion and science, and was a voracious reader of magazines, newspapers and periodicals. He was a member of the group that established the Honolulu Library and Reading Room, which he served as president from 1886 to 1892.[17] Cartwright, who'd been a volunteer fireman in New York, founded the Honolulu Fire Department, and introduced baseball to Hawaii, laying out the islands' first diamond in 1852.[18]

Despite his successful life in Hawaii, Cartwright never forgot his baseball roots. In 1865, as the Civil War came to its end, Cartwright penned a letter to old Knickerbocker colleague Charley DeBost. "What pleasant memories arise," he wrote, "as I read your dear, good letter."

He asked for his fellow Knicks and noted that he still possessed a baseball they had used. "Hurrah! For us," he wrote of the news of the fall of Richmond and Lee's surrender for despite his love of Hawaii, he retained his United States citizenship until his death.[19]

Cartwright died in 1892, at the age of 72, and was buried in Oahu Cemetery in Honolulu. In 1997, Anne Cartwright, widow of Cartwright's great-grandson, placed an advertisement in the bulletin of the Society for American Baseball Research, seeking to sell an adjacent 23 by 63 foot plot, which would allow a few baseball fans the opportunity to spend eternity next to one of the Fathers of the Game. Anne's son Alexander Cartwright IV quickly took the plots off the market and stated his own desire, at some hopefully distant date, to lie beside his famous ancestor.[20]

The Hawaiian Islands were isolated from the United States, and for many years little notice was taken of the old Knickerbocker and his role in baseball's early days. He was out of sight and, as far as baseball historians were concerned, out of mind. If they remembered the Knickerbockers, they were likely to think of men like James Whyte Davis, who remained active with the club for many years and left a lengthy record behind him. The Knickerbockers honored many of their pioneers by designating them honorary members, but Cartwright had not served the necessary five years and was not even carried on the club rolls in that capacity. While mentioning the Knickerbockers, the Mills Commission did not note Cartwright's contribution in its report.

In 1939, while baseball celebrated the centennial of Doubleday's "invention" of the game, Bruce Cartwright, Jr., Alex's grandson, wrote a letter outlining his ancestor's contributions to baseball and inquiring as to whether the newly opened Hall of Fame would like some "relics" of his grandfather.[21] At the same time the Hall of Fame dedication gala took place, there was an Alexander Cartwright Day[22] in which ceremonies were held at Cartwright's grave and at Honolulu Stadium. The Honolulu Chamber of Commerce lobbied for a stamp bearing Cartwright's likeness, similar to the one issued of Doubleday.[23]

At Ebbets Field, Cartwright was honored between games of a doubleheader with the players drinking pineapple juice to pay homage to Hawaii, but the program was so poorly executed that most of the fans had no idea who Cartwright was or why he was being feted.[24]

More importantly, Cartwright's contributions to the game were recognized by his election to the Hall of Fame. Cartwright's plaque read: "Father of Modern Baseball — Set Bases 90 Feet Apart — Established 9 Innings as Game and 9 Players as Team — Organized the Knickerbocker Base Ball Club of NY in 1845." Cartwright did not, of course, establish the distance between bases at ninety feet, the length of a game at nine innings or the number of players on a team as nine. The bases were 42 paces from first to third and home to second, and the game ended when one club scored 21 aces in even innings. In the early days of the Knickerbockers, the number of players on each side varied.

Cartwright was not the sole organizer of the Knickerbockers, and he was not the club's first president. Nor was he the father of "modern baseball," whatever that may have meant in 1939, but perhaps the distinction was necessary for Cooperstown to preserve the notion that Doubleday had been the father of all baseball.

While Bruce Cartwright's letter stirred some initial interest, his death shortly afterward shunted Alex into the background once more, and the Hall of Fame resumed its lionization of Doubleday. Henderson mentioned Cartwright in his history of early ball games, but Henderson's book was a scholarly work little read by the sporting public. It was not until Peterson took up the cause two decades later that the role of Cartwright was again thrust prominently into public view. The celebration of professional baseball's centennial and the appearance of Peterson's work in the mainstream publication *Sports Illustrated* brought Cartwright a popular prominence that Rankin and Henderson had not.

When Peterson went in search of Cartwright's journal and the old ball he had hauled across the country, he was gravely disappointed. The ball had disappeared, and the journal had been mutilated. Bruce had burned large portions of the original work, sections he believed were harmful to the reputations of some people Cartwright had mentioned. He also considered the baseball references superfluous and burned much of them as well, depriving historians of priceless data. Much of what Peterson reviewed was copied from the original by another descendant.[25]

Still, when the entire story was evaluated, there was enough to present a convincing case that Cartwright, if not the inventor of baseball, played a role in its early development. He apparently was the one who suggested the idea of organizing a formal club, as opposed to continuing the informal gatherings, and he clearly played some role in the development of the Knickerbocker rules.

On the other hand, there was evidence that Cartwright's contribution was no greater than that of his fellow club members. Historian George Kirsch claimed that Cartwright should share his laurels with Knickerbockers William Wheaton and William Tucker.[26] Frederick Ivor-Campbell suggested that the Knickerbocker rules were not the creation of a new game, but merely the written version of the game the Knickerbockers were already playing.[27] John Thorn, one of the most knowledgeable of nineteenth century historians, is even tougher on Cartwright ("I stripped the brevets from Cartwright's shoulders in a speech at the Smithsonian last summer") and the Knickerbockers ("who have received too much credit for a hundred years now").[28]

Cartwright, unlike Doubleday, was actually involved with the development of the game and, like the general, was a red-blooded American hero and pioneer. For a time after the publication of Peterson's book, Cartwright was recognized as the closest thing to an "inventor" of baseball that could be found.

In 1887, two decades before the Mills Commission issued its report, there appeared in the *San Francisco Examiner* an interview with the elderly William Wheaton, who described early baseball in New York. In 1837, Wheaton related, he and several others formed the Gotham Base Ball Club and played under a set of rules that greatly improved upon the game of three old cat. Two of Wheaton's teammates on the Gotham Club were James Lee, later a Knickerbocker, and John Murphy, a hotel-keeper who played for the New York Club in the famed 1846 match with the Knickerbockers.

The Gothams' rules differed from those of old cat principally in the establishment of the diamond and the elimination of "soaking" (putting a player out by hitting him with the ball). Ending the practice of hitting a player with the ball was important, for it allowed for the use of a harder ball, which could be hit farther, creating more action and greater excitement.

Wheaton claimed that he drafted the Gothams' first written code of rules, which included the provision that in order to register a putout on a fly ball, it must be caught on the fly and not on the first bound. If his assertion is true, he was eight years in advance of Cartwright's Knickerbocker rules. It would also indicate that Wheaton, having prior experience in rule drafting, probably worked with Cartwright in the development of the Knickerbocker rules. It was a distinct possibility, as Ivor-Campbell pointed out, that the rules drafted by the

Knickerbockers were not novel, but merely the formalized version of what had gradually evolved on the playing field. Cartwright and Wheaton were not inventing a new game in 1845, for one could not take their rules and play baseball without some prior knowledge of a very similar game, possibly the one created by Wheaton for the Gothams. What was important was that the rules were written, removing the game from the realm of those that were handed down by custom and oral tradition.

One thing the Knickerbockers have frequently been credited with was establishing the distance between the bases at ninety feet. The ninety foot spacing is considered one of the most miraculous aspects of Cartwright's conception for it is the ideal distance for creating close plays. The Knickerbocker rules did not indicate how far each succeeding base should be from the previous one; they measured diagonally across the infield. The distance between home and second and first and third was established at 42 paces.

The definition of a pace is the subject of much disagreement among historians. John Thorn believes that a pace was defined as approximately two-and-one-half feet in the 1840s, which would result in a distance of 74 feet between the bases. Tom Shieber believes that a pace was a pace, the average stride of an average-sized man walking at a brisk pace, or about three feet, which would place the bases approximately, although not exactly, at today's distance of 90 feet. Men were somewhat shorter in the mid-nineteenth century than they are today, but if the 6'2" Cartwright used his pace, it would be at least three feet. If a pace were the actual stride of the person laying out the diamond, the distance would, of course, vary from game to game. Sheiber supports his three foot theory with the supposition that if there had been a 16-foot alteration in the distance between bases from 1845 to 1857, it would have had a substantial impact upon the game and contemporary sources would certainly have commented on the change. He believes that the fact that there are no references to a change in distance supports his theory that the bases were always approximately 90 feet apart.[29]

While Wheaton's information, like that of Abner Graves regarding Doubleday, was several decades after the fact, we know that Wheaton was a Knickerbocker and clearly involved in the early development of the game. His Gotham Club of 1837 was also known as the New York Club, and played in two matches in the fall of 1845 against a team of cricketers from Brooklyn (see Chapter 4).

Wheaton disappeared from the Knickerbocker chronicles in early 1846 and, like Cartwright, migrated westward following the discovery of gold in California. Unsuccessful in his quest for precious metal, Wheaton returned to the practice of law and became involved in California politics.[30] His connection with baseball, like Cartwright's, was brief.

A third Knickerbocker pioneer was Dr. Daniel Lucius (Doc) Adams.[31] Once again, baseball's 1939 centennial celebration spurred a descendant, in this case Roger C. Adams, the son of the doctor, to write a letter on behalf of his father.[32] No one, not even his son, claimed Adams was the originator of modern baseball, but if no one person had touched off the spark, Adams was clearly one of the people who wielded significant influence in baseball circles during the game's formative years.

Adams was born in New Hampshire in 1814, the son of a doctor and noted author. The younger Adams attended Amherst College for two years and graduated from Yale in 1835. He earned a medical degree from Harvard in 1838 and, after practicing for a short while with his father in New Hampshire, found his way to New York City in 1839.

Adams began to play an early version of baseball during his first year in New York, and he joined the Knickerbockers about a month after they were formed. He substantiated the claims of Wheaton regarding the earlier activity of the Gotham/New York organization and noted that the original Knickerbockers included some old members of the New York Club.[33] Adams played in the famous match of June 19, 1846, at the Elysian Fields, the game generally recognized as the first between two clubs, and became president of the Knickerbockers in 1847. A shortstop (possibly the first shortstop) and left-handed batter, Adams took pride in the fact that he could sometimes hit the ball from home plate at the Knickerbocker's Elysian Fields grounds into the Hudson River.

Given the difficulty of obtaining baseballs, Adams' teammates were probably not as excited as he was when the doctor launched one of their precious balls into the water. Fortunately, Adams, who learned the art from a Scottish saddle maker, was the Knickerbocker in charge of making balls and supplied other teams as well as his own. He also said he supervised the manufacture of bats, which were equally scarce.

Prior to the mass manufacturing of baseballs, each one was hand-made and consisted of strips of rubber twisted into a round shape (or, earlier, any solid substance, such as a rock or bullet[34]), covered with yarn and then with leather or cloth. Needless to say, the quality and consistency of the early balls varied considerably. In the mid–1850s, two men, Harvey Ross, a sail maker who was a member of the Atlantics, and John Van Horn, a shoemaker who was a member of the Union Club of Morrisania, began to manufacture baseballs on a regular basis.[35] Van Horn took rubber strips from the old shoes in his shop and cut them up to provide the center for his baseballs.

In 1848, Adams, not Cartwright (although the latter was still a member of the club) headed the committee to revise the constitution and by-laws of the Knickerbockers. Adams served as president of the club for three years in the 1840s and again for three years the following decade.[36] In 1857, he was elected president of the convention that met to formalize the rules of baseball and was the first chairman of the Rules Committee, a position he retained until 1862. Regardless of who devised the original rules of the New York game, Adams was instrumental in amending those rules to keep pace with changing circumstances.

On March 26, 1862, Adams resigned from the Knickerbockers and was immediately named an honorary member and presented with a set of resolutions thanking him for his long and meritorious service to the club.[37] In 1865, he relocated his practice to Ridgefield, Connecticut, and, for all practical purposes, severed any meaningful connection with baseball. Adams became one of the leading citizens of the Connecticut village, served as President of Ridgefield Savings Bank and was elected to the Connecticut legislature. He continued to play baseball until he was in his seventies, appearing in a Knickerbocker old-timers game in 1875 at the age of 61.[38]

Adams died in 1899, largely unrecognized as a pioneer of the game, but not before he had given a lengthy interview to *The Sporting News* in 1896, titled "Dr. D. L. Adams; Memoirs of the Father of Base Ball; He Resides in New Haven and Retains an Interest in the Game." During the interview, he provided invaluable information on early baseball and the evolution of its rules and playing style. Like all old-timers, he noted the fact that players in his day played for the love of the game and had much more fun than the money-hungry professionals of the 1890s. Adams did admit that baseball, which he knew as a recreational pastime, had become pretty important. "[W]e pioneers," he admitted, "never expected the game so universal as it had now become."[39]

Despite his valuable contributions to the development of the rules, Adams was not the Father of the Game. He had much more influence than Cartwright on the form that baseball assumed by the 1860s, but Adams joined the Knickerbockers after they had begun playing the New York game. Although he had played some form of baseball prior to joining the club, he had certainly not been part of a creation event.

Who was the "Father of the Game?" An ancient proverb states: "Victory has a thousand fathers, while defeat is an orphan." If the proverb is true, baseball had arrived, for by the mid-twentieth century, it had many purported fathers. With the Doubleday myth consigned to Cooperstown, and Cartwright, Wheaton and Adams classified as collaborators, but not inventors, the Knickerbockers as a group became the most likely candidates as originators of the American version of baseball. In the 1860 edition of *Beadle's* Chadwick noted, "There was a club called the New York Club, which existed before the Knickerbocker, but we shall not be far wrong if we award to the latter club the honor of being the pioneer of the present game of Base Ball."[40] If none of the Knickerbockers had been struck with the vision that created the game in one bold stroke, however, the question at issue was what provided the club with the inspiration to draft the famous "Knickerbocker Rules?" Were there games that preceded baseball upon which the New Yorkers based their rules? Was rounders the game? If not, what was it?

CHAPTER 3

What About Rounders? What About Old Cat?

Two historians deserve immense credit for discovering and analyzing the ancient bat and ball games that preceded baseball. Robert Henderson, in 1947, and David Block, in 2004, produced voluminous evidence, drawn from primary sources, concerning games developed in America, Europe and Africa, all of which revolved around hitting something (a ball or a piece of wood) with something else (a bat or one's hand) and running somewhere (to bases, stools, or stumps) in either counterclockwise or clockwise sequence. Such activities are categorized by the Protoball project as "safe haven" games.

The plethora of bat and ball games include long ball, stool ball, goal ball, old cat (one old cat, two old cat and three old cat), feeder, squares, club ball, barn ball, northern spell, round ball, poisoned ball, tip cat, tut ball and the French game of *teque*. While the early games bore some resemblance to modern baseball, none had all of the essential elements, and most did not involve running to a sequence of bases. In many games, the ball was struck with the hand rather than a bat. Others, such as the old cat games, often involved hitting a piece of wood (the cat—short for catapult) rather than a ball.[1] The cat games were a necessity in sparsely populated areas as they required just three to eight players.

The primary linkage in most of the references prior to 1700 is the use of the word "ball." Historical figures, such as Ching Tsung, the young Chinese emperor in A.D. 824,[2] mentioned that they were playing at ball without explaining what such playing involved. It is probable that their correspondents knew what playing ball was, but we, several centuries after the fact, do not.

Block found a history of ball games in Asia and Africa and a group of Polish workers who brought a brand of baseball, which they called *pilak palantowa* (bat ball) to the British colonies in America in the early seventeenth century.[3] He repeated the oft-told tale of the Prince of Wales playing baseball in 1748 and found a reference to baseball in a 1755 diary entry of a young Englishman named William Bray.[4] There was an English game called baseball as well as a German one. A safe-haven game was reported in Innsbruck in 1600, played by Poles and Silesians,[5] and it is evident that by the seventeenth century, games similar to modern baseball were being played throughout Europe. In 1744, John Newberry published *A Pretty Little Pocket Book,* which described a number of games, among which was one called "base-ball."

One of the most popular of the old games was stool ball, supposedly originated by Sussex milkmaids in the fourteenth century. The maids used their milking stools in a role similar to that of wickets on the cricket field, and the game evolved into one which included bats.[6] On Christmas Day 1621, there was a stool ball game played in the Plymouth Colony, one of the first bat and ball games played by white men in America. Some colonists told Governor Bradford that religious scruples prevented them from working on the holy day, and he excused them. Bradford was horrified to find some of them, rather than worshipping, playing stool ball.[7]

Stool ball, which is still popular in Sussex and the surrounding area, bears greater similarity to cricket than it does to baseball. In its current form, two stools are placed opposite each other, with a batter defending each stool. Batters get runs by dashing between the stools or striking the ball outside set boundaries. They are put out by having their ball caught in the air, being run out between the stools or by having the bowler hit the stool. Sussex stool ball is played today almost exclusively by young ladies, which generates great consternation among cricketers who are told that stool ball is the ancestor of their sport.[8]

Another sport prevalent in the Old World was rounders. Henry Chadwick, of course, insisted that rounders was the direct antecedent of baseball, the claim which so infuriated Albert Spalding and John Montgomery Ward. Pioneer player Doc Adams also believed, according to his son Roger, that baseball had its origins in rounders.[9] The English game, which Chadwick said was played as early as 1600, took place on a field that had five bases, marked with stakes or bags. Four of the bases were in a square, while the fifth, home base, formed the tip of a triangle above the square. The distance between the bases varied, but was typically about forty feet. There was no foul territory, and balls hit anywhere on the field were in play.

Teams ranged from five to twenty players, who were stationed in varying positions, other than the pitcher, or feeder, who always stood about thirty feet from the batter. The pitcher tossed the ball overhanded and slowly, so the batter could hit it.

The batter was out immediately if he (i) missed the ball twice, (ii) tipped it at his feet or (iii) had his hit caught in the air. If the batter hit the ball and was not out, he ran the bases, attempting to go from one to the next, either on his own hit or that of a subsequent batter, without being hit by the ball. If the batter negotiated all four bases and attempted to go home, a fielder could put him out by rolling the ball to the home base before the batter/runner arrived. If all four bases were negotiated safely, and the batter proceeded to the home base before the fielders could get the ball there, he had made a run.

After a player was put out, he could no longer bat. Each team's turn at bat ended when all players had been put out, or when all the remaining players were on base, and there was no one left to bat. Therefore, if all of his teammates had been put out, no one was on base, and the last batter hit the ball, he had to try for home base, or the inning was ended. If there was only one player left, he could bring the whole team back to bat again if he was able to hit the ball and complete the circuit of all five bases without being put out. This equivalent of a home run was called a rounder.[10]

Those were the rules commonly used in rounders, but they were by no means the rules used in every game. Sometimes a batter was out if he missed the ball just once or if a hit was caught on the first bounce. Sometimes each base that was reached safely counted as a run, making a rounder worth five runs. Like so many of the early games, the methods of play were subject to local custom, necessity (the number of available players or the contours of the field) and whim.

To add to the confusion, the rules set forth above also applied to games other than rounders. In New England, they played a game called round ball, which employed rules very similar to those of rounders and town ball.[11] Round ball, according to the statement of Henry Sargent to the Mills Commission, was played at the time of the American Revolution.[12]

Until the end of his life, Chadwick insisted that baseball was a natural evolution from rounders. Early emigrants from England, he said, brought the game to America where it gradually evolved into town ball and then baseball. Chadwick had no documentary proof of this, but in the absence of any countervailing evidence, used his authority to press the claim. Historian Fred Ivor-Campbell attributes the disagreement to the fact that names were given to the various ball games depending upon local custom. What Chadwick knew as rounders, for instance, was a game Ivor-Campbell believes that others called base ball.[13] A sandwich on an elongated roll is known in various parts of America as a grinder, submarine, hoagie, wedge or po boy, and thus was the same game of ball referred to by different names in different regions.

Spalding and Ward disagreed vehemently with Chadwick but, like him, had no solid evidence. Block, with an abundance of documentary proof, sided with Spalding and Ward as to the doubtful nature of Chadwick's rounders theory. English baseball, Block said, had existed before rounders, and by the 1840s, when Chadwick claimed the transition from rounders to baseball was occurring, rounders was looking less like baseball. Block found little evidence of rounders played or mentioned in America and, as asserted below, in order to qualify as a direct ancestor, rounders not only had to resemble baseball, it had to be known to those who developed the new sport. There were a number of bat and ball games, in addition to rounders, that shared characteristics with baseball, and their claim to be the forerunner of the sport was equally strong. Rounders was the leading candidate only because Chadwick, by far the most influential sports journalist of his time, had seen the old game played in England. Had the pioneer baseball writer been a French immigrant, he might well have had Ward and Spalding chanting, "No *tecque*! No *tecque*!"

When did all of the old games become a new game called baseball? Noted baseball historian John Thorn found a reference to baseball in a 1791 Pittsfield, Massachusetts, newspaper, the earliest newspaper article in America specifically mentioning the sport by name.[14] The subject of the piece was an ordinance prohibiting a number of ball games as a nuisance, baseball being listed among them. The main concern was the preservation of the windows of the new meeting house. While no particulars were given to describe how the ordinance defined baseball, the article is evidence that, in the late eighteenth century, Americans were playing a game known as baseball, long before any American reference to rounders.

In 2001, George Thompson, Jr. published an article announcing his discovery of a letter that appeared in the New York newspaper *National Advocate* in the spring of 1823. The letter, signed with the pseudonym "A Spectator," described a game of "base ball" that Spectator had witnessed among a group of young men that took place in lower Manhattan at what is now Washington Place and 8th Street. Spectator also announced that the men were part of a formal organization that planned to play again the following Saturday. There was no description of the game, and no mention of what rules constituted "base ball." Was it rounders? Was it similar to the game the Knickerbockers played two decades later? We only know that the correspondent referred to it as base ball.[15]

In 1825, two years after the publication of Spectator's letter, a number of residents of Hamden, New York, published a notice in the *Delhi* (New York) *Gazette* challenging any and all comers to take them on in a game of "bass-ball."[16] Again, the letter gave no details, but several men, including famous ones like Oliver Wendell Holmes, William Cullen Bryant, journalist Horace Greeley, Kentucky abolitionist Cassius Marcellus Clay and New York politician Thurlow Weed, recalled playing baseball in their youth during the 1820s. Daniel Webster said he played "ball" at Dartmouth in 1797[17] and John Adams took part in bat and ball recreation as a youth in the 1740s.[18] Henry Wadsworth Longfellow recalled being encouraged to play ball at Bowdoin to improve his physical well-being. "[T]here is nothing now heard of, in our leisure hours," he lamented, "but ball, ball, ball."[19] Future Presidents Rutherford B. Hayes and Benjamin Harrison played ball at Kenyon College in 1839[20] and Farmer's College in 1848,[21] respectively. General Joseph Hooker, infamous loser of the battle of Chancellorsville, recalled playing ball in 1830 and related that he was quite good at catching the ball.[22] Hooker's commander-in-chief, Abraham Lincoln, was reported to have played town ball on many occasions in many sources, some of which may be true.

The old game that found the most favor in America was town ball, which was played extensively in Cincinnati and Philadelphia. Its leading exponents in the latter city were the members of the venerable Olympic Club, formed in 1833. Town ball bore some similarities to rounders in that the side was not retired until all were put out, and a "home run" by the last man could restart the process.

On October 22, 1845, at the Elysian Fields, in Hoboken, New Jersey, eight men from the New York Club played a match called baseball against eight players from Brooklyn. The game took place eight months before the Knickerbockers played the New York Club at Hoboken in what is generally acknowledged as the first modern interclub match and about six months after the Knickerbockers had written down the rules by which they would henceforth play ball. A number of the players for the New York Club later played for the Knicks, and their experience at baseball enabled them to beat the Brooklyn players, many of whom were cricketers of the Union Star Cricket Club, 24–4. Three days later, the two groups met again, this time at the grounds of the Brooklyn Star Cricket Club, and the New York Club won once more, 37–19.[23]

Given all of the new information available on the many games from which baseball might have evolved, several questions must be asked: Did anyone (either individually or collectively) invent baseball? Was it a tribe in Libya? Was it the Prince of Wales? Was it the Polish workers who brought their game to Jamestown? Which, if any, of the many bat and ball games was the one from which modern baseball was derived? Was a Knickerbocker-like form of the game being played in Pittsfield or lower Manhattan in 1791 or 1823? How do we define modern baseball? Is the name of a sport sufficient to claim ancestry? Did the modern game begin with the sports called baseball that were played in Europe? Did it encompass the games played in America in the 1820s that were called baseball? As historian Martin Hoerchner said when describing stool ball, "If you are interested in the genealogy of ball games, you quickly learn that it is easy to find similarities, but hard to prove ancestry."[24]

The only documented, unbroken line between baseball as played in its current form and any prior version of the sport begins with the Knickerbockers. Any connection between the Knicks and an older game can be based only upon conjecture for the differences are too great to claim direct descent. A case can be made for rounders, English baseball, German baseball, stool ball, the old cat games, and a few other ancient bat and ball games; however, nothing can be proven absent one key bit of knowledge, which is missing from all the comparisons.

What did the Knickerbockers know when they wrote down their code of rules in 1845? Clearly they had some prior game in mind, for using the Knickerbocker rules alone, one cannot determine how to play a game. The rules contain the inherent assumption that readers were aware of some form of baseball, a form the Knickerbockers made more attractive. The only circumstance in which an older game could have been the genesis of the Knickerbockers' new game, however, was if the Knicks were proven to be aware of a particular game and used its precepts in the development of their rules.

If a modern player has a batting stance like Joe DiMaggio, but never saw DiMaggio play nor saw pictures of him, DiMaggio cannot be given credit for the player's stance or for any success he might have. It is only a coincidence, two people independently reaching the same conclusion. Did the Knickerbockers know of the bat and ball games played in Europe and Africa during prior centuries? Probably not. Very little written information was available on the older games, and until Henderson and Block conducted their research during the last sixty years, even twentieth century baseball historians were unaware of the older forms of bat and ball games.

The Knickerbockers played some older version of baseball for a few years, probably without any idea how it had evolved. What they saw that led to the new rules and from what they drew their inspiration is difficult to ascertain, for although they recorded every bit of minutiae from their parliamentary proceedings, they left a cold trail as far as the rationale behind their initial rules. Interestingly, despite Roger Adams' statement of his father's opinion, there is no reference to rounders in the writings of Cartwright, Wheaton or Adams when discussing the genesis of the Knickerbocker rules. In the absence of the knowledge of the Knickerbockers, my conclusion is that if we are to call anyone the "inventor" of "modern" baseball, it must be the Knickerbockers as a group, with possibly Cartwright and Wheaton among those most responsible for the form of the new game.

No matter what pastimes may have had some influence upon the Knickerbocker rules, it is clear that the Knicks transformed the older versions, perhaps drawing on several different games, into a different sport, one that we know today as baseball. Prior to the 1840s, ball games were primarily children's affairs, played in open fields for amusement. The Knickerbockers developed a structure that converted children's games involving bat and ball into serious exercise and entertainment for adult males. According to Henry Chadwick, those who first saw the Knicks play at the Elysian Fields "used to watch the ball tossers with surprised and incredulous looks, as if astonished to find that grown men could be found to engage in what they thought boys' play."[25]

The Knicks, in addition to codifying the playing rules, turned baseball into a serious affair. They kept score and preserved the records for posterity. Children didn't keep tally and report the results to newspapers, and a child's game could never be a national sport on a par with cricket in England. The Knickerbockers created a new type of baseball, distinct from all that preceded it, and paved the way for the growth of the new sport. "With the birth of the Knickerbockers," wrote Frederick Ivor-Campbell, "baseball gained a public face."[26] Ivor-Campbell pointed to Rule 8 of the Knickerbocker code as perhaps the one that had the greatest impact upon the game. Rule 8 stated that the first team to score 21 aces would be the winner. Older ball games had usually been played for enjoyment without the concept that someone would win and someone else would lose. The game ended when the time for recreation was over, players had to leave for home, meal time had come or some other similar reason.

The 21 ace rule, eventually followed by the nine inning standard, made ball games competitive endeavors upon which pride, money and reputations could be staked.[27]

Should the Knickerbockers be considered the "inventors" of baseball? Does it matter? All one can say with certainty is that from the beginning of recorded history, men (and children) had been playing bat and ball games and that, for all practical purposes, all but two (baseball and cricket) have fallen by the wayside. No one plays old cat anymore, nor do they play long ball or northern spell. But they do play baseball in countries throughout the world, and it is the story of baseball we will follow through the end of the Civil War.

Chapter 4

The Jolly Old Knickerbockers, 1845–1856

On September 23, 1845, Alexander Cartwright, William Wheaton and a number of their friends, the group that gathered regularly together to play ball, held a meeting at McCarty's Hotel, at what is now Hudson and 12th Streets,[1] and formally became the Knickerbocker Base Ball Club.

Duncan Curry, an employee of Union Bank,[2] was elected president, and Wheaton and William Tucker, who were good friends and shared an apartment over Tucker's father's tobacco shop, were elected vice president and secretary and treasurer, respectively. Wheaton, a lawyer, drafted the club's constitution and bylaws. Cartwright was not an officer.

The Knickerbockers needed reinforcements if they were going to play interesting games for even if all the original members showed up, they would not have more than five on a side. During the succeeding years, many men joined the founders, and each season saw new members arriving and old ones departing. Outfielder James Whyte Davis became one of the most prominent, and certainly the most enthusiastic, Knickerbockers. "[W]e used to call him a fiend," recalled Doc Adams, "in the old days because of his enthusiasm."[3] Davis played with the club for the first time on September 12, 1850 and, sixteen years later, penned a nostalgic note on the old scorecard, "My first play with the good old Knicks."[4]

Davis played with the Knicks into the mid–1860s and took an active part in the club's affairs for a long time after that. In 1880, the club commemorated the thirtieth anniversary of his first match, and Davis and a number of his old mates took part in an old-time game.[5] He served as president, secretary and treasurer of the Knickerbockers at various times but was apparently not eager to assume either of the latter two posts. In 1855, Davis received the majority of votes for secretary but wanted to decline the position because "some dissatisfaction and ill-feeling had been expressed at the manner in which he had carried out the bylaws and it being a thankless office to hold."[6] Apologies were made and Davis consented to serve although he tried to resign a few months later.[7] In 1857, he gave up his position as treasurer in disgust.[8] The previous month, he had submitted his resignation as a member, which was tabled in order to allow him to reconsider.[9] In 1860, Davis was fined fifty cents for using improper language during a spirited discussion that became a bit too animated.[10] Despite the occasional quarrels, Davis was a Knickerbocker through and through. In 1854, he composed a song called *Ball Days* about the players on the three New York clubs,[11] and when he died in 1899, Davis was buried wrapped in a Knickerbocker flag.[12]

Another new member, Charles Schuyler (Charley) DeBost, joined the club in April 1846, and played with the Knicks in their second interclub match against the Washington Club in 1851. DeBost was new to the Knicks, but he had apparently been playing ball for several years on Long Island.[13] He was a Knickerbocker through 1860,[14] a spirited and enthusiastic performer often given to flamboyant moves that were not always appreciated by all. Yet, he was possibly the best catcher in New York in the 1850s. "This gentleman's appearance at the bat," said the *Times*, "is generally the signal for some demonstration of applause or hilarity."[15] "DeBost," the *Spirit of the Times* proclaimed in 1855, "as behind man, has no equal."[16] He was such a talented player that, on numerous occasions, the club declined to play matches in his absence.[17]

Cricketer Harry Wright was originally a member of the St. George Club, whose grounds were near those of the Knickerbockers. He joined the Knicks in 1858, and played with them until 1863 when he resigned and became a member of the Gothams. Wright was one of the best players on the Knickerbockers and was selected to play in the Fashion Course All-Star Series in 1858. Unfortunately, cricket took up a great deal of his time, and he was frequently an absentee at baseball matches. Wright played a major role in the history of baseball from the mid–1860s until the mid–1890s, but he was not a big story prior to 1865. In the 1850s and early 1860s, Harry was known more for his cricket skills as a round arm bowler than he was as a baseball player.

As new members arrived, many of the Knickerbocker pioneers departed. Cartwright and Wheaton were in Hawaii and California, respectively. Curry, the first president, resigned in 1856 and was immediately elected an honorary member. The peripatetic William Tucker, who was an original member, resigned in 1850,[18] rejoined the club and then resigned once more.

The Knickerbockers came from assorted occupations, but none from the world of physical toil. Historian Harold Seymour analyzed the professions of the members from 1845–1860 and listed seventeen merchants, twelve clerks, five brokers, four professional men, two insurance men, one bank teller, one cigar merchant, one hatter, one cooper, one stationer, a U.S. Marshal and several who identified themselves only as "gentlemen."[19] There were physicians, attorneys, bankers and business owners but none who gave any form of manual labor as their livelihood.

The Knicks were not formed for the purpose of competing with other baseball clubs. Their principal activity was to meet every Monday and Thursday afternoon and play a game (sometimes two) with whatever number of members happened to appear. The players, mostly businessmen who spent their days behind a desk or counter, sought exercise in order to regain the muscle tone of their more active ancestors. Although there was an occasional fine for profanity, there is little indication that the Knickerbockers expressed much competitive fire in the games amongst themselves. Exercise and good fellowship were the goals, and winning or losing the game was not of great consequence.

The Knickerbockers played ball, elected officers, and took attendance at meetings and on play days. They collected dues and, when, as often happened, the treasury ran dry, levied assessments on the members to cover the shortfall. They raised motions and voted on them, and the secretary took copious minutes of every meeting. While others may have played some form of ball prior to the Knickerbockers, none left the historical trail of the latter. The club scorebook contained the record of each game played among themselves as well as those with other clubs.

The financial condition of the club varied over the years. In 1853, receipts (consisting of dues and initiation fees) totaled $150.50, while expenses were $150.00, leaving fifty cents in the treasury at the end of the year. The principal expenses were the rent of the grounds ($75) and refreshments ($45.50).[20] The following year, an assessment of $62.50 was required to balance the books,[21] and in 1856, an assessment of $105 was needed.[22]

It was nearly a year after their formation before the Knickerbockers played against outside competition. On June 19, 1846, at the Elysian Fields, they lost ignominiously to a group known as the New York Club, 23–1. The box score of the game is set forth below:

KNICKERBOCKERS	Hands Lost*	Runs	NEW YORK	Hands Lost	Runs
Turney	1	0	Davis	1	3
Adams	1	0	Winslow	2	2
Tucker	2	0	Ransom	2	3
Birney	1	1	Murphy	0	4
Avery	0	0	Case	0	4
H. Anthony	2	0	Johnson	1	2
D. Anthony	2	0	Thompson	2	2
Tryon	2	0	Trenchard	2	1
Paulding	1	0	Lalor	2	2
	12	1		12	23

* Hands lost was the term used for an out.

Source: The box score can be found in a number of sources, including the Knickerbocker scorebooks and Orem p. 18.

Cartwright acted as umpire for the match, during which the New York Club took four innings to score more than the 21 tallies necessary to win. How, one wonders, could the Knickerbockers, who'd been playing ball for several years, lose so badly to a group of men who were not even organized as an official club? A perusal of the box score provides a clue for it includes several names at the top of the New York order, Davis, Winslow and Ransom, who were excellent players and later joined the Knicks. Although not a formal club, the New York players were not new to the game of baseball, apparently having played for at least three years,[23] and the result is not as surprising as it may seem at first. Duncan Curry, the Knickerbocker president, said later that his club took their opponents too lightly and underestimated the impact of their significant cricket ability.[24]

For four years after their first game, the Knickerbockers remained the only official baseball club in the United States and continued to meet on a regular basis for play days, typically fifty or more times each year. The Knicks traditionally opened the season in early April and played the last game of the season on Thanksgiving. On most occasions, two captains chose sides, but occasionally the split was "Married v. Single" or, on one occasion, "First Nine v. All That Come." There was a spirited debate as to whether members of other clubs should be allowed to participate in play days. Given the fact that there were often less than eighteen Knickerbockers on hand, it was decided that if there were openings, outsiders should be allowed to join. The name of their club was duly noted on the scorecard.

Finally, in 1850, a second baseball organization, the Washington Club, was formed.[25] On

June 3, 1851, the Knickerbockers, five years after their first outside match, played for the second time, defeating the Washington Club, 21–11. Two weeks later, they beat the Washington nine again, this time, 22–20, in an exciting contest that took ten innings to reach a decision.

In 1852, the Eagles, formed in 1840 to play an unspecified type of "ball,"[26] converted to baseball and joined the Knickerbocker and Washington organizations. That same year, a number of new players joined the Washington Club and changed its name to Gotham.[27] The Gothams played on the Red House Grounds in Harlem in their early years[28] before joining the Knickerbockers at Hoboken.

The membership of the Gotham Club was similar to that of the Knickerbockers. The shortstop for the nine, whose pedigree was typical of the Gothams, was Charles Commerford, born in 1833 to a socially prominent New York family. Commerford married Elizabeth Hamilton, a direct descendant of Alexander Hamilton, and eventually moved to Waterbury, Connecticut, where he became active in Democratic politics. He was appointed postmaster by President Grover Cleveland and corresponded with Victor Hugo regarding the exploitation of the working man. Despite his admirable sympathy for the working class, however, Commerford, like most of his Gotham teammates, was never part of it.[29]

In 1853, the Knickerbocker, Gotham and Eagle Clubs (each of which had about 30 members) met and standardized the rules by which each organization played the game. In December of the following year, in keeping with the social traditions that were such an important part of the early game, the three clubs held a dinner at Fijux's, which was attended by about 45 players and became an annual affair.[30]

In 1855, more clubs began to appear, and on Thanksgiving, the traditional finale of the season, there was a very impressive flurry of activity. The final day was much like opening day, as clubs met among themselves for friendly play, rather than competing against another club. Although the weather was chilly, the Continentals, a new club, played from nine in the morning until dusk came at five. The Putnams intended to play three complete games (63 runs), but lasted just twelve innings and 36 runs. The Knickerbockers, Eagles, Empires, Atlantics, Gothams, Baltics and other clubs also took the field during the first big holiday in the history of baseball.[31]

By the end of the 1856 season, a number of new clubs had been organized, and the Knickerbockers had taken part in 21 matches, 20 of which were against the Eagles or Gothams.[32] They won 13, lost 6 and played two ties. Twenty-one interclub games in eleven seasons is, of course, less than two per year, as the Knicks spent most of their time playing among themselves.

There were still not many clubs in New York, and the interclub match remained somewhat of a novelty. The records of New York and Brooklyn clubs through the 1856 season, which show the minimal level of activity, were as follows:

Club	Record
Knickerbocker	13-6-2
Gotham	6-8-2
Eagle	6-6-1
Empire	1-3-1
Union of Morrisania	4-2-0
Excelsior	1-1-0
Atlantic	6-0-0

Harmony	0–2–0
Eckford	2–0–0
Baltic	0–5–0
Putnam	1–1–0
Young America	0–1–0
Columbia	0–2–0

Source: Wright

The Gothams played seven games during their first three seasons without tasting victory before finally beating the Knicks in 1855. One of their most exciting games took place in 1854 when the Knickerbockers took 16 innings to score the 21 runs needed to defeat the Gothams.

The Atlantics and Eckfords, two clubs made up of artisans and workingmen, would be the dominant clubs of the early 1860s. Both got off to fine starts, but neither the Atlantics nor Eckfords played against the older clubs like the Knicks, Eagles or Gothams. First, the former clubs were from Brooklyn rather than New York, and second, they were a little different from the latter three organizations.

The Knicks were very particular about which clubs they would play. They declined numerous challenges, including those from the Eckford and Mutual Clubs, and in 1857 decided to play only against those organizations that occupied the Elysian Fields.[33] In 1857 and again in 1860, there was a debate over whether the Knicks should play *any* games against other clubs.[34] They played principally against the Eagles and Gothams and did not venture into Brooklyn until 1858 when they accepted an invitation from the Excelsiors.

As more clubs were formed in the New York area, interclub matches took place more frequently. In November 1856, surveying the recently completed season, the *Clipper* stated, "Base Ball has made rapid progress in this vicinity during the past year, and bids fair to become a formidable rival to the more scientific game of cricket."[35] Even the Knickerbockers were beginning to become just a little bit competitive. In the club's early days, members had been admitted based upon their social status and *bonhomie*. Before the 1857 season, it was suggested that before the applicants were voted on, they play a couple of games in order to determine whether they had the skills to compete effectively.[36]

The Eagles and Gothams looked to the Knickerbockers for guidance on rules and procedures for playing the game, and the three clubs met informally to clarify standards.[37] By December 1856, with more clubs appearing on the scene every month, the Knicks, Eagles and Gothams realized they could no longer decide the fate of the game among themselves. On the sixth day of the month, at their regular meeting, the Knickerbockers appointed a three-man committee, chaired by Dr. Adams, charged with the task of organizing a convention of the baseball clubs of New York and the vicinity. On January 22, delegates from the following fourteen clubs met at Smith's Hotel on Broome Street with the object of standardizing the rules of the game:[38]

Club	Date of Formation	Delegates
Knickerbockers	1845	Daniel Adams, William Grenelle, Louis Wadsworth
Gotham	1850	William Van Cott, Rueben Cudlip, George Franklin
Eagle	1852	W.W. Armfield, A.J. Bixby, John W. Mott
Empire	1854	R. H. Thorn, Walter Scott, Thomas Leary

Putnam	1855	Theodore Jackson, James Smith, Edward Walton
Baltic	1855	Phillip Weeks, Robert Cornell, Dr. Charles Cooper
Excelsior	1854	James Andrews, James Rogers, P.R. Chadwick
Atlantic	1855	Caleb Sniffen, W. Babcock, Thomas Tassie
Harmony	1855	R. Justin, Jr., G.M. Phelps, Frank Carr
Harlem	1856	E.H. Brown, John Riker, C.M. Van Voorhis
Eckford	1855	Charles Welling, Francis Pidgeon, James Gray
Bedford	1857	John Constant, Charles Osborn, Thomas Bagot
Nassau	1857	William Howell, J. R. Rosenquest, Ephriam Miller
Continental	1855	John Silsby, Nathanial Law, James Brown

The first order of business was to elect officers with the following gentlemen chosen to fill the positions:

President	Dr. Daniel Adams
Vice President	Rueben H. Cudlip and John Mott
Secretary	James Andrews
Assistant Secretary	Walter Scott
Treasurer	E. H. Brown

The purpose of the meeting was to standardize the rules of the game, which, contrary to legend, were not established for all time by Cartwright on a magical day in 1845. The rules were flexible and had been continually adapted to suit circumstances and changing conditions. In order to identify and codify the then commonly observed rules, the convention appointed a committee of fourteen to draft a code and present it to all the delegates. It was also agreed that each club would pay dues of two dollars per year to defray incidental expenses.[39] The meeting came off efficiently and harmoniously, adjourning at 9:30, having accomplished much.

Porter's Spirit of the Times began its account of the convention with praise for the game and its many physical and moral benefits, declaring that baseball "has been known in the Northern States as far back as the memory of the oldest inhabitant reacheth, and must be regarded as a national pastime, the same as cricket is by the English." "The gentlemen assembled last evening at Smith's Hotel," said the *Spirit*, "were engaged in a work not of that trifling importance which a casual observer might suppose," a statement followed by lengthy comments regarding the desirability of *mens sana* in *corpore sana* and the evils of the bars and gaming tables.[40]

The second meeting of the delegates took place in February at which time the committee appointed to make recommendations on the rules did so, and the entire convention voted to adopt them. The most significant change, which recognized the increased fielding skills of the players, established the nine-inning game rather than requiring a club to score 21 runs in order to win. (See Appendix B for a complete set of rules) The distance between bases was set at 90 feet rather than the original 42 paces from home to second and first to third. The number of players, which had not been specified in the Knickerbocker code, was set at nine.[41]

One of the rule changes, suggested by the Knicks at the urging of Jim Davis, was not adopted. Davis was enamored of the value of the "fly game" under which a ball had to be caught on the fly, rather than the first bounce, to be an out. The delegates felt otherwise and did not adopt the proposal, laying the groundwork for a battle that would be fought for the next seven years. A second change, proposed by *Porter's Spirit of the Times,* that would empower the umpire to call strikes on a batter who did not swing at good pitches, was also declined, but was adopted the following year.[42]

Baseball now had a set of rules, but no governing body for the officers had no meaningful authority beyond drafting the rules, and the group lacked a defined mission. Therefore, in March 1858, at a meeting called by the Knickerbocker, Eagle, Gotham and Empire Clubs, attended by delegates from 25 organizations, the National Association of Base Ball Players[43] was formed, with the following officers:

President	W.H. Van Cott, Gotham
First Vice President	J. B. Jones, Excelsior
Second Vice President	Thomas S. Dakin, Putnam
Recording Secretary	J. Ross Postley, Metropolitan
Corresponding Secretary	Theodore Jackson, Putnam
Treasurer	E.H. Brown, Metropolitan

The delegates adopted a constitution and bylaws and began the Association's governance of the game of baseball that would continue until the tumultuous convention of 1870 at which the amateur and professional classes parted ways, each forming its own association.[44]

The NA was not a league in the sense of the modern American and National Leagues, but more of a trade association in which membership was easily obtained. Its goal was to manage the game and its rules and hold members to certain standards. Admission was open to any club that made written application in the prescribed form and paid a five dollar admission fee and five dollars in annual dues (later reduced to two dollars per year). The Association met in convention each year, at which time new clubs were admitted, rule changes were evaluated, and everyone congratulated each other on the game's progress. The convention was held in New York each year through 1866; the delegates met in Philadelphia the following year, marking a milestone in the gradual shift of power away from the city in which the sport began.

When the National Association took form, however, New York was the undisputed center of baseball activity. The city was a rapidly growing metropolis in the 1840s and 1850s with its population increasing from 313,000 in 1840 to 516,000 in 1850 and 814,000 by 1860.[45] In both New York and neighboring Brooklyn, much of the population was foreign born, 47 percent in the latter city in 1855. Most of the immigrants were Irish and German. Blacks comprised less than 2 percent of Brooklyn's 1860 population.[46]

In retrospect, the good old days always seem better, and to some looking back on the city during baseball's formative years, there was nothing but bliss. Harold Peterson, the biographer of Cartwright, wrote, "Little Aleck entered a New York City whose doors were seldom locked and where 'it was not considered at all necessary that counters of banks should be shut by iron gratings, since sneak thieves and the like were seldom heard of.' Its entertainments were quilting parties, candy-pullings and conversation refreshed by hickory nuts, apples, new cider, and doughnuts.... Little boys were tantalized by visions of ice cream ... at the shops of Mrs. Usher or John Contoit where pound cake, lemonade ... were also to be had. Their fathers, though whiskey was unknown and champagne rare, could obtain rum at three cents the glass and ale at two cents...." There were pretty, well-dressed women, bakeries, sleigh rides and happy parents, all in all quite a wonderful place to grow up.[47]

To Peterson, writing in 1973, in Richard Nixon's America, recently removed from the turmoil of the '60s, the old days were better in every sense. "There are ways," he wrote in a shocking passage, "in which it was better to be a slave in 1849 than it is to be a free man in 1973."[48]

A reading of contemporary newspapers tells a far different picture than the idyllic portrait painted by Peterson more than a century later. In the late 1830s, the public drinking water in Manhattan was virtually unpotable.[49] The sweet smell of flowers Peterson depicted was often overcome by the odor of raw sewage running through the streets, offal stopping up the sewers and carcasses of dead animals floating in the Hudson.[50] In fact, the area in which the Knickerbockers originally played had become badly polluted by 1845.[51]

While members of the Knickerbockers and Gothams might have lived in relative ease and comfort, the majority of New Yorkers did not. The Lower East Side, in particular, was filled with overcrowded tenements. With public sanitation largely absent, cholera and typhus epidemics swept through the city in the 1840s and 1850s.[52] Violence, lawlessness and crime, including murders and robbery, were reported frequently in the press and not very sympathetically. Alcoholics were considered responsible for their own fate, and the victims were not the drinkers but the families they abandoned, mistreated or failed to support.

White collar crime was also prevalent with embezzlements and defalcations taking place throughout the city. With banks and states issuing their own currency, counterfeiting was a thriving activity.

After the Fourth of July celebration of 1856, the *Times* reported, "Much Noise, Little Drunkenness and Few Accidents—One Man Killed and a Woman Shot." "With the exception of the above cases," the paper observed, "the day may be said to have passed off finely and pleasantly."[53] Unless, of course, you were the unfortunate man or woman. A year later, there was wide-scale rioting in the city in early July, as eight were killed and more than thirty wounded. The Army had to be summoned to restore order.[54]

At Thanksgiving 1857, the *Times* felt it necessary to point out that New York was not all rapes and murders. "As all our provisional contemporaries," it reported, "have been greatly exercised by the few sporadic cases of murder and violence which have recently taken place here, we hope they will not fail to notice, and be comforted by the fact, that yesterday, the festival of Thanksgiving was kept up here with as much rational and quiet enjoyment as in any village in New-England. There were no mobs, no murders, no fires even, nor any unusual burglaries or street rows of any kind."[55]

New York was not all senseless violence, and the city offered much in the way of pleasure. In 1858, the *Times* sent a reporter on the town to discover what New Yorkers did for fun. He discovered that they went to circuses, beer gardens, saloons, theaters, museums and "Model Artist" studios. The choice of entertainment, according to the writer, was a function of ethnicity and economic and social status. The country people were the least sophisticated and could be amused by virtually anything, including the circus, and the Model Artists studios, where they could view seductively dressed, although not, according to the writer, attractive, women. Most of the drinking establishments visited by our correspondent came in for a great deal of criticism for their filth and overall depressing atmosphere. The places he liked the best were the German beer halls for he respected the Teutonic race more than any other group he encountered on his travels.[56]

All the candy and treats described by Peterson did not make the citizens sweet and sugary, and political correctness was a foreign concept. In 1862, the *Clipper* took umbrage when the competing *Tribune* failed to provide a complete account of a visit of Philadelphia ballplayers to the city and blamed the omission on an obsession with abolitionism. The tenuous connection was explained in an article titled *Too Much Nigger*.[57] The piece appeared approximately six months before the Emancipation Proclamation, an indication that perhaps New York sportsmen were not quite ready for emancipation.

Later, the *Clipper* published a lengthy article titled *The Dark Sports in Council* in which it described a picnic and outing of "the children of Africa." The writer noted from the "motley assemblage" that miscegenation was frequent and praised the beauty of the women. "To me," the author opined, "—and I confess it freely—there is a charm in the young Creole's guileless glance which I would vainly seek in the eye of the white girl, and I think the charm consists in that beseeching expression which seems to acknowledge the superiority of the white race, to deprecate the white man's anger, and to implore his protection."

The black men did not come in for much admiration, even on such questionable grounds. After commenting on their performance at a shooting gallery, the author noted, "Such shooting as the majority displayed would have done little towards winning the battle of Gettysburg—for the North."[58] And such language did little to advance the cause of racial harmony.

Some unusual language found in contemporary journals was the result of different usage, such as the advertisement touting "Gay Books for Gay Boys,"[59] and other comments were unkind in any era. In 1854, *The Spirit of the Times* published an article titled, "Ugly as Sin," which described "the ugliest, most pitiable specimen of humanity I have ever seen. One of his legs had been amputated above the knee, his right hand was withered and contracted as if by a severe burn, his shoulder had a curious hump, and the cords of his neck were so drawn and shortened that the cheeks seemed to rest upon it, as a pillow. His eyelashes were gone, and his bloodshot eyes were continually moving uneasily with their raw and inflamed lids."[60] Other journals were more kindly disposed toward the unattractive. "It is curious to observe," the *Clipper* noted in 1862, "that an ugly face is generally the indication of a humorous and witty mind."[61]

Advertising was as tasteless and mindless in the 1850s as it was in later centuries, as evidenced by the following written during the Crimean War: "The struggle is now going on, and thousands of warriors have probably fallen on the field of battle. Where such carnage is going on, and where a man does not know that another minute may be his last, it is of little consequence what kind of hat he wears, but in a great city like New York, it is absolutely necessary in order to make a good appearance that the head be covered with one of those fine Daguerrean Hats, which can be had only at the stores of Messrs. Rafferty and Leask...."[62]

There was one topic on which discretion was absolute, no levity was permitted, and no insults tolerated—the virtue of the Caucasian American woman. While journalists might write of ugly people and too much nigger, they spoke of their women in the most exalted and, when virtue was unquestionably compromised, obtuse terms. Creole girls might be sensual and alluring, but white women were not. They did not flaunt their sexuality, and ladies were never raped or sexually assaulted; they were victims of an "outrage."

New York was clearly not the paradise on earth portrayed by Harold Peterson, but it was a dynamic, exciting metropolis, taking in immigrants (welcoming would be an inappropriate verb), expanding, and bustling with activity.

As New York underwent great changes between 1845 and 1870, so did the Knickerbockers. By 1870, when the old National Association was no more, the pioneer organization had long since faded into the background. "The Knickerbockers," wrote Ivor-Campbell, "in sharing their game with the world, doomed themselves to irrelevance."[63] The club retained its traditional structure as time passed them by, never choosing to adopt the competitive tactics of the Atlantics and Eckfords. They had withdrawn from the NA, which they had been so instrumental in forming, in 1869. The Knickerbockers' last influential stand was the club's championing of the fly rule and the abolishment of the bound rule they had established in 1845.

The Knickerbockers continued in existence until 1882 but were principally a social organization in their later years. They still played baseball, but no serious ballplayer would consider joining the Knicks. If a man were serious about the game in the 1860s, he wanted to play for the Atlantics or Eckfords. Later, he wanted to become a professional. When the Excelsiors played the Knickerbockers in 1865, the *Clipper* said, "[T]he winning of a trophy is secondary to the playing of a jolly good game together."[64]

After the late 1850s, the Knickerbockers would never again hold a position of prominence in the baseball world, nor did they seem to want to. Given their revered position in the early days of the sport, however, many kept hoping they would once again play a leading role. In 1864, the *Clipper* stated, "We are glad to learn that the old Knickerbockers aim to revive the club, and endeavor to bring it up to its former standard of excellence and to do this they have determined to [inject] young and active blood into their veins by taking in several players of note. Had they done this all along, they would not have been so much in the rear of their more enterprising brethren."[65] A month later, the disappointed journal noted, "The veteran Knickerbockers have not waked up yet apparently, for we have neither seen nor heard anything of their having commenced play or when they intend doing so. We thought they had intended to rejuvenate themselves with some young blood, but it would appear that they are still in that lethargic state that has brought them to such a low ebb as a playing club."[66]

Hope sprung eternal, and no one could believe the pioneer club was no longer a factor in baseball circles. "We expected to see the Knickerbockers revive," reported the *Clipper* in 1866, "but the old fogies still retain control of its affairs."[67] In 1868, the veterans of the Excelsiors and Knicks, captained by veterans Joe Leggett and Jim Davis, respectively, played each other in a pleasant exhibition, but rarely, from the mid–'60s on, did the club play a competitive match. The older players fumbled and bumbled about the field while the younger ones played more seriously. By 1879, there was talk that the older and younger players should meet on separate days since the poor play of the old frustrated the young, and the good play of the young embarrassed the old.[68] The Knickerbockers no longer played a meaningful role in the game of baseball, but they had done their job, propelling the sport on a course they could not have foreseen. The task of carrying on was left to others.

Chapter 5

The Base Ball Club

Major league teams of the twenty-first century are generally corporate entities that pay players to perform on behalf of the company. While the players, primarily through union representation, have gained great influence — many believe too much — over the game of baseball, they have relatively little input into the business affairs of their club. They can opt for free agency or demand a trade. They can strongly suggest that management spend more money to upgrade the team's talent. Still, their role is strictly advisory as the individuals or entities that own the clubs have the final say over the manner in which they are operated.

Today's major league teams have come a long way from the baseball clubs that existed in the mid-nineteenth century. The first organizations — the Knickerbockers, Gothams and Eagles — began in the same fashion as clubs that pursued pastimes such as riding, hunting, or debating. A number of gentlemen would decide they wanted to gather together to play the game of baseball, just as a group of present day businessmen might decide they want to play golf every Thursday after work. In the 1850s, most baseball clubs had twenty to thirty members, but as the years went on, some grew substantially. In 1866, the Athletics claimed 371 active members,[1] the Excelsiors 370,[2] the Atlantics 220,[3] and the Eckfords 150.[4] Most of the members, of course, were not active on the ball field but participated in social events and supported the first nine financially and as cheerleaders.

Although the first clubs were primarily social and recreational in purpose, rarely were they organized on an informal basis. A constitution and bylaws were almost always drafted and adopted, officers were elected, and official-looking certificates were issued to members. Such formal processes propelled baseball a giant step beyond rounders and the old cat games played by youngsters. Anything governed by a constitution and bylaws must be serious business.

Prior to the 1860 season, Henry Chadwick provided his *Clipper* readers with sample constitutions and bylaws to assist them in the formation of new clubs.[5] He furnished advice on the selection of club members, balloting processes, dues, the roles of each officer and director, the setting of meeting dates and practice days and a process for amending constitutions. Bylaws typically included detailed procedures for holding meetings and a system of fines. Chadwick recommended no fines for failure to attend practice, "experience having shown that such are almost useless, partly from the difficulty attending the collection of such small amounts, but principally from the valid excuses rendered by the absentees."[6] "The fines should be light," Chadwick advised.[7]

Clubs that followed Chadwick's advice would have come a long way from their predecessors. The Olympic Club of Philadelphia, which was organized to play town ball in 1833, adopted a formal constitution in 1837. The preamble noted that field sports were very beneficial and enjoyable for the members "when exercised with decorum and moderation."[8] The matters of decorum and moderation (and obedience) were not left to chance or individual preference. While sport and recreation were in many ways contrary to the Puritan work ethic, their practice was to be partaken of in an atmosphere almost as strict as that of organized religion. Any member who did not benefit from and enjoy their town ball in the manner prescribed by the Olympic constitution was subject to a number of fines, including those for the following offenses:

Disorderly behavior at a meeting	not more than 50 cents
Absence from roll call	12½ cents
Absence from a meeting	25 cents
Refusal to perform assigned duties	50 cents
Neglect of duty	50 cents
Absence of Club Recorder (Scorer) from roll call	12½ cents
Absence of Club Recorder from meeting	25 cents
Neglect of the roll and minute books	25 cents
Failure to have the record book in proper order	25 cents
Failure to bring the record book to meeting	25 cents
Failure of Clerk to deliver notices	6¼ cents
Improper or unauthorized use of club equipment	one dollar
Failure to take good care of club equipment	50 cents
Failure to provide a proper uniform	25 cents per month
Failure to notify secretary of change of address	12½ cents
Absence from roll call on club day	6¼ cents
Absence from club day	12½ cents
Absence from special meeting	25 cents
Leaving meeting or club day without permission	25 cents
Disorderly behavior on club day	50 cents
Appearing on club day without uniform or with unclean uniform	12½ cents
Failure of committee to report at a meeting	12½ cents
Disobeying an order of the captain	not exceeding one dollar

The constitution also contained sections on expulsion, which could be effected by the affirmative vote of two-thirds of the members present for (i) moving out of the area; (ii) missing two consecutive meetings without being excused; (iii) breach of the constitution, improper conduct or breach of duty, upon a complaint signed by three or more members, or (iv) being three months in arrears with required payments. While expulsion and fines came relatively easily, admission did not. Unanimous approval of all members was required to admit a new applicant.

An inordinate portion of the constitution, which was not all that long (fifteen articles), is devoted to fines, punishments, expulsions, and the procedures associated with each. Precious little space was reserved for the supposed object of the club, which was stated to be enjoyment. Whether the Olympics enforced their draconian dictums religiously is not evident, but the written word is clear regarding the serious weight of responsibility that came with membership in a ball club.

Other constitutions were equally strict but not always unreasonable. In addition to the acts proscribed by the Olympics, the Harlem Club felt it necessary to impose sanctions on any member who was inebriated at a club function and prohibited the use of liquor at all times when engaging in baseball activities.[9]

The Knickerbockers were enamored of sanctions. They took attendance at each play day and meeting and noted the missing. Four consecutive absences from the field drew a fifty cent fine, and eight a warning to produce an acceptable excuse or be stricken from the club rolls. There was a fine for not wearing a proper uniform while playing unless the offender provided his captain with a suitable explanation. Apparently, improper language had become more prevalent since the Olympics had established their rules, for the Knickerbockers instituted fines for the use of profanity. The pre-printed scorecards of the club had a column on the left hand side for noting fines, and one on the right titled "Remarks" which was mainly used for describing the reason for a fine. In 1847, Alex Drummond, who later became president of the club, was fined, with the notation "Hell and Damn," placed beside his name. Drummond followed a respectable tradition, for Duncan Curry, the Knickerbockers' first president, was docked for using the expression "d — — d impudence."[10] Even Alexander Cartwright was assessed a fine for disputing a decision of the umpire.

In 1860, at a monthly meeting of the Board of Officers, President Jim Davis accused Norman Welling, one of the club's most respected members, of using abusive language during a heated debate at an earlier meeting. Davis stated that he had notified Welling of his intention of making the charge and requested his presence at the meeting. Since Welling had not appeared, Davis wanted him expelled. Cooler heads prevailed, and Welling was given the opportunity to present his defense at a future meeting. He admitted using the language, but apologized and said he had not meant to offend anyone, and the matter was dropped.[11]

Fines sometimes came about unexpectedly, without warning. In 1860, David Keeler, treasurer of the Knicks, reported that several members had not paid their dues, which created a deficit in the treasury. Two of the non-payers stood up and declared they had not been called upon to pay dues. Secretary Wenman then introduced a motion, which was carried, that Keeler be fined two dollars for neglect of duty for failing to diligently collect the dues.[12]

No organization was more obsessed with parliamentary procedure than baseball's first club. The bylaws called for the annual meeting to transpire in accordance with the following agenda:

1. Roll call
2. Reading of minutes from the prior meeting
3. Reading of minutes from the Board of Officers' meeting
4. Report of Committees
5. Treasurer's Report
6. Election of Officers
7. Miscellaneous
8. Roll call and adjournment

The second roll call was important for any member who left before the end of the meeting was subject to a fine. The Knickerbockers, as did most clubs, took the bylaws seriously.[13] They debated the procedure for accepting matches with other clubs. They held spirited discussions regarding the expulsion of members for non-attendance or failure to pay dues and assessments, and they carried on interminably about virtually any topic other than the playing of baseball.

The twin obsessions of the Knickerbockers appeared to be flags and lockers. The club held numerous discussions regarding procuring a flag and staff and getting the other clubs that used the Elysian Fields to share the expense. Surprisingly, for an organization comprised of "gentlemen," the club seemed unduly concerned about the possibility of said gentlemen breaking into each other's lockers or leaving unsightly piles of dirty clothing strewn about the room. Deliberative bodies frequently refer to "housekeeping items," which the Knickerbockers took literally. In 1857, they passed a number of rules governing the maintenance of the club room and lockers, including:

1. Every member must have his apparel marked with his initials placed in his closet after exercise and keep same locked.
2. Members shall not wear the apparel of a fellow member without his permission.
3. Members shall not attempt to open the closet of a fellow member.
4. All clothes found out of place in the room will be taken care of and the owner must pay fifty cents for the redemption of each article to the keepers of the room.[14]

On several occasions, the officers reiterated their intention to rigidly enforce the rules regarding lockers, and in 1860, President Jim Davis was fined for entering the locker of a fellow Knickerbocker in the latter's absence. Davis had merely opened the locker to get a ball that was needed for the game, but he had violated the rule, and the fine stood. At the same meeting, William Grenelle reported that someone had opened his locker and left it open. The matter was referred to Director Kissam for investigation.[15]

Even in this manly sport, feelings were important. In 1856, the minutes of a prior Knickerbocker meeting were amended to eliminate the expression "Old Fogy," which was used to describe one of the members and considered too personal and offensive.[16]

Agenda Item Six for the Knickerbockers' annual meeting was the election of officers. "The officers of the club," Chadwick continued in his 1860 article, "should be men of influence with the members thereof, and such as can always be present on the occasions appointed either for meetings or for field exercise. It is not necessary that they should be good players, beyond the ability to properly represent the club on all occasions."[17]

The Knickerbockers readily found men willing to accept the positions of president, vice president and director, but often had grave difficulty filling the jobs of secretary and treasurer. On several occasions, men elected to the position of treasurer declined to serve, and another election was required. The secretary was required to perform a great deal of work and the treasurer, who was required to collect dues, pay the bills, and account for the finances, seemed to encounter an undue amount of criticism from his fellow members.

The difficulties engendered by such controversy made it essential that clubs recruit the right kind of men. "In admitting the members," Chadwick counseled, "be sure that they are persons of good habits and character. A person of a quarrelsome disposition should never be allowed to enter or remain in any ball club, as he will not only destroy the harmony that should exist in such an association, but will also deter good men from joining, who would make perhaps fine players, as well as firm supporters of the club."[18]

Chadwick further defined the type of man who should be coveted as a player. "[O]ur model ballplayer," he wrote, "is never guilty of disputing an umpire's decision, even by his mere actions, which, in many instances, are just as expressive as words; but when the decision is rendered, he retires perfectly contented, and silently acquiesces in the decision, whatever it may be.... In short, the conduct of our model player, whether he be a cricketer or base ball player, is as much marked by a courtesy of demeanor, liberality of action, and thorough good nature, as it is by a practical and theoretical knowledge of the manly game he is so partial to and proud of."[19]

Later, in 1867, Chadwick expanded upon his notion of the ideal ballplayer. "The principal rule of action of our model base ball player," he wrote, "is to comport himself like a gentleman on all occasions, but especially on match days, and in doing so, he abstains from *profanity* and its twin and evil brother obscenity, leaving these vices to be alone cultivated by graduates of our penitentiaries [or the President of the Knickerbockers]. He never takes an ungenerous advantage of his opponents ... he plays solely for the pleasure it affords him ... he never permits himself to be pecuniarily involved in a match ... he values its welfare too much to make money an object in view in playing ball."[20]

Notably, Chadwick made virtually no reference to the model player's baseball skills although in other writings he listed the attributes needed to play the various positions on the diamond. Even when the game had changed and competition was fierce, Chadwick always preferred a gentleman of modest ability to a skilled hooligan.

In addition to good character, members of baseball clubs needed to have no small degree of disposable income. The principal expenses associated with membership were dues, the cost of a uniform and the expense of the social entertainment that was such an integral part of baseball of the 1850s and 1860s.

Anyone wishing to join the Knickerbockers had to be recommended by an existing member and receive no more than one negative vote. Later, when there were other baseball clubs, if an applicant had previously been a member of another organization, the secretary inquired of that club whether the man had left in good standing. Once elected, members were formally notified and provided with a copy of the bylaws. New members were to pay a two dollar initiation fee and, initially, fifty cent monthly dues during the season.[21]

Despite the ideals espoused by Chadwick, in reality the majority of clubs drew their members from limited sources, the way in which contemporary social clubs typically populate their organizations. Most baseball clubs, other than the most talented, had a common link. The Alpine Club of New York was composed principally of members of the Jane Street Methodist Church.[22] The Phantoms were mostly saloonkeepers, the Metropolitans schoolteachers, the Manhattans policemen and the Powhatans dairy farmers.[23]

There were far more than nine players in each club for in order to hold practice games, which constituted most of the activity of early organizations, at least eighteen were needed. When matches were held between two clubs, they were played by the first nine, who were the best players, the second nine, those not good enough for the first nine, or the muffins, too unskilled to play the game seriously. "Muffins," the *Clipper* explained, "are those whose awkwardness in fielding, induced by want of outdoor exercise, makes it almost impossible for them to play ball well, and the result of a match between such individuals as those is a most amusing and interesting game."[24] Muffin matches were similar to current day beer league softball (there was often beer available during muffin matches), and newspaper accounts were written in suitably comic fashion.

When the negative aspects of championship competition manifested themselves in the early 1860s, second nine and muffin games became the embodiment of the good old days of the 1850s. They were "fun-provoking" which was what baseball was supposed to be. "[Merrill's] attempt to catch balls by that portion of his body that goes through the door last," reported the *Atlas* after a second nine match between the Henry Eckford and Manhattan Clubs, "was really very fine."[25] "Indeed," observed another reporter on a similar occasion, "a more mirth-provoking or enjoyable game of ball is seldom seen."[26]

Muffin matches were, for some, a welcome relief from the gambling and ruffianism that pervaded the activity of the top clubs. "[B]all matches of late years," lamented Chadwick, "got to be quite serious affairs, and some have even intimated that ball playing has become quite a money making business, many finding it to pay well to play ball." By the mid–'60s, politicians had also become interested in baseball, and that could come to no good end. "All these things," Chadwick concluded, "have a direct tendency to retard the progress of the game and work against its best interests."[27]

The muffin matches, of course, had none of these troubling issues, and therefore represented the good that remained in the game. "Who can remember," the journalist continued, "the grand muffin match, Putnam vs. Excelsior, that took place on the Putnam grounds a few years ago without enjoying a good hearty laugh? ... Why cannot the Atlantic and Eckford muffins come together again?"[28]

"Where are the Eckford muffins?" Chadwick asked a day later, "and also those of the Excelsiors and Stars. Bring out your teams, gentlemen, and let those first nine fellows see how ball matches should be played."[29] As the 1864 season wound down, Chadwick became particularly enamored of muffin contests and stated his strong preference to them over the sordid championship games. Few others wanted to see the Atlantic and Eckford muffins, however. They preferred watching those sordid affairs in which the talented first nines played for the championship.

Clubs needed the men who played on the second and muffin nines for no one played ball as a profession, and the demands of business generally prevented one or more of the first nine from showing up for a match. It was not uncommon for four or five to be absent. If second nine players were on hand, they took the place of the missing men, and if no one were available, teams sometimes played short-handed or waited for late arrivals before agreeing to start play. "The Stars are lucky in having such a good second nine," observed the *Eagle*, "as they seem to find it necessary to play their first nine matches with them."[30]

Sometimes substitutes were members of the short-handed club, but occasionally they were recruited from those on hand to watch the game. If a star player was not present when the first pitch was thrown, but was believed to be in transit, the club often played short-handed and awaited his arrival for if a replacement were put in the field, the late arriving member of the first nine had to stay on the sidelines as no substitutions were allowed except for injury.

There were numerous occasions on which a club played with eight, seven or even fewer players. This led to mismatches and disappointed spectators although some clubs were able to compete quite well short-handed. In 1862, the Stars played the Resolutes with six men at first, then seven, but lost by the respectable margin of 35–27.[31] As always, Chadwick had a suggestion. "If you cannot get your old nine out," he said, "organize a new one. If the regular first nine won't attend to their duties replace them with those who will. Don't hesitate to cross every player off your nine that won't attend on practice days — any other course is unfair to those who are prompt in their attendance and ambitious of promotion."[32]

Games with other clubs were typically arranged by means of formal written challenges which sometimes led to unforeseen problems. On November 4, 1861, the captain of the Hamilton Club wrote a letter to the *Eagle* stating that although he had read in the paper that his club was to play the Star nine, he knew nothing of it and asked the paper to retract the story. The following day, the captain of the Stars replied that the match had been arranged and the Hamilton Club was to have given three days notice if they would be unable to play. Since no notice had been received, the Stars assumed the game was on.

Two days later the Hamilton Club responded, stating that several dates had been discussed, and the Hamilton Club was to have given three days notice if they *were* able to play. The Stars had done him an injustice by impugning his integrity, Captain Davenport fumed, for the "Hamilton Club never were or ever will be afraid to come up to the scratch against any club, and take their chances win or lose."[33]

In addition to the date of the game, there was a disagreement (or misunderstanding, depending upon whose version is accepted) about the location. The Stars showed up at the Hamilton's grounds on several occasions ready to play, only to find the opposition absent. The game finally took place on the Star grounds on November 8, with the Stars prevailing, 29–16.[34]

The previous year, the Lone Stars (not to be confused with the Stars) arrived at the grounds at 81st Street and 2nd Avenue, as arranged, to meet the Champion Club. The Champions were, however, at Hamilton Square, 17 blocks away. The Lone Stars made the trek to the Square and, foot weary and miffed, lost.[35] In 1863, the Stars were involved in another scheduling snafu. On August 26, the Empire Club showed up for a game, but the Stars, who apparently could not gather their first nine together for the occasion, did not.[36]

Clubs came in two varieties, senior and junior, the latter of which were generally composed of members 21 years of age or younger. Some junior clubs were composed of players much younger than 21, including the Little Zephyrs of 1858, whose members ranged from 11 to 18 years of age.[37] Other clubs had no members older than 14.[38] The first noteworthy junior club organized in Brooklyn was the Stars, who first appeared in 1856. The juniors played for their own championship and sometimes held all-star games among the best players. They emulated the seniors in their muddled idea of a championship, which led to continual disputes as to which club was superior.

Chadwick, when not touting the muffins, was perhaps the biggest champion of the junior clubs, repeatedly urging the senior organizations to give them equipment and encourage them for, as he pointed out, the future of the senior clubs lay in the grooming of young players to take the place of retiring veterans. "[U]nless we have plenty of junior clubs in our midst," he wrote, "we may look in vain for a perpetuity of the game of ball, for unless ball play is learnt in early life, no great degree of skill can ever by acquired at it."[39]

It would cost, Chadwick estimated, no more than five dollars for a senior organization to supply equipment to a junior nine. He beat Branch Rickey by more than half a century in espousing the control of young players by the top clubs. Chadwick hinted that financial support of the juniors would lead to the most talented young players joining their benefactors when they became older. He urged the Atlantics, Mutuals, Eckfords and all the other top teams to have their own junior organization from which to draw talent. The Atlantics had, in fact, such an arrangement with the Enterprise Club, but it was less formal than that advocated by Chadwick.[40]

Junior clubs were not allowed to join the National Association, but by 1861, there were enough of them to warrant a convention and the formation of the National Association of Junior Base Ball Players. The initial meeting of the junior association was held on January 9 at a building on the corner of Court and Jorolemon Streets in Brooklyn. Sixteen clubs paid their dues and were admitted, committees were established and manned and the playing rules of the senior association were adopted. Rules governing the championship were also set forth. Any club that won the title two years in succession was to be recommended for membership in the senior Association.[41] In succeeding years, many junior clubs converted to senior status as their players aged, regardless of whether they were champions.

The junior association was never able to generate a great deal of enthusiasm, perhaps much to the credit of the youngsters, who were more interested in playing baseball than forming associations and drafting bylaws in the fashion of their older brethren. As it had with senior clubs, the Civil War led to a decline in activity among the juniors. Just ten clubs sent delegates to the April 1862 convention.[42] At the March 1863 meeting, only seven clubs were represented and, the following May, just nine clubs showed up. By the late summer of 1864, however, there was a great deal of activity among junior players, even more than during "the palmy days of 1860."[43]

After generating a constitution and bylaws, making certain the men they admitted were gentlemen, and planning and financing a host of social activities, club members faced the weighty issue of choosing a name.[44] Chadwick's advice in this matter was to select a name that reflected the club's locale and noted, "Care should be taken to avoid if possible the selection of a name already adopted."[45] His latter instruction was roundly ignored. A correspondent to *Porter's Spirit of the Times* pointed out in 1858 that a number of clubs chose their names without realizing another club had already taken it.[46]

"Excelsior" was the motto of the State of New York, and a very popular name for baseball clubs. There were the famous Excelsiors of Brooklyn, of course, and other, less famous, groups of Excelsiors from New York City, Fort Hamilton, New Utrecht, Philadelphia, Baltimore, and Bloomfield, New Jersey. There were Excelsiors in New Haven, Connecticut, Chicago, Illinois and California, none of whose states had the motto Excelsior. There was even an Excelsior Club in Canada. In all, according to one historian, there were at least 23 Excelsior Clubs composed of white players and one made up of black players.[47] There was an Eckford Club in Albany and there were Atlantics in Chicago. There were Athletics in Newark as well as Philadelphia and Knickerbockers in Albany.

The identical names sometimes led to confusion, such as when the Hamilton Club of Jersey City played the Hamilton Club of Brooklyn. In 1864, the Clinton Club challenged the right of any other nine to use its name, claiming its members had investigated prior to forming and found no other club named Clinton. When a second Clinton organization turned up, the battle was joined, and not on the playing field.[48]

The Atlantics were named after one of the most prominent streets in Brooklyn as was the Rutledge Club. The Putnam and Clinton Clubs were also named after streets. There was a club named after the *Clipper;* in fact, there was an organization known as the Frank Queen Club, in honor of the *Clipper's* publisher. Clubs were often named after famous people, as in the case of the Joe Leggett Club of Cohoes, New York. Leggett, the catcher and captain of the Excelsiors of Brooklyn, was so honored by the use of his name that he sent the club a banner to be flown at their games.[49] The Henry Eckford Club and the plain Eckfords were named after a Brooklyn shipbuilder. Mort Rogers of the Resolutes had a junior club in Brooklyn named for him. There were two Ellsworth Clubs, which took their name from the first Union hero of the Civil War, Colonel Elmer E. Ellsworth. There was a Jefferson Club, a Hamilton Club, a Madison Club, a Franklin Club, a McClellan Club, a Garibaldi Club for international historians and, seemingly out of place in such exalted company, a Burnside Club. There was even a club bearing the unlikely handle of Benicia Boy for the champion American fighter John Heenan, and a Young Heenan Club. The former had been known as the Manhattan Club but decided to change their name to Benicia Boy following Heenan's fabled bout with Tom Sayers in April 1860.[50] After the Boy's loss to Tom King in 1864, the club reorganized under the name Pacific.[51]

Other names were more descriptive, such as Free and Easy, Blow-Pipe, Jr., Will Try, Fear Naught, Wild Wave, Wild Rover, Freethinking, Invisible and two clubs with opposing names, the Rip Van Winkle Club and the Wide Awake. Some names were patriotic, such as Young America and Union, while others appealed to the academic, such as *Semper Paratus*. Some were less than manly, such as Cinderella and Katy-did. A modest aggregation called themselves the Muffins.

The name of a club was not cast in stone. The Excelsiors of Brooklyn had begun their existence as the Jolly Bachelors Club, and we might have seen a proliferation of Jolly Bachelors Clubs had they not adopted their permanent moniker. The Rough and Ready Club, perhaps believing they were no longer one or the other, voted in 1859 to change its name to the Chelsea Base Ball Club.[52] The above mentioned Muffins, after defeating a club named Superior, decided they were muffins no more and changed their name to the J.C. Brevoort Base Ball Club of Bedford.[53]

Once a club had members, a constitution, bylaws, a healthy array of fines, equipment, and a name, it needed uniforms, a place to meet and a place to play. The Olympics, who played town ball in Philadelphia, had uniforms, consisting of dark blue pants, white shirts trimmed in scarlet, and a white cap with blue trim, as early as the 1830s.[54] When men first began playing ball in New York in the 1840s, however, there was no thought that they needed uniforms. They simply rolled up their sleeves and went at it. The development of baseball clubs, however, often paralleled that of fire companies, and fire companies wore uniforms. In 1849, the Knickerbockers adopted a uniform that did not, remarkably, include knickers. It consisted of blue woolen pantaloons, plain white flannel shirts and straw boaters.[55] An emblem on the shirt to identify a team would come later. Knickers and long socks were not worn until the mid–1860s when Harry Wright had them designed for his Cincinnati Red Stockings. Numbers were more than a half century away. The Knicks were, of course, subject to a fine if they did not wear the proper uniform.

The Knickerbockers made changes to their uniform over the years and, with their typical attention to detail and procedure, formed committees on caps, belts and other articles of clothing. The committees discussed styles and prices and dutifully reported to the members on their recommendations. In 1860, the club ordered belts for all at a cost of $49.45.[56] Caps were procured at $1.25 each.[57]

Uniforms came in a variety of colors and shapes but generally consisted of long pants, a shirt with (by the 1860s) an emblem across the breast and a cap. "Dark blue pants, and white flannel shirts trimmed in blue, are the most appropriate," advised *Wilkes*.[58] That was the uniform of the famed Excelsior[59] and Enterprise Clubs.[60] The Zouave Club of Brooklyn wore the colorful costume of the Zouave soldier with bright red billowing pants, a loose flannel jacket and a skating cap. *Wilkes'* noted that a number of the players were skilled gymnasts, which one imagines they must have had to be in order to play effectively in such attire.[61] While some clubs had less than manly-sounding names, others wore less than manly uniforms. The Charter Oak Club sported pink shirts and white pants with pink stripes.[62]

The Atlantics wore light blue trousers, a white flannel shirt with ABBC across the breast, and red and white caps.[63] In 1864 the Mutuals trotted out new white uniforms, which the *Clipper* thought would become too easily soiled. The pants should be dark, it advised.[64] The Continental Club committed the fashion *faux pas* of appearing in black pants and brown shirts.[65] As might be expected, the New Orleans players were snappy dressers. The Empire Club of that city sported blue jockey caps, white flannel shirts trimmed with black, white flannel pants trimmed in blue and black belts engraved with the club initials.[66]

Not all clubs were fastidious in their dress. Many junior clubs had no uniforms at all and played in street clothes.[67] In 1864, *Wilkes'* scolded New York and Brooklyn clubs for their careless attire. "We have observed," they wrote, "for a season or two past, that our ball-clubs have grown negligent in regard to their appearance in uniform, both in matches as well as in practice games."[68] *Wilkes'* made a valid point for not all players wore the team uniform, and some appeared in parts of them, wearing perhaps a club shirt with their own trousers. The Atlantics and Stars were cited as particularly egregious offenders against good fashion taste. By June, the Atlantics appeared in attractive new uniforms which passed *Wilkes'* stringent inspection. "[T]heir new caps are especially tasty and becoming," the journal noted approvingly.[69]

What caused the Atlantics' reversal? "We would simply ask the Atlantics," said the *Eagle*, "what it is that has led to this change? Surely it cannot be anything that has appeared in the papers, for what do they care what the papers say? It is a little singular, however, that these improvements should follow so closely upon the heels of certain suggestions which have emanated from a source they profess to regard with indifference."[70]

With the parliamentary tasks facing the top baseball clubs, each needed a meeting room. The Mutuals and Actives met at The Study, a Hudson Street saloon. The Knickerbocker club room was at a hotel near the Elysian Fields, but most of their meetings were held at Fijux's Hotel, 42 Murray Street in New York. The Excelsiors had a clubhouse on their Court Street ground.[71] In their early years, the Atlantics met at Willoughby's Shades, a tavern at which they maintained a collection of balls from their victories. They later moved to a saloon owned by club member Mike Henry.[72]

Virtually all clubs had their own grounds upon which they practiced and played interclub matches. As always, Chadwick provided helpful suggestions in the area of field selection. The ideal size for a ball ground, he recommended, was six hundred by four hundred feet, with at least seventy feet behind home plate. The ground behind the plate, he advised, should be cleared and tamped down to create a firm surface for the catcher. Ideally, the field should be rolled, particularly if new turf had been put down, to avoid irregular bounces, and it should be sprinkled to keep down the dust.[73]

The Knickerbockers first played, in 1842 and 1843, at 27th Street and 4th Avenue,[74] and later on a site near Murray Hill in Manhattan. The rapid development of the city soon drove them across the Hudson to the Elysian Fields, located in Hoboken, on a site now bounded by 10th and 11th, Hudson and Washington Streets.[75] Elysian Fields was a beautiful site, surrounded

The Hudson River Club played the Elmira nine on the former's field in Newburgh, New York, in 1865. The game was nothing special, except that it was the subject of the oldest known photograph of a baseball game in progress. The site is typical of the era, as a limited number of fans sat in the grandstands, while the remainder ringed the field or sat in carriages parked deep in the outfield. Generally, balls bouncing around the carriages remained in play.

on three sides by woods, a bucolic setting just minutes from the bustle of New York City. The fields were accessible by ferry, followed by a short hike (about a mile) up the footpaths which ascended the hill alongside the river.[76]

Many years before the grounds came into use for baseball, proprietor Colonel John Stevens established the first ferry service from New York to Hoboken, with boats regularly crossing the river from 1823 onward. By the 1830s, the ferries were carrying 20,000 passengers a day during the peak summer season. The Stevens family also ran ferries to Philadelphia and in 1832 built the Camden and Amboy Railroad, one of the nation's first rail lines. Although Stevens did not always charge for use of his facility for baseball, he was well-compensated by the ferry fares the players and their friends expended to reach Hoboken.

The Elysian Fields were much more than just a baseball park.[77] In addition to baseball and cricket grounds, there were picnic facilities, a deer park, a trotting course, a platform for fishing in the Hudson, and Otto Cottage Garden, a favorite of the German contingent. The Stevens family was active in yachting, and the New York Yacht Club built its clubhouse, the first such facility in the United States, on the grounds. Perry's Hotel was frequently visited by the players for nourishment after the games, and a number of organizations built clubhouses on the site.

The Hoboken park was the product of the vision, technical skill, and vivid imagination of Colonel Stevens, who had been a member of the Continental Congress and was a wealthy man who owned an estimated 35,000 acres in New York and New Jersey. In 1784, he acquired the 689-acre Hoboken parcel, which had been seized from loyalist William Bayard by the State of New Jersey during the Revolution. Stevens eventually expanded his holdings to give him a mile of Hudson shoreline and a monopoly on the ferry trade. In 1787 he completed construction of his elegant home, overlooking the Hudson, which was called Castle Point. Then Stevens began to execute his plan for a magnificent recreational facility that would give New Yorkers a reason to take his ferry across the river and perhaps purchase one of his 800 lots.[78]

The first phase of the new park was the River Walk, a scenic, beautifully-landscaped trail that opened in 1810. To finance the remaining improvements, Stevens, even in that era of libertarian self-sufficiency, sought government funding. After all, he was creating a public facility to be enjoyed by all, and the city dwellers' exposure to fresh air and nature would surely bring an improvement in public health. His request was denied, and the project continued on with private capital.

Stevens built a number of interesting attractions at the Elysian Fields, including a merry-go-round, a ferris wheel, and a "whirligig." The latter was similar to a current-day amusement park ride in which, for twenty-five cents, visitors could sit inside a basket which spun around on a sixty foot radius. In 1825, Stevens built a railroad with a track 200 feet in diameter, which carried patrons at the breakneck speed of six miles per hour. He also constructed a ride called "Aerial Ways," which appears to have been an early form of roller coaster. Stevens staged events such as hot-air balloon ascensions, boat races, boxing matches, and concerts which, in combination with the rides, caused authors James DiClerico and Barry Pavalec to refer to the Elysian Fields as the "Disneyland of its day."[79] In 1843, thirty thousand spectators attended a buffalo hunt orchestrated by P.T. Barnum, which proved quite profitable but a tremendous disappointment to the crowd when the animals turned out to be twenty young calves rather than the large plains buffalo they had expected.

The natural beauty of the site and the unique mechanical attractions drew a number of famous visitors, including Charles Dickens, Edgar Allan Poe (who based his story "The Mystery of Marie Roget" on an event that occurred at the Elysian Fields), Martin Van Buren, Daniel Webster and Washington Irving. John Jacob Astor constructed a villa in Hoboken in 1829.

In 1852, just six years after the historic game between the Knickerbockers and New York Club took place, there was a deplorable, most un–Disney-like incident at the Elysian Fields. A number of Germans were celebrating a holiday with a variety of athletic games when a New York gang known as the "Short Boys" appeared. One of the Short Boys stole a cigar, which precipitated a riot during which one of the Germans was shot dead. The fracas spread to the streets of Hoboken, and in the subsequent brawling, another man was killed.[80] Seven years later, death again visited the Elysian Fields. In 1859, while crossing the Hudson to watch the cricket matches of the All England Eleven, a young woman named Theresa Schultz fell out of a boat and was drowned.[81]

By the time baseball came to the Elysian Fields, the famous park had passed its prime, and was first under the management of the colonel's son, John Stevens III and, from 1856, John's brother Edwin. The site eventually became the most active and popular ball-playing facility in the New York area. In 1855, the Knicks played on Mondays and Thursdays, the Eagles on Tuesdays and Fridays and the Empires Wednesdays and Saturdays.[82] By 1860, there were eight baseball clubs that called it home: the Knickerbockers, Gothams, Eagles, Empires,

Mutuals, St. Nicholas, Jeffersons and Alpines, plus the St. George Cricket Club. There were often a number of games taking place simultaneously, which allowed spectators to wander from one to the other. There were no seats until 1862 when three rows of benches were placed behind the catcher's position on one of the fields, so spectators stood or sat on the ground.[83] The fact that the fields were not enclosed and no admission fee could therefore be charged eventually made them obsolete from the standpoints of both revenue generation and crowd control. By the mid–'60s, most of the important games took place at the Union Grounds and Capitoline Grounds, both located in Brooklyn although the Knickerbockers played at Elysian through 1871.[84] Today, the grounds are the site of the Stevens Institute of Technology.

There were a number of fields of varying quality throughout New York and Brooklyn, as set forth in Appendix C. The Red House Grounds in Harlem were a popular site, as were the famous Excelsior Grounds at "the foot of Court Street" in Brooklyn. When the Excelsiors were organized, they first played on a field at the corner of Smith and DeGraw Streets in South Brooklyn, moving to a ground near Carroll Park, bounded by Smith, Carroll, Hoyt and President Streets, in 1858. The following season, they acquired use of the grounds on Court Street.[85]

In 1862, the famed Excelsior ground was the site of a brutal stabbing. Two women, Bridget Conway and Johanna Ryan, both of whom resided in the vicinity, became embroiled in a bitter dispute over whose cows should be allowed to graze on the field upon which Captain Joe Leggett and his nine had played many memorable contests. Mrs. Conway stabbed her rival in the face and neck in a scene not in character with the fair play Leggett insisted upon from his men.[86]

Some facilities were not up to the standards established by Chadwick. The outfield at the Atlantics' ground in Bedford was uneven.[87] The field on which the Nassaus of Princeton played was a series of undulating waves. First base was uphill from home plate, second base downhill from first, and from second it was uphill all the way to home. Right field was on a hill.[88] The outfield of the Manhattans' grounds was sadly uneven.[89] The playing field of the Charter Oak Club was very narrow, and hits to right or left field often landed among the crowd.[90]

The most prominent recreation area in Manhattan, Central Park, was off limits to baseball players. The initial plans submitted for the Park in 1857 included a cricket ground "for the encouragement of and indulgence in athletic and manly sports."[91] At first, the baseball fraternity was outraged at its exclusion, then decided that the "manly sports" might include baseball. The January 1857 convention of baseball clubs appointed a committee to petition the city for a separate plot dedicated to baseball and was confident of success.[92]

On several occasions, clubs attempted to obtain use of the spacious facility, but they were never successful. In December 1858, the commissioners referred their request to set aside a plot in the eastern portion of the park for baseball to a special committee where it died.[93] In many ways, Central Park was similar to the Elysian Fields in that there were a number of activities taking place at any point in time of which baseball would be just one. Prior to the 1863 season, *Wilkes'* again urged the city to permit ball playing at the facility.[94] In 1864, the National Association formed a committee for the express purpose of attempting to get the city to allow clubs to play in the Park. Like previous attempts, this one was unsuccessful.[95]

As baseball matured, playing fields in Manhattan became increasingly scarce as a building boom absorbed much of the vacant space formerly available for ball playing. By 1863, the only significant field in the borough was that at 63rd Street and 3rd Avenue.[96] With limited open space available, it became necessary for the most active clubs to procure the use of an enclosed ground.

At the same time the real estate boom reduced the available playing fields in Manhattan, Brooklyn had problems of its own due not to the war-induced economic boom but to the conflict itself. In August 1863, the Star Club lost the use of its field, which was used as an encampment by the 110th Ohio Regiment.[97]

Once it had engaged a field, each club established its "play days," which were the staple of its activity. Practice generally took place two or three times per week, sometimes in the wee hours of the morning, as early as 5 A.M. Although first nines played a limited number of games by modern standards, second nines and muffins augmented the first nine's activities, and the first nine players were usually on hand to lend support, and in the case of the muffin games, to assist in the consumption of the beer than generally flowed on the sideline. In 1864, the *Eagle* noted when announcing an upcoming muffin match, "We need not inform our readers that the first nines of the two clubs will be among the spectators, and that a full delegation of reporters will be on hand, because both parties are always on hand on these occasions, not of course to partake in the lager and supper part of the proceedings — the idea of such a thing — but simply to give an account of these important games."[98]

By the mid-1860s, the most successful baseball clubs, measured by their victories on the playing field, were beginning to look more like the professional franchises they would eventually become. Second nine and muffin matches would soon become a relic of the past, and players who were not on the first nine, or who substituted for members of the first nine in their absence, slipped into the roles of financial supporters and cheerleaders, plus serving as critics when the first nine played poorly. By the 1870s, the term first nine would rarely be used. By then, most top baseball clubs, especially those who belonged to the professional National Association, were stock organizations, supported by contributions from the stockholders or members. Eventually, of course, professional ballclubs became corporations or partnerships, whose profits or losses accrued to the owners. There were no more Peter O'Briens or Joe Leggetts, star players who also participated in managing a team's affairs. The only task of the players was to play. The club era was over.

Chapter 6

The Transition Years, 1857–1859

Through the 1856 season, baseball had been dominated (although the word may be inappropriate in such a non-competitive environment) by gentlemanly organizations such as the Knickerbockers, Gothams and Eagles. It was not their success on the field that placed these clubs in the vanguard. Their influence over the rules, their relatively long experience with the game and the personal character of their officers and members caused the few other clubs to look to them for leadership. Doc Adams of the Knickerbockers, P.J. Cozans of the Eagles and Judge Van Cott of the Gothams were highly respected men who played significant roles in baseball's early years.

From 1857 through 1859, a new elite emerged, a group very different from the Knickerbockers, Gothams and Eagles. In 1854, the Eckfords were organized, followed by the Atlantics in 1855 and the Mutuals in 1857. The first two clubs were based in Brooklyn, the Atlantics from the Bedford section of the city, while the Mutuals, organized in New York, played at Hoboken. Over the next decade, these three clubs would be the best in the New York area and, for most of that period, the Atlantics were the best of the three. For one shining season, the Excelsiors of Brooklyn stood atop the baseball world, but through 1870, the Atlantics were the strongest team in the United States, holding the mythical national championship more than any other team in the baseball universe, which during that period meant New York.

Formed in the late summer of 1855 in the back room of a Brooklyn saloon[1] with the assistance of some of Brooklyn's Democratic politicians,[2] the Atlantics played two games that season and four the next without losing a single match. None of the teams they defeated, however, was formidable, two of the Atlantic wins being over the Baltic Club, which lost all five of its 1856 matches, two against the Harmony Club and two at the expense of the Columbia Club.

The Atlantics' first game was hardly a masterpiece, taking two hours to play the three innings that were needed for the Brooklyn club to score more than the 21 runs required to win, an indication of sloppy play and unskilled pitching. Their opponent, the Harmony Club, despite having some talented players, was not a good team. In 1856, following a Harmony-Continental match, the *Brooklyn Daily Times* noted of the nine, "The play was nothing to brag of on either side."[3] After the Harmony's game with the Continental Club the following season, the *Eagle* commented, "The play was miserably poor, neither party being entitled to be called good players.... They all require a good deal of practice before again attempting to play a match."[4]

The box score for the Atlantics' first game contained the names of a number of players who would star with the club over the next several years, but not all of them played for the Atlantics in that game.[5]

Atlantics	Pos.	Runs	HL	Harmony	Pos.	Runs	HL
Caleb Sniffen	p	2	2	G. Phelps	p	4	0
W. Whitson	c	3	1	L. Bergen	c	3	1
T. Powers	1b	4	0	F. R. Boerum	1b	3	1
Tice Hamilton	2b	2	2	J. Ireland	2b	3	1
L. Loper	3b	3	1	J. Price	3b	3	1
W. Babcock	ss	3	1	N.W. Robbins	ss	2	1
W. Bliss	lf	2	2	McKoy	lf	2	2
John Holder	cf	3	0	Jacob Sayles	cf	1	0
A. Gildersleeve	rf	2	0	P. Beckman	rf	1	2
Total		24	9			22	9

By 1857, Bergen, Price, and Folkert Rapeleye Boerum of the Harmony Club were regulars with the Atlantics, and the strengthened club was ready to test its mettle against top flight nines like the Eckford, Gotham and Putnam.[6]

Baseball commenced in leisurely fashion in the 1850s as clubs began to appear gradually during the uncertain weather of spring. The season unfolded in a very informal manner, the sport had not evolved to the point where the schedule was set in advance; that would not occur for another twenty years. Opening Day was typically in mid–April after the grounds thawed from the winter frost and dried up from the March mud. Opening Day didn't involve two opposing teams; it was the first practice for an individual club. The ball was thrown and batted around and, if there were enough members on hand, they might divide into teams of varying numbers and play a few innings. For several weeks or maybe a couple of months, clubs repeated the routine, dutifully appearing on the field for their practice days and a couple of hours of batting, fielding and throwing.

Matches between clubs began in May or June after club secretaries issued and accepted written challenges. When the Knickerbockers, Gothams and Eagles began to play against each other, they sent "invitations," for victory was a secondary consideration. By the late '50s, invitations had evolved into "challenges." Sometimes challenges were accepted quickly; other times it took months to receive a reply. If one or two key players were unavailable, matches were delayed or postponed.

While the season began much later than it does today, it also ended much later. Once the players finally got started, they didn't want to stop. The traditional end of the season was Thanksgiving Day when a number of social, non-competitive games were usually played. If the weather was mild, teams sometimes played into early December.

In 1857, when the commencement of games between rival clubs materialized slowly, the *Clipper* became anxious. "Through some untoward circumstances," it reported the first week in June, "our friends of the Base Ball Clubs of this vicinity seem rather backward in coming forward this season, as no regular match has yet been played, while our cricketing friends, on the other hand, are up and doing."[7]

The games finally began on June 8 when the Eagles and Knickerbockers met at the

Elysian Fields. The Atlantics dawdled about until July 24. In 1856, the Brooklyn club had issued a challenge to the Putnams, which the latter had not accepted. The following summer, the older club took up the challenge, and went down to a 19–3 defeat, one of the first significant victories for the Atlantics.

A month went by before the Atlantics took the field again, beating the Continental Club, 37–21. The Brooklyn nine won six more games before the season ended, losing only to the Gothams, 24–19, in their final match of the season on October 30. Although the Atlantics were a relatively new club, their reputation was such that, for the Gotham match, the Elysian Fields were so crowded with spectators that people nearly encroached on the playing field. The venerable Gothams, who lost, 41–11, to the Atlantics earlier in the season, got off to a 20–6 lead and barely held off their opponents from Brooklyn. Although they lost, the earlier victories over the Gotham, Putnam and Eckford Clubs were a portent that the Atlantics would be heard from again.

Two of the best players on the Atlantic nine were full-bearded outfielder Peter O'Brien, one of the club's batting stalwarts, and brother Matty, the pitcher. Peter was a slow-moving but hard-hitting outfielder who stroked many a home run and, although awkward and jerky in his movements, could also play the infield capably. He was known for his fine character and was one of the most respected ballplayers in the fraternity. "No man who plays ball,"

wrote one journalist upon O'Brien's retirement, "commands more of the general respect and regard of the members of the metropolitan clubs."[8] Like many of the players of the '50s, O'Brien was an officer of his club for many years and active in its management.

Although they had some very good players, the 1857 Atlantics had only one who would remain through the championship years of the mid-'60s. He was 21-year-old shortstop Dickie Pearce, who had joined the club the previous season. Standing just 5' 3½", Pearce weighed in at a stocky 161 pounds. Despite his bulk and consequent lack of speed, he was quick and a master of place-hitting.[9] Pearce was, according to his own account and that of Henry Chadwick, the first to employ the fair-foul hit.[10] He was also believed by some to have originated the bunt.[11]

While Doc Adams may have "invented" the shortstop position, it was Pearce who converted it from its relatively unimportant role of relaying throws to that of the most critical post in the infield. The little shortstop was well versed in the strategic points of the game, which endeared him to Chadwick, who always favored

Peter O'Brien was a long-time member of the Atlantics who played the outfield and the infield and was also active in the management of the club. He was a powerful hitter whose strong baritone voice could often be heard at postgame dinners of his club. O'Brien died tragically in 1874 when a gun he was cleaning discharged accidentally.

"scientific" players, as opposed to those who relied upon physical strength. In addition to starring at shortstop, Pearce was a skilled catcher, reportedly the first to give signals to pitchers. Since it was rare in the 1860s to throw anything but a straight pitch, Pearce's signals consisted of the intended location of the pitch.[12]

Pearce was in the early stages of a very lengthy career, the major league portion of which ended in 1877 at the age of 41 with the St. Louis Brown Stockings of the National League. He continued to play with a number of clubs after his big league tenure was over, finishing his active career as player-manager with the Quincy Club of the Northwestern League in 1884, at the age of 48. He also served as a National League umpire in 1878 and 1882, and in 1890 he was the groundskeeper for the New York Club of the Players' League.[13]

While the O'Briens were almost universally admired for their good humor and sterling reputations, Pearce was more controversial. He was known for displays of temper on the field and language that was not at all gentlemanly. Pearce was not the only Atlantic whose behavior did not meet the Knickerbocker standard of decorum. On the rare occasions when things went badly, the Brooklyn club often yelled at each other, as opposed to excusing teammates' errors as did clubs like the Knickerbockers and Gothams. In 1860, the *Clipper* censured Atlantic Johnny Oliver when he berated teammate Matt O'Brien for allowing a Star runner to steal against him. "Whatever loose play there may be in a match," the journal cautioned, "never allow the tongue to get loose...."[14] Sometimes, the Atlantic players even questioned the decision of the umpire, an unpardonable affront.

Such behavior was not a complete surprise for the Atlantics were not just better than most clubs; they were a bit different. Their members were chosen for ability rather than social class, and most were not "gentlemen"; they were workingmen. *Porter's* remarked after an Atlantic-Excelsior match on a chilly November day in 1858, "A majority of the members of the Excelsior club, being involved in mercantile pursuits, are not as fully prepared to withstand the severity of the weather when playing ball as the more hardy campers of the Atlantics, whose avocations necessarily oblige them to be weatherproof."[15]

Gentlemen were gradually becoming less desirable as baseball players. "Both clubs (the Independent and Stuyvesants)" reported the *Atlas* in 1860, "are composed principally

Dickie Pearce joined the Atlantics in 1856 and was with the club through 1870. He played in the major leagues until he was 41 and in the minor leagues at the age of 48. Pearce was a 5'3½" shortstop who pioneered the fair-foul hit and was credited by some with inventing the bunt.

of professional gentlemen, merchants, clerks &c., and are not considered strong in that kind of muscle that is generally thought to be necessary for first class ballplayers."[16]

When gentlemen departed, bad behavior often arrived. In 1858, the Niagara Club refused to play the North Stars, who allegedly arrived at the Niagaras' grounds in ill humor, stating, "If we cannot whip you with bats and ball, we can with fists."[17] This was a far cry from the jolly old Knickerbockers where the phrase, "Well struck, sir," was used to describe an opponent's good hit, not a roundhouse right to the jaw.

While there was more activity in 1857 than in any previous year, inter-club matches remained relatively rare. The Knickerbockers, never robust campaigners, played only four games, winning two. No team, in fact, played more than ten games. One of the reasons teams didn't play many games was because each was a major event. Before a match could take place, written challenges had to be issued and accepted, and the choice of grounds and time agreed upon. In addition to planning the game, club members (often a committee formed for the purpose) had to arrange for the entertainment that was such a vital element of 1850s baseball. The first mention of baseball in the *New York Times*, in fact, described the dinner at Fijux's in December 1854, rather than any on-field action.[18]

As soon as the final hand had been lost, the ceremony began, first with the post-game cheer. Cheers were a very important part of the gentlemanly ritual.[19] Win or lose, each club "huzzahed" the other and usually the umpire, if he had been impartial and gentlemanly, even if he made a few errors of judgment. In the proper antebellum era, it was important not just to salute one's opponents but to do so in an appropriate and sincere fashion.

"The last man of the Eagles had barely dropped his bat," reported the *Clipper* after an 1858 game, which the Eagles lost badly to the Excelsiors, "when we were perfectly electrified by some tremendous cheering by the two parties, which we were pleased to observe was not done in an exultant manner by the victors, nor in a dogged one by the defeated, but in a congratulating and jovial spirit, which invariably indicates the gentleman, and gives evidence that our friends of the base-ball fraternity are possessors of noble and generous dispositions. And know as well how to bear defeat, as how to wear the laurels of victory."[20]

"There was one thing very creditable to the Hoboken Club," the *Clipper* stated on another occasion, "and that was the manly way in which they bore their defeat, but they were beaten by gentlemen in every respect, and hence half the sting of defeat is removed."[21] Vince Lombardi was supposed to have said, "Show me a good loser and I'll show you a loser." His Packers didn't give a hearty three cheers to the winners. In the 1850s, they said, "Show me a good loser and I'll show you a true gentleman."

To fail to cheer one's opponents was an unforgivable outrage. As early as 1858, a time all later remembered as featuring the epitome of gentlemanly behavior, the Nassau Club, upset with their defeat by the Continentals, petulantly refused to reciprocate the cheers of the victors.[22] During a game on the Atlantics' home grounds, in which the Brooklyn nine defeated the Gotham Club, 31–17, Atlantic supporters crowded the field and got too close for the comfort of the Gotham players, often interfering with their efforts to catch batted balls. *Porter's Spirit* admitted that the crowd was ungentlemanly but claimed the Atlantics had used their best efforts to suppress the poor behavior. After the game ended, "[T]he Atlantics gave three cheers for the Gothams, but we regret to say that no response was made by the latter, much to their discredit, we think."[23]

The cheers were not necessarily the end of the post-game activity on the field. After an

1863 match between the Gotham and Eagle Clubs, following the cheering, there was a foot race between two of the heftier members of each club, President Phil Cozans of the Eagles and Burtis, first baseman of the Gothams. Burtis won the 150-yard sprint, which was followed by a race between sixteen club members, the last-place finisher to pay for the beer at Perry's Hotel. Haggerty of the Gothams ended up footing the bill.[24]

After the cheering and ancillary activity was over, players and non-playing club members generally repaired to a restaurant, hotel, club room, or private home for a bountiful "collation," speeches, the presentation of the ball by the losing team to the winner, and possibly music and other forms of entertainment. One of the favorite forms of musical entertainment was a lengthy song about one of the teams with a verse about each player on the nine. One of the members of the Niagaras of Buffalo drafted a 23-verse composition on the exploits of his club. A tortuous sample verse read:

> "Sidway's bat sends a rolling ball,
> And he makes his first base.
> As Demarest strikes an airy one,
> Sidway has gained a base."[25]

Not all entertainment was of original composition, and sometimes club members reverted to the classics. Following a game between the Active and Constellation clubs, there were readings from *Romeo and Juliet* in addition to the usual singing and speeches.[26]

During the game's early years, the press frequently devoted as much space to describing the entertainment as it did to the actual playing. A staple of the post-game ritual was the presentation of the ball to the winning club. A baseball was a valuable commodity, and most games were completed with a single ball. It was furnished by the challenging team and awarded to the winner as a fruit of victory, typically in a ceremony following the match or, if there was entertainment afterward, as part of the festivities. Some clubs, such as the Eckfords and Atlantics, maintained the balls, with the score and date of each victory neatly inscribed thereon, in trophy cases at their club room.[27]

The Eagles, who had been defeated by the Excelsiors in an 1858 game, and whose cheering was so rapturously described above, surrendered the ball on that occasion with appropriate gentlemanly spirit. "The ceremony of giving and receiving the trophy of the match [a ball] was then gone through," reported the *Clipper*, "to which A.J. Bixby, Esq., President of the Eagle, and J.B. Jones, M.D., President of the Excelsior, officiated, the remarks made by them being couched by them in terms eulogistic of their favorite game, and of the character and abilities of the clubs and gentlemen that had enjoyed and taken part in the exercise of the day."[28] Other speeches followed, as well as toasts, including one to Chadwick and the *Clipper,* both of which pleased the reporter to no end.

There was much more to come. "Speeches followed from the members of the various clubs there represented," continued the *Clipper,* "interspersed with some excellent singing, toasts, and jokes, which flew thick and fast, and at which it is needless to say bursts of hearty laughter were engaged in."[29] In addition to talking, ballplayers liked to sing. Peter O'Brien of the Atlantics was renowned as a comic singer, and often entertained at the post-game festivities of his club.[30] The Atlantics were a virtual vaudeville act with O'Brien and Johnny Oliver's singing, Fred Crane's piano playing and Jack Chapman's renowned whistling.

Speeches were sometimes spontaneous, and at other times strained in their attempt at melodrama. "May your innings at this fireside hearth," said Joseph Warren of the Niagaras of Buffalo following a game with the Flour City Club of Rochester, "be the best of all, and when the shortstop is put out by the great umpire, may he find his home base where celestial music is struck by angel bands on golden lyres."[31]

During the Civil War, the Star Spangled Banner might be sung, and toasts to President Lincoln, and, at least early in the war, General George McClellan, were common.[32] The Borax and Blow Pipe Clubs drank a toast to the Prince of Wales.[33] Occasionally, the press was saluted. On rare occasions, ladies were allowed to participate in the post-game activity, but for the most part, it was a male-only event.[34]

Sometimes the entertainment started early. At a California tournament in 1860, the players enjoyed a drink of wine before taking the field.[35] If a club were visiting from another town, it ran late, as the itinerary nearly always included a send-off at the pier or depot. When the Baltic Club of New York visited Newark, their hosts, following the obligatory feast, escorted the Baltic members to the dock to board the Jersey City ferry, "each cheering the other until their voices died away in the distance."[36] If the visitors were staying overnight, the ritual was extended, as the visiting club was treated to another meal the following day. And cheers.

Nothing dampened the appetites of the ballplayers, not even the "fast days" established during the war. On April 30, 1963, a day of abstinence proclaimed by President Lincoln, there were a number of games, followed by celebrations that, according to the *Clipper*, "will not be in accordance with the prescribed fast."[37]

The older, aristocratic organizations, such as the Knickerbockers, Gothams and Excelsiors, were the most diligent with their hospitality, but virtually every club, wealthy or not, did what it could to make their opponents, win or lose, feel themselves honored guests. With such elaborate fanfare associated with nearly every inter-club match, it is no wonder that no one played more than ten games in 1857.

As might be expected, the Knickerbockers were among the leaders in the entertainment league. Following the first game with the Washington Club in 1851, they hosted a dinner at McCarty's Hotel at the Elysian Fields.[38] Bureaucrats that they were, the Knickerbockers' entertainment was always authorized in the appropriate manner, and usually a committee was appointed to carry out the task. On one occasion, the Secretary was authorized "to provide brandy and sandwiches for the Putnam Club on the day of the match."[39] For other games, it was voted not to offer any hospitality.[40] After an 1858 match between the Knickerbockers and Excelsiors at Hoboken, the clubs adjourned to the Odd Fellows' Hall where they were joined by members of other clubs, totaling 200 in all, for dinner. Food and drink were consumed, the beauty of the game was extolled, the English were ridiculed for believing that the Americans were not good athletes, many, many toasts were drunk and a song about baseball, composed by James Davis of the Knickerbockers, was sung to the tune of "Uncle Sam's Farm." Dodsworth's Band then led a procession to the ferry from which the Excelsiors were sent off with more cheers toward Brooklyn.[41] The entire event was filled with "songs, laughter, etc. hilarity and good feeling."[42]

When the bills arrived, much of the hilarity and good feeling dissipated. Several Knickerbockers objected to a ten dollar per member assessment for the entertainment, which cost a rather exorbitant $340. When the assessment was approved, two longtime members resigned in protest. A resolution was quickly passed limiting entertainment expenses to forty dollars without the prior approval of the membership.[43]

Generally, newspaper accounts told of sumptuous fare in addition to good fellowship, but occasionally, fellowship was the only pleasure. In 1860, after the Eckfords dispatched the visiting Hudson River Club of Newburgh, the party, numbering about 75, went by omnibus to the Odeon where they anticipated a tasty repast. They were sadly disappointed, reported the *Brooklyn Daily Times,* which described, "meat ... decidedly unfit to eat; not to speak more unkindly of it than possible, we are forced to say that the ox who supplied the tongue, especially, must have been possessed of very bad-smelling breath. One person, we know, who ventured to eat a morsel, had to pay a pretty severe penalty for the sake of keeping it down, and was obliged to give it up at last before morning." Proprietor Sam Lewis arrived, observed the catastrophe in progress, apologized profusely, and set out to procure some palatable fare. By the time he returned, however, the party had left for Threall's.[44]

When the Excelsiors of Brooklyn commenced the practice of visiting cities far from New York, the level of hospitality moved up a notch, for an intercity visit was an occasion for major entertainment. When the Excelsiors arrived in Baltimore one fall morning in 1860, they were met at the depot by a delegation of Baltimore baseball men and taken to Guy's Monument Hotel for breakfast. After a pleasant visit, the visitors were taken in carriages to see the principal sights of the city. "[F]rom the time of their arrival," commented the *Clipper,* "to their departure, not a cent's expense were they allowed to incur, and whenever they desired to visit any place, carriages were at once placed at their disposal; in fact, nothing that the most generous hospitality could suggest, or yield, was wanting to make their time pass agreeably, and in this respect the Baltimoreans were most successful and victorious, taking the palm from every previous occasion the Excelsiors have hitherto enjoyed."[45] After the game, which the Brooklyn club won, 51–6, there was a dinner at the Monument House and more toasts and speeches acclaiming the Excelsiors the finest club in the United States.

Then it was on to Philadelphia where the Excelsiors dispatched a local all star collection, 15–4, and afterward dispatched bountiful helpings of catfish at The Falls at Schuylkill. There followed a series of cordial and self-congratulatory speeches. "The remarks of each person," Chadwick reported, "were in exceedingly good taste, and certainly very complimentary. The unanimity of good feeling and gentlemanly deportment of all in the field and elsewhere, was frequently expressed by many."[46]

Apparently, on some occasions, not all remarks were in good taste, according to *Porter's Spirit of the Times.* "We regret to notice," they wrote in October 1858, "that a marked feature of these social entertainments is a prurient taste for indecent anecdotes and song, a taste to be gratified at the cost of true dignity and self-respect. Especially objectionable is this practice when emanating from the lips of those advanced in years, its effect then being pernicious in the extreme."[47]

For the most part, however, sportsmanship, courtesy and gentlemanly behavior was the rule in all things. In 1861, the Exercise Club presented the Atlantics with a set of resolutions which began, "To the Atlantic Base Ball Club, from the Exercise B.B. Club, as a token of their appreciation of the many courtesies extended to them during the season of 1860, and to commemorate the friendly feeling existing between the two clubs." *Wilkes'* praised the beautiful penmanship and elaborate form of the document, which was read at the Atlantics' annual meeting.[48]

In 1862, *Wilkes'* commented after a game between the Jefferson and Eureka Clubs, "The games have been conducted in the most friendly and courteous spirit — in the manner which goes far to maintain base ball in its present position, as the out pastime of the United States. Generous, but not costly entertainment, have been provided on each occasion; and at the termination of the game the winners and losers have fraternized in that true spirit which is ever the characteristic of gentlemen."[49] No better summation could be given of the *desiderata* of mid-nineteenth century sportsmen. If all clubs acted in such a manner, baseball could not help but flourish.[50]

Even when good sportsmanship was absent, the rebuke was generally delivered in gentlemanly, if sarcastic, fashion. "Sir," Jack Purdy, President of the Gotham Junior Club addressed the *Clipper*, "We, the members of the Gotham, Jr. Base Ball Club do thank the Union Club, of Newburgh, for the courteous manner in which they treated us, on the 29th ult., by accepting our challenge, and then, when we arrived at Newburgh, sending us down to New Windsor, and giving us the pleasure of waiting there half the day, and then sending us a note stating that we were sold."[51]

During the late 1850s, the number of inter-club games increased, and the cost and time of the banquets became burdensome as each club sought to outdo the other. In 1859, the National Association voted to discontinue extensive entertainment following matches. It was agreed that festivities would be limited to those occasions on which clubs visited other cities, a restriction that was roundly ignored. The banquets continued although in its 1860 edition, the *Beadle's* handbook, in its sample bylaws, indicated that no general funds of the club should be used for entertainment, which was to be paid for only through individual subscription.[52]

Social activity didn't end with the playing season, for the Knickerbockers and their compatriots were social clubs in addition to sporting organizations. Many clubs held an annual ball during the winter, and the blend of baseball players and dancing tempted the *Clipper* to venture perhaps too far into the punning business. After the Waverly Club ball in 1859, the journal reported, "The dancing was kept up till an early hour, since none of the gentlemen were inclined to be so 'base' as to make a 'short stop' while the ladies were 'left' in the 'right field,' but not a few were evidently anxious to take the post of 'catch(h)er,' and we shall not be surprised to learn that there were more hearts gained than 'hands lost.'"[53]

The Atlantics' principal ball during the winter of 1860–61, held at Montague Hall, was described by *Wilkes'* in much greater detail than the journal covered most of the club's games, which were dismissed with a terse summary and a box score. Not only did club members and their female guests attend their own balls, they frequented those of other clubs as well, so that a ballplayer's social card could be quite full during the off-season. At the aforementioned Atlantic ball, in addition to the flag symbolizing the Atlantics' championship, the banners of several other clubs were hung about the ballroom, and many members of the Eckford Club were present, led by Captain Frank Pidgeon. Peter O'Brien's tenor voice belted out *Would I Were With Thee*, and brother Matty orchestrated the affair as floor manager.[54] In all, the Atlantics hosted eight dances during the winter, exactly half as many as the number of games they played during the summer.

Meanwhile, as the clubs wined, dined, sang and danced the evenings away, action on the diamond continued. In the spring of 1858, *Porter's Spirit* estimated that there were 30 to 40 teams on Long Island alone, and that more than 400 young men belonged to either cricket or baseball clubs.[55] The 1858 season, like the previous one, was slow in getting underway, and there was little action, virtually none between the top teams, during the spring. It was June 24 before the first major contest of the season between the Eagle and Excelsior Clubs took place. Even then, the months of June, July and August witnessed very few matches between prominent clubs.

The Atlantics, now acknowledged as the best nine in the New York area, won all seven of the matches they played in 1858. The club, as usual, got off to a late start, playing one game in June, one in September and the rest in October and November, finishing on November 16. Many of the stalwarts who paced the Brooklyn club during its triumphant next few years, including John Oliver, Matt O'Brien, Peter O'Brien, Dickie Pearce, and Charlie Smith, were already with the Atlantics by 1858.

Smith, who worked in his father's vegetable store,[56] had played with the Enterprise Club in 1856 and 1857.[57] He covered third base so well that in 1863 the *Clipper* opined, "There is no question about it, whatever, Charley Smith, of the Atlantic Club is the finest ball player in the country."[58] Harry Wright later called him the "king of third basemen,"[59] and William Rankin wrote, "[H]e was a born ball player — one of the most artistic and graceful I ever saw. I know of no player who had a greater following or was more popular in his day than Charles J. Smith ... when Smith would leave the clubhouse and start over to the diamond the great crowd, as soon as it would recognize him, would rise as one and cheer and applaud him. He was a wonderfully popular player."[60] Smith played with the Brooklyn club for 13 seasons before joining the Mutuals in 1871.

Oliver was an agile infielder with great speed who'd played with the Constellation Club in 1857. He was a flashy second baseman for a few years but later fell into dissipation and died of consumption while still a young man.[61]

Eighteen fifty-seven had witnessed the first appearance of the Atlantics in the front rank. The next year saw the emergence of two more strong clubs. The first was the Excelsiors. In November 1854, some spectators at a Knickerbocker-Eagle game, led by John H. Suydam,[62] decided to form their own club, which they did on Thanksgiving,[63] calling themselves the Jolly Bachelors. Shortly thereafter, the club assumed the name associated with the motto of New York State.

The Excelsiors started slowly, playing just two matches in 1856 and three the following year. "The club is composed," a journalist reported in 1856, "of merchants and clerks, who formed this association merely for the benefits of that healthful exercise which few other amusements can give, and not with the expectation of contesting, in this noble game, with older and abler clubs."[64]

In 1858, however, the Excelsiors were perhaps the most improved club in the New York area, winning eight of thirteen encounters. They beat established teams such as the Knickerbockers, Eagles, Gothams and the Unions of Morrisania, but on two occasions lost badly to the Atlantics, 22–10 and 27–6. "The Excelsiors," the *Clipper* wrote in September, "meteor-like, have rushed on to glory, allowing no obstacles to mar the lustre of their escutcheon, their chief delight being to single out the oldest and strongest, accumulate laurel upon laurel in grasping the victory from each, then hold out the right hand of fellowship, in a manner which will not admit of doubt as to its sincerity, while with the other they point to their best of mottoes, Excelsior."[65]

The Excelsiors' captain and best player was their catcher, Joe Leggett, who joined the club in 1857 after beginning his career with the Wayne Club the prior year. When the two clubs consolidated, he became an Excelsior, was elected vice president of the club and served as a delegate to the NA convention.[66] Leggett, who sported a prodigious set of sideburns in an era when they were called Dundreadys, demonstrated remarkable prowess behind the bat.

Like Peter O'Brien, he was not considered a "graceful" player, but he was nimble enough to catch foul bounds and ticks, and he had sufficient fortitude and tough hands to withstand the rigors of the position. Leggett was a great hitter with power, a catcher who rarely let the ball pass him and one whose strong arm discouraged would-be base stealers. In 1859 and 1860, no player on any National Association club scored more runs than Joe Leggett. In future years, nearly every promising young catcher was referred to as "another Leggett."

Leggett was the captain and leader of the club and was, in some ways, the Harry Wright of his era. Harry, a good player in his prime, is remembered primarily for his leadership ability and integrity. Leggett was likewise a much-admired figure in the late 1850s and early 1860s, a paragon of respectability on one of the leading teams of his time. The Excelsiors were well trained, disciplined on the field and off, and were good sports, even in their later years when they were not winning very often.

The other club to emerge as a potential competitor to the Atlantics was the Mutuals who, in their second year of competition, won their first eleven matches of the season. The Empires defeated the Mutuals in the latter's final game, but with eleven victories, the Mutuals had the most wins of any major team.

A young club, the Niagara, made little impression as a first-class nine, but they had a second baseman named Jim Creighton who was considered a pretty good player. Creighton, just 17 years old, often played cricket as well as baseball and sometimes played third base as well as second. He'd begun his career with the Young America Club, which he'd helped organize, in 1857.[67] The pitcher for the Niagara Club was the left-handed captain, John Shields, who was good enough to relegate young Creighton to the infield. One day, however, Shields was absent, and Creighton was asked to pitch, an event that would have a great impact on the game of baseball.

By 1858, the concept of playing for a championship was beginning to take hold, and the idea of winning and losing was being taken more seriously. The press began to speak more often of competitive skill and less frequently of gentlemanly behavior. They encouraged captains to place their men in the same positions in each game in order to refine their skills, to practice more frequently, and to replace older players with younger, more active men. After the Knickerbockers played on an unfamiliar field where the sun shone in their eyes, the *Times* advised, "[I]t ought to be strictly adhered to as a rule, especially when you are playing with clubs of equal strength, never to give away a point in the chances of winning a game, for courtesy, unless the concession should be dictated by an imperative sense of justice and propriety."[68]

While competition between the Mutuals, Atlantics, Excelsiors and other top clubs was intensifying, the old-line teams were becoming more social and less athletic. The Knickerbockers, as they had in 1857, played just four times, losing three and tying one. The Gothams lost six of seven and the Eagle Club three of five.[69] No clubs, new or old, were particularly active as only three (the Mutuals, Empires and Excelsiors) played ten or more games against other clubs.

The unquestioned highlight of the 1858 season was a series of three games between teams made up of the best players of New York on one side and the cream of Brooklyn on the other. The concept of an all-star game originated with the presidents of a number of clubs in the metropolitan area, which appointed a Committee of Arrangements to tend to the details.[70] The series was, according to the *Atlas,* "by far the most important event in the annals of this purely national and American game."[71] The site was the Fashion Race Course on Long Island, located near the present location of Shea Stadium in West Flushing along National Street.

The ground upon which the Fashion Course stood had originally been a farm before it was acquired by four wealthy southern racing aficionados for $100,000. The new owners expended an amount nearly equal to the purchase price and constructed a luxurious, first class facility, which they named after a famous horse of the 1840s. The half-mile, oval track was in the shadow of a brick grandstand with the entire parcel surrounded by a brick wall. For the comfort of racing patrons, the owners built Colton Mansion, a 22-room building featuring a bar and numerous meeting rooms. With its beautiful landscaping, the Fashion Course track was the finest in the New York area.[72]

At the time of the all-star series, the Fashion Course had been in operation for just two years. It was chosen because, first, it was a neutral site for the two nines; second, it was readily accessible by public transportation from New York and Brooklyn and, third, it was one of the few locations capable of accommodating the large crowds that were anticipated to watch the matches. "All New York nearly could be accommodated on the Fashion Course," *Porter's Spirit* explained.[73] Expectations were high, and the Long Island site was able to accommodate up to fifty thousand spectators, many times the largest crowd that had ever attended a baseball game. An awning was erected to shield the ladies from the sun, and thousands of seats were provided for both ladies and gentlemen.[74]

Clearly evident in the planning was a concern for the composition and deportment of such a large crowd. Gambling and alcohol were to be prohibited, impossible rules to enforce in such a large, open area, and the clubs were requested to contribute a total of 250 members who would be deputized for the occasion and charged with maintaining order under the direction of the police.[75] In order to defray the costs of preparing the field and maintaining order, a fifty cent admission fee would be charged,[76] the first time anyone paid money for the privilege of watching a baseball game. Other sports, such as boxing, horse racing and cricket, had charged for admission, but not baseball.[77]

The New York squad consisted of players from the Empire, Knickerbocker, Eagle, Union and Gotham Clubs, while the Brooklyn nine was composed of men from the Atlantic, Excelsior, Putnam and Eckford organizations. The first game of the series was to have taken place on July 13, but about noon a severe storm arrived, necessitating a postponement until the 20th. Despite the horrible weather, about two thousand spectators were on hand, and they had already made several wagers by the time the postponement was announced.

On the 20th, the weather was clear, and the long-awaited match took place. Chadwick's excitement was evident by the length of the first sentence of his article describing the opening game. "The great match which has been in contemplation for several weeks past, has, in connection with Base Ball," he wrote, "had the effect of directing the public mind to the great question of athletic sports for the people, and it has been growing and growing until the excitement has become so intense that it has been made the chief topic of conversation and every one met with has had opinions to express, as to who would be the ultimate victors in this grand contest."[78]

Chadwick then took a deep breath and told *Clipper* readers of the grand contest.[79] Interest in the game was as intense as the reporter had indicated with seemingly every ballplayer in the metropolis in attendance. Many clubs hired omnibuses to bring their members to the grounds. The Excelsiors' bus (ironically called the *Putnam*, the name of one of the Excelsiors' rivals) was pulled by fourteen grey horses festooned with feathered headgear while the Empires had two carriages of six horses each, and the Putnams, Unions, St. Nicholas and a number of other clubs had less impressive vehicles. Each was festooned with flowers and banners bearing the club name. Less stately conveyances, such as beer wagons and milk wagons, conveyed less-exalted spectators to the event.[80] Steamboats chugged across the water bringing spectators to Long Island all afternoon. The Fashion Course was accessible from New York principally by boats which embarked from the Fulton Street pier and deposited passengers at the Flushing railroad depot at Hunter's Point.

The weather was as grand as it had been forbidding a week earlier, and attendance was estimated at eight to ten thousand, well short of fifty thousand, but by far the largest gathering that had ever witnessed a baseball game. The crowd included four or five hundred ladies, whose presence was greatly coveted by admirers of the sport, for it brought respectability to the occasion. Many spectators sat in carriages lined three deep down the homestretch of the racetrack, some reclined on the grass surrounding the diamond that had been laid out in the infield, and others stood behind those who were seated.

To staunch supporters of baseball, numbers alone were not sufficient. The quality of the crowd was equally important as its quantity. The number of fine carriages parked around the field evidenced the fact that baseball appealed to the upper classes, and Chadwick was pleased to report, "The assembly was one of the most respectful character. It was composed, in the main, of staid citizens, sober business men of various callings."[81]

The business of some of those men, however, was picking pockets and the trade of others was running assorted games of chance. Three card monte was the most popular. "All the [gambling] paraphernalia was openly displayed," reported the *Eagle*, "and gambling went on under the eyes of everybody, and many a greenie from the interior of the Island was fleeced."[82] A police sergeant lost thirty dollars and obtained a refund in exchange for a promise of no arrest.[83] One man was expelled from a wagon for attempting to pass a counterfeit bill, and a number of wallets were lifted.[84] At the third game, a notorious pickpocket native to Manchester, England, named William Day, also known as "Squib" Dixon and by various other *aliases*, was arrested and later convicted of robbing a journalist of more than four hundred dollars. Four hundred dollars was a remarkable amount of money to carry on one's person, far more than was required for the fifty-cent admission and a refreshing glass of lemonade, and it is likely that the victim was intending to wager on the game, the very wagers that were prohibited in the name of order.[85]

The teams that played the first game were as follows:

	Brooklyn		*New York*	
Pitcher	Matt O'Brien	Atlantic	Tom Van Cott	Gotham
Catcher	Joe Leggett	Excelsior	Charles DeBost	Knickerbocker
1st Base	John Price	Atlantic	Louis Wadsworth	Gotham
2nd Base	John Holder	Excelsior	S.R. Pinckney	Union
3rd Base	___ Masten	Putnam	A. J. Bixby	Eagle
Shortstop	Frank Pidgeon	Eckford	M.E. Gelston	Eagle
Outfield	Peter O'Brien	Atlantic	Harry Wright	Knickerbocker
Outfield	A. E. Burr	Putnam	___ Benson	Empire
Outfield	J. Greene	Eckford	___ Hoyt	Knickerbocker

The game lived up to expectations as New York beat the Brooklyn all-stars, 22–18, in a close, exciting contest in which the lead changed hands several times. John Holder of the Excelsiors hit the only home run.[86] Afterwards, the players and the many club members present gathered for victuals in the club room of the Colton Mansion. The Brooklyn players cheered and toasted their New York counterparts and vice versa. The net profit of $71.10 was divided equally between the Widows and Orphans funds of the New York and Brooklyn Fire Departments.[87]

The second match, played throughout intermittent showers on August 17, was captured by Brooklyn 29–8, but New York took the rubber match and the series, 29–18, on September 10. Both clubs made numerous changes in their nines, and by the third game, the Brooklyn club consisted entirely of players from the Atlantics and Eckfords. Crowds at the last two games, although not as great as those who attended on July 20, were impressive (the second game attracted five to eight thousand[88] and the third about five thousand[89]) and, other than a few irritating Brooklyn youths who shouted at the umpire, well behaved. There was a considerable amount of wagering, which was dutifully reported, as were the odds. While players were forbidden from gambling, it was assumed that spectators, as they did at nearly every other form of sport, would put money on the outcome. Fortunately, as the crowds diminished in the second and third games, so did the number of pickpockets and con artists.

All in all, despite the gambling and petty crime, the series had been a great success, a major development in the growth of the relatively new sport. "The series of matches played at the Fashion Course this season," wrote *Porter's*, "have been extremely favorable to the progress and popularity of the game of base ball, thousands having been made thereby to become interested parties who otherwise would never have practically have [sic] known anything of the game at all."[90]

The all-star series was the highlight of the career of the Fashion Course facility. Despite their sizable investment, its owners were never able to realize a profit. In 1865, the Flushing Railroad ran tracks through the grounds, and the stately facility was no more.[91]

Sixteen new clubs joined the National Association at the annual meeting in March 1859, swelling the ranks to 37. During 1858, 1859 and 1860, it seemed as though a new club was being formed every week. "The Cry is Still They Come," read an August 1858 headline in the *Eagle*.[92] Most new organizations were insignificant, and few joined the Association, but each club meant twenty or so more young men were engaged in playing baseball. Not every new organization was noted in the press, but a reading of the sporting journals revealed notices regarding the formation of the following new clubs:

Month	*Clubs*
July 1858	National, Oriental, Phoenix
August 1858	American Star, Independent, Crystal, Columbia, Unknown, American, American Eagle, Constellation, Hudson, E Pluribus Unum, Bedford
September 1858	Oakland, Adriatic, Ivanhoe, Albion, Jackson, Dreadnought, Endeavor, Fulton, Nassau, Jr., Charter Oak, Franklin

October 1858	United, Tippecanoe, Lady Washington, Hickory
November 1858	Trainor, Wyoming
December 1858	Grammercy
April 1859	Morphy
May 1859	Grasshopper
June 1859	Manhattan, Neptune, Jr. Jem Baggs, Favorita, Alert, Wilson, Hudson
July 1859	Reindeer, Eagle, Young Mechanics, Lilly, Franklin, Madison, Pastime, Jr.
August 1859	Mechanics, Union, Exercise, Jr., Jefferson, Marion
September 1859	Waverly, National, Jr., Rough and Ready, Liberty, Wyandank, Eclipse, Portland, Henry Eckford
January 1860	Brooklyn
June 1860	Peconic, Champion, Matteno, Mystic, Crystal, Union, Seminole, Constellation, Excelsior, Jr., Marion, Jr.
July 1860	Junietta, Nassau
August 1860	Muffins, Active, Jr., Acme, Forrest, Zouaves, Mansion, Madison
September 1860	Auld Lang Syne, Sylvan, Eagle, Semper Paratus, Ariel, American

Note: The appearance of a name more than once is due to the fact that a number of clubs shared the same name. The data was compiled from the *New York Clipper, Brooklyn Eagle, Porter's Spirit of the Times, New York Atlas, The New York Times* and *Wilkes' Spirit of the Times.*

The press, which had fretted over the ill health of the American male (see Chapter 7), lauded the sharp increase in activity, which would undoubtedly "aid in the development of a robust national physique."[93] The *Atlas,* noting the attendance of nearly ten thousand at an 1859 Atlantic-Eckford match, stated, "[T]he gathering of so large a crowd of people, among which were a large number of ladies, is an unerring and practical indication that the American public, with singular unanimity of feeling and opinion, have decreed for the game of Base Ball, the top niche or head of the column of outdoor pastimes."[94]

Still, an impediment to the growth of the game and its establishment as the national sport was the fact that, despite the impressive proliferation of new clubs, none was far from New York and Brooklyn. In April 1858, as the NA was being formed, the *Clipper* chided, "National, indeed! Why the association is a mere local organization, bearing no *State* existence even to say nothing of a *National* one."[95]

The 1859 season witnessed the continued success of the Excelsiors, making them, along with the Atlantics and Eckfords, the three strongest clubs in the metropolitan area. The Excelsiors were 12–3, the Eckfords 11–3 and the Atlantics 11–1.

Since all three clubs were from Brooklyn, that city laid claim to supremacy over New York, whose nines were rarely able to beat their Brooklyn rivals. "If we are ahead of the big city in nothing else," said the *Eagle,* "we can beat her at base ball."[96]

The Atlantics' only loss was to the Eckfords. After falling to the Atlantics in early July, the Eckfords scored six runs in the eighth inning for a garrison finish that gave them a 22–16 victory on September 8. This set up a third game, played on October 12, which the Atlantics won, 22–12. Since the Atlantics beat the Eckfords twice in their three-game series, they retained the championship. The Excelsiors, although winning more games than either of the other two contenders, did not play the Atlantics (nor did they play the Eckfords) and therefore did not compete for the title. They lost to the Unions of Morrisania, the Star Club of Brooklyn and, shockingly, the unheralded Charter Oak Club. The latter defeat took place in the Excelsiors' first game of the season as several of the first nine, anticipating an easy win, failed to put in an appearance. Playing with a number of substitutes, the Excelsiors went down to an 18–17 defeat. Less than a month later, the two clubs met again and the Excelsiors mustered in force, winning, 62–13, scoring 20 runs in the eighth inning.

Another of the Excelsior defeats was administered by the young Star Club of Brooklyn. While the loss to the Charter Oaks had resulted from the Excelsiors' failure to take their opponents seriously, the defeat by the Stars was no fluke. The latter club, composed mostly of teenagers who had been playing baseball together since 1856, scored ten runs in the ninth inning for a 17–12 victory in a very well-played game.

The Stars were in an unusual position. As youngsters, and therefore underdogs, they were generally favorites of the spectators. They had two *bona fide* stars in infielder George Flanly and pitcher Jim Creighton, the former Niagara second baseman. Why weren't the Stars, who lost only once in nine games in 1859, contenders for the championship? The *Clipper* indicated that the youngsters were having difficulty getting the top clubs to answer their challenges,[97] a claim that highlighted a major weakness of the championship system, one that would become more marked as the title became more coveted.

The championship could only be lost by dropping a best-of-three series to a challenger. One certain way to retain the title was to decline all challenges from clubs that were likely to win a series. There was no schedule and nothing to compel a champion to go to the mat. The Stars lost to the Atlantics by the close score of 16–12, but they were not able to get the reigning champions to play them again and thus had no chance at the title.

During the 1860 season, the matter of the championship would play a very important role in the future of the game of baseball. The Atlantics wore the crown, but other clubs, particularly the Excelsiors, were in a position to wrest it away. Their effort to do so resulted in a most unexpected and troubling outcome.

Chapter 7

Mad Dogs and Englishmen: Other Antebellum Sports

During the 1850s and 1860s, while baseball was striving to establish itself as America's national game, there were a number of other pastimes that enjoyed some degree of popularity. Horse racing was the first American sport to gain wide acceptance, with roots extending to the middle of the seventeenth century.[1] The sport came to New York with the opening of the Union Course on Long Island in 1821, and there were a number of tracks throughout the South,[2] for much of the action took place in southern horse country. By the 1830s, horse racing was a popular diversion for the plantation class, including President Andrew Jackson, who both owned and wagered on horses.

Other old world sports, particularly cricket, were popular in Philadelphia and New York while some pastimes, including boxing, cock fighting (or cocking) and "canine sports" had a less savory reputation. In addition to the violent nature of all three activities, they had other undesirable elements in common. All offered cash prizes, all were accompanied by spirited betting on the outcome, and all had been the subject of numerous scandals.

Canine sport was a particularly brutal form of entertainment that was divided into two main categories — dogs fighting with each other and dogs competing against each other to see which could kill the most rats. Canine fighting was exciting, stimulating and bloody. Serious injury and death were common, and dogs that fought on despite broken bones, ripped skin and copious bleeding were particularly admired. In 1858, the *Clipper* described a match in New Orleans between a game animal named Snap and his opponent, Snow. Both dogs were badly bloodied, and by the end of the fight, one of Snap's front legs was broken and useless. Snow fared even worse, and his trainer carried him to his corner, apparently dying. Snow was revived, however, and Snap came out gamely on three legs to renew the scrap. Snap's other foreleg soon became disabled, and finally his handler picked him up and stopped the fight, which had lasted an agonizing hour and forty minutes.[3]

Other battles were equally revolting. In Canada, about the same time Snap fought Snow, two dogs named Danger and Major tussled for two hours and forty minutes after which Major won and Danger died.[4] In New Orleans, two dogs named Dan O'Connell and Lion fought to a draw over nearly six hours. It was intended to renew the contest at a later date, but both dogs died within two days of the fight.[5]

Needless to say, dog fighting was not the most reputable of sports, and every precaution was taken by the dog owners to be as certain as possible that they were not victimized by foul play. One of the common methods of cheating was feeding an opposing dog tainted meat before a match. Another tactic was to place poison on those parts of one's own dog that were most likely to come in contact with its opponent. In 1854, there was, as it was referred to in the press, a "dog dispute" between Red Jack and Connaught Lad at McLaughlin's Pit on First Avenue in New York. Prior to the match, proprietor McLaughlin, the handler of Red Jack, assumed the unenviable task of examining his dog's opponent by "tasting" Connaught Lad in the most likely places to look for poison. While McLaughlin tasted Connaught Lad, the dog broke free of its handler and decided to taste McLaughlin. His teeth clamped on the proprietor's cheek, and ripped the flesh until blood flowed freely. Finally, after fifteen or twenty painful seconds, McLaughlin managed to choke the dog and free himself from its clutches.

Once McLaughlin and Connaught Lad had repaired to neutral corners, the fight commenced, and the two champion dogs fought furiously for 25 minutes before Red Jack inflicted a serious wound on his opponent. John Marriott, handler of the Lad, picked up his dog, at which point McLaughlin picked up Red Jack and claimed victory. A heated dispute ensued, an imbroglio settled when the referee ruled that Marriott had violated the rules by picking up his dog and that the wounded McLaughlin and Red Jack were the victors.[6]

Rat killing was the other version of "canine sport." The number of rats killed and the period of time required to dispose of them were the criteria of excellence. Where could one obtain sacrificial rats? In 1858, the *Clipper* ran an advertisement headlined "Rats, Rats, Rats." For ten dollars per hundred, plus three dollars for the cage, Harry Jennings, operator of the most popular canine emporium in New York, would send all the rats one desired. "A good supply of rats always on hand," proclaimed an ad for Jennings' establishment, and he might not have been referring only to the four-legged variety.[7]

In 1853, Hubbard's Rat Pit in Cincinnati hosted a contest in which the object was to kill 50 rats in the shortest period of time. The "full terrier slut" Rose knocked off all 50 in two minutes and thirty-five seconds, while her opponent, Fanny, "killed thirty rats in six minutes and gave out, letting the rest go unharmed."[8]

Harry Jennings was the top dog in New York canine sport, operating at 22 White Street, and sometimes at 49 Madison Street where he put on exhibitions twice a month. On one occasion, to vary the entertainment, Jennings brought in a fighting pig to contest with a bulldog.[9] John Marriott was another force in the New York canine world with his Empire Rat Pit at 92 Crosby Street.[10] Matches were invariably well-attended by both man and beast, and on January 25, 1860, there were 21 dogs on hand at Jennings' establishment to contest for rat-killing honors. These were handicap matches in which a champion killer spotted rats to a less accomplished exterminator. The dogs, weighing from 10 to 25 pounds, put a sizable dent in the New York rat population that night. Topsy, who disposed of four rats in 27 seconds, was the winner.[11] Topsy couldn't hold a candle, however, to Lady Suffolk, the "celebrated rat-killing slut," who once knocked off 100 rats in nine minutes and 57 seconds.[12]

As expected, canine sport was not universally welcomed, and there were occasional protests about the cruel treatment of the animals. After the *New York Express* published such a condemnation, it was chided by the *Clipper* for reporting the results of recent bouts. Many protested, the *Clipper* claimed, but everyone wanted to know the winner of the rat-killing contests. "Considering the popularity of canine sports," the author said, "it is a wonder to me that our friends at Albany don't turn their legislative halls into canine pits."[13]

Cock fighting had a long history in England and the British colony of India, and while it never achieved the popularity of canine battles in the United States, the sport had its American followers. To assuage squeamish souls, the *Clipper* provided rational justification for the use of animals for human amusement. "It would be needless labor," the journal editorialized in November 1856, "formally to attempt a proof of the obvious truth, that universal Providence has submitted to the domination and care of man, the beast of the field, the fowls of the air, and the fishes of the water, indeed all brute animal existence, and that both for our serious indispensable use, and our diversion and sport; for, even the latter, in a secondary degree, is a necessary of life: a need in which the inferior animals share equally with man. They are also possessed of feelings, are capacitated by nature to enjoy pleasure, and to endure pain like ourselves; and, therefore, their right to compassion stands on the same foundation as our own. But they are destined to our use — it is on the condition, however, in the view of right reason, that we discriminate between the use and abuse." Besides, the *Clipper* informed its readers, it was the natural instinct of the cocks to fight each other.[14]

If Providence had ordained it so, how could man question? Let the cock fights begin. After all, what was the difference between shooting and eating game animals and letting them satisfy their natural desire for a little healthy competition before ending up on the serving platter? At least the opposing bird didn't have a gun.[15]

Cock fights usually took place in secret, one step ahead of the law. One such event occurred in January 1862 at Troy, New York. The date and location, the fourth story of a garret, were disclosed only to those in the know, yet cock fighting aficionados from New York, Chicago, Detroit and numerous other cities and towns attended. "What a scene!" exclaimed *Wilkes'*. "It well nigh baffles human language and description." For one dollar, spectators could climb three flights of stairs and cram themselves into the small room, reeking of human odor, that was to be the site of the "dispute."[16]

The men drank, watched and wagered. Perhaps the most enthusiastic bettor was Troy businessman and politician and former boxing champion John Morrissey, who placed large sums on each match. He bet on the cocks and also offered to put money on his ability to fight any man in the place, although no one was enthusiastic about accepting. After several rounds of bantams, the session ended at about six in the morning.

Canine, rat and avian lives were cheap, and human existence only slightly more precious. Boxing had been practiced as a sport in England during the days when the Romans ruled the Island, but then disappeared until the early eighteenth century, with the first British champion, James Figg, crowned in 1719. Fighting was a natural part of life on the American frontier. With formal justice generally unavailable, men resorted to their fists to resolve disputes over land, money, women, and pride.

Wilkes' claimed that the initial boxing match in America took place in 1816 when Jacob Hyer defeated Tom Beasley.[17] The first renowned American boxer was handsome James (Yankee) Sullivan, who fought in the 1840s and 1850s. Sullivan's background was unfortunately typical of the era's prizefighters. Born Frank Murray in Ireland in 1813, he had a few fights before being arrested for burglary and shipped off to a penal colony in Australia for a fourteen-year sentence. Murray escaped from Sydney in a ship under harrowing circumstances. He was hiding below decks with a fellow escapee when the authorities attempted to ferret out stowaways by drilling through the floorboards. When the augur penetrated the leg of Murray's companion, Murray pulled a knife and threatened him with death if he made a sound.

Despite the excruciating pain, the man remained mute although the augur went clear through his limb, and the ship put out to sea with both men aboard.

Murray arrived in the United States and changed his name to James Sullivan. He went to England, the country from which he had been deported, and had a few well-publicized fights that brought him to the attention of the English authorities. This brought about a return to America where he had more fights, including a drunken brawl with his wife. During the latter fracas, during which both parties were inebriated, a lamp was tipped over and ignited Mrs. Sullivan's clothing, burning her to death.

Following his wife's death, Sullivan was on the move once more, this time to San Francisco, where he once again found trouble and was jailed by local vigilantes. While in prison, he either committed suicide or was stabbed to death by an old enemy. Sullivan lived just 45 years but had enough experiences for several lifetimes.[18]

While Sullivan was generally acclaimed the best boxer of his time, there was no organized system for determining a champion and only a haphazard manner of arranging matches. Adherents of the various boxers ran from saloon to saloon, issuing challenges, staking prize money and arranging logistics.

The first acknowledged American champion was Jacob Hyer's son, Thomas, who fought in the early 1850s. Irish native John Morrissey, later a member of Congress, and a man who would have an infamous connection with baseball in the 1860s as a backer (frequently with large wagers) of the Unions of Lansingburgh, New York, was the next great American fighter. Morrissey was sometimes known as "Old Smoke" for during one of his matches, he was supposedly thrown on his back onto hot coals but continued to fight on with smoke rising from his burning flesh.[19] Morrissey emigrated to California and had a number of fights in 1852. In October 1853, he won the American championship by defeating Yankee Sullivan, who had taken the title from Hyer, in a 37-round bout that ended with Morrissey on his knees and the seconds trading punches in the ring.[20] After obtaining the crown, Morrissey didn't defend it until 1858 when he accepted a challenge from a sturdy young brawler from California who would become the most famous boxer of the mid-nineteenth century and one of the most renowned athletes of his time.

John Carmel Heenan, known as the Benicia Boy, was born in Troy, New York, in 1835, but had gone to California, as had Sullivan, Morrissey, Alexander Cartwright and William Wheaton, in search of the riches promised by the discovery of gold. The 6'1", 200-pound muscleman became a blacksmith in the iron works of the Pacific Mail Steamship Company in the town of Benicia where he gained his nickname and some backers through his skill in brawling. Heenan eventually moved back east, and his people got together with Morrissey's people. After many accusations of false dealing, the two men agreed to face off in the ring and signed a contract at the offices of the *Clipper*.[21] The match would take place in Canada rather than the United States, where the police were always on the prowl for prize fights and often broke them up. It was not unusual for an American fight to begin in one location, last a few rounds, move to a second and perhaps a third locale with the law in hot pursuit.

The law's concern with prizefighting was certainly justified for, with bare fists flying and little medical attention available, fatalities during prize fights were not infrequent. In England, there were a number of manslaughter convictions after fights that resulted in the death of the loser.

Prize fights rarely took place in cities, and, as with cock fights, the location was usually kept a secret until the day of the match to throw the police off the track. On the morning of the bout, often in the pre-dawn hours, the betting sports were put on a train or boat and taken to a remote location where a ring was hastily set up and the fight took place, hopefully before the police arrived to intervene.

In 1849, a fight between Yankee Sullivan and Tom Hyer was scheduled to take place at Rock Point, about 40 miles from Baltimore. Sullivan chose Rock Point because he'd heard jurisdiction of the area was in dispute between Maryland and the United States Government. Prior to the fight, both the City of Baltimore and the State of Maryland issued warrants for the arrest of the two boxers, and the police discovered Hyer's headquarters. When he realized the law was on his trail, Hyer immediately placed his second in his bed, went downstairs and hid under another bed. The police grabbed the second and left, after which Hyer made his escape, ran to the beach and hopped into a waiting boat.

Boxer John Heenan was perhaps the most famous athlete of the mid-nineteenth century. In the brawling, disreputable world of pugilism, the handsome Heenan was a favorite in England and the United States. He was a crude boxer and had limited success in the ring, but he achieved world renown for his few fights.

The police then proceeded to the house where Sullivan was staying, but the fighter jumped out a window and prepared to make a run for it. Confronted by two gun-toting lawmen, he switched to Plan B. Turning to his second, Tom O'Donnell, he shouted, "Run, Sullivan, run, as if hell had kicked you!" The police fell for the ruse and grabbed O'Donnell, while Sullivan dashed off and climbed a nearby tree. After the police left, he shimmied down, made for the beach and jumped aboard a boat. The police had now succeeded in taking both seconds into custody, while the two fighters remained at large, rowing toward their date with destiny.

Sullivan's and Hyer's boats took off up the Chesapeake with a police boat in pursuit. The police finished a poor third, and the two fighters decided "to drop upon the first convenient spot, whether it was in Maryland, or Delaware, or Virginia, or hell." Once they found a suitable venue, the spectators were brought on and the fight began. After all of the difficulties in getting the match underway, the actual event, which Hyer won in seventeen minutes, was anticlimactic.[22]

Morrissey and Heenan had no intention of having their contest interrupted, and they chose a site in Canada, opposite Buffalo. Canada was the site of many important fights of the era, the main impediment being the cost of transporting the fighters, their seconds and the spectators north of the border.

Both fighters trained religiously in the months preceding the bout, running, sparring and going through paces similar to those of modern pugilists. The most remarkable part of Morrissey's routine was his liquid intake in the course of a day. Every second morning before his three-mile walk, Morrison drank a "large glass of the finest sherry, with an egg beaten up in it." After a second walk, he partook of a "glass of Murphy's fine old ale." Then came more exercise, and dinner. "He is allowed but little water," reported the *Clipper*, "and after dinner he takes half a tumbler of sherry." The day ended with a half-glass of sherry.[23]

The fight was scheduled to take place on October 20, but a few days before Heenan was due to depart from his training site in New York City, he received word that a warrant had been issued for his arrest. He left straightaway for Buffalo, which was to be the jumping-off point for the as yet undisclosed site of combat.

Along with Heenan and Morrissey, there was a sizable entourage of spectators waiting in Buffalo, the nearest city of any consequence to the Canadian border at Niagara Falls. The fighters, who knew the destination, and the spectators, most of whom didn't, were loaded onto boats that would deliver them to the island of Long Point, just across the border. At 11 P.M. on the 19th, a steamer, the *Galena*, and a paddle boat departed for Canada.

When the boats arrived at Long Point, immediate difficulties arose. Apparently, the ground had been selected without an intimate knowledge of the topography of the island, most of which was covered with sand and marsh. Eventually, however, the parties found ground that was sufficiently solid to set up the ring and string the ropes.

The rules of boxing in the 1850s, which often varied from match to match based upon agreement between the parties, were quite different from modern regulations. There were no gloves, and the men pounded each other with bare fists. Clinching and wrestling were allowed. There was no predetermined number of rounds; the combatants continued until one or the other was unable to come to the scratch. In 1849, a fight between Bill Hayes and Mike Madden lasted over six hours.[24] A round ended when one of the fighters hit the ground, either as the result of a blow or by being thrown. There was constant suspicion that tired fighters fell intentionally to gain a respite, a tactic that was supposed to be prohibited by the referee.

The role of referee was not an enviable one. He was to watch for fouls, such as intentional falls, gouging, striking below the belt, etc., and prevent interference from the spectators, all under the watchful eyes of gamblers who had sizable wagers riding on the outcome. Since the main object in site selection was to avoid the police, the referee could expect no protection from the law.

After the months of preparation and the years of waiting for Morrissey to defend his crown, the match at Long Point was somewhat of an anticlimax. Heenan was hampered by a sore on his leg, which slowed his movements and left him vulnerable to Morrissey's powerful punches. Heenan was a brawler, and fell victim to the champion's superior boxing skills. Although Heenan started out strongly, Morrissey quickly wore him down and dominated the eleven rounds. The final round ended when Morrissey dropped the Benicia Boy with a left-right combination to the ribs and throat. Heenan was unable to come to the scratch for a twelfth round and the fight ended after just 22 minutes.[25]

Prior to the fight, Morrissey had announced that the match would be his last. After returning to New York, he reiterated his intention to retire and declined a rematch. After a suitable passage of time, Heenan, although he had never won an official fight, was declared the champion of America.

The most exciting boxing match of the era was the fight that pitted the Benicia Boy against Tom Sayers, the English champion, in 1860. A few years earlier, Morrissey had aroused the country's patriotic fever when he defeated George Thompson, then the British champion, and the match between Heenan and Sayers, which took place outside of London, again placed American pride on the line.

Having conquered one country by default, Heenan set out to capture another in the ring. He challenged Sayers, a 33-year-old miller and former bricklayer, in early 1859 and, following a prolonged series of machinations, negotiations, and broken agreements, managed to arrange a match. Heenan went to England to train, followed by George Wilkes, proprietor of *Wilkes' Spirit of the Times,* who was to cover the great event in person. Wilkes, who fancied himself a player in the world of sports, had been instrumental (or so he said) in arranging the match.[26]

A few days before the fight was to take place, Heenan was arrested by the British police on the grounds that he and Sayers intended to "breach the peace" with their proposed bout.[27] He was released on bail and, on April 17, 1860, the long-awaited match, publicized extensively in all the sporting papers in both countries for several months, finally took place at Farnborough, in the early morning hours. Among the spectators in the open field was John Morrissey, whose role in the affair would later be a matter of great controversy.

Both men came out fighting aggressively. Sayers bloodied Heenan's nose in the first round, but the Benicia Boy, with a tremendous size advantage over the 5' 8", 154-pound Sayers, soon gained the initiative and knocked Sayers to the ground several times. By the seventh round, although Heenan was getting the better of the exchanges, his right eye was puffed and nearly closed, and his lip was swollen and bleeding. By the 26th round, Sayers was also bleeding profusely and decidedly taking the worst of it. The 35th round ended when Heenan threw Sayers to the ground near his corner. Sayers' backers pressed upon the ropes and surrounded the two men, leading to an outburst from Heenan's supporters. By the 37th round, Heenan could barely see out of his swollen eye, and Sayers could scarcely stand from the brutal beating he had absorbed. Heenan pressed his opponent into the ropes, nearly choking him, which led to cries of "Cut the ropes! Cut the ropes!" from Sayers' supporters.

At this point, referee Dowling, editor of the British journal, *Bell's Sporting Life,* beat a hasty retreat from the ring, allowing the two men to finish the fray without his supervision. With his departure, almost total mayhem ensued. At one point a man rushed toward Heenan with a billy club, but he was intercepted before he could get inside the ring. Another man grabbed Heenan by the leg while someone else cut the ropes. During the 40th round, Sayers exited the ring to safety. He returned, however, for the next round, and continued to absorb a fierce beating from Heenan.

By the call for the 43rd round, two hours and twenty minutes into the fight, the crowd was heavily involved in the action. Heenan strode to the center of the ring, but Sayers remained seated in his corner, making no move to resume the hostilities. Finally, Sayers rose, but at that point, a number of men burst into the ring, preventing the two men from coming to blows. Heenan's seconds, fearing that his departure would cause the heavily partisan English crowd to declare Sayers the winner, made Heenan stay put until Sayers left.

With no referee, and the crowd milling about in the ring, the fight was declared a draw, much to the consternation of Heenan's adherents on both sides of the Atlantic. Sayers' backers were equally dissatisfied. Heenan, they claimed, had tried to choke the British champion

On April 17, 1860, American champion John Heenan met British titlist Tom Sayers in a greatly anticipated match at Farnborough, England. After 43 rounds and two hours and twenty minutes, spectators broke into the ring and disrupted the fight. It was declared a draw although Heenan's adherents insisted he had victory snatched from him by the unfortunate finish.

and should therefore have been disqualified. There were other factors clouding the outcome. Dowling, the referee who made an early exit (due to the unruly crowd, he claimed), had gone on record before the fight as saying that Sayers would win. Morrissey, it was claimed, was the man who had cut the ropes when Sayers was pinned against them.[28]

Bursting into the ring when one's fighter was losing was a time-honored boxing tradition, and it resulted in Wilkes and others declaring Heenan champion of the world. The Benicia Boy was perhaps the only world champion who had gained two titles without winning a fight.[29] He returned home to a hero's welcome, financed by nearly ten thousand dollars in donations.[30]

While he may have lacked victories, Heenan had no shortage of charisma and was much more famous than any baseball player of the mid-nineteenth century. Most of the fighters of his day were brawling, battered, frontiersmen, but Heenan, well-muscled, darkly handsome and mustachioed, made an impressive appearance. Before his fight with Tom King in 1864, the *Clipper* described the Boy's physique. "Heenan's magnificent form and muscular development," it reported, "seemed to have an immense effect upon the assembly. His muscles on the arms and chest stood out in large bosses, and, from the delicate color of his skin, he was the living Hercules, such as the ancient sculpture delighted to represent in marble."[31]

In 1858, Heenan had married the famous actress Adah Isaacs Menken, whose most notable role was performed in flesh colored tights and gained her the name of "The Great Naked Lady of the Stage."[32] Her liaison with the Benicia Boy was complicated by the fact that Ms. Menken was still married to her first husband. That soon proved of little consequence, as her relationship with Heenan was short-lived; allegedly the fighter treated his wife in the same rough manner he dealt with Sayers. Like Sayers, Adah declared the match a draw and moved on to the third of her five husbands.[33]

After the Sayers fight, Heenan embarked on the American carnival circuit, then returned to England, where he toured with Howes and Cushings' Circus for the munificent salary of five hundred dollars a week.[34] He had a song, titled "The Bold Irish Yankey Benicia Boy" written in his honor,[35] and he endorsed a number of products, including chewing tobacco and other manly items.

For three years following the Sayers bout, there was constant speculation regarding Heenan's next opponent. He challenged Jem Mace, who had succeeded Sayers as the British champion, and finally, in early 1864, he met Tom King, who had defeated Mace.

As so often happened in major prize fights, the most difficult task was avoiding the "beaks," as the police were affectionately known. On the morning of the fight, Heenan's brother Tim was disguised to look like the Benicia Boy and throw the constables off the trail. The plan worked, and as Tim rested in police custody, Heenan hightailed it across the fields to the train that delivered him to the battle scene. Once again, the police had gotten the wrong man. Given their difficulties corralling Sullivan, Hyer and Heenan, it would seem to have been helpful if the police had known what the fighters looked like, knowledge that could have been obtained from any of the sporting papers.

Heenan's three-year quest for a championship bout resulted in just 35 minutes of fighting, during which he managed to knock King out, but did not win. The muscular American's forte was wrestling, while King was a much better boxer. For the first seventeen rounds, the fight went about as expected, Heenan gaining an edge and throwing King on numerous occasions. At the end of the eighteenth round, Heenan slammed King to the ground head first, knocking him senseless.

During the interlude between rounds, several spectators entered the ring, causing great confusion and allowing King's seconds time to bring him back to a state of consciousness. He revived and charged Heenan and, during the ensuing rounds, inflicted a brutal beating on the American. Heenan's left cheek was swollen and blood ran profusely from his face. His left eye was also cut, and he was barely able to stand. When King dropped him to the ground at the start of the 25th round, Heenan's seconds threw a sponge into the ring, ending the fight. Heenan now had two losses, a draw, a battered face and a small fortune from his boxing career.[36]

Once again, John Morrissey, although he had long since retired from the ring, became the center of controversy. It was alleged that, through a straw man, Morrissey had wagered several thousand dollars on King, while wiring his friends in America to lay their money on Heenan. The latter's trainer, John McDonald, was alleged to have drugged Heenan before the fight, and Morrissey was thought to be an accomplice. The battle that was lost in the ring continued to be fought in the newspapers for months with the same result Heenan had received in the Sayers fight — a draw. It was the last significant bout of his career. Heenan, whose body was greatly damaged in his few fights, became involved in Tammany Hall politics and died at the age of 38 in 1873.[37]

Not all sports featured the brutality of dog fights, cock fights and boxing. The early 1860s witnessed a boom in a much more benign activity — ice skating. Skates were long used in America as a means of transport, but it was not until about 1858, when the lakes at Central Park were opened to the public, that skating became a popular recreational pastime. The Stars and Stripes flew over the Round House in the Park as a signal when the ponds were suitable for skating, and New Yorkers experienced the pleasure of the sport for the first time.

Within a year, skaters began frequenting the ponds in great numbers. The *Clipper* reported that the number of skaters increased from 483,000 in the winter of 1859–1860 to 1,086,000 the following season. On a single day, February 9, 1861, an estimated 105,000 people glided across the ice of Central Park.[38]

By 1862, as the skating boom gained momentum, the ponds at Central Park had become overcrowded, and more facilities appeared throughout New York and Brooklyn. Oscar Oatman opened Washington Park, Brooklyn's first facility, in 1860.[39] The pond covered twelve acres, was surrounded by a board fence and was named after the first President, who had established his headquarters on the site during the Battle of Long Island.[40]

Beekman Pond, Harlem Meadows, Lake Lincoln and Sylvan Lake at Hoboken were available to New York and New Jersey skaters, while the Washington Club Pond, the Communistic-sounding People's Independent Skating Club Pond, the Capitoline Pond and the Union Pond — the latter operated by William Cammeyer — were the most popular Brooklyn locations.

Cammeyer's Union Skating Association of East Brooklyn opened on Christmas Day, 1861. The pond was located on Marcy Street and Rutledge Avenue, covered more than five acres, was enclosed by a high board fence and was open only to members. A membership could be purchased for five dollars for the season, skates could be rented for ten cents per hour and clothing could be stored for ten cents per session. All in all, it was clean, affordable fun, and the tariff avoided the possibility of "a too miscellaneous crowd." Plainly stated, it kept out the riffraff. There were a number of buildings on the Union Pond site, including one for ladies who did not skate, one housing Cammeyer and his staff, another for the lamps used to illuminate the pond at night, one for refreshments, a cloak room, a facility for skate rental and a ladies' lounge.[41] A "Strephilation," a 35-key instrument similar to a calliope, provided musical accompaniment.[42] Cammeyer also owned a "patent freezing machine," a steam-powered condenser that allowed him to strengthen the ice with a cold blast.[43]

One of the most attractive features of skating was the presence of ladies and young girls. In 1862, one New York paper stated, "The feature of the season's demonstrations has been the extreme favor the sport has met with from the ladies. Three years ago a lady on skates was a rare sight; now they form the majority of the visitors to our club ponds."[44] Ladies were spectators at baseball games and other sporting events, but skating was one of the few public activities in which they participated. "We trust that the ladies will not be neglected in this matter [of exercise]," said the *Atlas*. "They require healthful exercise and recreation fully as much as the 'lords of creation.'" The journal, however, suggested archery and "similar English feminine sports" as appropriate activities for the weaker sex.[45]

When the skating furor erupted, archery went by the wayside. "[Skating] is just the exercise for them," proclaimed the *Boston Herald*. "It gives them strength, energy and beauty, developing their forms and planting roses and carnations upon their cheeks.... It expands the chest, strengthens the hips and invigorates the entire system." Women would make better childbearers if they spent more time on the ice, the *Herald* suggested, and that would be good for America. "[T]hey will not only do themselves good, but will enhance the glory of the American eagle, the star spangled banner and all that sort of thing," the writer concluded.[46]

Female participation brought ancillary benefits to male skaters. Women needed to keep their skirts short enough to give them clearance on the ice, and a gust of wind might display a fleeting glimpse of a stocking-clad ankle. If a man were extremely fortunate, a young lady might lose her balance in his vicinity, requiring the gentleman to catch her in his arms and right her. The *Clipper* compared the older pastime of sleighing with the newer one of skating and found the sexual allure of ice activity far more enticing. "True," the writer admitted, "it is delightful to sit beside a lovely girl, encased in warm fur robes, gliding along the glistening roadway of hardened snow, handling the reins attached to a fast-going horse; but then, it is not a very unpleasant task, you know, to teach the same lovely feminine how to skate, for in imparting the requisite knowledge, how often one has to keep the dear one from falling, and isn't it nice to have a rosy-cheeked, bright-eyed girl clinging to you for dear life."[47]

Apparently, the experience was consensual, for, reported one paper, "One laughing, blooming Hebe gave it as her opinion that it was rather pleasant than otherwise to fall on the ice and be picked up, with a perceptible squeeze, by a good looking youth."[48]

The ice pond was a veritable nineteenth century meat market, filled with attractive, helpless women skidding about in need of a strong man to steady them. "To intervene," added another journal, "just in the critical moment between her departure from the perpendicular and her assumption of the horizontal is to enjoy a combination of duty and pleasure not often within reach, and no relation is more calculated to produce tender attachment than that of pupil and tutor under such circumstances."[49]

Not everyone thought skating was a suitable activity for ladies and young girls. The *Brooklyn Daily Times* reported the story of a young woman who supposedly ruined her health by excessive skating and was confined to a sickbed from which she might never rise again.[50] The *Eagle* suggested that archery and croquet, both practiced by English women, were more suitable for American ladies.[51] The paper printed a series of letters from correspondents who debated the propriety of women on ice. A man who signed his name "G" was strongly against the notion, partly because of "the unsightly and inelegant attitudes assumed by the female novices," the aspect of the sport so greatly longed for by other men. "A Man Skater" claimed that the women were not skillful and therefore susceptible to injury. Rowing and pigeon shooting were more appropriate activities, he suggested.

The letters brought about a rebuttal from "A Father Who Takes His Wife and Daughters to the Skating Ponds" who called "G" an old fogy and insisted that, with appropriate attire and training, women were perfectly capable of learning to skate while maintaining their modesty. The distaff side was heard from in the person of "A Lady Skater" who proclaimed, "The lords of creation, in their proneness to insist on the eternal and inalterable supremacy of the male sex, are apt to become selfish in their appropriation of healthy amusements. Probably the writer of the article in question longs for the return of those days when American women shall become again the caged victims of disease, the hot house plants, whom a breath of the pure frosty air sent to consumptive graves.... The awkwardness we are accused of is not confined to ladies, not one man in a thousand is a graceful skater." The writer was a century ahead of her time, as she went on to protest the protective, condescending nature of men, and their insistence on dominating their wives. No doubt, many of the *Eagle* readers thought she deserved not only banishment from the ponds, but a good lashing besides.[52]

On February 4, 1862, a grand skating carnival was held on the Union Pond. Including the spectators, it was estimated that there were ten thousand in attendance. Thousands of costumed skaters made an appearance, including many New York and Brooklyn baseball players who dressed up as, surprisingly, baseball players. Members of the Atlantic, Putnam, Eckford, Charter Oak, Hamilton, Constellation, Resolute, Brooklyn and Favorita Clubs were present, as were numerous others dressed as Hungarians, Russians, Polish Princesses, and Quakers. Mr. John T. Barber sported the outfit worn by Dr. Kane on his original Arctic expedition. Cammeyer was dressed as Hamlet.

In that politically incorrect era, there were fugitive contrabands (slaves), several women dressed as Pocahontas, and Jacob Johnson, who appeared as Barnum's Fat Boy. S.P. Hicks and C.H. Nourse were Mr. and Mrs. Snowdrop "darkies of the first water," and "Mr. John Costigan made a capital drunken Irishman, with black eye and other accompaniments." Military costumes appeared on the ice in abundance, and Miss Pullus, who dressed as a ghost, stayed in character the entire evening, acting an eerie role to the great satisfaction of all. Chinese lanterns and, at the end of the evening, a fireworks display, illuminated the scene, which took place with the utmost decorum and good behavior. The crowd could be observed "deporting themselves only as a publicly educated North American crowd can do with credit to themselves and their country." That was a rather pretentious description of people skating around in carnival costumes, but tensions were great and patriotic feelings strong.[53]

Four days later, a second carnival took place, attracting five to six thousand skaters, again in costume. There were more baseball players and make-believe soldiers, and the *Clipper* published a lengthy list of attendees and their dress.[54] An 1864 carnival attracted a crowd estimated at twenty thousand.[55]

Not everyone was excited about the carnivals. The Reverend Wells of the South Third Street Presbyterian Church delivered a scathing sermon condemning the masquerade, based upon his reading of the Book of Romans and the laws of the State of New York.[56] The Christian Young Men's Association included ice carnivals, along with tobacco, intoxicating liquor, and baseball among evils to be avoided at all costs.[57]

The Reverend Wells and the Christian Young Men's Association notwithstanding, the carnivals continued. The war didn't dampen the ardor for skating, for the *Brooklyn City News* declared, "Never, in the annals of skating in this country, has there been such a brilliant and successful season as that of the winter of 1861–62."[58] Bands often performed beside the Union Pond and Cammeyer frequently delivered a ringing peroration in support of the Union. Perhaps the Army of the Potomac, having such difficulty with the overland route, could skate to Richmond. In 1864, Cammeyer held a particularly successful masquerade on ice. The following January, the event featured an impromptu fireworks display in honor of the capture of Fort Fisher.

The sporting press pointed out both the physical and *moral* benefits of skating. The *Eagle* touted the physical. "Sunken chests," it opined, "sallow cheeks, hollow eyes, defective breathing apparatus, and the wild range of pulmonary afflictions will be considerably diminished."[59]

Another journal cited the moral benefits. One should "ascertain what there is in skating," it declared, "that should lead its votaries to throw aside the ill-humor, the discourtesy and the uncharitableness which, as a general thing, marks the conduct of people when they assemble together on ordinary public occasions, but which is replaced by kind words, pleasant smiles, and good-natured deeds when they are in the enjoyment of skating on a good field of ice."[60]

"Methinks," said *The Brooklyn Daily Times*, "if the hot blood of the South could have been favored with this healthy recreation, their treason and folly would have been worked off by a more healthy and beneficial process, than is now displayed in their insane attempts to overthrow the best Government the world ever saw."[61]

Military maneuvers took place on the ice, as did cricket matches, trotting,[62] and baseball games, the latter a combination of batting, fielding and skating which was more a curiosity than a serious sport. Baseball on ice was first played at Rochester, in January 1860, and later in other areas of upstate New York. A game on ice took place in Detroit in February 1861,[63] and came to New York City for the first time the same month when the Atlantics played the Charter Oak Club on Litchfield's Pond, near 3rd Avenue and 5th Street in South Brooklyn. A reported crowd of twelve to fifteen thousand sport-starved spectators (including a couple of thousand ladies — give or take a few hundred), watched from the embankment surrounding the pond.[64]

In a concession to the difficulty of navigating the slippery surface, games on skates generally featured ten players, including a second catcher positioned behind the first. A runner did not have to stop at the bases, which, along with the positions of the players, were marked by paint, but merely had to skate beyond the line of the base to be considered safe. Because of the problems involved in playing on skates, it was expected that the pitcher, even after more liberal deliveries were allowed under baseball rules, would toss the ball, which was sometimes colored red for better visibility,[65] easily to the bat.

Matches on ice did not always proceed smoothly. In February 1864, a game between the Gotham and Empire Clubs had to be moved to dry land when the ice proved too thin to hold the players safely. In February 1862, an ice match between the Atlantic and Charter Oak Clubs was halted when members of the Nassau Club, upon whose pond the game was being conducted, unceremoniously booted the players off their ice.[66] In fact, many skaters resented the baseball players encroaching upon their territory, for twenty players crisscrossing the pond often inflicted severe damage upon the ice and made it unfit for recreational skating.

There were a number of games played on skates during January 1865, but baseball on ice, like the skating furor, proved a passing fancy. Although it continued into the 1880s, ice ball was more of a novelty and curiosity than a serious sport. "Let them go to Coney Island and play [baseball] on stilts," scoffed the *Eagle*.[67]

A number of other pastimes were mildly popular in the New York area. None were more civil than chess and checkers (the latter often referred to as draughts), both of which were reported extensively by the *Clipper*. The Scots played a game called golf, which was known but rarely played in America. College students played a brand of rugby they called football. Handball, quoits (horseshoes), curling, pedestrianism (track), gymnastics, bowling, yachting, billiards, and handball are familiar to modern sports fanciers, but other nineteenth century pastimes are not. Fire companies competed with each other to see whose engine could throw water the farthest. Pigeon shooting was a popular, well-reported activity. In 1862, there was a hog race in McClary, Illinois, that was deemed worthy of mention in the *Clipper*.[68] In

December 1853, a *Clipper* headline promised "Fun! Fun! Fun!" to those who attended a festival featuring a variety of winter sports, including hurdle leaping, a sack race and a wheelbarrow race.[69] Californians favored hare hunting and held wood-chopping contests. In February 1861, two New York butchers staged a sheep dressing match for $100 in prize money. The winner, Roger Gorman, dressed five sheep in the impressive time of 22 minutes and 8 seconds, besting his opponent by ten minutes.[70]

While boxing, canine sport, cocking, skating, draughts and even sheep dressing had their followers, it is difficult to imagine any of them becoming the national sport of a country that saw itself as a leader of civilization. The *Clipper* and *Wilkes'* did their best to defend boxing, but it was a difficult task. In 1859, the *Clipper* published two drawings side by side. One featured a pair of robust young men, stripping off their coats in anger, preparing to engage in "the manly art" in which "the best man may win." "They come out," the caption stated, "the victor and vanquished, better friends to each other, and more highly pleased with the doctrines of manual defense than when they went into the scrimmage." The other drawing pictured a hollow-chested, lank-haired, dispirited, downcast duelist who has been stripped of his sword and waits for his opponent to administer the *coup de grâce*. "Reader," the *Clipper* asked gravely, "which is the more humane?"[71]

Canine sport, horse racing and boxing were tainted by a number of unsavory incidents, including shootings over disputed results. Still, boosters of sport, such as the *Clipper*, took great pains to emphasize the "scientific" nature of such pastimes. The technical aspects of boxing were touted as sufficient to allow a smart fighter to overcome a powerful but unskilled brawler. While it was nigh impossible to attribute science to two dogs ripping each other to shreds or killing rats, the art of breeding and choosing cocks for battle was discussed *ad naseum*. Skating was reputable and civilized, but it was not particularly scientific, nor was it highly competitive, and Americans strove to be the best in the world at everything they did.

No sport was touted as scientific more often than baseball, but there was one more test to be passed before the value of baseball could be justified. It was not sufficient that baseball was fun. It was not enough that it tested the intellect. In order for the sport to be taken seriously, it had to be beneficial to human progress, a remedy to a serious issue that was troubling America.

Prior to the middle of the nineteenth century, sport had generally been considered a waste of time or worse. In 1726, an English official speculated that cricket was simply a way to gather a group of troublemakers together to foment rebellion.[72] In 1743, an article in *Gentleman's Magazine* cautioned, "The Diversion of Cricket may be proper in Holiday Time, and in the Country; but upon Days when Men ought to be busy, and in the Neighbourhood of a great City, it is not only improper but mischievous in a high Degree."[73] Students at Deerfield Academy in the late 1700s were subject to a fine for playing ball near the school,[74] and Etonian cricketers of the same era were flogged by their headmaster after he discovered they had played against the Westminster School.[75] Early town ball players in Philadelphia were often reproached by their friends for wasting time in such a frivolous pursuit.[76] Ironically, the Village of Cooperstown banned ball playing in 1816,[77] and as late as 1839, ball playing in any public place in New York City was punishable by a fine of five dollars.[78]

Sports and outdoor games were generally seen as a suitable entertainment for boys and an aid to their physical culture, but it wasn't until the 1850s that they were considered a productive activity for adults. As early as 1846, poet Walt Whitman had written, "the game of ball is glorious,"[79] but few others thought so.

Eventually, less lyrical writers joined the chorus. "[S]ports which are essentially manful in their nature," stated the *New York Times*, "we have, for some reason or other, given over wholly to boys, and come to regard as undignified in the full-grown man. This ridiculous prejudice is disappearing in great cities, but still prevails extensively throughout the country."[80]

No one praised the beneficial value of sport more than those who stood to gain from its growth, such as editor Frank Queen of the *Clipper*. In November 1856, the *Clipper* published an editorial titled *Mental Power vs. Bodily Health*. The healthy physical exertion associated with frontier life had given way to the sedentary habits of city life and business, the *Clipper* asserted. Something was needed to restore the robust health of the American male, and what was better than sport? "It is only by making all sporting exertion voluntary and pleasurable," the article stated, "that we can shake off the restraints of business and the stagnant blood generated while under their influence."[81]

"Half our citizens," the *Clipper* stated a few years later, "are killing themselves by neglecting physical exercise.... Hence come the consumptive forms, the pale or the bloated faces one sees in a ramble through the streets."[82] "We pay far too much attention," said the *Eagle*, "to our desks, counters and offices than the laws of Dame Nature will admit of without the accompanying penalty of ill health."[83] The health of women was even worse, claimed the *Eagle*, noting "the chalky complexions, the hollow chests and consumptive appearance of a majority of the pupils [of female academies and seminaries]."[84] Others saw "the Yankee as a slab-sided, lantern-jawed, spindle-shanked dyspeptic" and women as invalids as fragile as porcelain.[85] Sports would make them whole again. The Knickerbockers, said Chadwick, slept better and had healthier appetites after an afternoon's play.[86]

All the deficiencies noted in the American male, in fact, could be remedied by the game of baseball. "The game of base ball," wrote the *Atlas*, "is a most exciting and pleasant one, and the exercise is well-calculated to develop the muscle and expand the lungs. The clubs of this city and vicinity are composed exclusively of young men of the first respectability, an inducement for new members to come forward."[87]

Baseball "is a sport," said the *Brooklyn Daily Times*, "to practice which insures the finest training possible for the eye, the brain, the muscles, and every particle of the human body, eventuating in a healthy frame, a manly bearing, prompt action, activity of mind and body, and other benefits that no other sport does or can educe."[88] "[N]o athletic game," claimed a letter writer to the *Times*, "is better calculated to strengthen the frame, and develop a full, broad chest, testing a man's powers of endurance most severely."[89] "We should hail it as a favorable omen for the next generation," added *Porter's*, "if that great specimen of humanity yclept Young New York would join baseball or cricket clubs and quit his bar rooms and other night amusements and seek the open air."[90]

"In Boston," the *Clipper* reported, "the head quarters of divinity schools and Puritan preference, we find that there is a noble upheaval of free opinion which advocates the absolute necessity of providing suitable sports in which all classes may mingle and cultivate health in the pursuit of sociality or profit."[91] "The clergy," added another paper, "not only lend their countenance to, but many actively participate in the game, thereby stamping it as void of all objectionable practices."[92]

Although many of the ancient ball games originated in religious services, the clergy had not always been supportive of athletic activity. In 1330, William Pagula, Vicar of Winkfield, composed a Latin poem for his parish priests, instructing them to forbid the playing of all ball games in their churchyards.[93] Apparently, not all priests heeded the advice of Pagula, for half a century later, in 1385, there were complaints that young boys were damaging churches by playing ball inside them. Excommunication was the suggested remedy.[94]

In 1637, after King Charles had approved ball playing after church, Protestant clergy pointed out that a higher authority apparently disagreed with Charles' edict, for in one game a boy had been hit in the head with the cat and immediately fell down dead.[95] A year later, Bishop Mantague reinforced the prohibition against ball-playing in churchyards, along with other objectionable acts such as drinking and dunging cattle. There were to be no cow stools and no stool ball, and no combinations thereof.[96]

Magic moments of revelation, by Doubleday, Cartwright and Chadwick, had allegedly spurred the growth of baseball, but they also occurred among opponents to sport. It was difficult to determine which side God was on. John Bunyan, author of *Pilgrim's Progress,* was playing cat and just about to bat, when he suddenly recognized a voice from heaven, which said, "Wilt thou leave thy sins and go to Heaven or have thy sins and go to Hell?"[97] On the other hand, the Mormons, always non-conforming to other religions, apparently played ball in the 1830s as they migrated west toward the Great Salt Lake. "[T]he Prophet frequently took a hand in the sport," reported one of the entourage.[98]

Eventually, mainstream religion discovered and accepted the value of athletics. In 1858, the Reverend Thomas Wentworth Higginson, pastor of the Worcester Free Church, wrote an article in *The Atlantic Monthly* noting the benefit of exercise and giving Christians permission to partake in it.[99]

One can find support for just about anything in the Bible if one simply looks hard enough, and by the middle of the 19th century, clergymen were using scripture to prove virtue in athletic pastimes. The Reverend C. H. Everest, pastor of the Puritan Church of East Brooklyn, chose the 13th verse of the 16th chapter of Corinthians, "Watch ye, stand fast in the faith, quit you like men, be strong," as a segue to the value of sport. "It promotes godliness," Everest proclaimed, "as religious joy and comfort depend largely on the health of the individual, and a dyspeptic man makes a dyspeptic Christian."[100] The *Union & Advertiser* of Rochester referred to "muscular Christianity."[101]

Some citations preceded the time of the Savior. "Such manly exercise," said the *Clipper* at the start of the 1857 season, "and healthful amusement as this calls to mind the interesting sports of the ancients, the games of the Olympics, participated in by the Alexanders, and all the great men of those times whose names live in history."[102]

The formation of new baseball clubs, especially those composed of youngsters, frequently elicited praise for the noble nature of the venture. "These clubs [the Enterprise and Star]," said the *Clipper* in November 1856, "are composed of youths ranging from 15 to 18 years of age, who have organized, like thousands of others, for the purpose of perfecting themselves in the various physical exercises, which are so necessary for a proper development of the mental faculties."[103] It is doubtful that the youngsters, who simply enjoyed playing baseball, had such noble motives in mind, but it was all for the cause.

Even the rival Massachusetts version of baseball provided social benefits. "How much better it is," wrote a Boston correspondent to the *Clipper* in 1859, "for those who engage in these pleasant recreations, and the 'early birds' with their female mates who are attracted to witness their games to return home with light and happy hearts, and good appetites for breakfast, than for those who while away insensibly the lagging hours of a long summer morning in bed. The smiling face and cheerful look of the early riser through the day is the best certificat [sic] that can be offered in his favor."[104]

"The fact was," wrote one journalist, "that at that time our people were a regular target for the shafts of raillery and even of abuse from the out-door sports-loving people of England, in consequence of our then national neglect of field sports and our too great devotions to the pursuit of the 'almighty dollar.' But thanks to base ball — the entering wedge of the great reformation which has since taken place — we have been transformed into quite another kind of people."[105]

For every action there is, of course, a reaction, and there were still enough Puritans in America to object to a shift from desks, counters and offices to the playing field. In 1859, the *Eagle* quoted an unnamed "observer" who claimed, "If a stranger were to form a judgment of the productive industry of this country by what he sees in the newspapers in reference to cricket matches, base ball playing, and other amusements, he would take it for granted that ours is a country wherein people can live without labor, or that one-third of our population toiled for the other two-thirds."[106]

Woe to those, however, who objected to sport as a frivolous waste of time. "Who are our opponents?" the *Clipper* asked rhetorically in February 1857, in a column titled "The Morals of Our Opponents." "What are they like? If they are men, let them stand forward. This, however, is the very thing they will not do. No; their bravery is shown in the slander which is poured into the ears of bigoted ignorance or fashionable simplicity ... what a sickening state of depravity they exhibit."[107]

"A visit to the Elysian Fields at Hoboken any fine day," the *Clipper* said a few months later, "will convince those disposed to find fault with our sports and pastimes that our young men rapidly improve in a moral as well as a physical point of view by participating in such manly games as Base Ball and Cricket. Let the good work go on."[108]

One could fill page after page with published arguments touting the benefits of baseball that appeared in the 1850s. One is hard pressed, however, prior to the 1860s, to find many articles describing the *pleasure* of playing or watching baseball. It was part of the job of getting fit, and the pleasure derived from the benefits associated with an expanded chest and increased endurance. The seriousness of business, which was so uniformly criticized, was to give way to the gravity of sport and physical development. Baseball was not a delightful diversion; it was a method of building up the physical man to complement the intellectual component.

Most of the writing on the pros and cons of sport appeared in the late 1850s. By the early 1860s, two changes had taken place in America. First, sport had become accepted to the extent that it was no longer necessary to defend it. Second, the onset of war made the glorification of sport as the epitome of manliness somewhat embarrassing when millions of men were carrying rifles and hauling cannons in defense of their country.

In the mid-nineteenth century, none of the other sports that competed with baseball for the title of America's national game reflected the values that citizens of the United States believed to be their own. Horse racing didn't provide the physical exercise of other pastimes. Boxing was certainly physical, but faced a number of problems in gaining mainstream acceptance. In 1860, the *Clipper* spoke optimistically of the growth of boxing in the U.S. "With respect to the fistic art in general," it said, "we have welcomed what we considered to be indications of its progress, as a national sport among us."[109] It chided publishers, such as Horace Greeley, who excoriated the sport, but used it to sell papers. Greeley had written of the ring, "It is in the grog shops and the brothels and the low gaming hells," while filling six columns with details of the Heenan-Morrissey match of 1858.[110]

In 1853, the *Spirit of the Times* took the part of Yankee Sullivan, who was facing trial in Boston as a result of his boxing activity. "Whatever reputation Massachusetts may have as a supporter and patron of the arts and sciences," Porter wrote, "there is evidence that at least one art does not come in for its share of her patronage, and that is the 'manly art of self defence.'"[111]

Boxing might be *a* national sport, but it was clear that baseball was becoming *the* national sport. In the minutes of the Knickerbocker Club for 1855, there is a reference to the sport as the "National Game."[112] In August 1856, the *Clipper* said of baseball, "As it has had its origin on this Continent, and is now thoroughly established as an American game, equal, to a certain extent, to the English game of Cricket, we hope to see it grow in popularity as it increases in age among us."[113] The following year, the *Clipper* headlined a paragraph on baseball with the phrase "The National Game." It commented on the increase in interest in baseball and its belief that it would soon become the national sport of the United States.[114] In 1860, the journal apparently believed the mission had been accomplished. "This manly pastime," read the February 18th issue, "and excellent outdoor exercise has made rapid progress in popularity within the past year or two, and may now be considered as the National game of ball."[115]

While baseball was by no means a perfect reflection of American values, life is graded on the curve, and baseball certainly spoke to Americans more than brutal sports like boxing, canine sport or cocking. The *Clipper* called it a sport "entirely free from the objections that are urged against other outdoor sports."[116] Charles Peverelly wrote in 1866, "[I]n short, the pastime suits the people, and the people suit the pastime."[117] There was very little of America in American cricket, which was brought to this country and dominated for its entire existence by Englishmen. Other sports fell by the wayside. America was ready to embrace leisure and prepared to adopt a sport they enjoyed playing and watching, particularly one they considered their own. There was a void, and baseball stepped in to fill it.

CHAPTER 8

Why Not Cricket?

In the early nineteenth century, most bat-and-ball games were intended to be played by the very young. References to the old cat variations, stool ball and feeder were found in children's books such as *The Every Boy's Book, The Boy's Own Book* and *Youth's Encyclopedia of Health*. The only ball game taken seriously by adults was cricket, which had been played for a number of years in England (apparently originating sometime during the sixteenth century[1]) and was introduced in the United States, in primitive form, in the eighteenth century. The first written rules of cricket appeared in 1744,[2] and Benjamin Franklin brought a set of rules from Europe to America in 1767.[3] Documentation of early games is rare, for few would think of recording for posterity informal leisure activity among friends, any more than one would now think of memorializing a backyard volleyball game at a Fourth of July picnic. Newspapers were far less numerous in the eighteenth century, and there were no blogs lending themselves to the preservation of mundane everyday events. Blithely unaware of twenty-first century researchers' quest for knowledge, eighteenth century cricketers and stool ball players trooped out to an open field, played for a few hours and returned to their more practical and serious tasks in the fields and shops.

There are scattered accounts of eighteenth century cricket matches in America, including a game played in Virginia in 1709,[4] one in Georgia in 1737,[5] one in New York in 1751[6] and one in Hartford, Connecticut, in 1767.[7] A more common game was wicket, which was very similar to cricket and played mostly in Connecticut.

There were two cricket clubs in New York by 1779 and one in Richmond as early as 1795, and by late in the century there were a number of games played in the New York area. Boston's first club was organized in 1809[8] and the Union Club was formed in Philadelphia in 1832.[9] The first widely-reported "modern" cricket match took place in 1838 in New York between former residents of the English towns of Sheffield and Nottingham.[10]

That was one of American cricket's biggest problems. Virtually all of the top cricketers in the early years were English-born, and they so dominated the sport that native Americans were loath to take up a game at which they were likely to be embarrassed. When American-born cricketers played against native Britons, they were generally given a manpower advantage, typically 18 to 11, and were still delighted on the rare occasions they won. In 1860, after 18 Americans defeated 11 Englishmen at Philadelphia, Captain Stevens of the Americans said it was the proudest moment of his life and that he hoped to see the day when 11 Americans could defeat 11 Britons "although he would candidly confess he thought the time was far distant."[11]

Many Americans felt that, even with favorable odds, they were at a disadvantage, since most cricketers played for more than one club, and the Americans frequently faced an all-star combination of talent. In 1863, the *Times* noted the predominance of baseball over cricket and commented, "The main cause of this is, that few cricketers — who have become stale in the opinion of the public — play pretty much in all the matches for the few clubs (except St. George) that exist only in name; while Bass [sic] Ball Clubs play their matches with their *bona fide* members."[12]

The most prominent cricket club in America prior to the Civil War was the St. George Club of New York, which first played as the New York Club in 1838 before changing the name of the organization in 1840.[13] The club bore the name of England's patron saint, a name selected on his feast day,[14] and its key members were English businessmen. In England, the Marylebone Cricket Club towered above all others, codified the rules and set the standards. The St. George Club sought to establish a similar place in American cricket.

One of the leading players on the St. George eleven was Sam Wright, born in Sheffield, England, in 1812. Sam, whose sons Harry and George would become prominent in American baseball, came to the United States in 1836 when oldest son Harry was an infant, and he commenced playing cricket two years later. Sam was a good round arm bowler, a strong batter and a sure fielder. He played cricket well into middle age, but, unlike his sons, never played baseball.[15]

The St. George Club was hindered in its effort to rule American cricket by its heavily English orientation. Yet no Americans stepped in to fill the void. The New York Cricket Club, composed principally of American-born players affiliated with journalist William Porter, was formed in 1842, but lasted only a short time.[16] Thomas Melville in *The Tented Field*, his splendid and insightful history of American cricket, identified the Union Star Club of Brooklyn, formed just a few years after the St. George Club, as playing a pivotal, though fleeting, role in the development of the American game. While it held to a structure and style of play imitative of the English version of the sport, the Union Star Club made an effort to appeal to Americans and adapt its structure to fit American values. It was not successful, however, passing from existence in 1847 after only three years of play.[17]

"Americanizing the game" principally meant speeding up cricket's agonizingly slow pace. "The cricket season," reported the *Eagle* in 1862, "also promises very fair, but as this is not an *American* game, but purely an English game, it never will be in much vogue with the Americans, especially the New Yorkers, who are all for fast and not slow things."[18] Playing in the English style meant showing up fashionably late, perhaps an hour after the scheduled starting time, commencing the match well after the appointed hour, taking numerous refreshment breaks, and concluding play over a two- to three-day period. It was not uncommon to take a half-hour break between innings, each of which continued until all eleven batters were put out, and five to ten minutes between batters.

Even when play was in, there was not necessarily much action, for batters did not have to run and risk being put out each time they hit the ball. They left their wicket only when they thought they could score a run. A ball bowled toward the wicket could be blocked, which resulted in neither an out nor a run. Blocking and being a good judge of when to try for a run were considered key elements of scientific batting, which was admired much more than long hitting. Such tactics also led to a very long game with little action. One batter might hit for more than an hour while the other members of his team sat idly by. Less patient American players swung freely and were often criticized for their lusty style of batting, even when they were effective.

"Cricket," opined one writer, "is suited to the softer feelings of a refined age."[19] "Cricket may do for England," wrote another, "where the shops do not open until 10 A.M. and close at 4:30 in the afternoon; where the railroads in the city run underground at the rate of three miles an hour; where three weeks are required to play a game of billiards; where drug stores are 'chemist shops;' where crackers are 'biscuits;' where dry toast is 'muffins;' where shoes are 'boots;' and boots are 'Wellingtons;' where street cars are 'trains;' baggage 'luggage;' railroad tickets 'books;' and 'jays' juggins'—but it will never do for America."[20]

"In England," wrote Henry Chadwick, "there is a large class of wealthy people on whose hands time hangs heavily, for want of regular employment; and when this class takes hold of any sport as a means of getting rid of the *ennui* which too much leisure induces, they invariably drag into it their customary lazy mode of doing everything, and hence waste of time becomes habitual."[21] "Cricket is essentially an English game," he wrote on another occasion, "and is adapted to John Bull, and he likes it; he can sit and sip his porter at ease, and enjoy the game. He can spend hours this way."[22] A "game in such favor with the English," he claimed, "cannot well have much attraction for the American, the disposition of both people being as different as baseball is from cricket."[23]

Whenever the cricket community realized that American participation and interest were low, they talked about changing the rules. Some Americans suggested three outs per inning and six innings per game.[24] Chadwick urged cricketers simply to show up and start matches on time in the prompt manner expected by Americans.[25] Perhaps games could begin on Friday, after the close of business, and conclude on Saturday, which would allow for wider participation. Maybe the entire affair could be condensed to a single day.

Shortening the length of matches, however, would take much more than merely appearing on the grounds at the appointed hour. It would require changes of a type that the English cricketers were unwilling to consider. The rules of cricket had been established for several decades, and to alter them was much more difficult than to change the rules of baseball, which was new and continually evolving. "Cricket is an English game," opined one journalist, "and we have no more right to interfere with the regulations of the Marylebone Club by adopting new rules, than they to change the rules of baseball adopted by the American National Association."[26]

Even those who admired cricket admitted that baseball was becoming more popular among Americans, partly because it was easier to learn and understand. "Base ball is the favorite game," declared the *Eagle* in 1858, "as it is more simple in its rules, and a knowledge of it more easily acquired. Cricket is the most scientific of the two and requires more skill and judgment in the use of the bat, especially, than base."[27] "Baseball is the favorite game here," said the *Atlas,* "and always will be, we presume, from the simple fact of its having been to a great extent the only game of ball practiced by the youths of the city from childhood up."[28]

Despite its shortcomings, cricket enjoyed significant popularity in the United States. By 1850, there were a half dozen clubs in New York and about twenty around the United States.[29] At that time, the Knickerbockers and Washingtons were the only baseball clubs in existence. During the 1850s, cricket spread to virtually every populated area of the country, including the South, where New Orleans was the center of activity. "Cricket is becoming the fashionable game," claimed the *Washington Star* in 1855, "the national game, it might be said."[30] In the early 1850s, cricket was far more popular than baseball, but Melville claimed that American cricket reached its pre–Civil War peak in 1857.[31]

In 1859, American cricket received a stimulus from across the ocean when the All-England team, under the leadership of George Parr, arrived in North America for a visit that had been talked of for several years. American cricketers had gone to Canada as early as 1840, and there were several matches between clubs from the two countries during the next few years. Although the contests were ostensibly between the United States and Canada, the American eleven was generally comprised entirely of Englishmen. A successful Canadian visit to the United States in 1856 whetted the American appetite for the real thing from the old country. For three years, a correspondence was conducted across the Atlantic, which eventually resulted in the English cricketers' visit to America.[32]

The publicity that preceded the All-England tour increased American interest in the sport to heretofore unseen levels, and the actual visit itself was a rousing success. As soon as the British players arrived in Montreal in late September, they were overwhelmed with invitations from Cincinnati, Baltimore, Albany and St. Louis, and an offer of five thousand dollars to play a game of baseball in New York.[33] The visitors had no room on their schedule for additional games and little interest in playing baseball, but the enthusiasm was certainly encouraging.

The cricketers played before good crowds in Montreal, Hamilton, Philadelphia and Rochester, but the highlight of the visit was the three days the cricketers spent in New York where a total of nearly 20,000 spectators took in the performance at the Elysian Fields. The lowlight of the event was the fact that the Americans, even playing with 22 against the English 11, were soundly and embarrassingly beaten. Even worse, the best Americans were not even Americans, for most of the 22 were immigrant Englishmen. Fortunately for American pride, the matches at the next stop, Philadelphia, were much closer, with interest nearly as great, as seven to eight thousand spectators were present.

Naturally, the New Yorkers had wanted the cricketers to play baseball against a team gathered from the best players of New York and Brooklyn. Discussions were begun, but unfortunately they were conducted with the wrong party. Mr. W. Bolivar Davis, who came to Brooklyn to attempt to arrange a game and a large fee, turned out to have no authority from the All-English Eleven.[34] That did not prevent him from holding spirited negotiations and insisting that the cricketers would only play the "fly" game.[35] When the doubts concerning Davis's authenticity were confirmed by a telegram from the eleven, Dr. Jones of the Excelsiors journeyed to Rochester to try to arrange the match in person.[36] In late October, however, the cricketers sailed away from Quebec, and Jones returned to New York, empty handed.[37] Apparently the cricketers, who had originally said they could not postpone their return trip, upped the ante ($500 per man plus expenses) to a level the ball players would not accept.[38] Further, the cricketers had played a little baseball with some local players in Rochester, and Jones, who had been singularly unimpressed with their skill, did not feel they could play a competitive or interesting game in New York.[39]

Every aspect of the English tour and every detail of the matches was dutifully and enthusiastically reported in the American press. The publicity brought about a wave of new clubs, and it appeared that the tour might be the impetus America needed to make cricket as popular in this country as it was in England. The phenomenon was short-lived, however, for which Thomas Melville provides a plausible explanation. The large attendance at the All-English matches was not indicative of a deep interest in cricket, he declared, only of a great curiosity to see the skilled foreign players. When they departed, so did the thirst for cricket. The skill of the American players was not sufficient to draw the kind of crowds that came to see the English professionals.[40]

In September 1863, the Atlantics and Mutuals played a baseball game on the St. George cricket grounds in Hoboken. "[T]here were more persons present in the occasion," reported the *Times*, "than there have been during the entire season on the St. George, New-York and Manhattan cricket grounds combined. This shows that cricket has been almost obliterated by base ball, which, but ten years since, was in its infancy, and could only count a corporal's guard to witness a match, while a cricket match would be attended for a couple of days together by from 8,000 to 10,000 persons."[41]

The year after the English tour, New Yorkers formed an American Cricket Club comprised only of native Americans, including baseball players Jim Creighton, Dickie Pearce, Thomas Dakin, Aleck Pearsall, Sam Patchen, Asa Brainard, one of the Grum brothers, John Holder, one of the Oliver brothers and John Whiting. Dakin was named president. Baseball players played more baseball than cricket, however, and the American Cricket Club never amounted to much.[42] Following the 1861 season, it was absorbed into the Long Island Club.[43]

Although New York was the early center of cricket activity, the sport was taken up in other cities, including Baltimore where there was some activity just before the war. The most prominent organization was the Maryland Club, which boasted a hired English professional and a number of distinguished members. The visit of the English professionals in 1859 heightened interest, but the war, during which Maryland was a frequent battleground, put an effective damper on the sport. Only one club, the Hygeia, survived the conflict, a circumstance ascribed to the fact that most of its members were English.[44]

No city took to the sport with more avidity than Philadelphia where the game had been played since the 1830s by the Union Club. One of the root causes of the sport's success was the fact that, although cricket was initially played by Englishmen who emigrated to Philadelphia to take advantage of opportunities in the city's wool industry,[45] it was later controlled principally by Americans. The first organization composed mostly of American natives was the Philadelphia Cricket Club, formed in 1854. Before the war Philadelphia boasted three strong and active organizations, the Germantown, Philadelphia and Young America Clubs.[46] Tom Senior, a native of Yorkshire, was the professional of the Philadelphia Club. He was perhaps the most prominent cricketer in the city and one of the best fast round arm bowlers in America.

The onset of the Civil War impacted cricket as deeply as it did all sporting ventures. Both Union and Confederate soldiers played the sport in the army, but activity on the home front, with many club members off to war, was limited. For several years, cricketers had been talking of forming an association similar to that set up by the baseball fraternity. Despite several meetings, they had not done so. At the annual convention of 1862, the *Clipper* noted the meager attendance and proclaimed the gathering "a mere farce." It despaired of cricket ever becoming popular unless it was made more American in nature.[47] The disappointing convention was the last the cricketers would hold.[48]

By 1864, cricket activity in Philadelphia, as well as the rest of the country, was sorely depressed. "The breaking out of the war," a journalist wrote years later, "was the breaking up of cricket in Philadelphia."[49]

The conflict also cost the city one of its top players, Walter Newhall, a member of one of the most renowned families in the cricket world. In 1857, Walter, not yet sixteen, had scored one of the first recorded centuries (one hundred runs in a single at bat) in America.[50] He enlisted in the Union Army just a week after the fall of Fort Sumter and, serving as a captain in the 3rd Pennsylvania Cavalry, drowned in the raging Rappahannock River in 1863 when his frightened horse fell on him.[51] In death, his cricket feats were magnified, and he became the Creighton of his sport (for Creighton's death, see Chapter 16).

After the war, cricket experienced a resurgence in Philadelphia with interest returning almost to antebellum levels. The Newhalls, minus the unfortunate Walter, were the city's first family of cricket. After the death of Walter and the retirement from active play of Harrison, the four active Newhalls were George, born in 1845, Charles, born in 1847, Daniel, born in 1849, and Robert, born in 1853. Their skills were impressive and their dedication to the game even more so. They played until the late 1880s, and it was in large part due to their efforts that the sport rebounded after the war.[52]

For the rest of the century, Philadelphia took the lead among American cities in terms of cricket ability and activity. In 1866, the Young America Club, comprised of native Americans, defeated the New York and St. George Clubs, made up predominately of Englishmen. Still, American cricket made meager progress outside of Philadelphia. When the United States took on international competition, the majority of players on the American team were usually Philadelphians. When foreign teams came to the U.S., they typically found their stiffest competition in Philadelphia and were rarely challenged elsewhere.

Being the leading cricket city in America was a lukewarm honor, for in the rest of the country, the sport's popularity had fallen to the point where its leading practitioners were upper-class schools and teams organized by companies for their workers. Postwar American cricket never again reached the level of popularity it enjoyed prior to the conflict. It was not until 1878 that an American club managed as much as a draw against a foreign eleven, and the following year the Americans finally achieved their first win. Still, after forty years, American cricket was not even close to being competitive on the international level.

Chadwick expressed the wish that cricket would at least take hold among the American upper class since it was clearly not challenging baseball for the favor of the great unwashed. "[W]e have hopes," he wrote in 1868, "that the game has had the inaugural start given it which will, ere many years have passed, have placed it in equal rank in popularity with the National game, at least as far as the leisure classes of American society are concerned." He cited the barriers to acceptance as the length of the game, the fact that many of the cricketers were older, while the game was ignored by the young, and the fact that players played for various clubs rather than engendering loyalty to any one.[53]

While Americans were not very good at cricket, they could take comfort in the fact that cricketers were even more inept at baseball. Baseball clubs frequently played against cricketers, offering the same kind of odds the baseballers were given at cricket. In 1861, the St. George Club beat the Favorita baseball Club, but the Favorita was hardly one of the best nines in New York.[54] Two weeks later, nine top ballplayers beat eighteen cricketers at baseball, even though the latter club included George and Harry Wright.[55]

Late in 1863, nine Atlantics played seventeen cricketers and beat them, 22–8, despite a very crowded eleven-man outfield. This was only one of many games in which outnumbered baseball players beat cricketers. In 1864, the New York Cricket Club and the Eagle Baseball

Club played a doubleheader, the Eagles winning at baseball and the New York Club at cricket.[56] It appeared that neither could play the other's game. The shortcoming of most of the cricketers was their fielding. Chadwick urged more interaction between players of the two sports, believing that cordial relations would be to the benefit of both. It was not the feelings between the players that mattered, however, it was the apathy of American spectators that doomed cricket to second tier status.

By the end of the nineteenth century, cricket and baseball had moved in opposite directions. Baseball in the 1850s was played by gentlemen, with games frequently followed by extensive entertainment, which seemed nearly as important as the game itself. Cricket, which at the beginning of the 1850s was the game played by serious sportsmen, became by the 1880s a game played by gentlemen for their own amusement. While reporting a rare American victory over an English eleven in 1885, a journalist devoted nearly as much space to listing the prominent socialites in attendance as he did to describing the match.[57] Cricket was no longer taken seriously as a competitive sport while baseball had become the national game, whose season was climaxed by a World Series for the championship of the United States.

Why didn't cricket take hold in America? Scholars have advanced a number of reasons, some ethereal and others quite practical. Among the latter was the long-held contention that cricket was simply too long and drawn out. Only a privileged few had the luxury of spending the two or three days of recreation often required to complete a match. The length of the affair also resulted in long periods with little action, which many observers claimed was contrary to the American spirit of dash and derring-do. Historian Ian Tyrrell believed that the reason for cricket's lack of support in America was that it became a sport primarily of the upper class while baseball was adopted by the more populous working class.[58]

Another factor contributing to America's lack of enthusiasm for cricket was the belief that there was little hope, given Great Britain's long history of playing the game, that Americans could excel and become the best in the world. In baseball, which was an American game, native players *were* the best in the world. Cricket is a game with many subtle points, which cannot be mastered easily, and one in which mere physical strength does not ensure success. George Wright, the finest baseball player of the late 1860s, insisted that cricket required more skill than baseball. A number of the English cricketers in America were professionals who devoted all their time to the sport and for whom American amateurs were no match. In a country that saw itself as being the best in everything it undertook, one which had conquered the wilderness of the American frontier, and by the end of the nineteenth century had visions of dominating the entire planet, embracing a game in which they could never be the best was not appealing.

The reason put forth by Albert Spalding and others for cricket's demise is that it did not suit American values, while baseball did. This is a rhetorical argument, perfectly correct in hindsight, but difficult to prove. What can be proved, however, is that many influential commentators, including Spalding, drove their point home with such regularity that Americans became convinced that what they said was true. Perhaps baseball was American and cricket wasn't.

Some scholars felt that the interruption caused by the Civil War killed American cricket. If so, why didn't it kill baseball? Why did interest in baseball explode after the war while cricket floundered? One of the reasons is that Americans had never exhibited the interest in cricket that they had in baseball. Most of the early American cricket activity was initiated by Englishmen, with a limited number of Americans taking part. Baseball was a game that, European bat and ball antecedents notwithstanding, had originated in America, and was driven by Americans, not by a group of recent immigrants from any one nation. Further, baseball was a new sport that was on the upswing before the war while cricket was a stable sport with little growth.

There were too many factors working against cricket, too many handicaps that prevented it from becoming America's national game, or even rivaling baseball in popularity. During the 1850s and early 1860s, coverage of cricket in the sporting press generally exceeded that of baseball. While writers discoursed on cricket, however, spectators flocked to baseball games. As a serious competitor to the new sport, cricket was doomed, a fact that first began to assert itself during the early 1860s and became readily apparent by the late 1860s. Baseball was clearly America's national game.

CHAPTER 9

The Southern Front: Sporting Life in Antebellum New Orleans

The only Southern locale in which baseball thrived prior to the Civil War was New Orleans. The Louisiana city had a unique history with roots both French and Spanish, having been under the rule of each at some point after its founding by the French in 1718. In 1803, the United States, as part of the Louisiana Purchase, acquired New Orleans, but the city retained a culture all its own, not really Southern and certainly not like the industrial Northeast.

In 1850, New Orleans was the most populous city in the South, and the fifth largest in the United States, behind New York, Boston, Baltimore and Philadelphia, with a heterogeneous population of more than 116,000. About a quarter of its residents were African Americans, both free and slave, and forty percent of the inhabitants were foreign-born. The French Creoles were the most prominent ethnic group, but the city was a true melting pot of races and nationalities.[1]

With its fortuitous location as a Mississippi River and Gulf Coast port, New Orleans became a prosperous city. Both agricultural and manufactured products found their way to the wharfs from which they departed, after the city took its cut, to a variety of national and international markets. Wealth sought leisure, and even in the mid-nineteenth century, New Orleans was renowned for its fine restaurants and elegant social clubs. Theater, opera and dancing were popular, and less reputable entertainments, such as saloons and gambling dens, catered to baser tastes. Prostitutes plied their trade freely. They were concentrated in the Storyville section, which became a center for jazz and the parades which eventually expanded to become the Mardi Gras celebrations for which New Orleans became known in the twentieth century.

With gambling, dancing, and fornicating readily available, could sport be far behind? In the Puritan northeast, tortuous justification was necessary before sport was accepted as a worthwhile activity. Supporters of leisure constantly stressed its beneficial nature, and the way in which it helped men achieve success in academic and profit-making endeavors. A strong body, they insisted, was the only suitable temple for a nimble mind and virtuous character.

In New Orleans, no such rationale was necessary, for if one could go guiltlessly to the casino and play card games, were horse racing, cricket or ball play in need of moral justification? A weak conscience and amoral character might as well be housed in a strong body as a weak one, but who really cared? Sports were fun, and in New Orleans, that was enough.

When a Vermonter visited New Orleans in 1848, he wrote, "There is a great deal of business going on here & a great deal of Sin — There seems to be more Sin committed than I had apprehended."[2]

Given the rural nature of the American South, sport had been slower to catch on than it had been in the more metropolitan North. One of the earliest references to ball playing in the southern states was a 1797 item reporting that slaves in Fayetteville, North Carolina, were lashed for playing ball on the Sabbath.[3] Slaves rowed and boxed against each other for the profit and glory of their masters[4] and occasionally batted and threw balls around the plantations.[5] There are scattered reports of various types of ball games in the southern states, including town ball. Almost all activity was of the informal backyard variety. In 1858, *Porter's* noted hopefully that the members of the defunct cricket club in Richmond were attempting to organize a baseball club, but nothing further was reported.[6]

In 1854, a southerner who identified himself as "Cricketer" sent a letter to the *Spirit of the Times* decrying the fact that the young men of New Orleans preferred sedentary activities to cricket. The climate, he said, was perfect for the sport, and he was most disappointed that it had not taken hold.[7]

The aspect of New Orleans entertainment that was perhaps most shocking to visitors was that it frequently took place on Sunday. The English clergy had long deplored ball-playing on Sundays, and in 1676 the City of New York enacted a law under which playing games on the Sabbath was punishable by a fine of ten guilders.[8] The law apparently did little to stifle the activity of New York youngsters, for in 1801, *The New York Evening Post* condemned ball playing on the Sabbath with the rhetorical question, "Is this a Christian country? ... Are our magistrates asleep, or are they afraid of losing their popularity, if they should carry the laws into execution?"[9]

In the Northeast, they took the Sabbath seriously. In Brooklyn, Alderman Douglass, "observed with pain that many wicked boys were in the habit of playing base ball on the Sabbath in the spacious fields on 5th and 6th avenues."[10] On several occasions, youngsters were arrested and fined for playing ball on Sundays. Throughout most of the country, in fact, the Sabbath was the Lord's Day, its piety not to be defiled by business or, worse yet, fun.

When the Olympics first began playing town ball in Philadelphia in 1829, their Sunday activity caused them to run afoul of the matron of a local orphans' asylum. Horrified that her children were seeing such an outrage, she dressed down the men and shamed them into coming in and joining her group at services. She claimed that the following Sunday the Olympic players voluntarily joined her for services, for they had seen the error of their wicked ways.[11]

Disregard of the Sabbath in New Orleans was the result of the predominantly Spanish and French influence, untainted by the Puritan mores that reached the northeastern American colonies from England. Roman Catholic Creoles, for the most part, were free of the Protestant constraints that inhibited their New England brethren. Business and entertainment went on uninterrupted, seven days a week.

Sunday sport activities provided all classes, even those who worked six days a week, with the opportunity to participate. In New York, baseball practices took place in the early morning hours or late in the afternoon, any day of the week but Sunday. That was fine for professionals or the moneyed leisure class, but, for the most part, not suitable for workmen.

The sporting season in New Orleans was also a function of the climate. During the summer months, the humidity and heat drove many residents away and made for a very unhealthy environment. With little knowledge of public hygiene, residents were subject to epidemics, and those who could absent themselves from the city during the summer generally did so. Therefore, much of the activity took place in cooler months.

Sporting activity began in New Orleans as early as the 1820s in the form of horse racing, foot races and regattas. As might be expected, canine sport was also part of the New Orleans scene with large stakes riding on the result. Most of the sporting men were Anglo-American as the Creoles preferred sedentary diversions like music, theater and dancing.

Horse racing was the first truly popular sport in the Crescent City with the construction of the Eclipse Course in 1837 and the Metarie Course in 1838 and the establishment of a number of jockey clubs.[12] For many years, New Orleans rivaled New York as a center of horse racing and maintained a leading position until the outbreak of the Civil War.

Swimming also became quite popular during the antebellum era. While skating was the sport that excited the male libido in New York, swimming was the preferred aphrodisiac in New Orleans. A writer described a group of young female bathers, attired to display their many charms, as follows: "The troup [sic] was slim all over," he observed, "except the upper works."[13] Men were even more daring, leading to the passage of a law calling for the arrest of anyone who stripped naked to bathe in public. For the most part, however, men and women bathed together, in heavy flannel costumes, "and young ladies courted and flirt in the bath with as little inconvenience as in a drawing-room." They were dressed as if they were in a drawing-room, however, wearing, as Eliza Ripley wrote, "...hideous, unsightly garments, high neck, long sleeves, long skirts, intended for water only."[14] Men seemed to have the better idea.

Other water sports, including yachting and sailing, became equally popular. Huge, shallow, Lake Pontchartrain was a natural venue and the most frequented sailing location. In 1849, the Southern Yacht Club, with many New Orleans members, was organized in Pass Christian, Mississippi, just down the coast. As with New York baseball clubs, social niceties were an integral facet of the yachting world with lavish entertainments usually following racing day. The summer saw regattas from New Orleans to Mobile with Pass Christian becoming "something of a southern Newport in the 1850s." Yachting continued to be a favorite New Orleans pastime until it, like horse racing, was curtailed by the Civil War.[15]

For those who could not afford yachts, rowing was a popular alternative and flourished in the 1830s and early '40s until an 1844 flood destroyed many of the boats and boathouses. There was a brief revival just before the start of the war, but rowing never took hold of the local population to the degree that yachting did.[16]

Boxing made its appearance in New Orleans in the 1830s. The earliest proponent of the sport was Sam O'Rourke, the champion of Ireland, who fought several bouts and organized an athletic club. In the 1840s, New Yorker Chris Lilly came south and promoted a number of matches, but boxing suffered from the same borderline reputation it had in other sections of the country and never became popular with the New Orleans middle and upper classes.[17]

Ball games were very slow to appear in the South, lagging well behind horse racing and sailing. By 1859, there were reports of town ball and cricket being played in Georgia, but no momentum was generated prior to the war. The most popular ball game in New Orleans was the Indian game of *raquette*, a sport similar to lacrosse in which players wielded spoon-shaped *raquettes* and attempted to propel a ball through the opponent's goal. Any number of players could participate, and as many as eighty per side sometimes took part. New Orleans blacks dominated the game, which remained popular until the war.[18]

Cricket was first mentioned in the press around 1800,[19] and cricket activity was noted in Louisville in 1818[20] and in South Carolina in 1821.[21] The excitement generated by the tour of the All-England Eleven in 1859 led to the formation in New Orleans of the Crescent City Cricket Club and Pelican Cricket Club the same year. In Alabama, the Mobile Cricket Club, with 47 members, was organized in early 1860.[22] As in the northeast, cricket was limited principally to the upper classes due to the amount of time consumed by each game, and the number of days the clubs met for practice. In May 1860, the Crescent City Club journeyed to Mobile for the first intercity match in the South, but, as it had in other regions, the war put an end to cricket playing. The sport never regained popularity after Appomattox, and 1860 represented the high point of cricket activity in Louisiana.

Baseball appeared in New Orleans the same year in which cricket made its debut. There are some reports of German organizations forming baseball clubs during the 1850s,[23] but the first to leave its mark in the city was the Louisiana Base Ball Club, which started to play among themselves in July 1859. Before the year ended, six additional clubs had formed. In the first year of baseball activity, teams played both the Massachusetts and New York versions of the game, but by 1860 the latter version prevailed. The leading clubs in the city were the Empire, Magnolia and Louisiana nines, while others included the Pelican, Crescent City and Southern.

The summer of 1859 saw a great deal of activity, principally at the Delachaise Grounds in suburban Jefferson City. Most of the action was intramural, as the clubs split into sides and played friendly games against each other. The local press took the lead of their northern brethren in trumpeting the practical benefits of the sport. "Base ball is not inferior to any field game," said *The New Orleans Daily Crescent,* "in the points of excitement is [sic] its necessities of strength, skill and activity. It is pleasant to see our young men turning their attention to the healthful and manly sports of the field as such sports have been too long neglected in New Orleans."[24]

Interest in ball games became so intense that clubs began to fight over the few available grounds. The *raquette* clubs had been playing for so long that they assumed rights to the fields whenever they chose to play, crowding out the newer baseball clubs and players of *les quartes*, another game similar to lacrosse which, despite its French name, was played mainly by Irish immigrants. As was the local custom, all of the clubs wanted to play on Sunday, which exacerbated the situation. "The new clubs," reported the *Daily Crescent,* "have accordingly picked upon an open space of ground on Claiborne Street, but when they all went to the ground at the same time, there is some excitement as to which has the best right and there has been one collision and there is the prospect of another. A lot of youths who live in the vicinity of the square have organized a *les quartes* club and claim the square as theirs exclusively by reason of their being near it."[25]

Playing fields were fitted up with as much care as those in New York. Club members spared no pains to provide for the comfort of the ladies, erecting tents and lavishing attention on the female spectators. The *Daily Crescent* described the scene with the hyperbole typical of the era. "At the Delachaise Grounds," it reported, "the lady spectators were seated beneath the elegant tent of the club, and the gentleman spectators rolled on the grass in the shade of the live oaks. The turf was as fine as a velvet cushion. The sunshine was as pure as 20 carat gold and as warm as *café noir* and the shade of the live oaks slanting freely over the sward as the sun went to bed was as sweet and pleasant as nectar soda ... but of the outside business enough."[26] More than enough, but one can gather that the Delachaise Grounds were a fine place to enjoy a game of ball.

For most of the summer of 1859, the Louisiana and Empire Clubs played among themselves, a favorite pastime being to have the single members of the club play against the married members. The first interclub game reported from Louisiana took place on September 15, 1859, when the Empire Club beat the Louisiana Club, 77–64, a game which took two days to complete, the conclusion taking place on the 22nd. If low-scoring games were the principal criterion of excellence, clearly New Orleans baseball had a way to go, and the two-day affair was reminiscent of the leisurely cricket matches which generated little interest in America. On October 6, the Empires beat their rivals for a second time, this time by a slightly more respectable score of 56–26.[27] In 1860, the Magnolia and Southern clubs began interclub competition, and by that fall, several clubs had been organized and a number of games had been played.

Baseball in the South was every bit as contentious as in the North. In 1860, just a few weeks before the disputed Atlantic-Excelsior game in New York (see Chapter 12), a match between the Magnolia and Empire Clubs was halted when some of the Empires left the field in protest over a call of the umpire. The Magnolias maintained their positions and the umpire gave the captain of the Empires time to convince his recalcitrant charges to return. They refused and their captain offered the ball to his Magnolia counterpart, putting an end to the match.[28]

When Louisiana seceded from the Union, many New Orleans ball players enlisted in the Confederate Army, which put a serious damper on the game. The city was one of the first to be occupied by Union forces, and the hated General Benjamin "Beast" Butler served as military commander. Sporting activity was virtually shut down although it returned with equal fervor when peace came. During the postwar years, New Orleans once again became the center of Southern baseball. The Lone Stars and Magnolias played for the championship of the South, and by 1870, the Lone Stars had enough money to embark on a tour of the north.

Baseball slowly, very slowly, spread through the former Confederacy following the war, but prior to the outbreak of hostilities, New Orleans was the only southern city to embrace any type of ball games, holding forth as the undisputed leader in virtually every form of sporting life.

Chapter 10

Baseball in Philadelphia

In 1860, with a population of 565,000, Philadelphia was the fourth largest city in the world, trailing only London, Paris and New York. At 129 square miles, it had the largest land mass of any city in the United States.[1] Only ten years earlier, the city's residents had numbered just 121,000. The massive increase was the result of both a sizable population influx and a re-drafting of the city's boundaries. The entire county of Philadelphia, which had formerly included the distinct towns of Kensington, Moyamensing, Spring Garden, Northern Liberties, and Southwork, was now called the City of Philadelphia, and its residents were included in the city census.[2] The consolidation of 1854 allowed for more efficient use of fire, police and educational resources, and propelled the city to its status as one of the largest in the world.

Philadelphia's population was more patrician than that of other big cities, containing far more native-born citizens than New York. In the latter city, approximately 48 percent of the population was foreign-born,[3] while only a third of the 1860 Philadelphians were born outside the borders of the United States. The largest contingent of immigrants came from Ireland (16.7 percent of the total population) and Germany (7.5 percent). Blacks were scarce, accounting for just 4 percent of the residents.[4]

There was cricket activity in Philadelphia in the early 19th century,[5] and by the late 1850s, it was the dominant sport in Philadelphia, with town ball following close behind. Town ball was similar to rounders, and generally engaged teams of eleven players each. One of the unique aspects of Philadelphia town ball was that each batter was required to score on every at bat and could not stop at a base.[6] The bases, of course, were much closer than in the New York game, making the feat more achievable.

Town ball was pioneered in Philadelphia in the late 1820s by a group of young rope makers,[7] who were first heard from in 1829, while playing at 18th and Race Streets.[8] In 1833, through the merger of the Olympic Ball Club, formed two years earlier, and a club from Camden of equal vintage, the Olympic Town Ball Club came into existence. Prior to their merger, the two clubs engaged in the first interclub games of ball in America.[9]

The Olympic Club, which consisted of 47 members in 1833,[10] was more social than competitive, its activities consisting, as did those of the Knickerbockers a dozen years later, primarily of gathering together to play ball among themselves. Until 1860, they never played a match with another club.[11]

Like most early games, the rules of town ball varied, depending on the number of players available, the circumstances and the whim of the participants. In general, however, the game was played under rules very similar to those of rounders, which are set forth in Chapter 3.

For a number of years, because ball playing was prohibited in Philadelphia,[12] the Olympics took the Market Street Ferry to Camden, New Jersey, just across the Delaware River, to take their exercise. In 1857, after Philadelphia's laws were relaxed, the club relocated to Camac's Woods (at 17th and Columbia), which eventually became home to many of Philadelphia's baseball clubs. A highlight of each Olympic season was the Fourth of July, when the club met on the playing field for a reading of the Declaration of Independence, the singing of patriotic songs, and speeches extolling the virtues of the United States. The town ball was almost an afterthought. During the decades following the merger, the Olympic Club continued to grow, assimilating two additional organizations, both of which had been playing in Camden.[13] In 1857, town ball was reported in Germantown, a Philadelphia suburb and the site of a famous Revolutionary War battle.[14] Soon the Excelsior, Athletic and Camden clubs joined the Philadelphia town ball fraternity and began to play matches against each other.

Although Philadelphia had a long tradition of interest in cricket and town ball, the commencement of baseball activity lagged behind that in both New York and Boston. Although the Minerva Club was established in 1857,[15] its members lived a quiet and largely unpublicized existence. The first report of the New York game of baseball in the city was an item noting an 1858 Thanksgiving Day match between two teams composed of members of the Pennsylvania Tigers Social Base Ball and Quoit Club.[16]

About the same time, a group of Philadelphia printers connected with *The Pennsylvanian*[17] organized the Pennsylvania Base Ball Club, and other groups formed the Continental and Nonpareil Clubs. Both the Nonpareil and Penn Tigers (now known as the Winona Club) organizations played practice games among themselves in November of 1859, but by the end of the year, there had not been a competitive game between nines from two different clubs.

During the winter of 1859–60, more clubs began to appear. On November 30, 1859, the Keystone Club was organized, leading the *Clipper* to note growing interest in baseball in the city. In January 1860, the officers of the Winona Club put forth a call for a convention of all clubs (few though they were) "to establish rules and regulations for the government of [baseball] in Philadelphia."[18] A meeting was duly convened, an organization formed, and Theodore Bomeisler of the Winona Club elected president.

In 1860, Philadelphia baseball received a boost when the Olympic Club converted from town ball to the new sport, much to the chagrin of some of the older members, a few of whom resigned in protest.[19] The Excelsiors also converted from town ball. The Olympics played their first game under the New York rules July 24, 1860, against members of the St. George Cricket Club. In April, the Equity Club was formed and numbered former Knickerbocker R.F. Stevens among its membership.

Finally, on June 11, the first nines of the Winona and Equity Clubs met in the first baseball game ever played between two Philadelphia clubs with the Winona earning a 39–21 victory. The Keystones played their first game on July 4, beating the Continental Club, 26–11.

By the time the Winona and Equity Clubs played for the second time on July 5, the *Clipper* reported that there were at least twelve clubs in Philadelphia, including the Athletics — who would eventually field the strongest nine in the city — and that four games had been played between rival organizations. The newly minted clubs had a way to go, however, for, as the reporter noted, "there is plenty of room for improvement in the fielding — far more than in batting ... but how the result would be were the same parties opposed to first class pitching and fielding we cannot say.... Both parties occasionally showed some good play in fielding and batting, but on the whole they were far behind the excellence we are accustomed to see."[20] Yet, baseball was still new, and with practice, there was no doubt that the level of play in Philadelphia would get better.

The highlight of the 1860 season was the visit of the Excelsiors of Brooklyn. On the evening of September 23, the Excelsiors arrived from Baltimore, and the following afternoon, the famous club played at Camac's Woods against nine Philadelphians selected from the Equity, Olympic, Hamilton, Athletic and Winona Clubs. Fifteen hundred spectators, far less than appeared at the battles between the Atlantics and Excelsiors in Brooklyn, but a good crowd for Philadelphia, came to see the visiting club play.

The Excelsiors had been victorious on every stop of their tour, and the Philadelphians didn't harbor serious hopes of ending the streak. The game, however, would stir up interest in baseball and provide a measure of how far the local players had to go before they could match the level of play shown in New York. The result of the game, which the Excelsiors won, 15–4, was very encouraging. At their last stop, the Brooklyn club had beaten the Excelsiors of Baltimore, 51–6. Granted, the Philadelphia nine was an all-star combination of the best players in the city, and the Excelsiors might have been a bit tired after their journey, but losing by only 11 runs was quite an accomplishment for players who had played the game for only about a year.

One of the players on the Philadelphia nine was Weston Dickson Fisler, a 19-year-old member of the Equity Club. Fisler exemplified the cultured social background so valued by clubs like the Knickerbockers prior to the war. He was the son of Lorenzo Fisler, who served five terms as mayor of Camden, and the brother of Lorenzo, Jr., a globe-trotting photographer.[21] Wes was a quiet, well-mannered, well-dressed young man, who never griped about umpires' bad calls or misplays by his teammates. Educated in private schools, and nicknamed "The Icicle," Fisler was noted for his placid demeanor and calm reaction to the most heated situation on the diamond. "I was a cool sort of player," he said in an interview in the early twentieth century, "and never saw the necessity for getting all mussed up and covered with dirt. I never got excited about anything."[22]

The season of 1860 was the first of many for Fisler, who eventually became a star with the powerful Athletic teams of the mid– and late–1860s, and remained with the club through 1877, spanning the National Association and National League eras. He was a strong hitter, averaging .316 over five NA seasons, and despite his short stature (5'6") and slight build (137 pounds) was a capable fielder at first base and the other infield positions. Fisler and Al Reach were the last of the old Athletics to leave the club.[23] Fisler remained a fan his entire life and was often found at games of Connie Mack's Athletics.[24] He never married and, in his later years, was a haberdasher and a law clerk who worked until shortly before his death at age 81 in 1922.[25]

Opposite: **Weston Fisler played for a number of teams in the early 1860s before joining the Athletics, where he established his reputation. Fisler was a short, thin man known as "The Icicle" for his placid temperament and coolness under pressure. He was a strong hitter and a good fielder who played through the late 1870s and lived well into the twentieth century.**

There was a flurry of activity in Philadelphia following the Excelsiors' visit. In December 1860, five clubs (Equity, Athletic, United, Benedict and Winona)[26] sent delegates to the convention of the National Association, the first time any Philadelphia clubs had joined the organization. Colonel DeWitt C. Moore of the Athletics was elected first vice president.

With the onset of the war, the promise of 1860 was not realized during the next few seasons. Many members of the Winona Club enlisted, which caused a suspension of activity for 1861. The Equity and Hamilton Clubs were inactive throughout the war years. The Athletic, Olympic, Keystone, Mercantile, Adriatic and Columbian Clubs continued to play, however, and the sport remained alive. A game in mid–November 1861, between the Olympic and Athletic Clubs, the two best in the city, attracted a sizable crowd, including a number of the coveted ladies which, said the *Clipper*, "proved conclusively that the love for active, exhilarating sport is not on the wane in Philadelphia."[27]

The Athletic Club was emerging as the most talented of all the Philadelphia nines. Originally formed as a town ball organization in May 1859,[28] it became the Athletic Base Ball Club on April 7, 1860.[29] Many of the Athletics' members were also active in the Handel and Haydn Music Society (the original town ball club was established in their meeting room[30]), and the club exhibited the gentlemanly behavior so coveted by lovers of the sport. Colonel Moore was captain of the Athletics and also served as vice president. "The lovers of baseball in Philadelphia," said *Wilkes'*, "ought to feel grateful to him for the zeal which he has exhibited in pushing on the baseball column in that city ... may his shadow never grow less."[31]

A second supporter of the club, who became president and perhaps the foremost advocate of baseball in Philadelphia, was Colonel Thomas Fitzgerald, proprietor of the *City Item*. The *City Item* covered baseball and also served as a forum for progressive, liberal political philosophy. One of Fitzgerald's cherished goals was the racial integration of baseball. He achieved limited success in Philadelphia, but with little support outside of the city, there was no possibility of integration on a national basis.[32] Fitzgerald opened his home for entertainment and his wallet for club expenses and generously devoted his time to encouraging the progress of the sport.

The Athletics of the early 1860s included a number of players who would stay with them for several years, forming the nucleus of the strong nines of mid-decade, teams that would challenge the New York and Brooklyn clubs for the championship of the United States. Original member and first baseman Nathan Berkenstock, 29 in 1860, was a bit older than most of his teammates. He was a sturdy man and heavy hitter, who also fielded reasonably well. "He is not a pretty player," noted the *Clipper,* "being heavy and clumsy, but does good service — generally manages to hold any ball thrown to him."[33] Berkenstock also served as treasurer of the Athletics.[34]

Teenager Tom Pratt, a cricketer, was the Athletics' pitcher and perhaps the best player on the nine. He threw swiftly, in the manner of Jim Creighton, and had good control, which placed him above other would-be Creightons, who fired hard but wildly. Pratt joined the Winona Club in 1860 at the age of 16 and defected to the Athletics the following season. After Creighton's death in 1862, Pratt was generally considered the finest pitcher in the game.[35] He left Philadelphia and pitched for the Atlantics off and on from 1863 through 1869, a time during which the Brooklyn club was probably the best in baseball. Pratt left the sport at the age of just 27 after one game with the Athletics in the National Association's inaugural season, and returned to cricket, his first love. Although he no longer played baseball, he served as an umpire and was owner and president of the Keystone Club of the major league Union Association in 1884. Pratt's principal occupation in his maturity was in his family's paint business from which he supposedly earned a substantial fortune.[36]

Catcher Dan Kleinfelder, who began his career with the Excelsiors of Philadelphia and joined the Athletics in 1862,[37] was an indefatigable, tough receiver who was as good as most of the backstops in New York. Fergy Malone, who caught for the championship 1871 club, joined the Athletics in 1862.[38] Dick McBride, who had been a cricketer with the Chippewa Club[39] before joining the Athletics in 1861, full-bearded outfielder Elias (Hicks) Hayhurst and infielder Isaac Wilkins were talented performers who would anchor the powerful Athletic Clubs of the mid–1860s.

The lavishly side-burned McBride, who became one of the finest pitchers in the professional National Association in the early 1870s, played the infield and outfield when he first joined the Athletics at the age of 16. He did not begin pitching regularly until 1863. If Fisler was the Icicle, McBride was the Blowtorch. Like Dick Pearce of the Atlantics, he was a bit of a hothead with a sarcastic streak, who sometimes lost his temper on the field.[40]

Hayhurst, a strong hitter who usually played center field, had been a town ball player previous to 1860 when he began playing baseball with the Winona and Excelsior Clubs. He joined the Athletics in June 1861, when he was at least 33 years old.[41] Hayhurst remained active as a player for several years and participated in the management of the Athletics after his retirement from field duty. He was a director of the club for 13 seasons,[42] including seven as chairman of the board, and in 1867 was a staunch supporter of the attempt of the black Pythian Club to enter the Pennsylvania Association.[43] In 1871, Hayhurst, often given credit as the field manager of the National Association Athletics, was actually their business manager, making financial and scheduling arrangements for the first champion of professional baseball. In 1875, in a greatly expanded Association, he severed his long ties with the Athletics to back a third Philadelphia NA club, the Centennials, which lasted only a couple of months. Hayhurst managed the 1877 Athletics in the League Alliance, became president of the Olympics, and served on the Philadelphia City Council before dying of typhoid fever in 1882.[44]

The Athletics demonstrated their prowess as soon as they took to the field for their first official game, in their new white uniforms, trimmed in blue, with a script "A" across the breast.[45] On that day, September 22, 1860, they defeated the Pennsylvania Club, 29–19.[46] Although they won only one of the three other games they played that season, the new club had a formidable list of members and gave the impression of being an organization that would be heard from in future years. The onset of the Civil War caused the Athletics to lose members, but a merger with the United Club provided reinforcements and allowed the organization to continue on.[47]

Perhaps the best indicator that baseball fever was on the rise in Philadelphia was the emergence of a feud between the Athletics and Olympics. The Olympics were the older club and the champions of the city, having defeated the Athletics for the title in 1861. In 1860, there had been hard feelings, but the rift had been temporarily mended when the clubs combined for a Thanksgiving game in which they made up teams containing a mixture of players from both clubs.[48] The Athletics were gaining somewhat of a reputation as a troublesome group, for they had also had some difficulty during a game with the Equity Club in 1860 and walked off the field after the eighth inning.[49]

Two years later, the Athletics were in the midst of controversy once more. In the May 24, 1862, edition of the *Clipper*, a Philadelphia correspondent who identified himself as "Looker-on" claimed there was a lack of gentlemanly behavior among the players of his city. "Petty jealousies, unmanly criticisms and childish bickerings," Looker-on said, "not only between rival clubs, but members of the same club, exist and are indulged in, which, to the numerous spectators of ladies and gentlemen, are calculated to retard the popularity of the game, and injure the success of the clubs in which they are tolerated."[50] He pointed to the Olympics as the primary offenders, citing instances in which they had disputed the decisions of an umpire and played in an unsportsmanlike fashion.

In the same issue, probably anticipating the letter of Looker-on, a gentleman who styled himself "Fair Play" leapt to the defense of the Olympics, insisting the charges against them were nonsense. The Athletics were merely bitter, he claimed, because they could not defeat the Olympics on the playing field. He pointed to the fact that they attributed their loss to the Olympics to the decisions of umpire R.F. Stevens, the former Knickerbocker pitcher. How, Fair Play asked, could an umpire have cost the Athletics a game they lost by 16 runs?[51]

The following week, "Justicia" explained to Fair Play how Stevens had blundered repeatedly and how his incompetence had completely discouraged the Athletics. Besides, Justicia said, the Olympics had started an ugly rumor that the Athletics had disbanded, which forced the latter club to limit the players on their opening day to club members, in order to demonstrate their strength and refute the rumor of their demise.[52]

"Uncle Fuller" heaped further abuse on the venerable Olympic Club. He referred to their defense as "fulsome nonsense" and declared, "It is a well-known fact, and admitted by all base ball players, outside of its own organization, that the Olympic has degenerated in play, morals and standing..." and so on and so forth.[53] The next week, "Jasper" took off in a different direction, complaining that while all the attention was going to the Athletics and Olympics, his Keystones were just as strong as either club. In the same issue, Thomas Fitzgerald, President of the Athletics, and the first correspondent to use his real name, published a series of resolutions from his club which disavowed the remarks of Justicia, and indicated that the Athletics bore no ill will toward the Olympics. He also praised Stevens, the umpire so maligned by Justicia.[54] The Athletic resolutions, in addition to refuting Justicia, disassociated the club from the article in question and asserted the Athletics' desire for harmony with the Olympics.[55]

The exchange was entertaining, petty and telling. While a few years earlier no one in Philadelphia had been interested in baseball, rivalries were now as hot and heavy as those in New York. In November, the Athletics settled the issue on the field rather than in the newspapers, defeating the Olympics in the deciding third game of their series, 19–10, to claim the championship of the city for 1862. Although the second game of the series had been marked by disputes over the umpire's decisions, by the third game, both teams had gotten over their ill feelings, and the match was harmonious and without incident.[56]

Despite, or perhaps because of, the controversies surrounding the top clubs in the city, baseball continued to grow, even under the limitations imposed by the war. In May 1862, the *Clipper* listed the following Philadelphia clubs[57]:

Club	*Practice Days*	*Grounds*
Athletics	Thursdays	Fairmount Park
Adriatic	Tuesdays and Fridays	Camac's Woods

Atlantic	Wednesdays and Saturdays	Camac's Woods
Columbian	Mondays and Thursdays	17th and Master
Excelsior	Wednesdays and Saturdays	15th and Columbia Ave.
Franklin	Saturdays	Fairmount Park
Hamilton	Wednesdays and Saturdays	38th Street north of Market
Keystone	Thursdays	4th and Mifflin
Mercantile	Wednesdays and Saturdays	15th and Columbia Ave.
Minerva	Saturdays	15th and Columbia Ave.
Niagara	Mondays and Tuesdays	Fairmount Park
Olympic	Wednesdays and Saturdays	Camac's Woods
Roanoke	Tuesdays and Fridays	Fairmount Park

The grounds at Camac's Woods, used for both cricket and baseball, were improved during the early '60s. In 1864, a new ground, at 25th Street and Jefferson, adjoining the Spring Garden Reservoir,[58] was laid out and made available for play. The Jefferson Street facility, leased by the Olympics from the city for ten years, was the finest in the city. It included a comfortable clubhouse and was easily accessible by public transportation. The Jefferson Street grounds were the site of many exciting games the Athletics played with the Atlantics and other top New York clubs, those they played in the National Association in the early 1870s, and those that took place during the maiden season of the National League.[59] Today, the site remains an open park used for recreation.[60]

When the Jefferson Street facility first opened, it was used by the Olympic, Mercantile and Athletic Clubs, but the inscription over the entrance read, "The Olympic, 1833." Hopefully, Justicia, Looker-on and Fair Play would not take up their pens once more over the implied slight to the other two clubs. "[I]t is certainly not advisable," cautioned *Wilkes*', "for rival organizations to occupy the same locality, and hence we shall expect to see the Athletics priding themselves on the possession of a fine ground and clubhouse, and the Keystones another."[61]

Although baseball activity was increasing by the spring of 1862, none of the Philadelphia clubs had played a nine from another city, other than the visit of the Excelsiors in 1860. The *Clipper* urged the Philadelphia clubs to journey to New York, claiming it would do wonders for the progress of the game in their city.[62] In early June 1862, Colonel Moore took a party of Philadelphians — members of the Athletic, Adriatic and Olympic Clubs — north for a series of games against the players of New York, Brooklyn and New Jersey. Moore's letter announcing his intentions modestly indicated that he and his cohorts wished to learn the finer points of the game and get some practice against top players. "We want to have a social time," Moore wrote, "and to take the 'boys' by the hand and make their acquaintances.... We are of course in the hands of our New York friends, and hope that in the selection of players in the matches we hope to play together they will not put in their 'big guns' so as to annihilate us."[63] Moore was not so presumptuous as to think that his players would beat any of the New York nines; neither was Henry Chadwick, who predicted that after the games, "they will be well posted up in the 'points' of the game and, if we mistake not, especially in that point that is elicited by the practice of tendering balls to the victors."[64]

Before entering New York, the Philadelphians stopped in Newark to play a combined team from the Newark and Eureka Clubs. The Newark combination won, 13–4, as Philadelphia had some fielding breakdowns that cost them the game. The slick, experienced players from New Jersey also managed to show the Pennsylvania novices a trick or two. In the third inning, Loughery of the Adriatics hit a foul ball that fell untouched. Jersey catcher Osborne threw the ball wildly toward the shortstop position where Charlie Thomas threw to third, to which Philadelphian Johnson was returning. The third baseman missed the ball intentionally, which caused Johnson's teammates to yell for him to run home. As Johnson crossed the plate, the third baseman retrieved the ball, and threw it the pitcher, who returned it to third, where Johnson was called out. This was an old dodge in the New York area, for veteran players knew that a runner could not leave on a foul until the ball had first been returned to the pitcher. Chalk up one victory for New Jersey and one lesson for Philadelphia.[65]

The following day, the New Yorkers learned a lesson, as the Philadelphians defeated a team composed of members of the Eagle, Gotham and Knickerbocker Clubs by the score of 46–29. There were actually two lessons to be learned from the outcome. One was that some pretty good baseball was being played in Philadelphia. The second was that the three New York clubs represented in the game, three of the oldest and most respected clubs in America, were in eclipse, replaced in stature by the Mutuals, Atlantics and Eckfords.

During the final two days of the visit, the Brooklyn players redeemed the honor of the metropolis. A team from the Eastern District, representing the Enterprise, Excelsior, Star, Atlantic and Exercise Clubs, posted a 27–10 victory behind the pitching of Jim Creighton, while the Western District, with players from the Putnam, Eckford, Constellation and Resolute Clubs, won by a 23–16 score.

There were no losers, however, in the field of entertainment. From the moment Moore and his entourage disembarked in Newark, they were feted, wined, dined, sung to, toasted, driven around and entertained. As soon as the Philadelphians got off the train, they were taken to the Newark club rooms for lunch. After the game, many players from New York and Brooklyn arrived and, in concert with the Newark and Eureka club members, treated the visitors to supper at a local hotel. There was a series of toasts, including two to Lincoln and McClellan, the latter of whom was then approaching Richmond from the eastern peninsula. The fun could have gone on all night, but there was a game to play the next day, so the Philadelphians returned to their hotel at 9.

After the game with the Brooklyn Eastern District nine, the troupe went to Wild's Hotel, then proceeded to the Pierrepont House in Brooklyn for dinner. Again, the Philadelphians reminded their eager hosts that they had to play baseball the next day, and retired at a relatively early hour. Still, there were a number of toasts, perhaps the most tortured of which was delivered by Chadwick, who said, "May the *Athletics* of Philadelphia attain the skill shown in the *Olympic* games of old; and may their passage through life be as free from storms as that placid sea of Italy—the *Adriatic*."[66] Certainly, among the Philadelphians, the feeling was *Mutual*. Fortunately, Chadwick limited his praise to the Philadelphia clubs, and the gentlemen were spared his raptures about the bright *Stars* in the *Constellation*, and the vast *Atlantic*, etc.[67]

On June 7, nine tired ballplayers departed on the train to Philadelphia with one victory, a wealth of experience, and a plethora of goodwill. They would return often to New York during the ensuing years; at first they were greeted with hospitality and good wishes, but later, when they challenged the Brooklyn clubs for the championship, they would be less welcome.

The visit had been helpful to the progress of the game in Philadelphia, and it inspired those in Brooklyn as well. Since the beginning of the war, the baseball scene had been somewhat unexciting, but the presence of players from a distant city re-energized the New York and Brooklyn fraternity. Almost immediately after Moore's party had left, Brooklyn players formed a committee to plan a return visit.[68]

On June 30, 1862, the Brooklyn entourage, assembled from the Atlantic, Star, Exercise and Enterprise Clubs, went to Philadelphia. They encountered the same hospitable treatment that had been accorded the Philadelphians in New York, being shown the Zoological Gardens, the Schuylkill Water Works, local billiard parlors and shows at two Philadelphia theaters. On Thursday, July 3, the players were the guests of honor at a gala dinner at the Washington House, attended by 80 people. The hosts toasted everybody, including Chadwick, who had accompanied the players, and the evening ended at midnight with the playing of the "Star Spangled Banner."

Either the Philadelphians played better at home, or they had profited from their games in New York a month earlier for they showed marked improvement on the playing field. In the first game, they beat the Brooklyn players, 16–10, and repeated the feat in the second, this time by a score of 22–9. The third game was won by Brooklyn, 18–15, but the final game was a rout, won by Philadelphia, 41–5. Philadelphia scored nine times in the second inning and 14 in the sixth. The *Clipper*, which often described games in play-by-play detail, closed its brief account tartly with, "Comment on such a match is unnecessary," and then set forth the box score.[69] Over the course of the reciprocal visits, Philadelphia and New York had each won three games, while the former had outscored the latter, 120 to 92. Apparently, Col. Moore and his mates had learned more than how to present the ball to the winning club.

Visits between New York and Philadelphia continued on a regular basis. In August 1862, the Mutuals played three games in Philadelphia, beating the Adriatics and Olympics, losing, 17–10, to the Athletics (the first time a regular Philadelphia club — not a picked nine — had beaten a New York club), and absorbing all the hospitality they could stand. In October, the Eckfords, champions of New York, and therefore the United States, arrived and did even better, winning all four of their games, including a 32–25 win over the Athletics.

The following year, the Athletics and Keystones came to New York for six days and proved themselves the equal of the older clubs.[70] *Wilkes'* cautioned the New Yorkers to beware for the Philadelphians were better than they had been the previous summer.[71] The Athletics beat the Excelsiors (18–17) in a very exciting game, defeated the Stars (37–17), and lost competitive games to the Mutuals (17–11) and Eurekas (8–6). They were also defeated by the Atlantics (21–13) and Eckfords (10–5), the New York area's top two teams. When the Mutuals won the ball from the Athletics, William Tweed, the infamous New York political boss who would be incarcerated within a few years, accepted it on behalf of the club. On the social and patriotic front, the Athletics were taken to the Continental Iron Works where they saw the ironclad *Puritan* under construction.[72]

The Pennsylvanians were no longer novices trying to learn an unfamiliar sport. The Athletics were clearly in the same class as the New York clubs, and, with a little more practice, might surpass them. Baseball was well-established in Philadelphia with top-flight clubs like the Athletics, Olympics and Keystones, and several junior nines that could provide a flow of young players to the senior clubs. The Athletics, in fact, had their own junior nine.

In August 1864, Chadwick summarized the state of Philadelphia baseball. There were five principal clubs in the city, he stated, of which the Athletics and Keystones (who boasted

200 members[73]) were the best. The Camden Club was new but promising, the Mercantile not very active and the Olympic Club more devoted to their old pastime of town ball.[74]

That month, the Atlantics showed the city what the best of Brooklyn could do to their upstart teams. They visited Philadelphia and beat the Camden, Olympic, Keystone and Athletic Clubs by a combined score of 230–47. The closest call was a 43–16 win over the Athletics. There were extenuating circumstances surrounding the lopsided victories, however. First, while the Atlantics invaded from the north, there was a real threat of the Army of Northern Virginia arriving from the south. The Governor of Pennsylvania called for 30,000 volunteers for the state militia, and many young Philadelphia players, including 30 members of the Keystone Club, rallied to the colors, and were thus unavailable to play.[75] Second, the Athletics were in a state of turmoil that resulted in the resignation of President Thomas Fitzgerald.[76]

Shortly before the Atlantics visited Philadelphia, another visiting Brooklyn club, the Resolute, found themselves enmeshed in the Athletic-Olympic feud, which had once more boiled to the surface. "It has remained," lamented the *Clipper,* "for a Philadelphia club to be the first this season to mar the harmony which should characterize base ball matches."[77]

In 1862, when Brooklyn players visited Philadelphia, Charles Bomeisler of the Olympics had had harsh words with Pearce and Massey of the Atlantics.[78] Now, in 1864, the situation escalated. During a close game between the Resolutes and Olympics, the Philadelphia crowd became very partisan on behalf of the visitors. Apparently, the Athletic fans wanted the Olympics to lose. As the Brooklyn club was in the midst of a rally and threatened to tie the score, Bomeisler, the Olympic captain, after dropping a fly ball, ordered his club off the field on the presumption that it was too dark to continue play. It was approximately 7:00 P.M. on a July evening, and few believed it was too dark to see the ball. Further, the decision to call the game was the umpire's, not the Olympic captain's. A wrangle ensued, during which, to the dismay of the *Clipper,* "suffice it to say that one of the Resolutes failed to emulate the excellent example set them by their gentlemanly President, Mortimer Rogers."[79]

Bomeisler argued vehemently, but after ten or fifteen minutes, Umpire Duffy of the Keystone Club ordered play to resume. The Resolutes' momentum was stalled, however, and they lost by a single run, 24–23. Several of the Athletics, who were present as spectators, and whose animosity toward the Olympics still flamed, began jawing at Bomeisler. "[S]ome of the Resolutes," reported the *Eagle,* "were not slow in expressing their opinions on the treatment they had received, and but for the intervention of mutual friends, Bomeisler would have had his 'claret tapped,' his 'peepers closed' and his physiognomy in general pretty well damaged at the hands of our friend Stearns." Bomeisler was lucky, Chadwick remarked, that the Atlantics had not been the opposing nine.[80]

When the Resolutes returned to their hotel, they were greeted by a cheering delegation led by Messrs. Moore and Fitzgerald of the Athletics. Bomeisler tried to make amends for his behavior by taking the Resolutes on a trip to The Falls of Skuylkill, but when he saw the newspaper reports the following day, his anger returned. As Chadwick was about to board the train for home, he was greeted by a salvo of abuse from the Olympic captain. Bomeisler had no pen in hand, however, and the reporter did; thus the ballplayer's reputation took another bath in Chadwick's vitriol. Chadwick said he had spared his readers the worst of Bomeisler's behavior, believing his action to be an aberration, but when he was accosted at the train, he decided that Bomeisler was indeed a blackguard of the darkest hue. He would

Members of the Athletics of Philadelphia and the Resolutes of Brooklyn pose together, possibly during a visit of the Resolutes to Philadelphia in 1864. Journalist Henry Chadwick, who accompanied the Resolutes, stands at the far right with his beloved scorebook. Resolute captain Mort Rogers sits in the center holding a ball. The player seated at the lower left may be Athletic pitcher Dick McBride.

not be deterred from reporting the truth, Chadwick announced, despite threats he might receive from a ballplayer. Henry was also incensed when he heard that some of the Atlantics had taken Bomeisler's part.[81] A few days later, he confided that, "In order to oblige 'Charley'" the Atlantics would take it easy on the Olympics and attempt to pummel the Athletics."[82]

Chadwick was not about to let the matter rest. No one was more protective of the privileges of the press than he, from insisting upon comfortable accommodations to pursuing accurate box scores. Freedom of the press, of course, was the most cherished privilege of any reporter. Chadwick therefore wrote a letter to the President of the Olympics, asking whether he and his club endorsed Bomeisler's actions. When he received no reply, he reached the conclusion that the Olympics condoned their captain's outrageous behavior, and included the club in his strong condemnation. Anyone who threatened the press was bad enough, but those who damaged the reputation of the game he loved were doubly dangerous.

The difficulties in Philadelphia were temporary. In a couple of years, the Athletics would be the equal of the Atlantics, giving rise to a series of battles for the championship in which some of the most telling episodes took place off the field. The intercity rivalry was fierce, and the New York and Brooklyn teams utilized the unwieldy practices governing the national championship to keep the crown away from Philadelphia. The chicanery was the ultimate compliment to the quality of baseball in the latter city. In 1871, the Athletics captured the first title of the National Association, and before the league folded after the 1875 season, Philadelphia had had as many as three teams in the league. Although baseball hadn't taken root in the city until 1859, it had grown very rapidly. After the Civil War ended, clubs that had been rendered inactive during the conflict revived, and baseball fever was nearly as strong in Philadelphia as it was in New York.

Chapter 11

The Massachusetts Game

At the same time the Atlantics and Eckfords entered the New York baseball arena, the game was being played in Massachusetts in a slightly different form. All bat-and ball-games, no matter what they were called, were played under irregular rules. The early game New Yorkers played was not exactly the same from day to day or from club to club. Sometimes more or less than nine players took part, and some rules were enforced while others were not.

There were significant differences, however, between the style of baseball generally played in New England and that played in New York. The former, which became known as the Massachusetts Game, was closer to rounders and older ball games. The field was a square rather than a diamond, with four-foot-high wooden stakes marking the four bases. The distance between Massachusetts bases varied, but it was always much shorter than the distance used in the New York game. Under the rules adopted by the Olympic Club of Boston in 1857, the spacing between first and second and third and fourth bases was to be at least fifty feet, and that between first to fourth and second to third not less than forty feet.[1]

The batter stood midway between the first and fourth base. The pitcher generally positioned himself about 30–35 feet away, toward the middle of the rectangle, and threw, rather than pitched, the ball to the batter. The ball was smaller and lighter than that used in the New York game, between two and two and three quarters ounces, compared to six to six-and-a-quarter ounces, and could not be thrown or batted as far. In some games, each team used its own ball when it batted, for even among the Massachusetts clubs, the balls were different.[2] When Williams played Amherst in 1859 (see below), the *Clipper* reported, "The ball used by Amherst was small, soft, and with so little elasticity that a hard throw upon the floor would cause a rebound of scarcely a foot."[3] One of the reasons the ball was light was that a player could be put out by hitting him with it, an act sometimes performed with great enthusiasm. A softer ball would do less damage to the base runner, but the inability to hit it hard or throw it very far detracted from the excitement of the game.

The Massachusetts game was in advance of the New York version in one respect. If a batter repeatedly failed to swing at balls that were within his reach, the umpire was empowered to call strikes, an innovation that was not fully endorsed in the New York rules until 1864. There were no foul balls; every batted ball was in play. Under New York rules, a skillful batter could execute the fair foul, causing the ball to land first in fair territory, then bound into foul ground out of the fielders' range. In Massachusetts, the batter could hit the ball directly behind him, or in any direction, which made it very difficult to play defense. Some players gripped the bat well up on the handle and actually swung toward the catcher, to propel the ball in his direction. Sometimes, they hit the catcher while doing so. Others let the ball glance off their bat and continue past the catcher.[4] The countervailing advantage to the defense was that there were generally far more than nine players on a team. Ten to fourteen was the suggested number, and the latter seemed to be the most common, but sides often ranged up to 18, 20 or more. On many occasions, there were two catchers, one behind the first, and sometimes there were three.[5] A single out ended an inning (one out, all out).

New York players didn't think much of the Massachusetts version of baseball, nor did the New York press. "This is what Mr. ... Thompson calls a manly game," huffed the *Atlas* in response to an article touting the New England style, "namely, ball stuffed with mush; bat in the shape of a paddle about twelve inches wide; bases about ten feet apart; run on all kinds of balls fair or foul, and throw the ball at the player running the bases. This game will do exceedingly well for genuine ball players — to laugh at, as they did at the stupid article in the *Tribune*."[6]

A Buffalo paper came to the defense of the New Englanders with a feisty editorial quoting from the aforementioned *New York Tribune* article and decrying the New York game as "no more like the genuine game of base ball than single wicket is like a full field of cricket ... a bastard game, worthy only of boys ten years of age.... The only genuine game is what is known as 'The Massachusetts Game.'" It advised the visiting English cricketers that if they wanted to test their mettle in the game of base ball, they should play one of the Massachusetts clubs, which were the best in the United States.[7] The Buffalo editor was a voice in the wilderness, however, and rarely was a word of support for the Massachusetts game heard outside of New England.

Given the free-wheeling nature of batting, there were typically far more runs scored in the Massachusetts game than in its counterpart. In New York, a game was won by scoring 21 runs or, later, by scoring the most runs in nine innings. Under the rules of the Massachusetts game, one usually had to score 100 runs to win. Sometimes clubs would play a best-of-three or best-of-five series of 25 runs each. This led to some extremely long games, occasionally carrying over to a second day. A five- or six-hour game was not unusual. In 1860, Upton beat Medway in a game than lasted 172 innings spread over seven days between September 25 and October 5. The total playing time was 21 hours and 50 minutes. Including meal breaks and other delays, the total elapsed time exceeded 25 hours.[8]

In many ways, the pace of the Massachusetts game was similar to that of cricket. An 1858 match between the Rough and Ready Club of South Walpole and the American Club of Dedham was a best-of-five series to twenty-five runs each. The first game consumed an hour and twenty minutes, after which there was an intermission and refreshments for the contestants. The second match took an hour and forty-four minutes, and the third two hours and fifteen minutes. The Rough and Ready Club had won two of three, and the Americans declined to undertake a fourth and possibly fifth game. The two teams and their friends adjourned to dinner at Billings' Hall, where speeches and a round of good fellowship completed a very full day.[9]

The first organization to play the New England version of baseball was the Olympic Club, which was formed in 1854. The Green Mountain, Elm Tree and Bay State Clubs followed, and the four became rivals with the first inter-club game taking place between the Olympic and Elm Tree Clubs in 1855.[10] While New York clubs, despite several efforts, were unable to acquire use of Central Park, Boston clubs cavorted on the Common, the finest playing field in the area.

By the late 1850s, there were enough clubs playing the Massachusetts game to warrant a statewide convention, which was held at the Phoenix House in Dedham, in May 1858, just one year after the New York clubs held their initial meeting. Like their New York brethren, the Massachusetts players, who represented ten clubs, used the convention to formalize the rules of their game. B.H Hoyt, of the Olympic Club, was elected President of the Massachusetts Association of Base Ball Players.[11]

In August 1859, the Excelsior Club of Upton defeated the Union Club of Medway, 100–78, in a match that was billed as the championship contest for those clubs playing the Massachusetts game. The match took two days and eleven hours of playing time, encompassed 80 innings and was attended by about 10,000 on the first day and roughly 5,000 on the second.[12] Unlike the practitioners of the New York game, Massachusetts players competed openly for prize money, and there was $500 at stake for the winning team. The large sum attracted a great deal of attention, and the game, played at the Worcester Agricultural Grounds, drew many players from other clubs, who were led by the competing teams in a procession to the ground by Fiske's Cornet Band. While five hundred dollars was a substantial sum in 1859, it amounted to just over three dollars per hour for each of the fourteen victorious Excelsiors.[13]

A few weeks later, the Union Club, despite their defeat, played Winthrop in another match billed as a contest for the championship of the state, a game which took two days and 101 innings to reach a decision.[14] An admission fee had been charged for the privilege of watching the game, just a year after the precedent had been set in the Fashion Course Series.[15]

The most memorable game played under the Massachusetts code was a match at Pittsfield between teams made up of players from Williams and Amherst Colleges.[16] This was not the first time college students had played baseball; they had done so since the eighteenth century.[17] There were references to ball playing and cricket at Harvard and Princeton during the 1760s,[18] and some famous graduates, including Henry Wadsworth Longfellow, mentioned playing "ball" as one of their diversions during the early decades of the nineteenth century.

Sports rode a rocky and irregular path to popularity in the Ivy League. In 1771, Dartmouth President Eleazar Wheelock recommended that students spend their leisure time gardening or practicing manual arts rather than wasting their time playing games of ball.[19] Nine years later, the college banned ball playing near windows,[20] as did the University of Pennsylvania.[21] In 1787, Princeton prohibited ball playing as dangerous and "low and unbecoming gentleman students,"[22] Finally, in 1824, the Town of Hanover permitted the playing of ball on the common in front of Dartmouth College,[23] and in 1837, a Yale student reported that the green was covered with ballplayers.[24]

Over the succeeding decades, baseball became an accepted activity on campus. In May 1858, the *Clipper* reported a game between students at Kenyon College, with eleven on each side,[25] and in April 1859, announced that students at New York University had formed a baseball club.[26] Two different colleges, however, had never played against each other.

Thirteen players from Williams and an equal number from Amherst took the field on July 1, 1859, in the first intercollegiate baseball game in America.[27] The contest resulted from a challenge issued by Amherst and was played on a Friday, to be followed by a chess match between the two schools on Saturday. Neither college had a formal club, so each chose players by ballot.

The Amherst ball players wore a blue badge upon their shirts and their opponents sported belts with the school name on the back. Each club used its own ball when it was at bat, and each ball was a different size and weight.[28] There were few students in attendance; the crowd watching the game consisted mainly of residents of the town, plus some members of the North Adams baseball club.

Prior to the start of the game, it was decided that the first team to score 65 runs would be declared the winner. In the 25th inning, Amherst scored eleven runs to break the 65 mark easily, and was victorious by the score of 73–32. As might be expected from players with little experience, there were no individual standouts; the run-making was rather evenly distributed. No member of the winning team scored more than seven runs, and no Williams player tallied more than four. To complete the sweep, Amherst also won the chess match the following day.[29]

During the next several years, intercollegiate competition became more common. The first game played under the New York rules took place in November 1859, when Xavier met Fordham.[30] Other universities followed suit and many fielded teams capable of competing with the best in New York. The Harvard Club and the Nassau Club of Princeton were perhaps the best of the college nines, and both played a number of games against top clubs in New York and Philadelphia.

There was evidence of ball playing at Princeton as early as 1786,[31] but the Nassaus, formed in the fall of 1858 when Brooklyn ballplayers Lewis Mudge, H.S. Butler and Henry Sampson arrived on campus, were the first club at the university. Members were charged fifty cents annually and ten cents per month to defray expenses, and the obligatory series of fines was laid down. The students played among themselves until October 22, 1860, when they encountered a group of college graduates and played them to a 42–42 tie that was called because of darkness.[32]

Over the next few years, the Nassau Club became very good. In 1862, they defeated the Stars of New Brunswick twice to claim the championship of New Jersey and, in 1863, by which time the nine included former members of the Enterprise, Star and Hudson River Clubs,[33] the Nassaus twice defeated the Athletics, then the top club in Philadelphia, by one-sided scores of 35–16 and 29–13. They beat the Olympics of Philadelphia, then went to Brooklyn, the baseball capital of the world, and beat the Resolutes, Stars and Excelsiors, before losing a close game, 18–13, to the former champion Atlantics.

The Nassaus had fared much better than most teams against the Atlantics, and the trip established the college boys as one of the best nines in the country. The following year, the Princeton club again journeyed to Brooklyn where, despite beating the Star and Mutual Clubs, they suffered an embarrassing 42–7 loss to the Atlantics. Although they had beaten many top amateur clubs, the Nassaus didn't play another college nine until 1864, when they defeated Williams despite the fact that one of the Williams players referred to his opponents as "country jakes."[34]

By 1864, there were a number of college clubs, some representing the entire school, others one of the classes. The Harvard Club was formed in 1863 and, after a spirited debate, decided to play the New York game.[35] Harvard played Brown, Bowdoin and Williams that year, in addition to competing against non-college nines. In 1866, the Crimson nine went to New York and played the best clubs in the city. Yale also took up the game and played a number of local nines, including the Charter Oak Club, one of the best teams in Connecticut.

The Crimson did not wear crimson. James Lovett recounted how a Boston seamstress took the liberty of using magenta for the "H" which appeared on the chest of each Harvard player, claiming it was "much more fashionable and much prettier."[36]

While most Massachusetts clubs played under the unique rules of their own game, there was a parallel movement taking place in the state. In 1857, Edward G. Saltzman, a former New Yorker who had been a member of the Gothams and came to Boston the previous year, organized the Tri-Mountain Club, named after the three hills that dominated the early Boston skyline. His colleague, Augustus Margot, laid out a diamond (rather than a square) on the Boston Common,[37] for the Tri-Mountains would play under the New York rules. "This mode of playing," reported the *Clipper,* "it is considered, will become more popular than the one now in vogue, in a short time."[38] When the 1858 convention set forth the Massachusetts code as the rule of the game, the Tri-Mountains withdrew from the Association.[39]

The Tri-Mountains, said the *Clipper,* occupied a position in Boston similar to that held by the Knickerbockers in New York.[40] The major problem faced by the Boston club in its quest to popularize the New York game was that none of the local teams would play against them. Since travel was not yet a part of baseball, none of the New York teams journeyed to Boston. It was a year after their founding before the Tri-Mountains faced competition from another club.

Despite the fact that there were no interclub games, other Massachusetts organizations were following Saltzman's lead and taking up the New York game. In 1858, the Atwater Club was organized in Westfield, Massachusetts, and the Bowdoin Club of Boston sprung to life, both with the intention of playing under the New York rules. The latter had initially intended to play the Massachusetts game before deciding the New York version was superior.[41]

Again, the *Clipper* pressed the advantages of the New York brand of ball, publishing a letter from a Boston correspondent who claimed, "This game is fast gaining ground in this State, and I should not be surprised if, in the course of a few years, it should become the only game played in Boston. The smallness of the ball adopted by the Massachusetts Association is a great drawback to the popularity of that game."[42] The limited distance between bases also made the Massachusetts version of the game more like child's play.

Finally, on September 9, 1858, the Tri-Mountains played the New York game against an opposing club. They lost to a nine from Portland, Maine, 47–42, but finally succeeded in showing Boston the New York style of play. Soon, it would eclipse the Massachusetts version and become the dominant method of playing baseball. In September 1859, the *Clipper* counted 50 clubs in Massachusetts, 13 of which played under New York rules and 37 that favored the Massachusetts game,[43] but the tide would eventually turn.

In addition to Salzman, there was a second strong proponent of the New York game in Boston. John Lowell, for whom the Lowell Club was named, was the founder of the Lowell and Bret engraving business and president and catcher for the Bowdoin Club.[44] He was not a New York expatriate, but clearly believed the New York style of play to be superior to that played in Massachusetts.

In 1861, Lowell spotted some younger boys who showed aptitude for the New York game and sent his friend and teammate Horace Chandler on a recruiting mission to the house of James Lovett, who was one of them. Lovett became one of the best and well-known of the Lowells and the man who immortalized the club in a book published in 1908. Chandler convinced Lovett and his friends to form a club to play the New York game, bolstered by the promise of free equipment.[45] He supplied the Lowells, most of whose members were students

The team pictured in their snappy uniforms is the Atwater Club of Westfield, Massachusetts, in 1858, the year they were organized. The bats are big, and the hats are not aerodynamic, but the Atwater Club was one of the first in Massachusetts to play the New York version of baseball. By the end of the Civil War, the New York game was the dominant sport in New England as well as New York.

at English High and the Latin School of Boston, with equipment, a meeting place, and encouragement.

Lowell was a tireless supporter of the move toward what he believed to be the better game. "We understand Mr. Lowell's ideas," reported *Wilkes'*, "have been fully realized in the great increasing interest taken in baseball, especially in Boston and vicinity. Several of the old Massachusetts clubs are changing their style to the national game."[46]

In 1860, the Bowdoin Club became the first New England organization to join the National Association, and in 1862, a correspondent informed the *Clipper* that four first-class Boston clubs, the Tri-Mountains, Bowdoins, Lowells and Shawmuts, were playing the New York game.[47] That year, the Excelsiors of Brooklyn visited Boston and easily defeated the Bowdoins and a combined nine from the Lowells and Tri-Mountains.

In 1864, Lowell donated a silver ball to be awarded to the champion club of New England. His adopted club, the Lowells, for whom he eventually played, won the first title in 1864. The only teams that could compete for the silver ball, of course, were those that played the New York game.[48]

The Lowell Club of Boston is pictured in 1866. The Lowells were named after their patron John Lowell, who supplied the club with equipment and was a great booster of the New York style of play. James DeWolf Lovett, one of the leaders of the Lowells, who later wrote a book about his experiences, is fourth from left.

The major sporting journals, such as the *Clipper* and *Wilkes'*, were based in New York, and of course favored the game played in their city. With the press against it and some of Massachusetts' own leaders, such as Lowell and Saltzman, against it, the Massachusetts game was on precarious footing. There were isolated attempts to spread the game to other areas of the country, but none was successful. By the end of the Civil War, it was essentially dead.[49]

Before the war, with the Massachusetts game still alive and well, the clubs of New York experienced the finest season in the brief history of the game. Eighteen sixty was a year of record activity, of unprecedented travel, and of a bitter contest for the championship. It was the year of the Excelsiors.

Chapter 12

Year of the Excelsiors, 1860

On March 14, 1860, delegates from sixty clubs met at the Cooper Institute in New York for the second annual convention of the National Association.[1] Nineteen of the sixty, nearly a third, were sending delegates for the first time. Most delegates didn't have far to go, for twenty-three clubs were based in New York, and sixteen were from Brooklyn. Several of the remaining twenty-one organizations hailed from the greater New York area, including five from Long Island, six from New Jersey and five from other parts of the state, none farther north than Troy. The remaining five clubs were the Quinnipiacs of New Haven, Connecticut, the Bowdoins of Boston, the Excelsiors of Baltimore, the Potomacs of Washington, D.C. and the Detroit Club, all of which were new members.

Despite the novel presence of organizations from beyond the greater New York area, the best clubs were still in and around the metropolis. The Atlantics were the defending champions, but there were clubs that were expected to provide a serious challenge to their supremacy. The Eckfords and Mutuals boasted strong nines, but the toughest competition was anticipated to come from the Excelsior Club of Brooklyn.

During the winter between the 1859 and 1860 seasons, the Excelsiors, who had made such great strides in 1859, took further steps to strengthen their nine. During the summer of 1859, two members of the young Stars had favorably impressed the Brooklyn club. In September, Jim Creighton, in one of his earliest stints in the pitcher's box, had hurled the Stars to a victory over the Excelsiors. Infielder George Flanly also played well, and the latter club was able to persuade both youngsters to change allegiances in November. Their loss, in combination with other defections, weakened the Star nine, and the new acquisitions substantially boosted the prospects of the Excelsiors. Captain Joe Leggett advised Creighton to throw an iron ball the size of a regulation baseball during the winter to increase the speed of his pitches.[2]

Only the most diligent baseball historian will recognize the name of George Flanly, a very good fielder but a weak hitter, but that of Creighton may strike a spark with even those lacking a deep knowledge of mid-nineteenth century baseball. What was magical about Jim Creighton? He was a very talented player, but so were others. He may have been the first professional player, but that claim is open to challenge. What constituted a professional? Was it someone who accepted a salary for a season, or for a game? Was it someone who was given a job requiring little work in return for playing ball? Was it someone who had his club dues paid by other members? Since all of the above methods of compensation were illegal under the rules of the National Association, no one was eager to lay a trail that would identify the first professional.

There is no hard evidence concerning the professionalism of Creighton, only the supposition that there must have been *something* that caused him to change teams. The Excelsiors had plenty of money, and the theory that they gave some of it to Creighton and Flanly is certainly a viable one.

Creighton was an innovator. He was not the first swift pitcher, but those who saw him said he pitched faster than anyone else, and unlike those who attempted to emulate him, Creighton could throw the ball both fast and accurately. His delivery began just a few inches from the ground, and the ball seemed to rise as it reached the plate. The unusual angle, in combination with the speed of the delivery, resulted in a large number of popups and foul tips, which were outs if caught by the catcher on the fly or the first bound. Everyone wondered how Creighton could pitch so fast without snapping his wrist, which was a violation of the rules. Was his novel "pitch" actually a "jerk," which was illegal? A reporter for *Brooklyn Eagle* (probably Henry Chadwick, although he was not identified) watched him carefully and decided it was not.[3]

When he first started playing ball, Creighton, who was a good hitter, was a second baseman, and his renown as a pitcher was limited until he joined the Excelsiors, for it was not until he combined with catcher Leggett that Creighton's vaunted speed became effective.[4] In the modern game, great defensive catchers are known as such principally because of their powerful throwing arms. Catching the pitch is a given. In the 1850s, however, the title of catcher was far more appropriate, for the most difficult task of the bare-handed man behind the bat was to catch the ball. A catcher who could catch and not throw was more valuable than one who could throw but not catch. With no one on base, most catchers stationed themselves well behind the batter and, in order to save wear and tear on their hands, often caught the ball on the bounce or not at all. By standing far from the batter, they also had greater range when pursuing foul tips and bounds. Catchers only moved up close to the bat when a runner was on base.

In the late 1850s, no one could catch a pitched ball better than Joe Leggett. Although he had never worked with anyone who threw like Jim Creighton, Leggett adapted quickly, and the pitcher was soon free to unleash his fast pitches without fear that they would be turned into a succession of passed balls. Teaming with Leggett brought out the full measure of Creighton's talent. The two complemented each other marvelously and became the first battery to institute a set of signals to determine when the pitcher would throw to the bases.[5]

The Excelsiors played very good baseball in 1860, but their primary contribution to the game was a series of trips the Brooklyn nine took during the summer. There were a number of clubs in upstate New York, and the game was beginning to take hold in Washington, Baltimore and Philadelphia, but baseball was still a very parochial pastime, for none of the clubs ventured far beyond their city limits. That would change in 1860.

One reason for the lack of travel was the time and expense required to get from one city to another. For trips to nearby cities, clubs usually engaged horse drawn conveyances, or possibly took short train or boat rides. Even these could be problematic. In 1864, when the Excelsiors journeyed from Brooklyn to Newark, there was a collision between two trains, which blocked the tracks and caused the Brooklyn players to have to walk more than two miles in the August sun to reach the grounds.[6]

For somewhat longer journeys, clubs always traveled by train or boat. An intercity trip of any distance was a venture which required a great deal of time and not insignificant expense.

Philadelphia was four hours from New York by train[7] with a round trip fare of $4.50. Those visiting the city could get hotel rooms for a dollar per night and meals for about twenty-five cents each. Entertainment was generally provided by the host club, and a ballplayer could make the trip to Philadelphia, and stay long enough to play a few games for about ten dollars.[8] Ten dollars could represent a week's salary for many workers, which eliminated the possibility of their making too many road trips.

In addition to the ten dollar expenditure, a trip of any distance generally took several days. The concept of widespread professionalism was several years in the future, and most players held full-time jobs. They were not, for the most part, independently wealthy, as were many cricketers, and few could spare several days absence from their businesses. Another reason for the lack of mobility of New York players was the fact that, with all the best clubs in the same vicinity, there was plenty of competition available at home, and very little in other areas.

Travel, in addition to being time-consuming and expensive, could be dangerous. On an 1864 excursion to Philadelphia, a boat carrying a number of New Jersey players caught fire. Although the flames were put out without anyone suffering injury, it was the second time the vessel had been aflame in just a few months.[9] A few years later, when the Atlantics took a trip to the Midwest, they planned to travel by boat from Louisville to Cincinnati. At the last minute, however, their hosts convinced the party to stay over and attend a banquet in their honor. The *Patrick Rogers,* the boat the Atlantics were to have taken, caught fire en route to Cincinnati, and many were killed.[10]

Despite the inherent difficulties, cricketers, with more time and money, traveled relatively frequently. The Milwaukee, Cleveland and Chicago Cricket Clubs exchanged visits regularly, as did the Pittsburgh, New York and Philadelphia elevens. Prior to 1860, however, baseball remained a strictly local pastime.

The Excelsiors' 1860 season, as it had the previous year, began unpropitiously, with a 12–11 loss to the Charter Oaks, the same club that had sprung such a surprising upset in 1859. This time, the result was not quite as shocking for the Charter Oak Club had added a number of top players since the previous season. Still, it was not the kind of beginning that foreshadowed the impact the Excelsiors were to have upon baseball in 1860.

A month later, the Excelsiors avenged their loss with a convincing 36–9 win over the Charter Oaks, and, with six former Stars in their lineup,[11] defeated the latter club, 16–5. Then, during the first week in July, the Excelsiors embarked on the first lengthy tour ever taken by a baseball club. Initially, the Excelsiors had intended to take a more extensive journey, traveling through upstate New York, then continuing on to Boston, Providence, New Haven and possibly Baltimore, Washington and Philadelphia.[12] They talked about going to Detroit.[13] While the actual trip was much shorter, it was still, for 1860, a very ambitious undertaking. From July 2 through July 11, twenty-two members of the Brooklyn club journeyed through upstate New York, playing six games and winning them all. The results were as follows:

Date	*City*	*Opponent*	*Score*
7/2	Albany	Champion	24–6
7/3	Troy	Victory	13–7
7/5	Buffalo	Niagara	50–19
7/7	Rochester	Flour City	21–1

Date	City	Opponent	Score
7/9	Rochester	Live Oak	27–9
7/11	Newburgh	Hudson River	59–14

Ten days, six games, six victories, not a close call, and, of course, hospitable entertainment at every stop. Baseball fans in the hinterlands, who had never seen players the like of the Excelsiors, witnessed the sport in its finest form. A Buffalo reporter gushed, "It is safe to say that no such ballplaying was ever before witnessed in Buffalo. The manner in which the Excelsiors handled the ball, the ease with which they caught it, the precision with which they threw it to the bases, and the tremendous hits they gave it to the long field made the optics of the Buffalo players glisten with admiration and protrude with amazement."[14] The Excelsiors did not even have their best nine players on the field, as Reynolds and Flanly, likely kept in Brooklyn by the demands of business, did not accompany the team, and they were replaced by two players from the second nine.

At each stop, the club was entertained by the locals, and the utmost good cheer prevailed in every city. At the end of the journey, a number of New York players met the Excelsiors in Newburgh and accompanied them back to the city. The only sour note from the tour was the fact that playing six games in ten days (far more than any club had ever played in such a brief period of time) *sans* gloves left the Excelsior nine with eighteen very sore hands.

The Excelsiors had assembled a team of very skilled players. The battery of Creighton and Leggett was without question the finest in the land, and a number of their teammates were almost as good. Flashy first baseman Aleck Pearsall, a doctor who began playing with a group of physicians who called themselves the Aesculapeans,[15] was a fine fielder with sure hands. No first baseman from his era caught every throw that came his way, but Pearsall caught more than just about anyone else. In addition to being a sure fielder, Pearsall carried a big bat, literally, reportedly 50 inches long.[16] Tall, husky outfielder Harry Polhemus, who sported a flourishing set of sideburns around his balding cranium and a thick mustache, was a heavy hitter who homered frequently, as did fellow outfielder John Holder.[17] Asa Brainard, later the pitcher of the famous Cincinnati Red Stocking Club of 1869, played the infield and outfield.

Aside from the obvious talent of the players, there was an additional element which set the Excelsiors apart from ordinary nines. They had class. Their president, Dr. J.B. Jones, was also president of the National Association, and the well-respected Health Officer of New York City.[18] On the field, the club was handled by perhaps the most esteemed captain of his day. In the 1860s, there were no field managers, and the captain was responsible for strategy and positioning the players on the field. "[T]here is one feature of the performances of the Excelsior Club we noticed," reported the *Eagle*, "that must have a large share in contributing to their success as players, and that is the admirable manner in which they are disciplined. Their prompt obedience to the commands of their captain [Leggett] is highly complimentary to him, as it fully proves the high estimation in which he is held by those under his command."[19]

When a ball was hit in the air, Leggett called the name of the fielder who was to catch it.[20] He demanded that his men behave like gentlemen and held them to a strict set of standards. In contrast to many teams, whose members straggled in and caused the start of games to be delayed, Leggett's Excelsiors always arrived on time.[21] Discipline was "scientific," comparable to the strategy employed in cricket, and was therefore desirable if baseball were to become a national game. Americans were not just physically gifted, they were organized and disciplined, and their game needed to reflect it.

Americans were also honorable, and no one garnered more respect than the Excelsiors. "The contest," one paper wrote of a game with the Eagles, "as all expected it would be, was marked by the most friendly and gentlemanly conduct on both sides, and it was one of those enjoyable affairs that the Excelsiors seem to monopolize to themselves."[22] The Excelsiors were the Knickerbockers with more talent.

Returning to Brooklyn, the Excelsiors got down to the task of trying to wrest the championship from the Atlantics by beating them in a three-game series. The clubs had met twice in prior years, with the Atlantics winning both times. These were the new, improved Excelsiors, however, fresh off their remarkable tour and featuring the best pitcher and catcher in baseball. Further, the Atlantics did not appear to be as dominant as in previous years. They won their first four games, but none was against strong opposition. Their captain, Rapeleye Boerum, was in Europe and had not played all season.[23]

The excitement generated by the tour created intense interest in the Excelsior-Atlantic matches. Would there be too much excitement? The game "will be undoubtedly attended," wrote the *Clipper* of the first match of the series, "by the largest crowd yet seen on a baseball ground. No fears need be entertained in regard to disorderly conduct, whatever excitement the game may create, as the Excelsiors are noted for the order they preserve at their matches." But just in case, "A large police force will be in attendance and as the Excelsiors are proprietors of the grounds enclosed, they will promptly remove any person who may act in any objectionable manner."[24]

There was good reason for concern, for the Atlantic followers had acquired a somewhat unsavory reputation. In a game against the Gotham Club in October 1858, they surrounded the players and crowded them to such an extent that the Gothams complained. "It was certainly not the fault of the Atlantics," opined *Porter's Spirit*, "as they tried their utmost to put the crowd back and to check their partial comments and unfair actions as much as possible."[25] In October 1859, a second offensive incident occurred at a game involving the Atlantics, when a male spectator began using abusive language in the presence of female fans. "It is the first instance of the kind we have

In 1860, the Excelsiors were the toast of the baseball world, and Joe Leggett, their catcher and captain, was among the most admired players. A strong hitter, good fielder, and respected leader, Leggett had a relatively brief tenure at the top. In his time, however, he was the finest backstop in the game, and any catcher with promise was referred to as "another Leggett."

been called upon to notice," said the mortified *Clipper,* "and we trust it will be the last, as no ladies will grace these occasions with their desirable presence."[26]

Fans were not only supposed to be well behaved, they were expected to be non-partisan, applauding the good play of their opponents as well as that of their own club. To cheer only for one's own club was in extremely poor taste. In 1864, reporting on a game between the Empire and Union Clubs, *Wilkes'* complained, "We never saw a more partial crowd of spectators at a match than were present at this one. They were blind to the merits of any good plays that did not emanate from the club they favored, and the Empires would have but little applause but for that they obtained from the force of their friends present."[27] If the crowd became too partial, club members were expected to correct the injustice.[28] "We noticed with pleasure," a journalist noted approvingly on another occasion, "that the applause of the spectators was fairly distributed to both clubs."[29]

Early in the 1860 season, reporting on a game between the Eckford and Union Clubs, the *Clipper* noted unruly behavior and made it clear that it was the responsibility of the clubs to control their followers and keep them in good order. "We refer thus particularly to this matter, as it is yet early in the season," the journal stated, "and we wish to nip the evil in the bud this year."[30]

Keeping their supporters under control was not an easy task for any club. In 1860, none of the grounds were enclosed, with spectators scrambling for good vantage points alongside the baselines, behind the catcher and sometimes deep in the outfield. There were usually no restraints on their movements, and fans often crowded the players, especially the catcher. Sometimes they retrieved an errant throw and relayed it to a player.[31] At other times, balls bounced off them or their carriages parked in the outfield, and everything was in play. At many matches, a few unruly spectators, usually gamblers, let their opinions be known in a loud fashion when the play did not go their way. In the sport's early years, offensive fan behavior had been a rare event, but by 1860, the atmosphere at several games had been marred by loud comments or spectators encroaching upon the field.

There were no grandstands, and the typical method of crowd control was to plant stakes in the ground and string ropes between them to keep the fans away from the baselines. The Mutuals were managed by members of Tammany Hall, and had their own methods of keeping order. When they visited Albany in 1864 and found the crowd encroaching on the field, President John Wildey took matters into his own hands. "Capt. Wilder [sic]," reported the *Eagle,* "undertook to clear the field himself and the way he fetched men around for a short time rather astonished the visitors. The Captain is not to be trifled with when his dander is up."[32]

One of the reasons spectators tended to get out of control was the wagers they placed upon the games. A second was the fact that alcohol was available at most grounds. Liquor was prohibited at the Elysian Fields,[33] and rarely was there a disturbance at the Hoboken site, but the same was not true of other venues. "These matches are attended by crowds of people," said the *Eagle,* "including all sorts of characters of both sexes, betting is freely indulged in, and intoxication is becoming prevalent."[34] "Fancy colored tents," reported the same journal after the second Atlantic-Excelsior match, "headed the field, and in some of these King Lager held his levee, his court being pretty well filled with thirsty worshippers, and in others his potent rival, King Alcohol, offered all the temptations of his infernal concoctions, his tents emitting flashes of 'Jersey lightning' every minute or so, much to the ultimate increase of the business the large force of police present had on their hands."[35]

A countervailing effect to liquor and gambling was provided by ladies, whose presence was expected to curb the baser instincts of male spectators. Ladies had been encouraged to attend sporting events almost as soon as they began, starting with horse races that took place in the 1820s and 1830s.[36] During baseball's early days, in the mid–1850s, the number of ladies in attendance, and their perceived interest, was noted fastidiously. In 1867, the Knickerbockers held a ladies' day, attracting twenty females to watch them play, and spent three dollars for their refreshments.[37] Many baseball clubs provided special, comfortable accommodations for the fair sex in order to encourage their attendance.[38] "Ladies wishing to witness the match" between the Continental and Harlem Clubs, the *Brooklyn Daily Times* declared, "will be provided with seats [which were always limited] and will have proper attention paid them."[39]

The presence of women lent an air of respectability to the events. Further, the ladies' femininity, by its contrast, supposedly caused the masculine features of the ballplayers to shine even more brightly. After an Eagle-Gotham match in 1857, at which a number of ladies were in attendance, the *Clipper* commented, "The smiles of the fair imparted a tone of chivalry to the manhood so nobly yet harmlessly displayed."[40] The main role of the ladies, however, was to preserve decorum by their mere presence. As the *Clipper* noted, "None but the lawless dregs of society will misbehave themselves in the presence of the fair sex among an American assemblage."[41]

During an 1864 game between the Gotham and Enterprise nines, the *Eagle* noted "the presence of a bevy of the fair sex, friends of the members, whose bright eyes and attractive countenances did much to bring about the result [gentlemanly, sportsmanlike behavior by the players and spectators]. It is greatly to be regretted that the attendance of ladies at ball matches is not such as to their being numbered by hundreds instead of dozens only."[42] "The ladies," said the *Daily Times* of one gathering, "waved their handkerchiefs and cheered as well as their feeble voices were able."[43]

The first Atlantic-Excelsior game took place on July 19 on the Excelsior grounds at the foot of Court Street in Brooklyn. Showers fell in the morning, but by afternoon the rain had stopped and the weather was oppressively hot with a blazing sun scorching players and spectators alike. Roughly ten thousand spectators (about as many as attended the first game of the Fashion Course Series) braved the heat, including some who viewed the action from surrounding rooftops, some who climbed the masts of ships anchored nearby and others who watched from the balcony of the nearby clubhouse of the Brooklyn Yacht Club.[44]

In the first inning, the Atlantics looked helpless against the pitching of Creighton. Three went to bat and three hands were quickly lost, one on a strikeout and two on foul tips to the catcher. Much later, Henry Chadwick related a conversation he had with Atlantic veteran Peter O'Brien after O'Brien had been Creighton's strikeout victim in the first inning. "Why," O'Brien stated, "we can't hit that pitching, Henry. The fact is, it's underhand throwing."[45] During the remainder of the game, Creighton had very few strikeouts, but Leggett retired a number of the Atlantics on weak foul tips. The Excelsiors scored twice in the first inning and dominated the game, winning, 23–4. It was the worst loss ever suffered by the Atlantics.

Despite the one-sided score, the Atlantics took their defeat gracefully. "But above all," the *Clipper* noted proudly, "do we select the gentlemanly conduct of the respective contestants throughout the match, and the prompt manner in which all outside comments were suppressed, as being worthy of the highest commendation. In regard to the conduct of the players, the thorough good humor that characterized the proceedings, and the instances of ability that the players afforded in this contest, mark it as a model game, and one calculated to have a lasting and beneficial effect on the future interests of baseball. We were also gratified in noticing that the decisions of the Umpire were promptly and *silently acquiesced in,* in every instance, and we trust this notable example will be followed on all like occasions."[46] Although everyone joined in the chorus of praise for the orderly nature of the huge crowd, they were to be gravely disappointed by what happened in the third game between the two clubs.

The second game of the series took place on August 9 on the Atlantics' grounds at Bedford. The Atlantics and Excelsiors had each lost only one game during the summer, the Atlantics to the Excelsiors and the latter the opening game stunner to the Charter Oaks. A second Excelsior victory over the Atlantics would give them the championship. An enormous crowd, estimated at ten to fifteen thousand, was on hand, and vehicles of many sorts, including carriages, stages, grocers' wagons and peddlers' carts,[47] completely encircled the playing surface. Spectators came from upstate New York, New Jersey and as far away as Boston to see if the Excelsiors would take the crown. Betting odds were heavily in their favor, based upon the previous easy victory. Even though the Atlantics were not as bad as they had looked in the first game, the Excelsiors looked unbeatable. "In our opinion," said the *Atlas,* "the Atlantics never in their lives played so well as did the Excelsiors on Thursday last."[48]

After three innings, when the Excelsiors held an 8–0 lead, it looked as though the bettors were correct and the Excelsiors would be the new champions. After five innings, the score was 12–3. But the Atlantics scored three times in the sixth and, with one of their famous rallies, nine times in the seventh to take a 15–12 lead. During the Atlantics' big rally, Creighton was hit so hard that he was removed from the pitcher's box and replaced by Ed Russell. The Excelsiors scored single runs in the eighth and ninth, but the game ended when Leggett, after singling, was thrown out at second.

The Excelsiors' 15–14 defeat set up a decisive third game. Like the first game, the second was marked by good sportsmanship and fair dealing, save for one occasion when a fan yelled "foul" on a fair ball, causing two Excelsiors to be put out.[49] In all, however, the fans, under the careful watch of seventy policemen, were well behaved. "A fair field and no favor," reported the *Clipper,* "was shown their opponents by the Atlantics, in every respect, and it was fully appreciated by the gentlemanly Excelsiors, the cordiality and friendly feeling that was manifested by both parties, one to the other, at the close of the proceedings being highly indicative of those sentiments, which are those that should ever exist among our clubs."[50]

Under the championship rules, the third game of a series was to be held on a neutral ground which, while favoring neither club, was also under the control of neither. The Putnam Club generously offered their grounds, located in Brooklyn between Gates and Lafayette Avenues, for the game which took place on August 23. Chadwick, anticipating a crowd of up to twenty thousand, saw trouble ahead despite the good behavior of the crowd during the first two matches. "It is to be regretted," he wrote, "that East New York was not selected, as there are but poor accommodations on the Putnam ground for so large a crowd as will undoubtedly be present."[51] The *Atlas* and *Brooklyn Daily Times* expressed similar sentiments.[52] The Excelsiors, under Leggett, always managed the crowd effectively when the game was played on their grounds, but they would have no control during the decisive third game.

The Excelsiors, despite the illness and consequent absence of star first baseman Aleck Pearsall,[53] jumped out to a 5–1 lead in the first inning, but, as they had in the second game, the Atlantics fought back. In the fourth inning, there was a disputed call. The Atlantics' Joe

Oliver hit a foul tip which struck catcher Leggett on the neck. He failed to hold it on the fly, but after the ball hit the ground, Leggett scooped it up on the first bound. Umpire R.J. Thorne of the Empire Club didn't see Leggett make the bound catch and declared that Oliver was not out. Even though just about everyone but Thorne had seen Leggett catch the ball, Atlantic Archie McMahon told Oliver, who had begun to walk toward the bench, to go back to the plate and await the umpire's decision. Such behavior was clearly contrary to the gentlemanly practice of refusing to benefit from an umpire's erroneous decision, but this game was for the championship and these were the Atlantics, not the Knickerbockers. Leggett explained to Thorne that he had made the bound catch cleanly, and Thorne declared Oliver out.

In the Atlantic fifth inning, Dickie Pearce singled. Charlie Smith hit a long double to left field, which scored Pearce to make the score 8–5. McMahon singled in Smith to make the score 8–6. With McMahon on second, Peter O'Brien fouled out to first baseman Russell. McMahon lit out for third, beat the throw, but over slid the bag. When Excelsior third baseman John Whiting saw McMahon's hand come off the bag, he tagged him and looked to Thorne for judgment. Thorne called McMahon out and the latter, who had urged Oliver to dispute the prior call, argued vigorously that his foot had remained on the base.

The third out was quickly registered, but McMahon's theatrics had aroused the Atlantic supporters. Gamblers had been present at the first two games, but the clubs had done a thorough job of silencing them and keeping them under control. On this day, their control was slipping away.

The game had not begun until after three o'clock, and had moved along slowly. With sundown approaching, it appeared as though the full nine innings might not be played, giving the Atlantics less time to catch up. As the Excelsiors came to bat in the top of the sixth, the crowd became loud and disorderly. John Holder led off by grounding out to third, but Leggett reached when Mattie O'Brien fumbled his hit back to the pitcher. Creighton hit into a force play, which would have been a double play if first baseman John Price had held the relay throw.

The crowd redirected its enmity from the umpire to their Atlantics after the two errors, and the heckling grew even louder when Smith dropped a ball at third, and then threw to Price, who again misplayed it at first. Numerous boxing matches had terminated when an unruly crowd broke into the ring, and it appeared now that a baseball game might reach such a shameful termination for the first time. The police force, although it mustered more than a hundred strong, was totally inadequate to deal with the massive crowd, estimated at fifteen thousand. Players from both clubs implored the crowd to desist, but to no avail. With the spectators shouting loudly and pressing in on the players, Captain Leggett issued a warning, then removed his team from the field, as the spectators poured onto it. The Excelsiors walked to their omnibus and left the grounds, trailed by jeering fans and Atlantic captain Peter O'Brien. O'Brien caught up to Leggett and the two captains quickly decided to call the game a draw.[54]

Umpire Thorne rendering a puzzling verdict. "My decision on the matter," he stated, "is that the game was won by neither party, inasmuch as it was brought to an abrupt termination by influences entirely outside of the parties interested in the match. But as the stoppage of the game was not by mutual consent, I must decide, according to the rules, that the party refusing to play [i.e. the Excelsiors] forfeits the ball to their opponents."[55] He said that he had entertained no thought of stopping the game and that the crowd had not bothered him in the least. It was Leggett, Thorne claimed, who had taken it upon himself to end the proceedings. Although the first sentence clouded the meaning of Thorne's statement, perhaps he meant that neither team had won the game on the field. In any event, it appeared he had awarded the game to the Atlantics.

Chadwick claimed that the rules decreed no such conclusion, and was completely baffled by Thorne's statement. He said that a forfeit was in order only if the Atlantics had returned to their positions after the Excelsiors departed, which they did not, and if they attempted to get the police to clear the field, which they did not. He declared that the game should have been called a draw and supported the position of the Excelsiors in leaving the field.[56]

With the battle on the playing field having terminated without a conclusion, the contest moved to the newspapers. The *Times* stated plainly that the Atlantic fans caused the disturbance, and neither team was to blame although the Excelsiors were clearly the victims.[57] It praised Leggett for his bold stance in pulling his men off the field. An Atlantic supporter who styled himself "Home Run" wrote a long letter to *Porter's Spirit of the Times* claiming to have seen no disputing of the umpire, no support of the unruly crowd by the Atlantics, and the Excelsiors inexplicably leaving the field for no reason other than they feared defeat loomed on the horizon.[58]

"Apparently," reported one journal, "the crowd saw that the Excelsiors were not as ironclad against outside abuse on the field as the Atlantics were, the latter having fought their way through many a fight in which the opposing crowd were bitterly against them, at Hoboken and elsewhere. But the Excelsiors' experience was not of the same rough kind, and the outside remarks 'rattled' them."[59]

The *New York Atlas,* perhaps with a degree of partisanship, declared that umpires from New York had often been roughly treated by Brooklyn fans. The journal sympathized with the plight of Thorne, and stated that, "[W]hen the Brooklyn roughs and sporting men undertake to quarrel about their favorite clubs, let them have the fight to themselves, and let an umpire from Brooklyn be chosen to be the subject of the blackguardism of those who are likely to lose bets upon the games."[60]

"Both clubs this summer," the *Atlas* continued, "have been followed by crowds of dirty-faced and half-grown ragged-tailed boys, who have made it very disagreeable for decent spectators to witness the games. Mr. Leggett, it is reported, however, has made commendable efforts to keep order, and repress noisy proceedings on the Excelsior grounds. It is said that the Atlantics cannot say as much."[61]

Another paper supported the Excelsiors, claiming that "the game was interrupted by the scandalous behavior of an outside crowd of noisy vagabonds, who indulged in hooting, yelling, and insulting remarks toward a portion of the players; and by their disgraceful action, in seeking to intimidate and influence the decisions of the umpire, compelled a suspension of the game." The disorderly element, they claimed, were "betting" friends of the Atlantics.[62]

Chadwick exonerated the Atlantics of wrongdoing and came to the defense of the O'Brien brothers, whom he praised for their fine character. It was the fans, Chadwick reminded his readers, who had caused the disturbance, while the players had tried to restrain them and had certainly done nothing to encourage them.[63]

Five days after the game, the Atlantic Club held a meeting at Butt's Hotel and formulated a response to the publicity, mostly negative, which had followed the debacle.[64] On the 31st, the Atlantics issued a statement defending their position. The letter, signed by Secretary

F.K. Broughton, claimed that the club had done everything within its power to provide adequate crowd control, and if Superintendent Folk and his police couldn't stop the crowd, how could they? "What more can any club do?" Broughton asked. "Can we restrain a burst of applause or indignation emanating from an assemblage of more than 15,000 excited spectators, whose feelings are enlisted as the game proceeds, by the efforts of this or that player or players? He who has witnessed the natural excitement which is ever the attendant of a vast miscellaneous assemblage, whether called together by a regatta, an important trial of speed on the turf, or a match between noted base ball organizations, knows full well that it is an utter impossibility to prevent the crowd from expressing their sentiments in a manner and as audibly as they please."[65]

Broughton cited regattas and horse racing, two sports known for relatively genteel adherents, but failed to mention boxing, a disreputable pastime that had witnessed instances of bad behavior very similar to that seen on the Putnam grounds. Umpire Thorne said he was not bothered by the crowd, Broughton stated, and the Atlantics had told him they would support all of his decisions, a statement belied by the Oliver and McMahon episodes. It was the jittery nerves of Leggett, Broughton stated, that brought about the termination of the match, and nothing else. Leggett "seems to be getting exceedingly nervous of late," declared Broughton, to have been spooked by a mere fifteen thousand shrieking hooligans, and the Excelsior captain's precipitate action would inspire imitation and ruin the game. It would also drive away the ladies.

"We wish the public to understand," the letter continued, "that we do not win our battles in the newspapers, but on the green turf, and we are also firm in the faith that the club is yet to be organized which can deprive us of our toil-earned championship … we would recommend to those aspiring to the championship not to be too hasty in leaving the field, as it is a 'poor road to travel' and does not lead to that enviable and coveted position."

The Excelsiors, secure in Leggett's decision, sent a card to the press indicating that its membership supported the captain's actions. Had McMahon not disputed the umpire's call, they stated, the subsequent disturbance could have been avoided.[66]

That was the end of the incident. The fracas and near riot, the first affair of its kind in the relatively brief history of baseball, raised a number of questions. The most important concerned the effect the embarrassing episode would have upon the future of baseball. "[T]he result must affect the interest of the game," opined *Wilkes' Spirit of the Times*, "and materially retard its progress, as it will be impossible to find a gentleman willing to risk his self-respect by acting as Umpire in matches where such excitement is likely to occur."[67] "A little further decadence will reduce the attendance at the ball matches to the level of the prize ring and the race course" said the *Eagle*."[68] Would ladies dare attend a spectacle which might end in violence? With no umpires, and no ladies, baseball risked being stripped of its coveted respectability.

Shortly after the game, a package arrived at the club rooms of the Atlantics. It contained a baseball, the symbol of victory, on which was inscribed, "Atlantic vs. Excelsior, August 23, 1860; six innings played; Atlantic 6, Excelsior 8; game unfinished." It was not known whether the package was sent by the Excelsiors, but the Atlantics took offense and the rift between the clubs was widened.[69]

The third Excelsior-Atlantic game was never replayed. The bad feeling between the two clubs was such that they never met again, and the Excelsiors were so disgusted by the partisan spirit engendered by the competition between clubs that they determined never again to play for the championship. The *Clipper* also saw the evils inherent in the system. "[W]e now regard these matches for the championship," it wrote, "as anything but conducive to the best interests of the game."[70]

A few days after the unfortunate episode, the Excelsiors and Knickerbockers played a match which the Excelsiors, as expected, won handily. In his typically gracious remarks during the presentation of the ball, Dr. Jones, President of the Excelsiors, noted the fine sportsmanship that had prevailed, and condemned the gamblers who had disrupted the Atlantic match.[71]

Although the game was totally one-sided and unexciting, Chadwick also pointed out the contrast to the Excelsior-Atlantic match. "It was interesting," he wrote, "solely from the striking contrast it afforded to the proceedings of Thursday last, both in the character of the play exhibited and the conduct of the spectators, for on this occasion the utmost cordiality was manifested throughout, good humor and courteous conduct ruling the action of all who participated in it."[72] However, while such a game was pleasing to Chadwick, fans preferred the rough-and-tumble, more skilled and intensely competitive matches played for the championship, and the game was clearly moving in that direction, as much as the stalwarts of the 1850s wanted to believe otherwise.

The Excelsiors and Atlantics, although they didn't play against each other, each took part in a number of games before concluding their seasons. The Excelsiors won their remaining six matches, but the Atlantics, since they hadn't been beaten in a best-of-three series, were still the champions. In late October, they played a three-game series against the Eckfords, who had challenged them for the title. The *Atlas* assured prospective spectators that there would be no trouble, as the two clubs had a good relationship with each other, a relationship that would deteriorate over the next three years.[73]

The Atlantics won the first game, 17–15, the Eckfords the second, 20–15, and the Atlantics took the deciding match, 20–11 on October 29. It was a close, well-contested series, with the Atlantics winning the initial contest by scoring four times in the ninth inning. The attendance of eight thousand for the third game (five thousand were at the second) didn't approach the number that had witnessed the Atlantic-Excelsior games, but neither did it portend the end of baseball's popularity. Perhaps most important of all, the spectators were well-mannered (which was carefully noted by the press), betting was at a minimum, and the players displayed the good sportsmanship that had characterized the first two games of the Excelsior series.[74]

It had been an interesting season, the most exciting in the history of baseball. "The past [season]," said the *Brooklyn Daily Times*, "has been the most active and brilliant that was ever known in America, and, with a few exceptions, during the whole of it, has passed off harmoniously."[75] The growth of 1858 and 1859 had continued, as new clubs were formed each month. By the end of the year, there were more than 100 in Brooklyn alone, while New Jersey had about 130.[76] More importantly, there were hopeful signs that the game was beginning to spread beyond New York, thanks in part to the tour of the Excelsiors.

Philadelphia and Baltimore showed indications of adopting baseball with all the enthusiasm of New York. The latter city had been introduced to the sport by George Beam, a wholesale grocer who made the acquaintance of fellow grocer Joe Leggett. One day Leggett invited Beam, who was visiting Brooklyn, to watch the Excelsiors play ball. Beam was so enthusiastic that he returned to Baltimore and formed a club of which he was named captain and which he called, predictably, the Excelsiors. Harry Polhemus, hard-hitting outfielder of the Brooklyn Excelsiors, was the New York representative of Baltimore's Woodberry Mills, and thus was frequently in the city.[77] He helped teach the new club, most of whom were local merchants, how to play the game. They found grounds at Flat Rocks, near Madison Avenue, and began to practice.[78]

Just to the south, in Washington, D.C., future U.S. Senator Arthur Pue Gorman, then 21, helped organize the Nationals who, along with the Potomacs, were the first clubs in the nation's capital. The Nationals, who had been playing informally, officially organized in 1859.[79]

Those who later knew Gorman as a silver-haired senator and nearly a nominee for the presidency would have been astonished to read the description of his play against the Pastime Club of Baltimore in 1863. "Gorman did the big thing of the day," a correspondent reported, "taking the lead at the bat, and in the seventh inning making a bound-catch which astonished everybody. Not content with this, in the ninth inning he again made a most difficult bound catch, the height which he attained inducing the lookers-on to believe that he used a springboard."[80]

On June 6, 1860, the Potomacs met the Excelsiors of Baltimore on the White Lot, just behind the White House, in the first game between clubs from the two cities. The Excelsiors were victorious by the score of 40–24, before a crowd of several thousand spectators, and Beam was the winning pitcher.[81]

In September 1860, the *real* Excelsiors, Beam's old friends from Brooklyn, visited Baltimore and defeated their namesakes, 51–6. Asa Brainard, rather than Creighton, pitched for the Excelsiors. The locals were delighted to absorb the thrashing, which included six home runs, a 13-run inning and a 12-run frame. They applauded the good play of the Brooklyn players as well as their own, seldom though the latter occurred. The play of the visitors dazzled the crowd. "[T]heir expectations," reported the *Clipper,* "really fell short of the degree of skill that was exhibited. Their grace and ease of movement, their surety in catching and holding the balls sent to them, their perfect discipline, and the admirable skill shown in each and every position, marked them at once as masters of the game."[82]

The Excelsiors were likewise impressed with Baltimore, both with the hospitality of their hosts and the beauty of their women. According to the *Clipper,* Excelsiors Reynolds, Brainard and Whiting spent so much time ogling the pretty maidens that they had to be reminded by Captain Leggett to keep their minds on the game.[83] The defeat in no way discouraged the novice players, who expected to lose (and had those lovely women to go home to), and the game greatly raised the profile of baseball in Baltimore.

The Excelsiors of Baltimore lasted only one more season before merging with the Waverly Club to form the Pastimes, who were to enjoy a successful career over the next several years. By the time the pioneers ceded their identity, there were 38 clubs in the city, enough to warrant the formation of The Association of Base Ball Clubs of Baltimore.[84]

Even before the July tour of the Excelsiors, baseball activity in upstate New York had been increasing. In the southern part of the state, there were clubs in Albany and nearby Troy which regularly played against each other. The top Troy nines were the Victory and Champion Clubs while the Knickerbocker and Champion nines were the toast of Albany.[85] The Highland Club was the pioneer organization in Newburgh, followed by the Hudson River nine, formed in 1859. The latter was a strong combination that often played clubs from New

York and Brooklyn.[86] Farther north, the Utica Club had been formed in 1859,[87] Syracuse spawned the Syracuse Club, and Rochester's first club, the Olympics, was organized in the mid–'50s.[88] Soon, it was joined by the Flour City, Washington, Live Oak and Charter Oak Clubs.

Earlier forms of baseball, similar to the New England game, had been played in upstate New York since at least the early nineteenth century, but it was not until September 1857 that the New York game permanently arrived in Buffalo with the formation of the Niagara Club, the organization that would field the best nine in the city during the following fifteen years. Two former members of the Excelsiors of Brooklyn, Messrs. Bach and Oliver, were instrumental in the genesis of the new club, whose bylaws would be modeled after those of the Excelsiors. Like their Brooklyn counterparts, the Niagaras were predominantly respectable business men.

The formation of the Niagaras was the signal for others to follow suit, and soon a number of new clubs appeared in Buffalo. The best nines in the city were the Niagaras, Erie, Frontier, Star and Buffalo organizations. The first interclub match under New York rules took place in August 1858, with the Niagaras beating the Erie Club, 25–16, before a crowd of several hundred spectators.

Rochester and Buffalo quickly developed a spirited rivalry. Shortly after the Niagaras dispatched the Erie Club, they beat the Flour City nine on the latter's home grounds. In late September, the Flour City's returned the visit, and were beaten again, 35–20. On both occasions, the host city went out of its way to entertain their guests, and many toasts were drunk, songs sung and cheers rendered.

The following season, the Erie Club traded visits with the Live Oaks of Rochester after the Niagaras had declined the challenge of the latter club on the basis that the Niagaras were the best in their city and the Live Oaks were not. In the event, the latter nine was as good as the Eries, as the clubs traded victories in the two matches.

The 1860 season, as it was in so many locales, was a banner year in Buffalo, despite the fact that the Niagaras suffered the first defeat since their formation. The loss was to the visiting Excelsiors of Brooklyn, which was no disgrace, and came before a crowd of roughly three thousand. Before the summer ended, Buffalo clubs took the game to Canada, as both the Niagaras and Queen City Clubs beat teams from Ontario. In September, the Niagaras suffered a second defeat, this one to the Lone Stars of Rochester, which led to the latter nine proclaiming themselves the champions of Western New York.[89]

Baseball was also spreading, albeit slowly, to New England. They played baseball in Boston, although mostly under the Massachusetts rules, and they played in Maine, especially in the city of Portland. There were games in New Hampshire, reported as early as 1858, and in Connecticut.[90] The sport was adopted in Washington, Connecticut during the 1850s when the children of William Van Cott of the Gothams attended the Gunnery School.[91]

The West, which we now call the Midwest, was also beginning to warm to the new sport. The rules of baseball had been published by *Porter's* and the *Clipper* in 1856, and the spread of baseball no longer required a transplanted New Yorker to lead the way. In 1858, the Excelsiors became the first club in Chicago, quickly followed by the Union Club. A year later, the two pioneers were joined by the Atlantic and Columbia organizations.

The Atlantics and Excelsiors played the first interclub match,[92] and the former claimed the 1859 city championship by beating the Excelsiors twice in three games. The following year, the *Clipper* listed twelve Chicago clubs that played the New York game. In the tense political climate that surrounded the 1860 presidential election, the Excelsiors divided into two teams, the adherents of Abraham Lincoln on one and those of Stephen Douglas on the other. The Douglas men beat the Lincoln men, 18–16, the only battle Douglas won that year.[93]

On August 1, 1859, the first St. Louis club, consisting of 18 members, was organized, and by the following June there were five clubs in the city.[94] As in New York, the sport was commenced with great organization and documentation and a trumpeting of the virtue of the new game. On March 31, 1860, a number of men played a game in St. Joseph, a suburb of St. Louis, and decided to form the Franklin Club. They made motions, elected officers and delivered speeches "setting forth the benefits to be derived from such an organization, both physically and mentally; and in bringing together young and old, tend to cultivate a social feeling."[95]

Town ball had been the sport of choice in Cincinnati, but in the fall of 1860, a group of young men, led by druggist Matthew Yorston, organized a club of high school students and young businessmen and called themselves the Buckeye Club. In early 1861, the Buckeyes, the first baseball organization in the State of Ohio, announced plans to practice three days per week. A second club, carrying the obligatory Excelsior handle, converted from town ball to baseball. Both clubs disbanded during the war, with the Excelsiors re-organizing and taking the Buckeye name with the coming of peace. The old Buckeyes became the Live Oaks.[96] Baseball didn't thrive in Cincinnati, however, until Harry Wright left New York to take the job of professional with the Union Cricket Club in 1866. Wright would bring fame, if not fortune, to the Midwestern city before the decade was over.

Primitive forms of baseball had been played in Michigan during the '30s and '40s. The New York game did not appear in the state until August 1857, when the Franklin Base Ball Club of Detroit, the first known organization west of the Mississippi, was organized.[97] The Franklins got the notion to form their club after reading the rules printed in the *Clipper*.[98] The members of the new organization gathered and played a number of games among themselves but, since there were no other clubs in the state, never played a match against anyone else. The Franklins disbanded sometime in 1858, undefeated, untied and untested.

In the fall of 1858, a second organization, the Detroit Club, was organized. While the Franklins had been primarily tradesmen, many associated with the newspaper industry, the Detroit Club was composed of men of Knickerbocker caliber, a number of them from the cream of Detroit society.[99] Other organizations followed, with Michigan cornering the market on clubs that practiced early in the morning, and who were proud of it. The Early Risers of Detroit began at 4 A.M., and the Daybreak Club of Jackson and Red, White and Blue of Marshall at 5.

The first match in Detroit, between the Early Risers and the Detroit Club, took place on August 8, 1859, and was won by Detroit, 59–21.[100] Interest in baseball increased after the initial game, and more clubs took to the sport. The Brother Jonathan Wicket Club changed to baseball, and soon became one of the best nines in the state. The Franklins reorganized. By 1860, baseball was solidly established in Michigan, with three major clubs, one, of course, named Excelsior. The Detroit Club became the first from the state to join the National Association.

There was activity in Louisville, Kentucky, where the Eclipse and Louisville Clubs held forth,[101] and in Milwaukee where games were reported as early as 1859.[102] By 1860, they were even playing ball all the way out in California. Informal ball games had been reported in the state in the early 1850s,[103] but formal clubs did not appear until several years later.[104] *Porter's Spirit of the Times* reported on a cricket match in San Francisco in 1857,[105] and in early 1858, the San Francisco Base Ball Club became the first baseball organization in the state.[106] A former New Yorker, M.E. Gelston, one of the founders of the Eagle Club of New York in 1852, and a fine catcher on the first nine, had been a catalyst in bringing baseball to the West Coast. Like immigrants from Europe bestowing the names of their former residences upon the new, Gelston christened his California club the Eagles, and became their catcher. With only two clubs, there was not much opportunity for competition, but, in 1860, things began to get lively.

The *Clipper* reported in early March, "Baseball had been started there several times, but never amounted to much until recently, when the San Francisco Club gave an impetus to the game by issuing a challenge on the 28th of January, and before two days had elapsed, they received three letters of acceptance."[107] Finally, it appeared, there would be a match in California between two competing clubs. Sure enough, on February 22, before the *Clipper* even hit the streets, the first interclub game on California soil had taken place at Center's Bridge. Unfortunately, the game was a 33–33 tie between the Eagles and the challenging Red Rovers, which ended in a dispute when the Red Rovers insisted that Eagles' pitcher J.C. Willock was using an illegal delivery. When the umpire disagreed, the Red Rovers left the field.[108]

The *Clipper* reported a May 1860 match between the Union and Sacramento Clubs, with the comment, "We are pleased to notice that this manly game is making rapid progress in California, and we should not be surprised at seeing some future day a match between one of our clubs and a California one."[109] And if the Sacramento Club left right away, the *Clipper* might have added, they could have made it to the Elysian Fields in time to open the 1861 season, for with the transcontinental railroad nine years away, it was unlikely that California and New York clubs would be playing each other in the near future.[110]

The secretary of the Sacramento Club was E.N. Robinson, formerly of the Putnam Club of New York. Robinson did not bring the name of his New York organization to California, as had Gelston, but the Sacramento uniform was identical to the Putnam uniform.

In September 1860, the California clubs held their biggest event of the season, a tournament at the Centreville Race Course in Sacramento among the Sacramento, Stockton, Eagle and Live Oak Clubs. The Sacramento Club beat the Stockton and Live Oak Clubs easily, 48–11 and 73–7, but lost two close games to the Eagles, who traveled from San Francisco for the event. *Porter's Spirit of the Times*, the Sacramento *Evening Post* and the *Stockton Argus* each sent reporters to cover the action.[111]

The last section of the country to embrace the new sport was the South. On April 4, 1861, just a few days before the Confederates fired on Fort Sumter, a group of 18 young Texans met and formed the Houston Base Ball Club. Within a week, the membership rolls had grown to 35 and the club had set its practice days and the date of its first practice.[112]

Even African Americans, still enslaved in the Southern states, were beginning to play the new game. The first reported game involving blacks took place in July 1859 with one of the teams including Congressman Joshua Giddings, a fervid abolitionist who was white.[113] The Unknown Club was the first composed entirely of African Americans, and by 1860 it was believed that there were four black clubs in existence.[114] Whenever the mainstream press reported on a game with black players, they invariably related the pleasure taken in the play, whether it existed or not. The distinction was clear. Whites played for the physical benefits, while blacks played to have a good time.

By the end of the 1860 season, baseball was being played in nearly all parts of the United States, fueled to a large extent by former New Yorkers who had migrated west. The game these emigrants brought to their new lands was the New York version, for apparently Bostonians, at least the baseball playing variety, lacked the wanderlust of their New York brethren. Despite the flurry of activity in other sections of the country, however, the center of baseball was still New York, where the top clubs battled each other for the "national" title. Although the Atlantic-Excelsior incident had hurt the game, all in all, 1860 had been a very successful campaign. "This season," said the *Eagle,* "has been prolific of first class contests, and has been decidedly the most brilliant season in the annals of the game."[115] What would 1861 bring?

Chapter 13

Abner Doubleday Invents the Civil War, 1861

As Captain Abner Doubleday boarded the *Baltic*, the steamship that would transport him from Fort Sumter to New York, he wondered what would become of the American Union. He contemplated the possibility of perishing in combat. But most of all, Doubleday worried about the survival of the game he had invented just over two decades earlier.

Well, maybe not. But there were plenty of others who wondered what would happen to the newly popular sport of baseball with the country in a state of war. They had little precedent to look to, for during previous conflicts, the Revolution, the War of 1812 and the Mexican War, there had not been much organized sporting activity in the country. The only sport that enjoyed any popularity was horse racing, a pastime that was severely curtailed during the Revolution.[1] The situation was different in 1861, for during the last season before the beginning of hostilities, there had been more baseball played than ever before, and the sport was spreading rapidly throughout the country.

In early February, as baseball clubs danced at their balls, and some played the game on ice, the first sign of impending war reached New York when the wives and families of the Fort Sumter garrison arrived on the steamship *Marion*.[2] After the fort was surrendered in April, there was little doubt that there would be a war. At first, everyone hoped it would end quickly. They expected a big, exciting battle or two during which young men would earn glory and one side or the other would prevail decisively. A very few soldiers would earn everlasting fame by perishing in battle while others would acquire wounds they could proudly display for a lifetime. The rest would return home and North and South would return to everyday life, either as one nation or two.

Virtually no one anticipated the countless deaths and horrendous, maiming wounds that would be inflicted upon so many soldiers during the next four years. During America's two previous wars, battlefield casualties had been few, as one was hard pressed to hit the proverbial broad side of a barn with the ancient muskets. Disease was a far more deadly adversary. During the fifty years since America's last war, however, firearms had become much more accurate and deadly.

By May and June, New York was teeming with soldiers waiting to be dispatched to the front. Central Park, Staten Island and Riker's Island became large encampments, and tents sprung up on what had been playing fields. Officers who had yet to see the enemy marched around the city in magnificent uniforms unstained by mud, blood or grime, and enterprising merchants sold the troops cakes, pies, beer and other delicacies.[3]

The sporting press took up the Union cause with enthusiasm, reviling the Rebels and lauding the patriotism of men who enlisted in the Union Army. "Better join in, boys," the *Clipper* urged, "than be loafing the streets or hanging around bar rooms, and thus show the people you have some noble traits that atone for whatever bad ones you get credit for."[4]

That did not mean, of course, that *Clipper* proprietor Frank Queen was about to take the road to Richmond, for he intended to wield a pen rather than a rifle. "[It] only belongs to every true lover of his country," he stated, "to lend a helping hand some way or other, to aid that country in the hour of need. So far as a public journalist can assist that cause, through the medium of his columns, the *Clipper* will not be found wanting ... the *Clipper* will, at all times, be ready to record the valorous deeds of those who have so cheerfully girded on their armor to do battle for their country."[5]

Henry Chadwick, the *Clipper's* baseball editor, spent the early days of the conflict as a war correspondent in Richmond. Chadwick's wife Jane was from a prominent Virginia family, but she remained in Brooklyn for the duration of the conflict. Within weeks, her husband was back to report the events of the upcoming baseball season.

The *Clipper*, which had lauded the physical benefits of sporting activities, now pointed out that it had not only aided in the development of more fit businessmen, but also in the preparation of hardy soldiers. "We would that every volunteer," they said, "had been the pupil of athletic exercises, gymnastic schooling, and pugilistic science."[6]

As the war went on, other figures from the sporting world showed their patriotism. William Cammeyer, proprietor of the Union Grounds, which opened in 1862, supported the Union cause from Brooklyn. He offered his facility for a game between the lightweight and heavyweight players of New York and Brooklyn with the proceeds to be given to a fund that encouraged enlistment. He also donated the use of the Union Grounds for a patriotic rally to honor the 47th Regiment of the New York State Volunteers upon its return from its 90 day enlistment, an event attended by a reported 25,000.[7]

Boxer John Morrissey expressed his patriotism in the same manner as Queen and Cammeyer — from afar. He visited the Troy regiment's encampment and presented its colonel with a set of pistols, "which will prove very serviceable in keeping the rebels at bay." "Credit to whom credit is due," the *Clipper* wrote of Morrissey's generosity, "is our motto; hence our commendation of the above loyal act. Let every man show his colors."[8] When the draft was instituted in 1863, Morrissey showed his colors by paying the three hundred dollar fee that was required to obtain exemption and engage a substitute.[9]

The big question in sporting circles was how the war would affect activities such as cricket, baseball and horse racing. On April 11, the day before the Confederates fired on Fort Sumter, the *Brooklyn Daily Times* forecast the greatest season in the history of baseball, based upon the great successes of 1860 and the unprecedented number of teams in the field.[10] In its April 20 issue, the *Clipper* discussed the prospects for 1861. "Many important matches are in process of being arranged, we are informed. Enthusiasts in the game are looking forward to a brilliant season. We hope they will not be disappointed."[11] All Queen could do was hope, for neither he nor anyone else could predict with confidence whether the public would support baseball or cricket when there was much more serious business at hand.

"[A]s they all cannot go 'to the wars,'" said the *Daily Times*, "the stay-at-homes have very wisely concluded to indulge in their favorite recreation and we have no doubt but that we shall ere long have the gratification of chronicling many well-fought contests on the Brooklyn grounds."[12] The sporting journals took great care to point out the physical risks involved in baseball and document the injuries suffered by the players. Baseball might not be war, but it required tough men to play it.

On May 6, the Philadelphia cricketers held their annual meeting. Many of the local players had marched off to fight, and not much activity was anticipated during the summer. A planned trip to New York would almost certainly be a casualty of war. "Not much business of importance was transacted," reported the *Clipper*, "in the way of match making &c., as it was thought, doubtless, that it would be unwise to get too many engagements on hand, owing to the existing war commotion."[13] Other sportsmen were equally cautious. The New York Yacht Club, fearful of being preyed upon by Confederate raiding vessels, cancelled its annual regatta.[14]

Meanwhile, the baseball season got under way. On May 9, the Excelsiors held their first practice of the season, despite the fact that many of their members were serving with the Union Army. On June 5, the Eckfords played the Enterprise in the first big match of the season, a game viewed by an estimated three thousand spectators.[15] The *Clipper* observed, "We were gratified in witnessing the presence of so many spectators at this match, as it indicated that the popularity of our national game has not been diminished by the excitement incident to the 'pomp and circumstance of war' which, to a certain extent, has laid an embargo on outdoor sports, and especially ball-playing, thus far this season; but the blockade has at last been forced, and henceforth we may expect to see our ballgrounds well frequented by the admirers of 'ye noble game.'"[16]

"It was thought," added the *Eagle*, "that cannon balls would supersede base balls this season — that our meetings and delightful measures would be exchanged for the pride, pomp and circumstance of glorious war, but even in their ashes live the wonted fires, and though faint and few, we are fearless still."[17] The almost forced enthusiasm, however, over the playing of a single game, spoke to the doubt of its supporters that baseball would prosper, and activity in the early season was very slow. The first game at the Elysian Fields, normally bustling with activity in May and June, did not take place until July 12.[18]

Baseball was not dead, but it was not very lively. "Cricket and Base Ball clubs," reported the *Clipper* in June, "usually so busy in the field at this period of the year, are now enlisted in a different sort of exercise, the rifle or gun taking the place of the bat, while the play ball gives place to the leaden messenger of death. Men who have heretofore made their mark in friendly strife for superiority in our various games, are now beating off the rebels who would dismember this glorious 'Union of States.'"[19]

The Knickerbockers, who documented every act, no matter how insignificant, made limited entries in their minute book from 1861 through 1864. At several meetings in 1861, the club could not muster a quorum, and there are no entries after July 5. Likewise, there are a limited number of brief entries for subsequent war years. While the books were to some extent a function of the diligence and verbosity of the club secretary, the brevity and infrequency of the entries is striking. One, in March 1862, noted a motion from Jim Davis to waive the dues of Knick stalwart Beverly Clarke, who was serving in the Union Army.[20]

Many players who enlisted immediately after the battle at Fort Sumter signed up for only 90 days, and returned to their clubs in July with the baseball season in full swing. Late that month, the 13th Regiment, which counted Joe Leggett among its members, arrived in Brooklyn and was greeted by a parade that included members of twelve baseball clubs, all wearing badges which read: "Base-Ball, Fraternity."[21] Throughout the war, players became soldiers and vice versa, as few enlisted for the duration. In September 1862, the 13th and 47th regiments returned to Brooklyn, and the ballplayers in their ranks again took the field, though probably not for long. "[I]t must be known," noted the *Eagle*, "that to be a true ball player, one must be a patriot too, and of those who have returned few will remain home."[22]

Despite the high hopes, baseball activity in 1861 was limited and didn't approach the excitement generated in 1860. "Sporting interests have not been very lively," the *Clipper* stated, "for many of our sporting friends have enlisted in defence of the Union, while those that remained with us lacked the spirit to indulge in those recreations so rife among us in former seasons. As a general thing ... our sports have been dull, nor can we look for better things until the integrity of the Union shall have been fully established and peace declared. Till then, we must bide our time."[23]

Most of the top nines played but five or six times all season. The Excelsiors, who had traveled far and wide in 1860, did not partake of a single match with another club. In September, the Eureka Club of Newark was reported to have issued a challenge to the Excelsiors, but, if so, the latter did not accept. The Knickerbocker, Charter Oak, Powhatan, Liberty and Putnam Clubs were also inactive. They practiced, and a number of their members played in games of mixed teams, but their first nines did not encounter any outside competition during the summer.

The Waverly Club, a junior organization, disbanded during the winter of 1861–62, and its members were absorbed by the Stars and other clubs.[24] In Washington, where many of the players trudged off to fight, the Potomac Club disbanded.[25]

In areas of the country where baseball had very shallow roots, it became almost dormant. In Michigan, the Early Risers dissolved due to the loss of members, and only one game was played in Detroit in 1861. That contest took place only because the Hamilton Club of Ontario, Canada, crossed the border to play the Detroit Club in one of only two games the champions of Michigan played during the war.[26] The Jackson Club of Michigan lost fifty percent of its members to the Union Army.[27] When baseball was played in Michigan during the war, it was sometimes under old versions of the rules, for clubs could not muster nine to a side.[28] The Brother Jonathan Club, one of the top organizations in the state, lost so many members to the war that it was almost completely inactive.[29] By 1864, the Detroit baseball scene was very quiet, but it would revive in a major way after the close of hostilities in 1865.

A number of clubs from upstate New York did not send representatives to the wartime conventions, as the conflict had depleted their ranks to the degree that they did not play ball. The Excelsiors of Chicago were also severely weakened by enlistments. Clubs in Philadelphia and Baltimore, which had sprung up just before the war, suspended activity as their members trudged off to fight. In Philadelphia, that meant fighting for the Union, while in Baltimore, it could mean either side.

A number of sporting men enlisted in the Union Army, and some lesser known players gave their lives for the cause. Two months after the start of the war, John Butterworth, a member of the Social Baseball Club, was accidentally shot while on guard duty in Alexandria.[30] The following summer, Guy Holt, a member of the Henry Eckfords, enlisted along with his two brothers. Guy was a popular player, one who had frequently acted as an umpire late in the 1861 season. Corporal Holt was shot in the head and killed, also by his own comrades, as he was returning from picket duty in Suffolk, Virginia.[31]

Joe Leggett exchanged his Excelsior uniform for Union blue, as did 90 fellow Excelsiors, including John Whiting of the first nine.[32] Pitcher Simon Burns of the Mutuals enlisted and fought at Roanoke Island.[33] Thomas Dakin, pitcher of the Putnams and the original vice president of the National Association, became a brigadier general in Brooklyn's 5th Brigade.[34] Pitcher Bernard Hannegan of the Unions of Morrisania served for a portion of the war.[35] George Zettlein, future star pitcher of the Atlantics, fought in both the Union Army and Navy, serving in the battles of New Orleans, Vicksburg and Mobile.[36] Pitcher Brientnall of the Eureka Club enlisted in 1864,[37] and a number of the Resolute's, Jefferson's, Putnam's and Henry Eckford's top players went to war.

Joe Sprague, star pitcher of the Eckfords, enlisted for 90 days in 1863 and campaigned with the 13th Regiment in Virginia, returning in time for the match with the Atlantics that gave the Eckfords the championship.[38] Athletic pitcher Tom Pratt served in defense of Pennsylvania, then, after his tour of duty ended, went to Brooklyn to join the Atlantics.[39] When the Atlantics visited Philadelphia in 1864, Athletic pitcher Dick McBride obtained a three-day furlough to hurl against them.[40] Over fifty players from Boston clubs enlisted.[41]

Al Martin, who in the decade after the war would become one of the great slow pitchers, enlisted with Hawkins' Zouaves of the New York Volunteers. He was wounded at Antietam, but served until 1864. It was in army games that he began to perfect his renowned drop pitch.[42]

Despite the numerous enlistments, most of the leading clubs retained their top talent, for ballplayers in the more affluent clubs could afford to pay a substitute to serve if they were drafted, and there was nothing to prevent wealthier club members for paying for a substitute for a top player. The Athletics had two colonels, Field Captain Moore and President Fitzgerald, but in 1862, neither was facing the leaden messenger of death. Moore was defending center field at Camac's Woods and Fitzgerald was, like Frank Queen, fighting the war with his pen.[43]

Moore was not the only ballplayer who stayed home. The three top teams of the war years were the Atlantics, Eckfords and Mutuals. Of the nine Atlantics who played the most games in 1860, only one (Tice Hamilton) did not appear in a game in 1861. Seven of the 1860 nine played for the club in 1862. Of the eleven Eckfords who played most frequently in 1860, ten played the following season and nine in 1862. Nine of eleven 1860 Mutuals played in 1861, and six the following year.[44] Moreover, the turnover on the three teams was primarily a function of upgrading talent rather than wartime attrition. Joe Start, Fred Crane and John Chapman, stalwarts of the championship clubs of the mid–'60s, joined the Atlantics in 1862 to replace some of the older Brooklyn veterans, and none served in the army.

While many players enlisted in the Union Army, perhaps the most notable soldier was Aleck Pearsall, the renowned first baseman of the Excelsiors, who joined the Confederate Army as a surgeon. Pearsall played for the Excelsiors during the 1862 season, then left Brooklyn during the winter of 1862–63 without announcing his destination. It turned out he had gone to Richmond to become a brigade surgeon under General Morgan. While accompanying some Union prisoners in the city, he met an acquaintance from Brooklyn and asked about his old Excelsior teammates. The man passed word back to Brooklyn where the club, many of whose members were serving in the Union Army, voted unanimously to expel Pearsall.[45]

There were a number of soldiers in New York during the four years of the war, but all wore blue uniforms (or red in the case of the Zouaves), for Southern armies never threatened the city at any time. The troops that had been evacuated from Fort Sumter were stationed at Fort Hamilton, under the command of Captain Doubleday. The young officer made an impressive appearance and had established a reputation as a staunch patriot. "Capt. Doubleday," wrote the *Eagle*, "is a man of about forty years of age, of commanding presence and soldierly bearing. It will be remembered, from the newspaper reports of the time, that he was peculiarly obnoxious to the South Carolinians. It was understood by them that Doubleday was for holding out in every extremity.... A brave soldier, courteous, accessible and affable as an officer, he is popular with his men, and makes a very favorable impression on all who come in contact with him."[46] There was no mention of his having invented baseball.

All in all, life on the Northern home front wasn't bad. In the early years of the war, bounties were paid to those who enlisted, a total of $120 for New Yorkers in 1862.[47] There was no draft until 1863, and even then, a man could hire a substitute to take his place. With so many men serving in the military, jobs were plentiful. If one could handle the odium associated with remaining safely at home while others suffered and died on the battlefield, it was relatively easy to live a comfortable existence. The federal government authorized large bond issues to cover the expenses of the war, and there was abundant opportunity in government contracting.

During the first months of the war, New York was as patriotic as any other American city. On April 20, 1861, in the midst of the recruiting fervor that followed the declaration of war, there was a rally in Union Square that was attended by a half million citizens. Young men rushed to the colors, and former New York Congressman Dan Sickles, out of office and disgraced after murdering his wife's lover, had great success gathering both men and money for his Excelsior Brigade.[48] The Tammany Society, which would receive much deserved reprobation in just a few years, raised the 900-man Jackson Brigade to defend the city.[49]

New York had been occupied by the British for most of the Revolutionary War, and at that time had many Loyalists among its residents. Revolutionary sentiment had been much stronger in Boston and Philadelphia. As the Civil War dragged on, and Northern generals blundered badly in the field, antiwar sentiment blossomed, and as the nation's largest city, New York attracted many of the dissenters. Abolitionism was strongest in New England, which was located far from any slave states, and faded out as it moved southward. Rarely did criticism of the Union reach the level of treason, but it was hard to forget that, very recently, the warring nations had been one, with ties of commerce, family and social activity. Some politicians favored peace and reconciliation without victory and others wanted the controversy over slavery, which in their eyes had been the sole cause of the rupture, to be resolved short of abolition.

The most admired Union personality early in the war was General George McClellan. Long after McClellan had fallen out of favor with Abraham Lincoln, and despite his undue caution and lack of success on the battlefield, the New York press remained loyal. In 1863 and 1864, the *Clipper* defended the general, referring to Lincoln's relieving McClellan as his "persecution" and fostering the notion that he had been under-supported and left without sufficient resources, a claim the general pressed continuously.[50] At every battle, McClellan believed he was opposed by an overwhelmingly superior force. Confederate generals often reported the same situation, causing the Northern and Southern press to report simultaneously of battles in which each side was hopelessly outnumbered.

In the 1864 presidential election, when he was the Democratic candidate opposing Lincoln,

McClellan carried New York City easily. McClellan's running mate was New York governor Horatio Seymour, a severe critic of Lincoln's conduct of the war. Seymour and former New York mayor Fernando Wood, who in early 1861 stated that the Union was doomed and suggested that New York City consider secession,[51] were less than fervid supporters of the war, which led to a significant amount of peace activity in New York.

On June 3, 1863, anti-war forces held five rallies in and around the Cooper Institute. Clement Vallandingham, former Ohio Congressman and perhaps the most prominent copperhead in the country,[52] was cheered and praised, as was Wood, who delivered a speech, and McClellan, who was not present. Among the phrases uttered by the speechmakers were, "The war is the curse of the age in which we live," "[T]he war cannot succeed. We have been beaten. We cannot conquer the South," "Why not arrest Mr. Seward when he is in the state?" and "[G]od is against us." Speakers invoked the names of Washington, Jefferson, Stephen Douglas and God as favoring their cause and denounced Abraham Lincoln as a usurper and tyrant. The size of the audience and the vehemence, confidence and courage with which the statements were made spoke volumes of the sentiments of New Yorkers and of the freedom of expression which prevailed, despite the copperheads' claims of having been stifled by the administration.[53]

One of the reasons for wanting to bring a peaceful end to the conflict was the mounting casualty lists. In the early days of the war, which were marked by very minor skirmishes, each combat death was described in detail, and the heroic deeds of the deceased were described at length. By 1862, after bloody battles such as Shiloh, Antietam and Fredericksburg, the reports became simply column after column of dead and wounded, without comment or description. Enthusiasm waned as the number of widows grew and declined further with the institution of the draft in 1863.

In the midst of New York's discontent, the city's ball clubs contested once more for the championship. The Atlantics, based upon their successful series with the Eckfords in 1860, began the 1861 season as champions. As early as 1856, a correspondent to the *Clipper* had suggested that the Brooklyn ball clubs purchase a silver ball to present to the top nine[54] and, prior to the 1861 season, the Continental Club of Brooklyn did so. The Atlantics won five of seven contests and earned the silver ball since they did not lose twice to any club.

Even though they were champions, 1861 was not a memorable year for the Atlantics. They beat the Exercise and Newark nines, which were hardly powerhouses, and lost to the lightly regarded Liberty Club of New Brunswick. Even in the games they won, the club did not play well. Their victory over the Mutuals was a hard-hitting, sloppy 52–27 game in which they scored 26 runs in a single inning.

The Atlantics often had difficulty getting their best nine players together and played several games with a number of substitutes from the second nine. After splitting two games with the Mutuals, the Atlantics did not play a deciding third game, which might have been interesting, since the Mutuals lost only one other game all season. An encouraging note in one of the Atlantic-Mutual contests was the attendance, estimated between six and eight thousand. That was not as large as the crowds which came to see the Excelsiors and Atlantics in 1860, but they were very healthy wartime gatherings.[55]

With little interclub activity, the highlight of the 1861 season was an all-star contest in October. Frank Queen offered the prize of a silver ball if an all-star club from Brooklyn would face a nine drawn from the clubs of New York.[56] The individual club whose players scored the most runs for the winning side would retain the trophy. The most successful event in the history of baseball had been the Fashion Course Series of 1858, and Queen hoped his game could generate the same level of excitement.

In September, there had been a game between the best players among those clubs that occupied the north grounds at Hoboken (the Mutual and Gothams) and those that played on the south side (the Empires and Eagles).[57] Queen expanded the all-star concept and named those he thought should comprise the Brooklyn and New York clubs. He set October 7 as the date and the Gotham grounds at Hoboken as the place for the encounter. A week after the issuance of the challenge, the date was changed to October 21, and the location to the Mutuals' grounds at Hoboken. The composition of the nines had been altered somewhat, but the match was still on.

In the mid-nineteenth century, competition between the clubs of Brooklyn and New York was fierce. Until 1898, the former was an independent municipality, rather than a borough of New York City. In 1860, Brooklyn had a population of 266,000, making it one of the largest cities in the United States. Ten years later, there were 396,000 people living in Brooklyn, making it the fastest growing city in the country.[58] The New York clubs, such as the Knickerbockers and Gothams, were the first to take up the new game, but once the Atlantics, Excelsiors and Eckfords took the field, they rarely lost to nines from New York. From the time a champion club was recognized, and through 1866, the title was held by either the Atlantics or Eckfords. Other Brooklyn clubs, such as the Excelsiors and Stars, generally held supremacy over their rivals from Manhattan. During the war years, the Mutuals were the only New York club that had the ability to challenge for the championship.

The all-star nines had some practice together, and Henry Chadwick, delegated by Queen to handle the logistics, finalized the arrangements. Extra cars were arranged for the Hoboken City Railroad, and more boats for the Hoboken ferries, for visitors from Philadelphia, Boston and upstate New York were expected.

The match did for Queen exactly what he hoped it would: give him center stage in the sporting world and arouse the jealousy of his rivals. One competing journal spread a rumor that the game had been cancelled, in an attempt to discourage attendance. Other papers compared the battle for the silver ball with the disreputable boxing matches undertaken for large stakes and hinted that Queen was dragging baseball down to the same level as boxing. Queen, an avid supporter of pugilism, wrapped himself in the flag and pointed out that a number of prize fighters were serving in the Union Army. "The President, Cabinet, all are 'brought down to the level of the prize ring,'" said Queen in a painfully tortured analogy, "if our neighbor's theory holds good."[59]

The game took place on October 21, as scheduled, and was a success. Brooklyn won, 18–6, behind the fine pitching of Creighton. Much to the delight of Queen, the play on both sides was quite good, the players giving justice to the claim that they were the best in the New York region. Eight thousand spectators, the largest crowd of the first war year, went to Hoboken to observe the contest. Dick Pearce of the Atlantics, rather than Joe Leggett, caught Creighton. Leggett served as umpire. The Atlantics, whose players scored the most runs, took the ball.[60]

The *Clipper* summarized the 1861 season the following January. "[T]he base ball season of 1861 ... despite the interruptions and drawbacks occasioned by the great rebellion, has been really a very interesting year in the annals of the game, far more so than it was expected it would have been in the early part of it; but the game has too strong a foothold in popularity to be frowned out of favor by the lowering brows of 'grim-visaged war' and if any proof was needed that our national game is a fixed institution of the country, it would be found in the fact, that it has flourished through such a year of adverse circumstances as those that have marked the season of 1861."[61]

Baseball might have been surviving, but, despite the hopeful rhetoric, it was not prospering. In 1860, at the last prewar convention of the National Association, 60 clubs sent delegates. In 1861, the number of clubs dropped to 34 with none farther from New York City than Troy. The Potomacs of Washington, the Excelsiors of Baltimore and the other out-of-state organizations that had joined the Association in 1860 failed to appear the following year. In 1862, only 32 clubs attended the convention, and there was a further decline to 28 in 1863. In December 1864, even though the end of the war appeared imminent, a mere 34 clubs sent their representatives to New York's Clinton Hall for the annual meeting.

While less baseball was played in New York during the early '60s, a fair amount of ball playing was taking place in army camps. More than ninety years earlier, when bat and ball games were in their infancy, there is evidence that Revolutionary War soldiers played some sort of ball games, both in camp and in English prisons.[62] A French officer claimed he saw General Washington playing catch, displaying the powerful arm that had launched a silver dollar across the Potomac.[63] There are a couple of references to soldiers and prisoners playing some kind of "ball" during the War of 1812[64] and the Mexican War.[65] With baseball much more widespread than it had been at the time of the earlier wars, it was clear that Civil War soldiers would do the same.

Soldiers had a great deal of free time, which their officers hoped they would fill with wholesome activity rather than card playing, drinking or seeking out carnal pleasure in the nearest town. Baseball was one of the pastimes they recommended. "In fact," reported the *Eagle,* "in every army corps there are full clubs formed, whose members take advantage of every opportunity to have a good game together. Base ball has become the favorite game of our soldiers when not engaged in actual service."[66] Soldiers played many versions of ball, including the New York game, the Massachusetts game, town ball, and various iterations they had learned in their home towns.

Soldiers began playing baseball nearly as soon as the army mustered. In early June 1861, a recruit wrote to the *Eagle* of a game in camp at Annapolis in which Joe Leggett served as umpire.[67] On July 2, 1861, a match was played in Washington, D.C., between a team made up of players of the Potomac and National Clubs and a group of soldiers, a number of whom were former New York players. The most prominent were A.G. Babcock, president of the Atlantics, Theodore Van Cott of the Gothams and Van Valkenburgh of the Putnams.[68] In another match, the Nationals defeated the 71st Regiment, 28–17.[69]

An October 1861 game among the Mozart Regiment included a couple of old New York ballplayers, a former member of the Atlantics of Jamaica and a member of the Matanos, respectively.[70] The sport was especially popular among troops camped in the Baltimore area. The Excelsior Regiment attempted to celebrate the first Christmas of the war with a game in their camp in Maryland, but had to abandon the effort when the ground proved hopelessly inadequate.[71]

New York's 71st Regiment (the same unit that lost to the Nationals) celebrated the Fourth of July 1862 with a game between Companies D and K.[72] At Fredericksburg, Virginia, in May

While Union soldiers stand at attention, a baseball game is taking place behind them. The year was 1863, and the site Fort Pulaski, Georgia. Baseball was a frequent diversion for the Union Army during the Civil War.

1863, the 14th Brooklyn regiment, immortalized in Thomas Dyja's fictional *Play for a Kingdom*, took on the 30th New York volunteers.[73] In the spring of 1864, New York soldiers were playing ball in Louisiana[74] and at Culpepper Court House and Brandy Station in Virginia,[75] scenes of far more violent confrontations earlier in the war. The following spring, just four days before Lee's surrender at Appomattox, the 102nd Regiment of New York Volunteers played the 2nd Division of the 20th Army Corps at Goldsborough, North Carolina.[76] In addition to the games reported to the press, there were many, many unnoted matches that took place on campaign.

Southern troops played baseball although, since there were no prominent sporting journals in the South, their exploits were not well reported. Prisoners played in camp, most notably Union prisoners at Salisbury, North Carolina, and Confederates at Johnson's Island, located on a small inlet of southern Lake Erie at Sandusky, Ohio.

Ball playing as an activity for prisoners had gotten off to a rocky start during the War of 1812. Americans confined at Dartmoor Prison in 1815 continually hit a ball over the walls, and when their British guards refused to retrieve it, made efforts to do so themselves. That started a riot which resulted in a reported seven deaths and sixty wounded prisoners.[77]

Civil War baseball at Salisbury Prison, a converted cotton factory, was immortalized by a drawing of Union prisoner Otto Boetticher, a New York City commercial artist who was captured in 1862. Most ball playing in southern prisons took place in the early stages of the war before the South ran short of rations. With barely enough provisions for their own soldiers and citizens, they had little for Northern prisoners. Incarcerated Yanks were fighting starvation rather than boredom, and few were physically capable of exercise. At Salisbury, prisoners

Union prisoners play baseball at Salisbury Prison in North Carolina, depicted in a drawing by New York artist Otto Boetticher. Confederate captives played a number of games at Johnson's Island in Sandusky, Ohio.

were reduced to hunting dogs and cats, and forcing down makeshift bread concocted by the Confederates from sour milk, water and corn cob ashes. Historian Patricia Millen estimated that a third of all Union soldiers sent to Salisbury after October 1864 died in prison.[78]

Confederate prisoners were somewhat better provisioned and continued playing ball during the latter stages of the war. The prison on Johnson's Island was the only Union stockade designated specifically for captured Confederate officers. The fact that the prisoners were officers led to their being perhaps more knowledgeable about sports and certainly more literate and likely to leave a written record of their activities. Further, a number of them were from New Orleans, the only southern city in which baseball had taken root before the war.

In late August 1864, the Confederate Club of prisoners challenged the Southern Club to a match game.[79] The Confederates consisted of the higher level officers, and the Southern of those below the rank of captain. Lieutenant Michael McNamara, a southern prisoner, estimated that three thousand, roughly the same attendance that could be expected for an attractive game in New York, came out to witness the contest. The Southern Club was victorious by the score of 19–11, numerous wagers were placed upon the outcome, and the Rebel yell was frequently heard when one club or the other did something noteworthy.

The captain and catcher for the victorious club was Charles Pierce, who had quite an active prison life. In addition to being captain of the Southerns, he acted in prison minstrels and, when not otherwise occupied, participated in at least seven escape attempts.

Lieutenant McNamara indicated that the spectators enjoyed the game, but others thought the Rebels were having too much fun for prisoners, and public pressure caused the commander to forbid future baseball activity.[80] After the war, members of the Southern Club returned to New Orleans, where they kept the club intact and continued to play ball.[81]

There are unsubstantiated, and probably untrue, stories of Union soldiers playing against Confederates. George Kirsch reported games being interrupted by a call to arms prior to the end of the ninth inning.[82] A game played amongst the 114th New York came to an abrupt termination when Confederate snipers shot the right fielder and captured the center fielder and the baseball.[83] Another match between New York regiments in Virginia was ended by artillery fire.[84]

Henry Chadwick had trained his disciples well, and reports of many military matches, both baseball and cricket, were sent to the *Clipper* and other papers with complete box scores and descriptive detail. While most ball playing was of the informal pitch and catch variety that was reported only in letters to home, there were some matches which attracted a great deal of attention. The most famous was the Christmas Day affair on Hilton Head Island between members of the 165th New York Volunteer Infantry and players from a number of other New York regiments, supposedly witnessed by 40,000 soldiers, in which future National League presidents A.G. Mills and Nicholas Young were said to have taken part.[85]

Baseball was the most popular game among soldiers, but it was not the only one. Lieutenant William Moore of the 62nd New York Volunteers helped organize a cricket club among his comrades and, on a visit to New York, acquired a number of bats.[86] *Wilkes'* suggested a match between Brooklyn and New York clubs with the proceeds devoted to purchasing cricket equipment for the soldiers.[87]

As in New York and Boston, there was often money riding on the outcome of camp games. In a match played under the Massachusetts rules in 1863, the winning team gained a fifty dollar prize.[88]

Despite the reports of baseball among soldiers and the hopeful optimism in New York, there is no question that the Civil War had a serious dampening effect on the sport. Activity in 1861 was greatly depressed from that of 1860, which was to be the high water mark of baseball until after the war. The best the adherents of baseball could do was hope for an early peace and a renewed interest in sports. They would be forced to wait a few years, but it would be well worth it.

CHAPTER 14

The Sporting and Not So Sporting Press

The main reason it has been so difficult to trace the beginning of modern baseball is that very little was written about the game prior to the mid–1850s. During the first half of the nineteenth century, *The Spirit of the Times* was the only major sporting paper in the United States. Its publisher, William Porter, was born in Vermont in 1806, and became a reporter while in his early twenties. He founded a paper called *The Constellation*, which he claimed was the first sporting journal in America. *The Constellation* was merged into *The Spirit of the Times* in 1831, and the combined product provided the public with news of horse racing, field sports and, later, cricket.[1] Porter was not merely a journalist; he was also a participant in the sporting arena, serving as the first president of the New York Cricket Club.[2] His primary interest, however, was horses, which led to his purchase of the *American Turf Register* in 1839.[3]

By the 1850s, *The Spirit* covered the theater, horse racing, cricket, boxing, hunting and fishing, along with other sports. During the winter months, when there was a dearth of sporting activity in the north, Porter's columns consisted of filler material of general, and sometimes dubious, interest, such as *The Last Days of Napoleon*, *Italian Gesticulation*, *Advice Gratis to "Strong-Minded" Women*, and a story on a race of men that had tails. On July, 9, 1853, *The Spirit of the Times* mentioned baseball for the first time, printing a letter reporting a game between the Gotham and Knickerbocker Clubs.

There was little baseball reported in *The Spirit* until 1855, and what did appear was limited to terse accounts of games (with box scores) submitted by members of the competing clubs. The primary emphasis was on four-legged sport and cricket, which often received multiple columns of coverage. Apparently, Porter felt that baseball was less interesting to his readers than articles such as *The World's Ugliest Man*. As interest in baseball grew, *The Spirit's* coverage of the sport expanded. On May 12, 1855, the journal printed the rules of baseball for the first time and soon began to report more frequently on games that took place in New York and its vicinity.

Unfortunately, Porter's forte was journalism, not finances, and he suffered a number of reverses that put his publishing enterprise in dire straits. In 1856, to extricate himself from his fiscal dilemma, Porter joined forces with George Wilkes (who apparently contributed much-needed capital to the venture[4]) to produce *Porter's Spirit of the Times*. Porter died just two years after Wilkes joined him, uttering as his final words, "I want to go home."[5]

Wilkes, a somewhat shady character who founded the scandalous *National Police Gazette* and was once committed to the Tombs prison for libel, continued as editor after Porter went home, in partnership with attorney and New York State legislator Theodore Tomlinson. In 1859, however, Wilkes and Tomlinson had an unamicable parting of the ways with the former claiming that the financial management of the paper, for which Tomlinson had been responsible, had been abysmal. Wilkes left *Porter's Spirit of the Times* and immediately began publication of *Wilkes' Spirit of the Times*.[6]

By late 1862, Wilkes was in trouble again. He was sued for libel in a case he attributed to the malice of John Morrissey, whose shenanigans, most notably in the Heenan fights in England, Wilkes had purportedly exposed. Wilkes claimed in court that a number of Morrissey's associates had attempted to draw him into a fight at the Fashion Course Race Track, in order to have him arrested. The testimony revealed that all parties to the suit were of somewhat questionable morals, but the jury found Wilkes not guilty.[7]

Without Wilkes, Porter's old *Spirit* had barely survived the departure of his earthly corpus, leaving the field open to Wilkes and the *New York Clipper,* whose first issue was dated May 14, 1853.[8] The *Clipper* became perhaps the best sporting paper of its time. Frank Queen, a Philadelphian who had been a printer's apprentice and operator of a newsstand, was but 30 years old when he started the *Clipper* in partnership with Harrison Trent.[9] Queen announced that he would report on the ring, the turf, yachting, pedestrianism, cricket, rowing, theatricals and music. The paper also gave extensive coverage to the stage, and ran lengthy, serialized fiction. There was no mention of baseball, other than a general reference to "the various sports of the old world and the new."[10]

While the *Clipper* employed some paid correspondents, it relied initially to a great degree on information submitted *gratis* by participants in various activities in the metropolitan area. When cricket and baseball clubs played, they frequently sent reports to the *Clipper,* which printed the sometimes biased accounts submitted by adherents of one of the competing teams.

In the interest of educating the public about new pastimes, the paper often printed long explanatory articles on sports such as cricket, gymnastics and skating. Diagrams showed the reader how to execute skating maneuvers or gymnastic vaulting, and instruction along the "put your right foot in and put your right foot out" lines told *Clipper* readers exactly how it should be done.

In its July 16, 1853 issue, the *Clipper* reported on baseball for the first time, providing a report of a game between the Knickerbockers and Gothams. A terse paragraph reporting the result was followed by a box score that listed the players (but not their positions) and the runs and outs accounted for by each.[11]

The *Clipper* reported on a few baseball games in 1854, but none the following year. In 1856, there was much more coverage, beginning in mid–July and extending through early December. In its December 13, 1856, edition, the *Clipper* published a lengthy piece setting forth the rules of baseball and an explanation of how the game was played. As late as 1861, however, there were issues in which baseball was completely ignored. It was explained in the September 14, 1861, edition that, "Our reports of base ball matches in type are, in consequence of an unusual amount of other important news, unavoidably postponed."[12]

By 1857, when Henry Chadwick joined the *Clipper,* the paper was reporting the results of all the top games. Chadwick was an Englishman, born in Devonshire in 1824, who came to New York with his parents in 1837. He was an imposing figure, physically as well as intellectually, standing over six feet tall, somewhat heavyset, with a full beard.[13] Chadwick's father

James had been a fiery editor in England, a supporter of Thomas Paine, the French Revolution and numerous radical causes.[14] He was a great believer in education, and as a result, his sons received broad-based, rigorous schooling.

James Chadwick's oldest son, Edwin, was a law student and writer who developed a great interest in sanitation as the impetus to better public health and a consequent improvement of the condition of the masses of urban poor. His acquaintances included many of the most prominent British intellectuals, such as John Stuart Mill and Thomas Malthus, as well as politicians Robert Peel and Lord Palmerston. Edwin was eventually knighted by Queen Victoria for his great contributions to public health and sanitation. Like his Americanized sibling Henry, he encouraged exercise as a contribution to good health.

In the 1840s, Henry, who was Edwin's half-brother (Edwin's mother had died and James remarried) decided to follow his father's profession, although not his politics, first writing for *The Long Island Star* in 1844. He became expert in a number of areas, including music and drama, and developed a great knowledge of many sports, especially chess and cricket. Like so many gentlemen of his era, Chadwick was a well-rounded individual, displaying skill as a pianist, vocalist and composer in addition to his writing talent.[15] Chadwick's father had been a music teacher, and so was Henry when he was a young man. In 1847, he composed a march in honor of General Winfield Scott, hero of the Mexican War.[16]

The younger Chadwick's many skills did not extend to active participation in sports although he played in a few informal baseball games in the late 1840s. He took little interest in the sport, either as a participant or spectator, however, until the following decade.

One day in 1856, while covering a cricket match at the Fox Hill cricket ground, Chadwick stopped at the Elysian Fields and watched a baseball game between the Gotham and Eagle Clubs, a chance happenstance that forever changed his life and which had a marked impact upon the future of baseball. As befits baseball legends, Chadwick did not merely see a game he liked, he had an epiphany similar to that of Saul being blinded on the road to Damascus or at least like the miraculous revelations of Doubleday and Cartwright. "It was not long before I was struck with the idea," he wrote later, "that base ball was just the game for a national sport for Americans."[17]

In 1857, Chadwick had his first baseball article published by *The New York Times*.[18] Over the next five decades, until his death in 1908, he covered many sports, but primarily baseball, for a number of New York journals. He spent 45 years on the staff of the *Brooklyn Eagle*. Chadwick also served on the rules committee of both the amateur and professional National Associations and chaired the committee in some years. By the twentieth century, Chadwick had become a legendary figure, receiving congratulatory greetings on his 80th birthday in 1904 from virtually every major figure in baseball circles, plus prominent men in other fields, such as President Theodore Roosevelt.[19] The National League gave him a pension for life, and, in 1938, Chadwick was elected to the Hall of Fame.

While he wrote for many papers, the *Clipper* was Chadwick's pulpit. He first became associated with the paper in 1857, succeeding W.H. Bray as its baseball reporter,[20] and eventually became the baseball and cricket editor. The *Clipper* covered sports in much greater detail than most of the dailies and gave Chadwick the opportunity to pontificate about the great issues facing the game, and offer his opinionated suggestions. He was vehement regarding the need to replace the bound game in which fair balls caught on one bounce were out with the more skillful fly game. He deplored swift pitching, preferring the "strategic" slow pitching style. Chadwick admired the scientific nature of cricket and felt baseball would benefit by emulating the older sport.

Chadwick was for sportsmanship, a fair field and fair play, and against gambling, which had found its way to baseball almost as soon as the sport began to be played competitively. "Throughout the five decades he covered the game," wrote his biographer Andrew J. Schiff, "Chadwick was baseball's moral conscience."[21] At Chadwick's funeral, writer Ren Mulford eulogized, "There never was a word in all the miles of copy that Henry Chadwick has written that was not penned for the betterment of the game as he saw it."[22]

During its early years, one of the greatest threats to baseball's well-being was the wagering which was pervasive at all important games. Gambling on cricket, both in England and America, had been common. As early as the seventeenth century, English sources reported a cricket game for stakes of five hundred pounds,[23] and in the eighteenth, a journal lamented that the sport "has been too long perverted from diversion and innocent pastime to excessive gaming and public dissipation."[24] It was estimated that fifty thousand dollars was bet on a single match between Canadian and American elevens at Hoboken in 1844.[25] Even in baseball's infancy, money was part of the equation. The 1825 challenge from the Delhi Ball Club of upstate New York, one of the earliest mentions of the game of baseball, was for a prize of one dollar per game.[26] Men bet on virtually every sport that was popular in the antebellum years, including boxing, dog fighting and horse racing. When baseball gained in popularity in the 1850s, it was a foregone conclusion that betting would follow.

When Chadwick first became associated with baseball, he predicted grave danger if wagering on games continued. In 1860, after witnessing a match between the Eagle and Gotham Clubs in which players and spectators had bet on the outcome, he wrote, "The heavy betting by outsiders on the result of ball matches is sufficiently injurious to the interests of the game without adding the still worse custom of allowing parties playing in matches to indulge in it, especially when there are rules expressly prohibiting it."[27]

The fact that gambling took place on a game between two old-line, respectable clubs like the Eagles and Gothams demonstrated the pervasiveness of wagering in baseball. The NA rules forbade players and umpires from gambling, but there was no effective way, especially on grounds that were not enclosed, of preventing wagering among the crowd.

The *Brooklyn City News* drew a distinction between the occasional dollar staked to increase excitement and interest and the professional gambler who depended upon wagering for his income. "Any man who tries to *make money,*" said the *City News,* "by betting at a ball match, deserves to lose every cent he has."[28] "[T]hose who bet on the result of these baseball matches in the open, loud-mouthed manner many of them do," added *The Sunday Mercury,* "are anything but friends to the club they bet on."[29]

Wagers were placed openly, and newspapers frequently reported odds given by gamblers at various points of games. In 1860, regarding a Gotham-Mutual match that was tied 18–18 after nine innings, the *Clipper* stated, "It was first proposed that the 10th innings should be played, but at the earnest request of the scorer of the Mutuals, who had one hundred dollars bet on the result, it was allowed to remain a tie. Section 30 of the rules [which prohibited betting by anyone involved in a match] appears to be a dead letter, for it is entirely ignored by some clubs."[30] The Mutuals, with their Tammany influence, were frequently fingered when shadowy deeds were involved. At one of their games in 1861, it was reported that a wager of one thousand dollars changed hands on the outcome.[31] In 1864, many speculated that the Mutuals committed intentional errors in order to improve the odds in future games.[32]

When the Capitoline Grounds opened in 1864, the proprietors enacted rules against gambling, but none of the other grounds had similar prohibitions. Many feared that if gambling were banned, interest in the games, and thus paid attendance, might diminish.

One of the problems with gambling, of course, was that players might be tempted to throw a game. Prior to 1865, despite the constant presence of open gambling, no incident of that kind was proven. Another problem, however, which occurred frequently, was that gamblers became agitated and abusive, and tried to influence or intimidate the umpires and players. The disastrous Excelsior-Atlantic match in 1860 had shown the effect gamblers could have upon a game, and Chadwick realized how close that debacle had come to seriously damaging the sport.

The advent of enclosed grounds in 1862, while it did not eliminate the gambler, brought him under greater control. Admission could be refused to those who were likely to disrupt the proceedings and, at the very least, venues such as the Union Grounds attracted a better-behaved brand of gambler.

The day after the Eagle-Gotham match noted above, the Eagle Club met and passed a resolution stating that any member found to have bet on a contest would be promptly expelled.[33] Such a measure might have an effect on members of respectable clubs such as the Eagles, but gambling was too deeply embedded to be eradicated. The problem plagued baseball for many years, and contributed to the death of the professional National Association.

The *Clipper, The Spirit of the Times, Porter's Spirit of the Times* and, beginning in 1859, *Wilkes' Spirit of the Times* were the leading papers devoted principally to sports. Among the papers of general interest, the *Sunday Mercury, Herald, New York Times, Brooklyn Daily Times* and *Brooklyn Eagle* devoted the most attention to outdoor recreation. In 1863, *The Brooklyn Daily Union* was established and provided excellent baseball coverage.[34] William Cauldwell, the first reporter for the *Mercury*, who began covering baseball in 1853, and Charles Peverelly, who in 1866 published the first history of baseball, were, in addition to Chadwick, two of the most prominent early reporters.[35]

Each paper strove to outdo the other, and none was modest about its achievements. In November 1859, the *Clipper* made its case. "Never was the success of the *Clipper*," it proclaimed, "more clearly apparent than at the present time. As the recognized sporting and theatrical organ of America, it has reached a point far beyond the most sanguine anticipations of it projectors and friends."[36] "Our readers will note," the paper stated after publishing a lengthy statistical analysis of the 1860 season, "that the *Clipper* is the first paper to promote the welfare of the game by making these analyses."[37]

While the *Clipper* repeatedly urged fair play and gentlemanly behavior on the field, modesty and fairness were not mainstays of its editorial bombast. In 1862, Frank Queen's journal again proclaimed itself the superior of its erstwhile competitors. "Poor Porter!" it lamented sarcastically. "He is dead now, and may the turf lie gently on his mouldering frame. *The Spirit of the Times* was unable to stand up against the youth and spirit of the *Clipper*. It survived its originator but a little while, and the journal that held the sway on sporting matters for nearly thirty years is no more. *Porter's Spirit* is likewise dead; and the *Challenge*, which was also started some years ago to swamp us, was long since swallowed up in the *Clipper*. Sporting literature is more to the point now. You get the substance in a nut shell, and you get it so you can understand it, too. Old fogyism has given place to the swift and steady advance of Young America."[38]

During the Civil War, Queen appealed to the patriotic ardor of his readership, claiming that much of the *Spirit's* readership had come from the South, since the paper was "all horse" and aimed at the upper classes. The commencement of the war, he said, had spelled the doom of the *Spirit*. The *Clipper*, in contrast, was the paper of the "people."[39]

Queen had even surprised himself with the success of his paper. "Truly, we had no idea," he continued, "when we started the *Clipper*, that such a complete revolution would follow its teachings in so short a time."[40] The secret to his journal's success, the publisher confided, was the *Clipper's* steadfast quest to unmask dishonesty and treachery.

In 1864, Queen enlarged his paper, due, he claimed, to its tremendous popularity. "The *Clipper* is no longer an experiment," he declared. "It is a permanent institution — the oldest sporting and theatrical journal in America ... hard work and honest principles have made it the leading theatrical and show paper in the country. It goes everywhere."[41]

That same year, following the celebrated boxing match between John Heenan and Tom King, Wilkes and Queen squared off in a bout of their own. Wilkes accused Heenan's trainer John McDonald of drugging the Benicia Boy prior to the fight, and McDonald fired off an angry letter of denial, which he forwarded to the *Clipper* because, he said, of the journal's "well-known impartiality and love of fair play."[42] Queen dutifully reproduced the letter, along with a hearty denunciation of Wilkes' dastardly editorial style.

The *Clipper* was not alone in its bombast. Nearly every paper sniped at its competitors, accused them of stealing their material, and didn't hesitate to point out their faults. In 1863, the *Eagle* noted snidely, "The match between [the Knickerbocker and Excelsior Clubs] played on Monday last, and published in the *Eagle* last Tuesday, appeared in Thursday's *Herald*, and from thence was transferred to our wide awake neighbor over the way."[43]

"Several games of baseball," declared the *Spirit of the Times* in 1854, "have lately been played by clubs of this city and vicinity, but we have received no official reports of them and the scores given in the daily papers are so incorrect and incomprehensible that it would be worse than useless to give them in our columns."[44]

The *Mercury*, often the target of the sporting papers, was not overly modest about trumpeting its own virtues. "What the bright sun is in the world celestial," it boasted, the *Mercury* "aims to be, and is, in the World of News and Polite Literature. Were it blotted out, the masses would be left comparatively in the dark in relation to innumerable subjects connected with their interests ... for none of the twinklers that affect to compete with it could supply its place.... The *Sunday Mercury* is a public necessity."[45]

Sporting journalism was a contact sport in the mid-nineteenth century, as evidenced by the following passage from *Porter's Spirit of the Times* in 1858. "A decayed sporting paper of this city," the *Spirit* reported, "which pretends to be a rival of ours but which, through its wretched imbecility, and utter worthlessness, has been reduced to a circulation of about 800 copies, reflected upon this paper last week, with an opprobrious epithet. We were not surprised at an exhibition of mean spirited and groveling gratitude from such a source, but hardly expected that the blackguard who penned the article would attempt to render it additionally acceptable by a lying attack on us. We have always treated the unhappy fossil in which this attack appeared with ceremonious respect and we must therefore necessarily attribute its malice to envy at our great prosperity, stimulated perhaps somewhat by the fact that it was our misfortune once to be present when the writer of the paragraph in question was thrust from a tavern by an indignant gentleman after having a pitcher of water thrown over his head, an application of which, we are sorry to say, did not succeed in sobering him."[46]

Even the minor weeklies entered the fray. "We are not inclined," said the *Atlas,* "to engage in any angry controversy, but if parties wish to pick a quarrel by poking their nose into our business in a manner that becomes too offensive, we feel abundantly able to take care of ourselves."[47]

In 1861, when the *Clipper* sponsored the Silver Ball contest for the picked nines of New York and Brooklyn, the *Tribune* and the *Herald* each reported that the game had been cancelled. The *Mercury* claimed that the report of the upcoming game was just a rumor. The *Times,* apparently having obtained their information from the *Mercury,* also announced that the game would not take place.[48] The *Herald* corrected its mistake (later in the same issue), but the *Tribune* did not, which Queen thought was a deliberate attempt to discourage attendance and detract from his carefully planned event.

A perusal of the competing journals lends credence to Queen's claim of vindictiveness. One wrote, "We congratulate the baseball fraternity upon the fact that 'the great silver ball match'—which certain of the minor journals have endeavored to make their readers believe was a grand contest between New York and Brooklyn—is at length played out. This humbug affair was a long time coming to a head. The 'eventful day' had, in fact, so often been deferred, that almost everyone had given it up for a bad job." The paper went on to indicate it had tried to find out whether the game was going to take place, couldn't verify the fact, and when it was supposedly told by some of the Brooklyn players that the match would be postponed, announced the cancellation. "[I]t was a pet scheme of certain parties," the account continued, "upon a cheap investment of fifteen or sixteen dollars in a silver ball, to put two or three hundred dollars in their pockets, exacted from the Ferry Company and the saloon keepers of Hoboken."[49] The reporter went on to describe the game itself as tedious and dull. No wonder Queen was upset.

Rather than criticize Queen and the *Clipper* generally, the *Atlas* fired several shots in the direction of *Clipper* reporter Bunsby. It began the attack the week prior to the all-star match, stating that Bunsby made a spectacle of himself at the game between the Atlantics and Mutuals, and further that at the cricket match at Long Branch attended by Mary Todd Lincoln, he had gone out of his way to be noticed by the First Lady.[50]

It was Bunsby, the *Atlas* declared, who had convinced Queen to sponsor the game in order to ingratiate himself with the Atlantics, and also conspired to see that the Brooklyn club would win and the Atlantics would take the silver ball. The *Atlas,* which nearly always took the part of New York in any controversy, claimed that the nines were chosen by Bunsby in order to ensure a Brooklyn victory. "Not only were the New York clubs averse to it," it claimed, "but many of the most respectable players of leading Brooklyn clubs repudiated it as an unauthorized and disreputable affair forced upon a few players, for the purpose of furthering individual interests, and not that of the national game of Base Ball." It was Bunsby, the *Atlas* declared, who had spread rumors that the game would not come off, and then acted the aggrieved innocent when the other papers reported it.[51]

In addition to flogging each other, the press could be tough on players. In July 1859, the *Atlas* referred to the play of Knickerbocker catcher Charles DeBost as "clownish" due to his flamboyant style, referring to him as "a clown in a circus."[52] When DeBost took umbrage, the paper declared, "[W]e never intended to publish anything that was calculated to injure the feelings of the gentleman in question." An apology was offered, tempered by the assertion that those on the grounds had complained about DeBost's style of play. "We still fail to discover," the *Atlas* continued, "the extreme grace and refinement displayed, when a player in a match attempts to catch a ball with that portion of his body that is usually covered by his coat tail." In other words, what we said is true, but we're sorry if it hurt his feelings.[53]

Other than vitriol, the backbone of early baseball reporting was statistics, lengthy play-by-play accounts of important games, and pompous prose. Chadwick, of course, didn't hesitate to voice his opinion, but players' thoughts, as conveyed through an interview, which are a staple of today's coverage, were completely absent. Nobody asked Peter O'Brien whether he found swift pitching or slow pitching easier to hit, and no one knew much about the personal lives of any of the players.

Flowery prose was frequently the order of the day, as evidenced by the following passage from *Porter's Spirit* marking the end of the 1858 campaign. "The month of dark December has arrived. As the legend has it and Lord Byron has said it, that Leander slammed the Hellesport, yet nevertheless, it cannot be expected that either the votaries of baseball or cricket will take the field in such weather as we have experienced in the past week."[54]

A week later, the journal added, "The season for playing of this popular game may be now deemed to be closed until May puts forth her blossoms and makes the turf redolent of verdancy so much the admiration of poets and pedestrians. This year of grace now fast declining into the sere and yellow leaf will soon be numbered with the past ... the bat is lying up and the ball, which was so recently to be caught on the fly, is now suspended, but another kind of ball is opened which the sport of terpsichord are enjoyed in company with the belles, who in the out of door games could only look on with approving smiles and reward the most agile and stalwart of the players with their admiration."[55] In other words, the baseball season was over, and the dances were about to begin.

The flowery words did not always appear as planned. In the first press report of a baseball game, the *New York Herald* account of the 1845 matches between the New York and Brooklyn players, the *Herald* erroneously reported that Brooklyn was the winning team. They printed a correction the following day.[56] The typewriter and computer had yet to make their appearance, and information submitted for publication was hand written. Apparently, the writing of some reporters was difficult to decipher, which led to some errors. "It was stated," said a notice in the *Eagle* in 1858, "that the defeat of the Excelsiors was due to the *bad feeling* existing amongst them. It should have read that they were beaten in consequence of their *bad fielding*."[57]

Two years later, the *Eagle* commended Mr. Sonag for his role in controlling the crowd during the first Atlantic-Excelsior game. The next day, they indicated that Sonag was actually Mr. Young.[58] The paper later misidentified the Irvington Club as the Tronington Club, another error clearly attributable to sloppy handwriting.[59]

The *Atlas* also experienced difficulty with transcription, as evidenced by the retraction printed in July 1860. "By a vexatious typographical error, in the report of a match, we were made to say that two of the players of the Putnam Club had a leaning toward 'ruffianism' when the word in the copy was plainly written 'muffinism.'"[60]

Chadwick loved words, but he worshipped statistics, which had been an integral part of baseball since its genesis.[61] From the earliest games of the Knickerbockers in the fall of 1845, they faithfully maintained records of every contest. Each "play day" was memorialized in a scorebook, which listed the players' names, the number of "hands lost" and runs scored, along with columns for fines and comments. Eventually, the positions played were put into the fines column, which turned out not to be needed very often. In the column under each inning, there was placed a 1, 2 or 3, to indicate which player made the first, second and third outs of the inning.

Accounting for runs and outs was a carryover from cricket, in which they were the only important statistics. Baseball had many more nuances, and as the years went on, the way in which a player was put out — caught out, run out on bases, etc.— was added to the score. Occasionally, there were interesting notes written in the margins of the Knickerbocker score books, such as on September 25, 1854, "Day when the National Guard occupied our ground and played back of the house" and on May 26, 1857, "Broke up by the Dutch Fight."[62]

Rudimentary box scores appeared in newspapers almost as soon as games were reported in print. Even the first article in the *Clipper*, four years before Chadwick joined the staff, contained a box score. After Chadwick came aboard, the format was gradually expanded to include the positions of the players, runs scored, hands lost, and often great detail on the fielding. (A sample of a comprehensive box score is presented in Appendix D.)

Some box scores presented just the basics, while others contained many additional statistics, such as the number of pitches thrown and the manner in which players were put out. When Chadwick was pushing hard for the adoption of the fly game, he incorporated statistics such as balls caught on the bound that could have been caught on the fly, and bound catches missed. After the 1859 season, the *Clipper* began publishing season statistics for the major clubs, including significant detail on the fielding of each player. As Chadwick's biographer Andrew Schiff cogently pointed out, there were virtually no pitching statistics, for Chadwick did not consider pitching to be an integral part of the game.[63] It was only the method of putting the ball in play.

Chadwick encouraged scorers to adopt his system as the uniform manner of reporting their club's play so that he could present consistent statistics for each team at the end of the season. In March 1861, he set forth a detailed primer on scoring methods in order to standardize the reports he received from club scorers.[64] Invoking the example of cricket and its comprehensive system, he urged scorers to use his method in order to fully analyze the play and create data that could be utilized for player selection and placement. "As of now," he wrote, "each club has its own plan of keeping score, whereas there should be but one rule, like that adopted by the Cricket Clubs. They have but one method of scoring, and hence a complete analysis can always be obtained of the play of any member of a Cricket Club."[65]

Rather than the numbering system in place today, Chadwick used letters, as follows:

> A for first base
> B for second base
> C for third base
> H for home base
> K for struck out
> F for catch on the fly
> D for catch on the bound
> L for foul balls
> T for tips
> H R for home runs

R O for run out between bases
L F for foul ball catch on the fly
L D for foul ball catch on the bound
T F for tip catch on the fly
T D for tip catch on the bound

As can be seen above, Chadwick used either the first or last letter of a word in his abbreviations, explaining the mystery of why K is used to designate a strikeout. It is the last letter in struck. One will also note that, initially, while fielding statistics were myriad, the only offensive records that were kept were runs scored, hands lost and home runs. Hits and extra base hits were not noted until the 1870s, about the same time that reporter H. A. Dobson suggested calculating batting averages by dividing hits by the number of times at bat.[66]

Chadwick was well aware of the limitations of early box scores which listed only runs scored (a carryover from cricket) and hands lost. "When we see a player's name," he wrote in 1863, "in front of a small score of runs, we are apt to charge him with poor batting, but in many instances players make their bases by good hits but fail to secure the reward of their batting through the poor play of those that follow them."[67] He also recognized that judging a player by the quantity rather than quality of his fielding was erroneous, for players in certain positions, like first base and catcher, had far more chances than others.[68]

Chadwick was justifiably proud of his system. In 1889, when a colleague wrote an article contrasting the scoring system of his day with the primitive one that existed in the 1860s, Chadwick took considerable umbrage. He was further offended by the fact that the writer credited Harry Wright and Albert Spalding with developing the earlier systems. Chadwick wrote a long, detailed rebuttal, replete with examples of his score sheets of 1860 from *Beadle's* and a complete explanation of his old system with symbols and illustrations.[69]

Since the *Clipper* could not have a reporter present at every game, it had to rely on club scorers to send them information, and at the end of each season, Chadwick appealed to them, listing those games that were missing from his reports and asking for the information or to borrow the scorebooks for a few days in order to extract the statistics.

Even when Chadwick did attend the games, his statistics were sometimes deficient. "We are reluctantly obliged to close our detailed report of the game at this stage of the proceedings," he reported after an 1859 Atlantic-Star game, "from having mislaid our scorebook, and we therefore direct to the score for further particulars."[70] Later that same year, the *Clipper* couldn't last through a late October game, failing to exhibit the pluck it so admired in the players. "At this stage of the proceedings," read the account, "we succumbed to the cold weather, and sought shelter in the rooms of the Club House adjourning, from which place we finished our report, but we were unable to watch the game at that distance sufficiently to continue the details of each inning, and therefore we are obliged to abruptly leave off at the close of the third innings."[71]

In 1860, Chadwick edited *Beadle's Dime Base Ball Player,* the first annual baseball guide, which featured a description of the game, advice on playing it and recent developments. The actions of the National Association at its annual convention and any rule changes were reported, so that all teams had access to the most recent playing rules. In its first year, *Beadle's* was reported to have sold 50,000 copies, and the success of the baseball guide led the company to publish books on croquet, cricket, football and chess.[72] For the rest of the nineteenth century and into the first decade of the twentieth, Chadwick provided players and fans with his beloved statistics, becoming, in 1882, the editor of Spalding's Official Baseball Guide, the bible of baseball men in the latter part of the nineteenth century. He held the post until his death in 1908.

No one understood the importance of the press more than Chadwick, who carped at those clubs that did not accommodate him or his fellow reporters. "Every facility should be granted to the *authorized* representatives of the press," he scolded in 1860, "to whose assistance the various clubs are greatly indebted for the publicity given to their doings on the field."[73] Later that season, he issued a reminder, lest anyone had not seen the earlier notice. "The reference to the press is in bad taste," he fumed, "for it is to the press that they are mainly indebted for the present popularity of the game. Once let the press be silent on the subject, and baseball would soon be obsolete, except as a boy's game at bats."[74] In 1862, a passage, probably written by Chadwick, stated, "It should be remembered that the press is largely influential in promoting the welfare and advancement of the game, and were the papers to neglect publishing the daily proceedings of the ballplayers during the summer, the games they play would decline in popularity and ultimately be confined only to a glorious minority of the sport loving of the community."[75]

The value of reporting was not merely the objective recital of facts; by touting the sport, the press was shaping public opinion to the benefit of baseball, in addition to selling newspapers. "[I]f every journal that makes base ball a specialty were to confine their notices to merely giving the scores," Chadwick stated, "or were they to ignore the game altogether, it would not be the papers that would suffer, but base ball. It is the press that has made the game what it is, and it is to the aid of the press that base ball players should look to enable them to make it a permanent institution of the land."[76]

Several years earlier, following the Fashion Race Course all-star series in 1858, *Porter's Spirit of the Times* expressed a similar sentiment. The paper commended the organizers, particularly Dr. Jones of the Excelsiors, on the fine accommodations provided for the press and noted the growing popularity that had been instigated by the matches and the numerous press accounts of the games.[77]

Apparently not everyone had gotten the message. "We are obliged to confine our remarks on the play of the game," Chadwick reported after an Excelsior-Charter Oak match in 1860, "and our reference to particular details almost entirely to the first innings, for afterward the crowd encroached so much on the ground occupied by the scorers that we were unable to see the game, except for occasional glances. The accommodations for the press were very meagre and insufficient."[78]

Chadwick was the only reporter from the 1850s and '60s whose renown survived his lifetime, and he deserves the lion's share of the credit for the publicity given to the game. Without him and his fellow reporters, baseball would have remained little known — a small, localized affair relatively unnoticed by the majority of the public and of interest only to its practitioners. Other sports, particularly cricket and boxing, received ample coverage in the sporting press, and neither achieved the popularity of baseball by the end of the nineteenth century. This does not, however, diminish the press's impact upon baseball. While coverage did not ensure popularity, lack of reporting would certainly guarantee obscurity. Without the enthusiastic support of the press, baseball would never have become America's National Game.

CHAPTER 15

The Manly Fly Game vs. the Boyish Bound Rule and the Fair Pitch vs. the Jerk

One of the rules adopted by the convention of 1857 decreed that any batter whose fair or foul ball was caught either on the fly or on the first bound was out. Another stated that the ball should be pitched to the bat rather than thrown. There were many other rules pertaining to batting, pitching, fielding and running the bases, but during the next few years, none would become more controversial than these two.

When the bound rule was instituted in 1845, baseball was a new game, barely removed from the old cat and town ball phase. The players were not professional athletes; they were merchants, craftsmen and professionals, and they didn't play every day. For these amateurs, playing without a glove, it was difficult to catch the ball on a bounce, let alone on the fly. Without the ability to retire an opponent on the bound, teams would have scored more easily and, with the 21-run limit, games would have ended very quickly.

As the skill of the players improved through practice, it became rather easy to catch a batted ball on the first bounce, and many a good hit to the outfield was negated by a fielder who merely backed up and caught it on the bounce, rather than attempting the more difficult catch on the fly. The only advantage of catching the ball on the fly was that base runners could not leave their stations until after the ball had been caught. There was no similar restriction for balls caught on the bound. By the mid–1850s, the bound game had become anachronistic, and the increased skill of the players cried out for a requirement to catch the ball on the fly.

The rule that the ball must be pitched to the bat presumed that the pitcher, who in the first days of the game was playing merely for enjoyment and recreation, would do his best to give the batter a good ball to hit. The batter, with the same motivation, would swing at the first hittable pitch he saw. This rule worked well until the game began to get competitive, and pitchers realized they could throw teasing pitches just out of reach. Batters likewise found they could frustrate the pitchers by letting good pitches pass.

Tradition dies hard and, even though tradition in the early 1860s consisted of less than two decades, it was not easy to change the rules regarding either pitching or the bound catch. Strong proponents of the fly game, who wanted to require that a fair ball be caught on the fly, included the Knickerbockers and Excelsiors, two of the most respected clubs, and the *Clipper*, perhaps the most influential sporting paper.[1]

The Knickerbockers were particularly staunch advocates of eliminating the fair catch on the bound. Doc Adams, longtime president of the club and for many years one of its delegates to the annual Association convention, proposed the change each year, and each year he was rebuffed either in committee or by the vote of the convention delegates.

In 1858, after the convention upheld the bound rule, the Knickerbockers held a spirited debate on the issue. Alfred Vredenburgh introduced a motion that the rules approved at the convention, including the bound rule, be adopted as the rules of the Knickerbocker Club. Alex Drummond moved to table the motion, and someone else tried to put an end to the debate by calling for an adjournment. The latter motion was defeated, and Adams, echoing Vredenburgh, made a motion for the adoption of the Association rules, which was carried.[2] Even though Adams personally favored the fly game, he was the president of the new National Association and hesitant to refute the decisions made at the convention.

A week later, Adams called a special meeting "for obtaining more fully the sense of the club in regard to catching the ball on the fly if possible and if possible to obtain a reconsideration of the resolution introduced by Dr. Adams and passed at the last meeting." Vredenburgh introduced a resolution calling for the adoption of the rules of the Association *except for the bound rule*. The motion passed by a 12–5 vote. The club would play the fly game when competing amongst themselves or against like-minded nines and the bound game when playing all other clubs.[3]

The main problem with the bound catch was that it was simply too easy. Further, the fly rule prevailed in cricket, and if baseball hoped to rival the English sport, its players would need to exhibit the same level of skill. One of the most attractive features of the new sport — what separated it from rounders and the old cat games — was the skill required to play it, and the players' ability to execute plays that could never have been made in one of the older games. In the infield, a ball caught on the first bound eliminated the need for an accurate throw and a skillful catch by the first baseman. In the outfield, unfortunately, on too many occasions, a chance for a difficult and admirable catch on the fly was not undertaken because it was so much easier to step back and take the ball on a soft, gentle hop. While it was considered "unmanly" to do so, that did not prevent many players from taking the safe route.

Agitation against the bound rule became stronger in 1859. When the rules committee reported to the National Association convention that it was split evenly and therefore not making a recommendation to change the rule, the *Clipper*, appealing to the pride of the delegates, urged, "An alteration in that respect would seem necessary to make the game more manly, as all the little boys are now able to play the game on equal terms with the older clubs, whilst they may put a hand out by catching the ball on the bound."[4] The *Clipper* and, one can assume, Chadwick, since he was the paper's chief baseball correspondent, suggested that if the ball was too hard to be caught on the fly without injury, its weight should be changed. There was no need, he insisted, to lose a hand while losing a hand.

The Knickerbockers continued to press for change. At a meeting in early May 1859, a motion was made that the club refuse to play any game unless it was played "on the fly."[5] Although the motion was defeated, the Excelsiors and Knickerbockers agreed to observe the fly rule in games between their two clubs. The first match, on June 30, was reported in rapturous terms by the *Clipper*. "[N]ot a dozen players among the great number present," wrote Chadwick, "could have been found who would not have voted there and then for the immediate repeal of the boyish rule of the catch on the bound. The superiority of the others was so manifest, the play so much more brilliant ... the catch on the fly when adopted would make the game complete, and place it on a par, in fielding at least, with the best display of cricketing ever seen here."[6]

One of the most surprising aspects of the Knickerbocker-Excelsior game was that, contrary to the fears of many who supported the bound rule, it was played relatively quickly. Since it was more difficult to register a putout by catching the ball on the fly, it would seem that the fly game would result in more safe hits and make the game longer and more tedious. While Chadwick pointed out that fly games often took less time than bound games, one reason was that the fly game was generally played by better teams, who had more skillful fielders than the sloppier teams that played longer bound games.

Porter's Spirit was also enamored of the Knickerbockers' and Excelsiors' play and, like the *Clipper*, held up cricket as the game worthy of emulation. "[T]he result was such," it reported, "as to satisfy any unprejudiced mind of the superiority in every respect of the former method [the fly game]. In fact, this is the only material difference in the fielding seen in a first class cricket match that in any way gives the former any claim to superiority ... far better fielding is seen in a majority of our baseball matches than what the cricket clubs display and but for the catch on the bound ... we should certainly claim for baseball the merit of affording more opportunities for brilliant fielding in one match than can be had in a dozen cricket matches.... [W]e refer to the brilliant fielding we expect to see in all such matches, caused by the increased efforts to catch on the fly, every fielder being aware that unless he does so, his fielding is, in one respect, useless, whereas, with the present rule, if he has any doubt as to his ability to succeed, or is at all unwilling to make an effort to field a ball creditably on the fly, he has the childish effort on the bound to fall back on."[7]

The reporter referred to the Putnam-Eckford match in which 23 catches were made on the bound. In its reports, *Porter's Spirit* began noting catches made on the bound that should have been caught on the fly in an effort to shame unmanly performers. "The catch on the fly," it commented later in the season, "must, in every case, be the result of good judgment in calculating the movement of the ball; whereas that on the bound, in a majority of cases, must of necessity be the result of accident."[8] Still, the *Spirit* was doubtful that the fly rule had sufficient support to be adopted by the National Association. The most prevalent argument against adopting the fly game, other than the fact that it was difficult for unskilled players, was that it would eliminate skillful bound catches.

"All the best clubs now practice the catch on the fly," the *Clipper* said shortly afterward, "on their practice days, and we think that next season it will be the only rule adopted."[9] Even in games where the bound rule was in force, Chadwick insisted that a manly player should attempt to make the catch on the fly. In an 1859 match between the Excelsior and Baltic Clubs, the *Clipper* noted, "In catching on the fly, the Excelsiors surpassed their opponents, not in the number of catches, but in the method of taking them, every ball that could be caught on the fly being obtained, whereas the Baltic's several times fell back upon the easier catch on the bound ... we certainly think that no effort should be spared to obtain the ball on the fly, it being the only creditable way of doing it, generally speaking."[10] In cricket, form was nearly as important as the result, and Chadwick wanted to bring the same standard to baseball.

In 1860, Chadwick looked unfavorably upon a match between the Potomac Club of Washington and the Excelsior Club of Baltimore, noting that twenty-nine catches had been made on the bound and only twelve on the fly. He took every opportunity to denigrate the bound game, noting a fine crowd at a Gotham-Eckford game which was, however, "not as many as were present on the occasion of the 'fly game' between the Excelsior and Knickerbocker Clubs."[11]

Almost alone among the sporting press, the *Atlas* supported the bound game. "We ... failed to discover that the players in either of these clubs," it reported after the Knickerbocker-Excelsior game of which Chadwick had been so infatuated, "were more skillful at catching balls on the fly than those of other clubs who have not made so much noise in the matter, and are wholly opposed to the fly movement. We could discover no advantage in this game over the one prescribed by the National Association."[12] After the second fly game between the two clubs, the *Atlas* was even harsher. "To judge from the score (60–33)," it reported, "we should say this was positively the worst game of ball that has been played this year."[13]

Despite the efforts of the Excelsiors, the Knickerbockers and virtually all the sporting press, it was several years before the bound catch was eliminated. At the annual convention in March 1860, the rules committee unanimously recommended a change to the fly game, but the bound rule was retained by a vote of 55–37, a result received with a rousing cheer from the delegates. Chadwick, always a poor sport when his suggestions weren't accepted, reported the news under the headline, "Meeting of the Convention; Re-adoption of the Boys' Rule of the Catch on the Bound."[14] Chadwick's point was in this case well taken, for an examination of the votes indicated that, for the most part, the more skilled, experienced teams voted in favor of the change while the poorer clubs voted against it. The Excelsiors and Knickerbockers voted in favor, of course, as did the Star and Empire Clubs while the two Atlantic delegates were divided. The Eagles and Gothams were the only top clubs to vote in favor of the bound game, as most of the negative votes came from little-known teams such as the Chelsea, E Pluribus Unum, and Katydid Clubs.

The division of votes highlighted a growing concern. As the number of clubs attending the convention increased, the top clubs lost most of their ability to influence the Association, as each delegate had only one vote, and all a club needed to do to join the Association was to make application and show up.

Chadwick didn't let the defeat at the convention muzzle him, and he continued his crusade during the 1860 season. "The regular game does very well for the junior clubs," he wrote in June, "and for the parties who make up sides for a lively game, but for those who desire to witness the game skillfully played the fly game is the only one worth seeing, in our estimation, and we shall never consider the game perfected until that rule is adopted."[15] He lauded the formation of the Englewood Club of New Jersey, which announced its intention to play the fly game only. Interestingly, throughout the campaign to adopt the fly rule, the catch of a foul ball on the bound, including a foul tip, perhaps the easiest play of all, was never considered a problem.

Chadwick's advocacy notwithstanding, the bound game was upheld by a 51–42 margin in December 1860, and again in 1861, 1862 and 1863. At each convention, every recommendation of the rules committee was quickly accepted, except for its proposal to change to the fly game. The adherents of the fly game were making progress, however, losing the 1863 vote by a margin of just 25–22. One reason for the close vote was that the war had caused several of the lesser teams to disband, while the stronger clubs survived. *Wilkes'* noted that four delegates who would have voted for the fly game were not present, and echoed Chadwick's opinion that the progress of the game was being retarded by the stubbornness of the inferior clubs.

"It was a noteworthy fact," *Wilkes'* stated, "that all, or nearly all, of those opposed to it belong to the muffin fraternity, whose fun the fly rule would put a stop to altogether."[16]

The last statement was not completely true. As late as 1864, despite the *Clipper's* claim that all the best teams preferred the fly game, the Atlantics, the best team in the country, insisted on using the bound rule in all their matches. The Excelsiors and Stars, however, stated they would not play against any club that would not agree to play the fly game, and the tide appeared to be shifting in their favor. Even most of the junior clubs were abandoning the bound game.[17] Finally, on July 31, 1864, the Atlantics, the last major holdout, played their first fly game against another club.[18]

Before the December 1864 convention, Chadwick rallied the troops once more. "The question of the fly rule *versus* the bound is also again to be acted upon," he stated, "and the friends of each style of play should muster in force on the occasion. As the poor players of our clubs are largely in the majority, and as it is those mainly who favor the bound rule, those in favor of the more skillful style of the fly catch will have to exert themselves to secure a majority vote in the convention."[19] He suggested a compromise, under which the new rule would be tried for a single season, after which the results would be evaluated.

Finally Chadwick's hopes were realized, as the clubs voted, 32–19, to adopt the fly game. There was no one-year trial period. The rule was changed on a permanent basis although foul balls caught on the bound would be outs until 1884.

The second major rule change during the war years, which also modernized the game and accommodated the increasing skill level of the players, was a sweeping revision of the pitching rules. To curb wild pitching, umpires were urged to call a ball if a pitcher consistently refused to deliver the pitch within the reach of the striker. Likewise, a strike could be called if a batter consistently refused to offer at balls within his reach. In an unsuccessful effort to put an end to swift pitching, the movements of the pitcher were restricted.

Cricket bowlers were so named because they had initially rolled the ball to the wicket, as in lawn bowling, before adopting the thrown ball and eventually round arm (overhand) bowling.[20] Bat and ball games that preceded baseball all called for the position of pitcher, known as the feeder in some games, to be a relatively unimportant one. His role was to toss the ball, making what was known as a "square pitch," so that the batter could hit it and put it in play. The action took place around and behind him. The Knickerbocker rules did not even specify a position for the pitcher, or the distance he was required to be from home plate. In 1854, the distance was established at "not less than 15 paces" and, like the uncertainty as to the distance between the bases, the issue was resolved in 1857 by changing the requirement from paces to 15 yards.[21]

By the late 1850s, players began to realize that the pitcher could have a decided impact on the game, while bending the spirit but staying within the letter of the law. In the first match game the Knickerbockers played in 1846, Duncan Curry attributed their crushing defeat in part to the fast deliveries of the hurler of the New York club, who was a talented cricket bowler.[22] In 1856, Knickerbocker pitcher Richard Stevens was reported to throw the ball with some velocity, rather than lobbing it toward the batter.[23] By 1859, nearly all the top pitchers threw hard, and those who didn't were criticized (except by Chadwick, who despised swift pitching). In addition to speed, the pitchers had discovered other dodges. What if the pitcher frustrated the hitter by consistently throwing the ball where he could not hit it? Would he swing at bad pitches he couldn't hit squarely? What if the pitcher tossed the ball *at* the batter?

On the other hand, what if the hitter frustrated the pitcher by standing there while one good pitch after the other sailed past? Sooner or later, would the ball escape the bare-handed catcher, allowing the base runners to move up? The "waiting game" was also employed by a trailing club when darkness or rain was approaching.

The gamesmanship of the pitchers and hitters led to an astounding number of pitches being thrown, which lengthened games and made them very tedious. In the first game of the Fashion Race Course series in 1858, Matt O'Brien threw 264 pitches, while his counterpart, Tom Van Cott, threw 198.[24] In the second game, Van Cott threw 270 and Frank Pidgeon of Brooklyn 290.[25] Pigeon outdid himself in the third game by throwing 436 pitches, 87 in the first inning alone.[26] In a game between the Niagara and Resolute Clubs the same year, Canfield of the Resolutes threw 359 pitches, including 128 in a single inning. His counterpart, John Shields, threw 458. Each pitcher would have thrown more had the game not been called by darkness after eight innings.[27] The Resolute-Niagara match was not the rare exception, for about a week later the Osceola and Hiawatha pitchers combined to throw 628 pitches in just five innings.[28]

Since there was nothing in the rules to prevent erratic pitching or stalling at the bat, the only recourse was, as in the case of the bound rule, an appeal to the good sportsmanship of the players. "Hit the first good ball you get," said one reporter, "is the only fair and square game to play."[29] After watching a game between the Harlem and Charter Oak Clubs that was filled with batters taking pitches until runners on first made their way to third, another wrote, "It is not a kind of game ... which any club of the character and standing of either of the contestants should countenance."[30]

As winning became more important and teams were less concerned with character and standing, the results were predictable. Nothing short of a rule change would stop the chicanery. In 1860, Chadwick advocated such a move. "Again," he wrote, "when a striker has stood at the home base long enough to allow a dozen balls not plainly out of reach to pass him, he should at once be made to declare where he wants a ball, and the first ball that comes within the distance pointed out, if not struck at, should be declared one strike, the second two strikes, and the third, three. If this were done, a stop would at once be put to the unmanly and mean 'waiting game' frequently played, and the cause of much unpleasantness removed."[31] Letting good pitches pass was as unmanly as catching the ball on the bound, but if it helped the team win, what was more manly than victory?

In 1860, with the emergence of Jim Creighton as a star, the role of pitching as an integral part of the game became fully acknowledged, and swift pitching was more popular and controversial than ever. John Stebbins, a top hurler in Rochester, supposedly wore a tight bandage on his arm in order to achieve speed while still keeping his arm stiff as required by the rules.[32] The paramount question was which style of pitching was most effective. "[S]ince the advent of Creighton," said one journal, "there has been a sort of mania for swift pitching."[33] The *Clipper,* meaning Chadwick, who always touted the strategic approach rather than the use of mere brute strength, never liked swift pitching. Stimson of the Putnams, Chadwick reported in 1860, "pitched swiftly, but is not regular enough in his delivery. Speed, in pitching, is well enough, but without accuracy in delivery, it makes a game tedious. Jerome's pitching, on the part of the Excelsiors [second nine] contrasted favorably with that of all the others, for he pitches with judgment, sending in a slow but twisting ball, and one puzzling to the batsman."[34]

"Creighton's success in pitching," the *Clipper* observed a month later, "has induced many to imitate him, under the supposition that his chief merit lays in his speed. This is a mistake, his fast pitching being only one element of his strength as a pitcher."[35] The next year, the *Clipper* criticized Earl of the Enterprise Club. "[U]ntil he adds regularity of delivery," it opined, "and capacity to control the direction of the ball thoroughly, to the power he possesses of pitching a swift ball, he need never hope to become a second Creighton. Merely swift pitching is 'played out.'"[36]

Three decades later, in 1891, Chadwick was still cautioning against the use of speed in pitching. He contrasted the heady mound work of "Hoss" Radbourn with the "cyclone pitching" of Amos Rusie. There was nothing good about cyclone pitching, Chadwick insisted, even when it was effective. It destroyed the catcher, bored the fans, and left the fielders with nothing to do. With such a horrible style, it was nothing short of a miracle that Rusie managed to win 106 games over the next four years.[37]

Swift pitching utilized muscle and strength, not science and cunning, which were the traits Chadwick exalted when describing the ideal player. However, swift pitching, as Walter Johnson, Sandy Koufax and Nolan Ryan would prove, was far from played out, and as pitchers learned more control, nearly every top pitcher threw hard. When the catcher began using a glove, the last restraint was removed. The slow but crafty pitcher, so greatly admired by Chadwick, became an anomaly.

In the mid-nineteenth century, however, speed was not the only way to pitch effectively. "The Pitcher," said *Beadle's* in 1860, "who can combine a high degree of speed with an even delivery, and at the same time can, at pleasure, impart a bias or twist to the ball, is the most effective player in that position."[38] Bernard Hannegan of the Unions of Morrisania was one of those who imparted a twist to the ball which made it hard to hit squarely. Hannegan, who joined the Unions in 1859 and became their pitcher in 1860, was at first the darling of the press, particularly Chadwick, for his "scientific" pitching, but his lack of control soon made him the epitome of all that was wrong with pitchers. In July 1862, Chadwick called Hannegan's pitching the key to his team's victories over some strong opponents.[39] By October, however, his style had become odious. "In the end," claimed Chadwick, "it will injure ballplaying more than is thought."[40] The problem was that Hannegan threw his slow twisters beyond the batters' reach, thus delaying the game and making it a long, dull affair. "Hannegan pitched with his usual accuracy," the *Eagle* noted in 1863, "and we all know what that is."[41] When he pitched in a picked nine game later that season, the *Eagle* described it as "the most tedious, dull, and in fact stupid game we have witnessed this season." The fault, of course, was Hannegan's, for his damnable wild pitching.[42]

Alphonse (Phonny) Martin, who had been playing ball since his early teens,[43] rose from the junior ranks to the Empire Club late in the 1864 season at the age of 19 and would become the most renowned of the slow pitchers. Martin, like Hannegan, imparted a twist to the ball. He was the Stu Miller of the nineteenth century, varying his speed, but always delivering every ball slower than the swift pitchers. "Martin's pitching," observed the *Clipper* after he'd held the champion Atlantics to the relatively modest total of fifteen runs, "was not found as easy to knock about by the Bedford players as they anticipated."[44] There was much talk of Martin's curve, which was actually a vertical curve that dropped due to lack of speed as it approached the plate.[45] In 1864, no pitcher was throwing what we would now refer to as a curve or any form of breaking pitch. The deceptive deliveries were drop pitches, changeups or balls thrown with a twist that made them difficult to hit solidly. The goal of the slow pitcher was to induce popups and foul tips, which if caught on the bound by the catcher were an easy out.

A great advantage of the slow pitcher was that his deliveries seldom resulted in passed balls, for catching a swift pitcher, especially one who was wild, was one of baseball's most difficult challenges. In order to be effective, however, the slow pitcher needed good fielders behind him. Even if he prevented batters from hitting the ball solidly, the popups and soft grounders would not result in putouts without sure hands in the infield and outfield.

During the latter part of the 1863 season, Chadwick lobbied tirelessly for a change in the rules in order to eliminate swift pitching.[46] In nearly every game reported by the *Eagle*, for which Chadwick wrote regularly, any incidence of swift pitching was condemned and all slow pitching praised, with the need for change set forth repetitiously, and the anticipated glorious results explained *ad nauseum*.

Without swift pitching, the hitter had a much better chance of putting the ball in play, which Chadwick believed was far more exciting than watching the battery play pitch and catch. "As long as swift pitching remains in vogue," he stated, "just so long may we expect to see dull, tedious and uninteresting games, where two or three of the nine are worked to excess, while the remainder have not half enough to do."[47] Once the ball was hit, the seven men in the field would have the opportunity to demonstrate their skills. Fielding a ball without gloves was far from a certainty, and the skillful fielders (one couldn't use the current expression "glove men") would prove their worth. Fielding, Chadwick believed, was the greatest skill involved in baseball, far more difficult than batting or pitching. "Lively fielding," he wrote, "is the beauty of base ball, and the only feature of the game that makes it more attractive than cricket, and the moment anything is done to deprive it of this special attraction, as swift pitching does, that very moment it will cease to be the popular game it otherwise will ever be."[48] "Batting ought not ever to be placed upon the same scale with fielding," he wrote on another occasion. "Every 'muffin' almost, can bat well."[49] A further benefit of the proposed change was to even out competition and lessen the advantages of teams that had good pitchers.

The second bane of Chadwick's existence, in addition to swift pitching, was wild pitching. As early as 1858, umpires had been authorized to call strikes, but few did.[50] The first reported instance of a strike being called on a batter for failing to swing at a good pitch was during the third game of the Fashion Course Series by umpire Doc Adams.[51] Adams may have been a pioneer in regard to the shortstop position, but his lead was not followed in strike calling, and such an incident was rarely seen thereafter.

Prior to the 1862 season, umpires were given the power to call balls if a pitcher repeatedly failed to deliver fair pitches, but once more the option was rarely exercised. The power was purely discretionary, the notion of a ball or strike largely in the eyes of the beholder, and there was no thought that a call should be made on every pitch. Further, this did not solve Chadwick's problem, for he did not just abhor wild pitching; he disliked swift pitching even when it was accurate.

Finally, two years later, in 1864, the rules committee, greatly influenced by Dr. William Bell, pitcher and captain of the Henry Eckford Club,[52] took steps to try to arrest the trend toward swift pitching. The pitcher's freedom of movement was restricted to a three-by-twelve foot pitcher's box, which prevented him from getting a running start, and he was required to deliver the ball with both feet planted on the ground, which reduced his leverage. Any pitcher who stepped forward with a foot off the ground while delivering the ball was charged with a balk. Less speed would, the committee assumed, result in greater control and shorter games.

In addition, the umpire was strongly encouraged to call balls should the pitcher repeatedly fail to deliver the ball within the batsman's reach. Three called balls entitled the batter to first base. The concept of having to call a ball or strike on every pitch was several years in the future, and the decision of whether to call a ball or strike on a pitch was completely within the discretion of the umpire. Still, it was a major step.

The strike zone was loosely defined, as the concept of home plate as a target had not been part of baseball's early rules. Home plate was the base the players had to touch in order to make a run, not the boundary of the strike zone. It was not until 1857 that the rules declared that the ball must be pitched "over the home base" rather than "to the striker."

The new rule required the pitcher to direct the ball as near to the center of the home base as possible and "for the striker."[53] The batter could state a preference for high or low pitches, and the pitcher was required to throw the ball where the batter wanted it. By mandating slower and more accurate pitching, the rule makers intended to create more action and allow the game to be dominated by batters and fielders, rather than pitchers. "We hope to see swift pitching laid aside after this," wrote the *Times* in 1865.[54]

Once the season began, umpires enforced the new rule at their whim. Some either weren't aware of the change or chose to ignore it. Colonel Thomas Fitzgerald, president of the Athletics, who should have known better, failed to enforce the rules in games he umpired. Apparently, he thought he was only to call balls when the wild pitching was intentional, despite the fact that the rule explicitly imposed the penalty if the pitches were consistently wild for the purpose of delaying the game or "for any cause."[55]

Other umpires, such as Billy McMahon of the Mutuals, were overly strict. McMahon umpired a game between the Empire and Active Clubs and called numerous balls and strikes, which baffled players and spectators, who expected the rule to be enforced only in the extreme — when pitchers and batters tried to delay the game by throwing wildly or playing the "waiting game."[56] Chadwick indicated that umpires should be lenient in the first inning, while the pitchers got their range.[57] All in all, the discretion given to the umpire made the interpretation of the rule often muddled and almost always uneven.

In 1863, Chadwick's crusade had been to have new legislation passed, but the following year he shifted his unyielding focus to a proper interpretation and further refinement of the new rule. The greatest need, he believed, was for a more precise definition of an "unfair ball." He suggested that an unfair ball be any ball which was more than a bat length away from the hitter, over his head, struck the ground before reaching the plate, went on the opposite side of the plate, hit the batter, or was so close as to cause him to move out of the way.[58]

Despite the difficulties with the new rule, the die had been cast. Called balls and strikes would gain increasing importance in baseball and put an end to intentional delay. Chadwick's second goal, the return to soft tossing on the part of the pitcher, was not to be, for the benefit of swift pitching had become too obvious. The portion of the rule change intended to limit the speed of pitching would first be ignored, then modified in 1872 to allow the underhand snap throw, then sidearm pitching, and eventually unrestricted overhand pitching in 1884. The pitcher, who, in the 1850s, had been no more prominent than any of his teammates, would eventually become the most important man in the field.

The press advocated rule changes, the Rules Committee recommended them and the delegates to the annual NA convention voted on them. The implementation of the changes on the field, however, depended upon the efforts and inclinations of the umpires. As shown in the case of the new pitching rules, this was the part of the process that was often found wanting. There were no full-time, professional arbiters. Originally, the rules had called for two umpires and a referee to decide those points upon which the umpires were of divided opinion. In 1858, the system evolved to one umpire and no referees, giving the man in that position complete control over the way the game was played.

The only qualification to act as umpire was that the man be a member of a National Association club and that he be agreed upon by the captains of both competing nines. Members of the most respected clubs were in demand, and in the early days of the game, Knickerbocker players often served as umpires. As a member of a club, the umpire was presumed to know the rules, which was not always the case. He was expected to render decisions promptly, convey them in a loud voice so that all could hear, give his decisions according to his best judgment and not be influenced by players or spectators. The most admired characteristic in an umpire was impartiality. Errors of judgment were forgiven as unavoidable flaws, so long as the arbiter was well posted in the rules and didn't unduly favor one side or the other. "These errors," wrote one journal, "although always annoying to the party who suffers, should be overlooked without a murmur."[59]

The umpire was charged with deciding only those points he could see, and with but one man in the position, he was not expected to see everything. If an umpire did not see a man tagged and did not call him out, that was all right. "[I]n giving their decisions," the *Clipper* advised, "we would suggest to umpires that they be entirely guided by the *first impression* made on their minds, for, whether it be right or wrong, it is certainly the only impartial decision that can be given. Nor should they, ever, be guided by statements of the fielders or base players in reference to touching players when running their bases, but be guided solely by their own opinion."[60]

Umpires, believing that ballplayers were an honorable lot, often asked a runner whether he had been tagged, or a fielder whether he had done so. That practice was supposedly forbidden, but it was permissible for an umpire to ask players regarding catches in the outfield since he could not be expected to see the play clearly from his position near home plate.[61]

There were, of course, a number of honorable men playing baseball. In a game between the Utica Club and the Knickerbockers of Albany in 1864, umpire Anthony, who had a poor angle, erroneously called a hit to right field by the Knickerbockers fair, when all could see it was clearly foul. Although two runs had scored, Captain Winne of the Knickerbockers ordered his men to return to their bases, as if the ball were foul.[62]

Umpires never ejected players for bad behavior. If a situation became intolerable, they ejected themselves, refusing to serve if they were subjected to further abuse. It was the problem of the competing clubs to find someone to replace the umpire, and since there was no compensation, it was not always easy.

The press invariably supported the umpire, so long as he acted honorably, and castigated those who abused him or carped about his performance. After observing a minor row in 1862, the *Eagle,* in a statement that would not stand the test of time, commented, "We trust never again to see the columns of a paper, professing to any respectability, attributing the defeat of a club to the partial decisions of an Umpire."[63]

The press reminded the players that, acting without compensation, the umpire was performing a generous act by filling a position without which the game could not take place. He was also operating under difficult conditions, for it was nearly impossible for one man to observe everything that happened on a baseball field. While the ball was in the outfield, the umpire couldn't watch runners, who sometimes took advantage of the situation by choosing the most direct route between the bases. Under Philadelphia town ball rules, it was only necessary to run past the base, and many old townballers carried the habit over to baseball. In 1862, the *Brooklyn City News* scolded players who had adopted the rather common habit of running past the bases rather than touching them.[64] If there were multiple runners and the ball was in the outfield, the gentlemanly inclinations of the players were the only obstacles to complete mayhem.

Umpires, particularly less experienced ones, often enforced some rules but not others. The balk rule, which decreed that if a pitcher hesitated after starting his delivery, each runner was entitled to a base, was frequently ignored, as was the rule that required batters to stand on a line drawn through the center of the home base.

The heaviest cross the umpire had to bear was generally placed on his shoulders by the gamblers, who attributed every decision to partiality and whose pecuniary interest in the outcome often resulted in abuse that was quite ungentlemanly.

Some men garnered praise for their officiating skills. Peter O'Brien, well-respected outfielder of the Atlantics, was held in high esteem for his ability to umpire a game efficiently and honestly, as was his brother Mattie. John Lowell was considered by *Wilkes'* to be the best umpire in the Boston area.[65] Colonel Moore of Philadelphia was another man who filled the position capably, as was John Grum of the Eckfords. "[W]hen placed in a somewhat critical and extremely unpleasant position," *Wilkes'* said in 1863, Grum "acted the part of a man — thus practically illustrating his capacity and ability to officiate as a base ball umpire."[66] Grum was one of the few umpires who correctly and consistently applied the new pitching rules. Chadwick praised him for his understanding and application of the rule, which, coincidentally, "accorded exactly with the article on the subject in yesterday's *Eagle*."[67]

While the change to the fly game and the restrictions on pitchers were the result of lengthy debate and were followed by copious instructions, umpires were left to their own resources for those innovations that sometimes came about by accident. In an 1860 game, a Putnam player named Brown "hit with the bat in a similar manner to that in which a cricketer blocks a straight ball; judgment was asked, and as the Umpire deemed it an accident, it was decided 'no hit.'" The *Clipper* noted that if a teammate had been on first base, he could easily have made second; therefore the hit should have been fair, a strategy we now refer to as the sacrifice bunt.[68]

Baseball was still a relatively new game, and further changes would be necessary as the skill of the players improved and rendered certain plays ridiculously easy, and as smart players found ways to circumvent the rules. By the middle of the 1860s, however, with the fly game and the calling of balls and strikes, the game of baseball had become very much like the game we know today.

CHAPTER 16

The Eckfords Take the Championship, 1862–1863

After a somewhat limited 1861 campaign, most lovers of baseball thought 1862 would bring, if not a return to the peak of 1860, more activity than had taken place the previous summer. "The rebellion has culminated," the *Clipper* wrote optimistically of the war in March, "its rapid downturn is but a question of time."[1] Second Manassas, Fredericksburg and Chancellorsville lay ahead at that point, but, while sadly disillusioned as to the imminent demise of the Confederacy, the *Clipper* was correct in its premise that there would be more baseball in 1862. The season was nothing, however, like the years from 1858 through 1860, when new teams were forming each week, and games were taking place in every vacant lot. In 1862, there was no rush of new clubs, and some of the old ones were falling by the wayside. In April, the Waverly and Pastime Clubs announced they were disbanding.[2] The number of junior clubs attending the annual convention was down from 23 to 10.[3]

During the winter of 1861–1862, a strong rumor began to circulate throughout baseball circles. Jim Creighton, they said, was going to join the Atlantics.[4] With his Excelsiors inactive in 1861, Creighton had not played in a single match. The rumor proved false, but baseball would not be without its star pitcher for a second consecutive season, for the Excelsiors planned to take the field again in 1862.

In late March, before the season even began, the Mystic Club broke new ground by announcing its schedule. The club would play nine games, the first on June 5 against the Oraton Club and the last on September 18, against Benicia Boy.[5] This was the first time any club had announced its schedule in the sporting papers so far in advance.

The young Star Club of Brooklyn was invariably the first in the field each spring, and on March 26, its members gathered on their grounds to play the first nine against the second. As frequently happened on opening day, players from other clubs stopped by and joined in the play. March was very early to open the season, and much, much sooner than in 1861, when many clubs dawdled around until June before deciding to play ball. The early start was a harbinger of a better year.

Numerous clubs followed the Stars into action. The Favorita Club began play on April 2, and the next day the Jeffersons became the first of the Hoboken clubs to practice at the Elysian Fields. They were soon joined by the Knickerbocker, Eagle, Mutual, Empire, and Gotham Clubs, plus others across the river in Brooklyn and New York.

At the corner of Marcy Street and Rutledge Avenue in Brooklyn, William Cammeyer, proprietor of the Union Skating Grounds, spent the early spring converting his property for use as a baseball ground, the first enclosed baseball park in the United States.[6] Unlike today, when the planning and construction of a new athletic facility takes years, the first announcement of Cammeyer's plans was made in early March, and the grounds were ready two months later.

Cammeyer, 42, was a prosperous, second-generation leather merchant who had acquired a lease on the Marcy Street land a year earlier. "An energetic man," reported the *Brooklyn City News,* "is at the head of affairs, and one that will accomplish what he undertakes, at any cost."[7] Cammeyer, who apparently had some connections with New York's infamous Tammany Hall politicians,[8] obtained the property for $50,000 and spent an additional $10,000 on improvements, including the construction of several buildings and the erection of a board fence six or seven feet high.[9] One of the buildings was a clubhouse for the use of the players, and another was a pagoda which was placed in deep center field, within the confines of the playing surface.

The construction of the Union Grounds was Cammeyer's first connection with baseball, but in subsequent years he became quite active in the management of the Mutuals, continuing through their brief tenure in the National League in 1876. The facility he constructed in 1862 would be used for baseball through 1877 and is now the site of the 17th Corps Artillery Armory.[10]

The advent of fenced enclosures for ball playing had several consequences. First, it enabled the proprietor to charge admission since there were limited points of access. At the Elysian Fields, with its vast open spaces, it was difficult to restrict entry. Spectators often came by to watch for a spell and then moved on. At the Union Grounds, the gates could be manned and entry tightly controlled.

In addition to enabling revenue generation, greater dominion over the grounds provided a means for keeping out undesirable spectators who might disrupt play or discourage more respectable citizens from attending. "On the Union Grounds," noted the *Brooklyn City News,* "none will be admitted save those who know how to conduct themselves in an orderly manner, as all true ballplayers do."[11] Cammeyer, added the *Eagle,* "is not the man to hesitate in taking prompt measures to eject any one from the grounds who attempts to disturb the proceedings."[12] In the event any rascals managed to slip through the dragnet, a large police force would be on hand for all important games.

The ground surrounding the enclosure was elevated and offered a view of the proceedings *gratis,* but anyone on the embankment was unable to cause a disturbance within. This development ostensibly made baseball more attractive to the coveted lady fans, who were provided with special seating in a long wooden grandstand.[13] In the eyes of many, the ability to keep out potential troublemakers was the most important facet of the new enclosed facility.

Yet another change brought about by the construction of the Union Grounds was the introduction of capitalism to baseball. Cammeyer, with his own funds at stake and the opportunity to generate a profit, had every incentive to keep the grounds in top condition — in contrast to some of the fields that were in sorry shape — and to provide a safe, attractive environment for spectators.

When he opened his facility, Cammeyer offered free use of the grounds to the initial three first class clubs that contacted him. This countered the main objection to the charging of an admission fee — the possibility that the clubs would receive it and thus be professionals.

There was no objection to clubs obtaining free use of the grounds, with the admission proceeds retained by the proprietor.

On May 15, 1862, the Union Grounds were christened with a game between two teams selected from players of the Eckford, Putnam, and Constellation Clubs, the three organizations that were to occupy the site during the season. The opening was a gala event, with flags flying, bands playing and ladies cheering. Attendance was between two and three thousand, all admitted free of charge.[14] The opening song was the "Star Spangled Banner," perhaps the first time a baseball game was preceded by the now-obligatory rendition.[15]

In 1862, as in prior seasons, there would be a contest for the championship of the New York area, and thus the United States. The system, however, was becoming unwieldy. As the number of teams multiplied, and with few of them playing more than ten games a year, not every team had a chance to play a series against the reigning champion, and the latter had every incentive to avoid strong nines.

The disastrous Atlantic-Excelsior episode of 1860 had cast disrepute on the entire process, and the Continental Club attempted to remedy the situation in 1861 when it offered a silver ball to the champion. The Continentals suggested that clubs be paired off by lot in a single elimination process with the last two undefeated clubs meeting for the ball.[16]

The war effectively scuttled the plan, and the silver ball was awarded under the traditional method. "[T]here can be no champion club in base ball," Chadwick observed, "as the rules are now. There are no special rules for playing championship games, or any recognized trophy such as mark the contests for the championship in pugilistic circles." He reiterated his assertion that the spirit of competition engendered by a quest for the championship was injurious to the future of baseball.[17]

The defending champions, the Atlantics, did not begin practicing until May 12 and made their title more secure by announcing they would not accept any challenges presented after July 15.[18] The personnel of the Atlantics had changed significantly from the time they played their first game in 1855 against the Harmony Club. Shortly thereafter, many of the Harmony's top players, including Peter O'Brien, Rapaleye Boerum, John Price, L.M. Bergen and George Phelps, changed allegiances and joined the Atlantics.[19]

By 1862, many of the old Harmony players had given way to others the Atlantics had lured from a different organization. The Brooklyn nine shared their grounds with the Enterprise Club, the latter occupying the field on Wednesdays and Saturdays, while the Atlantics played on Mondays and Thursdays. The Enterprise was a junior club from its formation in 1856 until 1859 when it converted to senior status. Junior or senior, the Enterprise Club acted as an informal farm system for the Atlantics, producing first baseman Joe Start, third baseman Charley Smith, outfielders John Chapman and Sid Smith, and infielder Joe Oliver. By 1862, the youngsters were on the Atlantic first nine, while old stalwarts such as former captain Boerum, Tice Hamilton, and Matt O'Brien were playing in second nine matches.[20]

Since everyone was, at least ostensibly, an amateur, there were no contracts, and no trade or sale of the players. The two clubs merely shared a field, and it was said that the Atlantics provided financial assistance to the Enterprise.[21] When the Atlantics, clearly the better nine, saw an Enterprise player they thought was more talented than one of their own, they asked him to join their club. The Stars provided several young players to the Excelsiors in the same manner, including Creighton, Flanly, Asa Brainard, and John Whiting.[22]

First baseman Start, called by historian Peter Morris "a forgotten superstar,"[23] was in the early stages of a remarkable career. Nineteen years old in 1862, he had been playing on the Enterprise Club since 1859. In his early years, he sometimes played third base, but for virtually his entire career, Start was a first baseman. One of the stalwarts of the Atlantics during the glory years of the 1860s, he joined the Mutuals in 1871, the first season of the professional National Association. When the shadowy Mutuals were tossed out of the National League following the 1876 season, Start, then 33, spent a season with Hartford and one with Chicago before arriving in Providence to play with the National League Grays from 1879 through 1885. In 1884, he was on the winning team in the first World Series. Finally, in 1886, at the age of 43, he ended his major league career with Washington of the National League. Over a 28-year span, Start was part of the gentlemanly era, the semipro decade of the 1860s, open professionalism, the formation of three major leagues and the first World Series.

A left handed batter and thrower, a rarity in his era, Start was known for his power, which may seem odd to anyone perusing one of the baseball encyclopedias, for Start hit just fifteen home runs in sixteen major league seasons. No one hit home runs in the 1870s, but Start hit many in the 1860s, before leagues were formed and statistics memorialized. In those days, with no outfield fences to aim at, extra-base hits were a function of both power and speed. Start had both, and he was one of the fastest of the Atlantics.[24]

Start's batting average for eleven National League seasons was an even .300, and he was an excellent fielder at first base. In 1865, the *Clipper* said that only Aleck Pearsall of the old Excelsiors of 1860 was his equal.[25] Today, receiving a throw from an infielder is considered a routine task, but in the gloveless era, Start's ability to catch the ball stood out. By modern standards, Start, just 5'9", would not appear suited to first base, but in his time, at 165 pounds, he was not considered small. He was almost always among the National League leaders in putouts and fielding average and was known for ranging far from the base, in contrast to many of his peers. Further, like teammate Peter O'Brien, Start had character. In 1862, just before Joe joined the Atlantics, a reporter claimed, "Start has no superior as a base player, and, withal, possesses that quiet self-command, which is as commendable a characteristic of a ball player, as it is a rare one."[26] Although many of his Atlantic and Mutual teammates came under suspicion of fraudulent play, Start, known as "Old Reliable," was never accused of doing anything less than his best.

John Chapman was a stocky, powerful,

Joe Start played baseball from 1859 through 1886, spanning several distinct eras. He was one of the finest players of the 1860s, combining power, speed, and fielding ability at first base. Start was also admired for his integrity and even temper, the latter quality setting him apart from many of his Atlantic teammates.

strong-armed outfielder who could also pitch. In his prime, he was a fine fielder known for his running catches,[27] although, as the years went on, he was limited in the outfield by his increased girth. Chapman joined the Atlantics in 1862 and played with them through 1866. After a season in Philadelphia with the Quaker City Club, he was an Atlantic again from 1868–70, and again in 1874 when the Brooklyn nine was a member of the National Association. Chapman played with St. Louis in 1875 and briefly with Louisville in the National League's first season. For many years after his retirement as an active player, he managed in the major leagues, piloting clubs in Milwaukee, Buffalo, Detroit, Worcester and Louisville. His 1877 Louisville Club was the unfortunate team that was involved in the National League's first major gambling scandal, but a second stint in Kentucky was much more successful, as he won the American Association pennant in 1890. Despite his success in Louisville, Chapman's overall record as a major league manager was a poor 351–502.

The players of the '50s and '60s who survived the longest had the opportunity to tell the tale of the game's early days, sometimes to their own benefit. They granted interviews, compiled scrapbooks and told stories, in which they rarely showed to disadvantage. Al (Phonny) Martin lived until 1933, Al Reach until 1928 and Wes Fisler until 1922. Chapman lived until 1916 and became one of the grand old men of the game with a sterling reputation for honesty and fair dealing (and incredible whistling). By the 1880s, he looked the part of a major league manager with "a pleasant face, a double chin, [and] a handsome black mustache."[28] Chapman was always an enterprising business man, selling sporting goods while managing Louisville, later working for a liquor distributor and owning a couple of minor league clubs. He spanned even more eras than Start. Hughie Jennings, star Detroit player and later manager of the club, was his protégé, and he signed twentieth century stars Jimmy Collins and Bill Dineen. Chapman also managed pioneer black infielder Frank Grant in Syracuse.

The Oliver brothers, Joe and John, were also stalwarts of the champion Atlantic Clubs. Virtually every mention of the latter noted the fact that he was very handsome and a favorite of the ladies. Johnny was known for a fine singing voice, his fielding skill as an infielder and his quick temper.

The Star Club had been the first to begin practice, and was also the first to commence match play in 1862, beating the Powhatan Club, 45–11, on May 21. The opening game of the season had taken place two weeks earlier

John Chapman played several seasons for the Atlantics as an outfielder, pitcher and first baseman. After his playing career ended, he served as manager for a number of teams and had ownership interests in a couple of minor league clubs. In addition to his batting skill, Chapman was known as an incredible whistler who often entertained at club dinners.

than it had the previous year, and, as other clubs soon followed the Stars and Powhatans into combat, it was evident that more baseball would be played during the second year of war than during the first. The visit of the Philadelphia clubs in early June was the undisputed highlight of the summer and served to kick off the season in grand style.

The Atlantics' defense of their championship began poorly, as they lost the first game of their series to the Eckfords 20–14 in mid-July. It was an exciting contest, as the Eckfords rallied from a 14–9 deficit to score the last 11 runs. The gate proceeds of $120 were donated to the Sanitary Commission, which saw to the well-being of wounded soldiers.[29]

The Eckfords and Mutuals were the two teams most likely to challenge the champions, as the old-line clubs like the Knickerbockers and Gothams now played principally for enjoyment, and none of the newer organizations had enough talent to topple the top three clubs. The Excelsiors, chief rivals of the Atlantics in 1860, did not intend to play them in 1862 — or ever. The Excelsiors were also estranged from the Eckfords over some unknown dispute which arose during the all-star series in 1858.[30]

A ten cent admission charge was imposed for the second game between the Atlantics and Eckfords at the Union Grounds, also to be donated to the Sanitary Commission. With such a worthy cause, *Wilkes'* hoped "upon this occasion that there will be a greater number within the enclosure, and far less 'dead heads' upon the surrounding embankments." During the first game, while 1200 had paid, about 5000 remained outside the enclosure to avoid the admission charge.[31]

At the second game, there were five to six thousand in attendance, but much to the disappointment of *Wilkes'*, most were not paying customers. The journal lamented, "[W]e regretted to see so large a proportion of the audience gathered upon the surrounding embankments, as the admission fee was very trifling (one dime) and the proceeds of each game ... is to be paid over to the United States Sanitary Commission."[32]

The Atlantics' overwhelming 39–5 win necessitated a third contest. The second game was highlighted by a series of the big rallies for which the Atlantics were famous. They scored seven times in the third inning, seven more in the fifth, six in the sixth and six more in the ninth. "The Eckfords," opined *The Sunday Mercury,* "seemed to play as if they wished to see how badly they could be beaten."[33]

Although the second game took place in late July, the deciding contest was not scheduled until mid–September at the Union Grounds. Since anyone had taken notice of the championship, the Atlantics had worn the crown. On September 18, they ceded the title to the Eckfords, who defeated them, 8–3, in a well-played match, the "Greatest Score on Record" according to *The Brooklyn Daily Times*.[34] The attendance of ten thousand indicated that baseball, unlike the Confederacy, would survive the Civil War. For their efforts, the Eckfords were awarded the silver ball that had been donated by the Continental Club.

The Eckfords, like the Atlantics, were a working class club, made up initially of shipwrights and mechanics and named after the late Brooklyn shipbuilder Henry Eckford.[35] In addition to building a number of vessels that served the U.S Navy during the War of 1812, Eckford constructed the famous steamship *Robert Fulton*.[36]

Nearly all of the Eckford players were from Brooklyn. In its first year, due to the members' difficulty in leaving work, the club was able to practice just once per week. According to Frank Pidgeon, a dock builder who was one of the Eckfords' founders and the leader of the club during its early years, his nine thought their lack of practice time would make them an easy mark for the clubs that played more frequently. Trash talk was not in vogue among the gentleman clubs of the 1850s, and while the Eckfords were mostly working class men, no one was more gentlemanly than Pidgeon, who later reminisced about the debut of his nine. He spoke of his club's modest aspirations, gave a humble accounting of its ability, and recounted how the Eckfords challenged the winner of a Baltic-Union match for their first game.

The Unions won, and agreed to meet the Eckfords. "Well," Pidgeon wrote, "we had got what we wanted — a match; and then what! Why, we would have to do the best we could." Pidgeon dramatically described the dread of meeting another club and the disastrous consequences to the future of the Eckfords if they were badly defeated.[37] Of course, the Eckfords played splendidly and defeated the Unions, 22–8, starting them upon a course that would eventually make them the champions of the United States.

The Eckfords' best player was Waddy Beach, their catcher, who was quick and agile behind the bat, "the beau ideal of a ballplayer, cool, plucky and skillful."[38] "His ease and grace of manner," noted the *Eagle*, "and his agility places him in the front ranks as a catcher."[39] The Brooklyn club also had left-handed hitting second baseman Al Reach, later to become a baseball executive and founder of the sporting goods empire that bore his name. Reach was born in England in 1840, the son of a cricketer, and he came to America at the age of one.[40] His playing career began in 1861 with the Jackson Club and ended in 1875 with the Athletics of Philadelphia, but his involvement with the game did not terminate when he left the playing field.

In 1883, A.G. Mills, president of the National League, who knew Reach from the days when both played baseball in the early '60s, convinced him to take ownership of a Philadelphia franchise that, along with a club in New York, would replace the struggling Worcester and Troy franchises. Philadelphia had not held an NL franchise since the Athletics, the direct descendant of the club formed in 1860, were expelled in 1876 for failing to complete their schedule. Reach became owner and president of the new club and, despite a 17–81 record in his first season, remained in his position for twenty years, building the franchise that still survives as the Phillies. He constructed two ballparks, the initial one the first in the United States made of steel and brick rather than wood.

Reach had begun making baseballs as early as 1861[41] and eventually parlayed his ability into a company that competed with Spalding for the patronage of the sporting world. Reach's firm was later absorbed by Spalding's, but for many years afterward it supplied the American League ball and published the American League Guide.[42]

The Eckford shortstop was 15-year-old, curly-haired Tom Devyr, who was to acquire infamy as one of three Mutual players banished in 1865 for conspiring to throw a game. Unlike many of his working class teammates, Devyr was the product of a prominent Brooklyn family, son of the well-known proprietor of a local newspaper.[43]

Infielder Jimmy Wood, who began playing with the Harlem Club in 1856[44] and had been an Eckford since 1860, was another fine athlete, who played with the club through 1869, then became captain of the Chicago White Stockings of the professional National Association. Wood's playing career ended tragically prior to the 1874 season when his infected right leg had to be amputated.[45]

The final member of the infield was John Grum, an Eckford veteran of many years who was esteemed for his integrity. The outfield was patrolled by Wesley Campbell, Harry Manolt and Marty Swandell (whose real name was Schwendel),[46] who played for several years in New York and Brooklyn and later became a prosperous baker.

The Eckford pitcher was twenty-year-old Brooklyn native Joe Sprague. Sprague was a big, strong hurler who began playing ball in 1857 at the age of fifteen with the junior National Club. He was well known in his native city, where his grandfather, also named Joseph, was a former Brooklyn mayor and his father Horace was a major in the 13th Regiment. After three seasons with the Nationals, Sprague joined the Exercise Club although he courted controversy by simultaneously playing with other teams. In 1862, he briefly joined the Enterprise, but defected to the Eckfords for whom he pitched in six games.[47] Sprague was known, as were most of the top hurlers, for his speed, and when he gained control, the youngster became one of the best pitchers in baseball.

The Eckfords' old pitcher and their first president, the veteran Pidgeon, rarely played in first-nine matches. When he took part in a game on July 29, 1862, it was his first appearance since 1860.[48] He remained active, however, in club affairs and almost always showed up to cheer for his club. As a pitcher, Pidgeon was a practitioner of the pre–Creighton style, tossing the ball to the plate in a "fair" manner, and he strove to be fair in all matters. "What a genial old fellow he was," proclaimed a writer after his death, "and what an enthusiastic admirer of the game. Then, too, he was integrity itself."[49]

Pidgeon, surprisingly, was known for grumbling on the field and, despite his gentlemanly demeanor, was a fierce competitor, exactly the kind of ballplayer Chadwick admired. He was also exceedingly loyal to his Eckfords. During the winter between the 1859 and 1860 seasons, at about the same time Creighton and Flanly left the Stars for the Excelsiors, it was rumored that Pidgeon had joined the Atlantics. He issued an angry denial, stating, "All the true and tried, all who love old times, old acquaintances and old friends, will stand by the club they have belonged to and gained their reputation in."[50]

Pidgeon, like Alexander Cartwright, was a man of multiple talents. Born in 1825, he was a shipbuilder, an entrepreneur, an inventor (he conceived the only successful steam traction plow and a machine for making thimbles), a musician and a painter. Like Cartwright, Pidgeon went to California in 1849 in search of gold. Unlike the old Knickerbocker, however, Pidgeon went by way of Cape Horn, and also unlike Cartwright, he came back to New York. He later visited San Francisco, but again returned to the New York area.

Pidgeon suffered an accident which ended his playing career prematurely in 1863 and left him with a severe limp, but he remained active as an avid defender of amateurism (see Appendix A) and all the old time values associated with baseball of the 1850s. In 1857, he had served on the committee that drafted the first comprehensive set of baseball rules, and at times Pidgeon seemed forever anchored to that decade.[51] At the tumultuous convention of 1870, Pidgeon, in amateurism's last stand, gave an impassioned speech in support of the resolution banning professionals, arguing that paying players gave an unfair advantage to wealthy clubs.[52] When professionalism took root in his old club, Pidgeon disassociated himself from the Eckfords in protest, faded from view and was no longer prominent in baseball circles.

Pidgeon was quite active, however, in the New York construction industry, and he completed a number of government contracts before falling on difficult times. In 1881, he was forced to file for bankruptcy and lost his expensive homestead. Three years later, Pidgeon, then 60 years old, was supervising sewer work on the Astor property near the Harlem River, and, while walking on a stretch of railroad track between High Bridge and the bridge of the Northern Railroad, was struck and killed by an oncoming train.[53] Pidgeon's death was described as an unfortunate accident, caused in part by the fact that his game leg had prevented him from avoiding the train. Some historians, including Trey Strecker, believe the old Eckford's death may have been a suicide. Pidgeon had suffered severe business reverses, lost his fortune and seemed to have sufficient reasons to end his life. He was facing the oncoming train as it approached him, walking with his head down, and ignored the whistle and warning shouts of the crew. Could he possibly have been so distracted that he failed to notice them? It seems unlikely.[54]

When the 1862 season ended, Pidgeon's Eckfords were the champions, and the records of the top clubs were as follows:

Eckford	14–2
Excelsior	4–1–1
Gotham	6–3
Mutual	8–5
Atlantic	2–3

Source: Wright

The Atlantics played just five games and won only two, losing to the up-and-coming Mutuals as well as their two losses to the Eckfords. Despite their poor record, however, had the Atlantics beaten the Eckfords in the final match, they would have retained the championship. The concept of starting the season even and awarding the crown to the team with the most wins or the highest winning percentage would not be accepted until the formation of the professional National Association in 1871.

The Mutuals, who were a contender for the title, defeated the Atlantics shortly after the latter club lost to the Eckfords, so the victory brought the Mutuals no closer to the championship since the Atlantics had been dethroned and the Mutuals now had to chase the Eckfords. They played them twice, losing 28–24 and 28–14.

For the first time, baseball had a champion other than the Atlantics, which boded well for the spirit of competition. Uncertainty is what makes any sport exciting, and 1862 had clearly brought some surprises. "Who would have thought," asked the *Eagle*, "the famed Excelsior would be defeated by the Union club? That the Atlantic would be deprived of the championship by its old ally the Eckford?"[55]

The Excelsiors may have been "famed," but they were not the Excelsiors of 1860 although some papers still referred to them as the "Champion Club."[56] While they may not have been champions, at least they were not the inactive club of 1861. The Excelsiors played six games, including two in Boston, wining four, tying one and losing one. True to their word, they did not compete for the championship, nor was it likely they could have. "The Excelsiors," the *Eagle* reported, "have now come to be regarded as a half dead club."[57] The following season, the Excelsiors were even less active, and the *Eagle* noted, "[I]t appears the Excelsiors have gone to sleep again for their ground is nearly deserted now, even the muffins being to [*sic*] sleepy too [*sic*] turn out."[58]

Never again would the Brooklyn club reach the heights to which it had ascended in 1860, their one shining moment of glory. The match with the Atlantics had not been a watershed event, as so many had feared, for baseball, but it had been for the Excelsiors. Rather than moving forward, the Brooklyn club journeyed backward, playing the Knickerbockers in matches that were reminiscent of the games of the late '50s, filled with jokes, cheering and errors, and followed by dinners and speeches. Although they remained in existence for a number of years, the Excelsiors competed with the Knickerbockers for lager and chowder, rather than against the Eckfords and Atlantics for championships.

Perhaps the most momentous event of 1862 occurred on October 18 when Jim Creighton, the great Excelsior pitcher, died at the age of 21 at his father's house on Henry Street in Brooklyn. A giant monument was erected to his memory, and he was laid to rest in Green-Wood Cemetery where he lies with such diverse luminaries as Samuel Morse, Horace Greeley, Joey Gallo and Henry Chadwick.

How and when Creighton suffered his fatal injury is the subject of much conjecture. For years, the accepted story was that Creighton ruptured himself while running out a home run in a game against the Unions of Morrisania, collapsing into the arms of his teammates as he crossed home plate. That story took hold despite the fact that, not long after the pitcher's death, it was duly reported that he had received his mortal injury while playing in a cricket match for the St. George Club against the Willow Club. At the National Association convention, Dr. Jones, President of the Excelsiors, stated in an address to the delegates that, contrary to reports that had been circulating about his dramatic death after hitting a home run, Creighton had been injured in a cricket match rather than a baseball game. Yet the baseball version of the story persisted for more than a century.

Was it cricket or baseball that sent Creighton to his grave? The baseball story is such a wonderful way for a hero to die that it doesn't seem likely that the cricket explanation was contrived. Historian John Thorn thinks it might have been, however, for perhaps the Excelsiors didn't want people to think that baseball was a dangerous sport. Better to place the blame on cricket.[59] Andrew Schiff has a third theory; Creighton was first injured playing cricket and aggravated the injury in the baseball game.[60]

Yet, there is so much evidence in support of the "death by cricket" theory that it is hard to ignore. Cricket professional Henry Sharp wrote of Creighton's death in *Wilkes' Spirit of the Times* and repeated the assertion that the fatal injury occurred during the St. George vs. Willow match. Sharp also shared his sentiment that "in the great innings of life, that we all pray, however 'well in' we may be, none of us can keep the grim bowler, Death, from our wicket."[61]

In any event, whether he died playing cricket or while hitting a home run, Creighton's fatal injury, now believed to be a ruptured inguinal hernia,[62] sent him into a test match with St. Peter and catapulted him instantly into baseball immortality. Any pitcher who showed promise would henceforth be referred to as "another Creighton." As the years went by, Creighton's pitches became faster and his feats more gargantuan. In life, he was a very good pitcher. In death, he became a legend, struck down in his prime and never to be subject to the inevitable decline of the living.

Generally, those who suffer a tragic death are extolled, all faults are forgiven and all earthly flaws forgotten. Creighton was no exception. "As a base ball player," the *Clipper* eulogized, "Creighton had no equal."[63] Nor did he as a cricketer, according to the tribute written by Sharp five months after Creighton's death. "[W]e can bear testimony," Sharp wrote,

Opposite: Jim Creighton pitched just one complete season but revolutionized the art of pitching. He threw fast and accurately, and the battery of Creighton and Joe Leggett led the Excelsiors to a great season in 1860. Creighton was also an excellent cricketer, and his tragic death at the age of 21 assured him a place among baseball's immortals.

JAMES CREIGHTON,
Pitcher of the Excelsior Base Ball Club of Brooklyn, N. Y.

"to the high esteem in which he was held by all who came in contact with him, either in the cricket-field or in social intercourse, his quiet, unassuming manners and demeanor being in strong contrast to his great and unquestionable ability both as bat and bowler and, but for his untimely end, he would have taken — and that speedily — the most prominent position among the leading cricketers of America."[64] Sharp went on to list the details of each of the 22 matches Creighton played in from 1860 through his death in 1862, concluding with the fateful St. George vs. Willow contest.

Shortly after Creighton's death, the Excelsiors drafted a resolution praising the late pitcher and extolling his virtues. "Possessing an amiable disposition," said *Wilkes'*, "a quiet and unobtrusive manner — and a genial and warm heart — he was indeed a young man to make himself beloved by all with whom he came in contact."[65]

When separated from his legend, how good a pitcher was Jim Creighton? He played only one complete season, the magnificent summer of 1860, during which he pitched 20 games. In 1859 with the Stars, he played the infield part of the time and pitched in just six games. In 1861, the Excelsiors did not play any games, relegating Creighton's activity to the cricket ground and the October Brooklyn-New York picked nine match. The next year, Creighton's final season, the Excelsiors played just six games before Creighton died in the middle of October. Thus, in his entire career, he pitched a total of only 32 games. Virtually his entire reputation was established in 1860 when the Excelsior Club undertook its ground-breaking travels to upstate New York, Baltimore and Philadelphia.

Pitching statistics for the years Creighton pitched are very rudimentary. One can determine how many runs a pitcher surrendered, which was generally many, and little else. In 1860, the Excelsiors, with Creighton doing virtually all of the pitching, gave up 7.95 runs per game. That's not very good by twentieth and twenty-first century standards, but not bad for 1860. The Eckfords surrendered an average of 14.24 runs in their 17 games and the Atlantics 13.38 in 16 games. The number of runs surrendered by a pitcher was often, as well as an indication of his ability, a function of the batting skill of his opponents, the fielding ability of his teammates and the talents of his catcher. Creighton clearly owed a great deal to Leggett. One day in 1862, when the catcher's hands became sore and swollen, Creighton was forced to slacken his pace and gave up nine runs in one inning.[66]

Batting skill was very uneven, and many low-scoring games came at the expense of greatly inferior clubs, such as the ones the Excelsiors encountered on their tour. During his fine 1860 season, Creighton held the St. George Cricket Club scoreless, limited the Flour City Club of Rochester to a single run, and he gave up only four runs to a picked nine from Philadelphia, many of whom were playing their first season of baseball.

Further, the Excelsiors were among the most skillful fielders of their time, and Leggett was the best catcher. "It is entirely unnecessary," said the *Atlas* after an 1860 game with the Independent Club, "to criticize the fielding of the Excelsiors, as it is always good."[67] Creighton clearly allowed significantly fewer runs than his contemporaries, but comparison is difficult at best, and any claim of immortality cannot be made based upon statistics.

Creighton's contribution to the game of baseball lay in the fact that he changed the art of pitching forever. Baseball had inherited the guiding principles of the ball games that preceded it, which established the role of the pitcher as the man who put the ball in play so that the batter could hit it. In the cat games, the ball had been sent into play by a catapult, and the pitcher in other games was the flesh and bones version of the cat.

Creighton was not the only pitcher to try to throw the ball in a manner that made it difficult to hit squarely, nor was he the first to employ swift pitching, but he was the most effective. Others were wild, or they didn't have a catcher like Joe Leggett who could handle fast pitching. Creighton didn't strike out many opponents and rarely got them to swing and miss, but batters didn't often hit the ball squarely. A foul tip frequently occurred when the hitter didn't hit the ball solidly, and a tip caught on the fly or the first bound was an out.

The combination of Creighton's inclinations, his ability, favorable rules (no called balls and foul tips caught on the bound counting as an out) and his advantageous situation in terms of catching and fielding made him the only one capable of revolutionizing the art of pitching.

Creighton never threw a curve, and his pitching bears no resemblance to that of modern day hurlers, but his impact on the game was the popularization of a philosophical change from letting the batter hit the ball to trying to make him miss, and his effectiveness in doing so. Others had tried before Creighton, but none achieved the same degree of success. Creighton set baseball upon a path that was irreversible, and, by the 1870s, virtually every pitcher was throwing hard. Some had begun to experiment with a curve ball and other trick pitches. By the 1880s, when overhand pitching was legalized, the groundwork for modern pitching was in place.

In 1864, two years after Creighton's death, the National Association instituted rule changes intended to negate the advantage of swift pitching. There was no escaping the revolution, however, for there had been a change in strategy that was beyond the scope of the regulations. When the rules committee tried to limit the pitchers' impact, hurlers found ways to overcome the disadvantage. The pitcher was no longer the passive "feeder" of the old games. He was a defensive weapon.

Although there had been more activity in 1862 than during the previous summer, the war still put limits on sporting affairs. "Although for a time," reported the *Clipper* in September, "there was a prospect of a revival in sporting matters, yet the fresh call made by the President for troops has interfered with many outside recreations. Once the war is over, we may look for an avalanche of recruits for our army of sports, for the campaign in Virginia and elsewhere has made many converts to our creed."[68]

Although the winter of 1862 was not a good one for Union military fortunes, baseball reared its head again in the spring of 1863. "Although the past season has been one of gloom and despondency," *Wilkes'* noted, "rather than one of joyful merriment and recreation, we are pleased to note that the young men composing our various base-ball organizations have gallantly stood by their noble pastime, and have not permitted even an adverse tide to cripple or stay the growth and prosperity of their favorite sport."[69] While Frank Queen of the *Clipper* was trying to shame young men into enlisting, *Wilkes'* praised their courage for standing by baseball during the national emergency and predicted the greatest season in the history of the sport.

The Eckford Club, which had wrested the championship from the Atlantics in 1862, defended their crown rather easily, beating back the challenge of the Atlantics by defeating them, 31–10 and 21–11. For the second game, played on the Eckfords' grounds on September 8, the crowd was estimated at eight thousand, one of the largest gatherings of the wartime era.[70] The match consumed four hours and was called by darkness after eight innings had been completed. The Eckfords played ten games during the summer and won them all, never facing a third and deciding game with any club. They beat the only other contender, the Mutuals,

10–9 and 18–10. The Eckfords also defeated the Resolutes and the tough Unions of Morrisania twice each.

The Atlantics were 8–3, losing to the Mutuals in addition to the two defeats inflicted by the Eckfords. The Mutual game, decided when the New York club scored nine times in the ninth inning for a 27–26 victory, was marred by unpleasant feelings between the two clubs, including frequent chaffing between the players and an attempt by the Atlantics to stall and have the game called due to darkness. The third out was finally made when Mutual catcher William Wansley, later a participant along with Tom Devyr in the first documented instance of players throwing a game for money, swung and missed three pitches intentionally. Pearce, catching for the Atlantics, purposely let the ball pass him. Wansley began to walk around the bases, waiting for someone to tag him. Finally, Charley Smith applied the tag and the game was over.[71]

The Mutuals, backed by Tammany Hall politicians and led by fiery captain and outfielder Billy McMahon, were known for their strong batting and unimpressive fielding. They finished the year 10–4. The remaining teams played each other without any real hope of challenging for the championship. The Athletics of Philadelphia visited New York in June and played six games in as many days, winning two. They then took a lengthy hiatus, not playing an interclub match from June 20 until September 4. For the season, they won seven of twelve games.

The Champion Club of New York made perhaps the most ambitious journey of the war era, traveling to Lowell, Massachusetts, to play the Union Club, then west to Schenectady, New York, and north to Buffalo. The three games were played on consecutive days, demonstrating the efficiency of the northeast rail system.

The prewar era had ended with the Excelsiors, Atlantics and Jim Creighton atop the baseball world. The third year of the war saw a new champion, new heroes, and a fresh start.

CHAPTER 17

The Evils of Championship Play, 1864

By the time the 1864 season began, it was apparent that the Union would win the war, and after playing three seasons under wartime conditions, it was also evident that baseball would survive the conflict. The *Eagle,* noting some large crowds that had appeared to watch games during the previous three summers, was optimistic, noting that, "for the past three seasons, base ball has had to contend with obstacles, resulting from the war, that would have entirely destroyed a less objectionable and less popular sport. Under these circumstances, it must be confessed by the most despondent that the game has flourished to an extent that its most sanguine friends could not have expected."[1]

Still, activity had never approached the level of 1860. At the end of the 1863 season, one paper scolded the clubs for the paucity of matches, urging them "to play at least five games between May and November. One game a month is little enough for a club to play."[2]

At a special May meeting of the NA, the number of delegates in attendance was three short of a quorum.[3] Those delegates who did appear accomplished little. Only one member of each of three committees was present. P.J. Cozans of the Eagles, representing the Committee on Incorporation, reported that, since the NA was neither a scientific, religious nor moral organization, it could only be incorporated by the legislature during its next session. Cozan's committee was therefore dissolved.

J. Seaver Page, of the committee appointed to examine books, papers and credentials, reported that the recording secretary had not delivered the documents he had promised, and therefore the committee was unable to perform its task. Action was deferred to the next annual convention. A few relatively unimportant issues were dealt with, after which Cozans, preaching to the assembled choir, stressed the importance of clubs sending delegates to the meetings and acting in the interest of the Association rather than just their own clubs.

Like the convention, baseball was stagnant, but still, the *Clipper* anticipated the greatest season since 1860. The Atlantics, about to begin playing in the newly constructed Capitoline Grounds, looked forward to winning back the championship.

For several years, the Capitoline Association of Brooklyn had organized various outdoor and indoor sports, as well as social activities. The club took its name from the Roman Capitoline Games, which were in turn named for the pagan god *Jupiter Capitolorus*. The club's combination of baseball, cricket, literary readings and social events merged the physical and intellectual in a manner similar to that enjoyed by the ancient Romans.

One of the winter activities of the Capitolines was skating on their enclosed ten acre pond.[4] In the spring of 1863, the *Eagle* reported that the Capitoline Skating Pond would be drained and used for baseball,[5] but the conversion did not take place until the following year, with the new park opening on May 5. Even then, there were many improvements that remained undone, including seating for the ladies, but they were added gradually over the next year. The Capitoline Grounds, located in the Bedford area of Brooklyn between Marcy, Nostrand, Putnam and Halsey Avenues,[6] were, along with the Union Grounds, two of the best fields in the New York area. As at Union, admission fees would be charged to pay for the maintenance of the facility. The principal tenants would be the Atlantic and Enterprise Clubs.[7]

One of the main advantages of playing in an enclosed ground, of course, was the ability to exclude undesirables and maintain order. As a further inducement to a calm environment, liquor and gambling were forbidden at Capitoline.[8] Occupancy of the new facility would provide the Atlantics with the opportunity to prove their assertion that they could control their more rambunctious followers if given a fair chance.

The 1864 season began later than usual, with the eager Stars, of course, leading the way.[9] The first game didn't take place until June 11, which was even later than in 1861. Although Brooklyn was the most active city in baseball circles, no games were played there until the end of June. Chadwick became impatient with the lack of activity. "Here we are," he chafed, "near the middle of July, and only two of the six principal clubs of Brooklyn have been engaged in matches yet."[10]

There were a number of "picked nine prize games," also called "Union Games," early in the 1864 season. Prizes were awarded to the best players, but without the partisanship associated with interclub matches, more sporting behavior was expected. Chadwick, disgusted with the gambling, disturbances and unsportsmanlike conduct that plagued championship contests, had been a driving force behind the prize games. He believed that, with little at stake other than pride, the matches would provide a return to the good times of the 1850s.[11]

The object of the Union games was not realized. "Unfortunately," wrote Chadwick, "there are too many individuals in the ball playing community who never can see anything in its proper light that is not immediately connected with their own pet club, and it is this over-jealous and selfish minority who are the chief promoters of all the jealousy and ill-feeling that exists between members of rival organizations."[12]

There were other problems. The Atlantics, who hosted one of the affairs, refused to play the fly game, which had previously been agreed upon, and insisted upon controlling the manner in which the match was conducted.[13] So much for nonpartisan spirit. Chadwick was disgusted. He said only the Stars and Eckfords had supported his efforts and wanted no further part of the entire business. "It being of no personal benefit to us," he huffed, "we have dropped these prize games entirely, and henceforth those who wish them must get them up for themselves."[14] The 1850s were gone, and despite the good example set by the Excelsiors and Knickerbockers, competition, healthy or not, was with us forever.

Despite the lack of success of the Union games among senior organizations, the junior clubs decided to follow suit. After his experiences with the senior prize games, Chadwick was only too happy to tell the juniors to make the arrangements themselves. "[W]e desire to have nothing to do with any more prize games," he declared.[15] The junior games were not just an opportunity for the players to collect prizes for their performances. The senior organizations were watching, and the best players in the prize games would have the opportunity to join those clubs.

After their undefeated season of 1863, Chadwick speculated that, since the Eckfords could not improve upon their undefeated season, they might consider bowing out of championship competition.[16] The Atlantics appeared to have an excellent chance of dethroning the Eckfords, who were much weaker in 1864 than they had been the two previous seasons. Pitcher Joe Sprague defected to the Atlantics and eventually left baseball to concentrate on cricket.[17] Catcher Waddy Beach was involved in a brutal fist fight with a fireman in the early morning hours one Sunday in January 1864 and was badly injured.[18] Later, he left New York for Tennessee and did not return until August.[19] Tom Devyr and Ed Duffy, the shortstop and third baseman, joined the Mutuals.

The 1863 champions were strengthened by the addition of several new players, a number of whom would later achieve some degree of renown, such as Charley Mills and Wes Fisler, but the massive turnover made it unlikely that they could retain their laurels. With so many of their top players gone, the Eckfords didn't take the field until most of the other clubs had been practicing for several weeks. They did not play an opposing club until late July. In early August the *Eagle* lamented, "What are the champions about? They keep pretty quiet now-a-days."[20] Chadwick suggested the club needed the old time inspiration provided by Frank Pidgeon. "We can almost imagine him," he wrote, "telling the boys to practice well together, make the best efforts they can to win, and to go in and play a fair, manly game, win or lose."[21] "What is the occasion of the lassitude that seems to have come over the club," Chadwick asked later. "Truly Frank Pigeon [sic] or some energetic successor is needed at the Eckford helm, for they appear to be drifting on a lee shore very rapidly at present."[22]

The Eckfords failed to answer the challenge of the Atlantics and played but four games all season, winning just one of them. They even lost to the Eagles, who hadn't been taken seriously by anyone in years. With the Eckfords out of the championship picture, the race fell to the Atlantics and Mutuals.

By the end of the season, the Atlantics left no doubt as to the identity of the best club in the New York area. The Brooklyn team still had difficulty getting their best nine players on the field at the same time, but their substitutes were often better than the opponents' first nine. When the young stars didn't appear, the old veterans of 1860 and 1861 took their places. As they had done in the early 1860s with the addition of the young players from the Enterprise Club, the Atlantics continually added fresh talent to the nine. They were a dynasty from 1857 through 1870, but with a continually changing cast — a rare accomplishment for a sports team.

In 1864, the Atlantics' most important addition was Tom Pratt, the excellent young pitcher of the Athletics, who replaced Mattie O'Brien.[23] Pratt pitched in 20 games, and posted a 19–0 record. During the season, the Atlantics played 21 games, far more than any club had played during the previous three years, and won 20 of them, the lone blemish on their record being a 13–13 tie with the Empire Club on June 30 in a game that was halted after five innings due to a rainstorm.

The tie game was the first time the Atlantics and Empires had played each other since 1856, and the good sportsmanship that prevailed indicated that the rupture that had kept them apart had healed. The previous year, the Atlantics, who were making efforts to improve the negative image they had established by the Excelsior debacle in 1860 and other incidents, mended a rift with the Mutuals, playing a cordial game, the proceeds from which were given to Harry Wright. Although the Mutual fans, who were nearly as raucous as the Atlantic followers, taunted the Brooklyn club throughout the match, the players got on well and relations were restored.

The Atlantics, of course, did not play the Eckfords, with whom they had maintained a chilly relationship since the 1862 season. After the first Eckford victory that year, the Atlantics had committed the mortal sin of failing to cheer their conquerors, and had not partaken in the time-honored ritual of presenting the game ball. The Eckfords took umbrage, and the situation was exacerbated when there was an unpleasant scene during one of the games between the two clubs in 1863.[24]

The Eckfords and Atlantics notwithstanding, one of the highlights of 1864 was the reconciliation of a number of clubs that had been estranged for years. The Atlantics, in addition to the Empire game, played against the gentlemanly old Eagles, whom they had never met before. They played the Gothams and even challenged the Excelsiors, whom they had not met on the field since that infamous August day in 1860. The Excelsiors did not respond.

The new, friendly Atlantics even played the fly game, to which they had been adamantly opposed for years. Playing in an enclosed ground for the first time, the Atlantics were prepared to show other clubs they could control their gambling supporters as capably as more well-mannered clubs. "Admission to [Capitoline]," noted the *Eagle*, "is only secured on condition of proper conduct, and this is the one great advantage of enclosed ball grounds, and it is well worth twice the fee charged for admission to enjoy a game witnessed by an orderly and respectable assemblage."[25]

The Mutuals played even more often than the Atlantics, and won 20 while losing just 3. Unfortunately for the Mutuals, two of the losses were to the Atlantics, which cost them an opportunity to win the championship. On June 27, the Atlantics beat the Mutuals easily, 26–16, paced by veteran Peter O'Brien's fine play. The second game of the series did not take place until September 12, when the Atlantics won again, by the score of 21–15. The second victory clinched the season's series, and with the Eckfords declining to accept the Atlantics' challenge, gave the 1864 championship to the Brooklyn club.

"The contestants in base ball circles for the questionable honors of the Championship," reported the *Clipper*, "have gradually decreased season after season, until this year the number is confined to two clubs only, the Atlantics of Brooklyn and the Mutuals of New York."[26] The *Clipper* commented unfavorably upon the factors that surrounded the decline, including the monopolization of talent by the leading clubs and the reported distaste with which many clubs regarded the quest for the championship. The Mutuals and Atlantics, they claimed, had 20 first-class men each, which prevented other clubs from employing players good enough to beat them. Chadwick advocated that clubs follow the example of the Excelsiors, who declined to participate in any championship matches.[27] "[T]he unfriendly feelings engendered thereby in these championship contests," he wrote, "was beginning to lead every well wisher of the game to see them put a stop to."[28] "It is on this account," he added several months later, "that we have regarded it as advantageous to the best interests of the game to give as little prominency to the series of contests for the championship in base ball as we possibly could."[29]

The previous year (1863) after an unpleasant match between the Mutuals and Atlantics, a paper commented, "The discreditable scenes that took place towards the close of the game leads us to hope that this will be the last season that any of these championship games are played. It is unquestionably for the best interests of the game that matches for the championship,

17. The Evils of Championship Play, 1864

The 1864 Mutual Club of New York. John Wildey, coroner of the City of New York and president of the Mutuals, stands in the center of the back row in the dark suit. To his immediate right is catcher William Wansley, who was implicated in baseball's first scandal. Wansley was involved in fixing a game against the Eckfords, as was Tom Devyr, sixth from right. Devyr was the shortstop for the Eckfords, champions of 1862 and 1863, but defected to the Mutuals in 1864. Anson B. Taylor, one the stalwarts of the Mutuals during their early years, is seated directly in front of Wansley.

with the title of champion, should be entirely done away with, and the sooner the leading men in the fraternity frown this class of matches down the better."[30]

Even in areas far from New York where the value of the title was dubious, clubs bickered over which was entitled to claim local championships. Michigan witnessed a bitter war of words between the Daybreak and Jackson Clubs in 1863, a battle eventually won on the playing field by the Daybreaks.[31]

Although the Mutuals and Atlantics were the only serious contenders for the New York championship, a number of other clubs played well. The Excelsiors, still weakened by the war and the death of their star pitcher, were 8–3, but lost twice to the Mutuals, the only strong club they encountered. There were different players in almost every game, as the club had severe difficulty getting their first nine up to scratch. In Asa Brainard, who became a star with the 1869 Red Stockings, the Excelsiors had a fine pitcher, but he was not Jim Creighton. Joe Leggett returned from the Army, but he was not the old Joe Leggett. "He must remember," the *Clipper* said in 1863, "that he is not nor will ever be again the Leggett of 1860, when he touched the highest point of the ladder. He has been descending since then, and though still a good player, he is not A No. 1 now, his inability to throw weakening his play exceedingly."[32]

During the winter between the 1863 and 1864 seasons, Leggett suffered a broken leg and, although he returned to the field occasionally in 1864, his days as a top player were over.[33] He played just twice in 1865, but returned to regular action in 1866, which was his final season as a ballplayer.[34] After his playing days ended, Leggett suffered some business reverses and fell upon hard times. In an article written in 1889, Chadwick related the whereabouts of many old ballplayers, stating only of Leggett: "Well, I will be silent for old times' sake."[35]

The departure of Leggett from the scene was a loss to the game, not just for his playing ability, but also for the leadership he provided to his team. In October 1863, in his absence, an incident occurred during an Excelsior game with the Nassau Club of Princeton, the likes of which had never taken place under Leggett. As darkness approached, the Excelsiors squandered a lead and were trailing. The club, "becoming excited by the fact of having the victory taken from their hands when almost secured, and also through the effect of sundry attentions to a pail of claret punch, indiscreetly placed at the disposal of the players, forgot the teachings of their worthy Captain Leggett," and began to stall, hoping the game would be called and the score would revert to the previous inning. Pitcher Brainard threw wild pitches, and his fielders disdained to put out the Nassaus. Chadwick was always incensed by such behavior and horrified that it came from his beloved Excelsiors, the men who had abandoned the opportunity for the championship in favor of honor. "Had Leggett been present," he wrote, "no such actions as took place would have been permitted." The absence of alcohol would have helped as well, Chadwick admitted.[36]

In 1864, the Excelsiors, as they had the previous two seasons, started languidly, not playing their first match until mid-July. Although their record was good, they played mostly against second rate competition. When the Excelsiors played clubs like the Knickerbockers, it was as if it were 1858 again. The men cheered each other, never exchanged a harsh word during the match and repaired to a sumptuous meal afterward. Perhaps the highlight of the Excelsiors' year came on December 8 when they invited the Knickerbockers to a festive dinner to celebrate the tenth anniversary of the formation of the club.[37] It had been a most eventful decade during which the baseball world had inalterably changed.

One of the best clubs in New Jersey was the Eurekas of Newark. In 1860, the *Times* said that the only club better than the Eurekas was the Excelsiors.[38] The New Jersey nine had the distinction of being known as one of the finest fielding clubs in the New York area, a quality that greatly endeared them to the scientific Chadwick. "The Eurekas aim at perfection in fielding," he wrote in 1864, "that being alone the criterion of skillful play, for any country club of stout built farmers can play a batting game with the best in the city."[39]

In 1863, the Eurekas lost to the Atlantics by just one run, and in September of that year journeyed to Philadelphia, where they played very well, beating the Keystones and leading the powerful Athletics before the game was rained out. Perhaps the best player on the Eureka nine was their captain, a left-handed shortstop named Charlie Thomas, who was a teller at one of the leading New York banks. Thomas was the epitome of the old time ballplayer, skilled, gracious and sociable.[40]

Another New Jersey club, the Irvington nine, was also beginning to play good ball. The Irvingtons began their existence as a junior club, but as the players matured, they became a senior organization and began to compete with the top clubs. They had a star player in Andy Leonard, who joined the Red Stockings for their triumphant 1869 campaign, and also featured the Campbells, Hugh and Mike, a top pitcher and first baseman, respectively. By 1866, the club would be one of the best in the New York area.

There were a number of clubs from outside the immediate vicinity of New York City that showed impressive results. The Athletics of Philadelphia won eight of nine games, and baseball in Washington and Baltimore was still alive, even as war raged not far across the Potomac. The Nationals and Unions of Washington and Pastimes of Baltimore played each other as well as nines within their own cities. Many members of the Nationals were employed by the Treasury Department, and the club played its games on the President's grounds behind the White House, an excellent site that was enclosed by a fence and shaded by tall trees. The Pastimes, Baltimore's best team, were generally considered the champion of the South.

By the end of 1864, baseball was not only the national game of America, it had been adopted north of the border as well. There were scattered reports of various games of "ball" played throughout Canada as early as the 1830s, but they were so vague it was impossible to tell what kind of games they were. The most credible report was of a game played in Beachville, Ontario, on June 4, 1838.[41] The information on the game was provided by Dr. Adam Ford in 1886 in a scenario eerily prescient of Abner Graves. Ford, like Graves, had relocated to Colorado, leaving Canada after being accused of poisoning a temperance leader in Ontario. Also like Graves, Ford was but seven or eight years old at the time he witnessed the first game.[42] Unlike the claim of Graves, however, that of Ford has some adherents, for he provided a significant amount of detail, including the dimensions of the field and the names of several of the players, some of which could be corroborated. Ford's game took place, coincidentally, one year before the game described two decades later by Graves.

David Block evaluated Ford's tale and opined that it could be true — or it might not be. There were some obvious defects in the claims of Abner Graves, the principal one being that the future General Doubleday wasn't in Cooperstown at the time Graves had him inventing the game. There were no "smoking guns" in Ford's tale — nothing that could definitively prove it false. On the other hand, there was no credible second witness to confirm what Ford had said fifty years after the fact.[43]

The game played in Canada in the 1850s was similar to the Massachusetts version of baseball. There were eleven players to a side, with a fourth baseman and second catcher added to the nine provided for in the New York rules. Pitchers were allowed to throw overhand, and an inning was not over until all eleven men had been retired.

By the late 1850s, teams had been organized in Hamilton (1854) and London (1855),[44] but the growth of the game truly began with the formation of the Young Canadian Club, of Woodstock, Ontario, in 1860.[45] The Young Canadians, who began their existence playing the Canadian brand of baseball, switched to the New York game and, in 1862, adopted the fly game for their practice matches. They claimed to be the best club in Canada, but in 1860, when they crossed the border to play the Niagara Club of Buffalo, they discovered that the best club in Canada was far from a match for a so-so club from the United States, as they were defeated, 87–13.[46] Two years later, the Canadians ventured to Detroit, where they beat the Brother Jonathan Club, and over the next two years, they played a number of games without losing one, thus becoming the unofficial champions of Canada. The club offered the traditional silver ball to any opponent that could wrest the championship from them.

In 1859, the first known game under New York rules had been played in Canada, and, one by one, virtually all clubs abandoned the Canadian version. By 1861, there were a number of Canadian clubs, and by 1864, there were enough to form an association. That same year, the champions of Canada challenged the champions of the United States, the Atlantics. The game took place at Rochester, on September 22, during the state fair. The Canadian champions were no match for the Atlantics, and fell behind, 26–1, after two innings. The final score was 75–11. A Canadian team would not be the champions of baseball until 1992.

Meanwhile, back in New York, a few players who would later become stars debuted toward the end of the war years. Bob Ferguson, captain of the fabled Atlantics of the late '60s, and a fixture in baseball as player, captain and umpire through the 1880s, played with the junior Frontier Club in 1864. His talent caused him to move very quickly to the senior ranks with the Enterprise nine. Ferguson was selected captain of the junior all-star team in the 1864 prize game series and also acted as umpire in games in which he was not a participant. As was obligatory for all promising young players, he was compared to Creighton. Dave Birdsall, a stalwart of the champion Union Club of 1867 and a player for the Boston Red Stockings of the National Association, also made his initial appearance during the early '60s.

Many clubs that had flourished in the 1850s and early 1860s had, by 1864, become insignificant, at least in a competitive sense. The Putnams had combined with the Brooklyn Club in 1862.[47] The Resolutes were 3–11 and had difficulty getting their first nine on the field. The Stars were 3–4 and the Enterprise appeared only rarely. In their early years, the young Stars had been unable to get teams to play them because they were too good. Now, they couldn't get anyone to answer their challenges because they were too weak.[48]

The Eagles were just 3–6. "The Eagles," reported the *Clipper*, "are going in for fun this year, and will be having 'a real jolly time of it, you know.'"[49] Fun would have to substitute for success, for the previous year they won only one of five games. The Henry Eckford Club (not to be confused with the Eckfords), which was founded in 1859 by a few disgruntled members of the Eckfords,[50] folded after the 1863 campaign and merged with the Empires, another old line organization that was no longer competitive.[51] During the war, many of the Empire stalwarts left the club to join other organizations, which led the *Times* to refer to them in 1862 as "the once famous Empires."[52] The Empires were not terribly successful in 1864, but they were extremely busy, playing 22 times (7–13–2). The Knickerbockers made not the slightest pretense of competing with the Atlantics, Eckfords or Mutuals. They barely even met for field practice in 1861 and 1862.[53] In 1864, *Wilkes'* declared, "The veteran organization keep on the even tenor of their way as an exercise club."[54]

Other clubs made a pretense but little else. "We are glad to learn," reported *Wilkes'* in May, 1864, "that the Gotham Club of 'ye olden time' memory are preparing to make a bold effort to regain the prominent position which they once occupied. We remember them well in the days of their Red House playing, when for them to engage in a game was but another name for their winning it."[55] Not only was *Wilkes'* view of the future overly optimistic, their perception of the past was as well, for it was not until the Gothams' fourth year of existence that they won a match (albeit they played very few) and they were 15–21 during the 1850s. Even in 1864, however, the good old days were remembered fondly, if inaccurately.

The period of friendly competition was clearly over, as the top clubs became more desirous of holding the coveted, if empty, championship. Despite the numerous reconciliations that occurred in 1864, there remained a number of unresolved disputes. The Excelsiors and Atlantics had been estranged ever since the tumultuous season of 1860. The Eckfords were feuding with both the Excelsiors and Atlantics, and played neither in 1864. Was competition the cause? The *Clipper* admired the lack of acrimony present at an exhibition between the Star Club and a field nine, and encouraged more such amicable events, rather than the bitter contests for the championship, which so often engendered bad feelings and encouraged heavy gambling.[56]

All in all, the 1864 season fulfilled the promise predicted before the start of the campaign. In the last war season, there were far more games played than in 1861–63, and large crowds came out to see the top clubs in action. *Wilkes'* called the season one of the best ever. "[C]onsidering the state of the country," they opined, "the success has been surprising. It shows conclusively that base-ball is now fully established as the national game of America."[57]

One certain sign that baseball had arrived was a longing for the "good old days." In 1862, *Wilkes'* spoke rapturously of "an awakening of the old *furore* for the game that marked the years 1857–8 and 9."[58] When the Atlantics lost to the Eckfords, the *Mercury* lamented, "several of the 'old-stylers' were among the missing. Price, Hamilton and Boerum had given way to younger flesh and blood and the 'muckle' which on other occasions been so effective, wasn't there."[59]

Of course, 1862 quickly became the good old days, for in 1871, the *New York Times* recalled fondly the honorable state of the game from 1860 to 1866, when clubs played first, second and muffin nine matches, society ladies watched from the sidelines, employers took no exception to players leaving work and there was no betting. They contrasted those idyllic days with "the deplorable state of the game as it stands."[60] A week later, the *Times* decided that 1859 was even better. "Those were the days when baseball was played in its integrity," the paper proclaimed.[61]

In 1895, former player John Morrill claimed that "there is no man today in any position who can excel the players of 20 years back. It is the conditions that have made the averages higher, in which gloves, mitts and smoother grounds are the chief factors."[62] In 1901, Chadwick noted that pitchers didn't work nearly as often as they had in 1875 when most pitched nearly every game and completed the full nine innings.[63] Now, a mere 26 years later, Joe McGinnity worked only 382 innings and was called an iron man.

"[M]en hit as hard, caught as well and threw as accurately and strongly thirty years ago as they do today," claimed Al Reach, many years after he retired. He said catcher Nat Hicks, who played in the '70s, was the equal of any big league catcher of the early twentieth century.[64] "There was more pleasure in ball in those early days," said Joe Start, "than there has been since. Each man was his own boss and did not abuse it."[65]

In order to return to the good old days, Jack Chapman suggested that only the catcher and first baseman be allowed to wear gloves.[66] Former Boston player James Lovett, writing in 1908, decried the sissified use of gloves. "What credit is there," he asked, "in catching a ball in such a trap? ... There is no more call for this mitten in the outfield today than there was forty years ago, as balls are batted there no oftener, no harder and no farther.... *O tempora, O mores!*"[67]

Chadwick, so fond of the old days, deserves credit, however, for realizing that the longing for the past was what psychologists describe as "retrospective bias." In the mid-'70s, he referred to an article lauding the old time players and clubs and declared it evidence that the game had passed the old timers by. There was no doubt, Chadwick declared, that the players of the '70s were younger, stronger, faster and more skilled than their counterparts of twenty years earlier.[68] The old games, while replete with bonhomie, were also filled with errors. The best players of the late '50s, most knowledgeable observers agreed, could not hope to compete with the amateurs of the 1870s.

Despite the enthusiasm shown during the 1864 season, only 34 clubs were represented at the annual convention in December. Seven clubs that had been members the previous year failed to send delegates and were dropped from the rolls. The Hamilton Club had not played since 1861, and the Charter Oak since 1862. The Constellation and Exercise Clubs were also inactive.[69]

During the preceding summer, there had been further disquieting trends. First was the dearth of clubs capable of competing for the championship. With the weakened state of the Eckfords, the Atlantics and Mutuals were head and shoulders above the other New York and Brooklyn clubs. Other than the Athletics, there were no competitive teams beyond the New York area. If baseball were to grow, competition would need to be more even. Despite the numerous concerns, the most positive harbinger at the end of 1864 was the near certainty that the war would soon be over. With the coming of peace, the baseball community hoped to equal or even surpass the glorious season of 1860. They would not be disappointed.

Chapter 18

The Road to Professionalism

The 1864 season was the last played under wartime conditions. By the time the 1865 campaign got underway, the last major military operations had been concluded with General Lee's surrender at Appomattox Court House. The end of the war marked the start of a baseball boom that would bring the sport to all populated areas of the country, and, within six years, result in the formation of the first professional league. Eighteen sixty-five saw more baseball activity than any previous year, far surpassing the landmark 1860 season in both the number of teams that were active and the number of games that were played.

With the exponential growth in activity, the increasing emphasis on winning that had unnerved Chadwick in 1864 was beyond reversing by 1865. Competition between clubs was fierce, and rivalries between cities had emerged now that baseball was being played beyond the confines of New York and Brooklyn. The Athletics of Philadelphia and the Atlantics of Brooklyn staged numerous battles, both on and off the field, in the late 1860s, and when top-flight players began to migrate to the Midwest, Chicago and Cincinnati developed a healthy dislike for each other.

With competition in full swing and the popularity of the sport increasing annually, it was inevitable that professionalism would follow. In 1969, major league baseball celebrated a 100th anniversary, marking the beginning of professionalism from the point at which the 1869 Cincinnati Red Stockings fielded an admittedly all-paid nine. The Red Stockings, following a ruling at the 1868 convention of the National Association that professionalism was legal, made no pretense that they were amateurs. While they were the first avowed professionals, however, the Reds were certainly not the first baseball players who were paid for their services.

Prior to the Civil War, men had been compensated for playing other sports. Cricketers were open about their status as paid performers, and each club generally employed a professional who performed a task similar to that of current golf or tennis club professionals, teaching the game to others. Prize money was sometimes offered to the winner of a cricket match, and admission fees were occasionally charged for walking or running races in order to cover the expenses of the participants.[1] In 1860, the St. George Cricket Club announced that it would charge fees to cover the cost of its grounds.[2]

Speculation as to the identity of the first professional baseball player focused for many years on Al Reach, the infielder who allegedly accepted expense money to leave the Eckfords and play for the Philadelphia Athletics in 1864. Four years earlier, however, Jim Creighton and George Flanly left the young Star Club to join the Excelsiors, and it is now commonly believed that some money changed hands in order to induce the two players, especially

Creighton, to leave the Stars. At the time of the first Atlantic-Excelsior game in 1860, the *Atlas* minimized the accusations that Creighton and perhaps others had been paid. "Malicious rumors," it reported, "were circulated that these men were induced to join the Excelsiors for a 'consideration,' but such reports, of course, could only arise from the envy and jealousy of unsuccessful rivals, and are not worthy of the least credit."[3]

The *Brooklyn Daily Times* thought there was substance to the rumors, and declared, "Though so successful as the [Atlantics] have been, money and influence have at length conquered. The Excelsiors, for the past four years, have been mowing with a powerful scythe among the clubs of Brooklyn, and to-day their nine is composed, principally, of players obtained from the Star Club, five being from that bright luminary, and one from the Atlantic."[4]

There were varying forms of professionalism. The earliest was simply for wealthier club members to pay club dues and expenses for men who were good players but couldn't or didn't want to pay dues. In 1858, this practice was the subject of a sharp exchange between *Porter's Spirit of the Times* and Eckford captain Frank Pidgeon (see Appendix A). Another form of compensation, practiced extensively by the Mutuals, and later the Nationals of Washington, was giving a top player a job, for which he was liberally paid and from which he was generously granted time off for baseball activity. The Atlantics supposedly convinced Athletic pitcher Tom Pratt to join their club by obtaining a political job for him.[5]

A third form of payment, openly practiced in the early 1860s, was the benefit game for which admission fees were charged and the proceeds given to one or more players. On November 7, 1861, friends of Atlantic Dickie Pearce and Excelsior pitcher Creighton arranged such a game after which the admission fees of ten cents per spectator were divided between the two players. The proceeds had initially been intended for Pearce, but the Atlantic shortstop insisted on including his friend Creighton.[6] The weather was chilly, and attendance, both from players who had promised to participate, and spectators, was disappointing. "Indeed," said the *Clipper,* "from the comparatively slim attendance of spectators, we should judge that these benefit matches do not find favor in the ball playing community, free matches being the order of the day among them ... when we ... bring other influences to bear, in which self interest, in a pecuniary point of view, is likely to become prominent, an element is at once introduced that is undoubtedly injurious, in its results, to the best interests of the game."[7]

While the benefit, if not popular, was acceptable, paying a salary, under the rules of the National Association, clearly was not. When admission fees were first charged, the funds were used for the maintenance of the grounds, thus subsidizing clubs indirectly, but in the mid-'60s, clubs began playing for a share of the gate. The funds were used to defray expenses, such as equipment and travel, but little by little, step by step, the sport moved toward paying players for their efforts.

Massachusetts clubs that were not members of the National Association, and thus not bound by its prohibition against playing for money, occasionally offered cash prizes to the winner of a game. In October 1859, the Excelsior Club of Upton, Massachusetts beat the Union Club of Medway and claimed a five hundred dollar prize.[8] The following July, the same Excelsiors offered a purse of one thousand dollars to any New York club that would challenge them to play the Massachusetts game. There were no takers from New York, so the Excelsiors played the Unions once more.[9]

A week after the second Massachusetts prize game, the Knickerbockers of Albany published a resolution against the playing of baseball for money, claiming it would ruin the sport and lead to bad feeling among the clubs, due to the large amounts at stake.[10] One of the troubles with boxing, everyone knew, was the chicanery that often occurred when one party or the other was about to lose, and cost his backers their substantial wagers.

Another form of compensation, admittedly nominal, was awarding prizes, such as balls and bats, to the best players in a game.[11] Occasionally, the award was a cash prize.[12] The value of the gifts was generally five to fifteen dollars, not a significant sum, but compensation nonetheless.[13] In 1864, after a game against the Eckfords, a backer of the Mutuals gave four or five of his club's players prizes, aggregating one hundred dollars, for their performances.[14]

After the Union Grounds opened in 1862, and gate money was being charged on a regular basis, the issue of paid players rose to the forefront. Prior to that time, the only source of paying players was the pockets of the club members, which although often deep were not bottomless. Gate money was much more plentiful, and provided a source for salaries. The initial use of the funds, however, was for proprietor Cammeyer's maintenance of the field, while he allowed the clubs free usage. This was not direct compensation, for while reducing the expenses of the members, the money did not flow directly to the players.

Once gate money was available, rationalization of professionalism quickly followed. Why should wealthy club members be expected to foot the bills, when spectators could just as easily be made to provide the funds to cover costs? After all, the idea was not to make money, but to pay expenses and break even.

By 1864, the *Eagle* was referring to some players as professionals and others as amateurs. What they meant, the paper indicated, was not that the professionals were paid for their services, which would have been in contravention of the rules of the National Association. Professionals, the *Eagle* explained, were those players with a high level of skill, generally the first nines of the top clubs. Amateurs were second nine players and those from second-rate clubs.[15] Clubs distinguished themselves between those whose players were nearly full-time ballplayers and those who had responsible jobs and played only for recreation.[16]

The Athletics lured Al Reach to Philadelphia for the 1865 season with the promise of twenty-five dollars per week in "spending money." Apparently several teams had bid for the Eckford infielder, at least one offering more money than the Athletics, but Reach preferred Philadelphia.[17] He maintained his home in Brooklyn and commuted for the first year of the arrangement before moving to Philadelphia the following year. Reach was the only player, however, whose compensation was common knowledge. If others were being paid, the secret was closely guarded.

As the decade progressed, there were more hints that compensation in some form was being paid, and the prevalence of the tales makes them hard to dismiss. Teams were playing so many games and taking so many tours that it was difficult to believe that top players could actually have the time to hold a full time job other than ballplayer.

Predictably, as surreptitious compensation crept into baseball, disputes over players arose. There were, of course, no written contracts, since paying salaries was illegal, and clubs sometimes had disagreements over the membership of certain players. The first reported dispute over the legitimacy of a player occurred in 1856, long before the rumors of paid players commenced, and prior to the formation of the National Association. The Unions and Knickerbockers objected to S. R. Pinckney playing with the Gothams while he was still a member of the Unions. Pinckney stated that, the previous Tuesday, he had become a member of the Gothams. On that same day, however, he had voted at a meeting of the Union Club.[18] The

NA later enacted a guideline requiring a 60-day waiting period before a player could take part in a match on behalf of a new club. There was no such rule in 1856, however, leaving the press wondering, even if it were legal, was it ethical?

There were similar episodes during the next few years. During a relatively short period of time, Joe Sprague pitched for the Oriental, Exercise and National Clubs.[19] In 1859, the *Clipper* noted that Boyd and Beers of the Pastime Club played against each other in a game between the Enterprise and Powhatan nines, even though they were not members of either club.[20] Often, "revolving" was merely a matter of a club being short a player or two and enlisting one who happened to be on hand. There was no evil intent, but the practice violated the rules of the National Association. Sometimes members of a junior club played with a senior organization and vice versa in the belief that "revolving" was only illegal if it involved two clubs within the NA. If a member of a non–Association club played with an Association club, many thought no harm had been done. Both of these instances, however, were contrary to the rules.[21]

In 1861, a player giving his name as Brown appeared in the lineup of the Free and Easy Club. He was the best hitter on the team and bore a remarkable resemblance to Joe Start of the Enterprise Club. It was, in fact, Start, playing under an assumed name, perhaps the only occasion on which the intrepid first baseman was ever accused of unfair dealings. "A victory obtained under such circumstances," the *Clipper* said, "is never creditable, and a defeat (which the Free and Easy nine suffered by a 28–10 score), as a matter of course, is doubly the reverse." The journal was shocked that the Free and Easy Club, as members of the National Association, could employ such a dodge and that Start, as an honorable player, would agree to it.[22]

One of the most celebrated "revolvers" of the early 1860s was Weston Fisler, the Philadelphia player who later became a stalwart of the strong Athletic nines of the early 1870s. In July and August of 1864, he played for Camden, the Eckfords and the Olympics, although he could hardly have been a member of all three clubs. While such behavior was frowned upon in New York, it was commonplace in Philadelphia. The practice of players of one club playing with another was accepted in cricket, which was, of course, more popular in Philadelphia than in any other American city.

At the annual convention of the Association in December 1861, a delegate asked what could be done if a club violated the rule against playing men who were members of other clubs. It was re-affirmed that if charges were brought against any club for breaking the rule and the allegations were proven, the club would be expelled from the association. Everyone knew that such violations took place, but no one was willing to step forward and proffer charges; therefore the issue remained unresolved.[23]

Finally, at the 1863 Convention, the NA established a Judiciary Committee, which was to pass judgment on any complaint submitted in writing to the Association Secretary. The decision of the committee was binding, subject to being overturned at the next annual meeting by a vote of two thirds of the members.

The formation of a Judiciary Committee was a step in the right direction, but as time would demonstrate, it would not solve the problem of clubs violating the rules. First, any complaint was to be submitted in writing within three days of the alleged violation, a difficult time frame. Second, members of the committee were also delegates of clubs, and self interest rather than justice frequently drove the committee process. As the game expanded beyond New York, regional rivalries pitted clubs against each other, and any complaint brought before the Judiciary Committee was liable to be influenced by regional bias.

During the first four years of the postwar era, the Judiciary Committee and everyone else looked the other way as players were paid *sub rosa*. Finally, in 1868, when everyone connected with the game realized that the pretense of amateurism was a sham, professionalism was made legal. The game had changed, and it would be better to regulate open professionalism than continue to pretend it did not exist. With gate money now a factor, and top clubs playing 40 or 50 games a year, it was impossible to expect that the players of 1868 would be like the Knickerbockers.

With the advent of open professionalism, another problem arose. How would amateurs and professionals coexist within the same association? In the old National Association, each club, whether professional or amateur, and no matter how insignificant, had equal representation. The Atlantics and Eckfords could send three voting delegates as could the most obscure club from Brooklyn, provided the latter had applied for membership and paid its dues. In the mid–'60s, Chadwick pointed out Association members who hadn't played a game in over a year, and he urged that membership at least be restricted to clubs that had nine or more members, on the grounds that smaller clubs couldn't possibly be active. If they weren't active, why should they have a voice in the Association?

Although the problems were obvious, it was not until the end of 1870 that the structure of baseball was formally changed. The professional clubs realized they could not be members of an organization, the vast majority of which consisted of amateur clubs, many of them small, and others, such as the Gothams and Eagles, who were part of an era long since ended. The professionals formed their own association for the 1871 season and left the amateur clubs to pursue good fellowship and partake of chowder suppers. The professionals set their own course in pursuit of championships, glory and profits.

One by one, the old clubs faded from the scene. The Eckfords played briefly and ineffectively in the professional association before eventually dropping baseball and becoming strictly a social club.[24] The Gothams lost five members of their first nine in 1866, which severely weakened the club[25] and led to its dissolution in the late 1860s.[26]

The Atlantics joined the National Association in 1872 as a co-operative team, a structure under which the players shared in the gate receipts rather than receiving salaries. They were a poor team from 1872–74, and a terrible one in 1875, finishing 2–42, losing their final 31 games. Through 1882, the once-proud Brooklyn club played sporadically in a number of leagues as a semipro organization before disappearing from sight.

The Excelsiors played regularly through 1871, then took the field just once or twice per season during the next few years. Like the Eckfords, they became a social organization. Their last influential act in the world of baseball was leading the amateur movement that separated from the professionals in 1871. The meeting which led to the formation of the amateur association was called by the Excelsiors and held in their club rooms.

Although the decline of amateurism was not officially recognized until 1870, the die was cast by the end of the 1865 season. The latter half of the 1860s was a mongrelized era in which professionals pretended to be amateurs and amateurs pretended that the mores of the 1850s still existed. Had the Civil War not intervened, it is probable that the change would have come sooner, spurred by the momentum generated by the exciting season of 1860. With the growth of the sport dampened by the war, there had been four more years of old style baseball. Although no one knew it at the time, the 1864 season was the last in which the game was played the way the Knickerbockers, Eagles and their friends had played it. An era had ended.

Appendix A:
Letter from Frank Pidgeon of Eckfords re: Professionalism

In its March 19, 1859, edition, *Porter's Spirit of the Times* commented harshly on the action of the National Association rules committee, claiming, among other things, that the association paid too much attention to rules, when they should be allowing the players to enjoy the exercise of playing the game. *Porter's Spirit* was especially critical of the rule which prohibited any player not current with his dues from participating in a game, and prohibited compensation for playing in a match. "Now we humbly opine," said the *Spirit*, "that as the Scottish poet [Robert Burns] hath said, no matter about the poverty or the rank of the individual, 'a man's a man for a that.' If from any circumstance, personal or pecuniary, a lover of the sport cannot afford a day to travel from his home to play a match of cricket or base ball, and his brother members of the club are able to remunerate him for his time and expenses, why should they not be permitted to do so? It is a good democratic rule and tends to level the artificial distinction between wealth and poverty in the 'Old County.' The peer and the peasant are on a level on the cricket ground. The former, it is true, may be styled a gentleman *par excellence* but the latter is more often the player who takes the stumps of my lord at bowling, or puts out the squire by his superior skill as a wicket keeper or a long stop."

The following week, Frank Pidgeon, the architect of the rule, responded.

Dear sir:

My object in sending this communication is to give you the reasons why the committee on rules of the National Association of Base Ball Players thought it necessary to recommend the passage of Section 36 of the Rules and Regulations. I am the parent of the bantling and am still unable to see anything ungentlemanly or unsportsmanlike in expecting every person to pay his dues and play ball for pleasure and not for profit. I suppose you will admit that a man who does not pay his obligations and has it in his power to do so is a knave and not fit to be trusted in the game of ball or anywhere else, and if he has not the money his time would be much better spent in earning the same than playing ball. Business first, pleasure afterward. This is all that may be said on that subject. I trust I have made it plain. As to compensation, you must state the object of the rule entirely, when you attribute the passage of it to snobbish inclinations. On the contrary, quite the reverse. We will suppose, sir, you belong to a club composed mostly of mechanics and you had taken great interest in helping to build it up — had shared in their victories and defeats and become attached to them and they to you by those friendly ties, the existence of which is one of the charms of ball-playing. How would you like to see those you depended upon to uphold the name of the club bought up like cattle, or if not bought, would you like to see the bribes repeatedly offered to them to desert their colors. These things have occurred and it was thought best to nip them in the bud, and it was done without one dissenting voice. You say you do not want to depreciate or throw cold water upon our intentions. I believe sir, you do not. But could anything be more unjust to our kind than to attribute snobbishness to us when this rule was passed to protect ourselves against the influence of money and give "honest property" a fair chance and in a struggle for supremacy between clubs to let skill, courage and endurance decide who shall be the victors. You also tell us that in the old country the peer and the peasant are on a level on the cricket ground, and why not, pray. But does it end there? I'm afraid it does. I agree with you sir that a man's a man for a that and I am rather surprised to see that so soon after such a quotation the remarkable act of condescension on the part of the "berkieca'd a lord" should be held up for the admiration of ballplayers. These things may do well enough for the "old country" but in this country "the man" allows no one to tolerate nor patronize him but knows and feels that "the pith's a sense and pride's worth are higher ranks than a that."

Frank Pidgeon
Captain
Eckford Base Ball Club

Source: *Porter's Spirit of the Times*, March 26, 1859

INSTRUCTING THE NAHUAS IN JUDEO-CHRISTIAN OBEDIENCE

A *Neixcuitilli* and Four Sermon Pieces on the Akedah

Viviana Díaz Balsera

In this essay I will compare the *neixcuitilli* "The Sacrifice of Isaac" with exegeses of the Akedah episode (the binding of Isaac) in four sermons from the beginning of the seventeenth century. The sermons are by three of the most distinguished *nahuatlatos* (experts in Nahuatl; translators) in New Spain at that time. A basic assumption of the article is that cross-cultural colonial contexts of reception alter, hybridize, and multiply semantic possibilities as messages are translated into indigenous languages and cast into the target culture's modes of conception and expression. The effects of hybridization that are produced as beliefs and practices from the foreign colonizing culture are imposed on the target culture can be more or less unexpected, more or less unpredictable. Frequently they may produce what Miguel León-Portilla calls "cultural nepantlism," or straddling the border between the two cultures, with the old ways obfuscated and the new ones not yet assimilated (León-Portilla 1974, 24, 33). Or these effects may paradoxically contribute to the survival of the old in spite of attempts to implement the new. They may even result in the alteration of the new by the traces of the old. And although it is sometimes impossible to know how certain messages were actually received by the intended colonial audience (without any direct contemporary testimonies about the matter), it is worthwhile to explore the apparent ambiguities, contradictions, and problems the texts present, if only to the modern reader. This gives us a better sense of the difficulties involved in the colonization of the imaginary (Gruzinski 1988), and a better sense of the possibility that the colonizer might not have always been totally present to himself, and in full control of his discourses, as he strove to reshape and control the will and desire of the colonized-to-be.

The representation of the Akedah episode to a Nahua audience presents two main issues to the modern critic, regarding the admixture and hybridization of cultural discourses in the colonization of the imaginary. The first issue is to explore how this foundational episode is depicted to a community that in its own not-so-remote precontact past had practiced human sacrifice as part of its essential duty to feed the gods and conserve the world. This fact must have been integral to how the audience read the episode of Abraham's obedience and thus must have affected the universality of its meaning as posited by the colonizer. Second, and closely related to the first issue, there is the interest in exploring the problems inherent in presenting this episode to the Nahuas in order to establish radical differences between the precontact gods, so harshly condemned by the spiritual colonizers, and the new colonial deity they should obey. These issues taken together dramatize in an exemplary way some of the uncertainties, ironies, and ambiguities of the Spanish spiritual colonization, which imposed a new god in the lands of Anahuac, but whose discourses were never powerful enough to eradicate the old.

In the first part of the article I will outline briefly the important place allotted to the episode of the Akedah in the religious traditions of the spiritual colonizer, Christianity, and in Judaism. In the second part of the article, I will examine how this controversial episode is depicted to the Nahuas in the *neixcuitilli* "The Sacrifice of Isaac." I will bring some aspects of the prehispanic religious practices of the audience to bear in my discussion, in order to show the similarities and differences that the text produces between such practices and the Akedah episode. These similarities and differences produce hybridization effects whereby the episode acquires new and unanticipated meanings, which make it slightly other to itself. In the third part of the article, I will examine the exegesis of the Akedah episode in sermons by fray Juan Bautista, fray Juan de Mijangos, and fray Martín de León. We will see how the interpretations of this controversial episode involving human sacrifice, although articulated from the perspective of clearly authoritative Christian voices, did not fully differentiate themselves from the cultural memories of prehispanic religiosity that they sought to obliterate.

Abraham in the Judeo-Christian Tradition

Abraham is a key figure in Judaism, Christianity, and Islam. His name comes either from the Babylonian *Abam-rama*, "he loves the Father," that is, God, or from the Canaanite name *Ab-ram*, "the Father is exalted" (*New International* 1:76). The name Abraham signifies "father of a multitude" and was given by God himself to the patriarch-to-be in Genesis 17:5. Because of Abraham's unwavering belief in the seemingly implausible promises of Yahweh, his faith was counted for righteousness and thus he was the man with whom God sealed a covenant that changed the course of history. The extraordinary promises that would be the basis of Abraham's life figure in Genesis. Being one hundred years old and having a wife who was ninety, he was promised a son and descendants that would be as numerous as the grains of sand on the seashore (Genesis 17:19–22, 22:16–18). God pledged to Abraham, a foreign nomad and wandering shepherd, that his descendants would inherit the rich land of Canaan (17:8) and, although he came from an insignificant tribe, that all nations would be blessed through him. Abraham's faith was manifested in a life of utter obedience. He left his father's house and constantly moved from one place to another at God's command. Most important, he was tested "to see whether in his person the people of God would esteem God enough to be willing to offer human sacrifice" (*New International*

1:76), and he was thus asked to sacrifice the beloved son that had been finally granted to him in a supernatural way. The ultimate act of obedience that was the binding of Isaac at Mount Moriah moved God not only to promise but to actually take an oath to bless Abraham and all his descendants. The stature of Abraham is thus of epic proportions for Judaism. He is the great mediator, the patriarch and father of Israel and of multitudes. He is the first man to have left behind the cult of false gods. He is the one who, if stood by, guarantees that God will not go back on his promise (Kuschel 1995, 19). God saw in Abraham "the innermost reality of the human soul" (Buber 1968, 42) and he was the first man in Scripture to whom God let himself be seen (43).

The Christian tradition had to come to terms with the figure of Abraham early on because of his central importance in Jewish theology. In his Epistle to the Galatians, Paul notes that Abraham justified himself through his unwavering faith, not through the Law, which came later. This allowed him to extend the promise of salvation and of the covenant to the Gentiles. In his letter to the Romans, Paul reiterates this call to the universality of the structure of Abraham's faith, "hoping against all hope, not doubting in the promise of God" (Kuschel 1995, 88), in the belief that Christ is the son of God and that he was in fact resurrected from the dead. He did not exclude Israel because of her unfaithfulness in Christ (she remains "loved by God, for the sake of the fathers" [Romans 11:28]), but with the advent of Christ, Israel is no longer the exclusive mediator of humanity for salvation. God's promise to Abraham has been fulfilled in Christ and Abraham remains the father of the Jews, but in faith. For his part, Matthew the Evangelist insisted on the carnal descent of Christ from Abraham, thus emphasizing that salvation and blessings for humanity would indeed come from the patriarch's lineage. However, Matthew, still without excluding the Jewish community, starts broaching the topic that carnal descent is inferior to spiritual kinship and that "a purely formal appeal is nothing to God" (Kuschel 1995, 94). In this sense, God's covenant with Abraham has not been derogated by Christ: it has been fulfilled by him in a faith that is the true essence of Israel.

James's epistle differs from Paul's in that he considers deeds to be a necessary evidence of faith. If there is faith, it will show in works, but faith alone will not be enough for salvation. James refers to Abraham, "our father" (2:20–24), in order to support his argument that faith and works are inseparable. James's position not only seeks to redefine Christianity vis-à-vis Judaism (actually not too difficult considering the Jewish stance on faith and acts) but also considers the offering of Isaac on the altar as a deed: "Was not Abraham our father justified by works, when he offered his son Isaac upon the altar?" (2:21) Much like Philo of Alexandria (c. BC 20–50 AD), James thinks that, although the sacrifice was not carried through, Abraham's acts—of taking Isaac up to Mount Moriah, tying him up, and drawing the knife—were already complete acts, not merely an internal disposition to do something (this will be important for our discussion of "The Sacrifice of Isaac" later on).

In John's Gospel, the relationship between Judaism and Christianity starts to break apart. John declares there cannot be knowledge of God without Christ (8:31–59). Thus the Jews, because of their hardness of heart and desire to kill him who had come from God and who had existed before Abraham was born, and in spite of being carnal descendants of the patriarch, were not his real children but children of the devil. As Jeffrey Siker observes: "The Jews who staked a special claim on their self-designation as 'descendants of Abraham' conceded by John, find themselves abandoned in the Fourth Gospel" (1991, 142). This will be the beginning of the exclusion of the Jews from the Christian ecumenical community, and the appropriation of Abraham as son of Christ.

With Augustine's theology of Abraham three centuries later, John's seizure of the father of Judaism would be consolidated, backed up by the patriarchs of the early Christian Church—Barnabas, Ignatius, and Justin. In book 16:32 of the *City of God*, Augustine treats the episode of the sacrifice of Isaac as God's temptation of Abraham to prove his obedience not to him, but rather to the world. In perhaps not the most convincing argument, Augustine states that "Of course Abraham could never believe that God delighted in human sacrifices; yet when the divine commandment thundered, it was to be obeyed, not disputed. Yet Abraham is worthy of praise, because he believed all along that his son, on being offered, would rise again" (1950, 554). That is, Abraham obeys God's awful command, represented by Augustine as a "not blameworthy temptation," knowing that God does not desire human sacrifices, and always believing that his son would be restored to him once offered. On this count, Augustine openly incorporates Hebrews 11:17–19. Augustine then reads Isaac as a type of Christ, as Isaac carries to Mount Moriah the wood upon which he is to be sacrificed, and once Isaac's father is forbidden to smite him, the ram then typifies Christ, who is sacrificed for the sake of humanity. According to Saint Augustine, in this figural relationship that anticipates Christ, the promise to Abraham (in terms of the blessing of the nations through his seed) is fulfilled. In terms of the old covenant between Abraham and God, Augustine follows John in stating that it has been superseded by the advent of Christ. The only reason for the existence of the Jews is the fact that their scriptures give testimony of the truth of Christianity (Kuschel 1995, 127). Insofar as Jews refuse to do this or misunderstand it, they are excluded from the plan of salvation. This position regarding Abraham and Judaism was passed on through Church tradition up to the twentieth century. And certainly, it was the prevailing one in Mexico during the sixteenth and seventeenth centuries.

"The Sacrifice of Isaac" and the Violence of Obedience

Critics are in agreement that the Nahua theater of evangelization had a clear didactic function from the perspective of the spiritual colonizers (Horcasitas 1974, Burkhart 1996, Lopétegui y Zubillaga 1965, Arróniz 1979, Williams 1992). This theater was supposed to teach the Nahuas regarding the new deities and narratives of origin they were henceforth supposed to believe in and claim as truth. The codification of the term *neixcuitilli* or "something that sets an example" (Burkhart 1996, 46) to refer to this dramatic colonial genre indicates that the Nahuas certainly did not miss the point of the friars' edifying intent.

Although the friars never elaborated on why they chose theater as a technology of evangelization, it may be posited that the religious dramatic tradition that had emerged in Europe since the tenth century helped to persuade them that spectacle was a great supplement to the verbal doctrine regularly received by the faithful from the pulpit.[1] The friars must have realized the vital role public rituals held in preconquest society. As is well known, the Nahuas believed in a large pantheon of gods. Scholars of Aztec studies have identified at least 128 major deities, making regular yet overlapping appearances, to whom worship was rendered (Nicholson 1971, 408–10). Each of the eighteen months of their solar calendar was dedicated to one or several deities, to whom a specific ceremony had to be carried out in order to influence their supernatural activities or to guarantee their survival.

These ceremonies or rituals were not merely a random group of religious activities. They followed an elaborate script meticulously overseen by priests. They would generally be celebrated in open public places such as the temple plazas and platforms. Often an individual, usually the sacrificial victim, wore the regalia of the deity in question and enacted a sacred narrative, supported by priests, penitents, and the more or less active participation of the people. Thus, as Ángel Garibay has suggested, it might well be that the friars felt compelled to transplant some of Spain's own traditions of public religious celebrations in order to fill the void created by suppressing the busy calendar of prehispanic pagan festivities (1953–1954, 2:155–56). Perhaps, to attract large masses of Nahuas to the new religion, "the most effective—indeed, the only—way . . . was through the use of song, dance, plays, processions, and their accompanying pageantry and paraphernalia" (Burkhart 1996, 43).

The Nahua theater of evangelization may have been conceived to introduce the new religious discourses, without breaking away from the prehispanic public ways of worship, as long as these ways were not incompatible with Christianity. The Nahuas themselves were in charge of the mise-en scène of the actual performances of the *neixcuitilli*, and even of a good deal of the commitment to paper of the dramatic scripts, which underscores the fact that the theater of evangelization, albeit an idea coming from the spiritual colonizer, could not possibly have been realized without active Nahua collaboration. This theater must be studied therefore from a double perspective: from the point of view of the colonizer, as an evangelization device whose realization largely depended on prehispanic ways of constructing spectacle, and as a theater that legitimized the colonized-to-be (Burkhart 1996, 48) by the display of their great capacity to appropriate the new gods, a capacity that harked back to precontact times, as Sahagún pointed out in his exasperated comments in the prologue to the *Arte adivinatoria* (in García Icazbalceta 1954, 382–83).

Furthermore, as James Lockhart has pointed out, given the understandable problems of the friars' linguistic competence in Nahuatl, it is difficult to know how much of the dramatic texts in the extant *neixcuitilli* they actually composed. Lockhart speculates that perhaps the Spanish ecclesiastics actually wrote in Spanish and the Nahua amanuensis would then translate into Nahuatl. An isolated unfinished phrase in Spanish that appeared in a sixteenth-century manuscript playlet entitled "Holy Wednesday" suggests to Lockhart that the Nahua aide did not understand what it meant but copied it down anyway. Several misspelled words in Spanish lead Lockhart to propose that the dramatic script was never again supervised by the friar: "It is as though the directing Spaniard, although in a sense probably deserving to be called the author of the play, never looked at it again once he had given it to a Nahua to translate and realize as he saw fit" (1992, 403). Needless to say, this hypothetical situation implies, at the material level of the dramatic script itself (not to say of the theatrical performance), enormous possibilities for inflecting the authority of the colonizing discourses.

There are some unsettling ambiguities brought about by the way in which the Akedah episode is represented to the Nahua audience in the *neixcuitilli* "Del naSimiento De iSaac del Sacrificio q.e habrahan Su Padre quiso por mandado de Dios hazer."[2] The 1760 extant manuscript of "The Sacrifice of Isaac" attests that it was copied from a 1678 "original." Fernando Horcasitas, the Mexican translator of many of the extant plays of the Nahua theater of evangelization, proposes that the date of composition of this specific *auto* must probably be located in the first half of the sixteenth century. He argues that Motolinia mentions in his *Historia de los indios de la Nueva España* the representation of an *auto* of this title in Tlaxcala in the religious festivities of 1539 and that no other chronicle mentions it again. The metaphorical language and certain speech patterns of the play seem to hark back to prehispanic usage. The inclusion of the episode of Ishmael and Hagar would indicate for Horcasitas an interest on the part of the friars in fighting the institutionalized polygamy that then prevailed among the Mexica nobility (1974, 191).

Of the three arguments supporting an early sixteenth-century composition of the play, the latter is perhaps the weakest, since the fact that Ishmael was Abraham's son is never directly stated (Williams 1992, 73). It can only be inferred through an oblique allusion to Ishmael's birth in a scene between Hagar and Ishmael.[3] Although the other two arguments may also be contestable, still there is some good reason to treat in this essay the *neixcuitilli* as if in fact it preceded the sermon pieces. The *neixcuitilli* does not show the theological refinement, discernment, and precision of the sermons, and herein lies the crux of some of its fascinating problems. Such "shortcomings" may certainly be from a problem of genre, or even from a contingency of composition, but it is not unreasonable to situate the less sophisticated text temporally before others showing more complexity, so without any decisive evidence to the contrary, we will proceed with what seems the most sensible scenario.

"The Sacrifice of Isaac" is clearly divided in two parts.[4] The first deals with the expulsion of Hagar and Ishmael from Abraham's household and, following the biblical episode, represents a banquet offered in honor of Isaac. Although there are several important moments of cultural translation that make this first part more readable and familiar to a Nahua audience, I will focus only on the representation of the controversial episode of God's demand for the human sacrifice of Isaac in the play's second part. If the dates of the *neixcuitilli* are the ones proposed by Horcasitas, it could be hypothesized, as many critics have done, that "The Sacrifice of Isaac" may possibly have been intended to show the Nahua audience the difference between the recently repudiated prehispanic deities, who demanded human sacrifices, and the new Judeo-Christian one, who did not (Horcasitas 1974, 198–99; Potter 1986, 312; Williams 1992, 73–74). If the play was written at a later period and was aimed at new Nahua generations, raised under the strict prohibition of human sacrifices, the urgency to establish such a difference might not have been so great. In either case, however, "The Sacrifice of Isaac" shows features that can seem inconsistent with the representation of the Christian God as truthfully good precisely because he does not desire human sacrifices: "The true God that we preach to you because he is good he loves well the Christian people and you too if you'd like to be his friends; and for all of this he does not want you to kill your children nor your slaves . . . . nor that you improperly shed your blood (Córdoba 1988, 35; translation mine). This statement appears in fray Pedro de Córdoba's *Doctrina cristiana*, printed in Mexico in 1544. Thus, it can be reasonably assumed that the Nahuas had already been introduced to this basic difference between the Christian and prehispanic deities by the first half of the sixteenth century, if not soon after the Twelve set foot in Mexico and human sacrifices were prohibited in 1525 (Motolinia 1951, 99).[5] But in the attempt to secure the continuing subordination of the indigenous audience to the authority of the Christian god, the latter will be portrayed in the *neixcuitilli* in a very different light. Far from being depicted as a merciful "Father who does not want to sadden us, who does not want to afflict us, but who wants to gladden us" (Sahagún 1993a, 137; translation mine), He is represented as demanding a total obedience and subjection similar to those rendered to the prehispanic deities by the Nahua ancestors.

The second part of the play opens with the dramatic figure of God the Father. He claims to have properly prepared all things of heaven and earth and declares that "all people on the Earth" will obey his consummate will ("Sacrifice," 31v). Abraham then comes onstage, politely and earnestly praying for Isaac's fate, since he is very worried his son will not obey God as he should. Abraham conveys a strong fatherly concern for the fulfillment of his son's religious duties, and great fear and deference to his God. In answering his prayers and devoted concern, however, God the Father calls on Abraham and requires him to sacrifice his beloved Isaac: "If it is true that you can carry out my sacred commands, seize your child named Isaac whom you greatly love and take him to the top of the mountain in the place named Moriah. There you are to kill him. If truly you carry out my sacred command my heart will be satisfied." (32r)

The violence of the demand being put forth by the Judeo-Christian god can be orthodoxically explained away as a test of obedience of an evidently righteous man. Abraham's instant acquiescence is thus represented in the *neixcuitilli* as part of the *pilli*/patriarch's exemplary faithful demeanor: "I will carry out your command. I intend to do it for you, the All-powerful, whose words I hear, are eternally worthy of being believed" (32r). This accords with the Jewish theology of Abraham as a faithful and honorable man, "deeming that nothing would justify disobedience to God and that in everything he should submit to his will" (Josephus 1.225, quoted in Siker 1991, 23). It also conforms with the Pauline conception of Abraham as father of all those who have faith in God (Romans 4:16–19) and all those who never doubt his promises.

In the colonial context of sixteenth- or even early seventeenth-century Mexico, however, this demand for a human sacrifice by the Christian god acquires unexpected, hybrid meanings, because it resembles the former exaction of human victims by the Nahua prehispanic deities as enacted in the old calendrical rituals. Abraham's piety as shown in his acquiescence to sacrifice his son to his God would not have been particularly extraordinary or new in the lands of Anahuac. In the first treatise of Motolinia's *Historia*, where he will later refer to the 1538 Corpus Christi festivities and to the only recorded performance of a "Sacrifice of Isaac," the friar discusses the feast celebrated in honor of Tlaloc, god of rain and water, to whom the Nahuas sacrificed children:

> Once a year when the corn was a palm high, a feast was held in the towns where the chief lord resided and where his house was called a palace. On the appointed day the Indians sacrificed a boy and a girl about three or four years

of age. *These were not slaves, but the children of chiefs, and the sacrifice was performed on a hill out of reverence to the idol who,* they said, was the god of water and who gave them the rain, and whom they invoked when there was lack of water. (Motolinia 1951, 118–19; emphasis mine).

Later on, Motolinia states that as the corn grew higher, children up to seven years old would also be sacrificed, the idea being that there was a correlation between the height of the corn and that of the children. However, he specifies that the older children were the sons and daughters of slaves, whereas the younger ones were the children of noble men and women, as if to imply a greater sacrificial value during the initial stages of the corn cycle. Contemporary anthropologists have not been able to verify Motolinia's claim on the noble provenance of the little children sacrificed to Tlaloc (Román Bellereza 1987, 139). Nonetheless, it is significant that he brought up the issue, even if erroneously, because of the many coincidences broached for the Christian imagination between this sacrifice and Isaac's—who, although not the son of a nobleman, was nonetheless the son of a prominent free one. The fact that, in the *neixcuitilli*, Abraham's social status is raised from that of a desert seminomad to that of a *pilli*, "nobleman," (and sometimes even *tlatoani*, "ruler")[6] suggests that the coincidences brought up by Motolinia's passage were being alluded to in the play.

On the other hand, Isaac's age goes unmentioned in the first and second parts of the play. In the opening scene, Sarah refers to him as "a young fellow" who has been raised up with her breast milk (24v). So he is already weaned, although we are not given a clear clue as to how recently. Inga Clendinnen has observed that the Nahuas usually weaned their children by age three (1991, 188–9). We could thus surmise that the "young fellow" Isaac must be at least four years old or more. It is not mentioned whether the banquet celebrated in Isaac's honor is to commemorate his weaning, as in the case of the biblical story. Also, in that story, Isaac seems to be around thirty years old when he goes to Mount Moriah to be sacrificed. Abraham opens the second part of the play with his worries over his child Isaac not carrying out his proper duties to God, and God the Father also refers to Isaac as "your child." This might suggest that Isaac is the same age in the first part of the play as in the second. Only at the moment of the representation, however, would the audience be able to discern his age, from the physical stature, voice inflection, and so on, of the actor playing that role. Needless to say, the smaller the child, the more likely he could be associated with the little children sacrificed to Tlaloc on the mountaintops, according to Motolinia the offspring of noblemen and noblewomen.

A couple of scenes later, Abraham, as a Nahua *pilli* or nobleman, arrives on the hilltop with his beloved Isaac. Much like the people crying for the little children taken to be slaughtered for Tlaloc (according to Sahagún 1989 1:107–8), the disconsolate lord sheds copious tears as he explains to Isaac that God has asked for his death in order to see if the people would really obey His orders. He then adds, "Now receive death with great humility, for he speaks thusly: I will be able to raise the dead for I am eternal life everywhere in the world" (33v).

In this exhortation to Isaac we may see a reference to Hebrews 11:17–19 and to Saint Augustine's claim that Abraham had unwavering faith that God would fulfill His promise of numerous descendants even as he demanded the sacrifice of the only beloved son. However, in spite of such faith, the depiction of Abraham's immense sorrow (an *amplificatio* of the biblical story) also reveals the inordinate suffering provoked in Abraham by the violence of the deity's command. In the pain inflicted upon loyal worshippers, the god of the spiritual colonizers seems to resemble the arbitrary god Tezcatlipoca, about whom it was said that "he was the only one who ruled the world, and that only he gave prosperity and wealth, and that only he took them away whenever he pleased. . . . That is why he was greatly feared and respected, because they believed it was in his hand to raise and bring down" (Sahagún 1989, 1:38; translation mine).

Similar to the biblical story, it is only when the sword is already falling over Isaac, when Abraham has started to slaughter his son, that an angel finally appears to seize his hand. The angel explains that God "has thus seen how you love him and carry out his sacred commands so that you do not violate them" (34v). The angel declares that Abraham must sacrifice a lamb instead, which is never represented dramatically. Horcasitas points out that the restatement of the Franciscans' prohibition of human sacrifices would explain the dissimulation of the animal sacrifice (1974, 189). With the angel's intervention to stop the slaying of Isaac, the friars may indeed have intended to proclaim to the Nahua public that the Christian god rejected human sacrifice.[7] They seriously overlooked the fact that, as Robert Potter points out, "the original story implicitly credits the idea of sacrifice, as a fitting response to a divine command" (1986, 312).[8] Moreover, as though God were not content with Abraham's initial disposition to perform the sacrifice, only at the very moment that the slaughter is to be consummated is it finally interrupted. As Abraham slowly walks to and climbs up Mount Moriah, as he dutifully cuts the firewood and ties and blindfolds Isaac, as he draws the knife, in his heart and imagination Abraham has already slaughtered his beloved son not once, but over and over again. This is what Philo of Alexandria saw when he stated that Abraham's sacrifice "though not followed by the intended ending, was complete and perfect" (*De Abrahamo* 62–68, quoted in Siker 1991, 23), and what James the Apostle meant when he considered the offering of Isaac on the altar as works that justified Abraham, along with his faith (James 2:21–22).

In the biblical episode, a deeply moved Yahweh sends the angel back to tell Abraham that he has sworn by himself, that is, by the highest being that he can conceive, that because Abraham has not withheld from him his only son Isaac, his seed will bless all the nations on earth (Genesis 22:18). But in the play God takes no oath at all. The character of Abraham is rewarded only by being released from his son's execution at the very last moment. As they descend from the peak of Mount Moriah, Abraham admonishes Isaac:

> Now may the honored name of the All-powerful, God the Father, whose compassion is very great, be eternally praised everywhere in the world. If all we people of the earth would carry out his precious sacred commands we would greatly please him. And as for you, my beloved child, you have seen how he saved you from death. Now as long as you live, always love him with all your heart and do not take in vain the name of God, and love your neighbors. Such are his orders. (35r–v)

There is no sense that Abraham has accomplished anything extraordinary, unique, and irreversible for all the peoples of the world. He is represented as having only fulfilled—albeit remarkably well—his duty to obey God's command. Although there is mention of Isaac as a prefiguration of Christ in an angel's passage at the very beginning of the play, the paramount epic dimension of the covenant between the patriarch of the Jews and of all nations and Yahweh is all but suppressed in the rest of the *neixcuitilli*.[9] With his act in extremis, Abraham generates only authority enough to establish himself as an example of obedience for Isaac and for the Nahua audience. And if the passage was intended to show the audience that although Abraham's ordeal was onerous, the orders spelled out to Isaac to follow from that moment on would be easy and nongrievous, the *neixcuitilli* gives no reason to think that such commandments were entirely new. Abraham had already mentioned to Isaac in the first part of the play that there were three things he should always follow and remember.[10]

Abraham's model behavior seems to be underscored in the dramatic text by the angel's ambiguous closing admonishment to the audience:

> All of you who are here have now heard this *marvelous thing*. And as for you, may you live entirely according to his sacred commands, may you and your children not violate a single one. Take good care that they will not go about playing and wasting time, so that they will serve with goodness our lord, God, and so that they will also merit the kingdom of heaven. May it so be done. (35v–36r; emphasis mine)

Although the angel defines what the audience has seen as a "marvelous thing," something that causes admiration, it is impossible to determine what such a marvelous and unheard-of thing refers to specifically. It could as easily be God's order to sacrifice Isaac, Abraham's willingness to carry out such a command, God's sparing of the human victim, or all of the above. The angel then edifies the audience by saying that the marvelous thing they have witnessed in the *neixcuitilli* has instructed them to keep God's commandments. But by linking the undecidable marvelous thing to the exhortation to obey the divine commandments and to keep children from playing and wasting time, the angel's passage certainly does not give much indication of anything exceptionally achieved for ages to come. Such a link between the marvelous and the ordinary opens up the possible interpretation that any of the spectators could be required to undertake and readily submit to Abraham's horrific ordeal. This didactic exemplariness of "The Sacrifice of Isaac" dangerously splits the Judeo-Christian God's unique, tremendous, perhaps most controversial request in the Scriptures into an iterative, duplicable one. Thus, with the loss of the epic dimension of the Akedah episode, the God that emerges in the dramatic text of "The Sacrifice of Isaac" becomes Nahuatized, hybridized, somewhat other to itself.[11] By being depicted as not having given up forever the demand for human sacrifice, if only just to test the obedience of his creatures, He is not *radically* differentiated from the violent, frightening prehispanic deities of the audience to whom all had also to be offered unhesitatingly in order to keep cosmic time alive. In this sense, the friars involved in the production of the dramatic text of "The Sacrifice of Isaac" partially betrayed the difference between the violent Tlaloc, the arbitrary Tezcatlipoca, and the all-loving, benevolent Christian god they proclaimed in their writings, in their pulpits, and in the very prohibition against human sacrifice that had been issued in 1525.

Along with many critics of the play, one may argue that, in spite of any similarity with the prehispanic deities, the God of "The Sacrifice of Isaac" is ultimately posited to the audience as not desiring human sacrifice (Horcasitas 1974, 189; Cornyn, quoted in Horcasitas 1974, 198–99; Ravicz 1970, 97; Williams 1996, 73–74; Potter 1986, 312). However, it should be recalled that, particularly for Christians, an act does not necessarily need to be fully performed in order either to be sinful or to bring blessings. In fact, the possibility that lustful thoughts and yearnings may be already sinful, independently from their materialization, is one of the constitutive aspects of the Christian moral subjectivity that the missionary agents were assiduously trying to implant in the Nahuas.[12] Christ's warning that whosoever looked lasciviously at a woman had already committed adultery with her in his heart (Mat: 5:27–28) clearly reflects this point. What is relevant to "The Sacrifice of Isaac" about such a specific mode of sinfulness and the interiority that it broaches is that the *neixcuitilli* indeed shows this new Christian form of subjectivity to the Nahuas while ironically creating strong continuities with their religious past. The *neixcuitilli* displaces the utter materiality of the final, external act of human sacrifice, but it retains as desirable the thought and internal disposition to perform it. It emphasizes that Abraham was ultimately spared of having to execute the actual immolation of the human body. But the violence and the yoke of having to submit to such a command is not lifted. For only by his unquestionable readiness to surrender to such an atrocious demand (not unlike the Nahua ancestors' obligation to perform human sacrifices), only after having carried out all the necessary steps for the slaughter, was Abraham rewarded by being freed from acting.

The Nahuatization of Abraham and of the colonial god that our reading has suggested may not only be imputed to the ardent desire of domination of the friars conceiving of "The Sacrifice of Isaac." It may have also been an effect of the participation of the Nahua scribes, as was mentioned above. The erasure in "The Sacrifice of Isaac" of the radical difference between the violent Tlaloc, the arbitrary Tezcatlipoca, and the all-loving, benevolent Christian god championed by the friars may have been a subversive intervention by the scribes to signal to the audience that the colonial god did not utterly condemn the prehispanic practices of human sacrifice. Or, such an erasure and hybridization may have been the result of an unwitting cultural projection through which the Nahua aides made sense of the new by making it look familiar to the known. Or finally, the omissions that hindered the epic transcendence of the Akedah episode as well as the weakness of the text's formulation of Isaac as a prefiguration of Christ may point to "the large field of Nahua discretion and independence in translation, extending to numerous adaptations and additions" (Lockhart 1992, 403), that in this case perhaps resulted in a less adequate grasp of the foreign theology's subtleties.

In any case, by not breaking decisively with the religious violence of the prehispanic past, "The Sacrifice of Isaac" transformed Abraham's seminal act of total surrender to the deity into something less than extraordinary for the Nahua audience. After all, the men and women in Anahuac had also been capable of sacrificing the most precious and beloved to their gods, believing these gods to be true. And from a Christian perspective, it may be argued that the *neixcuitilli* hybridized the

Akedah episode by portraying God the Father as expecting from the Nahua masses a form of absolute surrender that in the Judeo-Christian tradition had been demanded only from Abraham, Jesus, and Mary.

Abraham Revisited by a Star Team of Early Seventeenth-Century *Nahuatlatos*

Sermons by three of the most prominent *nahuatlatos* of the seventeenth century—fray Juan Bautista, of the Franciscan order; fray Juan de Mijangos, an Augustinian; and fray Martín de León, a Dominican—provide commentaries to the Akedah episode.[13] Bautista's and Mijangos's texts were carefully revised by the outstanding Nahua *letrado* and trilingual teacher at the Colegio de Santa Cruz in Tlatelolco, Agustín de la Fuente.

It may be perhaps more than an exceptional coincidence that these three salient contemporaries would have written exegeses on the binding of Isaac for the edification of the Nahua faithful around the same period of time. Besides the *neixcuitilli* and some occasional references to Abraham sprinkled in sermons here and there, the Akedah episode is not commented on much by any other friar-*nahuatlato* in print.[14] Were exegeses on the binding of Isaac shunned by less audacious spirits—both before and after Bautista, Mijangos, and León—because of fears of possible misunderstandings by the Nahua audience of the thorny issue of the demand for human sacrifice by the Judeo-Christian God? Needless to say, much archival work and research must still be done in order to venture any hypothesis on why this prominent trio of *nahuatlatos* decided to take on the Akedah episode during the first two decades of the seventeenth century, other than it being merely a fortunate coincidence or collegial theological rivalry. It could very well be the case that future scholars may find in presently unknown manuscripts of devotional literature exegeses of the binding of Isaac spread throughout the colonial period. Until such new evidence is found we will have to work with what we have, which already offers interesting possibilities for textual analysis. For one thing, such analyses of the commentaries will show how the exacting and controversial demand for a human sacrifice by the Judeo-Christian God was represented by these friars' official voices, and how the Nahuas were expected to think about it. In each sermon piece we will see how the didactic thrust of the episode mirrors discursively in one way or another the violence of the ordeal portrayed. And as with the *neixcuitilli*, we will be able to appreciate that the violence of the depicted Christian sacred in these sermons was not totally alien to that of the prehispanic past.

Bautista and the Violence of God's Favors

Fray Juan de Bautista is considered by some to be perhaps the most eloquent, influential, and prolific *nahuatlato* of his time. According to Ángel Garibay, "nobody in his time . . . took the Castilian language to the heights to which fray Juan Bautista elevated the Mexican one" (Garibay 1953–1954, 2:171; translation mine). Since Bautista was associated during the last decades of the sixteenth century with the trilingual Colegio de Santa Cruz, and he was published in the seventeenth century, Ascensión H. de León-Portilla considers Bautista an important figure of transition (1988, 1:51). The extant imprints of his work, although only a part of his total output, are notorious both for the wide range of topics they cover and because of their impressive volume. His extant imprints are the trilingual *Advertencias para los confesores de los naturales* (1600a); a book of *huehuetlatolli* associated with fray Andrés de Olmos, which Bautista edited (1600b); a book of ascetic meditations entitled *Libro de la miseria y brevedad de la vida del hombre y de sus cuatro postrimerías* (1604); a life of Saint Anthony of Padua (1605); and his monumental *Sermonario en lengua mexicana* of 1606. This sermonary contains sermons only for the four Sundays of Advent[15] and the feast days of Saint Andrew and the Conception of Our Lady. Thus it has only a fraction of what Bautista intended to publish and is, according to Sell, the longest single extant Nahuatl publication (1993, 31n.110).

I now turn to two short sermon sections that refer to the Akedah episode in Bautista's massive *Sermonario*. In order to make the sermons more manageable and useful for many occasions, there was the long-standing practice of dividing long sermons into pieces or units that could be read independently from each other. Since there was no fixed length, either for the sermon or for each of its constituent units, it is difficult to know how many sections were read to the faithful in a single occasion. The piece to which our section on the Akedah episode belongs is the second sermon written for the feast of the Apostle Saint Andrew.[16] This feast belongs to the calendar of saints,[17] and not to the principal cycles of the life of Christ, but it falls on November 30 and is thus part of the Advent period. The (tenuous) connection between Saint Andrew's feast and the treatment of the Akedah episode is established through a commentary on Matthew 4:18, where the evangelist talks about Jesus walking along the shore of the Sea of Galilee and calling upon Andrew and Simon to become fishers of men. The point that Bautista highlights to the Nahua brethren is how saints have a clear memory of the circumstances of their calling: "Because those who are saints take good care of and remember well, not only what mercies are done to them that they receive, with which people are benefited, but likewise where, in what place, the time, when, in which they received them" (Bautista 1606, 288). The ancient saints remembered in similar fashion, Bautista continues, and he then brings up Abraham the patriarch as an example of the proper way to remember God's favors.

The Christian God that fray Bernardino de Sahagún portrayed to the Nahuas in his *Apéndiz a la Postilla* as a good father who never wanted to afflict people (1993a, 135–37) is very different indeed from the one who, in this sermon, orders Abraham "to lay out an offering of, to make an offering of, his beloved son, his firstborn . . . Isaac" (Bautista 1606, 288). Abraham obeys and after he has everything ready for the sacrifice, has bound Isaac, and has drawn the knife to slay him, God finally stays his hand in order to prevent the slaughter, saying: "That is enough, O Abraham, let that be all, for the people of the earth have already seen, are already satisfied, that you are most obedient" (Bautista 1606, 288).

This representation of Abraham's obedience as evidence to be shown to the people rather than to God is a reference to Saint Augustine's interpretation of the Akedah episode in the *City of God*.[18] But Bautista's particular take is not so much that Abraham was tested by God to show the world an unimaginable proof of piety, but rather that the people of the world needed to be convinced of Abraham's unfaltering obedience. Once they were persuaded he would actually carry out the slaying, the execution could be stopped. Although there is no further elaboration on this point, the people's satisfaction with the Akedah would suggest it is their standards of maximum obedience (rather than or not only God's) that have been met. And the insinuation that they were (just) convinced of Abraham's piety by his offering of Isaac rather than profoundly impressed or shocked would imply that the people's expectations of total submission to the deity were severe in the extreme. The communal aspect of the people's criterion adds then to its harshness, since Abraham's proof of utmost obedience is now not something unique, generated within the inscrutable realm of the sacred, but rather something over which there is a human consensus and an expectancy: something not utterly unimaginable, but heard of, and talked about. There is then an erosion of the stature of Abraham's act. It is admirable and worthy, yes, but the fact that it is within the bounds of people's standards situates it below the marvelous, below what is almost humanly unbearable. In this downgrading of the patriarch's exceptional act—by making it meet human expectations of the proper measure of extreme piety—we may find a similarity with the *neixcuitilli* on "The Sacrifice of Isaac," which also lessened the uniqueness of Abraham's act, albeit by the implication of its possible repeatability.

In contrast to the *neixcuitilli*, the sermon does bring out the epic dimension of Abraham's act: "By my praiseworthy name I promise you that from your beloved child your lineage will emerge as a mercy to the people of the world" (Bautista 1606, 288). The passage gives a clear sense that God's solemn promise to Abraham will have important consequences for the whole of humanity. But rather than underscoring the greatness of the patriarch's act that moved God to take an oath, the emphasis shifts to the favors God imparts upon Abraham: "And so that Abraham would always remember the very great favor our Lord, God, had done for him there, he named the top of the mountain where he would have made an offering of his child: *Dominus videt*. It means: our Lord watches" (Bautista 1606, 289). It is important to point out that, whereas Saint Augustine fully acknowledges the Genesis passage in which the causal relationship between Abraham's act and God's oath is established,[19] Bautista downplays the merits of the former by focusing only on God's promises and mercy, as if they had been freely bestowed upon Abraham, as if Abraham had not done anything to deserve such favors. In this second moment of lessening the merits of Abraham's perfect yet terrifying obedience there is a violence not totally dissimilar to the downgrading of his act in the *neixcuitilli* from the singular and unique to the merely exemplary. Bautista then shifts points of view and takes on Abraham's perspective:

> It means: our Lord watches. It is as though it means that our Lord, God, saw that quickly, right away, I obeyed him, I did what he ordered me to do. And so he was merciful to me, he had pity on me and on my child when he ordered me not to kill him, not to make an offering of my child. Most especially he favored me by declaring to me a belief in the Savior of the world, that he will be my descendant. (Bautista 1606, 289)

Bautista's *inventio* of Abraham's monologue evidently sidesteps the agony inflicted on the patriarch by God's awful demand. For the Lord allegedly did *not* see right away, quickly, that Abraham would obey, as the sermon claims he thought out loud. The Lord waited and watched how Abraham woke up that fateful morning and walked with Isaac for three long days until they reached Mount Moriah. God looked on as they slowly climbed the mountain, as Isaac was burdened by the wood he carried. God saw how Abraham tied up the lad and blindfolded him, and how the disconsolate father finally drew the knife to stab him. Not until the very last possible moment, not until there was no hope left that he would give up on his command did he finally feel pity and stay Abraham's hand. There is then a great deal of rhetorical violence in declaring that God saw immediately that Abraham would obey and in defining as merciful the patriarch's release from his gruesome imperative.

Because the sermon is more theologically precise than the *neixcuitilli* in representing the universal scope of the Akedah episode, the so-called favors conferred to Abraham are not limited to the physical restitution of Isaac. The promise that the Savior of the world will come from his lineage is something exceptional indeed, although not wholly incommensurable with or unrelated to the patriarch's singular piety. The sermon winds up by reminding the audience that, as the patriarch remembered where and when he had been shown favor and mercy, so the Nahua faithful should always be mindful to acknowledge gratitude to God because of the constant benefits he bestows upon them. The displacement of God's oath and covenant with Abraham by the Christian economy of grace, favors, and mercy moves the patriarch's willingness to sacrifice his son from the realm of the meritorious and relocates it in that of the due. The lack of emphasis and recognition of the immensity of Abraham's act as motivating the promise of the Savior would seem to suggest that, in the Christian religion, everything God does for his creatures is ultimately a favor and a gift, independent of people's acts. It is ironic, however, that in this sermon piece this incommensurate economy of gifts, mercy, and favors becomes more oppressive than that of the superseded reciprocity of the covenant and the law. For Abraham, in spite of his extraordinary act in extremis, is represented as not entitled to receive anything in return except his eventual salvation, on the condition that he always keeps obeying God.[20] The life of Isaac and the promise of the Savior as his descendant are not depicted as things Abraham either earned or deserved. They are represented as favors that the Lord freely and mercifully conferred upon him, and that he could have just as easily withheld without any detriment to his justice. The sermon section then concludes with its initial reference to Saint Matthew and his insistence on retrieving the circumstances of the calling of the apostles.

The second sermon fragment from fray Juan Bautista also deals with the Christian economy of love and favors, but its interpretation of the Akedah episode is very different from the first. This fragment is part of a long sermon based on the Epistle of the Second Sunday of Advent, Romans 15:4–13. The exegesis of the Akedah episode is inspired by Romans 15:9: "So that the gentiles might glorify God for his mercy." The point of the sermon piece will be to persuade the Nahua brethren of the gratitude they owe God, since as Gentiles they have been given the Savior for free: "We who are gentiles did not earn it, we were not promised it, wherefore it is very necessary that we be grateful and thankful" (Bautista 1606, 346). Bautista brings in as contrast the children of Israel, whose father Abraham had to do "a great many things" (346) in order to receive the promise of the Savior. The Franciscan then relates in detail the story of Abraham, closely following the biblical version. He represents how God tested the patriarch by calling upon him to offer his beloved firstborn, and how Abraham dutifully obeyed, preparing an ass, cutting wood for the holocaust, and going off very early in the morning with two servants and Isaac. Bautista narrates how, while they climbed the mountain God had singled out, Isaac asked where the offering was and a devastated Abraham answered that the Lord would provide the lamb. Bautista tells how Abraham bound the hands and feet of his beloved son, how he drew the knife "in order to decapitate his child" (347), and how the angel finally prevented him from continuing. Bautista departs from the biblical episode at this point, as he elaborates on the great docility and subjection of Isaac, who, in spite of being thirty years old, in no way tried to prevent or dissuade his father from carrying out the offering:

> Nor did he say to him: O my father, look. Perhaps you are fooling yourself or you are deceiving yourself . . . for God is not giving you [such] orders. Perhaps it is just that your fasting and vigils are making your head faint and confused. Has someone [else] killed, has someone [else] made an offering of his only child, his firstborn? Absolutely no one! He [Isaac] absolutely did not respond in that fashion. (347)

The driving force of the arguments Isaac could have raised but never did, according to Bautista, is based on the horror of what Abraham was willing to do in obedience to the deity. In sharp contrast with the *neixcuitilli* and with the earlier fragment analyzed, in this section Bautista focuses on the singularity of Abraham's act. He emphasizes how the patriarch's unheard-of obedience was the high price paid for God's oath to have the Savior of the world, God's own beloved son, come from Abraham's lineage.[21] But whereas this sermon section fully acknowledges Abraham's great merits, it also reveals that the violence of the test he was subjected to by God was almost beyond human endurance, and hence the great promise made to the patriarch, and through him to the children of Israel, in exchange for his great act.

The sermon then picks up again the theme of the gratitude owed by the Gentiles, since they did not do any penance, did not pay any price in order to receive the grace of Jesus Christ. The piece concludes by exhorting the Nahua brethren to be patient and receive consolation from the divine words, which oblige the Nahuas to consider all the good they have received from God, having been delivered from the false "people-eating beasts of hell" their ancestors not so long ago worshipped (Bautista 1606, 349). Whereas in the *neixcuitilli* the exhortation to the Nahua audience to emulate Abraham's obedience could be (mis)read as a demand to be ready and willing to offer up a son if God would so command, in this sermon piece it is clear that the Nahua faithful will never be required to undergo Abraham's onerous ordeal in order to receive the Savior's gifts. As Gentiles, they have received the latter under the superabundant economy of grace, in which things circulate freely and not as payment or expenditure.

By reminding the audience of the concrete historical iniquity of their not-so-remote ancestors, the sermon may also have reminded Nahuas of the annihilation and destruction that came upon them as they were delivered from their supposed servitude. Thus, in focusing only on the spiritual participation of the Nahuas in this Christian universal economy of superabundance, favors and release, there is great violence in dismissing the material reality of the millions of lives that were lost as the Nahuas received the redeeming Word. Abraham had to pay the cost of slaughtering Isaac for the sake of the deity, whereas the price the Nahuas paid for being freed from eating and drinking their own "bodies, their blood and their hearts" (Bautista 1606, 349), was the actual loss of legions of Isaacs, most precious jewels, in the great sixteenth-century *cocoliztli* (diseases; epidemics) that God had sent, not so long ago, together with the arrival of Christianity. The great gifts, favors, and mercies of God as depicted by Bautista in his two sermon fragments on the Akedah, allegedly free, actually came with a high price tag for humanity, perhaps not totally unlike the toll paid by the Nahua worshippers for the prosperity and affluence conferred by the prehispanic deities.

Mijangos and the Appeasement of God

Our third sermon piece comes from another outstanding *nahuatlato* of the early seventeenth century, the Augustinian fray Juan de Mijangos. His two major works are the *Espejo divino*, published in 1607 and reprinted in 1626, and a sermonary published in 1624. Both of these works are extremely long,[22] and their explicitly intended audiences were clerics and literate Nahuas (Sell 1993, 75). Both books fall under the genre of devotional and ecclesiastical literature, widespread in Spain during the first half of the sixteenth century but closely watched by an increasingly suspicious Inquisition after 1559 (Nalle 1999; Bataillon 1966).

The voluminous *Espejo divino* is noteworthy because it is written as a dialogue between a father and his son. This is remarkable because it weds European and Nahua cultural traditions. The *Espejo* harks back to the dialogue form that was characteristic of the humanistic spiritual literature of the sixteenth century widely diffused by the printing press,[23] as well as to the oratorical prehispanic genre of the *huehuetlatolli* or "words of the elders." Both genres had in common the intention of edifying their audiences in the art of proper social and religious conduct. As Barry Sell has pointed out: "Mijangos explicitly states in his prologue that he wrote the book in this form in order to make it more understandable to his Nahua readers" (Sell 1993, 75). This desire to make spiritual advice and reflection accessible and real to a secular, literate, and cultivated readership is precisely what had moved reformers and, later, counterreformers, to adopt the lively dialogue form.

Trying to engage the Nahua readership to which the *Espejo* is directed, Mijangos makes extensive use of the vintage figural language of the *huehuetlatolli*, employing characteristic metaphorical doublets and many stock idioms and expressions. In the sermon fragment dealing with the Akedah, this characteristic figural language of the prehispanic genre is further complemented, wittingly or unwittingly, by casting the mediation of Christ the Savior in terms that resonate with prehispanic ways of relating to the sacred. The sermon fragment opens with an invitation to the reader to understand God's ways and works "in the time of the ancient way of living" (262). But first, Mijangos tackles the issue of Christ's redeeming role in the very present time of the reading audience:

> First know that how today in our time . . . we lay out and make an offering to our Lord, God, of the honored body and of the precious blood of his beloved honored child, our Lord Jesus Christ, in mass, it is as though with it we appease, we calm, our deity and ruler, God, if he is angry with us because of our great sins, because there [i.e., in mass] is remembered how for our sake he was crucified, how he was made to suffer burning pain because of our sins and faults, our great and abominable sins. (262)

The doctrine of transubstantiation, which proclaims that the bread and wine are transformed into the body and blood of Christ when consecrated by the priest in the mass, is surely what allows Mijangos to say that the people make an offering in the mass in order to placate God the Father's anger for their sins.[24] By alluding to the iterative nature of Christ's sacrifice that is implicit in this doctrine, the terms "offering," "blood," "sin," and "appeasement of the deity" are linked together in the passage in ways not totally alien to the sacrificial economy of prehispanic times. As scholars of Aztec studies have pointed out, the people of Mesoamerica believed there had been a time of "intranscendent existence of the gods" (López Austin 1984, 1:68; my translation), a time that was interrupted by a violent, creative mythical period when the deities sacrificed themselves and destroyed each other in order to give birth to the different suns, the last being the fifth, under which humans currently lived. This turbulent mythical or creative time of the gods did not cease with the creation of humankind: it constantly impinged on human time, but now according to cycles, patterns, and rotations, which were fixed by the calendar devised by the primeval pair of humans or semi-divine entities, Oxomoco and Cipactonal (Sahagún 1989, 1:233–35; Nicholson 1971, 398; López Austin 1984, 1:264–65). Rituals had the important function of reenacting this mythical time in a controlled way, so that its thrust would be beneficial to the community rather than deadly (López Austin 1984, 1:70; Matos Moctezuma 1984, 135). Prehispanic gods were given steady ritual service by human beings in order to appease, feed, and placate them and thus ensure "the return of reproduction through the channels that human beings needed for living" (López Austin 1977, 244).

For her part, Louise Burkhart explains that, for the Nahuas, sin or *tlatlacolli* was conceived of not so much as a state of internal degradation (as in Christianity), but more as the material effect of damage brought about "by any sort of error or misdeed . . . from conscious moral transgressions to judicially defined crimes to accidental or unintentional damage" (1989, 28). *Tlatlacolli* could also be damage caused by breaches of the all-important rituals, by improper sexual conduct, by stealing, intoxication, and even unintentional acts that spoiled something. All of the above sins were forms of disruptions of order that destabilized and upset the delicate cosmic balance. These disruptions, in their turn, could cause the anger of the gods, or the unmanaged unleashing of their influences, which could be harmful to the individual and to the community. Lockhart argues that during prehispanic times there was the belief that the anger of the gods or supernatural beings was the basic cause for disease (1992, 259), which was a dreaded form of damage and imbalance affecting human beings. Taking all this into account, we can conjecture that in prehispanic times there was a systematic relation between blood offerings and the placating of the destructive anger or hunger of the gods; the rupture of this relation was a form of sin that could be fatal to the individual and to the human community at large.

In Mijangos's passage, the relations between the offering, sin, and the appeasement of the deity are not ordered in the same way as in the Nahua prehispanic system, but the relation among the three terms is nonetheless present. Thus, the blood of Christ appeases the anger of God that has been aroused by the awful sins of the human community. It is as if the sins did not give God his due, what belongs to him, what he expects as creator of the universe. This offends him, stirring his anger and his desire to make his creatures suffer. This is why it is said that Christ "was made to suffer burning pain because of our great sins" (Mijangos 1607, 262), that is, a pain commensurate with the grave transgressions of humanity, which otherwise would be inflicted on the creatures themselves.[25] The difference is that, whereas in the prehispanic system the divine anger may be conceived of in terms of hunger (see Read 1998), in the Christian system the anger is markedly moral. And whereas in the prehispanic system divine anger is likely to be aroused by the sin of a sacrifice improperly performed, in the Judeo-Christian system the sacrifice is offered so as to placate the wrath caused by sin.

Mijangos proceeds to discuss the sacrificial practices of "our fathers and our grandfathers [i.e., our ancestors]" (262). The Nahua readers must thus understand their ancestors to be Judeo-Christian as well as Mesoamerican, an identification quite unlikely to take place in the context of this sermon. The practice that Mijangos discusses as belonging to the "time of the ancient way of living" was the spilling of the blood of a lamb in order to placate God's anger for the sins committed by people. Although also propitiatory, according to the passage this ancient sacrificial economy involved no human sacrifice. Mijangos then declares that when Christ was tormented and crucified such "ancient usage" came to an end, and "our consummately good way of making offerings" (262) emerged, which is the mass: "There we lay out and make an offering to our Lord, God the Father, of the honored precious body and precious blood of his beloved child, our Lord Jesus Christ" (263). It is ironic that, since this new, superior Christian sacrificial economy is clearly centered on human sacrifice, it would seem closer to the prehispanic system than to the Jewish one left behind. However, since such human sacrifice is constantly reenacted in a highly mediated way, namely, in the transubstantiating ritual of the mass, it also evidently implies significant differences with the Mexican sacrificial economy. In any case, once Mijangos has established how the old sacrificial practices were superseded by the new Christian way of making offerings, he brings in the episode of the Akedah.

Thus the Lord orders Abraham to cut the neck of his child Isaac on top of the mountain, where he will show him a miracle. As Abraham is ready to strike his son, the angel appears and stops the slaughter, saying: "Now he knows that you truly love him ... and that you want to please him, for you do not want to make him angry, you do not want to bother him" (265). The angel's representation of Abraham's act in extremis as just a desire to please, as a desire not to make angry or to bother God, although compatible with Nahua standard linguistic usage, is nonetheless an understatement, to say the least. As in the *neixcuitilli*, the epic dimension and awful singularity of Abraham's act is reduced to the ordinarily devout, to not wanting to upset the deity. Again, there is no sense here of something transcendental, never heard of, as we saw in the second sermon fragment of Bautista analyzed above. The great violence of God's test in the biblical story is further increased in the sermon with the lessening of the patriarch's extraordinary act into the familiar and the quotidian.

But in contrast to the *neixcuitilli*, Mijangos will not try to exhort the Nahua readers to take Abraham as an example to follow. A lamb appears in a thicket, which Abraham will be able to offer in lieu of his son: "It is just as though with the lamb he paid the price for, he bought, and saved his beloved honored only child Isaac, whom our Lord, God, had ordered him to make an offering of to him, so that he did not die, so that his throat was not cut" (265). The miracle promised by God was, then, to allow Abraham to perform the awful sacrifice he had demanded with a lamb that he himself provided, so that, in the end, Isaac could go free. A wonder of a bargain indeed! Mijangos interprets Isaac as the "very sign and example of our Lord Jesus Christ" and the lamb as the "sign and example" of the sinner (265). It is relevant to point out that Saint Augustine interprets both Isaac and the ram as figures of Christ.[26] Mijangos clearly takes a different exegetical route in order to illustrate God's love for humankind through a dramatic reversal of the Akedah story:

> Thus it is clear how very much the deity and ruler, God, loves us, for that we will escape, that we lousy sinners defend ourselves, he cast and left his beloved only child, his beloved honored son, in the hands of the utterly wicked and very oppressive Jews. . . . He was made to suffer [so that] finally he was hung on the cross, crucified. Thus the deity and ruler, God, greatly favored and had mercy on us for if his beloved honored son would not have suffered for our sake, would not have died for our sake, if not: we would suffer, we would be killed. (265–66)

That is, if in the Akedah episode the lamb is sacrificed in lieu of Isaac, with Christ's crucifixion it is the beloved son who is sacrificed so that the lambs (i.e., the sinners) may go free. Clearly, in contrast with the great pain inflicted on Abraham by God's test, this astonishing reversal should show the readers evidence of God's great love for humanity. Still, the sacrifice of Jesus does not abolish or supersede the violence of God the Ruler, or the economy of debts, payments, and retributions that He presides over and enforces, according to the sermon. It is as if God's wrath, once aroused, had necessarily to be appeased in one way or another. And rather than hurting or killing the lambs who kindled his anger with their sins, he enigmatically (incomprehensibly?) chose to spare them by upgrading the offering and having his own son, who was also himself, be sacrificed to him.

The violent cosmic economy of sacrifice, debts, payments, and retributions upon which Mijangos founds his exegesis in this sermon is not something he draws only from the Nahuas, if he does at all. It is a tradition received from apocalyptic Judaism by Paul, the authors of the Synoptic Gospels, and the Fathers of the Church (Daniélou 1964; Lachowski 1967, 851; Cilveti 1977, 67–94, and 1989). Origen, Saint Gregory of Nisa, Saint Leo the Great, and even Saint Augustine concede to the devil a certain juridical entitlement over humanity (Cilveti 1977, 71). With original sin, humankind became indebted to God and enslaved to the devil, and thus the Prince of the World gained rights over humankind.[27] And indeed, there is a clear reference to these teachings in our sermon fragment when Mijangos writes how "with his precious blood he saved us, he paid the price for us, since we were the slaves, the captives of the devil" (262).

This is, however, the only mention of the devil in the sermon piece. Although Mijangos is alluding to this Jewish-Christian tradition of debts, payments, and sacrifice, his emphasis is not so much on how Jesus sacrificed himself in order to liberate humankind from the devil. Rather, the focus is on how Jesus appeased God the Father's anger with his blood and then on how the Father allowed his beloved son to be crucified by the Jews (not the devil), so that the people would not be killed. This shift of emphasis could be explained as Mijangos's desire to downplay the notion of Christ's sacrifice as ransom for humanity to the fallen angel. The patristic notion was dramatic and moving indeed, but it risked transforming the devil into a stupendous power that God the Ruler and his beloved son seem almost forced to satisfy in order to save humanity.[28]

With the shrouding of the role of the devil in this Judeo-Christian economy of debts, payments, and sacrifice, the prehispanic sacrificial regime all of a sudden does not look so utterly alien. For when Mijangos emphasizes God and not the devil as the supernatural entity to whom payments are due, the demand for blood sacrifice is not portrayed as something expected only by evil forces. Here we should note again that even though the sermon identifies the ancestors of the Nahuas as those who practiced animal sacrifices, such an identification carries little rhetorical force. The most outstanding commonality between the Akedah and the Crucifixion episodes is human sacrifice, and human sacrifice was much more readily associated with precontact religious practices than with Jewish ones, as any minimally educated Nahua would know.

The representation of God's pleasure over Abraham's disposition to slay his son as a proof of his devotion, the representation of the human sacrifice of the honored precious Christ as what saved sinful humankind from being killed, and finally, the representation of the mass as a new mode of repeatedly offering the son's flesh and blood in order to placate the Lord's wrath, may not necessarily have been interpreted by the Nahua readers as a radical break with their ancestors' sacrificial universe, in which the anger of life-giving deities had also to be appeased with offerings and entreaties, and in which the constant enactment of sacrifice by gods and humans is what spares time from destruction. What Mijangos's sermon certainly suggests is that the Christian "consummately good way of making offerings" was superior and more efficacious than any other sacrificial regime that had come before. But the need to placate the anger of the deity with the most precious offering of blood and flesh lest great misfortune befall people (not totally unlike the Nahuas of prehispanic times had believed) had not been abolished. Thus, wittingly or unwittingly, in Mijangos's exegesis of the Akedah episode and of the Crucifixion, a violent hybrid cosmic economy emerged in which prehispanic conceptions of the relationship between humanity and the sacred, although greatly modified by the colonial present, had not been fully left behind.

The Virgin Mary as the New Abraham

Our last sermon piece comes from the most prominent Dominican *nahuatlato* of the early seventeenth century, fray Martín de León. In 1611 he published the first devotional manual of the seventeenth century, entitled *Camino del cielo en lengua mexicana*.

This manual contains also a cathecism, a calendar of the prehispanic year, and a guide for the dying (León-Portilla 1988, 1:83). His second published work, to which our sermon piece belongs, is a long sermonary in Nahuatl with sermons for Sundays and holidays running from the first Sunday of Advent to Holy Week. The sermonary was originally conceived in four parts to cover the whole year, but only the first was published (León-Portilla 1988, 2:228). His other important work was a short manual published in 1614 entitled *Manual breve y forma de administrar los Santos Sacramentos a los indios universalmente*. Its three reprints in 1617, 1640, and 1669 are evidence of its widespread use in Mexico.

The piece concerning us here is conceived as part of Christ's farewell to his mother, Mary, the Wednesday before his death. This episode has no basis in the Gospels, canonical or apocryphal. It was conceived by a thirteenth-century Franciscan from San Gimignano named Giovanni da Cauli (Peck, quoted in Burkhart 1996, 25) as part of a book of meditations about the life of Christ, appropriately entitled *Meditationes vitae Christi*. The episode in question takes place in Mary Magdalene's house. The Virgin implores Jesus to stay with them for Passover, since she realizes that her son's intent to go to Jerusalem and thus bring redemption to humanity actually means his death (26). In a somewhat chauvinistic way, Jesus rebukes her, claiming that he must follow his father's desire. The overwhelming pathos and potential beauty of da Cauli's episode made it a likely candidate to be borrowed and rewritten by ecclesiastical writers, playwrights, and preachers dealing with Holy Week.[29]

In our sermon piece by fray Martín de León, Jesus's riposte to the Virgin's entreaties also displays the patriarchal privileging of the Father's will and the placing of it over the mother's. Jesus brings in Abraham, who was ordered by God to offer him Isaac, as an example for the Virgin to follow. Jesus emphasizes the horror of Abraham's test by pointing out how he carried in his own hands the very knife with which he would slay Isaac "and the fire with which he would be burned" (León 1614b, 316r). Jesus admonishes his mother to consider how Abraham utterly disregarded his agony in order "to comply fully with the wishes of God the father" (316r). He then tells her that "if God the father had wanted you yourself to kill him, thus your great love would have been revealed. But such was not necessary. God just wants you to endure patiently" (316r). The violence inherent in Mary's ordeal is augmented by the suggestion that God is requiring less from her than from Abraham, since she is only expected to witness the horror of her beloved son's death rather than actually carrying it out. Finally, however, Jesus concedes that just by willingly offering her child (that is, himself) to God, "you greatly surpassed Abraham's obedience and love" (316r), for, contrary to Isaac, we should add, her beloved son did indeed die.

The image of God the Father as a frightening deity who expects total and uncompromising submission from humankind is reinforced in León's passage, since God is represented as having demanded the sacrifice of a beloved son for a second time. In spite of the acknowledgment that God's command has caused Abraham anguish and will be terribly painful for the Virgin, the focus is clearly on the necessity to obey unquestioningly, regardless of the enormous personal cost his commands may entail. And if the Nahua faithful felt that these exacting demands were made by the colonizer's god only to the most pious and loving saints of Christianity, namely Abraham and Mary, and would no longer be required of them, maybe they would remember with secret satisfaction that these insuperable deeds of obedience were not that different from what their ancestors had also been capable of doing for their gods, who in exchange for their absolute submission had for a long time showered the lands of Anahuac with much food, wealth, and prosperity.

Conclusions

The Akedah is an episode that speaks about something beyond reason and even beyond the ethical. It speaks of the uncanny mysteries of faith that perhaps only those within the Jewish and Christian communities can fully grasp and understand. Yet, it is also an episode that exalts the capacity of human beings to defy their own earthly nature and give up what they cherish most for the sake of an otherly divinity. As soon as the focus of the episode shifts to this profound human dimension of Abraham's deed, the enormous spiritual violence of the Akedah comes to the fore.

In these readings of "The Sacrifice of Isaac" and the sermon pieces on the episode of the Akedah, I have focused primarily on the severity, not only of the enunciated story, but also of the different positions the Nahua audience is expected to take on the Judeo-Christian episode of the ultimate test of the human soul. Of all the pieces analyzed, perhaps the *neixcuitilli* is the most problematic, since the audience is asked to model behavior on Abraham while scarcely considering the singularity of the patriarch's perfect deed of obedience. The demands made on the Nahua faithful by the sermon pieces vary, as we have seen. But all of them coincide in representing God the Father's awful request as something righteous, which ought not to be questioned but only accepted. There is nothing theologically improper in these pieces, even when the emphasis on the episode may change depending on the moral lesson the friar intended to transmit to the faithful. All four sermon pieces, even Mijangos's, could conceivably have been addressed to a Spanish audience. Yet, the episode of the Akedah could never have meant the same culturally for a Spanish audience as it did for a Nahua one. And by thus meaning something different, these representations put into question the posited universality of the Judeo-Christian Word. This is where the forces of hybridization come into the play.

By representing the Akedah episode to the Nahua audience as a model to follow, as exemplary of the colonial God's difference, and as harbinger of a new cosmic economy of human sacrifice, the episode acquired meanings it did not have before. Far from its representing a decisive break with the prehispanic past, there is little that the Nahuas could have learned from the Judeo-Christian patriarch's epic piety that their ancestors' devotion to their gods had not already taught them. True, at the very end of the episode, God stopped the offering of Isaac, which indeed marked a significant difference from the prehispanic deities. Human sacrifice was no longer portrayed as being essential to the preservation of the world, as was believed during prehispanic times.

And yet, even if no actual material sacrifice ever took place, the Judeo-Christian God's demand for human sacrifice presupposed an expectation of utter service and obedience that was not incongruent with the unquestioning submission required of the Nahua ancestors by their prehispanic gods. If to this onerous expectation of obedience we add the downplaying of God's absolute commitment to bless Abraham and his descendants that we see in the *neixcuitilli* and in several of the sermon pieces discussed, an even more pronounced degree of mixture and hybridization becomes apparent. By scaling back God's oath into merely an expression of satisfaction with the fulfillment of his commands, the spiritual colonizers emphasized even more the severe expectancy of unconditional submission, thus Nahuatizing even further the figures of Yahweh and Abraham from what could be argued was already available in the biblical episode of the Akedah.

Thus, as Homi Bhabha has observed about colonial discourse, "Hybridity intervenes in the exercise of authority not merely to indicate the possibility of its identity but to represent the unpredictability of its presence" (1994, 114). In their ardent desire to subject the Nahua audience to Christianity by parading Abraham as an example of obedience, the spiritual colonizers partially betrayed the difference between their Judeo-Christian God and the prehispanic deities. As a result, they may also have unwittingly opened up a space for the audience to accommodate memories of the old prehispanic disposition to sacrifice the most precious to the gods, in order to placate divine anger and prevent the onset of misfortune. This is not to say that the Nahuas thought the Judeo-Christian God to be a Tlaloc or a Tezcatlipoca in disguise. Instead, as William Taylor has suggested, the great site of continuity between prehispanic and colonial Nahua religiosity may have lain "in habits of conception—in ways of representing and entering the sacred" (1996, 5). With "The Sacrifice of Isaac" and these four sermon pieces, rather than showing the way to break away decisively from these prehispanic forms of relating to the sacred, the friars may well have contributed to their preservation in the brave new world of Spanish colonialism.

Notes

1. It has long been held that medieval religious drama was born in the tenth century with the liturgical tropes *Quem quaeretis?* and the *Visitatio sepulchri*. These were short dialogues in Latin, interpolated in the Easter mass, in which an angel appeared to the three Marys in order to announce to them Christ's resurrection. Little by little, this simple dialogue would grow with the addition of characters and more complex scenes.

2. These are the opening words of "The Sacrifice of Isaac" (23v).

3. This scene occurs as Abraham's servants are preparing a banquet to introduce Isaac to his blood relatives. Says Hagar: "Today the great ruler Abraham has yet again invited people to a banquet because of the great esteem he has for his child. But as for us, since we are lowly servants, we are held in no regard. And as for you, my child, you are doubly luckless. Would that I could find relief in you, that you could give relief to all my earthly torments, for in truth your birth and your lot are eternal weeping" (28v). Although Hagar's sense of being wronged by Abraham's neglect toward her and her child would seem to indicate that Abraham's relationship to Ishmael was more than that of a master, the point is not made sufficiently clear and is not ever mentioned again in the play. Thus, it is difficult to claim that the *neixcuitilli* was taking an open stance against polygamy. What will be emphasized is Hagar's ineptitude for bringing up her son properly.

4. I am using the translation in this volume, and I will adopt the abbreviated title, "The Sacrifice of Isaac."

5. The destruction of temples and idols commenced in 1525, a year after the first Twelve arrived in Mexico (Motolinia 1951, 99; Mendieta 1980, 226–30). According to fray Juan de Zumárraga's letter of June 1531, already five hundred temples and twenty thousand idols had been destroyed (Israel 1975, 7–8). Although scholars have questioned these numbers and accounts

as being inflated by a partisan interest in promoting the evangelizing achievements of the orders (Lockhart 1991, 204), it seems that the Mexica priesthood and human sacrifice were eliminated almost immediately (Gibson 1964, 100).

6. This class upgrading is pointed out in John Cornyn's preliminary notes on "Sacrifice" (Horcasitas 1974, 198–99).

7. These are the positions of Jerry Williams (1992, 73–74) and Marlyn Ravicz (1970, 97).

8. Potter then adds that "having established this, the story decrees . . . the end of human sacrifice in the tribe of Abraham, and the forging of a new relationship with divine power" (312). But then, in the next paragraph, he arrives at the conclusion that by dramatizing these events for the Nahua audience the anonymous playwright "recapitulates . . . [the] message of hope—that divine power has ceased to exact such sacrifices from its subjects" (312). This was only partially the case, and herein lies the striking contradictions of the position of this play vis-à-vis the practice of human sacrifice.

9. The passage reads as follows: "Listen, you people of the world: in the example of this child Isaac will be seen everything that will happen to the beloved son of God when he will save people everywhere in the world, for through his blood and his death he will open up heaven where sits his beloved honored Father. But meanwhile, before it happens to the son of God, it will first happen to the precious and blessed child Isaac" (25r–v). The passage is ambiguous. Since ultimately Isaac's blood will not be shed, it is not clear what those things are that will happen to Isaac and that the audience must take as an anticipation of those that will happen to Christ.

10. Abraham declares to his son in the first part of the play that God's commands are three, and that Isaac should not violate a single one ("Sacrifice," 27v). These commands are not specified in the passage, nor is it clear why the playwright chose the number three instead of ten (for the commandments) or two (for the commands all Christians must follow). However, the number does coincide with the three commands represented to Isaac as he and his father walk back home after the gruesome episode.

11. I have written more extensively about the *neixcuitilli* "The Sacrifice of Isaac" in "A Nahua Yahweh or a Judeo-Christian Tlaloc? Domination, Hybridity and Continuity in the Nahua Theater of Evangelization," *Colonial Latin American Review,* 2001.

12. Here I turn once more to Sahagún's additions to the *Postillas,* or the gospel and epistle commentaries to be said in Mass every Sunday of the year. Writes Sahagún: "Y sabe que cuando andas pensando en algún pecado mortal, aunque no consientas en que lo cometas, pues tan sólo te alegre el pensar en ello y en tu más íntimo ser bien sepas que no lo deseas cometer, pues tan sólo el pensar en él te da placer, ya has pecado" (And know that when you are thinking about some mortal sin, even if you do not consent to commit it, just because by thinking about it you become happy, and in your innermost being you know well that you do not desire to commit it, just because by thinking about it you receive pleasure, you have already sinned; Sahagún 1993a, 43, translation mine).

13. I am grateful to Barry Sell for his generosity in allowing me to use for this article his unpublished translations of the Bautista and Mijangos sermon fragments on the Akedah. I also thank Louise Burkhart for permitting me to use her translation of León's fragment, which is published in Burkhart 2001, 94.

14. I owe Barry Sell the valuable information that, from his examination of many imprints and manuscripts of the sixteenth and seventeenth centuries, he has found no further mention of the Akedah episode. Among the key imprints he has examined besides Bautista's and Mijangos's works are fray Juan de la Anunciación's *Sermonario* (1577), fray Juan de Gaona's *Colloquios de la paz y la tranquilidad Christiana* (1582), and Sahagún's *Psalmodia christiana y sermonario de los sanctos del año* (1583). He has found nothing, either, in the work of the eighteenth-century Jesuit Father Ignacio de Paredes (email, December 8, 2000).

15. Advent is the period that precedes the festivity of Christmas or the Nativity. It commences with the Sunday closest to November 30 (Nacar Fuster and Colunga 1961, 16) and ends on December 25. It is supposed to be a time of expectancy and of spiritual preparation.

16. I owe this information also to Barry Sell, who as translator of these sermon pieces has had firsthand access to Bautista's imprint, and thus to the organization and distribution of the

sermons among the four Advent Sundays and among the calendar of saints corresponding to the Advent period.

17. The calendar of saints was incorporated into the liturgical year by the Church soon after the cycles of the Nativity and Easter were established, which commemorated the principal events of the life of Christ. The calendar of saints is divided into four hierarchical categories according to their importance. The feast of Saint Andrew belongs to the second category, which includes the less principal feasts of the lives of Christ and of the Virgin Mary, the lives of the Apostles, and of other significant saints (Nacar Fuster and Colunga 1961, 15–19).

18. "Among other things, of which it would take too long time to mention the whole, Abraham was tempted about the offering up of his well-beloved son Isaac, to prove his pious obedience, and so make it known to the world, not to God" (Saint Augustine 1950, 554). Saint Augustine's canonical exegesis of the Akedah must have been an indispensable intertext of our three star *nahuatlatos'* sermon pieces on the subject, and this exegesis will be important in this article also as an authoritative point of reference against which to compare the different inflections given to the episode by Bautista, Mijangos, and León.

19. "And the Angel of the Lord called unto Abraham from heaven the second time, saying, By myself have I sworn, saith the Lord; because thou hast done this thing, and hast not spared thy beloved son for my sake; that in blessing I will bless thee, and in multiplying I will multiply thy seed as the stars of heaven, and as the sand which is upon the seashore" (Saint Augustine 1950, 556).

20. "Paul insists that man does not earn reward in the same full and fundamental sense in which he earns punishment. He merits in a lesser, secondary sense, since the graces that make him holy and move him to do good are a gift: 'The wages of sin is death, but the gift of God is life everlasting in Christ Jesus Our Lord' (Romans 6:23)" (Most 1967, 674). In other words, according to this economy of grace and gifts, Abraham is owed nothing by God because the patriarch's willingness to sacrifice his son is already a gift that will eventually obtain him salvation, unless he were to decline such a gift to do good in the future, not repent about his refusal, and thus be punished.

21. "Right because of me, for my sake, I make an oath because after you did it you did not destroy your beloved child, your firstborn, on my account. Behold, I will favor you, thus I will show you mercy. I will multiply your lineage, such that it will be . . . like the sand lying spilled on the seashore" (Bautista 1606, 348).

22. The *Espejo divino* has "7 preliminary pages + 552 numbered p. + 3 final ones" and the *Primera parte del Sermonario y santoral* has "15 preliminary pages without numbers + 564 numbered p. + 93 with tables and misprints" (León-Portilla 1988, 2:275; translation mine).

23. In fact, the famous dialogues of *De los nombres de Cristo* by the renowned Augustinian fray Luis de León (published in Salamanca in 1583 with four subsequent editions in 1585, 1587, 1595, and 1603) may have been a humanist model for fray Juan de Mijangos, along with fray Juan de Gaona's *Colloquios de la paz y tranquilidad en lengua mexicana*. Mijangos's emphasis on the elegance and style of the Nahuatl as a vernacular language would seem to emulate fray Luis de León's efforts in elevating the Castilian language. Fray Bermúdez Pedraza, a contemporary of fray Luis, declared that "[he] wrote the books *Del nombre de Dios* [sic] and *La perfecta casada* with such a chaste and graceful language that they may be useful to learn phrases, rhetorical colors and soft ways of speech" (quoted in Cuevas García 1982, 63; translation mine). The Ciceronian style of fray Luis de León's dialogues in which one speaker-master develops his thoughts in long doctrinal arguments without being interrupted by his interlocutors (Cuevas García 1982, 53) are quite in line with the monological style of the *huehuetlatolli*. Most important is perhaps fray Luis's invitation (to those who felt up to the task) to write in the vernacular about things closely related to the Scriptures, since the Church had prohibited reading the Bible in the vulgar languages (Cuevas García 1982, 37). We should remember that Mijangos was quite intent on defending the richness of Nahuatl for expressing the subtleties of scriptural thought. Just like the *Nombres* and the *Perfecta casada*, "the *Espejo divino* is a series of meditations inspired by the Bible and by the teachings of the Fathers of the Church" (León-Portilla 1988, 2:275; translation mine). According to Robert Ricard, the learned friar Alonso de la Veracruz

had been a close friend of fray Luis (Ricard 1991, 12). Fray Alonso was elected provincial of the Augustinian province four times (Grijalva 1985, 402). He founded the Colegio de San Pablo and its library. He was professor of Scriptures in the Universidad de México (Grijalva 1985, 179–80; 396–403). When fray Luis de León was incarcerated by the Inquisition for his propositions, fray Alonso declared (albeit not publicly) that he was in agreement with them (Grijalva 1985, 400). Although fray Alonso died only one year after the *Nombres* and the *Perfecta casada* were published, it can be surmised that copies of these books were received in Mexico, and that the renowned and now-vindicated fray Luis de León would be widely read (and emulated) by his Augustinian brothers.

24. This doctrine had been reaffirmed by the Council of Trent on October 11, 1551, in chapter 4 of session 13: "It has always been the conviction of the Church of God, and this holy Council now again declares, that by the consecration of the bread and the wine a change takes place in which the entire substance of the bread is changed into the substance of the body of Christ our Lord and the entire substance of the wine into the substance of His blood. This change the holy Catholic Church fittingly and properly calls transubstantiation" (quoted in Vollert 1967, 260). Now, the way Mijangos presents the offering of Christ—as a way to placate God the Father whenever he is angry with the sinner—underscores the iterability of the actual sacrifice of flesh and blood, which is what transubstantiation means, and not its one-time occurrence.

25. Later in the sermon piece, Mijangos writes: "Thus the deity and ruler, God, greatly favored and had mercy on us for if his beloved honored son would not have suffered for our sake, would not have died for our sake, if not: we would suffer, we would be killed" (265).

26. Saint Augustine writes: "In order, then, that the children of the promise may be the seed of Abraham, they are called in Isaac, that is, they are gathered together in Christ by the call of grace" (1950, 555). Later on, Saint Augustine establishes a similarity between Isaac carrying the wood for his execution and Christ carrying the cross. Since Isaac was not slain, after all, but the ram: "What then did he [the ram] represent but Jesus, how, before He was offered up, was crowned with thorns by the Jews?" (555).

27. "The Synoptics further described sin as resulting in slavery to the devil, an idea that entered into their concept of guilt. Thus, Christ's victory over the devil led to freedom from sin and guilt" (Lachowski 1967, 851).

28. This may possibly be why the theologian L. Lercher calls the Church Fathers' quasi-dramatic representation of humanity's liberation from its servitude to the devil "minus convenientium," that is, less convenient (quoted in Cilveti 1977, 70n.4).

29. Burkhart (1996) analyzes a sixteenth-century Nahuatl adaptation of a Spanish play that dramatizes and elaborates on this episode.

PART 2

The Plays

TRANSCRIPTION GUIDELINES

The editors of *Nahuatl Theater* have attempted to reproduce as closely as possible the spelling, punctuation, capitalization, and other orthographic features of the original Nahuatl manuscripts. This practice extends to including expected marks like crosses (often resembling plus signs above or in proximity to the word for cross) as well as unexpected marks like those resembling equal signs whose function is unclear. In order to make the transcriptions as suggestive as possible of the handwritten originals, later additions to the main text, typically written in smaller charcters above or below the main text, are placed in corresponding superscript or subscript positions. This is reflected in the formatting of the corresponding English. The growing number of those studying early Nahuatl will find the foliation of the transcriptions included in the English translations, which will facilitate matching the longer Nahuatl passages with their English interpretations.

While there will always be some differences between handwritten manuscripts and their modern printed counterparts (like those in this set), we hope that our renditions will be of great help to those searching for reliable versions of these early Nahuatl writings. One of the more obvious minor areas of disputed interpretation will be our resolution of characters of various sizes into lower- or upper-case letters. Sometimes the intentions of the original scribes were unclear, at least by current orthographic conventions, so our decisions may be legitimately disputed by those who compare the originals with our versions.

Our one major departure is in the spacing of letters into the familiar units of "words." Here our practice generally follows that established by fray Juan Bautista and the Nahua teacher Agustín de la Fuente in their extensive published corpus (1599–1606); fortuitously, it usually anticipates and coincides with current scholarly norms. Notwithstanding our approach, most of those who wrote early Nahuatl texts thought more in terms of those elements most obvious in speech, i.e., the syllable and the utterance, than of the word and the sentence. Thus transcriptions and translations are closely linked since our renderings of the originals ultimately reflect our understanding of what we think the authors of the texts meant to say. There should be little dispute most of the time given the content of the plays and the relative brevity and formulaic nature of much of the dialogue, but extended speeches always involve deciding what is more—or less—probable given what preceded and followed a dubious passage. This is further complicated by Nahuatl's complex system of affixes: in certain cases does a particular syllable end one item or begin a new one? While we are confident that the majority of our choices will stand the test of time, there will inevitably be advances in the study of early Nahuatl and Nahuas that will render some of our decisions less probable.

Present Location
William L. Clements Library, University of Michigan
Ann Arbor, Michigan

[1r]
+

Nican pehua nican tzinti inninnemilitzin[1] in yeintin tlatoque Reyesme in quenin Oquimotlapalhuitzinoque in tlaçomahuisteopiltzintli yn ipiltzin D.^{S} in toteCuio. Jesu x$\overline{\text{po}}$ in onpa Ohualeuhque in iquiçayanpa in tonatiuh Auh nican pehua nican motlalia i nexcuitilmachiotl in quenin omochiuh huallehuasque in yeintin tlatoque reyesme onpa in iquiçayanpa in tonatiuh quihualyacantias in intitlan in inteyacancauh yhuan Citlali Oc achi huel tlayacanas. auh in icuac ye hualaçisque in yeintin tlatoque reyesme in ixtlahuacan inahuac yn iAltepeuh in ERodes motlatis in [1v] Citlali auh niman onca tlatos in

Gaspar = Ye huecauh in nontlachixtiuh in aocmo nicnotilia in mahuistic Citlali in tomahuisteyacancatzin in ixquich cahuitl in techmoyacanilia huel iuhqui nicmati iuhqui niquilnamiqui Ca ye otaçico in canpa Omotlacatilitzino in mahuistic piltzintli in tictotemolia Ca huel nelli Ca iscatqui in huey Altepetl in Jerusalem ca ninomati ye otictonextilique in tlein tictotemolia = Auh xihualauh in tehuatl in titotetlayecolticauh Xonyauh Xoncalaqui in ip$\bar{\text{a}}$ huey Altepetl Jerusalem iuhqui xiquilhui Xicmelahuili in canpa Otihualeuhque iquisayanpa in [2r] tonatiuh auh ca çentzonpa ticontēnamiqui[2] in imatzin in icxitzin ma techmomaquili in itlatocahuelitzin inic huel tictixpantilitihue in tlein tonetequipachol auh i ni=can ixtlahuacan in ihueyAltepetzin Jerusalem nican ticonchie in itlatocahuelitzin inic huel onpa tonyasque tictixpantilitihue in tlein tonetequipachol—

Titlantli = Ma nicneltili in amotlatocatlanahuatiltzin ma nicchihua in annechmonahuatilia Canel namotlacauhtzin—

Yas in titlantli yquiahuatempa in ERodes quitlapalos in Calpixqui quilhuis

Titlantli = Tlatohuanien ma mitzmochicahuilican in teteo Oticmiyohuilti [2v] ma xicmomachilti ca nintetlayecolticauh in yeintin tlatoque—Reyesme—

---

1. inninnemilitzin: read *in innemiliztzin*.
2. ticontēnamiqui: standard *tocontennamiqui*. Here and below can be found *ticon-* for standard *tocon-* and *xicon-* for standard *xocon-*. See Carochi 1983, 42v–43v.

The Three Kings
Translated by Louise M. Burkhart, with assistance from Barry D. Sell

[1r]

Here begins, here commences the life[1] of the three rulers, kings, how they greeted the precious and wondrous sacred child, the child of God, our lord Jesus Christ. They came from the east.[2] And here begins, here is placed the exemplary model, how it happened that the three rulers, kings, came from the east. Their messenger, their guide comes leading them. And the star goes a bit ahead. And when the three rulers, kings, are about to reach the plain next to Herod's altepetl,[3] the star will be hidden. [1v] *And then speaks*

CASPER: I have been looking around for quite a while. I no longer see the wondrous star, our wondrous guide, that has been leading us the whole time. What I really think, what I reckon, is that we have reached the place where the wondrous child whom we are seeking was born. Truly indeed, here is the great altepetl of Jerusalem. I think that we have now found what we are seeking. But come, our servant. Go forth, go enter into the great altepetl of Jerusalem. Tell him, explain to him, that we came from the east [2r] and that we kiss his hands, his feet, four hundred times.[4] May he give us his royal authorization so that we can go put before him what our problem is. And here on the plain of his great altepetl of Jerusalem, here we await his royal authorization so that we can go there, we can go put before him what our problem is.

MESSENGER: Let me carry out your royal command, let me do what you command me, since I am your servant.

(The messenger goes to Herod's door. He greets the steward. He says to him:)

MESSENGER: O ruler, may the deities[5] give you health.[6] Greetings.[7] [2v] Know that I am the servant of three rulers, kings.

---

1. The term is used as if this were a biographical story, such as a saint's life.
2. Literally, "where the sun comes out." The biblical basis for the story is in Chapter 2 of the Gospel according to Saint Matthew. It begins (verse 2:1): "Now when Jesus was born in Bethlehem of Judea in the days of Herod the king, behold, there came wise men [Magi in the Vulgate] from the east to Jerusalem." Matthew states that there were three gifts but does not specify the number of wise men. According to Farmer (1992, 312–13), since the time of Origen (third century) they have traditionally been numbered at three and were subsequently given the names Casper or Jasper, Melchior, and Balthasar. An iconographic tradition represents one as an old man, one as middle-aged, and the third as young. The practice of depicting one as a dark-skinned African dates from the fifteenth century.
3. altepetl: the largest sociopolitical unit to survive Spanish conquest and colonization. During colonial times the word was translated in many ways including *ciudad* (city) and *pueblo* (people, settlement).
4. Here and below, *four hundred* is a common idiom in the vigesimally based traditional counting system for "countless, innumerable." Where it occurs in the phrase "four hundred times" it could be construed as meaning "countless or many times over."
5. Here and below, the messenger is the only character in the play who professes belief in multiple deities.
6. Here and below, formulaic statement about—or inquiry into—someone's health (literally, "strength") that forms part of polite greetings, similar to statements in the *Bancroft Dialogues* (Karttunen and Lockhart 1987).
7. Formulaic polite greeting, literally, "You have expended breath on [unspecified object]" or "You have fatigued yourself."

Calpixqui = Ma nican tihuitz nocniuhtzinē ma te[l?] huel huey in monetequipachol huel mixco nestihuitz—

titlantli = Tlacatlen tlatohuanien ma mitzmochicahuilican in teteo – Oticmiyohuilti ma xicmomachilti ca onpa nihualehua in iquiçaianpa in tonatiuh auh ca onpa noChantzinco in itocayocan Prençia auh yeintin tlatoque Oniquinhualnoyacanili auh nican ononaçico in ipan in mohueytlatocatlaltzin auh in mohueytlatocauh in ERodes ma ixpan xinechmohuiquili Ca intencopatzinco in tlatoque in pipiltin inic nicnotlapalhuico— [3r]

Calpixqui = Ca ye cualli nocniuhtzinen ma oc nican Xinechie ma oc nicnotili oc nicnolhuili in tlatohuani ERodes—

Auh niman yas tlecos in Calpixqui ixpan in ERodes quicopinas in insombrero yexpa motlancuacolos El fragmento agrega: **auh ixpan motlanquaqueztietzi çe ynca ytlanquateuh, auh nima etc**[3] **auh niman quitos—**

Calpixqui = Totecuiyoyē Tlacatlen tlatohuanien teuctlen huel ye nohuianpa Oquis oaçic Omoteneuh O^{n}caquistia in motenyo in momahuisyo in ixquich in mohuelitilis in ixquichtin Cm̄c tlaca Pipiltin tlatoque teteuctin mitzmimacaxilia^n mitzmomahuistililia^n Auh Çe huey^n tlamahuisolli^n in ^{axcan} topam quimochihuilia^n in toteotzin totla^{to}catzin in nican motecpanchantzinco motlatocachantzinco Ohualla [3v] intitlan in yeintin tlatoque Reyesme huel çenca hueca in ohualquisque Ohualeuhque ca niman ayac iuhqui hualmaxitia in ipan in motlatocaAltepetzin huel Çentlamantli in itlatol huel tlaque yn ixayac auh ninomati ca tlateotocani^{me} auh mixpantzinco tlatosnequi Onca quiahuac quichie^n in motlatocatlanahuatiltzin Cuix nicnotzas Cuix calaquis Cuix mixpantzinco neçi(quiuh)(quihui)—

ERodes = huey tetzahuitl huey tlamahuisolli^n in tinechtenehuilia^n ma calaqui ma nixpan neçiqui inic nicmatis Canpa^n agrega inchan, campan in Ohualeuh tlein quinequi—

temos in calpixqui quinotzas ^{auh} **in titlantli——expan motlanquacoloz yn ixpan Erodes——namiquilis**[4] **in iman in icxin nima huallemos**[5] **in calpixquin quitos** [4r]

Calpixqui = Ma ximocalaquitzino nocniuhtzinen Ca mitzmonochilia^n in tlatohuani in ERodes—

titlantli = Ca ye cualitzin nocniuhtzinen =—

yxpan yas in ERodes——in titlantli motlacuaquetzas

titlantli = tlacatlen tlatohuanien ma xinechmomaquili in momatzin in mocxitzin in nimotlacauhtzin $^{inic\ nictennamiquis}$__

Yc moquetzas in ERodes oc cecpa[6] **motlalis—**

---

3. Here and below, the superscript additions/corrections/changes appear to be in a different hand.
4. namiquilis: read *quitennamiquiliz*.
5. huallemos: evidently to be read *hualtemoz*.
6. oc cecpa: here and below can be found this and other variants of standard <u>oc ceppa</u>.

STEWARD: Welcome, O my friend. Your problem must be very great, as it is quite evident on your face.

MESSENGER: O personage,[8] O ruler, may the deities give you health. Greetings. Know that I come from the east. And my home is there in the place called Persia. And I have led here three rulers. And I have arrived here in your great and royal land. And as to your great ruler, Herod, take me before him. By order of the rulers, the noblemen, I come to greet him. [3r]

STEWARD: Very well, O my friend. Wait for me here for a bit. Let me see and tell the ruler, Herod.
(And then the steward goes, going up[9] before Herod. He takes off his hat. He bends his knees three times. The fragment adds: and before him he kneels on one knee, and then, etc. And then he says:)

STEWARD: O our lord, O personage, O ruler, O lord, in all places has your fame and your renown gone out, arrived, been declared, been pronounced. You are all-powerful. All the people of the world—nobles, rulers, lords—fear and respect you. But our deity, our ruler is performing a great wonder upon us today. Here to your palace, your royal home has come [3v] the messenger of three rulers, kings, who have come, who have ventured here from very far away. Absolutely no one like this has come [before now] to your royal altepetl. His speech and his face are quite distinct.[10] And I think that he is an idolater.[11] And he wants to speak before you. There in the doorway he awaits your royal command. Shall I summon him? Shall he enter? Shall he come appear before you?[12]

HEROD: It is a great omen, a great wonder, that you declare to me. Let him enter, let him come appear before me so that I will find out where add: his home is, where he came from, what he wants.
(The steward goes down. He summons the messenger. And he bends his knees three times before Herod. He kisses his hands, his feet. Then the steward comes down. He says:) [4r]

STEWARD: Do enter, O my friend. The ruler, Herod, summons you.

MESSENGER: Very well, O my friend.
The messenger goes before Herod. He kneels.

MESSENGER: O personage, O ruler, give me your hands, your feet, so that I, your servant, may kiss them.
(Thus Herod stands up. He sits down again.)

---

8. Literally, "O person," or "O human being," this term was used frequently in formal speeches as a vocative and title denoting respect for the addressee (see the *Bancroft Dialogues* [Karttunen and Lockhart 1987, 34–35] and the *Florentine Codex*, book 6 [Sahagún 1969]).

9. Stage directions suggest that the set for Herod's palace has an upper and a lower level, with Herod's hall or throne room raised above the stage.

10. Tentative translation. The speech is distinct; the face is *huel tlaque* [?].

11. Emendation in text makes this plural, referring to the kings as well, but it probably should remain singular, referring only to the messenger.

12. Here again, text is emended to plural, as if to include the kings, but it should refer only to the messenger.

titlantli = — Ma xicmiyohuilti pilen tlatohuanien in titlacatl in tiERodes ma mitzmoChicahuilican in teteo ma xicmomachilti ca onechhualmotitlanique in yeintin tlatoque pipiltin in nican ixtlahuacan ynahuac in mohuey[n]Altepetzin Omaxitico auh [ca] Onca nechmochielia[n] [4v] Onpa Ohualquisque ynyn campa in iquisayanpa in tonatiuh huel Çenca hueca auh Çentzompa[n] qui(hual)tennamiqui quitennamiqui solamte in momatzin in mocxitzin auh çenca necnoma(ti)[chi]listica mitzmitlanililian mitz(hual)falta hualmotlatlauh(tilia)tiliyan ma xiquinmomaquili in motlatocahuelitilitzin inic mixpantzinco neçiquihue mitzmixpantiliquihue in tlein intequipacholtzin tlacatle tlatohuanie.—

ERodes = Nocniuhtzinen ic otimaxitico ma mitzmochicahuili in totecuio D.[s] tiquinmolhuilis in moteachcahuan in motlatocaycniuhtzitzinhuan in moteucyohuan Ca çentzompa nictlasocamati in intlatocamahuistetlaçotlalitzin inic Oquimomahuistililico in noAltepeuh in nochan in nocalitic ma nican hual[5r]mohuicacan ma hualmocalaquican ca yntlatocachantzin ma nicnomaçehuis in inMahuisXayacatzin ma nicmatis in tlein innetequipacholtzin ca niquinnochielia—

titlantli = Ca ye cualitzin tlatohuanien nopiltzintzinen—

Auh niman (quinotzas) quinnahuatiz[7] **in ipilhuan ERodes**

ERodes = Auh yn amehuantin in antlatoque in anpipiltin in anteteuctin Xihuian Xiquimonamiquiliti Xiquinçiauhquetzacan tlapitzalos netotilos Xiquinmahuistililican XiquinXochitican Ca nican niquinnochielia—

Auh niman yaS in titlantli (quinnotzatiuh in tlatoque in ixtlahuacan Altepetenco) Variante auh niman yaz in titlantli yhuan tennamiquisque yn ipilhua Erodes ycan xochitl yhuan tlapitzalin achtopa yaz yn titlantlin quitoz_____

[5v]

titlantli = Ononaçito in canpa Oannechmotitlanique ixpan Ononneçito in ERodes in huey pilli in huey tlatohuani auh Ca huel Çenca quitlaçocamati in amotetlaçotlalitzin Ca quimitalhuitzinohua ma hualmocalaquican ma hualmohuicacan ma moçehuitzinoqui yn incalitictzinco Ca mochi intlatquitzin Ca mochi intetzinco pohuis in quexquich noaxca notlatqui—

Achitzin nenemisque in—tlatoque hualtemosque—ȳpan yn iCaballohuan—auh onca tlapitzalos quinXochitisque auh in ERodes niman hual=temos quintlapalos ymixpam motlanquacolo[tie]s quitos Erodes_____ [6r]

ERodes = Anquimiyohuiltique in oanmaXitico in oanhualmohuicaque in anmahuistililonime in anteteuctin in antlatoque Ma amechmochicahuilitzino in teotl in tlatohuani totecuio D.[s] Cuix achitzin amechmochicahuilia in tloque nahuaque D.[s]—

---

7. To the right in the margin: *auh*. It is unclear whether this was meant to be included in the text.

MESSENGER: Be welcome,[13] O nobleman, O ruler, you personage, Herod! May the deities give you health! Know that three rulers, noblemen, have sent me as a messenger. They have arrived here on the plain next to your great altepetl. And they are waiting for me there. [4v] They came from the east, very far away. And four hundred times they kiss your hands and your feet. And very humbly they ask of you, they beseech you, may you give them your royal authorization so that they may come appear before you, they may reveal to you what their problem is, O personage, O ruler.

HEROD: O my friend, welcome.[14] May our lord God give you health. You are to tell your masters, your royal friends, your lords, that I thank them four hundred times for their royal and wondrous affection, with which they have come to honor my altepetl, my home, the inside of my house. Let them come [5r] here, let them enter their royal home, let me be deserving of their wondrous faces, let me learn what their problem is. I await them.

MESSENGER: Very well, O ruler, O my nobleman.[15]

(And then Herod summons gives orders to his noblemen.)[16]

HEROD: And, you rulers, you noblemen, you lords, go, meet them, greet them! Wind instruments will be played. There will be dancing. Honor them, adorn them with flowers! I wait for them here.

(And then the messenger goes to summon the rulers on the plain at the edge of the altepetl. Variant: And then the messenger goes, and Herod's noblemen[17] go, to meet the others with flowers and flutes. The messenger goes first. He says:) [5v]

MESSENGER: I reached the place you sent me to. I appeared before Herod, the great nobleman, the great ruler. And he is most grateful for your affection. He says: "Let them enter, let them come, let them rest inside their house, for everything is their possession, for everything will belong to them, whatever is my property, my possession."

(The rulers move on a bit. They get down from their horses. And then wind instruments are played. They adorn them with flowers. And Herod then comes down, greeting them, going on bended knee before them. Herod says:) [6r]

HEROD: Greetings! You have arrived, you have come, you honored ones, you lords, you rulers. May the deity, the ruler, our lord God, give you health. Does the Lord of the Near, the Lord of the Nigh, God, give you a little health?

---

13. This is an optative statement, literally, "May you have expended breath on [unspecified object]" or "May you have fatigued yourself," the pragmatic thrust (probably uppermost in a typical Nahua's mind) being a formulaic polite greeting.

14. Welcome: literally, "so you have come to arrive."

15. The possessed form of *pilli* normally means "child" rather than "noble" (see Carochi 1983, 9v–10r). However, the doubling of the honorific suffix here, as in later speeches by Casper and Balthasar, indicates that "my noble" is the intended meaning (Karttunen and Lockhart 1987, 39–40). This can also be found in Molina 1977, 73v: "Nopiltzintzine. a señor. vel. o señor. vel. señor. [dize el que habla con persona de calidad]" (Nopiltzintzine. Ah Lord, or O Lord, or Lord [says one who speaks with a person of high rank]).

16. Literally, "his children," in this case meaning the high-born subordinates of Herod.

17. See previous note re "his children."

Melchor = Ma ximehuiltitie tlacatlen tlatohuanien in tiERodes Ca çenca ticmahuiço-
hua in motetlaçotlalitzin Otlacauhqui in moyolotzin Ca in timotlacahuan in timomaçehualhuan Ca achitzin Otictomaçehuique in techiCahualistli Ca çenca
ticontennamiqui in motlaçomatzin in motlaçoicxitzin—
ERodes = Ma ximotlecahuican yn a[6v]mochantzinco in amaltepetzin ma Ximo-
calaquican anmotlacualtisque Canel amochantzinco in anmaxitico—
Calaquisque in tlatoque moçehuisque huel Çenca quinmahuistilisque———
ERodes = = Ma xicmitalhuican in anteteuctin in antlatoque in anmahuistililonime in
anpipiltin tle ica in ixquichica in anhualmohuicaque Çenca nicmahuiçosnequi in
amotetlaçotlalitzin—

Melchor = Ca çenca Otictomaçehuique Çenca otitechmocnelili tlacatlen tlatohuanien
ERodese Canel tipilli Ca titlatohuani—Ca tiquinmomahuistililia in mo[7r]tlahuan
auh ma xicmomachilti Ca ye huecauh in inmacpa in toColhuan in ye huecauh huehuetque Oquimopielique in çenca huel ye huecauh in huey in huey tlamatini
Oquicahuilitehuaque y.n achtopaittalistli auh yn achtopaitohuani itoca catca Balan
Auh Oquimitalhuitzino in tetatzin Jacob tlacatis Çe mahuistic Çitlali itech isRael
tlecos moquetzas hueyas Çe pilli Çe tlatohuani quinmococolhuis quinmotlatza-
cuiltilis in itlayacancahuan in mohuap quinmoçenpolhuis in ipilhuan Çet auh in
achtopaittalistli Ca huel Oquimoyolotique in huehuetque in tocolhuan inic huel
quimochielisque in pilli in [7v] tlatohuani ihuan in iCitlaltzin inic machos
mahuiçolos in iquin maxitiquiuh in machiotl in tetzahuitl in anoço Citlali in ipan in
ilhuicatl Oquixquetzque in toColhuan in matlactin omome ixtlamatque huehuetque tepeticpac Çemicac yesque iquiçayanpa in tonatiuh itztiesque in iquin
mahuiçolos in mahuistic Citlali. Auh in axcan ye nauhtzonXihuitl in ye
quimochielia Cemicac tepeticpac tlachieloya auh in axcan ye quesquilhuitica in
oquimonequilti in ipalnemohualoni in tloque in nahuaquen totecuiotzin yohualnepantla in icuac ye nohuianpa Cochihualoticatqui in Altepetl Auh Oquimotilique
çe huel mahuistic Çitlali. in matlactin omome huehuetque [8r] huel pepetlaca in
Çitlali huel quiçenpanahuia in tonatiuh in nohuianpa Otlanes Otonameyotic ihuan
çenca huel huey tlamahuiçolli in itic in Çitlali in oquimotilique Ocatcaya çe huel
mahuistic chipahuac Çenca ylehuiloni in piltzintli in itic Ocatcayaya Auh niman
nochantzinco Onmehualtique Omotlaloque Onechmoxitilito Auh inniscate[8] in tlatoque in pipiltin nonahuac Ocatcayaya Onechmotlapalhuito auh niman Oniquin-
notz Oniquimixiti Otictotilique in Çitlali auh in mahuiztic teopiltzintli Ca
iuhquima Otechmoyolehuili Ca niman Otitoyecnonotzque Otitocohuanotzque Oti-
tochichiuhque Otitotacatique Auh Auh niman Otli otictopehualtili[9][8v]que inic tic-
totemolisque in piltzintli Auh in mahuistic Çitlali ca niman Otechhualmoyacanili

8. inniscate: read *in iz cate*.
9. In anticipation of the following page: *que*.

MELCHIOR: Do remain seated, O personage, O ruler, you who are Herod. We marvel greatly at your hospitality. Your heart has been generous. We are your servants, we are your vassals. We have enjoyed a bit of health. We fervently kiss your precious hands and your precious feet.

HEROD: Ascend to [6v] your home, your altepetl. Enter. You are to eat, since it is at your home that you have arrived.

(The rulers enter. They rest. They treat them with great honor.)

HEROD: Tell, you lords, you rulers, you honored ones, you noblemen, why you have come all this way. I want very much to honor your affection.

MELCHIOR: We have been very fortunate. You have shown us great favor, O personage, O ruler, O Herod. Since you are a nobleman, you are a ruler, you honor your [7r] uncles. And know that our grandfathers long ago, the elders of long ago, kept in their hands a prophecy that the great sages of ancient times bequeathed to them. And the name of the prophet was Balaam. And he said that from father Jacob would be born a wondrous star; that from Israel would ascend, would arise, would grow a nobleman, a ruler, who would wound and would punish the leaders of Moab, who would destroy the children of Sheth.[18] And the elders, our grandfathers, took much to heart this prophecy by which they would await the nobleman, the [7v] ruler, along with his star, by which he would be known, he would be noted, when a sign, an omen, or a star would appear in the sky. Our grandfathers appointed twelve prudent elders to be always on a mountaintop in the east, to be watching for when the wondrous star would be observed. And now it has been sixteen hundred[19] years that they have been waiting continuously for the star in the observatory on the mountaintop. And now some days ago He by Whom All Live, the Lord of the Near, the Lord of the Nigh, our lord, wanted it to happen, in the middle of the night, when people were asleep everywhere in the [various] altepetl. And the twelve elders saw a very wondrous star. [8r] The star was shimmering so brightly that it surpassed the sun. It was bright everywhere, full of rays, and it was a very great wonder that within the star they saw that there was a quite wondrous, pure, very appealing child who was inside it. And then they set forth, they ran to my home, they went to wake me up. And the rulers, the noblemen who are here were with me, had gone to greet me. And then I summoned them, I woke them up. We saw the star. And it was as if the wondrous, sacred child inspired us. Then we came to an agreement, we dined together, we adorned ourselves, we gathered our provisions. And then we took to the road [8v] in order to search for the child. And

---

18. Balak, ruler of the Moabites, engaged the seer Balaam to curse the Israelites, who were traveling through his land during their exodus from Egypt. But Balaam saw that the Israelites were blessed by God and he defied Balak. The prophecy recounted here, which Christian exegetes applied to Christ, is from Numbers 24:17: "I shall see him, but not now: I shall behold him, but not nigh: there shall come a Star out of Jacob, and a Sceptre shall rise out of Israel, and shall smite the corners of Moab, and destroy all the children of Sheth." As a prophecy attributed to an ethnic group other than the Israelites, it could be assigned to the non-Jewish ancestors of the Magi.

19. In the traditional vigesimally based Nahua counting system this is literally "four units of four hundred," that is, 4x(20x20). This has a distinctly ideal ring to it within the framework of prehispanic Nahua culture. In the cellular or modular structure characteristic of *altepetl* and song/poetry (among others), one finds a tendency for Nahuas to construct symmetrically balanced wholes out of four pairs.

Oticualitztiaque auh nican Otihualaque Otonaçico in ipan in moAltepetzin Jerusalem Otictopolhuique in tomahuisteyacancatzin in aocmo tictotilia Auh ipampa in axcan Oticmatque aço nican ipan in mohueyAltepetzin tictonextilisque in tlein tictotemolia Çentzompa teuctlen tlacatlen ERodesen ca timitztotlatlauhtilia ma xitechmolhuili—in canpa Omotlacatili in canpa mohuetztica in intlatocauh in Judiosme Ca ye nelli ca ye Oticcquitaque[10] in iÇitlaltzin in ompa in iquiçayanpa in tonatiuh Auh ca Otihualaque Otictoteotitzinoco ixpantzinco[11] [9r] Otitopechtecaco Otictomahuistililico—

ERodes = = Tlatohuanie Cuix timotlapololtia tlein ticmotenehuilia aquin tlatohuani aquin intlatocauh in Judiosme intlacamo nehuatl Onechmotlauhtili in tlatocayotl in Roma Enperador Çesar de Agusto Cuix amo nohuaxca Cuix amo notlatqui Cuix amo nitlatohuani Cuix amo nitlatocati Cuix ye onipoliuh Cuix ye Onimic Cuix ye onitlan Cuix acmo nicmati Cuix amo—niERodes Cuix acmo nipilli aquin nopan tlatocatis in axcan ᵐᵃ içiuhcan A̶n̶nechmelahuiliqui in a̶n̶noteyacancahuan in a̶n̶Judiosme in a̶n̶noteopixcahuan in a̶n̶tlamatinime in a̶m̶amoxhuaque[12] in teoyotica pipil[13][9v]tin in teoyotica tepachohuanime ma nechmelahuiliqui in tlein Citlali tlein piltzintli tlein tlatohuani in quimoteⁿᵉhuilia in tlatoque iÇiuhcan Ca ye nimiquiznequi ye niçotlahua̶s̶ iyoyahuen ninotolinia Ay Ay Ay—

Calpixqui = Ca ye cua̶l̶litzin tlatohuaniē ma niquinnotza macamo Ximotequipachotzino—

niman yas in calpixqui quinnotzatiuh in teopixque̶̶̶̶̶̶̶̶̶̶̶

Calpixqui = = Ca ye huitze tlatohuanien macamo titotlapololtican in tixquichtin timotlaᶜᵃhuan in timomaçehualhuan in tiJerusalem tlaca—

1º teopixqui = = Ma mitzmochicahuili in Çe nelli teotl tepachohuani D.ˢ tlacatlen tlatohuanien ERodesᵉt̶z̶i̶n̶[14] [10r] [m̶a̶] ca mitzinco tontlachie in timotlaᶜᵃhuan Ca çenca tipaqui titotlamachtia titoyolalia Ca neçi ca mitzmochicalia[15] in totecuio D.ˢ ma xitechmomaquili in momatzin in mocxi.tzin ma tictennamiquican tlein ticmonequiltia ma ticoncaquican ma timitztotlaᶜᵃmachitiˡⁱcan—

10. Oticquitaque: standard *otiquittaque*.
11. In anticipation of the following page: *O*.
12. The preceding crossed out subject prefixes (second-person plural) anticipate dialogue by Herod that appears on 10r.
13. In anticipation of the following page: *tin*.
14. In anticipation of the following page: [m̶a̶].
15. mitzmochicalia: read *mitzmochicahuilia*.

the wondrous star then led us in this direction. We came along watching it. And we came here, we reached your altepetl of Jerusalem. We lost our wondrous guide. We no longer see it. And therefore we now have realized that perhaps here in your great altepetl we will discover that which we seek. O four-hundred-times lord, O personage, O Herod, we beseech you, tell us where the ruler of the Jews was born, where he is seated.[20] For it is true that we have seen his star there in the east. And so we have come, we have come to worship him, [9r] we have come to bow down before him, we have come to honor him.[21]

HEROD: O ruler, are you confused? What are you talking about? Who is the ruler? Who is the ruler of the Jews if not I? The Emperor of Rome, Caesar Augustus, granted me the rulership. Is it not my property? Is it not my possession? Am I not the ruler? Do I not rule? Have I already perished? Have I already died? Have I already been finished off? Am I no longer mentally competent? Am I not Herod? Am I no longer a nobleman? Who will rule over me? Now let my Jewish leaders, my priests, the sages, those who keep the [sacred] books, those who are noblemen in regard to sacred things, [9v] those who are governors in regard to sacred things, come quickly to explain it to me. Let them come to explain to me what star, what child, what ruler the rulers are talking about. Quickly, for I am about to die, I am about to faint! Alas! I am afflicted! Ay! Ay! Ay![22]

STEWARD: Very well, O ruler. Let me summon them. Do not be anxious!

(Then the steward goes to summon the priests.)

STEWARD: They are coming now, O ruler. Let us not become confused, all of us, we who are your servants, we who are your vassals, we people of Jerusalem.

FIRST PRIEST: May the one true deity, the governor, God, give you health, O personage, O ruler, O Herod. [10r] We gaze into your face, we who are your servants. We are very joyful, we are happy, we are contented for it appears that our lord God gives you health. Give us your hands and your feet that we may kiss them. What do you want? Let us hear it, let us obey you.

---

20. "Seated" with the connotation "in all his authority and majesty." Alternatively, "where he is fallen [to earth, or from the womb?]."

21. Parallels Matthew 2:2, in which the wise men say to Herod: "Where is he that is born King of the Jews? For we have seen his star in the east, and are come to worship him."

22. Matthew 2:3–4: "When Herod the king had heard these things, he was troubled, and all Jerusalem with him. And when he had gathered all the chief priests and scribes of the people together, he demanded of them where Christ should be born."

ERodes = Yn amehuantin in anJudiosme in anteopixcatlatoque in antlamatinime in amamoxhuaque Ça çentzompa antetlapololtique teca anmocaca^{ya}uhtime[16] çenca anteistlacahuitinemi in neltilistlatolli aocmo anquiximati in aocmo antenehualo Cuix amo çemicac namechilhuitinemi Ca namotlatocauh huel annechtlaçotla quenin huel amistlacati Ca in yeintin tlatoque Oma[17][10v]xitico Ohualeuhque ompa in iquiçayanpa in tonatiuh inchantzinco Onpa yohualnepantla Oquitaque in Citlali quilmach in Citlali in intlatocauh in Judiosme ca ye Otlacat aquin piltzintli aquin tlatohuani in nopan tlatocatis içiuhcan Xinechmelahuilican Cuix amo anquitaque in yancuic Citlali Cuix çeçenyohual in ancochi Cochmiquinime tlatziuhque pitzome Cuix amo anquipohua in maytines in yohualnepantla Judiasos Diablo ipilhuan içiuhcan xontlatemocan xinechyolpachihuitican amo namechçenpopolos tlahueliloqueyen—

2.º teopixqui = Macamo ximocualanalti totecuioyen tle çan nen Camo tomachispan camo totlatlacol [ma in?] mo[11r]chihua ma ticmomachiltis Ca in totecuio Otechmotenehuilili Ca techmomaquilis in quemanian in itlaçopiltzin in D.s in nican tlalticpac in quihualmihualis in topanpa monacayotitzinoquiuh auh intla ye Ohualmohuicac Cuix tictoquixtililisque in iteotlanequilitzin Cachtopaittalistli[18] Oquimotenehuili Oquimotecpanili in tetecuio[19] D.s—

ERodes = Xontlatemocan tlahueliloqueyen in teoamoxpan canpa in tlacatis in amotlatocauh yes isquime[20]—

1.º teopixqui = Xicanati in teoamoxtli ma tontlatemocan ma techmonextilili in D.s aquin quimotemolia in piltzintli ic moyolçehuis in tohueytlatocauh ERodes—[11v]

3.º teopixqui = = Ca iscatqui ma tontlatemocan ma techmonextilili in tlacatl

oncan tlatemosque ipan in teoamoxtli in Judio teopixque⸻

1.º teopixqui = tlacatlen Erode^{es}tzinen ca nican quimitalhuia in achtopaittohuani Ysayas capitulo in inelhuayo in çenquiças ixhuas moscaltis Çe tlacatl tlatocapilli auh ixhuas cueponis çe mahuistic Xochitl ic necis Ca pilli ca tlatohuani ipan tlacatis ca itech pohuilis in itlacamecayo in David—

ERodes—Ye nicmati tlahueliloqueyen in titlapaltontli Ca itech pohuis yn itlacamecayo in David canpa in tlacatis tlein ipan Altepetl içiuhcan xontlatemocan xinechmelahuili[12r]can amo namechichinos namechxipehuas chicharones namechcuepas Judiasos—

---

16. teca anmocacayauhtime: read *teca anmocacayauhtinemi* or *teca anmocacayauhtique*.
17. In anticipation of the following page: *Xi*.
18. Cachtopaittalistli: read *ca achtopaittaliztli*.
19. tetecuio: scribal error; standard *totecuiyo*.
20. isquime: see note in translation.

HEROD: You Jews, you priestly rulers, you sages, you keepers of the [sacred] books, four hundred times you have confused people. You go about mocking people, you go about deceiving people greatly. You no longer recognize truthful words, you are no longer acclaimed. Am I not forever going about telling you that I am your ruler? You sure do love me. How well you do lie! Three rulers have arrived, [10v] have come from the east. In their home there in the middle of the night they saw a star. It is said that the star is[23] the ruler of the Jews who has been born. Who is the child? Who is the ruler who will rule over me? Quickly, explain this to me! Didn't you see the new star? Are you asleep every night? Sleepyheads! Lazy ones! Pigs! Don't you recite matins[24] in the middle of the night? Rotten Jews,[25] children of the devil, quickly, go find out, satisfy me, and I will not destroy you, O scoundrels!

SECOND PRIEST: Do not be angry, O our lord. What's the use? What is happening is not our concern nor our fault. [11r] Know that our lord declared to us that he will someday give us God's beloved child. He will send him here to earth. He will come to take on flesh for our sake. And if he has come, are we to tamper with[26] his sacred will? Our lord God declared and established the prophecy.

HEROD: Go look up, O scoundrels, in the sacred book, where he will be born, the one who will be the ruler of all of you.[27]

FIRST PRIEST: Go get the sacred book. Let us look it up, may God reveal to us him whom they seek, the child, so that our great ruler, Herod, will be appeased. [11v]

THIRD PRIEST: Here it is. Let us look it up, may the personage[28] reveal it to us.

(At that point the Jewish priests will search in the sacred book.)

FIRST PRIEST: O personage, O Herod, here the prophet Isaiah, chapter,[29] says: "From his root will emerge, will sprout, will grow, a certain royal child. And a wondrous flower will sprout, will blossom." By this it would appear that the nobleman, the ruler, will be born from and belong to the lineage of David.

HEROD: I already know, O scoundrels, you pip-squeak, that he will belong to the lineage of David. Where will he be born? In what altepetl? Quickly, look it up, explain it to me, [12r] and I won't singe you, flay you, turn you into pork rinds, rotten Jews.

---

23. That the star indicates that this ruler has been born may be the intended meaning.
24. An anachronistic reference to the observance of the canonical hours, a series of eight daily offices of devotion practiced by friars, monks, and other pious Catholics, including the indigenous students at the Franciscan College of the Holy Cross in Tlatelolco. The first hour, matins, falls at midnight.
25. *Judiazos*, here and below literally means "big Jews," an augmentative Spanish loanword with deprecatory meaning.
26. *Tictoquixtililisque*: tentative translation; literally, "we will cause it to go out in regard to him (honorific applicative of *quixtia*)."
27. The last word in this speech is *isquime*, a plural form of "all." Logically, this would refer to the priests, or Jews in general, but it lacks the *am-* subject prefix it should have. Tentative translation.
28. That is, God.
29. No chapter number is given. The playwright may be mimicking priests' readings of weekly Bible lessons at church services. The prophecy cited is Isaiah 11:1–2: "And there shall come forth a rod out of the stem of Jesse, and a Branch shall grow out of his roots: And the Spirit of the Lord shall rest upon him," interpreted by Christian exegetes as a reference to Christ's birth from the lineage of Jesse's son David.

3.º teopixqui = Ma techmopalehuili in totecuio D.ˢ ma techtolini in tlatohuani ca huel cualani axcan techichinos chicharrones techcuepas—

2.º teopixqui = Yn timahuistic titlatohuani in çenca tiylehuiloni in tiERodes iscatqui yn oquimotecpanili in totecuio D.ˢ in ticmotemolia Auh Xicmomachilti in tlein quimitalhuia in achtopaitohuani in tehuecapaittani Meçias in ipan Çe capitulo auh in tehuatl tiBelem in tiJudiatlalpan Camo titepiton in ipan yn iteyacancahuan in pipiltin in ~~in~~ Judia huel motechpa quisas in teyacanqui in tepachohuani tlatohuani—[12v] in teoyotica quinpachohua yn iAltepeuh isrrael ic neçis in tlacatl tlatohuani ca onpa Otlacat yn ipan in Betlem in Judiatlalpan ma onpa contemoti intla ticmonequiltia—

ERodes = Ypan Betlem xontlatemocan tlahueliloqueen axcan namechichinos quenin aic annechilhuique pitzome diablo ypilhuan

oJo niman oncan quintocas in ERodes in Judio. teopixque Oc Cecpa onca quiçocohuasque²¹ in teoamoxtli oJo

ERodes = YSiuhca xinechtlalcahuican oncan niquinnonotzas in tlatoque—

Calaquisque in teopixque auh in ERodes inhuicopa mocuepaS in tlatoque huel mocnomatis—[13r]

ERodes = Yn çenca anmahuistililonime in anteteuctin in antlatoque ma xinechmotlapopolhuilitzinocan Çenca tepitzin Ononnocualanalti amixpantzinco intechcacopan in nopilhuan yeicca²² amo Onechmelahuilique in quenin tlamahuiçoltica mochihuas Auh in axcan ca huel çenca namechnotlatlauhtilia ma xinechmolhuilican ye quexquich cahuitl in ones in omotac in Citlali in onpa amochantzinco in oanquimotilique Ma xinechmolhuilican Ca çenca namechnotlatlauhtilia—

Gaspar = Tlatohuanien nopiltzintzinen in timahuiztic titlatohuani in tiERodes ma xicmomachiltitzino macamo timitztocualantilisque amo motechtzinco toncualani Ca ye Oticma[13v]huiçoque in motetlaçotlalitzin auh amo timitztostlacahuilizque in Çenca timahuistililoni in titlatohuani ma xicmomachiltzino Ca ye matlactli yhuan yeil~~tica~~huitica in otictotilique in çe mahuiztic Citlali in onpa in iquiçayanpa in tonatiuh amo huecauhtica inic Oticualtotilitiaque Auh in axcan yohuatzinco Otictopolhuique in tomahuisteyacancatzin inic nican icalaquian in moaltepetzin Jerosalem Çentzompa teuctlen ERodesen—

ERodes = hoannechmocnelilique in anteteuctin²³ in antlatoque Otlacauhqui in amoyolotzin in axcan ma ximohuicacan in onpa in huey Altepetl Betlem Camo hueca Ca çan nican inahuac in Jerusalem Ma çenca [14r] huel yca in piltzintli Auh in iCuac anquimotilis~~ti~~que Ma annechmolhuilitiquiçasque inic no nehuatl in nicnotlapalhuitiuh nicnoteotitiuh in teotl in tlatohuani nicnotlatocatitiuh ma onpa ximohuicacan—

---

21. quiçocohuasque: read *quiçoçohuasque*.
22. yeicca: read *yehica*.
23. There is a written indication of some kind above the letter *c* but its intent is not clear.

THIRD PRIEST: May our lord God help us! May the ruler [not] torment us! He is really angry. Now he will singe us, he will turn us into pork rinds.

SECOND PRIEST: You honored one, you ruler, you very appealing one, Herod, here is what our lord God established, which we are seeking. And know what the prophet, the seer Micah says, in one chapter: "And you, Bethlehem, you land of Judea, you are not small among the governors and nobles of Judea. From you will come the leader, the governor, the ruler [12v] who in a sacred way will govern[30] the altepetl of Israel."[31] By this it would appear that the personage, the ruler has been born there, in Bethlehem, in the land of Judea. Let them go look for him there, if you wish.

HEROD: In Bethlehem! Go look it up, O scoundrels! Now I will singe you! How can it be that you never told me, O pigs, children of the devil?
(Note Then at that point Herod drives out the Jewish priests. Note: *Again they open the sacred book.*

HEROD: Leave me at once! Then I will consult with the rulers.
(The priests enter. And Herod turns toward the rulers. He is very humble.) [13r]

HEROD: Pardon me, you very honorable lords and rulers. I got a bit angry at my noblemen[32] in front of you because they did not explain to me that it would happen in such a wondrous manner. And now I fervently beseech you, tell me how much time it has been since the star appeared, was seen, when you saw it there in your home. Tell me, I fervently beseech you.[33]

CASPER: O ruler, O my nobleman, honored one, ruler, Herod, be informed of it. Let us not make you angry. We are not angry at you. For [13v] we have marveled at your hospitality. And we will not lie to you. You are very honorable, you are a ruler. Be informed that it has been thirteen days since we saw a wondrous star there in the east. It was not long ago that we came along watching it. But this morning we lost our wondrous guide here at the entrance to your altepetl of Jerusalem, O four-hundred-times lord, O Herod.

HEROD: Thank you, lords, rulers. Your hearts have been generous. Now, go to the great altepetl of Bethlehem. It is not far away. It is right here close to Jerusalem. May it be very [14r] well with the child. And when you have seen him, come by to tell me so that I too may go to greet and to worship the deity, the ruler, I may go to take him as a ruler. Go there.[34]

30. Verb is present tense but future is presumably intended.
31. In Matthew 2:5–6 the priests' response is as follows: "And they said unto him, In Bethlehem of Judea: for thus it is written by the prophet, And thou Bethlehem, in the land of Juda, art not the least among the princes of Juda: for out of thee shall come a Governor, that shall rule my people Israel." The Nahuatl text gives the prophet's name as Meçias, or "Messiah," but the text in Matthew derives from the book of the prophet Micah (Spanish Miqueas, Latin Michaea), verse 5:2: "But thou, Bethlehem Ephratah, though thou be little among the thousands of Judah, yet out of thee shall he come forth unto me that is to be ruler in Israel."
32. Literally, "my children," in this case meaning the high-born subordinates of Herod.
33. Matthew 2:7: "Then Herod, when he had privily called the wise men, inquired of them diligently what time the star appeared."
34. Matthew 2:8: "And he sent them to Bethlehem, and said, Go and search diligently for the young child; and when ye have found him, bring me word again, that I may come and worship him also."

Balthasar = Ma motlaçonahuactzinco mocauhtzino in tlamatcayelistli ihuan ma mitz-mochicahuilie~~an~~tzinocan in tloque nahuaque in ipaltzinco nemohualoni in totecuio D.ˢ nopiltzintzinen teuctlen tlacatlen tlatohuaniē Ca ticontennamiqui in momatzin ihuan in mocxitzin Ca ye titohuicatihui tlatohuanien nopiltzintzinen—

Niman quincahuatiuh in ERodes, in tlatoque tlatzintla icaltenpa. [14v] auh niman yasque calaquisque ᵃᵘʰ ipā theopan ixpan quinextisque in Cjtlali niman tlatos in Balthasar huel quimotetzahuis ʸᵗˡᵃⁿ ᵃʳᶜᵒ in Citlali quitos———

Balthasar = honotlaçoicniuhtzitzinhuanē ma xiconmitilican in otechhualmoyacanili-aya in tomahuisteyacancatzin in mahuistic Citlali Ca ye no cuel techmoyacanilia ho tla xiconmotilican notlaçomahuisicniuhtzitzinhuanen—

Melchor = Ma çemca ic titopapaquiltican yeica ca ye Otictonextilique Otechmonex-tililitzino in tloque nahuaque in ipaltzinco nemohualoni in tomahuisteyacancatzin in quenin Ohualmelauhtia ye moquetza ye motzicohua [15r] yn ipan Çe xacalçolli Omoquetz Omotzico itech Omopacho auh tlein quitosnequi Cuix amo çe huey tec-pancalli itech mopachosquia in niCan Altepetl icalaquian—

Melchor = = Xihualauh in tehuatl in titotetlayecolticauh xoncalaqui xontlachie xon-tlatemo tlein tlamahuiçolli Onca quimopielia in totecuiotzin in totlatocatzin—

titlantli = Ca ye cualitzin tlatoqueyen ma oc noncalaqui ma oc nontlachie—

OnCan calaquis in theopan in titlantli tlachietiuh oc çecpa hualquisas quitos— Oraçion

BALTHASAR: May peace be with your precious self, and may the Lord of the Near, the Lord of the Nigh, He by Whom All Live, our lord God, give you health, O my nobleman, O lord, O personage, O ruler. We kiss your hands and your feet. Now we are going to go, O ruler, O my nobleman.

(Then Herod escorts the rulers below, outside of his house.[35] *[14v] And then they go, they exit. And in in front of the church they discover the star under the arch.*[36] *Then Balthasar speaks. He is quite astonished at the star. He says:)*

BALTHASAR: O my beloved friends, look! Our wondrous guide that led us this way, the wondrous star, is leading us again! Oh, do look, O my beloved honored friends!

MELCHIOR: Let us be very joyful for this! For we have found it! The Lord of the Near, the Lord of the Nigh, He by Whom All Live has revealed to us how our wondrous guide came straight in this direction. Now it is stopping, now it is halting. [15r] It has stopped, it has halted, above a shack. It has drawn near to it. But what does it mean? Would it not draw near to a great palace, here at the entrance to the altepetl?[37]

MELCHIOR: Come, our servant. Go in, go look, go find out what marvel our lord, our ruler is keeping there.

MESSENGER: Very well, O rulers. Let me go in, let me go look.

(At that point the messenger enters the church. He goes and looks. He comes out again. He gives a speech.)

---

35. That is, he will escort the Three Kings down to the lower level of the stage setting representing his palace, seeing them off.

36. The phrase "under the arch" appears in the manuscript in the margin after the verb *quimotetzahuiz*, but it would seem to refer to the placement of the artificial star, which could have been suspended from an arch. The stage directions indicate that the actors move the drama right into the church building. Upon leaving Herod's palace, which could be a stage set erected in the churchyard or open chapel, the kings may go into an "offstage" space, then come out again and ride to the church. The "shack" is probably meant to be represented not by the church building itself but by a manger scene set up inside of it. According to the Franciscan chronicler fray Gerónimo de Mendieta, indigenous people customarily erected such crèches, with statues of Mary, Joseph, the infant Jesus, and shepherds, in their churches from Christmas to Epiphany (Mendieta 1980, 432). As Mary and Joseph do not speak in the drama, they may be represented by the statues rather than by living actors.

37. Matthew 2:9–10: "When they had heard the king, they departed; and, lo, the star, which they saw in the east, went before them, till it came and stood over where the young child was. When they saw the star, they rejoiced with exceeding great joy."

titlantli = Yn antlatoque in āReyesme ca onicchiuh in tlein Oannechmonahuatilique Ca onontlachieto auh ca niman [15v] atle iuhqui niquitoz ca niman atlein iuhqui nicnenehuiliz in ononcalac in onontlachix Ca huel çenca tlanestoc huel iuhqui in ye hualquiças in tlanextli in tonameyotl in nohuianpa quiquistoc auh Onicnotili çe tlaçomahuistic Çenquiscatlateochihualichpotzintli quimonapalhuitica çe tlaçomahuistic tlateochihualpiltzintli Auh ynahuactzinco mohuetznoticatqui Çe huehuetlacatzintli Auh quimoyahualhuiticate in tlaçomahuispipiltzitzintin aastlacapaleque auh Onca inahuactzinco cate Omentin manenencatzitzintin Auh yn ilhuicac tlaçoÇihuapilli Ca huel quimoçenpanahuilia yn ixquich nepapan tlaçoXochitl y nestic in costic in tlaçoXochitl Camopalpopoyauh[16r]tic ye mochi in nepapan tlaçoXochitl in tlauhqueCholtic in onpa quiquistoc Auh in tlaçomahuistlateochihualpiltzintli in itlaçomahuizÇenquiscatlaçomahuizqualtilispepetlaquilisXayacatzin Ca huel Çenquizcachipahuac Auh in itlaçomahuisÇenquiscatzomtzin yuhqui in Costic teocuitlatl inic pepetlaca in anoço iuhqui in çepayahuitl inic chipahuac Auh ca huel ÇenquiscaCualcan in omotlacatilitzino Çacaxacaltzinco in omotlacatilitzino in tlaçomahuizteopiltzintli Auh tlatoqueyen Ma tihuian ma tictotlapalhuiti ma tictomahuistililiti ma ixpantzinco titocnomatiti ma ixpantzinco titopechteca[can][24] tlatoqueyen—

_____ [25] [16v]

Melchor = Ma çemicac yectenehualo in tomahuizteotzin in totlatocatzin D.[s] Ca ye Otictonextilique in tictotemolia ma ticalaquican tlatoqueyen nocniuhtzitzinhuanen ma tictoteotitzi.noti ma ixpantzinco titopechtecati ma tictotlahuenchihuililiti—
onca motemohuisque in tlatoque inpan yn icaballohuan moCalaquis[26] in teopan huel mocnomatisq[e] tlatocanenemisque motlācuaquetzatihue Altar itzintla in canpa mochihua in Missa yhuā ipan Euangelio tla otlan in Credo quimotlapalhuitzinosque in tlaSomahuisteopiltzintli—[17r]
ÇeÇenyacan yca Oraçiones tlapehualtis in

---

24. The three superscript letters, *can*, were themselves overwritten with *ti=*. This seems to anticipate the "titopechtecati" uttered by the next speaker, Melchor, on the following page.
25. In anticipation of the following page: *Melchor*.
26. moCalaquis: read *mocalaquizque*.

MESSENGER: You rulers, you kings, I have done what you commanded me. I went and looked. And I cannot [15v] describe it at all, I cannot compare it with anything at all. I went in, I observed. It is very bright. It is like when the light, the sunlight, is about to come forth. It is issuing out in all directions. And I saw a precious, wondrous, and utterly blessed maiden holding in her arms a precious, wondrous, and blessed little child. And next to her is seated an elderly person.[38] And surrounding them are precious and wondrous little children with wings. And there beside them are two animals. And the heavenly precious[39] noblewoman greatly surpasses all the various precious flowers, ash-colored and yellow precious flowers, deep-purple-tinted ones, [16r] all the various precious flowers, like roseate spoonbills, that lie issuing forth there.[40] And the precious, wondrous, utterly precious, wondrous, good, and shimmering face of the precious, wondrous, and blessed child is utterly pure. And his utterly precious and wondrous hair is like gold, the way it shimmers, or like snow, it is so pure. And the precious and wondrous sacred child was born in an utterly good place, he was born in a hut. And, O rulers, let us go, let us go greet him, let us go honor him, let us go humble ourselves before him, let us bow before him, O rulers! [16v]

MELCHIOR: May our wondrous deity, our ruler, God, be forever praised! We have found what we are looking for. Let us enter, O rulers, O my friends! Let us go worship him! Let us go bow before him! Let us go make offerings to him!
(At that point the rulers get down from their horses. They enter the church. They humble themselves quite a bit. They proceed in a regal manner. They go and kneel at the foot of the altar where mass is being performed, and in the Gospel, when the Creed is finished,[41] they will greet the precious and wondrous sacred child, [17r] one at a time, with orations. He begins:)

---

38. Joseph, elderly according to a medieval tradition based on apocryphal gospels, which by the sixteenth century coexisted with a newer interpretation that regarded him as a young man.

39. precious: also has the connotation "high-born."

40. Filling Christ's birthplace with flowers is a Nahua innovation seen also in the *Psalmodia Christiana*'s Christmas text (Sahagún 1993b, 372–73) and the *Cantares Mexicanos* (Bierhorst 1985, 254–57); the latter work also compares the flowers to roseate spoonbills. The *Psalmodia Christiana*'s Epiphany text adds many types of flowers to the gifts brought by the three kings, elaborating upon a Latin antiphon that speaks only of gifts and tribute (Sahagún 1993b, 40–41).

41. These stage directions suggest that the drama is integrated into the church service.

Gaspar = Tlacatlen toteCuioyen tlaçochalChihuitlen quetzalen teoxihuitlen maquistlen ca ye nican Otihualmohuetzititzino in nican Omitzhualmotlalilitzino in motlaçotatzin D.^{S} tloq̄yen nahuaqueyen ipaltzinco nemohualonien Ca ye nelli ye oyaque Omotecato in motechicatzitzinhuan[27] in machcocolhuan in prophetasme in patriarcasme in ye nechca onmatihui in tlacatl in tlatohuani David Auh in tlacatl ⊬ in tlatohuani Abraham Oconcauhtehuaque Oconquetztehuaque in caCaxtli in tlatconi in tlamamaloni in Çenca yetic in amo Ehualistli = in amo huel ixnamiconi Can mach [17v] oc qualmati[28] oc quihualytta in imicanpa in intepotzco Can mach Oqualmati[29] in imauh in intepeuh in ye iuhtimani in ye iuh inencauhyan mochihua Can mach Oc quihualmati in çequi Cuauhtla Sacatla inon çeçenmantiuh in tlatconi in tlamamaloni auh canel aocmo nane aocmo taye in cuitlapilli in atlapalli Auh canel aocmo ixxe in aocmo nacaçe in iuhqui nontiticac in amo nahuati in amo tlatohua inɐniuhqui[30] quechcotonticac in ayocac. itzonteco mochihua in iyacac onicatiuh yn axcan Noteotzinen Notlatocatzinen in titlaçomahuisteopiltzintli Ca tehuatzin ticonmanilitzinos momactzinco mocahuas in itequipanolocatzin in motlaçomahuistatzin D.^{S} yhuan ca mixpantzinco nicnoCuitia ca ye ixquich [18r] Cahuitl in

27. motechicatzitzinhuan: read *motechiuhcatzitzinhuan* (as below).
28. qualmati: read *quihualmati* (as below).
29. Oqualmati: read *oc quihualmati* (as below).
30. inɐniuhqui: read *in iuhqui*.

CASPER[42]: O personage, O our lord, O precious jade, O quetzal plume, O fine turquoise, O bracelet! You have seated yourself here. Your precious father, God, has placed you here, O Lord of the Near, O Lord of the Nigh, O He by Whom All Live. It is true that your progenitors, your great-grandfathers, the prophets, the patriarchs have gone, have gone to lie down, and the personage, the ruler, David, and the personage, the ruler, Abraham, who go along further back. They left behind, they set aside the carrying frame, the instrument of carrying, the instrument of bearing,[43] which is very heavy, which cannot be lifted, which is unbearable. [17v] Is it possible that they still come to know, that they still come to see what is behind them, in back of them? Is it possible that they come to frequent their water, their hill,[44] which lies now as in the beginning,[45] which now is becoming like his[46] desolate place? Is it possible that they still frequent some forest or grassland, where the instrument of carrying, the instrument of bearing lies scattered?[47] And truly the tail, the wing[48] no longer has a mother, no longer has a father. And truly it no longer has eyes, it no longer has ears.[49] It is as if it stands mute. It does not speak, it does not talk. It is as if it stands beheaded. No longer is there anyone who is its head, who goes in front of it.[50] Now, O my deity, O my ruler, precious and wondrous sacred child, it is you who will grasp, in your embrace[51] will remain the work for your precious and wondrous father, God. And I confess before you that up until now [18r] I was living in darkness, in gloom, since I did not know you. But

---

42. Casper's speech, through the word "beheaded," closely parallels the beginning of the *Florentine Codex* oration for the installation of a new ruler (Sahagún 1950–1982, 6:47). After greeting the new sovereign, the speaker notes the passing of the rulers of old who will return no more and laments the sad plight of the leaderless vassals. The playwright inserts Old Testament leaders for the departed rulers. The plight of the vassals becomes the plight of all humanity, awaiting Christ's arrival. The texts are not identical, but they are so similar that the playwright must have had access to this text or a close cognate. There is also a similar speech in the *Bancroft Dialogues* (Karttunen and Lockhart 1987, 133).

43. Metaphor for government: the common people are "carried" by their rulers like a burden (Sahagún 1950–1982, 6:246; Karttunen and Lockhart 1987, 54).

44. their water, their hill: here and below, a metaphorical diphrase that often appears as the quasi-compound *altepetl*, the largest sociopolitical unit to survive Spanish conquest and colonization. During colonial times it was translated in many ways including *ciudad* (city) and *pueblo* (people, settlement).

45. The *Florentine Codex* here has *iooatimanj*, referring to darkness. *Iuhti* refers to the original condition of something. See Siméon 1977, 212, entries for *yuhti* and *yuhticaua*.

46. In the *Florentine Codex* this place belongs to "our lord" (Sahagún 1950–1982); the possessor is not specified here.

47. That is, the city has reverted to a wild state in the absence of rulership.

48. Tail(s), wing(s): prevalent metaphor for common people or vassals. There are numerous references to this in colonial Nahuatl texts. The following Spanish gloss by the famed Nahua Latinist, don Antonio Valeriano, appeared in fray Juan Bautista's sermonary of 1606 (559–60): "Cuitlapiltin, atlapaltin (cuitlapilli, *es la cola*, atlapalli, *el ala del aue, y junto* cuitlapiltin, atlapaltin, *en el singular,* cuitlapiltin, atlapaltin, *en el plural, significa la gente menuda plebeya, y comun*)" [cuitlapiltin, atlapaltin (cuitlapilli *is the tail and* atlapalli *a bird's wing, and together* cuitlapilli atlapalli *in the singular and* cuitlapiltin atlapaltin *in the plural mean the lesser, plebeian and common folk*)]. See also Molina 1552, 204r: "Pueblo de menudos. cuitlapilli, atlapalli. ytconi, mamaloni. maceualtin" and 240v: "Vassalos o gente plebeya. per metaphoram. cuitlapilli, ha,tlapalli. ytconi. mamaloni. quiltica nemi. quauhtica nemi. yn haualnecini ycochca yneuhca. ycemiluitica. yomilhuitica." Note that *cuitlapilli atlapalli* is the first diphrase in the Molina entries, as if indicating that it is the most widely used and accepted.

49. That is, with no one to govern them, the people lack prudence.

50. That is, the people lack a leader.

51. embrace: here and below, tentative translation.

tlayohuayan mixtecomac Oninemia Canel amo Onimitzniximachilitzinoaya auh in axcan ca Oticmotlanextililitzino in noyolia in noaniman ihuan in ixquichtintzitzin in ilhuicatl itic monoltitoque in motlachihualtzitzinhuan in otiquinmotlanextililitzinoco Auh noteotzinen Ca huel nimitznotlatlauhtilitzinohua ma huel xicmoçelilitzino in noyolia in noaniman ihuan in nonemilis inic huel mochihuas ynic nimitznohuenChihuililitzinohua inin Copaltzintli itocan inÇiençio Ma huel xicmoçelilitzino Noteo[31] notlatocatzinē = **oncan tlācuanenemis quimotlahuenchihuililitzinos ihuan quimomotennamiquiliz**[32] **in tlaçomahuisteopiltzintli oc çecpa hualtzinquisas qui**[33] [18v]

Gaspar = Auh noteotzinen notlatocatzinen ca no mixpantzinco nicnocuitia Ca tinelli titeopixcatzintli tinelli tiSaçerdote ca ticmocuitlahuitzinos in itlayecoltilocatzin in motlaçotatzin D.^{S} Auh noteotzinen ihuan Ca timonomahuenchiuhtzinos ytech in Cruz inic ticmoyolçehuilitzinos in motlaçotatzin D.^{S} Auh notlatocatzinen noteotzinen tloqueen nahuaqueē ipaltzinco nemohualonie ma huel xicmoçelilitzino in noyolia in noaniman ihuan in nonemilis—

Melchor = Notlaçomahuisteotzinen notlatocatzinen in tihuel nelli Oquitzintli in tihuel nelli teotzintli Ca moch ica in noyollo nimitznoneltoquititzinohua Ca oticmochihuilitzino Oticmoyocolilitzino in ilhuicatl in tlaltic[19r]pactli in ittalo in amo ittalo Ca huel tehuatzin motetzinco ca in tlatocayotl inic ticonmoyacanilis in Cemanahuatl inic ticonmopachilhuis auh. in ixquichtin motlachihualtzitzinhuan Ca ixquich cahuitl in timitztochielitzinohua ye ixquich cahuitl mohuicpatzinco tonelçiçiuhtinemi Ca ye Otimaxititzinoco ca ye Otihualmohuicatzino in omitzhualmihuali in motlaçomahuistatzin D^S auh ca tehuatzin mopantzinco Oya in iyotzin in itlatoltzin in motlaçomahuistatzin D.^{S} Auh Ca oc tehuatzin tonmetiçihuitis Auh Ca oc tehuatzin itlan tonmaquiltis in cacaxtli in tlamamalli Canel Omitzmotenehuilitiaque in motechiuhcatzitzinhuan in machcocoltzitzinhuan ȳ Patriarcasme in Prophetasme [19v] in

---

31. Noteo: given the context, evidently scribal error for *noteotzinen*.
32. quimomotennamiquiliz: read *quimotennamiquiliz*.
33. In apparent anticipation of the following page: *tos yn*. However, this does not repeat on the following page so it properly belongs to the last item on 18v, to be read: *quitos yn*.

now you have illuminated my spirit, my soul, along with all those who live in heaven, your creations, whom you have come to illuminate. And, O my deity, well do I beseech you, receive well my spirit, my soul, and my life, so that it may be done, so that I may make an offering to you of this copal called incense. Receive it well, O my deity, O my ruler.

(At that point he goes about on his knees, he makes the offering, and he kisses the precious and wondrous sacred child. He withdraws again. He says:) [18v]

CASPER: And, O my deity, O my ruler, I also confess before you that you are the true priest, you are the true clergyman. You will look after the serving of your beloved father, God. And also, O my deity, you will make an offering of yourself on the cross in order to appease your beloved father, God. And, O my ruler, O my deity, O Lord of the Near, O Lord of the Nigh, O He by Whom All Live, receive well my spirit, my soul, and my life.

MELCHIOR: O my precious and wondrous deity, O my ruler, you who are a really true man, you who are a really true deity,[52] with all my heart I believe in you. You made, you created heaven, earth, [19r] that which is visible, that which is invisible. You are the one incumbent upon whom is the rulership, by which you will govern the world, by which you will rule it. And as for all your creations, until now we have been waiting for you, until now we have gone about sighing toward you. Now you have arrived, now you have come. Your precious and wondrous father, God, sent you. And it is you upon whom has gone the breath, the words of your precious and wondrous father, God. And you will yet become weary from burdens.[53] And you will yet go putting your effort into the carrying frame, the load. Truly your progenitors, your great-grandfathers, the patriarchs, the prophets, [19v]

---

52. The pairing of *oquichtli* ("man" or "male") and *teotl* was common in Nahuatl in reference to Christ's dual status as human and divinity.

53. Beginning with this sentence and ending with the phrase "No longer," Melchior's speech resembles a later passage in the *Florentine Codex* oration cited above (Sahagún 1950–1982, 6:48–49). The playwright identifies the past rulers with Old Testament figures, the vassals with unredeemed humanity, and Christ's city with the Church. The cross, like the vassals, is a burden Christ must bear.

YsRael tlatoque in teteuctin in omitzmotenehuililitiaque in itechpa Otimoquixti in ye nechca Onmatihui Ca oc tehuatzin tonmotlatquilis ticonmomamalis in moCrutzin +: in temaquixtiloni moCuitlapantzinco ticonmotequilis Auh cuexantzinco[34] momalhuatzinco[35] quimotlalilia in motlaçotatzin D.S in itcoca ymamaloca in—Cuitlapilli in atlapalli in maquixtilos Ca iuhqui in piltontli monenequi mosuma auh ca Cuel achitzinca Ca huel tehuatzin momacotzinco[36] ticonmotlalilitias in matzin in motepetzin Yn tonantzin Santa Ygleçia Ocuel[37] tehuatzin Ocuel achitzinca ticonmonapalhuis ticonmotlahuitequililis mopan[20r]tzinco Oya in iyotzin in itlatoltzin in motlaçotatzin D.S tloqueyen Nahuaqueyen Ca omitzmomapilhuili Omitzmixquechili Cuix huel Oc timotzinquixtitzinos Ca niman aocmo Auh yn axcan Notlaçomahuisteotzinen Notlatocatzinen Ma çenquiscayectenehualo in motlaçomahuistocatzin in tinotlatocatzin Ca çenca Onicnomaçehui in momahuiztetlaçotlalitzin Auh tlein inic nimitznoCuepililitzinos Ca mixpantzinco ninopechteca nimitznoteotitzinohua nimitznoçenmacatzinohua nimitznoçenmaquilia in noyolia in noaniman ihuan in nonemilis ihuan inin Costic teocuitlatl Ma huel Xic[20v]moçelilitzino noteotzinen notlatocatzinen Ma xinechmotlapopolhuilitzino = Amen

OnCan tlatennamiquis yhuan tlahuenchihuas aocmo tlein quitos in Melchor Auh niman Oncan tlatos in Balthasar—

---

34. cuexantzinco: scribal error; read *mocuexantzinco*.
35. momalhuatzinco: read *momamalhuaztzinco*.
36. momacotzinco: read *momacochtzinco*; parallels similar wording in the *Florentine Codex* (Sahagún 1950–1982).
37. Ocuel: here and below, read *oc huel*; in parallel passages in the *Florentine Codex* (Sahagún 1950–1982), these are rendered *oc cuel achic*.

the rulers and lords of Israel made you known. Those from whom you descended, who go along further back, made you known.[54] You will yet go to carry something, you will go to bear on your shoulders your cross, the instrument of salvation, which you will place on your back. And in your lap, in your backpack[55] your beloved father, God, places the carrying of, the bearing of, the tail, the wing, who is to be saved. It is as if it is a little child, who has to be cajoled, who becomes angry, but only for a moment. It is indeed in your embrace that you will go place your water, your hill,[56] our mother holy church. Soon you will go carry her in your arms, you will go lull her to sleep.[57] On you [20r] has gone the breath, the words[58] of your beloved father, God, the Lord of the Near, the Lord of the Nigh. He has pointed his finger at you, he has encharged you. Perhaps you can still back out of it? No longer! And now, O my precious and wondrous deity, O my ruler, may your precious and wondrous name be utterly praised, you who are my ruler. I have benefited greatly from your wondrous love. And what will I do for you in return? I bow low before you, I worship you, I give myself entirely to you, I give entirely to you my spirit, my soul, and my life. And this gold, receive it well, [20v] O my deity, O my ruler. Pardon me. Amen.

(At that point he gives a kiss [to the child] and makes an offering. Melchior does not say anything more. And then at that point Balthasar speaks.)

---

54. This alludes to the Old Testament texts interpreted as prophecies regarding Christ.

55. This diphrase refers to responsibility for governing others (Karttunen and Lockhart 1987, 53; cf. Molina 1977, 72v: Nocuexanco nomamalhuazco yeloatiuh. tener el cargo de regir y gouernar a los otros). This *mamalhuaztli* contrasts in vowel length with the name of the constellation *Mamalhuaztli* (Karttunen 1983, 135).

56. your water, your hill: as before, a more high-sounding version of the quasi-compound *altepetl*.

57. The imagery here is of the ruler's city or subjects as a metaphorical child who must be cuddled and coddled. Sahagún's Spanish gloss in the *Florentine Codex* speaks of "making for them the sound so that they sleep" (Sahagún 1950-1982, 6:49n.6). The corresponding Nahuatl verb, *tocontlaviviteequiliz* in the *Florentine Codex* and the reverential *ticonmotlahuitequililis* in the drama, literally mean "you will go to beat on things for him/her" (applicative of *huitequi*). Based on Sahagún's gloss, we take this to refer to the making of some rhythmic sound to help a child sleep.

58. A similar phrase occurred earlier in Melchior's speech. Here it parallels wording in the *Florentine Codex* (Sahagún 1950–1982). It has the sense of God appointing him; in other words, "You are the lord's anointed."

Balthasar = tlacatlen tlatohuaniē in ticmopielitzinohua in ilhuicatl ihuan in tlalticpactli in pilotl in tlatocayotl auh ca huel nelli tiD.^{s} tloqueyen nahuaqueyen ipaltzinco nemohualonien Auh Ca ^{ni}mitznoçenneltoquititzinohua moCh ica in noyolia in noaniman ihuan in nonemilis Auh Ca huel tehuatzin topampatica[38] Oticmocahuilitzino in motlaçomahuistla[21r]tocayotzin ihuan in motlaçomahuistlatocaicpaltzin Auh yn axCan Ca topampatica timoCauhtzinos in nican Tlalticp^c timotemachtilitzinos ihuan topampatica Temimiltitech mitzmomailpilitzinosque Mitzmomecahuitequilitzinosque in moyaotzitzinhuan in Judiosme Auh Ca topampatica pinahuistica Cruztitech + Mitzmoma^{ma}çohualtilitzinosque timomiquilitzinos Auh Ca san inpanpa in C$\bar{m}$c tlaca auh Canel motlachihualtzitzinhuan momiquilisticatzinco tiquinmomaquixtilitzinos Auh in axcan tlein nel nimitznomaquilitzinos tlein nel ONimitzte^{no}huenChihuililitzino~~que~~^{co} Ca niman atlein Ca çan ix[21v]quich nican catqui nimitznohuenChihuililitzinohua Çenca tlaçotli chichic Paatl in ito^{ca} Mirra Auh in icuac tepetla^{a}calco tocos in motlaçomahuisnacayotzin Ca ic quimamatilosque Auh in axcan notlaçomahuisteotzinen tlein nel O~~niti~~mitz~~nito~~^{to}huenchihuililitzinoco Ca san ixquich in toyolia in toaniman ihuan in tonemilis Ma huel Xitechmotlapopolhuilitzino notlaçomahuisteotzinen = **oncan tlatennamiquisque no quichiuh in GaSpar ihuan in Melchor oc çecpa tzinquiSaS quitos** =

Balthasar = = Auh in tehuatzin tlaçomahuistlateochihualichpotzintlen in aic motetzinco Oaçic in tla[22r]tlacolpeuhcayotl Auh Ca huel Çenquistoc in motlaçomahuisGraçiatzin in onpa in ilhuicatl itic y.huan nohuian C$\bar{m}$c in aic tlamis in aic tzomquisas in moÇihuapiltlatocamahuisyotzin[39] Auh tlein nel nimitznohuenChihuililitzinos tlein nel Otimitztomaquilitzinoco Ca niman atlein Ca san ixquich in toyolia in toaniman ihuan in tonemilis Ma huel xitechmotlapopolhuilitzino notlaçomahuisnantzinen Ca ye titohuicatihui Ma iuh mochihua in—Amen Jesus Maria y Joseph =

Niman oncan monextis in Angel quimmonahuatilis in yeintin tlatoque quitos

---

38. topampatica: here and below, standard *topampa* for the early colonial period. However, our initial impression is that this form is occasionally seen in the later colonial period.
39. moÇihuapiltlatocamahuisyotzin: standard *moçihuapillatocamahuizyotzin*.

BALTHASAR: O personage, O ruler, you have in your keeping the sky and the earth, nobility and rulership. And it is indeed true that you are God, O Lord of the Near, O Lord of the Nigh, O He by Whom All Live. And I believe in you utterly, with all my spirit, my soul, and my life. And you are the one who, for our sake, has left your precious and wondrous realm [21r] and your precious and wondrous royal seat.[59] And now, for our sake you will remain here on earth, you will teach people, and for our sake your enemies, the Jews, will tie you by the hands to a stone column, will flog you. And for our sake they will shamefully stretch you by the arms on the cross. You will die. And it is just for the sake of the people of the world. And truly, as for your creations, through your death you will save them. And now, what, truly, will I give to you? Of what, truly, have I come to make you an offering? It is nothing at all. It is only [21v] of this here that I make an offering to you, a very precious bitter potion, called myrrh. And when your precious and wondrous body is buried in the sepulcher, they will anoint it with this. And now, O my precious and wondrous deity, of what, truly, have we come to make you an offering? It is only our spirits, our souls, and our lives. Pardon us fully, O my precious and wondrous deity.

(At that point he[60] gives a kiss like Casper and Melchior did. He withdraws again. He says:)

BALTHASAR: And you, O precious, wondrous, and blessed maiden, original sin never reached you.[61] [22r] And your precious and wondrous grace lies gathered all together there in heaven and everywhere in the world. Your queenly honor will never be finished, will never come to an end. And of what, truly, will I make an offering to you? What, truly, have we come to give you? It is nothing at all. It is only our spirits, our souls, and our lives. Pardon us fully, O my precious and honored mother. Now we are going to be on our way. May it so be done. Amen. Jesus, Mary, and Joseph.[62]

(Then at that point an angel appears. He gives instructions to the three rulers. He says:)

---

59. *Icpalli*: the basketry seats on which indigenous rulers sat; by extension, rulership. Often appears as part of the metaphorical diphrase *petlatl icpalli* "reed mat, basketry seat" (seat of authority, rulership, and so on). A common idiom attested early, for example, in Molina 1555, 131, the last item under "Gouernar" (and one of a number of explicitly marked metaphors for governing) is "petlapan, ycpalpan nica" (I am on the reed mat, I am on the basketry seat). See also Molina 1977, 33v and 81r (Nahuatl-Spanish) and 108v (Spanish-Nahuatl).

60. Verb is plural but singular seems to be intended.

61. A reference, using wording typical of Nahuatl texts, to Mary's immaculate conception, or conception free from original sin.

62. Matthew 2:11: "And when they were come into the house, they saw the young child with Mary his mother, and fell down, and worshipped him: and when they had opened their treasures, they presented unto him gifts; gold, and frankincense, and myrrh."

Angel = Yn antlatoque in AnReyesme oçenquizcatlacauhqui ~~t~~anquimocnelilitzi[22v] noque in tlaçomahuiztlateochihualichpotzintli yhuan in itlaçomahuizpepetlaquilizÇenquizcaÇenteconetzin in ixquichica anhualmohuicaq^e anquimotlapalhuitzinoco anquimotlahuenchihuilitzinoco Auh Ca huel namechnotlatlauhtilia maca acmo onpa ic amocueptzinozque in canpa ic anhualmohuicatzinoque ma oc çe otli inic anmohuicazque inic amo imac anmohuetzititihue in ERodes huey tlahueliloc ca çan amechmoztla^{cahuili} inic oquito Ca no nehuatl niaz nicnoteotzinotiuh Auh ca huel cualani quimomiquiztlatzomtequililiznequi auh ca niman ayānmo inma in momiquilitzinos Ca ac quinmomaquixtilitzinos in C̄m̄c tlacca⁴⁰

yntla otla in MiSSa oncan quimotzatzaliliz n⁴¹ San Joseph quimonahuatiliz in Angel quitoz————[23r]

Angel = = Josephtzinen Josephtzinen Josephtzinē ma xicmochololtilitzino in tlaçomahuizteopiltzintli ca ye huitz in ERodes in tlahueliloc ca quimotemolitinemi ma onpa xicmohuiquilitzino in egipto itzintla in huey Çoyama[~~hui?~~]itl ma onpa xicmotlatilitzino inic amo quimomiquiztlatzomtequililitzino^s[~~quihui?~~] ca ye ixquichtin pipiltzitzintin quinmictitihuitz ma içiuhca ximototoquiltitzino Santo Josephtzinen————————

---

40. tlacca: read *tlaca*.
41. quimotzatzaliliz n: read *quimotzatzililiz yn*.

ANGEL: Rulers, kings, you are most generous,[63] you have shown favor [22v] to the precious, wondrous, and blessed maiden and her precious, wondrous, shimmering, perfect, and only child ever since you came, you came to greet him, you came to make offerings to him. And I do beseech you, do not return the way you came. Go by another road, so that you do not go to fall in the hands of Herod, the great scoundrel. For he just lied to you when he said: "I too will go, I will go to worship him." And he is very angry. He wants to sentence him to death. But in no way is it time yet for him to die. Who will save the people of the world?

(When mass is over, at that point the angel cries out to Saint Joseph, giving him instructions. He says:) [23r]

ANGEL: O Joseph! O Joseph! O Joseph! Flee with[64] the precious and wondrous sacred child! For Herod, the scoundrel, is coming. He is going around searching for him. Take him to Egypt under a large palm frond, hide him there so that he will not sentence him to death! He is coming to kill all the little children! Go speedily, O Saint Joseph![65]

---

63. The word *amoyolloh*, "your hearts," which would complete this idiomatic phrase, seems to be missing here.

64. Literally, cause him to flee.

65. Matthew 2:12–13: "And being warned of God in a dream that they should not return to Herod, they departed into their own country another way. And when they were departed, behold, the angel of the Lord appeareth to Joseph in a dream, saying, Arise, and take the young child and his mother, and flee into Egypt, and be thou there until I bring thee word: for Herod will seek the young child to destroy him." The playwright attributes both warnings to the angel.

Present Location
William L. Clements Library, University of Michigan
Ann Arbor, Michigan

[23v]

Del naSimiento De iSaac del Sacrificio q.ᵉ habrahan Su Padre quiso por mandado de Dios hazer de la Prime=ra Jornada = Hualquiçaz Abraham Yhuan ynamic Saram = = = =

Abrahan = Yn cemicac timohuetznotica[1] in timoçenhuelitiliani in tiDios tetatzin in oticmochihuili in Ylhuicatl in tlalticpac:tli in tonatiuh in metztli yhuan in çiçitlaltin auh in ixquich ittalo yhuan in amo ittalo in nohuian Çemanahuac onoc auh in ixquichtin in Ylhuicac chaneque in çemicac mitzmoyectenehuilia in motlatochantzinco[2] [24r] in Ylhuicatl ytic canel ic otiquinmoChihuili in çemicac moChantzinCo motlamachtizque auh in tehuātin in timotlaChihualtzitzinhuā in otitechmoChihuili in otitechmoyocolili Ca tehuatzin mohueliticatzinco in titotolinia i nican tlalticpac = Auh in tehuatzin notlaçonamictzinen in motechtzinco = oquiz in moconetzin in meezço in motlapallo macamo ytla ic quimoyolitlacalhuiz in iteyocoxcatzin in moçenhuelitiliani Dios tetatzin—

Saran = = Yn titlaçopilli in ye ixquich cahuitl in ye timonemiltia in nicā tlalticpac in omitzmochihuili in ixquich Yhuelitzin in Dios tetatzin Auh in nehuatl in çenca[3] [24v] ic ninotequipachohua in axcan =

oncan choca Yca ce paño ic mixpopohuaz = = =

habraham = Amo çenca ximochoquili tlein mitztequipachohua ma xi=nechmolhuili—

Saram = = Ynic nichoca in nehuatl Ca ytechcopa in nochalChiuhconetzin iSaac in ipepetlaquiliz in itlanexyo in naniman Canel neezyo notlapallo oquinoqui Auh nochichihualayotica nomemeyālotica onicnohuapahuili auh in axcan Ye ixco Ye icpac tontlachie ye chamactzintli aquin huel techilhuiz in Cuix onca tocnopil tomaçehual in itechcacopa = in toconetzin cuix quimotlayecoltiliz in Dios inic nemiz in tlalticpac[4] [25r] acaçomo quichihuaz in itenahuatiltzin in iuhqui ic techmonahuatilitzinohua in titlachihualtzi=tzinhuan intla moztla huiptla Ximomiquili aquin quihuapahuaz aquin quititiz in mahuiztic nemiliztli in Ylhuicac tehuicac—

oncan chocas

Yc choca in nanimantzin ça çan : nenpolihuiz in nochichihualayo in nomemeyallo oc achi qualli macamo nitlacahuapahuani nitlacaChihuani—

= Oncan monextia Angel

---

1. timohuetznotica: here and below, a nonstandard item. Perhaps the intention (in standard orthography) was *timoyetztzinotica*.
2. In anticipation of the following page: *in.* motlatochantzinco: read *motlatocachantzinco*.
3. In anticipation of the following page: *ic.*
4. In anticipation of the following page: *a.*

The Sacrifice of Isaac
Translated by Barry D. Sell, with assistance from Louise M. Burkhart

[23v]
Of the birth of Isaac and of the sacrifice that his father Abraham wanted to make by order of God. Of the first act.

Abraham enters along with his spouse, Sarah.

ABRAHAM: You the All-powerful, God the Father, are eternal. You made heaven and earth, the sun, the moon and the stars, and all that lies seen and unseen everywhere in the world. All the residents of heaven eternally praise you in your royal home [24r] in heaven since for that reason you made them eternally rich in your home. But as for us, we your creatures whom you made and created, we suffer here on earth by your authority. And as for you, O my beloved spouse, out of you emerged your child, your offspring. May he offend in nothing his Creator, the All-powerful, God the Father.

SARAH: You high-born nobleman, whom the All-powerful God the Father made, have been living here on earth for some time.[1] But as for me, I am very [24v] anguished now.

(At that point she weeps. She wipes her face with a cloth.)

ABRAHAM: Do not weep so much. What is bothering you? Tell me.

SARAH: The reason I am weeping concerns my precious child, Isaac, who is the light and radiance of my soul, which gave me my offspring.[2] I raised him with my breast milk, my milk, and now we gaze into his face already a young fellow. Who can tell us whether we are fortunate and deserving concerning our child? Will he serve God while he lives on earth? [25r] Perhaps he will not carry out his commands in the way in which he orders us, his creatures, [to do]. If you die soon, who will raise him? Who will show him the honorable way of living that conducts people to heaven?

(At that point she weeps.)

For that reason my soul weeps. My breast milk, my milk, will have been spent in vain. It would have been better if I had not raised children, if I had not given birth.

(At that point Angel appears.)

---

1. Tentative translation. The entire utterance seems incomplete, as if the Nahua scribe simply left out a line or two of text.
2. Tentative translation. Evidently "neezyo notlapallo oquinoqui" is an unattested metaphorical phrase. It literally means "it/he [soul/Isaac] spilled my blood, my dye," the diphrase "blood, dye" being a metaphor for "offspring" often with connotations of noble birth (e.g., on the Nahuatl-Spanish side of his dictionary see Molina 1977, 93v: "Teeço, tetlapallo. hijo o hija `d nobles cauallerros" and on the Spanish-Nahuatl side, 71r: "Hijo de principal o senador. pilconetl. tecpilconetl. teeço, tetlapallo. teoxiuh. tetlapanca. tetzicueuhca.").

Angel = Ylhuicac ocaquiztic in moneyolnonotzaliz ixpantzinco in ixquich yhuelitzin in Santissima Trinidad Xicaquican in āçemanahuactlaca in itechpa mottaz inin piltzintli iSaac in quexquich[5] [25v] ypantzinco mochihuaz in Dios itlaçopiltzin inic motemaquixtiliz in nohuian çemanahuac ca yyezçoticatzinco imiquizticatzinco quimotlapolhuiz in ilhuicatl in ompa mehuiltitica in itlacomahuiztatzin[6] auh in oquic ayāmo mochihua ipantzinco in Dios itlaço=piltzin yehuatl yacachtopa ypan moChihuaz in tlaçotlateochihualpiltzintli iSaac auh in titetatzin in titenantzin ic ximoyollalican—

Polihuiz in Angel

habraham = = Amo cenca ximoyoltequipacho Ca ixquich yhuelitzin ca yehuatzin quimochicahuiliz quimohuapahuiliz in nochalchiuh in nocozticteocuitlapiltzin auh in axcan ma oc ticalaquican ma oc tepitzin titoçehuiti

_____[7] [26r]

Saram = Ma yuhqui mochihua ma ximoCalaquitzino—

y Calaquizq.ᵉ tlapitzaloz hualquiçaz iSmael çan yçel

iSmael = Çenca tonehua chichinaca in nix in noyollo in itechcopa in piltontli in iSaac in çenca huel qualnemiliçe in aic quinequi in nechmocniuhtiz in manoço notlan mahuilti in iuhqui oc çequintin pipiltotontin in titoçepanahuiltia ca in quexquich in quinahuatia yn itatzin in inantzin mochi quichihua in itenahuatil amo tlein = ma ytla quitlacohua auh inin queni huel nicchihuaz tla oc nonnonotza

y Hualquiçaz Demonio = veStido de Angel o de vieJo[8] [26v]

Demonio = Tlein ticchihua telpochtlen iuhqui nimitzitta çenca huey in monetequipachol—

Ismael Ca quemaca miec in nechtequipachohua auh quen ticmati intla itla onca nonetequipachol ac omitzilhui—

Dem.ᵒ = = Amo tiquitta ca ylhuicac niChane onpa onihualyhualoc inic nimitzilhuiz in tlein ticChihuaz in nican tlalticpac—

iSmael = Auh ma niccaqui in motenahuatil—

Dem.ᵒ = Xicaqui in axcan inic timotequipachohua ca nican ca Ca yehuatl itechcopa in tlaçopilli iSaac inic huel qualnemiliçe in çemicac quineltoquilia in itenahuatil in itatzin auh iuhqui tiquilnamiqui tiquilehuia inic acmo quitlacamatiz[9] [27r] yn itatzin in inantzin ca nimitzilhuiz in quenin ticChihuaz—

iSmael = Queni Çenca ninoyollalia in niCaqui in motlatoltzin ma nicnomaçehui in motepalehuilitzin Canel ilhuicac tichane Ca timotepalehui=liani—

Dem.ᵒ = Huel xicmoyolloti in notenahuatil xiquitta in axcan Ca yn i=tatzin yhuan ynantzin tecohuanotzatzque Çenca neyolaliloz papacohuaz auh in tehuatl ticcuitlahuiltiz inic quintlalcahuiz yn itatzin yn inantzin inic cana anmahuiltitihue auh intla ça nen omiztlacama ca ic quitelchihuazq.ᵉ in inconeuh in manel huel quitlaçotla—

iSmael = Yuhqui nicChihuaz in motlanahuatiltzin—

---

5. In anticipation of the following page: *y*.
6. itlacomahuiztatzin: read *itlaçomahuiztatzin*.
7. In anticipation of the following page: *Saran*.
8. In anticipation of the following page: *D*.
9. In anticipation of the following page: *y*.

ANGEL: Your concerns have been clearly heard in heaven before the All-powerful, the Most Holy Trinity. Listen, you people of the world: in the example of this child Isaac will be seen everything that [25v] will happen to the beloved son of God when he will save people everywhere in the world, for through his blood and his death he will open up heaven where sits his beloved honored Father. But meanwhile, before it happens to the son of God, it will first happen to the precious and blessed child Isaac. And you who are fathers, you who are mothers,[3] console yourselves with that.
(Angel disappears.)
ABRAHAM: Do not be so anguished, for the All-powerful will strengthen and raise my jade, my golden child. But for now, let us enter, let us rest a bit. [26r]

SARAH: May it so be done. Enter.
(They exit. Wind instruments are played. Ishmael enters alone.)
ISHMAEL: Deep within me there is great burning pain concerning the boy Isaac, who is of very good life. He never wants to make friends with me nor play with me as do the other boys with whom I play. However many orders his father and his mother give him, he carries them all out. He is at fault in absolutely none of their orders. Now then, what can I do? Let me figure this out.
(Demon enters dressed as an angel or an old man.) [26v]
DEMON: O young man, what are you doing? You appear to me to have very great cares.
ISHMAEL: Yes, there is much that worries me. But how do you know if I have some cares? Who told you?
DEMON: Do you not see that I am a resident of heaven? I was sent here from there in order to tell you what you are to do here on earth.
ISHMAEL: Let me hear your commands.
DEMON: Listen, here is what has you so occupied today. It concerns the high-born noble Isaac, who is of such good life. He always gives credence to the commands of his father. But you have been thinking that you want him to no longer obey [27r] his father and his mother. I will tell you how to do it.
ISHMAEL: How very content I am to hear your words. Let me enjoy your help since you are a resident of heaven and you are a helper of people.
DEMON: Take right to heart my commands. Look. Today his father and his mother have invited people to a banquet. There will be great contentment and enjoyment. But you are to oblige him to abandon his father and his mother by you and him going somewhere to play. And if he so ruinously obeys you they will despise their child for it even though they greatly love him.
ISHMAEL: I will carry out your command in that fashion.

---

3. father(s), mother(s): in this order or reversed, a common diphrase that means "parent(s)" A staple of polite speech, it is often not gender specific.

Demonio = Auh in nehuatl Ca ye niauh Yn ilhuicatl itic Ca onimitzyolalico yhuan onimitznahuatico = in tlein ticChihuaz—[10] [27v]

Calaquizq.ᵉ çeçecni huetziz truenos = hualquicaz[11] Abrahan yhuan ypiltzin YSaac huel hualmoyecchichiuhtiazque—

Abra.ᵃ Yn tinocozticteocuitlacozqui in tinochalchiuhmacuex in tinoztacteocuitlaneapan tinotlaçopiltzin xihualmohuica çenca noneyolaliztica nimitznahuatia in quen nimitzmalcochohua canel omitzmochihuili in moçenhuelitiliani in Dios teTatzin in ixquich in itlachihualtzin in tlalticpac yn ittalo ihuā in amo ittalo =. Auh xicmocaquiti notlazomahuizpiltzinē, ma nen itla quemanian itla ic ticcatzauh in moyolia in moaniman Ma çemicac Xicchalchiuhmati Xicepyollomati canel ytlachi=hualtzin in Dios auh in itlaçomahuiztlatocatenahuatiltzin in totecuiyo Dios in etlamantli in itlanahuatiltzin macamo çentlamantli tiquitlacoz huel moyollo itech XicquiCuilo Çemicac Xicquilnamiqui Ca onmohuetznotica in motechiuhcatzi[12] [28r] in moteyocoxcatzin in omitzmochihuili in çemicac yectenehualoni Yn ilhuicac in tlalticpac, auh in axcan Xicmomachilti notlaçomahuizpiltzinen Ca nican hualmohuicazq.ᵉ in motlacamecayohuan mitzmotiliquihue yhuan quimatiquihue in quenin çenca nimitznotlazotilia in tinotlaçopiltzin————

ISaac = Yn tinotlaçotatzin in tlalticpac tinotechiuhcatzin ca ye ochicahuac in motlallotzin in moço:quiotzin ixquich tlatequipanoliztli tlamaçe:hualiztli ye nimitznomaquilitzinohua in nican tlalticpac inic ye tinechmohuapahuilia auh tinechmomaquilia in nocochca in noneuhca Auh inic nictlapachohua in notlallo in noçoquio mochi tehuatzin motetlaocoliliztlachihualtzin ticmochihuilitzinohua auh cocoliztli temoztli[13] nimitznomaquilitzinohua in tinotlaçotatzin Ca çenca onicnomaçehui in motlaçomahuiztlatoltzin inic tinechmononochilitzino:hua, motzontecontzin nictlapana melchiquiuhtzin niquehuaz notlazomahuiztatzinen Ca[14] [28v] yn ixquich tinechmonahuatilia, ca mochi nicchi=huaz—

Abraham = Ximohuica[15] Xiquinnahuati in notetlayecolticahuan ma yçiuhca tlaçencahuacan in oncan notlaquayan in oncan tepitzin titoyollalizq.ᵉ—

ISaac = Ma niman, niauh nicneltili in motlaçotlanatiltzin[16] notlaçotatzinen————

<u>y</u> Calaquizque in iSaac Yhuan habrahan hualquiça Agar la esclava yhuan iconeuh iSmael = = = = = = = = = = = =

---

10. In anticipation of the following page: *Ca*.
11. **hualquicaz:** read *hualquiçaz*.
12. In anticipation of the following page: *in*.
13. temoztli: standard *temoxtli*.
14. In anticipation of the following page: *y*.
15. Ximohuica: originally written *Ximohuicacan*. The last three letters are obscured by the X that immediately follows.
16. motlaçotlanatiltzin: scribal error; as elsewhere in this text, read *motlaçotlanahuatiltzin*.

DEMON: As for me, I am going into heaven for I came to console you and to tell you what you are to do. [27v]

(They exit. Thunderclaps sound in various places. Abraham enters along with his son Isaac. They come well dressed.)

ABRAHAM: You my golden jewel, my jade bracelet, my silver necklace, you my beloved child, come. With great contentment I give you orders as well as embrace you since All-powerful God the Father made you, he by whom everything on earth, the seen and the unseen, was made. Listen, O my beloved honored child, do not sometime soil your spirit and your soul with something. Always regard it as a jade, as a precious pearl, since it is a work of God. And as to the precious honored royal commands of our lord, God: his commands are three; do not violate a single one. Inscribe them well on your heart. Always remember them, for there exists your Engenderer [28r] and Creator who made you and is eternally worthy of praise in heaven and on hearth. Now know, O my beloved honored child, that those of your lineage will be coming here to see you and to know how very much I esteem you, my beloved child.

ISAAC: You my beloved father and engenderer on earth, your earthly body has already become old with all the work and penance I give you here on earth raising me. You give me my daily sustenance and what I cover my body with. All are your works of mercy which you do for me. I [do not wish to] make you ill, my beloved father, [with my importunities] for I have greatly profited from the precious honored words with which you counsel me. I [do not wish to] give you headaches and stomachaches [with my bothersome chatter]. O my beloved honored father, [28v] all you order me, all I will do.

ABRAHAM: Go, order my servants to quickly prepare my dining area where we will console ourselves a bit.

ISAAC: O my beloved father, let me go right away to carry out your precious command.

(Exit Isaac and Abraham. Hagar the slave enters along with her child Ishmael.)

Agar = Yn axcan in no cuel oc cecppa[17] tecohuanotza in huey tlatohuani habraan in ipampa in ipiltzin in çenca quitlaçotla, auh in tehuan = Canel titetlannenque atlei ypan tittoni auh in tehuatl in tinoconeuh yn atle mocnopil yn atle momaçehual ma tehuatl motech oniçehuini ma oxicçehuiani in ixquich in nochichinaquiliz tlalticpac canel motlacatiliz momaçehual in çemicac Choquiztli =

y oncan chocazq.ᵉ innehuan yn iconeuh = [18] **[29r]**

iSmael = : Yn titonatiuh in çenca huecapan in tica ma xi=techhualtotonili yca in çenca huey in motlanex ic in nohuian, C͞m͞C, inic huel tiquihueltlamachtia[19] in ixquichtin in tlalticpac tlaca Auh in tehuantin, Ca tomextin titolinia in atle tolhuil in atle tomaçehual Auh in axcā xicmomachilti nonantzinen in tlein nicchihuaz in axcan yn iquac intla ye tlaqualo azo huel nicnahualquixtiz inic cana titahuiltitihue ynic quitlacoz in itenahuatil in itatzī inic acmo yca yyollo, quitlaçotlaz—

Agar, = Ca huel qualli in tiquilnamiqui ma yuhqui XicChihua—

oncan hualquiça YSaac =

iSaac = tlein anquichihua nican Cuix ye mochi Omoçēcauh in ixquich in monequiz ma motlali in mesa =—

iSmael = Ca yehuatl in axcan nican ic titononotza macamo ytla itlacahuiz itechpa in tecohuanotzaliztli ma mochintin monotzacan in tlapitzq,ᵉ in tlatzotzomque ma mochintin hualhuian—[20] **[29v]**

iSaac = Ma yuhqui mochihua yçiuhca Xitlaçencahuacan

y oncan tlaçencahualo in oncan tlaqualoz motlaliz Sillas mesa = miec xochitl intla otlaçencauh oncan tlapitzaloz tlatzotzonaloz hualquiçaz Abraham = Sara yhuan omentin pipiltin tlatoque tenamiquiz = YSaac = =

iSaac = = Ma nican timohuicatz notlaçomahuiztatzinē yhuan in tehuatzin in tinotlaçonantzin = Auh in amehuantintzitzin in antlaçomahuizpipiltin ma ximoçehuitzinocan ca nican tamechtochieli=ticate———

1.º Pilli = O quenin çenca tetlamachti in inezcaliliz inin telpochtzintli ma oc miec quimomaquili in itechicahualitzin in Cemicac mohuetznotica in Çemanahuac tlatohuani Dios—

2.º Pilli = huel çenca itech neçi in çenca huey in inezcaliliz canel tlazoeztli[21] mahuiztique tlaca in in omoquixti[22]—

Abraham = Ma ximoçehuitzinocan yn antlaçopipiltin =

oncan motlalizque tlatzotzona[23] **[30r] tlapitzaloz oncan ycaz Agar auh in iSmael conmati=lanaz Yn iSaac—**

iSmael = Xihualmohuica, nocniuhtzinen y nocuie[24] neyolalilo ma no cana tontaahuiltiti Cuix aca mitzhualmottilia Cuix can çemicac ticmoteoti=tiez in motatzin in monantzin tihuian ti:toyolaliti intla, oc çequintin topilicnihuā, = =

---

17. oc cecppa: here and below can be found this and other variants of standard *oc ceppa*.
18. In anticipation of the following page: *iS*.
19. tiquihueltlamachtia: standard *tiquinhuellamachtia*.
20. In anticipation of the following page: *ysaac*.
21. tlazoeztli: the first z has a cedilla, a feature I have never noticed in any other Nahuatl text.
22. in omoquixti: perhaps to be read *intech omoquixti*.
23. In anticipation of the following page: *loz,*. However, it does not appear on the following page. Therefore read the item as *tlatzotzonaloz*.
24. nocuie: evidently scribal error for *notecuiyoe*.

HAGAR: Today the great ruler Abraham has yet again invited people to a banquet because of the great esteem he has for his child. But as for us, since we are lowly servants, we are held in no regard. And as for you, my child, you are doubly luckless. Would that I could find relief in you, that you could give relief to all my earthly torments, for in truth your birth and your lot are eternal weeping.

(At that point she and her child weep together.) [29r]

ISHMAEL: You, sun, who are very high up, warm us with your very great radiance everywhere in the world, with which you are able to please all the people of the earth. But as for us, the two of us are suffering. We are doubly luckless. But now know, O my mother, what I will do today when all are eating. Perhaps I can sneak [Isaac] out so that we will go play somewhere. Thus he will violate the orders of his father so that he will no longer love him with his heart.

HAGAR: What you are thinking is very good. Do it so.

(At that point Isaac enters.)

ISAAC: What are you doing here? Have all necessary preparations been made? Let the table be set.

ISHMAEL: That is what we were just talking about here. Let nothing be amiss concerning the banquet. Let all the players of wind instruments and drums be summoned; let them all come! [29v]

ISAAC: May it so be done. Make swift preparations.

(At that point all gets prepared in the dining area. Chairs and a table are placed. Next to them are many floral arrangements. At that point wind instruments are played and drums are beaten. Enter Abraham, Sarah, and two high-ranking nobles.[4] Isaac greets them.)

ISAAC: Please be welcome here,[5] O my beloved honored father, and you, my beloved mother. And as for you high-ranking honored noblemen, do rest, for here we are awaiting you.

FIRST NOBLEMAN: O what a great joy it is [to observe] the upbringing of this young man! May God, ruler of the world who is eternal, give him much health.

SECOND NOBLEMAN: His very great upbringing is readily apparent since he is the high-born offspring [of] the esteemed people whom he takes after.[6]

ABRAHAM: Rest, you high-ranking noblemen.

(At that point they sit down. Drums are beaten. [30r] *Wind instruments are played. Hagar is standing there. Ishmael goes pulling Isaac along by the hand.)*

ISHMAEL: Come, O my friend, O my lord. All are content. Let us also go somewhere to play. Will someone [important] see you [fooling around]? Are you always to be adoring your father and your mother? Let us get going, let us go enjoy ourselves with our other childhood friends.

---

4. Literally, "two noblemen [who are] rulers" In this instance Nahuatl *tlatoque*, "rulers," is almost certainly not meant literally but to heighten their noble status.

5. Ma nican timohuicatz: see Carochi 1983, 67v, 80r, and Sahagún 1997, 296.

6. Tentative translation.

iSaac = Yn nehuatl, amo nonahuatil in nicnotlalcahuiliz in notlaçotatzin yhuan in notlaçonantzin Xinechcahua, tehuatl moçel ximahuilti—

Oc çecppa tlapitzaloz, auh in iSaac, onmicuaniz itla in = Messa huel mocnomaticaz =

Sara = Yn tehuatzin in titlatohuani in çenca timahuictic[25] in tinotlaçonamictzin çenca nimitznotlatlauhtilitzinohua Yhuan in nican mohuetzticate in çenca mahuiztililoni, ma xicmocaquiltican in nocnotlatol in itechcopa in nochalchiuhconetzin ca yn iquac in timotlaqualtiticaca in[26] [30v] tlaçoÇihuatl[27] yn iconeuh imatitech ocan in motlaçopiltzin ynic oquiquixti quiahuac inic mahuiltizque, Auh huel çenca ic nichoca = yn ahuilli Camanalli ca ic mahuizpolihui in motlaçopiltzin = = =

Abraham = Xihualauh in tehuatl in titlaçotli[28] yhuan in mocone:uh nican Ximomemanacan[29] =—

y oncan momenazq.^e[30] **Agar yhuan ismael**———

Abraham = Xicaqui in titenan in moconeuh in ticpaccayta in çemicac mahuiltia in amo tictlacahualtia Ca tehuatl motlatlacol Ca moztla huiptla mic=tlan tictzauctiaz——

1.º Pilli = = Melahuac in ticmitalhuia yn ahuilli yn camanalli, huel ypeuhca in tlahuelilocayotl, intlacamo tiquintlacahualtizque in topilhuan Ca tehuantin ^{totla-}tlacol mochihuaz in moztla huiptla—

Sara = Yntlacamo tiquinmototoquiliz in quitlalcahuizque in totlaçomahuizconetzin ca quimachtizque in ahuilnemiliztli yhuan in atlei ypā teittaliztli—

Abraham = Yuhqui mochihuaz in motlanequilitzin—[31r]

2º Pilli = Ma niman Xiquinmototoquili Cuix yuhqui tlaçotlaloni yn aqualnemiliçeque yuhqui in nantli yuhqui in iconeuh aço mach oanquimitalhuique aço yehuatl itla, qualnemiliztli quittitiz, ye quicuitlahuiltia yn imahuizpopololocatzin in Dios yhuan in amehuantzitzin—

Abraan = Xihuian, xinechtlalcahuican acmo nican namechittaz xictlalcahuican in taltepeuh amo anquinmachtizq.^e yn amaqual:nemiliz in oc çequintin tlaçotepilhuan =—

y oncan chocaz in Agar—

Agar = = = Onohueytlahueliltic yn ahuel nitlacahuapahua, in aqualli inic onimitzhuapauh in tinotlahuelilocaconeuh axcan mohuan nictzaqua in motlahuelilocayo omochiuh onotlahueliltic—

y oncan chocazq.^e innehuan in AGar yhuan yn iconeuh iSmael—

1.º Pilli = Xihuian xitechtlalcahuican amo oncan xichocatimanican—[32] [31v]

iSmael = Omochiuh, onotlahueliltic yn atle onechonquixti in noxolopiyo———

y Calaquizq.^e AGar yhuan in iconeuh, Ysmael———

2.º Pilli = Ma ximocalaqui, tlacatlen tlatohuaniē = =

---

25. timahuictic: read *timahuiztic*.
26. In anticipation of the following page: *tla*.
27. tlaçoÇihuatl: scribal error for *tlaçocihuatl*.
28. titlaçotli: scribal error for *titlacotli*.
29. Ximomemanacan: read *ximomamanacan*.
30. **momenazq.^e**: read *momamanazque*.
31. In anticipation of the following page: *2º*..
32. In anticipation of the following page: *iSmael*.

ISAAC: I am not supposed to leave my beloved father and my beloved mother. Leave me, play by yourself.

(Wind instruments are played again. Isaac moves over next to the table. He stands very humbly.)

SARAH: You, my beloved spouse, are a ruler and very esteemed. I greatly implore you and those here who are very worthy of esteem. May you hear my humble words concerning my beloved child. When you were eating [30v] the child of the slave woman grabbed your beloved child by his hand in order to take him outside that they might play. I weep copiously over the trivialities and jokes, for by them your beloved child is dishonored.

ABRAHAM: Come, you slave, along with your child. Here you two will kneel.

(At that point Hagar and Ishmael kneel.)

ABRAHAM: Listen, you who are a mother. Your child, whom you look at with such approval, is always playing. You do not restrain him; the fault is yours. Soon you will pay the penalty for it in hell.

FIRST NOBLEMAN: What you are saying is correct. Wickedness begins with trivialities and jokes. If we do not restrain our children [their flaws] will soon become our fault.

SARAH: If you do not exile those who will forsake our beloved honored child, they will teach him waywardness and to have no regard for others.

ABRAHAM: Your will be so done. [31r]

SECOND NOBLEMAN: Run them off right away. Are those of a bad way of life such as to be worthy of esteem? Like mother, like child.[7] Will they say you said that perhaps a good way of life will show her something?[8] [However] now it constrains her to dishonor God along with you.[9]

ABRAHAM: Get going, leave us, I will see you here no longer. Abandon our altepetl.[10] You will not teach your evil way of life to the other children of high-ranking people.

(At that point Hagar weeps.)

HAGAR: I am very unfortunate! I am unable to [properly] raise children given the bad way I raised you, my malicious child. Now along with you I pay the penalty for your iniquities. Woe is me!

(At that point Hagar and her child Ishmael weep together.)

FIRST NOBLEMAN: Get going, leave us! Do not lie down there crying! [31v]

ISHMAEL: Woe is me! My stupidity didn't do me any good!

(Hagar and her child Ishmael exit.)

SECOND NOBLEMAN: Enter, O personage, O ruler.

---

7. Literally, "such is the mother, such is her child."

8. That is, that she will make proper amends if given a good example.

9. Tentative translation. Alternative translation for the last two lines: "They say that perhaps you said that a good way of life would perhaps show her something, but the way she dishonors God and you keeps her from it."

10. altepetl: Nahuatl term applied to various kinds of sovereign sociopolitical units; most of those existing in central Mexico at this time were of approximately city-state dimensions During colonial times the word was translated in many ways including *ciudad* (city) and *pueblo* (people, settlement).

Abraham = = Ma yuh mochihua, mahuiztiq^e tlacaen ma tihuian—

Calaquizque mochintin oncā = tlapitzaloz motlapoz in Ylhuicatl hualmoquixtiz in Dios Padre motlatoltiz—

Dios Padre = Ye mochi onicçencauh, Yn ilhuicatl in tlalticpactli auh atle itech polihui auh in ixquichtin in Ylhuicac chaneque in noyectlachihualhuan çemicac nechhueltlamachtia³³ aic qui=tlacohua in notlaçotenahuatiltzin auh canel, yuh nitlanahuatia inic quichihuazque quineltilizque in notenahuatiltzin in quichihuazq,^e in ixquichtin, tlalticpac tlaca yn iuhqui quinequi = in noçenquizcatlanequilitzin—

v = oncan hualquizaz Abraan³⁴ [32r]

Abraham = Yn çemicac timohuetznotica in çenca huecapan in Ylhuicatl itic in nohuian tiquinmotztilitica in ixquichtin in motlachihualtzitzinhuan auh in nehuatl, in nimitznixpantilitzinohua in itechpa in motlachihualtzin in otinechmomaquili, in nican tlalticpac in notlaçopiltzin YSaac ca intla nican nemiz tlalticpac ca yuh ca in nix no:yollo aço mitzmoteopohuiliz acaçomo quichi=Chihuaz in motlaçoteotenahuatiltzin in iuhqui timotlanahuatilitzinohua—

Dios Padre = Abraham, Abraham, nimitzonnotza—

Abraham = Ac tehuatzin, in tinechmonochilia—

Dios Padre = Yntla nelli, in huel ticchihua in noteotlanahuatiltzin xiconana³⁵ in mopiltzin in çenca tictlaçotla in itoca YSaac = Xichuica in icpac tepetl yn itocayocan Moria ompa ticmictiz ic noyollo pachihuiz intla nelli in ticchihua in noteo=nahuatiltzin—

Abraham = Nicchihuaz in motlanahuatiltzin, ca yuhqui ca in in noyollo, Ca tehuatzin in çemicac tineltoconi in ixquich mohuelitzin in niccaqui in motlatoltzin—³⁶ [32v]

v Motzaquaz in Ylhuicatl tlapitzaloz, calaquiz in Abraham oncan Cuicoz, mehuaz te de³⁷ = laudamoz = hualquicaz³⁸ in Abraham Yhuan YSaac ihuā omentin, ytlannencahuan =

Abraham = Yn axcan, xicmomachilti, Ca nimitzhuicaz in icpac in nepa ca huey tepetl ompa titla^{tla}tlauhtitihue—

iSaac = Ma yuhqui mochihua in motlanequilitzin notlaçomahuiztatzinen————

Abraham = Auh in amehuantin Xiqualquixtican in tlatlatilquahuitl, yhuan mecatl yhuan çe teposmacquahuitl = =

1.º Criado = Ca ye qualitzin, tlatohuanien—

v Niman Yazque quicuitihue çe tlalpilli quahuitl, Yhuan mecatl ihuan alfange tlapitzaloz tepitzin—

2.º Criado = Ca ye nican, catqui in ticmotlania—

Abraham = Ca ye qualli ma tihuian Xinechhualtocatihuian in canin niaz ompa anyazq.^e amo anmoXiuhtlatizq.^e—³⁹ [33r]

---

33. nechhueltlamachtia: standard *nechhuellamachtia*.
34. In anticipation of the following page: *A*.
35. xiconana: standard *xoconana*; see Carochi 1983, 42v–43v.
36. In anticipation of the following page: *Mo*.
37. de: read *deum*.
38. **hualquicaz:** read *hualquiçaz*.
39. In anticipation of the following page: *isaac*.

ABRAHAM: May it so be done, O honored people. Let us be on our way.

(At this point all exit. Wind instruments are played. Heaven opens. God the Father enters. He speaks.)

GOD THE FATHER: I have already prepared all of heaven and earth. Nothing is lacking in them. All the residents of heaven, my good creatures, eternally please me. They never violate my precious commands. And since I have given orders such that they will perform and realize my commands, all the people of the earth will perform them in the way my consummate will wants.

(At that point Abraham enters.) [32r]

ABRAHAM: You who are eternally very high up in heaven see all your creatures everywhere [they are]. But as for me, I make a declaration before you concerning your creature you gave me, my beloved child here on earth, Isaac. I am of the opinion that if he will live here on earth perhaps he will offend you, perhaps he will not carry out your precious orders you have commanded.

GOD THE FATHER: Abraham, Abraham, I am calling you.

ABRAHAM: Who are you that calls me?

GOD THE FATHER: If it is true that you can carry out my sacred commands, seize your child named Isaac whom you greatly love and take him to the top of the mountain in the place named Moriah. There you are to kill him. If truly you carry out my sacred command my heart will be satisfied.

ABRAHAM: I will carry out your command. I intend to do it for you, the All-powerful, whose words I hear, are eternally worthy of being believed. [32v]

(Heaven closes. Wind instruments are played. Exit Abraham. At that point all sing. The te deum laudamus is raised up [in song]. Enter Abraham along with Isaac and two of his lowly servants.)[11]

ABRAHAM: Now know that I will take you to the top of that big mountain that is some distance away. There we are going to pray.

ISAAC: May your will be so done, O my beloved honored father.

ABRAHAM: And as for you, bring out the firewood and rope and a sword.

FIRST SERVANT: Very well, O ruler.

(They go right away, taking a bundle of wood along with rope and a sword. Wind instruments are played a little.)

SECOND SERVANT: Here is what you are requesting.

ABRAHAM: Very well, let us go. Come following along after me. Where I will go, there will you go. You are not to be impatient. [33r]

---

11. While grammatically there is ambiguity, contextually the lowly servants would seem to be those of the father.

iSaac = Ca mochihuaz in motenahuatiltzin yn iuh tinechmonahuatilitzinohua, notlaçomahuiztatzinen =

<u>v</u> Niman tlapitzaloz inic yazq,ᵉ in canin ca Tepetl—

Abraham = Ye otaçico in intzintlan tepetl in oncan titlatlatlauhtizq.ᵉ Auh in amehuantin nican ximocahuacan amo antechhuicazq.ᵉ Xiqualhuicacā in notepozMauhcuauh yhuan in tletl auh in tlatlatilquahuitl Xiquechpanoltican in notlaçopiltzin ca ytech monequiz—

<u>v</u> Tlapitzaloz tepitzin oncan quiquechpanoltizqᵉ in quahuitl, in iSaac niman, yaz tlecotiaz Yn itech Tepetl niman oncan ᵐᵒquetzaz in iSaac tlatoz =

iSaac = = Notlaçomahuiztatzinen, Ca çenca huel, ye nechçianmictia in nichuica ynin tlatlatilquahuitl auh tlein ticmochihuiliz—

Abraham = Ca motech monequiz ic nextli mocuepaz in monacayo ic nimitzhuenchihuaz—.

iSaac = Auh notlaçomahuiztatzinen Cuix çan ye⁴⁰[33v]huatl in tichuenchihuazque in quahuitl yhuan in tletl = =

Abraham = Notlaçopiltzinen, çenca tinechpatzmictilia in noyollotzin ca in tley itlanequilitzin in Dios ca yehuatl mochi mochihuaz canel yuh nechmonahuatilitzinohua ma tihuian—

<u>v</u> Tlapitzaloz. Yatiazque niman quitlaliz in quahuitl, Yn iSaac in habraham oncan tlatoz—

Abraham,⁴¹ = Xiqualhuicacan in tlatlatil,quahuitl nican Xictemacan—

<u>v</u> Niman oncan quixeloz in habraham in quahuitl—

Abraham = Xihualauh nican ximotlanquaquetza, yuhqui onechmonahuatili in Dios, inic nicchihuaz, in itlanequilitzin—

iSaac = Ma mochihua, in itlatocatlanahuatiltzin in Dios yn iuh quimonequiltitzinohua yhuan in tehuatzin = = = = = =

Abraham = Xicaqui yn axcan, notlaçopiltzinen, ca huel iuh. onechmonahuatili in moçenhuelitiliani, in Dios, ynic neltiz yn itlaçoteotenahuatiltzin inic quiMotiliz intla tictotlaçotilia in titlalticpactlaca intla ticchihua, Yn iteotenahuatiltzin auh ca intlatoca⁴²[34r]tzin in yolque Yhuan in mimicque auh in axcan ma huel monecnomachiliztica Xicçeli in miquiztli = Ca yuh quimitalhuia ca in nehuatl nihuelitiz in niquimizcaliz in mimicque ca in nehuatl çemicac niyoliliztli in nohuian Çm̄C auh ma mochi=hua yn itlanequilitzin—

<u>v</u> oncan chocaz in Abraham Yhuan mopitzatz⁴³ Missericordia

iSaac = Amo ximochoquili notlaçomahuiztatzinen Ca çenca huel nopaquiliztica in nicçelia in miquiztli, ma mochihua yn itlaçoteotenahuatiltzin, in Dios = Yn iuh omitzmonahuatili—

Abraham = Xiqualhuican in moman nicYlpiz inic amo timoliniz—

<u>v</u> oncan quimailpiz yn itatzin Yn isaac——

---

40. In anticipation of the following page: *huatl*.
41. Here and in two other instances below there is no underlining.
42. In anticipation of the following page: *tzin*.
43. mopitzatz: standard *mopitzaz*.

ISAAC: Your command will be done as you order, O my beloved honored father.

(Wind instruments are played when they get to where the mountain is [located].)

ABRAHAM: We have now arrived at the foot of the mountain, where we will pray. As for you, you will stay here; you will not accompany us. Bring my sword and the fire. As for the firewood, put it on the shoulders of my beloved child, for he will need it.

(Wind instruments are played a little. They make Isaac carry the wood on his shoulders. He immediately ascends the mountain. Once there Isaac stands up. He speaks.)

ISAAC: O my beloved honored father, this firewood that I am carrying makes me extremely tired. What are you going to do?

ABRAHAM: You will need to turn into ashes [for] I am going to make an offering of your body.

ISAAC: But, O my beloved honored father, [33v] are we [not] to make an offering of just the wood and the fire?

ABRAHAM: O my beloved child, you greatly anguish my heart. All that which is the will of God must be carried out since such are his orders to me. Let us be on our way.

(Wind instruments are played. They go along. Then Isaac sets the wood down. At that point Abraham speaks.)

ABRAHAM: Bring the firewood. Lay it down here.

(Once there Abraham splits the wood.)

ABRAHAM: Come, kneel here. God has ordered me to carry out his will in a certain fashion.

ISAAC: May the royal commands of God be done in accordance with his will and yours.

ABRAHAM: Now listen, O my beloved child: The All-powerful, God, has strictly ordered me to [make sure] that his precious sacred commands are realized so that he will see if we people of the earth love him and if we carry out his sacred commands, for he is the ruler of [34r] the living and the dead. Now receive death with great humility, for he speaks thusly: I will be able to raise the dead for I am eternal life everywhere in the world. May his will be done.

(At that point Abraham weeps and the Misericordia is played on wind instruments.)

ISAAC: Do not cry, O my beloved honored father, for it is with very great happiness that I receive death. May the precious sacred commands of God be done as he has ordered you [to do them].

ABRAHAM: Give [me] your hands. I will bind them so that you will not move.

(At that point Isaac's father binds his hands.)

iSaac = Notlaçomahuiztatzinen Ma yhuan xinechmixquimilhui ynic amo ninomauhtiz in iquac ticmacoCuiliz in momatzin⁴⁴ in motepozmacquauhtzin ma xinechmotlapachilhuilili⁴⁵ in nixtelolo—⁴⁶ [34v]

<u>Abraham</u> = Ma yuhqui mochihua, notlaçopiltzinen = = =—
oncan quixquimiloz in habraham in i,piltzin, niman huel cacocuiz, in ialfange in habraham =—

<u>Abraham</u> = Ytencopatzinco in Dios, inic timomiquiliz in tinotlaçopiltzin—
<u>v</u> **oncan monextiz Çe Angel q:tzitzquiliz, Yn iman in habraham Ynic ahuel quimictiz Yn ipiltzin isaac—**

<u>Angel</u> = Abraham, Abram,—
<u>v</u> **Quitzitzquiliz in iman v**

<u>Abraham</u> = Ac tehuatzin in tinechmonochilia—

<u>Angel</u> = Yn axcan xiccaquican, yhueli^ti catzinco in Dios, yhuan ytencopatzinco ca ic oquimottilitzino in quenin ticmotlaçotilitzinohua, Auh inic ticchihua yn iteotenahuatiltzin, ynic amo tiquitlacohua ca in motlacopiltzin⁴⁷ in çenca ticmotlaçotilitzinohua in axcan, nican Tepeticpac in otiqualmohuiquili in oticmohuenchihuililico in moçenhuelitiliani, in⁴⁸ [35r] Dios tetatzin, Auh in axcan ytlaçotlanequilizti=catzinco, Ynic onihualla inic nimitznolhuilico ynic ticmocahuiliz inic amo momiquiliz in motlacopiltzin,⁴⁹ YSaac—

<u>Abraham</u> = Ma mochihua Yn itlaçotlanahuatiltzin yn iuh quimonequiltitzinohua = Xihualmohuica Notlaçopiltzinen ca ye otimomaquixti, Yn imacpa in miquiztli—
<u>v</u> = **oncan quitomiliz in paño inic oixquimiliuhticatCa Yhuan, in mecatl ic mail=pitica quitotomaz,—**

<u>Angel</u> = Auh in axcan xicmomachilti ca in ixiptla in motlaçopiltzin, Ca çentetl, ichcaconetzintli ticchichihuaquiuh Yn iuh quimonequiltitzinohua in Dios, ma tihuian Ca nemechcahuatiuh,⁵⁰ in amochan—

<u>Abraham</u> = Ma yuhqui mochihuan, ma tihuian—
<u>v</u> **tlapitzaloz, niman hualtemozq,ᵉ Yn icpac tepetl = =**

<u>Abraham</u> = = Yn axcan Ma çemicac moyectenehua y⁵¹[35v]n imahuiztocatzin in moçenhuelitiliani in Dios, tetatzin in nohuian CmC in çenca huey in itetlaocolilitzin intla timochintin in titlalticpactlaca, in ticchihuacan Yn itlaçoteotenahuatiltzin ca çenca ic tictohueltlamachtilizque⁵² = = Auh in tehuatl in tinotlaçopiltzin otiquittac, in quename ic omitzmomaquixtili yn ihuicpa in miquiztli Auh in axcan yn oquix⁵³ cahuitl timonemiltiz Ma çemicac ticmotlazotiliz = yca mochi moyollo Yhuan amo tictlapictenehuaz in itocatzin in Dios, Yhuan tiquintlaçotlaz in mohuanpohuan yn iuh motlanahuatilitzinohua = = =

---

44. momatzin: perhaps to be read *momactzinco*.
45. xinechmotlapachilhuilili: tentative transcription because the end is obscure due to blotting.
46. In anticipation of the following page: *A*.
47. motlacopiltzin: read *motlaçopiltzin*.
48. In anticipation of the following page: *Dios*.
49. motlacopiltzin: read *motlaçopiltzin*.
50. nemechcahuatiuh: read *namechcahuatiuh*.
51. In anticipation of the following page: *ni*.
52. tictohueltlamachtilizque: standard *tictohuellamachtilizque*.
53. oquix: read *oc ixquich*.

ISAAC: And, O my beloved honored father, wrap up my eyes so that I will not be afraid when you raise up your sword in your hand. Do cover my eyes. [34v]

ABRAHAM: May it so be done, O my beloved child.
(At that point Abraham wraps the eyes of his child, and then Abraham raises his sword right on up.)
ABRAHAM: It is by order of God that you, my beloved child, will die.
(An angel appears there. He seizes the hand of Abraham so that he cannot kill his child Isaac.)
ANGEL: Abraham! Abraham!
(He seizes his hand.)
ABRAHAM: Who are you that calls me?
ANGEL: Now listen up! By the power of God and by his orders, he has thus seen how you love him and carry out his sacred commands so that you do not violate them. For today you brought your beloved child, whom you greatly love, to the top of the mountain here in order to make an offering of him to the All-powerful, [35r] God the Father. Now it is by his precious will that I have come to tell you to leave him alone so that your beloved child, Isaac, will not die.

ABRAHAM: May his precious commands be done as is his will. Come, O my beloved child, for you have now been saved from the hands of death.
(At that point he loosens the cloth with which the eyes are wrapped and he undoes the rope with which the hands are bound.)
ANGEL: Now know that the substitute for your beloved child will be a little lamb you are to make ready. Such is the will of God. Let us be on our way, for I am going to leave you at your home.
ABRAHAM: May it so be done. Let us be on our way.
(Wind instruments are played. They immediately descend from the top of the mountain.)
ABRAHAM: Now may [35v] the honored name of the All-powerful, God the Father, whose compassion is very great, be eternally praised everywhere in the world. If all we people of the earth would carry out his precious sacred commands we would greatly please him. And as for you, my beloved child, you have seen how he saved you from death. Now as long as you live, always love him with all your heart and do not take in vain the name of God, and love your neighbors. Such are his orders.

iSaac = = Ca mochi nicChihuaz, Yn itlanahuatiltzin = in Dios, Yhuan in tehuatzin = Auh ma ximocalaquitzino Ca ye otaçico in tochan, ma oc ximoçehuitzino—
v Calaquizque oncan tlatoz Angel =—

Angel = Yn amixquichtin in nican ancate Ca ye oanqui=mocaquiltique Ynin tlamahuiçolli, Auh in amehuantin ma huel xicmonemiliztican, in iteote[54][36r]nahuatiltzin Macamo çentetl, anquitlacozque yhuan in amopilhuan huel Xiquinmocuitlahuican inic amo ahuilnemizque inic qualyoti:ca inic quimotlayecoltilizque in totecuiyo Dios inic no quimomaçehuizque in Ylhuicac tlatoCayotl Ma yuh mochihua =

v = finis Laus Deo, de 1678 A^s Oçencauh[55] inin Neixcuitilli omotrasladaro axcan Ypan tonalli Viernes 1 de febrero, de 1760 Años, auh inic melahuac nehuatl onictequipano inin Neixcuitilli Bernabe Vazquez [simple rubric]

JESVS MARIA Y
JOSEPH
NEIXCVITILLI, I
TECHPA TLATOHua[56]

---

54. In anticipation of the following page: *na*.
55. Oçencauh: read *omoçencauh*.
56. To either side of **JOSEPH** are simple drawings (three to the left, two to the right). At the bottom of the page in a different hand: *pa. Neixkuitilli maxiotl* ^{vj} *Tlatolmaxiotl (Mol)*.

ISAAC: I will perform all the commands of God and you. Do enter, for we have reached our home. Please rest a while.

(They exit. At that point Angel speaks.)

ANGEL: All of you who are here have now heard this marvelous thing. And as for you, may you live entirely according to [36r] his sacred commands, may you and your children not violate a single one. Take good care that they will not go about playing and wasting time, so that they will serve with goodness our lord, God, and so that they will also merit the kingdom of heaven. May it so be done.

Finis. Laus Deo.[12] *This moral example was prepared in the year 1678. It was copied today, Friday, the first of February of the year 1760. And as to whether in truth I worked on this moral example, [I affix my signature]: Bernabé Vázquez.*

JESUS, MARY AND JOSEPH.
MORAL EXAMPLE WHICH SPEAKS ABOUT[13]

---

12. *Finis Laus Deo.*: The End. Praise God.
13. There is no indication why there is such an incomplete and abrupt ending.

Present Location
William L. Clements Library, University of Michigan
Ann Arbor, Michigan

[36v]
YN ANIMASTIN Y:HVAN ALVACEAS:ME, HVALQVIZAZ. IN DON PEDRO
I:HVAN INAMIC TLatZOtZONALOZ TLaPItZALOZ—

D. Pedro = Tla xihualmohuica notlaçonamictzinen ca izcatqui in cenca nechtequipachohua ninentlamatinemi in ixpantzinco in Dios yn intechcopa in mimiccatzitzintin in macan,[1] nicalpixcatzin in teotl, tlatohuani Dios Auh ca ye oquimotlapohuililique Ca ye ixpantzinco otlatemoliloque yn itechpa yn intlachihualiz in i nepapan[2] [37r] tlatlacolli yhuan ye otlatzomtequililoque intla oc cecpa[3] nican tp̄c hualani ca techmelahuilizquia in quenin omelauhcatlatzomtequililoque acaçomo çan quexquich, in ipalehuiloca yezquia in animasme Auh in tehuantin Ca ye ticmomachitia Ye ixquich cahuitl in tiquinpalehuia in ica MiSsa yhuan ResponSo = Ca çenca ye icnoyohua tonehua in noyollotzin Yn iquac in niquimilnamiqui, in canpa oquimoyeyantlalili in totecuiyo Dios, Aquin huel quimatiz notlaçonamictzinen, auh in axcan, ye totech pachihui tonehuiztli chichinaquiliztli aocmo hualnezini in tocochca toneuhca tlein ynic ticpalehuizq.^{e} Auh ma tehuatzin Xicmitalhuitzino, notlaçonamictzinen—

Cihuatl = Notlaçonamictzin in ticmotenehuilia ca no çenca, Ye patzmiqui inaniman[4] ca nican Catqui in niquilnamiqui ma ticnamacacan in çentetl caltzintli in onca ticate ma yehuatl inic mochihuaz yn inMissatzin in animasme Yehuatl quimati çaço tlein tiquizque Cuix oncate ytlachihualtzitzinhuan in totecuiyo Dios, Canel ayac techmomaquilia in [37v] Dios, ma oc tixpan tomattian mochihua maca tlein tiqualnacazitztiazque in moztla huitlpa[5] intla, otechmopolhui in totecuiyo Dios—

D. Pedro = Ca melahuac in ticmitalhuia nonamictzinen ma tihuian in teopan Ma tictotlatlauhtilitzinoti, in totecuiyo Dios, Ca ye pehuaz in MiSsa ma ticchihuati Çentetzintli Responso in inpa[6] in animastin motoliniticate purgatorio inic quinmocnoittiliz in Dios, in campa mohuetzticate—

Cihuatl = Ma yuh mochihua notlaçonamictzin ma ti=huian—

v **Calaquizque hualquizazque albaçeas, quihualhuicazque in Testamento quipohuazque**

---

1. macan: probably to be read as *ma çan* or *maca çan*.
2. In anticipation of the next page: *tla.* in i nepapan: read as standard *yn nepapan*.
3. oc cecpa: here and below can be found this and other variants of standard *oc ceppa*.
4. inaniman: read *in naniman*.
5. huitlpa: read (as elsewhere in this text) *huiptla*.
6. inpa: if not read as *inpa(h)* "their medicine" then read as *inpan* or *inpampa*.

Souls and Testamentary Executors
Translated by Barry D. Sell, with assistance from Louise M. Burkhart

[36v]

Souls and Testamentary Executors. Don Pedro enters along with his spouse. Drums are beaten, wind instruments are blown.

DON PEDRO: O my beloved spouse, please come.[1] Here is what greatly distresses me. Although I am just a steward of God the deity and ruler I go about discontent before God concerning the unfortunate dead people. They have already given an accounting to him, already been examined before him concerning their deeds, the various [37r] sins, and already been judged. If they were to come again here to earth they would explain to us how they were rightly judged. Perhaps it would be no small help to the souls. As for us, you already know that we have been helping them all this time with masses and prayers for the dead. My heart is very compassionate and suffers burning pain when I remember where our lord God has placed them. O my beloved spouse, who can know [his will/where they are]? Torment and pain now press down upon us and we are miserably poor. With what will we help them? O my beloved spouse, speak.

WOMAN: O my beloved spouse, what you are saying also greatly grieves my soul. Here is what I am thinking. Let us sell the little house where we are and with it let the souls' mass be performed. They know whatever it is we will succeed.[2] Since God has given us no one [that is, children], are there creatures of our lord God? [37v] Let it happen before our eyes and in our time. Let us look at nothing [earthly] with affection since tomorrow or the next day our lord God may have effaced us.

DON PEDRO: O my spouse, you speak the truth. Let us go to church to pray to our lord God, for mass is about to begin. Let us go make a prayer for the dead for the sake of the souls who are suffering in purgatory so that God will have pity on them where they lie fallen.

WOMAN: So be it, O my beloved spouse. Let us go.

(They exit. The executors enter bringing a testament. They read it.)

---

1. Concerning the optative/imperative particles *ma* and *tla*: the former is used far more frequently in this text than the latter, reflecting general usage in the colonial Nahuatl corpus. In several instances, I have added "please" to the translation in order to convey the stronger sense of pleading that *tla* apparently imparts. The most complete and authoritative contemporary explanation of these particles is in Carochi 1983, f. 25:

> Este *mā*, es nota de imperatiuo, y de Optatiuo, y suele dexarse en la segunda persona singula[r], y plural del imperatiuo; y mas quando se mande à algun inferior, si no es que se le quiera mostrar amor; y assi el amo à su criado dize, *xitlachpāna* barre; y con el *mā*, parece, que se ruega, ò se anima à que hagan algo; y en lugar del se vsa tambien del *tlā* que aun es mas comedido, que el *mā*, y con el se ruega, ò anima mas que con el *mā*.

2. Tentative translation.

1º Albacea = Notlaçoteycauhtzinen quenin huel mochihuaz in iuhqui oquitotiaque in mimicque inic teopā calaquiz in imaxca in intlatqui inic palehuilozque in oc çequintin, Animas, auh ca nican catqui in oqui=cauhtiaque in teocuitlatl huel çenca ic ninotlamachtia quenin huel mochihuaz—

2º Albacea = Macamo mitzmotequipachilhui, Ca nehuatl nicmati in quenin huel mochihuaz, ca huel mone⁷[38r]qui axcan nictlaliz amatl in ixquich in oquitecpantiaque in mimicque mochi niquiquaniz mopopoloz cannoço⁸ mocuiz inic titoyolalizque—

<u>v</u> **Calaquizque hualquizazque Demonios luçifer,**————

Lucifer = Tlen⁹ amay tlein anquichihua yn amo anquimocuitlahuia in tp̄c̄ tlaca, ca ça izquilhuitl ma nen anquixichcauhti ma huel ypan Xitotocacan in intech omocauhtiaque in mimicque ma xihuian ma xiquincuitlahuiltican inic huel mochi quipopolozque in miccatlatquitl inic amo huel tomacpa quiçazque in = Animastin in techquixtilizque ma niman nelti moChihua in notenahuatil—

2º Dem,º = Macamo Ximotequipachotzino ca niman ye tihui axcan inic tiquintlapololtizque—

3º Dem,º = Ma niman tihuian ma tiquimittati in tomaçehualhuan in tocnihuan ma tihuian—

<u>v</u> **Yazque itzintla Mesa mo=tlalizque tlacuilozque in Demonios hualquiçazq,ᵉ albaçeas—**

1º Albacea = Yzcatqui in niquilnamiqui ma tlaco Xicmo¹⁰[38v]çelili Auh in oc tlaco nicCui ma ytlatzin ie ticonixtlapanacan¹¹ ma çatepan ic palehuilozque in animas, Cuix oc quihualmati Ca ye omimicq,ᵉ—

2º Albaçea = Ynontzin, Çenca huel teyolquima ma yuhqui mochihua intla noço popolihuiz anquin¹² tlatoz Cuix aço çeme oncate yn imezçohuan intlapalohua in techtequipachozque, macamo Ximotequipachotzino notlacoteachcauhtzinen¹³ ma oc titoyolaliti. ma tihuian Ca ye onca in tohuaxca totlatqui yhuan yn iquac omicque Ca ayocac ixpan ca za tehuatzin yhuan in nehuatl—

1º Albaçea = Ca melahuac yn oticmotalhuitzino¹⁴ ma tihuian tipapaquilti notlaçoicniuhtzinē—

<u>v</u> **Yazque connamiquizque in Viuda quitlaliz luto quihualhuicazque demonios—**

Viuda = Yn amehuantzitzin yn antlaçopipiltin campa in ammohuica ma nicaqui in amotlaçotlatoltzin = = =

1.º Albacea = TlaçoÇihuapillen ca otimitztonamiquilico Canel Domingo in axCan tontahuiltitinemi Auh in tehuatzin campa timohuica ma timitztohuiquilican = =

Viuda = Ca ychantzinco in tonantzin S,ᵗᵃ Yglesia Missa niconcaquiz¹⁵—[39r]

7. In anticipation of the next page: *qui*.
8. cannoço: read *ca noço*.
9. Tlen: here and below, standard *tlein*.
10. In anticipation of the next page: *çe*.
11. ticonixtlapanacan: standard *toconixtlapanacan*; see Carochi 1645, 42v–43v (in Carochi 1983).
12. anquin: read *aquin*.
13. notlacoteachcauhtzinen: read *notlacoteachcauhtzinen*.
14. oticmotalhuitzino: elsewhere in this text standard *oticmitalhuitzino*.
15. niconcaquiz: standard *noconcaquiz*; see Carochi 1983, 42v–43v.

FIRST EXECUTOR: O my beloved younger brother, how can it be done as the dead left ordered, that their goods and property would enter into the church in order to help other souls? Here is the gold they went leaving behind. I will be very rich with it. How can it be done?

SECOND EXECUTOR: Do not let it bother you. I know how it can be done. It is very necessary [38r] that now I compose a document [concerning] all that the dead left ordered. I will move all that is to be spent from one place to another. Thus will be taken that with which we will console ourselves.

(They exit. The demons and Lucifer enter.)

LUCIFER: What is wrong with you,[3] you who do not take care of the people of the earth? It has just been a few days! Do not uselessly lose it through neglect; really go after those in whose hands the dead left themselves.[4] Go, induce them to dissipate absolutely all the property of the dead so that the souls they are to take from us will not escape from our hands. Let my command be realized and done.

SECOND DEMON: Do not be anxious for we are going right now in order to confuse them.

THIRD DEMON: Let us go right away to see our subjects and friends. Let us go.

(They go and sit down at the foot of the table. The demons write. The executors enter.)

FIRST EXECUTOR: Here is what I am thinking. You take half [38v] and I will take the other half. Let us lend some out at interest and afterwards the souls will be helped with it. Do they still frequent [the earth]? They are already dead.

SECOND EXECUTOR: That is very greatly pleasing. Let it be so done. If perhaps it comes to ruin: who will speak up? Will one of their offspring bother us? O my beloved older brother, do not be distressed. Let us go console ourselves. Let us go, for it is already our goods and property, and when they died it was before no one but you and me.

FIRST EXECUTOR: What you have said is the truth. O my dear friend, let us go enjoy ourselves.

(They go meet Widow. She puts on mourning clothes. The demons enter.)

WIDOW: You dear nobles, where are you going? Let me hear your precious words.

FIRST EXECUTOR: O dear lady, since it is Sunday we came to meet you. Now we are going about enjoying ourselves. As for you: Where are you going? Let us accompany you.

WIDOW: I am on my way to hear mass in the home of our mother holy church. [39r]

---

3. *Tlen amay tlein anquichihua* / What is wrong with you (literally, What oh what are you doing): here and below this doublet, and perhaps either half of it, can mean "What is the matter with you?" See Carochi 1983, 116v, "*Tle ōtimāilī? mach huel ōchīchīliuh in mīxtelolo?* que tienes? parece, que tienes los ojos muy colorados" (What is the matter with you? Your eyes seem very reddened) and 124v, "*tle ōtax? aoc ticmati?* ... que tienes, as perdido el juyzio?" (What is the matter with you? Have you lost your mind?)

4. That is, the executors. Tentative translation.

Dem.º 1.º = Xicahua tlein tiquitohua MiSsa xiccahua xiauh xipapaqui yn intla[16] momecahuan—

2º Albacea = Tla xihualmohuica tla nican totlan ximohuetziti tla nican tonpapaquican =—

v conanaz ymatitech inic ome albaçea motlalizque⎯⎯⎯⎯⎯⎯

Viuda = Notlaçotelpotzitzinhuan Ca çenca huel ye nicnoyohuatiuh inic niuah in teopa[17] yehica in axcan Yohualtica oniquittac, yn ipan notemic çenca tlayohuia[18] in nonamic in onpa purgatorio auh nicnequi nicchihuaz Missa yn ipanpa Oc çecppa niquitohua ca tel ayanmo huecauh innomomiquili[19] ma oc motelChihua—

1º Albaçea = Xicmocahuili on, Çihuapillen ca quitohua in tlamatinime = in aquin quinequi yaz teopā ma yauh = auh in aquin quinequi papaquiz tlalticpac ma papaqui ma moyollali yehica Ca moztla huiptla momi=quiliz tla xicmottili Cuix amo ye neltiliztli melahuac auh inin ma oc tonpapaquican—

Viuda = = Ca melahuac in ticmitalhuitzinohua oquichpilli ma tipapaquican—

v tlatzotzonazque auh in teopan[20] **[39v] tziliniz miccatepoztli, cuicoz mehuaz Responso—**

2º Albaçea = Aquique in oconchiuhque MiSsa ca ontzilin in miccatepoztli auh in tehuatin tlein tay tlein ticchihua—

Viuda = Ca yehuatin inniz[21] tocalepohuan tla oc yehuan quimati ma quipopolocan in intomin ca ymixco=yan ic mochamahua = Auh in tehuantin ma ye ic ōçehui in tix in toyollo—

1,º Albacea = Ca melahuac in ticmitalhuitzinohua camo[22] totequiuh in MiSsa moztla huiptla intla titomiquilizque Cuix ocecppa tihualazque ma oc titoyolalican—

2,º Dem,º = Ye qualli in anquilnamiqui xiquincahuacan in animas, ma ye Xatlican Xitlaquacan Xitecohuanotzacan ma ximoteicniuhtican ma vinotica Ximoçentlalican macamo ximamanacan—

Viuda = Auh in axcan notelpotzitzinhuan ma oc niccui in nechcahuilitihui in miccatomin ma ic titoçepanyollalican—

1.º Albaçea = Ca ye Cualitzin ma oc ticalaquican ma tihuian = = =

v Quihuicazque in Demonios hual[23]**[40r]quiçazque D,ⁿ Pedro yhuan, y=namic—**
⎯⎯⎯⎯⎯

---

16. intla: read *intlan*.
17. niuah in teopa: read *niyauh in teopan*.
18. tlayohuia: here and below, read *tlaihiyohuia*.
19. innomomiquili: read *in omomiquili*.
20. In anticipation of the next page: *tzi*.
21. inniz: read *in iz*.
22. camo: here and below, read *ca amo*.
23. In anticipation of the next page: *qui*.

FIRST DEMON: Leave it. What are you saying? Leave mass. Go, enjoy yourself among your consorts.
SECOND EXECUTOR: Please come and sit down here with us. Let us go on enjoying ourselves here.
(Second Executor takes her by the hand. They sit down.)
WIDOW: O my dear young men, I am going to church in an extremely compassionate mood for last night I saw my spouse in my dreams greatly suffering over there in purgatory. I want to make a mass on his account. Again I say that he only died recently. Let [your invitation] be disregarded.
FIRST EXECUTOR: O lady, leave that, for the wise men say: "He who wants to go to church, let him go, and he who wants to enjoy himself on earth, let him enjoy himself and be consoled, for tomorrow or the next day he will die." Please consider. Is it not a veritable truth? And now, let us go on enjoying ourselves.
WIDOW: You speak the truth, O manly noble.[5] Let us enjoy ourselves.
(They beat drums. [39v] Bells are rung in church. A prayer for the dead is raised in song.)

SECOND EXECUTOR: Who put on a mass? The bells have rung. As for us, what oh what are we doing?
WIDOW: As for our neighbors here, let it be their responsibility, let them spend their money for it is their very own. They brag about it. And as for us, let our spirits be appeased with it.
FIRST EXECUTOR: You speak the truth. Mass is not our business. If tomorrow or the next day we die, will we come back again? Let us still console ourselves.
SECOND DEMON: What you are thinking is good. Abandon the souls. Eat, drink, invite people to feasts, make friends, gather together with wine. Do not get worked up.
WIDOW: And now, O my young men, let me take the dead people's money they left to me. Let us console one another with it.
FIRST EXECUTOR: Good. Let us enter. Let us go.
(The demons accompany them. [40r] Don Pedro and his spouse enter.)

---

5. oquichpilli: this compound is composed of *oquich(tli)* "man" here serving as the adjective "manly" modifying *pilli* "noble." If the reverential suffix *–tzin(tli)* were added it would mean "male child" (see Carochi 1983, 9r).

D.ⁿ Pedro = Notlaçonamictzinen, Çenca otictotlamachtique inic ypan otaçique in inMissatzin animas auh, in axcan çenca nimitznotlatlauhtilia macaic tiquinmolcahuiliz in motoliniticate, Purgatorio, in ahuel monomapalehuia momaquixtia ca yuh ca, in itlatoltzin in totecuiyo Dios, ca in Christiano, yn oc tp̄c. monemitia teoyotica mopalehuia tlamaçehualiztica yhuan tlahuenchihualiztica inic huel momaquixtiz yn itech[24] in tlayohuiliztli Auh Cuix oc çecppa hualmohuicazque tlamaçehuaquihue in nican tp̄c. ca niman amo ca ic çenmayan oquinmocaltzacuilitzino in totecuiyo Dios, auh in tehuantin in oc tp̄c. inpampa tihuenmanazque aço quinmocneliliz, anoço amo Ca yehuatzin quimomaChiltia in totecuioyo[25] Dios, auh yn axcan ma oc ninoçehui Ca çenca, Yetiye in tlalli Çoquitl—

Çihuatl = Otlacauhqui in motlaçoyollotzin notlaçonamictzin yehica Ca tehuatzin motechtzinco nicanaz in qualtlachihualliztli[26] inic tinechmozcaltiliz Ca niuhqui, nimopiltzin yn ipan tinechmomachiltia Ca mochi nicneltiliz in ixquich tinechmonahuatilia ma ximochi[27][40v]cauhtzino ma ixquich motlapaltzin Xicmochihuilitzino ma ticalaquican—

v Calaquizque hualquiçazque albaceas, Yhuan, Viuda, ihuan tercero Demonio—

Viuda = Yn axcan notlaçotelpotzitzinhuan Ca çenca nipapaqui ninoyollalia ca nican Catqui in onechcahuilitiaque in mimicque ma ic ximoyolalitzinocan tle yez Cuix totonalÇiahuiliz ca niman amo—

1.º Albacea = Ma oncan on, Xicmotlalili auh ma mocui in totech monequiz ynic titotlamachtizque—

2.º Albaçea = Ma oc motelchihua noteachcauhtzinen ma oc ticaquiti in temachtilli ca ye inman in pehuaz notlaçoicnihuanen ma tihuian—

3.º Dem.º = Ximocahua tlen tiquitohua aocmo oncan molnamiqui Ximotentzaqua—

1.º Albaçea[28] = Xitechcahua amo Xitechmoçihui Ca tipacticate oc oncan titoyolalia Cuix amotequiuh, in Sermon noço Xiauh xitechtlalcahui ma xiauh amo motequiuh in = tlein ticChihuazque—

v tlatzotzonaloz hualquizaz D.ⁿ Pe.º ihuan ynamic— [29] [41r]

24. itech: probably a scribal error because *itechpa* seems more appropriate here.
25. totecuioyo: standard *totecuiyo*. The same item can be found below on 50r.
26. qualtlachihualliztli: because of assimilation and loss (abundantly illustrated in this and other texts) read as standard *quallachihualiztli*.
27. In anticipation of the next page: *cauh*.
28. Here and in one other instance below there is no underlining.
29. In anticipation of the next page: *D.ⁿ Pedro*.

DON PEDRO: O my beloved spouse, we have been so fortunate that we have arrived during the souls' mass. Now I greatly implore you to never forget those who are suffering in purgatory, who cannot help save themselves. For such is the word of our lord God: the Christian who still lives on earth spiritually helps himself through penance and offerings to save himself from suffering. Will they come here again to earth to do penance? Absolutely not! Our lord God has imprisoned them once and for all. As for those of us still on earth, we are to make offerings on their behalf. [Only] our lord God knows whether he will favor them or not. Now let me rest for the earth and clay [that is, my mortal body] is very heavy [with illness].

WOMAN: Thank you, O my beloved spouse, because I take from you the good works with which you raise me, me whom you regard as your child. I will carry out all you order me [to do]. Be strong, [40v] exert all your effort. Let us enter.

(They exit. The executors and Widow and Third Demon enter.)

WIDOW: Now, O my dear young men, I am very happy and content. Here is what the dead went leaving me. May you be content with it. What is it to be? Is it our blood and sweat? Absolutely not!
FIRST EXECUTOR: Set it down over there. Let what we will need be taken so that we will be happily rich.
SECOND EXECUTOR: O my older brother, let it be scorned! Let us go hear the sermon for it is high time for it to begin. O my dear friends, let us go.
THIRD DEMON: Shut up. What are you saying? It is forgotten. Be silent.
FIRST EXECUTOR: Leave us alone. Do not upset us for we are still happy and content there. Is the sermon perhaps your business? Go, leave us. Go, what we do is none of your business.
(Drums are beaten. Don Pedro enters along with his spouse.) [41r]

D.ⁿ Pedro = Notlaçonamictzinen ma yhuiantzin tiatihuian³⁰ in teopā ynic nicnoçeliliz in itlaçomahuiznacayotzin in totecuiyo Jesu christo Ynyoyahuen canin ye niaznequi canin ye ninotlaça Cuix ahuilpa camanalpa notecuiyoen notlatocatzinen ma xinechmocnoittilitzino ma xinechmopalehuilitzino macamo xinechmolcahuilitzino in nitlacatl in çenca nihuey tlatlacohuani ma xinechmotlaocolili in ica in mohueytetlaocolilitzin in mohueyteicnoittalitzin ma xinechmoyolchipahuili Xinechmopapaquili miecpa Xinechmaltili in itechpa in aqualli ayectli in tliltic Catzahuac in notech ca in notlahuelilocayo in çenca tecatzauh teyçolo in notlatlacol yuhquima Çe huey tlamamalli nechyetiçihuiltia in maca çan huey cacaxtli inic tlalla nechaquiaya ma xinechmocnoytilitzino in nitlatlacohuani totecuiyoyen Diosē = =

Chocaz =—

Cihuatl = Notlaçonamictzin ma ximochiuhcauhtzino ma yçenmactzinco Ximocauhtzino in toteyocoxcatzin in Dios, ma tihuian in teopan

v Calaquizque hualquiçaz animas hualp[oç?]auhtiaz tlecuecalli³¹ inic micuiloz mehuaz Peccata tlananquiliz anima nu³² [41v] nula es. Responsion =—

3.º Anima = Ay inyoyahuen totecuiyoen Diosē. moteicnoytiliniyen motetlaocolilianien ma xinechmotlaocolilitzino yn ica in motetlaocolilitzin moteopohua in nix = in noyollo, yn ipampa in izquitlamantli onicChiuh in moyolitlacolocatzin, Ca ypampa nichoca, ca onimitznoyolytlacalhuitzino in tinoteotzin tinotlatocatzin ca huel tlapanahuia inic titlaçotlaloni ma xinechmotlaocolilitzino in ayac nechtlaocoliani in nican tp̄c. auh Ca tehuatzin in tinotlaçotatzin in otinechmochihuili innotinechmoyocolili³³ Ca tinotepalehuicatzin tinotemanahuicatzin in tlalticpac ca oniccauh in maxcatzin in motlatquitzin inic nipalehuilozquia atle nomaçehual in nitlatlacohuani amo nechilnamiqui in nohualyoque³⁴ in oc nemi tlalticpac, ca tehuatzin ticmomachiltitzinohua—

v calaquiz mehuaz Responso hualquizaz Cihuatl quitlaliz Luto, quihualhuicaz Candela xochiqualli = inic quichihuatiuh Missa quihualhuicaz Angel—

Cihuatl = Noteotzin notlatocatzin omochiuh onotlahueli³⁵[42r]tic³⁶ inic ça nocel otinechmocahuili inic omomiquili nonamictzin auh macamo nican nihuecahuaz in motlalticpactzinco in axcan ma niauh in teopan ynic nicChihuaz Missa inic mopalehuizq.ᵉ animas—

1.º Angel = Ma ximochicauhtzino ma ixquich motlapaltzin Xicchihua macamo ximocahua ma xiauh Xicneltili in motlahuenmanaliz yn inpalehuiloca, in Purgatorio, Cate macamo Xiquincahua—

v connamiquiz, Demonio Segundo

---

30. ma yhuiantzin tiatihuian: perhaps to be read as *ma yhuiantzinco tiatihuian*.
31. **tlecuecalli**: read *tlecueçalli*.
32. **nu**: apparently anticipates the first syllable of "**nula**," which immediately follows on the next page.
33. innotinechmoyocolili: read *in otinechmoyocolili*.
34. nohualyoque: read *nohuanyolque*.
35. In anticipation of the next page: *tic*.
36. onotlahuelitic: read *onotlahueliltic*.

DON PEDRO: O my beloved spouse, let us go calmly and peacefully to church so that I will receive the precious honored body of our lord Jesus Christ. Alas! Where am I about to go now? Where will I cast myself now? Will it be in frivolities and jokes? O my lord, O my ruler, have pity on me, help me, do not forget me, very great sinner that I am. Be merciful with me through your great mercy and your great compassion. Purify my heart, scour me, cleanse me many times of the bad and evil things, my black and dirty iniquities, my befouling and besmirching sins,[6] that are in me. It is as though a great burden weighs me down, as though a great packframe plants me in the earth. O our lord, O God, have pity on me, a sinner!

(He cries.)

WOMAN: O my beloved spouse, be strong. Leave yourself entirely in the hands of God our Creator. Let us go to church.

(They exit. A soul enters, coming smoking, painted with tongues of fire. The Peccata[7] is sung. The soul answers. [41v] Nula est responsio.)[8]

THIRD SOUL: Oh, alas! O our lord, O God, O compassionate one, O merciful one! Have mercy on me with your mercy. My spirit is tormented because of all the things I did in offense to you. Wherefore I cry, for I have offended you, my deity and ruler, surpassingly worthy of being loved. Have mercy on me, whom no one else on earth would have mercy on. You my beloved Father, who made and created me, are my aid and defense on earth. I relinquished your goods and property with which I would have been helped. I am an undeserving sinner. You know that my relatives who still live on earth do not remember me.

(He exits. A prayer for the dead is raised [in song]. Woman enters, wearing mourning clothes. She comes bringing candles and fruit with which she will make a mass. An angel accompanies her.)

WOMAN: O my God and ruler, woe is me, [42r] that you left me alone when my spouse died! May I not tarry long here on your earth. Let me go now to church in order to perform a mass with which the souls [in purgatory] will be helped.

FIRST ANGEL: Be strong, exert all your effort. Do not stay, go, make your offerings, which will help those who are in purgatory. Do not abandon them.

(Second Demon meets her.)

---

6. in çenca tecatzauh teyçolo in notlatlacol: although *tecatzauh teyçolo* might be considered transparent metaphors for sin, they are not so treated here or in other texts that I have seen. First, the seemingly redundant *in notlatlacol*, "my sins," is added as if in necessary explanation. Second, in Carochi's treatment of similar items, he explicitly states that "*nopotōnca*, mi hedor" means "por metaphora mis pecados" but not the closely related forms of *tecatzauh* (1983, f49).

7. This is apparently from the Office for the Dead, Psalm 24, the verse that begins with Peccata—"Peccáta iuventútis meæ et delíxcta mea ne memíneris; secúndum misericórdiam tuam meménto mei tu, propter bonitátem tuam, Dómine" (*Breviarum romanum* 1961, 1:242). This is Psalm 25, verse 7, in the King James Bible: "Remember not the sins of my youth, nor my transgressions—according to thy mercy remember thou me for thy goodness sake, O Lord."

8. *Nula est responsio*: There is no response.

2.⁰ Dem,⁰ = Çihuatzintlen campa tiaznequi tlein taiz: in teopan tlein ticchihuaz Cuix onpa neçiz in motech monequiz ca amo Cuix noço ompa timo:tlayecoltiz intla teopan tiaznequi ompa tapizmiquiz macamo ompa Xiauh—

Çihuatl = Ca niman amo nihueliti notlaçotelpotzin Ca niaz ma xinechmocahuili ca ytencopatzinco in Dios, inic niquitlaniz MiSsa—

2⁰ Dem,⁰ = Cuix amo titlacaqui, Çihuatzintlen Ca melahuac atle onca MiSsa = Yhuan ayaque, in teopixque quen huel axcan ompa onihualla ma ximocuepa ca nimitznotza tle ipā tinechmati Xiauh in mochan amo miec ic Xiquintla³⁷[42v]pololti in mohuanpohuan xiauh xiquiça—

1,⁰ Angel = Xiccahua tlacatecolotlen ma^(ca)mo xicnotza in D.ˢ ytetlayecolticatzin Xiauh camo monemac in ichuic tihualmiquaniz Ca nican nica in nitepixcauh inic mochipa nicnocuitlahuitinemi ma xictlalcahui yn itlachihualtzin Dios,—

v Quitocaz hualtzatziz mictlā,caltenco

2.⁰ Dem,⁰ = Cuix amo nimitznotza Çihuatlen, Xihualmocuepa Ca intla tihualmocuepaz mochi ni=macaz³⁸ Yn ixquich axcaytl tlatquitl inic timoyollaliz tipapaquiz—

1⁰ Angel = Xicahua in Dios, Ytlachihualtzin—

Calaquizque mitoz ReSponso intla omito hualquiçaz teopixqui yhuan Çihuatl—

teopixqui = Notlaçopiltzinen ma çan ypaltzinco in Dios, ma moChipa, Çemicac XiquilnamiquiCa in oamechyaCanque = miquiztica ma amechtlaocoltican in achtopa omomiquilique, ma xiquintlaocolican in ixpantzīco in Dios, Ca çenca tlayohua in ompa nechipahualo³⁹[43r]yan = in Purgatorio ca quihualtemachitoque yn amohuen in ican inMiSsa⁴⁰ = anoco⁴¹ tlatlatlauhtiliztica anoço tlahuenchihualiztica in ye oncan Ca oc tleyin inhueli inic mopalehuizque Ca quichixticate, quitemachiticate in tepalehuiliztli inic huel momaquixtizque auh yn iquac tlaocolilo Ca çenca ic mocnelilmati Çenca quitlaçocamati in imicneliloca, Auh ynintzin yn iuh otinechmolhuili in amo huel neçi in mocochca in moneuhca auh macamo ximotequipacho notlaçopiltzinen macamo ic tiquinxicahuaz in ixquichtin Animas ma motlatlauhtiliztica mochoquiztica ixpantzinco in Dios, xicmotlatlauhtili inic quinmotlapopolhuiliz inic quinmocaxahuililiz in intlayohuiliz yhuan inic amo huecahuazque in Purgatorio Auh yn iquac tlamiz in tp̄c. monemiliz ca no mopan motlatoltizque ynic mitzmocneliliz in Dios, ynic ticmaçehuaz Yn ilhuicac papaquiliztli Gloria—

Çihuatl = Notlaçomahuizteopixcatzin otlacauhqui in moyollotzin otinechmocnelili ma oc nimitznotlalcahuilitzino ca tel oc cecppa nihualaz ma oc ytlatzin nicontemo⁴² inic tiquinmopalehuiliz = in Animas ma oc nimitznotlalCahuilitzino—

---

37. In anticipation of the next page: *po*.
38. nimacaz: read *nimitzmacaz*.
39. In anticipation of the next page: *yan*.
40. ican inMissa: read *ica in inMissa* (as below).
41. anoco: read *anoço*.
42. nicontemo: standard *nocontemo*; see Carochi 1983, 42v–43v.

SECOND DEMON: O woman, where are you about to go? What oh what will you do in church? Will you find what you need there? No! Or will you make a living there? If you want to go to church you will suffer from hunger there. Do not go there.

WOMAN: O my dear young man, I absolutely cannot refrain from going. Leave me, for it is by order of God that I ask for a mass.

SECOND DEMON: O woman, don't you understand? Truly there is no mass and there are no priests.[9] I just came from there. Turn back for I summon you. What do you take me for? Go to your home. Do not confuse [42v] your neighbors with [so] many things. Go, leave.

FIRST ANGEL: Leave her alone, O demon, do not summon God's servant. Go, for you do not deserve[10] to move over here to her for I am here, I her guardian [angel] who always goes about taking care of her. Relinquish God's creature.

(*He pursues her, crying out from outside the house of hell.*)

SECOND DEMON: Oh woman, am I not summoning you? Turn back, for if you turn back in this direction I will give you everything, all the goods and property with which you will be content and enjoy yourself.

FIRST ANGEL: Relinquish God's creature!

(*They exit. A prayer for the dead is said. When it is over Priest enters along with Woman.*)

PRIEST: O my beloved child, let it just be through the grace of God that you always and forever remember those who preceded you in death. May those who have died first have mercy on you, and may you have mercy on them before God for they suffer greatly over there in the place of self-purification, [43r] purgatory. They rely on your offerings, through the masses performed for them, or prayers, or the making of offerings. What else is there with which they can help themselves? They are waiting and relying on help so that they can be saved. When mercy is shown they are very grateful for the favors done them, they are very thankful for the benefits shown them. And as for this matter, as you have said to me, that you cannot find enough to eat, O my beloved child, do not be distressed. Do not therefore abandon all the souls [in purgatory]. Before God with your prayers and weeping, implore him to pardon them so that he will relieve them of their burden of suffering and so that they do not tarry long in purgatory. When your earthly life comes to an end they will speak on your behalf so that God will favor you, so that you will enjoy heavenly bliss, glory.

WOMAN: O my beloved honored priest, I give you many thanks for the favor you have shown me.[11] Let me take leave of you for now. I will come again. Let me first go seek a little something with which you will help the souls. Let me take leave of you for now.

---

9. Here used in the plural, the singular *teopixqui* is defined in Carochi 1983 [1645], 52r, as "el sacerdote, o religioso, que guarda lo que toca à Dios." This parellels the abstract collective noun *teoyotl* covered in a footnote below.

10. camo monemac: "*ahmo monemac*—no mereces" (Arenas 1982, 106); "Nonemac. la merced, o don que se me hizo o dio" (Molina 1977, 73r).

11. otlacauhqui in moyollotzin otinechmocnelili: below appear two other variants of this typical doublet of thanks. My phrasing in all three cases is based on Molina 1984 [1569], 118v, "¶ Notecuiyoe tlatohuanie, otlacauhquin moyollotzin otinechmocnelili" / "¶ Señor mio, hagoos muchas gracias, por los beneficios q̃ me aueys hecho." See also the dictionary, Molina 1977, 115v, "Tlacaua noyollo. otorgar a conceder algo." as well as 78r, "Otinechmocnelili. doyte gracias por la merced que me heziste."

teopixqui = Ma mitzmoyacanilitzino in totecuiyo Dios ca tel[43] [43v] nimitznoChieliz notlaçopiltzinen—

v calaquizque hualquiçazque albaçeas yhuan, Viuda————

1,⁰ Albaçea = Yn axcan huel monequi ynic çenca huel tipapaquizque inic amo tlein techtequipachoz auh in tehuatzin ma oc Ximoyollali in tinotlaçoicniuhtzin Auh in nehuatl ma oc niccui in totech monequiz inic tipapaquizque titoyollalizque =—

2.⁰ Albaçea = Ca ye qualli ma tihualmoçihuitiz auh in nehuatl Ca nican catqui in teocuitlatl ynic titoyalalizque[44] Cuix mochipa in t͞p͞c. ma tihualmoçihuitiz nocniuhtzinen———

Viuda = Auh in nehuatl, notlaçotelpotzin ca no nican calqui[45] in tomin, çan ixquich = Caxtolli pesos = Auh in oc çequi ca notzotzomatzin yc onicouh, Cuix yuhqui teixpan ninemiz—

2⁰ Dem,⁰ = Ca ye qualli ye mahuiztic ca mochi yehuatl om, monequi Cuix mohuaxca motlatqui ma xicpopolocan Xahuiecan xipapaquican—

1,⁰ Albaçea = Ca ye onihualla ca nican catqui, ynic onçehuiz in totlaçoyeliz ma tlatzonalo ma cuico tlen anmaylia tocniuhtzitzihuanen—[44r]

v tlatzotzonazque auh in Viuda coniz = vino yc onmotenpopohuaz in luto çatepan quiquixtiz contlaçaz mesapan onca yez Xochiqualli cui=cazque papaquizq.ᵉ oncan tzili=niz animas = auh çan içel in anima quiçaz—

1,⁰ Anima = Ay ma xitechmolnamiquilican yn antocnihuan in oc annemi t͞p͞c. macamo xitechmolcahuilican in ixpantzinco in totecuiyo Dios, yn antohuayolque in oc annemi t͞p͞c, ma çan ypampatzinco in Dios, ma çe Pater noSter, çe Ave maria Xiquitocan topampa = = = =

Viuda = Jesus tlen moChihua ma oc ticalaquican ma oc titoçehuiti Ca ye teotlac—

2⁰ Dem,⁰ = Amo Ximotequipachocan ca ytzatziliz in cahuitl inic yauh Yohualli auh camo cocoliztli ma ximoyollalican—

2,⁰ Albacea = Xicmocahuili matzatzin Cuix motequiuh ca tipacticate—

v tlatzotzonazque oc çepa tzatziz anima çan ye yehuatl quitoz ocpa[46] [44v] cruz + auh motlapoz Yn ilhuica[47] auh in oc çequintin ᵃⁿⁱᵐᵃˢ motlancuaquetzazque ixpantzinco D,ˢ

2,⁰ Anima = Ay yoyahuen totecuiyoen Diosē, ma xitechmocno=ittilitzino in titoteyocoxcatzin in mochipa çemicac timohuetznoticatqui yn imayeccanpatzinco in motlaçomahuiztatzin Dios, Ca mohuicopatzinco tontzatziticate, in inpanpa in t͞p͞c. motlachihualtzitzinhuan in oc nemi in aic techilahua in motlacoixpantzinco[48] in momoztlae, inpampa tlahuenchihua yn ica in intlatlatlauhtiliz inic techilnamiqui macayāmo in ma inic ontlamiz tzomquizaz in tlalticpac in innemiliz ma oc Xiquinmocnoyttilitzino xiquinmotlaocolilitzino = =

= = **v**= tziliniz animas———

---

43. In anticipation of the next page: *ni*.
44. titoyalalizque: read *titoyollalizque*.
45. calqui: read *catqui*.
46. In anticipation of the next page: *cruz*. It is unclear whether *ocpa* should be read as *oc ceppa* or *oppa*.
47. ilhuica: read *ilhuicatl*.
48. motlacoixpantzinco: read either as *motlaçoixpantzinco* or (as several times below) *motlatocaixpantzinco*.

PRIEST: May our lord God guide you. [43v] O my beloved child, I will await you.

(They exit. The executors and Widow enter.)
FIRST EXECUTOR: Now it is very necessary that we will be extremely happy so that nothing will bother us. You, my dear friend, be content. And as for me, let me take what we will need to enjoy ourselves and be happy.
SECOND EXECUTOR: Very well, hurry. As for me, the gold with which we will be happy is here. [Will we live] forever on earth? O my friend, hurry.

WIDOW: And as for me, O my dear young man, there is also money here. It is only fifteen pesos. And as for the rest, I bought my rags with it. Am I to go around in public [dressed] like that?
SECOND DEMON: That is good and estimable, for that is all that is necessary. Is it your goods and property? Squander it, pleasure yourselves, enjoy yourselves!
FIRST EXECUTOR: I have come now. Here is what our precious being will be calm with. Let drums be beaten, songs be sung. O my friends, what is wrong with you? [44r]
(They beat drums. Widow drinks wine, cleaning her lips with the mourning clothes. Afterwards she casts them off, flinging them on the table where there is fruit. They sing and enjoy themselves. Bells ring there for the souls [in purgatory]. A lone soul enters.)
FIRST SOUL: Oh! You our friends who still live on earth, remember us. Do not forget us before our lord God. You our relatives who still live on earth, for God's sake say an Our Father or Hail Mary on our behalf.

WIDOW: Jesus, what is happening? Let us enter, let us go rest for it is already afternoon.
SECOND DEMON: Do not grieve, for it is the cry of time as the night goes. It is not sickness. Be content.
SECOND EXECUTOR: Leave your rags.[12] Is it your business? We are happy.
(They beat drums. The soul cries out a second time, that very one speaking twice [in prayer?] [44v] to the cross. Heaven opens. The other souls kneel down before God.)

SECOND SOUL: Oh, alas! O our lord, O God, have pity on me! You our Creator always and forever sit on the righthand side of your beloved honored Father, God. We are crying out to you on behalf of your earthly creatures. Those who are still alive who never forget us in your royal presence make offerings every day on their behalf, remembering us with their prayers. Let it not be that their earthly lives should come to an end and conclusion yet. Have pity on them! Show them mercy!

(Bells ring for the souls [in purgatory].)

---

12. Tentative translation.

3.º Anima = Ay in tiçenquizcahuecapanoloni in titotemaquixticatzin in tiJesu x̄p̄o = Ca titocnoitohua in motlatocaixpantzinco = ma xitechmotlahuel,caquitilitzino ma çan ypanpatzinco in moMiSericordiatzin xiquinmotlaocolili in ixquichtin tlalticpac techmolnamiquilia in techquixtilia in Santa Bula, yhuan in yca in inMiSsa = yhuan ReSponso inic mixpantzinco tlahuēmana auh intla moztla huiptla Xiquinmotlatzom⁴⁹[45r]tequilili totecuiyoen Diosē, aquiq.ᵉ techpalehuiz aquiq.ᵉ in oc techicnoittazque Ca niman ayac Xpiano in tp̄c. inic topan tlahuenchihuazq.ᵉ in mixpantzinco ma oc : xiquinmocahuilitzino in ixquichtin tp̄c. tlaca

y = = tziliniz animas = = = v

4.º Anima = Ay in timºçenquizcateicnoittilitzinohuani in timotetlaocoliliani ma çan ipanpatzinco in motlaçomahuiznantzin Santa Maria, inic omitzmotlacatililitzino yhuan in ica yn imemeyalotzin inic omitzmohuapahuilitzino ma xiquinmocnoyttilitzino in tlalticpac oniquīhualcauhtehuac inic nopan tlatohua in ica in neçahualiztlaquemitl ynic qualyotica quichihua in tohuanyolque yhuan inic ÇeÇenmetztica tlaçelia ma çan, no yuhqui Xiquinmotlaococolilitzino⁵⁰ = = = = = = = =

y = tziliniz, animas = = =

5º Anima = Ay MiSericordia ynYoyahuen totecuiyo Diosē, quenin Çenca nitetlaocolti nitechocti in yca in ayac nechilnamiqui onoçentzomtlahueliltic inic ayac nechiximati in tlalticpac, aço notatzin nonantzin, aço noteachcauh, aço noteicauh, aco⁵¹ nohueltihuatzin aço huecapan nohualqui⁵² inyoyahuen noteyocox⁵³[45v]catzinen ma çan ipanpatzinco in moMiSericordiatzin xitechmocnoittilitzino in tiçenquizcatlateochihualYchpochtzintli ma xitechmolnamiquilitzino in timotlachihualtzitzinhuan yn ayac techylnamiqui ma çan ipampatzinco in motlaçoRoSariotzin in motlatlauhtilocatzin. Ca yn oc tp̄c. ninemia aic onimitznolcahuili ma ye Xinechmopalehuilitzino in ninotolinia tlalticpac oniqualcauhtehuac in no=namic acmo nechilnamiqui, amo nictlaocoltia aoctle onca nopalehuiloca in mixpantzinco ma çan huel çe MiSsa, anoço tlatlauhtiliztica ye nechilnamiqui auh in oniqualcahuilitehuac in nopalehuiloca mochihuaz axcan mochi, cahuilquixtia auh in neçahualiztlaquemitl in luto çan ipan xocomictinemi momecatitinemi Cahuilquixtitinenemi ma ixquich ma tlami ma tzomquiza in tp̄c ynemiliz Ca çenca ye miec inic mixtzinco mopactzinco⁵⁴ nemi—

y — Motlapoz Ylhuicatl—

S,ta M,ª = Yn tinotlaçomahuizçenteconetzin in tiJesu x̄p̄o, ca mixpantzinco ninixtlapachtlaça yn inpanpa in motlachihualtzitzinhuan in tlayohuiticate in tetlechipahualoyan = Purgatorio = ma xiquin⁵⁵[46r]mocnoittilitzino Xiquinmotlaocolilitzino notlaçomahuizconetzin ma yehuatl xicmottilitzino = in nochoquitzin nixayotzin notlaocoltzin Ca in oc tlalticpac onenque notlaçomahuizconetzin aic omitzmolcahuilique Cm̄C omitzmotepotztoquilique Ca yn iquac quilnamiquia yn ipampa in motlayohuilitzin ynic otiquinmomaquixtilitzino—

---

49. In anticipation of the next page: *te*.
50. Xiquinmotlaococolilitzino: standard *xiquinmotlaocolilitzino* (as above and below in this text).
51. aco: read *aço*.
52. nohualqui: read *nohuanyolqui*.
53. In anticipation of the next page: *ca*.
54. mopactzinco: here and below can be found this variant and others of standard *mocpactzinco*.
55. In anticipation of the next page: *moc*.

THIRD SOUL: Oh, you our savior Jesus Christ, perfectly exalted, we humbly speak in your royal presence! Listen with approval and grant us that just because of your compassion you have mercy on all those on earth who remember us, who get holy bulls for us, and with their masses and prayers for the dead make offerings before you. O our lord, O God, if it be tomorrow or the next day, judge them. [45r] Who will help us, who will still have pity on us? For there are no Christians at all on earth who will make offerings on our behalf before you. Abandon all the people of the earth!

(Bells ring for the souls [in purgatory].)

FOURTH SOUL: Oh, you the perfectly compassionate one, you the merciful one! Let it just be on account of your beloved honored mother, Saint Mary, who gave birth to you and who nurtured you with her milk, that you have pity on those whom I left behind on earth so that they would speak on my behalf with fasting garments, so that our relatives would do things virtuously and take communion every month. May you likewise have mercy on them.

(Bells ring for the souls [in purgatory].)

FIFTH SOUL: Oh mercy! Alas! O God our lord! How very much I aroused grief and tears because no one remembers me. I am unfortunate four hundred[13] times over that no one knows me on earth, whether it be my father and mother, or my older brother or my younger brother, or my older sister or my more distant relatives. O alas! O my Creator! [45v] Have pity on me just because of your compassion. You the perfectly blessed maiden, remember us your creatures whom no one [else] remembers. Let it just be because of your precious rosary and prayers to you. While I still lived on earth I never forgot you. Help me. My spouse, whom I left on earth, no longer remembers me, I do not make her sad. There is no longer any help for me before you. Let [my spouse] just remember me [with] one complete mass or through prayers. All of what I left behind to [my spouse] to become a help for me [in purgatory] she now sells for cash, and the fasting garments, the mourning clothes—[my spouse] just goes about in them drunk and taking lovers, selling them to raise cash. Enough![14] Let [my spouse's] life on earth come to an end and conclusion for she offends you in many things.

(Heaven opens.)

SAINT MARY: You, Jesus Christ, my beloved honored only child, I cast myself down before you on account of your creatures who are suffering in the place where people are purified by fire, purgatory. [46r] O my beloved honored child, have pity on them, show them mercy. See my weeping and tears and sorrow, for while they still lived on earth, O my beloved honored child, they never forgot you, they always followed you for at the time they remembered it was on account of your suffering that you saved them.

---

13. The number *four hundred* is a common idiom in the vigesimally based traditional counting system for "countless, innumerable." When it occurs in the phrase "four hundred times," it could be construed as meaning "countless or many times over."

14. ma ixquich: "*no mas*—ma ixquich" (Arenas 1982, 88).

X͞p͞o = = Çemicac, ychpochtzintlen notlaçonantzinen macamo inpampa Ximochoquili in motetlayecolticatzitzinhuan yehica in oc tlalticpac nemiaya ca mochipa notech mo^{tla}canequia notech motemachiaya manahuilozque palehuilozque maquixtilozque notemanahuilitica yhuan oquiximachilique in notlaçotatzin Dios, auh in iquac nechmotzatzililizque ca niquinhualcaquiliz in intlatlatlauhtiliz yn iquac moyolteopohuazque in atlamatizque in imelel açiz auh in nehuatzin niquinyollaliz niquintēyotiz niquinmahuizyotiz niquinhuecapanoz Çemicac nemizq.^e yollalilozque niquinnextiliz in nopapaquilitzin Gloria = =

S,^{ta} M,^a = Ma xicmocnoytilitzino, notlaçoconetzin inic motlaçohuicopatzinco hualmotzatzititicate ma xiquinmo⁵⁶[46v]tlahuelcaquililitzino in motolinia in motlachihualtzitzinhuan—

v := tlatzotzonazque no tziliniz = animas =

3⁰ Anima = Ay omochiuuh⁵⁷ onotlahueliltic ma xitechilnamiquican yn oc tlalticpac annemi in antocnihuan macamo xitechcahuacan in ixpantzinco in totecuiyo = Dios, Ay Ay intla mochi tlacatl in quenin huel titotolinia ynic titlatlaticate titlayohuia Ca huel nelli ca techtlaocolizquia aquin amehuantin yn antohuayolque, Cuix monequi antechilcahuazque macamo itla ic Xitechilcahuacan aquin techtlaocoliz ma icnoyohua yn amoyollotzin ma xitechtlaocolican ca çenca titotolinia inyoyahuen totecuiyoyen Diosē, ma y=çiuhcan xiquinmotlatzomtequilili in tlalticpac, otiquinhualcauhque in totepantlatocahuan yezque in motlatocaixpantzinco, auh amo techilnamiqui ca tlaqualtica atica quinenquixtia in otiquinhualcahuilitehuaque ma xicmonequiltitzino inic içiuhca nican mixpantzinco neçizque totecuiyo Jesu x͞p͞oe =

x͞p͞o = Yn tehuatzin in tiSan Miguel archangel ma ximotlanahuatili inic hualyoltiazq.^e in t͞p͞c tlaca—[47r]

Sn Mig,^l = Ma mochihua in motlatocatlanahuatiltzin ma Xihualquiçacan in mictlan antlan antlatelchihualtin motlanahuatilitzinohua in melahuacamotetlatzomtequililiani = Jues = inic hualyoltiazque inic anquihualhuicazque yn ipanpa miccatlatquitl tlaixquetzaltin inic oquipopoloque in imaxca intlatqui in animas in motoliniticate in onpa = Purgatorio inic aocac quimilnamiqui = = = =

v hualquiçaz Luçifer ihuan in oc çequintin = Demonios =

Luçifer = Otlacauhqui in mo in moyolotzin⁵⁸ otechmocnelilitzino ma tihuian ma tontocacan tocnihuanen = = =

3,⁰ Dem,⁰ = Ma yçiuhca, tiquimanati in totetlayecolticahuan tocnihuanen, ca motlanahuatilia in totecuiyo Dios—

Calaquizque mochintin calitic quimanatihue nacateme in Viuda tliltic yez mochintin tzatzizque, = tlacueponiz in iquac hualquizazque albaçeasme = =—

= anima = [47v]

1,⁰ Albaçea = Ay omochiuh onotlahueliltic, Ay Ay Ay omochiuh ototlahueliltic in titlatlacohuanime—

---

56. In anticipation of the next page: *tla*.
57. omochiuuh: standard *omochiuh*.
58. in mo: repeats in the manuscript.

CHRIST: O maiden eternal, O my beloved mother, do not cry for your servants because while they still lived on earth they always trusted in me, relied on me. They will be defended, helped and saved with my protection, and they recognized my beloved Father, God. When they cry out to me I will hear what they say, their prayers when their hearts are anguished, when they are unwise and in great pain and affliction. As for me, I[15] will console them, make them famous, honor and exalt them. They will live forever, content, and I will reveal to them my bliss, [glory].

SAINT MARY: O my beloved child, show pity when they are crying out to your precious [personage], listen with approval to [46v] those of your creatures who suffer.

(They beat drums. Bells also ring for the souls [in purgatory].)
THIRD SOUL: Oh! Woe is me! You our friends who still live on earth, do not forget us, do not abandon us before our lord God. Oh! Oh! If everyone suffered as we are suffering, burning and languishing, they would certainly have mercy on us. [Where] are you our relatives? Is it necessary that you will forget us? Do not forget us for anything. Who [else] will have mercy on us? Let your hearts be compassionate, have mercy on us, for we are greatly afflicted. Alas, O our lord, O God, quickly judge those on earth. We left them to be our intercessors before your royal presence but they do not remember us. They waste with food and drink what we left them. O our lord Jesus Christ, let it be your will that they promptly appear here before you.

CHRIST: You, Saint Michael the Archangel, order that the earthly people come hither alive. [47r]

SAINT MICHAEL: Your royal command be done. Come out, you accursed ones of hell! The just sentencer, the judge, orders that they will come hither alive, that you will bring them hither because they—as the ones encharged with the property of the dead—used up the goods and property of the souls suffering over there in purgatory such that there is no longer anyone who remembers them [with offerings].
(Lucifer enters along with the other demons.)

LUCIFER: We give you many thanks for the favor you have shown us.[16] O my friends, let us go, let us be on our way.

THIRD DEMON: O our friends, let us quickly go seize our servants for [so] orders our lord God.
(They all enter the house. They go seize the [condemned?].[17] Widow is in black. All cry out. There are fireworks when the executors and a soul enter.) [47v]

FIRST EXECUTOR: Oh! Woe is me! Oh! Oh! Oh! Woe to us who are sinners!

---

15. I: the Nahuatl reads "nehuatzin" (46r), that is, *nehua(tl)+-tzin(tli)*, the intent being the first person singular reverential. This seems to violate traditional Nahua cultural norms. See Carochi 1983, f. 7, where he discusses the uses of *-tzin(tli)* and adds, concerning this very usage, that it cannot be employed "en la primera de reuerencia, y estimacion, porq̄ nadie deue mostrar estima de si mismo" (7v).

16. In the original Nahuatl "in mo" repeats; this may be no accident. See Sell essay in *Nahuatl Theater, Volume Three*.

17. nacateme: here very tentatively translated as "condemned," it also appears in "Final Judgment," tentatively translated there as "fully fleshed." As far as we know this item appears nowhere else.

2.º Albaçea = Ca tehuatl motlatlacol inic nican titla^(tza)cuiltilo in titlayohuiltilo ca onimitzilhui inic teopan calaquiz in imaxca in intlatqui in animasme inic opalehuilozquia yn iuhqui axcan yc topan mochihua—

1.º Albaçea = tlacatecoloÇihuatlen ca tehuatl motlatlacol inic oticahuilquixtique in teaxca tetlatqui ca mochi tehuatl ^(motlatlacol) in tiquiyohuia—

Viuda = Ay omochiuh onotlahueliltic macamo titlacatini ynic amo iuhqui topan omochihuazquia, in temamauhti teyzahui in axcan topan mochi=hua—

Luçifer = Xitotocacan Cuix quin oanquilnamique in amotlatlacol acmo onca ca ye antohuaxcahuan ye antotlatquihuan—

<u>v</u> **Yazque in ixpantzinco in x$\overline{po}$, = oncan quiçohuazque in imamauh, Lucifer yhuan mochintin in Dem,^(os) motlaquaquetzazque**

Luçifer = Yn tiçenquizcamelahua^(c)tl, Jues in timotetla^59[48r]tzoomtequililiani^60 Ca nican mixpantzinco otiquinhualhuicaque in çenca huey tetlayecoltique in amo omitzmotlacamachitique in amo oquichiuhque in motlanahuatiltzin maçonelihui motlaçoezçoticatzinco otiquinmomaquixtilitzino in tlahueliloque in yollopoliuhque in aic omitzmolnamiquilitzinoque ma xiquinmotlatzomtequililitzino ca totech pouhque yehica ca çemicac Otelchihualoque auh in teoyotl mochi oquitecococamatque atle ypan oquittaque in motlayecoltilocatzin izcatqui in intlatlacol ma xicmottili=tzino in intlachihual, Ma xicmopohuilitzino in tehuatzin tiAngel in intlatlacol—

S,^n Mig,^l = Yzcatqui in itenahuatiltzin yn içel teotl in Dios, in matlactetl, in etetl, in itechtzinco pohui in imahuiztililocatzin in yehuatzin Dios, auh in chicontetl itech pohui in intlaçotlaloca in tlalticpac tlaca—

S,^n Mig,^l = Ynic Çentetl, ticmotlaçotiliz in içel teotl D,^s ica mochi moyollo—

Luçifer = Ca niman aic Omitzmotlaçotilique in nican mani, aic omitzmoteotitzinoque—

S,^n Mig,^l = Ynic ontetl, amo tictlapictenehuaz in itocatzī in Dios,—[48v]

Lucifer = Mochipa Juramento quichiuhtinemia omitzmotlapictenehuilitinemia ypan in imahuil in intlaelpaquiliztlatlacolpa =—

S,^n Mig,^l = Ynic yetetl, in Domingo, yhuan Ylhuitl ipan atle taiz çan tiquixcahuiz in titlateomatiz—

Lucifer = Yn ixquich cahuitl, in oc tlalticpac nemia aic omitzmoteomachiltique aic omitzmolnamiquilique auh in ilhuitl ipā ye quintequipachohuaya^61 in innemecatiliztlatlacol oquichihuaya—

S,^n Mig,^l = Ynic nauhtetl, ticmahuiztiliz in motatzin in monantzin—

Lucifer = Quenin quimahuiztilizq,^e in tehuatzin otiquinmomaquili in qualli yectli yhuan Otiquinmochihuili in īpanpa Cruztitech otimomiquili amo omitzmomahuiztililique, in çan mixtzinco mocpatzinco onenque = Auh yequene in oc çequintin tetahuan quinyacantinemi quinhuicatinemi yn inpilhuan yn ocnamacoyan, Vinocalcohui in inpilhuan in çan nequiza = in motlanahuatiltzin. totecuiyoyē Diosē,—

---

59. In anticipation of the next page: *tzom*.
60. timotetlatzoomtequililiani: standard *timotetlatzontequililiani*.
61. quintequipachohuaya: given the context this must be scribal error; read *quintequipanohuaya*.

SECOND EXECUTOR: It is your fault that we are punished and made to suffer here for I said to you that the goods and property of the souls with which they will be helped should be entered into the church. That is why these things are happening to us now.

FIRST EXECUTOR: O devilish woman, it is your fault that we sold other people's goods and property for cash. It is all your fault that we are suffering.

WIDOW: Oh! Woe is me! Would that we had not been born so that the frightening and scandalous things now happening to us would not have happened.

LUCIFER: Run along. You just now remembered your sins? No longer anything for it, for now you belong to us.

(They go before Christ. There they spread out their document. Lucifer and all the demons kneel down.)

LUCIFER: You the perfectly righteous judge, you the sentencer, [48r] here before you we brought those who greatly served [us] and did not obey you. They did not carry out your commands even though through your precious blood you saved [these] scoundrels and lunatics who never remembered you. Judge them. For they belonged to us because they were eternally despised. And as for that which pertains to God,[18] they regarded it all as torment and had no regard for service to you. Here are their sins. Look at their works. You, angel, read their sins.

SAINT MICHAEL: Here are the ten commands of God the only deity. There are ten. Three pertain to the honoring of God and seven pertain to the loving of the people of the earth.

SAINT MICHAEL: First, you shall love God the only deity with all your heart.

LUCIFER: Those who are here absolutely never esteemed you, never regarded you as a god.

SAINT MICHAEL: Second, you shall not take the name of God in vain. [48v]

LUCIFER: They used to go about taking oaths all the time, speaking vainly and falsely about you in their useless idleness and in their sins of filthy carnal delight.

SAINT MICHAEL: Third, on Sundays and feast days you shall just occupy yourself in spiritual pursuits.

LUCIFER: All the time while they lived on earth they never acknowledged you as god, never remembered you. On feast days what used to preoccupy them was their sinful love affairs that they used to carry out.[19]

SAINT MICHAEL: Fourth, you shall honor your father and your mother.

LUCIFER: In what way did they honor them? You gave them good and virtuous things, you made them, you died for them on the cross. They did not honor you for that but just showed you disrespect. Moreover, other fathers go about leading and taking their children to the place where pulque is sold, go to the house of wine. O our lord, O God, your command is just in vain!

---

18. teoyotl: depending on context this has many meanings including "that which pertains to the divine cult" such as mass, Christian doctrine, and the sacrament of marriage; see Carochi 1983, 52v–53r.

19. Tentative translation.

S,ⁿ Mig,ˡ = Ynic macuiltetl, ayac momac miquiz in teyolia—

Lucifer = Quenin. ayac in imac miquiz Ca huel miec teaniman [49r] oquixpoloque inic otetlatlacolcuitique inic nezia tp̄c. ca qualnemiliçeque Ca miecpa otemiquizylehuique = = =

S,ⁿ Mig,ˡ = Ynic Chiquaçentetl, amo taahuilnemiz in tlaticpac⁶² =—

Lucifer = Ca huel axcan ypan in oanoloque in imahuilpapaquiliz in innemecatiliztlatlacol—

S,ⁿ Mig,ˡ = Ynic Chicontetl, amo tichtequiz amo ticylehuiz in teçiahuiliz—

Lucifer = Auh ca huel yez tecalotica in oanaloque in oquitzquiloque⁶³ Camo tiquimiztlacahuia—

S,ⁿ Mig,ˡ = Ynic Chicuetetl, amo titetentlapiquiz amo tetech tictlamiz tlatlacolli—

Lucifer = Ca huel teixpa inic oquintētlapique in inhuanpohuan inic tetech oquitlamique in tlatlacolli—

S,ⁿ Mig,ˡ = Ynic Chiucnauhtetl, amo tiquilehuiz in teçihuauh yhuan tenamic—

Lucifer = Ca miequintin Oquinmahuizpoloque in ica mani in intētlaximaliz aic Omitzmomauhcaittilique = amo oquimauhcaittaque in moteotenahuatiltzin Ca çan Oquihuetzquiliaya ca zan ahuilcamanalli ypan quimatia in motetlatzomtequililitzin manel moyolcuitizque Ca niman amo ic momaquixtizque in mo=⁶⁴[49v]tlatocaixpantzinco totecuiyoyen Diosē,—=

S,ⁿ Mig,ˡ = Ynic matlactetl, amo tiquilehuiz in teaxca tetlatqui—

Lucifer = Auh quenin amo quilehuizque ca in mimicque in imaxca in intlatqui ca mochi Oquixpachoque Camo, oquinpalehuique in ixquichtin Animas, Ca amo oquinquixtilique in Bula in manel zan = MiSsa = anoço ReSponso, anoso RoSario, ic quintepotztocani amo oquiChiuhque Auh yn iquac otzilinia = Animas, in imilnamicoca, çan innemecatiliztica onenque, in aic Oquimilnamicque Auh ma xiquinmotlatzomtequililitzino—

S,ⁿ Mig,ˡ = Yzcatqui in itenahuatiltzin in tonantzin S,ᵗᵃ Ygl,ᵃ ca macuiltetl = Ynic Çentetl in Domingo, yhuan ylhuitl ipā huel Çentetl MiSsa mocaquiz

Lucifer = Aic inyollocacopa oquittaque MiSsa, momoztlae Vinonamacoyan moçentlaliaya amo otlateomatia in motlatocaixpantzinco—

S,ⁿ Mig,ˡ = Ynic ontetl, neyolmelahualoz yn ipan in axcan tlamaçehualizCahuipan Quaresma—

Lucifer = Ca niman aic Omoyolmelauhque yn iquac onemia in tlalticpac amo ic omoyolcocoque in tlamaçehualiztli = = [50r]

S,ⁿ Mig,ˡ = Ynic yetetl, Çeliloz in itlaçomahuiznacayotzin in totecuioyo⁶⁵ Jesu xp̄o. yn iquac huey pasqua anoço Xochipasqua.—

---

62. tlaticpac: here and below, read as standard *tlalticpac*.
63. oquitzquiloque: appears to be scribal error; we read as *otzitzquiloque*.
64. In anticipation of the next page: *tla*.
65. totecuioyo: standard *totecuiyo*. The same item can be found above on 40r.

SAINT MICHAEL: Fifth, no one's spirit shall die at your hands.

LUCIFER: In what way did no one die at their hands? They ruined the souls of many people, [49r] they caused people to take up sin, so that it would seem on earth that they had good lives.[20] Many times they desired the death of others.
SAINT MICHAEL: Sixth, you shall not live licentiously on earth.
LUCIFER: Right at this moment they were seized in their carnal delights and their sins of concubinage.
SAINT MICHAEL: Seventh, you shall not be a thief, you shall not covet the labor of others.
LUCIFER: They were seized and taken hold of right on the path to someone's house.[21] We are not deceiving them.
SAINT MICHAEL: Eighth, you shall not slander others nor impute sin to them.
LUCIFER: Right in public they slandered their neighbors and imputed sin to others.

SAINT MICHAEL: Ninth, you shall not covet someone else's wife and someone else's spouse.
LUCIFER: Those here defamed many people with their adulteries. They never looked at you with fear nor your sacred commandments with fear. They just laughed at them, regarding your judgments as just frivolous jokes. O our lord, O God, even if they confess they will absolutely not thereby be saved in your [49v] royal presence.
SAINT MICHAEL: Tenth, you shall not covet the goods and property of others.
LUCIFER: And how did they not covet the goods and property of the dead? They hid it all, they did not help all the souls [in purgatory], they did not take out for them the [papal] bulls and would not even follow up for them with just a mass or prayer for the dead or a rosary. They did not do it. When the bells rang in remembrance of the souls [in purgatory] they just lived in their illicit unions and never remembered it. Judge them.
SAINT MICHAEL: Here are the five commands of our mother holy church. First, on Sundays and feast days an entire mass will be heard.
LUCIFER: They never willingly heard mass. Every day they used to gather together in the place where wine is sold. They did not occupy themselves in spiritual matters in your royal presence.
SAINT MICHAEL: Second, all will confess now in the time of penance, Lent.

LUCIFER: They absolutely never confessed when they lived on earth and they were not repentant with penance. [50r]
SAINT MICHAEL: Third, the precious honored body of our lord Jesus Christ will be received when it is great Easter or the flowery Pasch.[22]

---

20. Tentative translation.
21. Tentative translation.
22. These terms for Pasch are discussed in Burkhart 1996, 172–73.

Luçifer = Ayc inyollocacopa otlaçelique Ca mochipa tlatlacolpan Omitzmoçeliliaya, Auh in quemanian intla otlaçelique niman ye connamiqui otlica mahuiltia teixyle- huia nepohualiztica quichihuaya inic oomoqualnextiaya[66]—

S,[n] Mig,[l] = Ynic nauhtetl, neçahualoz in iquac motenahuatilia in S,[ta] Ygl,[a]

Luçifer = Quenin moçahuazque momoztlae atlitica = tlaqualtica mocohuanotzaya moçentlaliaya yn ica in micCatlatquitl oquinenquixtiq.[e]—

S,[n] Mig,[l] = Ynic macuiltetl, tlamanaloz in tlamatlactetilia inic motenahuatilia in S,[ta] Ygl,[a]—

Luçifer = Ca niman, atle qualli oquichiuhque quenin tlamanazque tlahuenchi- huazque ca manel temachtiltica nonotzaloya çan quihuetzquiliaya = in inteopix- cahuan Ca quitohuaya Cuix nelli melahua[c] ca çan ic techmamauhtia Auh ynin Ca zan Xolopitli aic oquimahuiztiliaya in neçahualiztlaquemitl in Luto = mochipa ocnamacoyan tecohuanotzaloyan[67] [50v] tlacatlatolli ypan quichihuaya ypan teca tlatohuaya ipan tetlanximaya aquetztinemia yn iuh momatia azo catle tetla- cuiltiliztli[68] ytech ca auh ca tiquinmoçenquizcaitztiliticatqui in timelahuac Jues = Camo tlen tiquintetlapiquia Ca oc çequi in nican yn iCuiliuhtica yn intlatlacol ma yÇiuhcā Xintechmomaquili macamo nican mixpantzinco neçican in tlahueli- loque—

Xp̄o = Ca çemicac inpan nixtoçotica in ixquichtin notlaChihualhuan camo niquin- cahua ca mochipa niquimitztica in tlatlacohuanime Ca yn iquac tlatlacohua in tlapilchihua Ca nictamachiuhtica in intlachihual ynic niquintlacuiltiz[69] niquinçen- manaz niquintzitzquiz niquinchichinatzaz = auh in yehuantin quenin zan tlael- paquiliztica Oquinenpoloque in teaxca tetlatqui auh in amoyolia in amaniman quenin oanquinenquixtique Ca inic onicyocox onicChiuh Ca çemicac notloc nona- huac nochantzinco oannemizquia oannechmotlayecoltilizquia = Auh çannimac[70] in Çemicac Zentetlayohuiltianime oanquicauhq.[e] ynic çemicac quitonehuacapo- lozque anchichinatzazque in ompa = Çentlani mictlan apochquia[71] [51r] huayocan oanmomomayauhque = Auh canpa oanquicauhque in miccatlatquitl inic amotech omocauhq[e] in ompa tlayohuia = Purgatorio = quenin amo anquinpalehuique ma xinechnanquilican = Auh in axcan, ma xiquinhuicacan in oanquītequipanoque ma amechtlaxtlahuilmacacan in amehuantin in mictlan anchaneque ma xiquinhuica- can Canel Oamechtlayecoltique—

1,[o] Dem,[o] = Otlacauhqui, in motlaçoyollotzin otitechmocnelilitzino ma niman tiquin- huicacan in ompa Çentlani, mictlan, oamotlahueliltic tlacentelchihualtinen ma tihuian in ompa toçenchan xitotocacan ca amechhualchie in totlatocauh in Luçifer, Ca amechmottiliz—

---

66. oomoqualnextiaya: standard *omoqualnextiaya*.
67. In anticipation of the next page: *tla*.
68. tetlacuiltiliztli: read *tetlatzacuiltiliztli* (see footnote immediately below).
69. niquintlacuiltiz: read *niquintlatzacuiltiz*.
70. çannimac: read *çan imac*.
71. In anticipation of the next page: *hua*.

LUCIFER: They never willingly took communion for they always took you in sin. If at times they took communion they later met on the road wasting time, desiring women, and pridefully trying to make themselves look beautiful.
SAINT MICHAEL: Fourth, all will fast when the holy church orders.
LUCIFER: In what way did they fast? Every day they invited themselves to feasts, gathering together with drink and food [obtained with] the property of the dead that they squandered.
SAINT MICHAEL: Fifth, offerings of a tenth will be made as the holy church orders.

LUCIFER: They did absolutely nothing properly. In what way did they give and make offerings? Even though they were admonished with sermons they just laughed at the priests, saying: "Is it true and correct? They are just frightening us with [all that talk]." And as for this one, he is just an idiot. He never honored the fasting garments, the mourning clothes. He was always in the place where pulque is sold, the place where people are invited to feasts, [50v] doing bad things in vulgar words, speaking out against others, being adulterous and going about with his head held high, thinking that no punishment attaches to it.[23] But you the true judge had a perfect view of them. We bring no false testimony against them for their other sins are written here [too]. Give them to us promptly. Do not let the[se] scoundrels appear here before you.
CHRIST: I keep eternal vigil on all my creatures. I do not abandon them. I am always looking at sinners.[24] When they sin and commit failings I am measuring their deeds so that I will punish them, rule them, take hold of them and make them suffer pain. As for them, how did they just squander the goods and property of others through filthy carnal pleasures? And how did you uselessly use up your spirits and souls? I created and made them so that you would eternally live next to and with me in my home, and so that you would serve me. But you have left them in the hands of the eternal torturers of everyone so that they will always torment them. You will suffer pain over there in the depths of hell, [51r] you flung yourselves down into the place without a chimney. And where did you leave the property of the dead that they who suffer over there in purgatory entrusted to you? How did you not help them? Answer me! And now, take those on whom you have worked. Let them make restitution to you residents of hell. Take them for they served you [well].
FIRST DEMON: We give you many thanks for the favor you have shown us. Let us take them right away there to the depths of hell. O accursed ones, woe to you! Let us go there to our eternal home. Run along, for our ruler Lucifer is waiting to see you.

23. Tentative translation.
24. ca mochipa niquimitztica in tlatlacohuanime: this might also be translated as "I always dwell/live with sinners." See Molina 1977, 72r: "Niquimitztica. biuir, o morar en compañia de algunos."

S,ⁿ Mig,^l = Motlanahuatilia, Yn melahuac Jues, inic tlequauhtemalacatitech anquintlalizque auh tlepopochatitla anquinmayahuitihue yhuan tleapas:calco anquinmayahuitihue tletemazcalco anquin:calaquizque huel anquintonehuacapolozque inic tlatzomtequililo ma xiquinhuicacan—

Quinhuicazque, motzaquaz in Ylhuicatl———————[51v]

1,º Albaçea = Ay ay ay omochiuh ototlahueliltic ma oc tic=tecuepiliani ~~in teaxca~~ in teaxca tetlatqui yn imaxca in mimicque, Ay Ay Ay omochiuh ototlahueliltic macamo titlacatini Campa tica in titlacatecoloteta macamo xinechtlacatiliani yn tlaticpac—

Viuda = Yehica omochiuh onotlahueliltic tlein onechonquixti in notlaelpaquiliz Auh catlique in oticçenpopoloque in teocuitlatl ma xinechpalehuiqui ma xinechmaquixtiqui—

1º Dem,º = Acmo onca inic antzatziticate axcan anquimetizque in oanquixpachoque in miccatlatquitl ma tihuian ca huel ye antechhuecahua Xitotocacan tlahuelíloque—

v Yazque niman quintlalizque quauhtemalacatitech in animatin tlachichihualtin yezque auh in condenados tlatic tzatzizque quinmalacachozque Cueponiz bonbas oc çecppa quinhualquixtizque quintlayahualochtizque mopi[72][52r]**tzaz trompeta cuacuauhomitl**

2º Albaçea = Ay Ay Ay in timictlan calli ma ça çepa Xitechtolo macamo timitzittacan auh in amehuāntin in antlatlacatecolo ma ça çecpa Xitechtzatzayanacan inyoyahuen ototlahueliltic ma totech ximixcuiticā in antlalticpactlaca ma xictecuepilican in teaxca tetlatqui inic amo no yuhqui amopan mochihuaz = yn iuh topan omochiuh in tehuantin—

Viuda = Ay. Ay. Ay. in amehuantin in anquipiezque in neçahualiztlaquemitl, luto camo ahuilli camanalli ypan anquimatizque ca ynic tinahuatillo tlamaçehualiztica tlatlatlauhtiliztica neçahualiztica yhuan Çeçenmetztica tlaçeliloz Auh camo yuhqui onicChiuh ca yehuatl nictzaqua in axcā ma mochi tlacatl notech mixcuitican yn annoÇihuapohuan macamo yuhqui anquichihuazque ay ay ay ay ay ay—

3º Dem,º = Ça ye Xiquintotoquiltican tocnihuanen aocmo oncan in manel tlein mach anquitozque Xicalaquican tlatelchihualtinen axcan anquittazque = = =

---

72. In anticipation of the next page: *tzaz*.

SAINT MICHAEL: The true judge orders that you place them on a wheel of fire. You will go casting them down into the place of fire-blackened water, into the house with tubs of fire.[25] You shall enter them into the sweatbath of fire. You will greatly torment them. That is the judgment. Take them.
(They take them. Heaven closes up.) [51v]

FIRST EXECUTOR: Oh! Oh! Oh! Woe is us! Would that we could still return the goods and property of others, the property of the dead. Oh! Oh! Oh! Woe is us! Would that we had not been born! Where are you, you demonic father? Would that you had not caused me to be born on earth.

WIDOW: Wherefore, O woe is me, what did my filthy carnal pleasures avail me? And what has become of all the gold we spent? Come help me! Come save me!

FIRST DEMON: There is nothing to cry about. Now you will make yourselves heavy [with] the property of the dead you concealed. Let us go for you have greatly detained us. Hurry along, scoundrels!
(They go. Then they attach to wheels the effigies of souls. The condemned cry out from inside. They turn them. Fireworks go off. Again they bring them out and parade them around. [52r] *A trumpet, [that is,] a horn trumpet,[26] is blown.)*

SECOND EXECUTOR: Oh! Oh! Oh! You who are the house of hell, swallow us up once and for all. Let us not look at you. As for you devils, just rip us to shreds once and for all. Alas, woe is us! You people of the earth, take an example from us. Return to others their goods and property so that what befell us will not also befall you.

WIDOW: Oh! Oh! Oh! You who will have fasting garments, mourning clothes, do not regard them as frivolous for you are ordered to it through penance, prayers, and fasting, and communion will be taken each month. I did not do this and now I am paying the penalty. Let everyone take an example from me. You who are women like me: Do not do likewise! Oh! Oh! Oh! Oh! Oh! Oh!

THIRD DEMON: O our friends, make them run along now. There is nothing for it now no matter what you say. Enter, O accursed ones! Now you shall see!

---

25. Tentative translation.
26. horn trumpet: literally, "head-stick-bone," from a colonial Nahuatl circumlocution for European horned animals, *quaquahueque*, "head-stick owners."

Present Location
Library of Congress
Washington, D.C.

[1r]
+

Nexcuitilmachiotl. motenehua Juiçio final—
tlapitzalos motlapoz yīh.^{c} hualmotemohuiz S.^{n} mig.^{1} =

S.^{n} miguel = v̄ Dios ytlachihualtzitzinhuane. ma xicmatican. yhuan Ca tel ye anquimati. Ca ypan Ca yn iteotenahuatiltzin ȳ tt.^{o} D.^{s} Ca quimotlamilliz quimopo^{l}huis yn oquimochihuilitzino. yn itlaçomahuiztatzin Dios. ȳ Senmanahuactli. Ca quimopolhuis. quimotlamilliz. yn ixquich yn oquimochihuilitzino. ȳ nepapan totome. y nepapā yoyolime. yhuan yn amehuantin. Ca hamechmopolhuis. yn ansemanahuac tlaca. auh ma yuh ye yn amoyollo. ca moscalizque y mimicque. y qualtin yecti. yn oquimotlayecoltilique. ȳ melahu^{a}caJuez motlatzontequililiani D.^{s} Ca quinmohuiquiliz yn onpa yn itlatocachantz.^{co} ȳ Semicac neSentlamachtiloyan. y gloria. yn inneSentlamachtiaya. yn ixquichtin S.^{tos} S.^{tas} auh yn amo qualtin. yn amo hoquimotlayecoltilique yn tt.^{o} D.^{s} ma yuh ye yn inyollo. Ca quimomasehuizque. yn mictlan tla^{i}yohuiliztli. auh ynin ma xichocaca. ma xiquilnamiquiCan. xiquimaCasiCan. ximauhCamiquiCan. Ca hamopan mochihuas. y tetlatzontequililizylhuitl. y senca temamauhti. y seca teiysahui. temauhcamicti. temauhcaçotlahualti. auh ynin ma ximonemiliz[yectilican?^{1}] [1v] ye amopan mochihuas. ȳ tetlatzontequililizcahuitl. ca ye ocan. ca ye hinma yn axcan—
Tlapitzalos Tlecos S.^{n} miguel hualquisas. Tlamasehualiztli.
Cahuitl: Sta ygl.^{a} : Tlachpanaliztli: miquistli—

Tlamasehualiztli = Ȳ niman ayoc huel mitos: anoçe motenehuas: yn innetlapololtiliz: yn ixquichtin çemanahuac tlaca: y çenca huel yhuicopa oquayxihuitique:^{2} nepapan tlatlacoltica: tlei mach ohuaxque: tlei mach yn quichihua Ȳ niman ahuel quicahua: yn intetzauhtlatlacol: yn inyollo:tepitzahuilliz: yn imixpopoyotilliz: oyçen^{tzon}tlahueliltic: aca nel ypam miquisque: yn intlatlacol: y nacatzonteme: y nacastapaleque: yn ixpopoyome: yn atlachianime: huel mitos tlatlacoltica: oyxtepapatzauhque: huel oquitzopelicamatque: ~~oquiya~~cahuiyacamatque: yn tlatlacolli: yuhquima oquimocaltique: oquimoquentique: yn ahuilnemilliztli: Ça yuhqui yn imauh yn intlaqual: ypan quimati: auh yn inteotzin yn intlatocatzin D.^{s} ye omolcahuillique^3: oyçentzotlahueliltic: Ca ye tlami yn innemilliz: yn tlpc̄:—

---

1. This part of page torn and missing. Could also be read as *ximonemilizcueppan*.
2. oquayxihuitique: originally read *oquayxihuiteque*.
3. omolcahuillique: read *oquimolcahuilique*.

Final Judgment
Translated by Louise M. Burkhart, with assistance from Barry D. Sell

[1r]
+

Exemplary model called Final Judgment.
(Wind instruments are played. Heaven opens. Saint Michael descends.)

SAINT MICHAEL: O creations of God! Know, and indeed you already know, for it is in the sacred commands of our lord God, that he will finish off, he will destroy the world that his precious and honored father, God, made. He will destroy, he will finish off all that he made, the various birds, the various living creatures, along with you. He will destroy you, you people of the world. But be certain that the dead will revive. The good and proper ones who served the just judge, the sentencer, God, he will take to his royal home, the place of eternal and utter bliss, glory, the place of utter bliss of all the male and female saints. But the bad ones who did not serve our lord God, may they be certain that they will merit suffering in the place of the dead.[1] So then, weep, remember it. Fear it, be scared to death, for the day of judgment will happen to you. It is very frightening, it is very shocking, it scares people to death, it makes people faint with fright. So then, emend your lives. [1v] The day of judgment is about to happen to you. It is the time, it is the moment, now.

(Wind instruments are played. Saint Michael ascends. Penance enters [along with] Time, Holy Church, Sweeping, [and] Death.)

PENANCE: It is still impossible to say or declare the confusion of all the people of the world. They are thoroughly dizzy in the head from the various sins. Whatever is wrong with them, whatever is the matter with them, that they are in no way able to abandon their ominous sins, their hard-heartedness, their blindness? They are four hundred times[2] unfortunate. Some will die in their sins. The recalcitrant, the deaf, the blind, the unobservant: it can be said that with sin they have destroyed people's eyes. They have considered sin to be quite sweet, they have considered it to be pleasing to the nose. It is as if they housed themselves and dressed themselves with lustful living. It is just as if they consider it to be their drink, their food.[3] And they have already forgotten their deity, their ruler, God. They are four hundred times unfortunate! For their life on earth is about to end.

---

1. mictlan: here and below translated as "the place of the dead" (locative senses such as "in" or "at" are already contained in the Nahuatl term), it was usually rendered by colonial translators as *infierno* (hell).
2. Four hundred times: here and below, *four hundred* is a common idiom in the vigesimally based traditional counting system for "countless, innumerable."
3. drink, food: here and below, this common diphrase often carries the sense "daily sustenance."

Cahuitl: y Ȳ nehuatl y nicahuitl: y niçemilhuiteotlatoltillizcahuitl: yn onechmomaquilitzino: onechmixquechillitzino: yn tt.⁰ D.ˢ ynic momostlaye: niquinpixtica niquinnoCuitlahuitica: niquintzatzilitica: niquintlalnamictiti[ca y çeçem?⁴]ilhuitl: y çeçeyohual: yn amo achitō cahuitl: [2r] nonnotencahua: yn innacastitla nitzatzitica: ynic quimolnamiquillizque: yn inteyocoxcatzin: yn intechiuhcatzin ȳ teotl: tlatohuani D.ˢ niquinCuitlahuiltia ma quimotzatzililican: ma quimoyectenehuilica: ma quimotlayecoltilican: ma quichihuacan: yn iuh quimonequiltia yn tt.⁰ D.ˢ ca niquintzatzillia: ma huian yn ichatz:ᶜᵒ ma quimoyectenehuillica ma quimotlaytlanililitin: ynic quinmomaquilliz: yn itlaçograçiatzin: auh ⁱⁿ yehuantin çan quinenquixtia: ȳ nonemilliz: ȳ notlatequipanolliz: yeçe tel niquitoa: ca ye yc ninoquixtia: yn inhuicopa atle notechcopa: yc moᵗᵉmapatlasque yn ixpantz:ᶜᵒ yn D.ˢ yniᶜ çeçēme notzalosque: tlatemolilosq̄ yehuantin quimati: yn tleyn ic tlananquilizque: auh ȳ nehuatl: ca Cuenta nicnomaquilliz: yn D.ˢ tetatzin: yn ixquich yhuellitzin: yn otechmoyocolili: auh ynin atle yc notech motlamizque: Ca ye ynman yn notzalosque =

S.ᵗᵃ ygl.ᵃ = y Yn nehuatl. ȳ nitetlaocoliliztenantzin: yn onechmixq̄.chilli: y notlaçotelpotzin Jesu xp̄ō: ynic nican ȳpampa yn tlp̄c̄ tlaca: Ca mochipa ypampa ninochoquilitica: oc çenca yn iquac yn ˢᵉme momiquilia: ypampa nicnoquia: ȳ nixayo nicnotlatlauhtilia: ȳ notlaçoçenpapaquillizteoameyalnantzin: ȳ ma quinmotlaocolili: ma quinmotlanextilili: yn itlachihualtzitzinhuan: maeamo nenquisas: yn chicontetl:[2v]tetl⁵ SaCram.ᵗᵒ y niquinpialitica: yn iuhqui quenmanian conelehuisque: quiteoçihuisque ca niquintlaqualtiz niquimatlitis: yntla amiquisque: auh ca yn axcan ca niquinchixtica: ynpampa nitlaocoxtica: ma hualhuian: ma monemilizyectilliqui: ma tlatlatlaᵘʰtican: ca tlaocolilosque: yhuan ma chocacan: yhuan ma tlaocoyacan: ypampa yn intlatlacol: yn intla<u>pilchihual</u>

Tlachpanaliztli = y yn tiçenquiscaçentlaneltoquiliztenantzin: ca mochi melahuac: yn ticmitalhuitzinoa: Camo quilnamiqui ynontzin: amo quelehuia: çan ye quinequi ȳ ma çan ontlatlacocan: Cuix amo tel yxquich notlapal nicchihua: yn nehuatl ca mochipa niquintzatzilia: momostlaye: niquinCuitlahuiltia: ma tlachpanacan: ma yxtoçocan. ma yohuatz.ᶜᵒ mehuᵉcan: ma tlaᵗˡᵃmaçehuacan ma çecmiquican: quitosnequi ma teoyotica quitlachpanilican: yn inyollia yn imanima: ma moçahuacan: ma tlaCuallizcahuaca: ynic huel tlaocollilosque tlapopolhuililosque: auh yntlacamo ca niman amo huel calaquisque: yn itlatocachantz.ᶜᵒ yn tt.⁰ Dios: ca hahuel tlapopolhuililosque: yntlacamo oc achtopa tlamaçehuasque: ca yn tlamasehualoni niqualhuiCa: Ca quimicmic[3r]nellia:⁷ ca ypan pohui yn ilh̄.ᶜ Ecahuastli: ynic huel calaquisque yn ilh̄.ᶜtl itec: Ca tel ayocmo huecauh Ca ye notzalosque yn ixpantz.ᶜᵒ yn tt.⁰ Dˢ: ynic çeçenmē quimomaquilizque Cuenta yniᶜ onenque yn tlp̄c̄: macamo toteᶜʰ motemapatlasque yn ixpantz.ᶜᵒ yn D.ˢ—

---

4. Corner of document is torn off here.
5. chicontetltetl: read *chicontetl*.
6. mehuᵉcan: read *mehuacan*.
7. quimicmicnellia: read *quimicnelia*.

TIME: I am time. I am one day's time[4] of the sacred word. Our lord God gave and assigned to me the charge that every day I be guarding them, taking care of them, calling out to them, reminding them of things day and night. Not for an instant do [2r] I close my lips. I am crying out into their ears so that they will remember their creator, their maker, the deity, the ruler, God. I induce them to cry out to him, to praise him, to serve him, to do as our lord God wants. I cry out to them to go to his home, to praise him, to ask him to give them his precious grace. But they just waste my life and my work. Even so, I say, I have thus fulfilled my obligations toward them. There is nothing in regard to me with which they will defend themselves before God, as they each are called and examined. They know how they will answer. And as for me: I will give an accounting to God the father, the all-powerful one, who created us. So then, there is nothing for which they will excuse themselves by blaming me. It is time that they be called.

HOLY CHURCH: I am the compassionate mother of the one who appointed me, my precious son Jesus Christ, so that here on account of the people of earth I am always weeping, especially when one of them dies. Therefore I spill my tears. I beseech my precious mother, sacred fountain of utter happiness, to have compassion for them, to illuminate his[5] creatures. May the seventh [2v] sacrament, which I am keeping for them, not come to naught. Sometimes it is as if they will desire it, they will hunger for it. I will feed them, I will give them drink if they are thirsty. And now I am waiting for them. I am sad for their sakes. May they come, and may they come to emend their lives, may they pray. They will receive compassion. And may they weep and be sad because of their sins, their defects.

SWEEPING: You are his mother of perfect and complete faith. It is all correct, what you say. They do not remember what they do not desire; they just want to go on sinning. Do I not exert all my effort? I always cry out to them, every day. I induce them to sweep things, to keep vigil, to arise in the morning, to do penance, to suffer cold, that is, in a sacred way[6] to sweep their spirits, their souls, to fast, to abstain from food so that they will receive compassion and be pardoned. And if not, there is no way at all that they will be able to enter the royal home of our lord God. They will not be able to be pardoned if they do not first do penance. I bring the instrument of penance.[7] It does them favor, [3r] for it is considered the ladder of heaven, by which they will be able to enter into heaven. For it will not be long until they are called before our lord God so that each of them will give him an accounting of how they lived on earth. May they not use us to defend themselves before God.[8]

4. Perhaps "an entire lifetime" is meant.
5. "His" is probably intended rather than "her" as it is God/Christ who is the creator.
6. teoyotica: used by priests and their native aides as an equivalent for "spiritual," means "through divinity" or "by means of sacredness." In actual usage it tended to confer not divine instrumentality as much as a broader sense of holiness or an association with Christianity. Translated here and in "How to Live on Earth" as "in a sacred way"; as the more traditional "spiritual" in "The Merchant."
7. Perhaps this refers to an actual broom that Sweeping is supposed to be holding.
8. That is, as Time stated above, humanity cannot blame anything on us.

Miquistli = v̱ Yn nehuatl ȳ nitopilecatzin: ȳ nitlayxquetzaltzin: ȳ nitititlatzin: yn ilh̄.ᶜhuicac⁸ mehuiltitica yn ixquich yhuelitzin yhuan y nican tlp̄c̄: nohuian tentimani ynic motonameyotitzinotica yn ilh̄.ᶜtl itec: yhua nohuian çemanahuac auh ma yuh ye yn inyollo yn tlp̄c̄ tlaca: ca sa mostla huiptla yn hualmotemohuis: yn D.ˢ hitlaçopiltzin ȳ quinmotlatzontequililiquiuh yn yol⁹ yhuan yn mimicque: auh y qualtin Ca quinmohuiquiliz yn itlatocachantz.ᶜᵒ yn ilhuicatl îtec auh yn amo qualtin yn amo oquimotlayeColtilique y nican tlp̄c̄: Ca quinmotlaxiliz y çentlan ȳ mictla: auh ma yuh ye yn inyollo yn tlp̄c̄ tlaca: Ca ynpan mochihuas yn tetlatzontequililizylhuitl: y çenca temamauhti yn inpan mochihuas: auh ynin ma monemilizyectilica yehica Ca ye oCan Ca ye ynma yn tlatzontequililosque: ynic tlatemolilosq̄. ynic oquimotlayeColtilique yn tt.ᵒ D.ˢ =

Santa ygl.ᵃ = v̱ Ca huel melahuac yn oticmotenehuillitzino: yn oticmotenquixtillitzino: Canel amitetlayecolticatzitzin[3v]huan yn amitlatequipanocatzitzinhuan: ȳ notlaçoneyolalilizçenteconetzin: ȳ notlaçonamictzin teoyotica Jesu x̄p̄o: yn ohuamechmixquechillitzino: ynic anquimotzatzililizque: anquinmotlayxpantililizque: yn itlamaquixtitzitzinhuan: yn tlp̄c̄ tlatlacohuanime: y huel çenca tlatlacoltica: oquixtlalteuhpachoque oquiçoquineloque yn inyolia yn imanima: auh yn axcan ma tihuian: ma tiquimontzatzilitin: ynic hualasque teoyotica moçencahuaquihue:¹⁰ choquistica yxayotica: auh yn nehuatl: ca niquinchixtica ynic niquinchipahuas: niquimaltis teoyotica niquinchipahuas: yca yn chiContetl SaCram:ᵗᵒ nenamictiliztli: ca niquinpialitica—

Cahuitl = v̱ Ca niman axcan ye niauh: niquintzatzililiz: niquintlalnamictis: yn ipan çeçen ora quilnamiquisque: yn tley quichihuasque: ynic amo quinenpolosque: amo quinēquixtisque: ȳ nemilizcahuitl: yn onechmopialtilitzino ȳ tt.ᵒ D.ˢ:

Calaquiz cahuitl çan içel—

S.ᵗᵃ ygl.ᵃ = v̱ Ȳ niçentlaneltoquilizteotlanextli. Ca niquintlanextilia: teoyotica niquintlahuillia: yn ixquichtin x̄p̄.tianome: ynic hualasque yniquinchipahuas:¹¹ ca çenca tlatlacoltica oCuayxihuitique: ca yntla chocasque tlaocoyasque: Ca quinmotlapopolhuililiz: ȳ notlaçotelpotzin Jesu xp̄o. Ca quinmomaquiliz yn ilh̄.ᶜ tlatocayotl:—[4r]

Calaquis Santa ygl.ᵃ çan içel

Miquistli = v̱ Ca huel tetlaocoltique yn tlp̄c̄ tlaca: yxpopoyome yn amo quilnamiqui yn iquin quenman tlatzontequililosq̄. çā yehuatl yn ahuilnemiliztli: tlatlacoltica quicatzahua yn imanima: tel niquitoa yehuantin quimati: yn tlp̄c̄: tlaca yxpopoyome: yn atlachianime: ȳ huel tlatlacoltica omixtlilmatoCaque: auh yn īyollia yn imanima: amo quintequipachoa: ma mopapacacan. ma maltican Cualtilizteotlanextiliztica: Cuix quin iquac yn inpā mochihuas yn̄ tetlatzontequililizylhuitl: yn molnamiquisque ᶜᵘⁱˣ quin iCuac yn chocasque Ca nelli melahuac Ca niman ayocmo huel tlaocolilosque oyçentzontlahueliltic: yn tlp̄c̄ ⁱ ᵗˡᵃᶜᵃ. ca ça mostla yn ipan mochihuas ȳ tetlatzontequililizylhuitl: Ca ye oCan Ca ye iman =

Tlapitzaloz Calaquizq̄: miquistli Tlachpanaliztli: hualquisas Luçia hualmotequipachotas =

    8. ilh.ᶜhuicac: read *ilhuicac*.
    9. yol: scribal error; in context (and as elsewhere in this play) read *yolque*.
    10. moçencahuaquihue: the final vowel appears to be an *i* corrected to *e*.
    11. yniquinchipahuas: read *ynic niquinchipahuaz* or perhaps just *yn niquinchipahuaz*.

DEATH: I am the constable, I am the appointee, I am the messenger of the all-powerful one who is seated in heaven and here on earth. He is sending out sunbeams, filling up everywhere in heaven and everywhere in the world. And may the people of the earth be certain that tomorrow or the day after[9] the precious child of God will come down. He is coming to judge the living and the dead. And the good ones he will take to his royal home in heaven. But the bad ones, who did not serve him here on earth, he will throw into the depths of the place of the dead. And may the people of the earth be certain that the day of judgment will happen to them. What will happen to them is very frightening. And so, may they emend their lives because it is time, it is the moment when they will be judged, when they will be examined as to how they served our lord God.

HOLY CHURCH: It is fully correct what you have declared, what you have uttered, for you are the servants, [3v] you are the workers of my precious consolation and only child, Jesus Christ, who in a sacred way is my beloved spouse. He appointed you so that you would cry out to, you would reveal to those he has rescued, the sinners of the earth, that through sin they have thoroughly covered their spirits, their souls, with earth and dust, they have filled them with mud. And now let us go, let us go cry out to them so that they will come, they will come to prepare themselves in a sacred way, with weeping, with tears. And as for me, I am waiting for them so that I will purify them, I will bathe them, in a sacred way I will purify them with the seventh sacrament, marriage, which I am keeping for them.

TIME: Right now I am going. I will cry out to them, I will remind them each hour [so that] they will remember what they will do so that they will not squander and not waste the lifetimes that our lord God entrusted to me.

(Time exits alone.)

HOLY CHURCH: I am the sacred light of the complete faith. I illuminate, in a sacred way I shed light for all Christians, so that they will come and I will purify them. They are very dizzy in the head with sins. If they will weep and be sad my precious son, Jesus Christ, will pardon them and give them the kingdom of heaven. [4r]

(Holy Church exits alone.)

DEATH: The people of the earth are really piteous. They are blind. They do not remember that one day, sometime, they will be judged. It is just lustful living. They dirty their souls with sin. But I say the people of the earth, the blind ones, the unobservant ones, know that with sin they have really masturbated themselves black in the face.[10] And their spirits, their souls do not worry them. May they scrub themselves, may they bathe themselves with the sacred light of goodness. When the day of judgment happens to them, will they remember then? Will they weep then? It is true and correct that there is no longer any way that they can receive compassion. Four hundred times unfortunate are the people of the earth! For tomorrow the day of judgment will happen to them. It is time, it is the moment!

(Wind instruments are played. Death and Sweeping exit. Lucía enters. She comes anxiously.)

---

9. tomorrow, the day after: here and below, a common diphrase that often means "soon, in the near future."

10. Although this may seem graphic, the root verb is *matoca*, which means "to masturbate" (see Molina 1977, 53v: "Matoca. nino. palpar o tocar sus partes vergonçosas").

Luçia = y O noteotzin notlatocatzin Jesu xpō: omochiuh onotlahueliltic: yn axcan tlei nopan mochihua: yn iuhqui ye patzmiqui: y nanima yn iuhquin ye mextitlan i calaqui auh tlei nicchihuas yn axCan: ma niyauh ma ninoyolCuiti [4v] aço tepitzin yc çehuis y nanima: ma niyauh ma nicnotemoli: y noteyolCuiticatzin: Ca huel tonehua ȳ nix noyollo =

yaz Luçia contzotzonas puerta hualquisas teopixq̄:

Luçia: = y Ma motlaçonahuactz.ᶜᵒ moetzinotie: yn tt.º D.ˢ notlaçotatzin:—
hualquisas teopixqui tlatos = y teopixqui = Ma mitzhualmoyacanilli yn tt.º D.ˢ notlaçopiltzine: ma nican timohuicatz: tlein ticmonequiltia—

Luçia = y Ma xicmomachiltitzino: notlaçotatzin y tlein ic onihualla: macamo yc nimitz-noCualanilliz: notlaçoᵗᵃtzin—

Teopixqui = y Tlein ticmonequiltia: noᵗˡᵃᶜᵒpiltzine ma xicmitalhui ca yc otechmix-quechillitzino: y tt.º D.ˢ ynic tamechyolmelahuasque: yn ansemanahuac tlaca—

Luçia = y Notlaçotatzin: Ca nicnequi nimoyolmelahuas:¹² yxpantz.ᶜᵒ yn tt.º D.ˢ yhuan yn tehuatzin notlaçotazin—

Teopixqui = y Notlaçopiltzine: Ca Senca tinechhueltlamachtia:¹³ ȳ nicaqui mitztequipachoa: mitzyolpatzmictia: ȳ motlatlacol ma tihuian: yn iteopanchantz.ᶜᵒ yn ttº D.ˢ—

Niman moyolCuitiz Luçia auh yntla ye moyolCuititica niman moquetztehuas teopixqui huel momauhtis

---

12. nimoyolmelahuas: standard *ninoyolmelahuaz*.
13. tinechhueltlamachtia: standard *tinechhuellamachtia*.

LUCÍA: Oh, O my deity, O my ruler, Jesus Christ! How unfortunate I am! What is happening to me now? It is as if my soul is now oppressed. It is as if it is now entering among the clouds![11] And what am I to do now? Let me go, let me confess. [4v] Perhaps thus my soul will be a bit calmed. Let me go, let me look for my confessor. For my face, my heart are really aching![12]

(Lucía goes and knocks on a door. Priest enters.)

LUCÍA: May our lord God be lovingly with you, O my beloved father.

(Priest enters. He speaks.)

PRIEST: May our lord God guide you, O my beloved child. Be welcome here.[13] What is it that you want?

LUCÍA: Know, O my beloved father, what I have come for. Let me not make you angry with it, O my beloved father.

PRIEST: What is it that you want, O my beloved child? Say it. For our lord God appointed us to straighten the hearts of you people of the world.[14]

LUCÍA: O my beloved father, I want to straighten my heart before our lord God and you, O my beloved father.

PRIEST: O my beloved child, what I hear pleases me greatly. Your sins worry you, they oppress you. Let us go into the temple-home of our lord God.

(Then Lucía confesses. And as she is confessing, then Priest stands up. He is very frightened.)

---

11. That is, into sinful and/or terrifying darkness or maybe just a state of confusion?

12. The possessed metaphorical diphrase *-ix, -yollo* (face, heart) has many connotations. The first "by itself often has to do with presence, perception, wisdom" while the second "is associated with emotion and volition" (Karttunen and Lockhart 1987, 54). In combination they often refer to one's "spirit, spirits, mood, state of morale" (54), which is the sense present here (for a more extended discussion see 54–55).

13. ma nican timohuicatz: see Carochi 1983, 67v: "mā nicān timohuīcatz, venga V.m. en hora buena," as well as Arthur J. O. Anderson's rendition of same in Sahagún 1997, 296.

14. Here and below, "to heart-straighten" was commonly used in colonial Nahuatl texts to mean "to confess." The more literal gloss is used here in order to distinguish between this and *yolcuitia* (to acknowledge one's failings), which is translated as "confess" (or sometimes "profess," depending on context).

Teopixqui = y Jesus: Jesus: Tlein tiquitoa: tleyn oticchiuh: Cuix amo tixpāna:[14] Cuix amo ticmati ca çentzonpa huey tlatlacolli [5r] yn oticchiuh: omochiuh omoçentzontlahueliltic: ma xicmaquixtiani ma ᵒxicchipahuani yn manima: Tle yca yn aic oticcelli yn teoyotl: yn çā diablo otichuicalti: yn chicontetl S.ᵗᵒ SaCram̄.ᵗᵒ yn teoyotica nenamictiliztli: omochiuh omoçentzontlahueliltic: yn axcan yn aic oticnec yn timonamictis yn tlp̄c: auh ma yuh ye ȳ mix ȳ moyollo: Ca timonamictitiuh: yn onpa y çentlan yn mictlan: Ca momasehual mochihuas: yn mictlan tlayyohuilliztli: auh yn axcan tlei Cuenta ticmomaquiliz ȳ moteotzin motlatocatzin ca niman ahuel timopalehuis yn axcan: yehica ca ye yman ca ye ohuaçic: yn itetlatzontequililitzin: yn D.ˢ axcan ticmahuiçoz: ynic hualmotemohuis: yn tla D.ˢ ytlaçopiltzin: ȳ quinmotlatzontequililiquiuh: y yolque yhuan yn mimicque ynic çeçenyacan Cuenta quimomaquillizque: yn intechiuhcatzin D.ˢ Auh no yhuan tehuatl: tinesis yn ixpantz.ᶜᵒ yn ᵐᵒmelahuacatetlatzontequililiani hin D.ˢ hitlaçopiltzin: Jesu xp̄ō =

Calaquis teopixqui mocahuas Luçia—
Luçia = y A yoyahue Diose: omochiuh onohueyçentzontlahueliltic: yn tlp̄c. tleyn onicac tleyn onechmolhuilli: yn itlaçotzin D.ˢ quenin çenca temamauhti: tetequipacho. yn iuhqui quimitalhuia yn itlaçotzin D.ˢ ma noçᵒ honicaquini: onicneltocani yn tleyn onechmonahuatiliaya: y nodios[15] yhuan y notatzin y nonantzin: yhuan yn ixquichtin nohuanpohuan: yn ix[5v]n ixquich[16] ynic onechyolmaxiltiaya: y ça notlahuel omoCuepaya: y çan onictlatelchihuiliaya: y S.ᵗᵒ SaCram.ᵗᵒ teoyotica nenamictiliztli: omochiuh onoçentzontlahueliltic yn axcan: ma sentelchihualo yn atlamachiliztli: tlen onax tleyn onechonquixti: yn atlamachiliztli: ma sentelchihualo yn tlp̄ctli: yhuan i cahuitl: yn axcan ye tzonquisas ye tlamis: yn çemanahuactli: omochiuh onohueyçetzontlahueliltic ȳ nihueytlatlacohuani—
Tlapitzalos hualquisasque yolque motlallizque tlaltitech: yhuan Luçia mocamachalpachotiesque: hualquisas amtexp̄o: tlatec quitlaliz tlahuelilocatilmatli: pani quitlaliz tunica quihualquetztas[17] yn iopochmapil: TlaCueponiz ynic hualquisas—
Amtexp̄o= y Notlaçopilhuane: Cuix amo annechiximati: ca nehuatl: yn amopampa oⁿⁱtotoneuh tlp̄c. amopampa onitlayyohui: auh yn axcan ma yuh ye yn amoyollo ca nictlamis: nicpopolos yn tlp̄ctli: ma xinechneltocacan notlachihualhuane: ca namechpopolhuis: yn amotlatlacol: yn amotlapilchihual: ma xinechneltocacan: ma xiquitacan y noᵗˡᵃezⁱᵒyotzin[18]: yʰᵘᵃ noᵗˡᵃçᵒnacayotzin—[19]
1ᵒ yolqui = Camo tehuatl. yn ticmitzchia[20]: ca hualmohuicas yn toteotzi yn totlatocatzin: ca huel yehuatzin topampa omotlayyohuihuiltitzino omo[6r]omomiquillitzino:[21] Cruztitech oquimomāmaçohualtillique: ypampa yn toʰᵘᵉⁱçentzontlatlacol:[22]—

14. tixpāna: read *ticristiana.*
15. nodios: it is extremely rare for the Spanish loanword *Dios* (God) to be possessed.
16. yn ixn ixquich: read *yn ixquich.*
17. quihualquetztaz: read *quihualquetzaz* unless *quihualquetztiyaz* was meant.
18. noᵗˡᵃezⁱᵒyotzin: read *notlaçoezyotzin.*
19. The superscript in the preceding lines is in a slightly different hand.
20. ticmitzchia: read *timitzchia.*
21. omoomomiquillitzino: read *omomiquilitzino.*
22. toʰᵘᵉⁱçentzontlatlacol: the superscript characters are in a different hand.

PRIEST: Jesus! Jesus! What are you saying? What have you done? Are you not a Christian? Do you not know that four hundred times you have done great sins? [5r] Four hundred times unfortunate are you! If only you had saved, if only you had purified your soul! Why did you never receive the sacrament of marriage?[15] Just to the Devil you sent the seventh holy sacrament, marrying in a sacred way. Four hundred times unfortunate are you! Now you never wanted to get married on earth. But be certain that you are going to get married there in the depths of the place of the dead. What you will merit will be suffering in the place of the dead. And now what accounting will you give to your deity, your ruler? For in no way can you help yourself now, because it is already time, God's judgment has already arrived. Now you will marvel at how God's beloved child will come down. He is coming to judge the living and the dead, such that they each will give an accounting to their maker, God. And you, too, will appear before the just judge, God's beloved child, Jesus Christ.

(Priest exits. Lucía remains.)

LUCÍA: Ah, alas! O God! Four hundred times greatly unfortunate am I on earth! What did I hear? What did God's precious one say to me? How very frightening and worrying it is, what God's precious one says. If only I had listened, if only I had believed what my God was commanding me, along with my father, my mother, and all my neighbors. All of this, [5v] which they used to certify to me, used to just turn into my indignation. I used to just scoff at the holy sacrament, marrying in a sacred way. Four hundred times unfortunate am I now! May presumptuousness be despised! What have I done? What did presumptuousness avail me? May the earth and time be despised! Now the world is about to come to an end, about to be finished off. Four hundred times unfortunate am I! I am a great sinner!

(Wind instruments are played. The living enter. They sit on the ground, along with Lucía. Their jaws hang open. The Antichrist enters. On the inside he wears a cloak of wickedness; on top he wears a tunic. He raises the fingers of his left hand. Things explode as he emerges.)

ANTICHRIST: O my beloved children, do you not know me? It is I, who endured pains on earth on your behalf, who suffered on your behalf. And now, be certain that I will finish off, I will destroy the earth. Believe me, O my creations, for I will pardon you your sins, your defects. Believe me. Look at my precious blood, and my precious body.

FIRST LIVING PERSON: It is not you whom we are awaiting. Our deity, our ruler will come. It is he who suffered and died on our behalf. [6r] Because of our four hundred great sins they stretched him out by the arms on the cross.

---

15. teoyotl: this abstract collective noun can be rendered in many ways depending on context. For the single best explanation of this specific item, see the celebrated grammar of Father Horacio Carochi of 1645, 52v–53r (in Carochi 1983). He specifically states on 52v that Nahuatl speakers use *teoyotl* as meaning "el Sacramento del matrimonio" (the sacrament of marriage) and that they use it "quando dan palabra à vna muger de casarse con ella" (when they promise a woman that they will marry her).

Luçia = v Ca quemecatzin. Ca tehuatzin yn timitztochialia: noteotzin notlatocatzin: ma xitechmopopolhuililitzino: yn totlatlacol =

Amtexp̄.to = v Ca quemaca namechpalehuis: Cuix amo anquimati ca yxquich nohuelitzin: y çemanahuac—

MoCuicaehuas christos factus es: motlapos ylh̄.c hualmoquixtiz xp̄o Cualmoyacanilliz San miguel Cualmohuiquilliz pexotli: auh yn xp̄o quihualmohuiquilis Crus: ylh̄.cuicatenpa²³ moquetzinos: auh yn amtexp̄o calactehuas tlaCueponiz—

xp̄o: = v ma xihualmohuica: yn tinoyaotlayacancatzin yn tiS.n migel: y nican ylhuicatl itec: yn axCan Ca ye ynman y nictlamiz nicpolos yn cahuitl: yn motenehua Juicio final: yn tetlatzontequililizylhuitl: Ca yuhqui ypan onictlalli: y noteotenahuatiltzin: Ca nitlachpanas: Ca nicchipahuas yn ylh̄.c yhuan yn tlp̄ctli: ca huel otlaCatzauhque: yn tlp̄c. tlaca: yn yolque yhuan yn mimicque: ypampa yn imaCualnemiliz: auh yn axcan ma xiquinmixitilli:²⁴ yn yolque yhuan y mimicque: y qualtin yhuan yn amo Cualtin: auh y~~n amo~~ Cualtin: ca niquinomaquiliz yn ylh̄.c yn inxochinetlamachtil: yn ylh̄.c chalchihuitl: neapantli: yn ylh̄.c çoyatl: auh yn amo Cualtin ma yuh ye yn inyollo: ca ymaxcā mochihuas: y mictlan calli: yhuan y mictlan tlayyohui[6v]liztli: yehica camo huel oquipixque: ȳ noteotenahuatiltzin = hualmotemohuis xp̄o. S.n migel motlalitzinos xp̄o =

xp̄o: v Ca ye onimitznonahuatillitzino: yn tlein ticmochihuillitzinos: yn tinoyaotlayacancatzin

S.n miguel = v Ca ye Cuallitzin notlaçotemachticatzine: ma yolican yn mimicque: ma mosCallican yn yolque: ma quiCuican yn inmomio: yhuan ma quinechicocan: yhuan ma conanacan: yn intlalo yn inçoquio: ma xiquinmomaquillitzino: ȳ nescaliliztli: yn espiritu S.to yhuan yn imanima: ynic huel mitzmonanquililizque: ynic quitosque yn tley qualli: oquichiuhque yhuan yn tlen amo qualli: oquichiuhq̄. yn intlachihual =

xp̄o = v Ca ycan y nohuellitzin: ca moscallizque ioliz q̄.²⁵ ca niquinmaca: ȳ nescaliliztli: yn iuhqui onimoscallitzino:²⁶ yn yeilhuitica çan no yuhqui ma moscallican: y notlachihualhuan—

Tlapitzalos. mocalaquis xp̄o: oc çe puerta ayocmo motlecahuis ylh̄.c niman motlapichilliz Sn. mig.l =

1o Angel = v Ximoscallican yn anyolque: Ca ytencopatzico: yn D.s xicCuiCan yn amonaCayo—

Oc çepa motlaPichiliz S.n miguel y canin yesque mimicque quinmotzatzililiz—

2o Angel = v Surgite mortui benite a yudiçio: ximosCallican yn anmimicque: xihualquisacan: yn tlalan ancate xicCuiCan yn amonacayo: Ca ytenCopatz.co yn tt.o D.s

Ni[can²⁷ h]ualquisasque yn mimicque: nacateme²⁸ [7r] oc çepa motlaPichiliz San miguel—

---

23. ylh̄.cuicatenpa: read *ilhuicatenpan*.
24. xiquinmixitilli: originally read *xiquinmexitilli*.
25. The superscript characters are in a slightly different hand.
26. onimoscallitzino: standard *oninozcalitzino*.
27. Torn corner; text in brackets may be all that is missing.
28. nacateme: while *nacatzonteme* suggests itself as a written possibility (see 1 verso above), it is not a logical choice given the context.

LUCÍA: Yes, it is you whom we are awaiting, O my deity, O my ruler. Pardon us our sins.

ANTICHRIST: Yes, I will help you. Do you not know that I am all-powerful in the world?

(Christus factus est[16] is raised in song. Heaven opens. Christ enters. He leads forth Saint Michael, who brings scales. And Christ brings forth a cross. He stands at the edge of heaven. And the Antichrist rushes in. Things explode.)

CHRIST: Come, my war leader, Saint Michael. Here in heaven it is now high time that I bring time to an end, that I destroy it. It is called Final Judgment, the day of judging people. As I set down in my sacred commands, I will sweep things, I will purify heaven and earth. The people of earth, the living and the dead, have greatly dirtied things because of their bad lives. And now, awaken them, the living and the dead, the good and the bad. And to the good ones I will give their heavenly flowery riches, heavenly jades and garments, heavenly palm fronds. But as for the bad, may they be certain that the house of the place of the dead and the sufferings of the place of the dead will become their possessions, [6v] because they were not able to keep my sacred commands.

(Christ descends; [also] Saint Michael. Christ sits down.)

CHRIST: I have already given you orders as to what you will do, my war leader.

SAINT MICHAEL: Very well, O my beloved teacher. Let the dead come to life, let the living rouse themselves. Let them take their bones and collect them, and let them take on their earth, their clay.[17] Give them reviving, [through] the Holy Spirit, along with their souls, so that they will be able to answer you, so that they will say what they did that was good and what they did that was bad, their deeds.

CHRIST: Through my power they will revive, they will come to life. I give them reviving, as I revived on the third day. In just the same way let my creations revive.

(Wind instruments are played. Christ exits by another door; he will no longer ascend to heaven. Then Saint Michael plays a wind instrument.)

FIRST ANGEL: Rouse yourselves, you living ones! By order of God take your bodies.

(Saint Michael again plays a wind instrument. He cries out to the dead where they will be.)

SECOND ANGEL: Surgite mortui venite ad judicium.[18] Revive, you dead ones! Come out, you who are underground! Take your bodies, by order of our lord God!

(Here enter the dead, fully fleshed.[19] [7r] Saint Michael again plays a wind instrument.)

---

16. *Christus factus est*: short for *Christus factus est pro nobis obediens usque ad mortem* (Christ became for us obedient even unto death). Antiphon sung on Holy Thursday, Good Friday, and Holy Saturday in the reformed breviary (see *Breviarium romanum* 1961, 1:837, 842, 859, 861, 873).

17. earth, clay: a standard diphrase (often found in testaments) that means "earthly body/bodies."

18. Surgite mortui venite ad judicium: Arise, O dead, and come to judgment. Apparently not a biblical passage; provenience unknown. This passage is inscribed on a relief sculpture of the Final Judgment at San Andrés Calpan, Puebla.

19. Tentative translation of *nacateme*.

Sⁿ. Miguel = v yn axcan Ca ye ᵒanmosCallique: ma ximosentlallican ca axcan anquichihuasque Cuenta: yn ixpantz.ᶜᵒ yn momelahuacatetlatzontequililiani Jues: macayac motlapololtiz xicmochialican: yn amoteotzin yn amoteyocoxcatzin D.ˢ = Tlapitzalos mocalaquis S.ⁿ mig:ˡ hualquisas antexp̄ᵒ quincacayahuaquiuh yn yolque yhuan mimicque: achi huecauh hualmoquixtiz xp̄.ᵗᵒ—

Antexp̄ᵒ = v Ca ye onihuala ma xicneltillican: ȳ notlaçotlatolltzin²⁹ = Mehuas te deū laudamos calactehuas antexp̄ᵒ: tlaCueponiz. niman hualmoquixtiz xp̄ᵒ: hualahuitiasque ᵒ1 Angel y ᵒ2 Angel: motlayacanilliz S.ⁿ miguel—

xp̄.ᵗᵒ = v xihualmohuica yn tehuatzin: yn ylh̄.ᶜ tiepyollotzintli ȳ tiSan mig.ˡ arcangel: ma xiquinmonochilli: yn yolque yhuan yn mimicque: oCatCa ma niCan nixpan: moçentlalican: ynic niquinchihuilliz Cuenta <u>yn oc onenque ȳ tlp̄c̄</u> =

S.ⁿ mig.ˡ = v ma yuh quimochihua: notlaçotemachticatzine: ma niquintzatzilli =— Motlapichilliz S.ⁿ mig:ˡ niman çeçenyacan yasque yn ixpantz.ᶜᵒ ȳ xp̄ᵒ: motlalitzinos auh yn angel tlapexohuis motlanquaquetzas primero micqui—

xp̄ᵒ: v xihualauh yn tehuatl: Cuix oticchiuh y notenahuatiltzin [7v] yn oc tlp̄c̄. otinemia: otipapatlātinenca: ma xitlato xinechnanquilli: yn iuhqui otitlatohuaya: yn tlp̄c̄: San no yuhqui xitlato yn axcan—

ᵒ1 micqui = v noteotzine notlatocatzine: Ca onicchiuh onictequipano: onicneltilli ȳ moteotenahuatiltzin: Ca onicchiuh ȳ motlanahuatiltzin: ma xicmotlatlanilli y noangeltzin: notlaçotemachtiCatzine—

xp̄ᵒ = v Otinechmocnelili: ca ylh̄.ᶜ timoçentlamachtiz timoCuiltonos yn aic tlamiz tzonquisas: yn mopapaquilliz—

quimoteochihuilliz: conmotopehuiliz yn S.ⁿ miguel ymayecācopatz.ᶜᵒ yn xp̄ᵒ—

xp̄ᵒ = v xihualauh yn tehuatl: yn tiyolqui aquin oticmahuistilli yn tlp̄c̄: yhuan aquin otictlaçotlaya—

ᵒ1 yolqui = v Ca tehuatzin yn tinoteotzin: yn tinotlatocatzin—

xp̄ᵒ = v Yntla nelli nimoteouh: nimotlatocauh Cuix oticchiuh ȳ noteotenahuatiltzin: Cuix oticneltilli—

ᵒ1 yolqui = v Camo onicchiuh noteotzine: ma xinechmotlapopolhuililitzino ȳ nitlatlacohuani—

xp̄ᵒ = v yn axcan Ca niman ayocmo ōca ᵗᵉtlapopol<u>huiliztli xiyauh</u>—

Conmotopehuilliᶻ yn S.ⁿ mig:ˡ yn yolqui oc çentlapal niman³⁰ motlaCuaquetzas 2 micqui yxpantz.ᶜᵒ yn xp̄ᵒ =

xp̄ᵒ = v xihualauh yn tehuatl: yn timicqui otiCatca: Catli yn oticchiuh yn oᶜ tlp̄c̄.tzᶜᵒ: otinenca: Cuix otinechtequipano Cuix otinechtlayeColti yn tlp̄c̄ <u>ma xinechnanquilli</u> = [8r]

2ᵒ micqui = v Ca niman amotzin: ma xinechmotlapopolhuililitzino: notlatocatzine: notemachticatzine Diose—

xp̄ᵒ = v yn axcan Cayocmo onca yn ipan yn tetlatzontequililiztli: cayocmo onca yn tetlapopolhuililiztli: xiyauh—

Conmotopehuilliz San mig:ˡ ȳ micqui auh yn demonios contilanasque quinmanasque. oc çentlapal motlāquaquetzas 2 yolqui Luçia—

---

29. notlaçotlatolltzin: read *notlaçotlatoltzin*.
30. Something illegible follows in superscript.

SAINT MICHAEL: Now you have revived. Gather together. Now you will make an accounting before the just sentencer of people, the judge. Let no one be confused. Wait for your deity, your creator, God.
(Wind instruments are played. Saint Michael exits. The Antichrist enters. He comes jeering at the living and the dead. In a little while Christ enters.)
ANTICHRIST: Now I have come. Fulfill my precious words.
(The Te deum laudamus[20] is raised [in song]. The Antichrist rushes in. Things explode. Then Christ enters. First Angel and Second Angel enter. Saint Michael leads the way.)
CHRIST: Come, you heavenly pearl, Saint Michael the Archangel! Summon the living and those who were dead. Let them gather together here before me so that I will make an accounting of them, of when they still lived on earth.
SAINT MICHAEL: May it so be done, O my beloved teacher. Let me cry out to them.
(Saint Michael plays a wind instrument. Then they each go before Christ. He sits down. And the angel weighs things on a scale. First Dead Person kneels.)
CHRIST: Come, you! Did you carry out my commands [7v] while you were still living on earth, you were flitting about? Speak. Answer me, the way that you used to speak on earth. Speak in the same way now.
FIRST DEAD PERSON: O my deity, O my ruler, I carried out, I worked at, I fulfilled your sacred commands. I carried out your orders. Ask my [guardian] angel, O my beloved teacher.
CHRIST: Thank you. In heaven you will be utterly happy, you will prosper. Your joyfulness will never be finished or come to an end.
(He blesses him. Saint Michael pushes him to Christ's right-hand side.)
CHRIST: Come, you living one. Whom did you honor on earth, and whom did you love?
FIRST LIVING PERSON: You, you who are my deity, you who are my ruler.
CHRIST: If it is true that I am your deity, I am your ruler, did you carry out my sacred commands? Did you fulfill them?
FIRST LIVING PERSON: I did not do it, O my deity. Pardon me. I am a sinner.

CHRIST: Today there no longer is any pardon at all. Go!
(Saint Michael pushes [First] Living Person to the other side. Then Second Dead Person kneels before Christ.)
CHRIST: Come, you who were dead. What did you do while you still lived on earth? Did you work for me? Did you serve me on earth? Answer me! [8r]

SECOND DEAD PERSON: Not at all. Pardon me, O my ruler, O my teacher, O God!

CHRIST: Today in the time of judgment there is no longer any pardon. Go!

(Saint Michael pushes [Second] Dead Person away. And the demons drag him off. They lay him on the other side. Second Living Person, Lucía, kneels.)

---

20. *Te deum laudamus:* "'We praise you as God.' This is the famous hymn simply known as Te deum. It was used in ceremonies of thanksgiving" (personal communication, Stafford Poole, C.M.).

x͞p.^to = v xihualauh yn tiyolqui Cuix otícchiuh y noteotenahuatiltzin: yn matlactetl: Cuix otiquintlaçotlac yn mohuanpohuā yhuan y motatzin yn monantzin—

^o2 yolqui Luçia Ca quemacatzin ca oc achtopa tehuatzin: yn tinoteotzin tinotlatocatzin: onimitznotlaçotilli: ca çatepan y notatzin y nonātzin—

x͞p.^to = v yntla nelli nimoteouh yhuan otinechtlaçotlac: achtopan çatepan yn motatzin yn monantzin: Cuix oticchiuh y notenahuatiltzin: yhuan yn itenahuatiltzin: y notlaçomahuiznantzi yn ipan chicontetl: S.^to SaCram̄.^to teoyotica nenamictilliztli: Cuix teoyotica otimopix: ynic otine yn tl͞p͞c: catli yn otiqui^xnexti =

Luçia = v Ca hamotzin Camo onimitznotequipanilhuitzino: yhuan amo honicmiximachilli:[31] yn motlaçonantzin: ma xinechmotlapopolhuililitzino: noteotzin notlatocatzin—

x͞p͞o = v Yn axcan Canel ayc totechcacopa otlato: yn moyollo yn tl͞p^c: yn san yehuatl: yn mahuilnemilliz: otictequipanohuaya - ma xiyauh ma xicchihua: aço hoquitla[32] tiquilcahua: yn mahuilnemilliz: ma xictequipano: ma yuh ye yn moyollo: Catle ic timotemachiz: yn ylh̄.^c omotlahueliltic yn axcā [8v] yn aic oticnec otimonamicti: yn tl͞p͞c. Ca otictlan yn mictlan calli: momasehual omochiuh: ma xiyauh ma xiquimita: yn aquiquen otiquintlayecolti: camo nimitzyximati =
Conmotopehuilliz ynhuicopa yn Demonios =

x͞p͞o[33] = v xihualauh yn tehuatl: yn tiyolqui oticatca yn tl͞p͞c: Tlein huel omitzyolcocohuaya: Cuix yehuatl y noteotlatoltzin: Cuix otinechtzatzilitinenca: ȳ mocochia ȳ monenemia =

^o3 yolqui = v Ca niman ayc onimitznolcahuilli: y notlaCuayan ȳ natlian: y nonenemiyan: yhua nocochia: notlaçotemachticatzine:—

x͞p͞o = V Ca hotinechmocnelili: notlachihualtzine: ca çā no yuhqui yn nehuatl: ca semicac onimitzylnamictinenca: auh ca nimitzpialitica: yn moxochicoscauh =
Conmotopehuilliz S.^n mig.^l yntlan yn qualtin =

x͞p͞o = v xihualhuian: yn mictlan anchaneque: ma xiquinhuicacan: yn amotetlayecolticahuan: yn sentlani mictlan: auh ȳ çihuantlahueliloc: ma onpa xichuicaca: yn itec—yn tletemascalli onpa xictoneuhcapolocan—

^o2 Dem^o: v tt^oE: otitechmocnellillitzino: Ca ye yuh ca yn toyollo: Ca san oticchixticnemi[34]: yn mohuanlalilitzin: otomasehualtic otlaçotlacauhqui: yn motlaçoyollotzin: ma tiquintomasehuican: yn motlachihualtzitzinhuan = Ma xoconCuitihuetzin: yn tletepozmecatl: yhuan yn tletepoztopinlli:[35] yc tiquinhuitequisque: yhuan xicmolhuilli: yn totlatocatzi[9r]catzin[36]: Lusifer ca ye onpa tiquinhuica: yntetlayecolticatzitzinhuā ma yçiuhcan quihualmotitlanilli: yn tletepostzatzastli: yn ocan tiquinhuicasque: yn itetlayecolticatzitzinhuan—

Calaquis Satanas: canatiuh tletepostzatzastli: =

---

31. honicmiximachilli: standard *onicniximachili*.
32. hoquitla: read *oc itla*.
33. It appears that someone first wrote *yolqui*, crossed it out, and then put an *x* before the *y*, changed the *y* to *p* and added an overbar, with the intent of creating the *x͞p͞o* we show in this transcription.
34. oticchixticnemi: perhaps to be read as either *oticchixtinenque* or *ticchixtinemi*.
35. tletepoztopinlli: read *tletepoztopilli*.
36. totlatocatzicatzin: read *totlatocatzin*.

CHRIST: Come, you who are a living person! Did you carry out my sacred commands, the ten of them? Did you love your neighbors, and your father and your mother?

SECOND LIVING PERSON, LUCÍA: Yes. It is you, my deity, my ruler, whom I loved first, afterwards my father and my mother.

CHRIST: If it is true that I am your deity and you loved me first and afterward your father and your mother, did you carry out my commands, and the command of my beloved honored mother, in the seventh sacrament, marrying in a sacred way? Did you guard yourself in a sacred way[21] when you lived on earth? What have you accomplished?

LUCÍA: No. I did not work for you and I did not recognize your beloved mother. Pardon me, O my deity, O my ruler!

CHRIST: Now, truly your heart never spoke to us on earth. It was only your lustful living that you used to work at. Go, do it. Perhaps you are forgetting something else of your lustful living. Work at it. Be certain that you may hope for nothing in heaven. How unfortunate you are now, [8v] that you never wanted to get married on earth. You have won the house of the place of the dead. You have merited it. Go! See those whom you served. I do not know you.

(He pushes her toward the demons.)

CHRIST: Come, you who were a living person on earth. What is giving your heart such pain? Is it my sacred word? Did you go about crying out to me when you were sleeping and when you were going about?

THIRD LIVING PERSON: I never ever forgot you, in my eating, in my drinking, in my going about, and in my sleeping, O my beloved teacher.

CHRIST: Thank you, O my creation. It is just the same with me: I always went about remembering you. And I am keeping your flowery necklace for you.

(Saint Michael pushes him among the good ones.)

CHRIST: Come, you residents of the place of the dead. Take your servants to the depths of the place of the dead. And the wicked woman, take her into the sweatbath of fire. Torment her miserably there!

SECOND DEMON: O our lord, we thank you. We are certain that we have just been going about waiting for your coming. We are fortunate! Your precious heart has been very generous. May we merit your creations. Grab up the fiery chains and the fiery metal staff with which we will beat them and tell our ruler, [9r] Lucifer, that we are taking his servants over there. Let him quickly send the fiery metal warping frame[22] there where we will take his servants.

(Satan enters. He goes along grasping the fiery metal warping frame.)

---

21. That is, practiced chastity.
22. yn tletepoztzatzaztli: see Sahagún 1997, 278.

Satanas = v̱ Ca ye nican niqualhuica mochi ynic tiquimilpizque: ynic amo çe tomac cholotehuas: axcan ye ticpia tauh totlaqual: yn onpa y sentlani mictlan: yn ixquich totlapal oticchiuhque: ynic tomac ohuetzque: yn totetlayecolticahuan =

Mochtin quitosque tt.ᵒE ma xi^{te}chmopalehuilli =

xp̄o = v̱ Ayoquic anmotemachizque: ma yuh ye yn amoyollo: ca semicac amechtoneuhcapollosq̄: yc çenmayan yn onpa y sentlani mictlan—

Oc çepa mochintī quitosq̄: ttᵒE: Diose ma San xitechmomaquixtilli: yn titlacohuanime³⁷ = niman quincalaquisque TlaCueponiz tzatzitasque: auh ȳ qualtin quimaquisque xochicoronaçoyatl: motlecahuis xp̄o: ylh̄.ᶜ nepantla escalera quinmolhuiliztin³⁸—

xp̄o = v̱ NotetlayeColticahuane: ma xihualmotlecahuican: xicmoCuilliqui: ȳ namechpialia yn amonetlamachtil yn ayc tlamis: yn ayc tzonquisas—

Tlapitzalos tlecosque yn angeles ˣp̄ᵒ yhuan yn Cualtin niman quihualquixtizque Luçia: tlepapalome yn ipipilouh: çe cohuatl ycozqui yhuan ςᵉ yc quicuitlal[9v]pisque: hualtzatzitias quinanquilizque Demonios =

ᵒ1 Demᵒ: v̱ xinenemi tlahueliloque: Cuix amo tiquilnamiqui yn tlein oticchiuh yn tlp̄c. axcan timitztlaxtlahuisq̄. yn onpa y sentlani mictlan: xinenemi xitotoca =

Luçia = v̱ omochiuh onoçentzontlahueliltic: ȳ nihueytlatlacohuani: o nomasehual omochiuh yn mictlan calli =

Satanas = v̱ Cuix quin axcan yn titzatzin: yn titlahueliloc axcan timitzpapaquiltisque yn onpa y sentlani mitlan³⁹: axcan timitznamictisq̄. yn onpa yn totecpanchan ypampa yn ayc otimonamitin: yn tlp̄c. xitotoca xine^{ne}mi: Ca mitzhualmochialitica yn totlatocauh Luçifer—

Luçia Ay: Ay: omochiuh onotlahueliltic: ȳ nitlatlacohuani: o nomasehual omochiuh yn mictlan yyohuiliztli:⁴⁰ ma noço camo onitlacatini yn tlp̄c: ay: ay: ma çentelchihualo yn tlp̄ctli: yhuan yn Cahuitl, yn ipan onitlacat: ma no çentelchihualo y nonantzin yn quinin onechiuh: ay. ma sentelchihualo yn chichihualayotl, ynic oninohuapauh: ma no çentelchihualo yn tlein oniCuaya: yhuan yn tlein oniquiya yn tlp̄c: ay ma sentelchihualo yn tlalli yn onictelecçaya: yhua yn tlei tzotzomatli onicnoquentiaya Ca mochi tletl: omecuep.⁴¹ ay. çenca ye nechtlatia: yn ⁿⁱcan nonacaztitech pilcatihuitze: yn tlepapalome: Ca quinescayotia ynic oninoqualnextia[10r]tiaya:⁴² y nopipilol auh ȳ nican noquechtlan teCuixtihuitz: çenca temamauhti tlecohuatl, ca quinescayotia y noquechcozqui onictlaliaya: auh y niCan ic niCuitlalpitihuitz: çenca temamauhti tlecohuatl: yyollo yn mictlan calli: ca yehuatl quinescayotia ynic oninotlamachtiaya yn tlp̄c: ay ay. ma noço onino^{na}mictiani ay. omochiuh onotlahueliltic—

ᵒ1 demᵒ: v̱ axcan mochi tictzacuaz ticyxtlahuas: yn amo tlen ipan otiquimitaya: yn mohuanpohuan yn tlp̄c. = quihuitequisque =

37. titlacohuanime: read *titlatlacohuanime*.
38. quinmolhuiliztin: perhaps *quinmolhuilitzinoz* was meant.
39. mitlan: read *mictlan*.
40. yyohuiliztli: read *tlayhiyohuiliztli*.
41. omecuep: read *omocuep*.
42. oninoqualnextiatiaya: read *oninoqualnextiaya*.

SATAN: I am bringing everything right here with which we will tie them up so that not one will flee from our hands. Now we have our drink and our food, there in the depths of the place of the dead. We exerted all our efforts so that our servants fell into our hands.

(All of them say "O our lord, help us!")

CHRIST: Never again will you be hopeful. Be certain that they will torment you miserably forever, eternally, there in the depths of the place of the dead.

(Again they all say "O our lord, O God, just save us sinners!" Then they make them go in.[23] Things explode. They go crying. And the good ones put on flowery crowns of palm fronds. Christ ascends. In the middle of the ladder he says to them:)

CHRIST: O my servants, come on up! Come and take what I am keeping for you, your riches which will never be finished, which will never come to an end!

(Wind instruments are played. The angels, Christ and the good ones ascend. Then they bring out Lucía. Fire butterflies are her earrings, a snake her necklace, and they tie one around her waist. [9v] She comes crying out. The demons answer her:)

FIRST DEMON: Get moving, O wicked one! Do you not remember what you did on earth? Now we will repay you there in the depths of the place of the dead. Get moving, run along!

LUCÍA: Four hundred times unfortunate am I! I am a great sinner! Oh, I have merited the house of the place of the dead!

SATAN: Not until now do you cry out, you wicked one? Now we will make you joyful there in the depths of the place of the dead. Now we will get you married, there in our palatial home, because you never got married on earth. Run along, get moving! Our ruler, Lucifer, is waiting for you.

LUCÍA: Ah! Ah! How unfortunate I am! I am a sinner. I have merited suffering in the place of the dead. If only I had not been born on earth! Ah! Ah! May the earth be entirely cursed, and the time in which I was born. May my mother who made me also be despised! Ah! May the breast milk with which I was nurtured be despised! May that which I used to eat and that which I used to drink on earth be despised. Ah! May the earth I used to kick be despised, and the rags I used to wear, for they all have turned into fire! Ah! Greatly do they burn me, the fire butterflies that come hanging here from my ears. They signify how I used to beautify myself [10r] with my earrings. And here, wound around my neck, is a very frightening fire serpent. It signifies my necklaces that I used to put on. And here I come girded with a very frightening fire serpent, the heart of the house of the place of the dead. It signifies how I used to enjoy myself on earth. Ah! Ah! If only I had gotten married! Ah! How unfortunate I am!

FIRST DEMON: Now you will pay a penalty, you will make restitution for everything. You had no esteem for your neighbors on earth.

(They beat her.)

---

23. That is, take them offstage.

Sathaz = y xinenemi tlahueliloq̄. Cuix quin axcan yn tiquilnamiqui ma oximonamictiani: quenin amo otiquilnamic yn oc tlp̄c. otinemia: Ca tel axcan mochi tictlaxtlahuas: yn motlahuelilocayo Xitotoca xinenemi = Quihuitequisque Ça ic quicalaquisque: TlaCueponiz. quitlapichilitasque Demonios niman hualquisas teopixqui—

teopixqui = y Notlaçopilhuane x̄p̄tianomeE: D.ˢ ytlachihualtzitzinhuane: Ca ye ohuanquimotillique yn tetzauhtlamahuiçolli: Ca melahuac Ca teoamoxpan yCuiliuhtoc: ma ximimatican ximosCalica ximotesCahuiCan: yn iuhqui ypan omochiuh yn amoanpo auh macamo no yuhqui amopan mochihuas. Ca machiotl: octacatl. techmomaquilia yn tt.º D.ˢ Ca mochihuatiuh yn mostla yn huiptla yn tetlatzonquililizylhuitl:[43] ma çā xicmotlatlauhtilican: yn tt.º Jesu xp̄o: yhuan yn yehua [10v]tzin yn çihuapilli S.ᵗᵃ m.ᵃ ynic quimotlatlauhtiliz yn itlaçomahuiconetzin[44] Jesu xp̄o ynic çatepan anquimomasehuisque anquicnopilhuisque yn ylh̄.ᶜ papaquiliztli: yn gloria ma y mochihua =

Abe maria[45]

---

43. tetlatzonquililizylhuitl: read *tetlatzontequililizylhuitl* (as above).
44. itlaçomahuiconetzin: read *itlaçomahuizconetzin*.
45. Abe maria: in a different hand. This is actually at the bottom of 10v, with approximately three-fourths of the space on the page separating it from the last line of this drama.

SATAN: Get moving, O wicked one! Not until now do you remember that you should have gotten married? How is it that you did not remember it while you were still living on earth? But now you will make restitution for all your wickedness. Run along! Get moving!
(They beat her. Just thus they make her go in. Things explode. The demons play wind instruments. Then Priest enters.)
PRIEST: O my beloved children, O Christians, O creations of God! Now you have seen an ominous marvel! It is correct. It is written in the sacred book. Be prudent! Rouse yourselves, look at yourselves in the mirror, the way that it happened to your neighbor.[24] And may it not happen to you the same way. It is a model, a measuring stick,[25] which our lord God gives us. Tomorrow or the next day, the day of judgment is going to happen. Just pray to our lord, Jesus Christ, and to the [10v] noblewoman, Saint Mary, that she pray to her beloved honored child, Jesus Christ, so that afterward you will merit and obtain joyfulness in heaven, glory. May it so be done.
Ave Maria.[26]

---

24. The implication is that the play is the mirror. What happened to Lucía is what they are supposed to see in the mirror, applied to themselves.
25. model, measuring stick: metaphorical diphrase for example after which one should pattern oneself.
26. *Hail Mary.*

Present Location
Library of Congress
Washington, D.C.

[11r]

tlatolpepechtli:[1]
~~Ma moCenquizcayecteneuhtzinno yn Cenquizmahuiztilli~~[2]

---

v. Ma huel yehuatzin ȳ. cenquizCamahuiztililoni ȳ teotl tlatohuani Dios amotlantzinco quimotlalili ȳ teyollalilitzin[3] ȳ toçihuanpillatoCatepatlatoCatzin yn axCa techmotintilia techmomaquillia ȳ tlaçōmahuiztlaoncoyalizCahuitl ȳ nōhuia çenmañahuac tentimani tlaōCoxtimani y tlaçomahuizCahuitli yn axCa ȳpā tiCate tlaçomahuiztlaCaye Ca niCan aquihualmotepotztoquilia ȳ cenCa Chipāhuac ȳ cēCa tlanextia y nohuia Cenmanahuac yn itlāçonmahuizteoxayaCatzin ytech quiçan y[?]tech meiya y teoyotiCa neÇentlalinliztli ȳ teoyotiCa netlaçontlaliztli yn iuhquin techmonahuatilia y tonāntzin Sancta yCleçia y niCa quimotepehuillia yn iuhqui tlaçochalchihuitl CozCatl y costic yn istac teocuitla.tl yn çenCa penpetlaCa yn inpenpenyocyo yuhqui tlaçoatl: ye chipinniz auh yn tehuantin Ca çan ticnequixtia ticnepollohuan yuhqui xochitli yntla oCuitlahuix[4] tixpā oquiztiquiçan Ayocmo totech moneq̄ auh ynin Cuix çan xochitli y ticnepollo y ᵗⁱᶜnequixtiz y tixpa quimotlalilia yn dios ytlaçonnatzin yn itlaocoyallitzin nepeñchtequiliztiCa necnomachilliztiCa y tixpa quimotlalilia yn itlaocoyallitzin yn inChoquizçotlanhuallitzin: Auh y tehuatin Ca çan ticnequixtia yn itlaçonmahuizyxayotzin niCan tlalᵗⁱᶜpac no ñonquihtoc ypampa y totlatlaCol Auh no çan io y niCa tlal[11v]-tlalticpāc[5] yn onepolliuhCa yhua yn intlaçoezyotzin y totlaçomahuiztemaquixtiCatzi ttᵒ xᵒ yn axCa tēchmom̄aquillia tēchmotintinlia yn itlaçomahuizpaçiōntzin y tinmochitin y titlatlacohuame[6] Auh yn aqui quimotlaçōtlayecoltilli y çenCa mochinpahuaCanemitia y niCa tlalticpac y çenCa quimomahuiztillilia Ca quimomaquilliz yn cenmicactli panpaquilliztli yn iuhqui axCa anquimotinlilizque tlatlaçomahuiztlaCaē[7] ma oC achitzin Cahuitl xonmotlapaCayocaᵗⁱˡⁱ+Ca—
tlapitzaloz hualquiçaz lurenso yhua yçihuauh yhua Agel y nepanᵗˡᵃ moq̄z[8] tlantozque—

---

1. tlatolpepechtli: practice letters to the left and the right.
2. ~~Ma moCenquizcayecteneuhtzinno yn Cenquizmahuiztilli~~: read *ma mocenquizcayecteneuhtzino yn cenquizcamahuiztililoni*.
3. teyollalilitzin: read *iteyollaliliztzin*.
4. oCuitlahuix: read *ocuetlahuix*.
5. tlaltlalticpāc: read *tlalticpac*.
6. titlatlacohuame: read *titlatlacohuanime*.
7. tlatlaçomahuiztlaCaē: read *tlaçomahuiztlacae*.
8. moq̄z: read *moquetzaz*.

How to Live on Earth
Translated by Louise M. Burkhart, with assistance from Barry D. Sell

[11r]

Prologue

~~May he who is utterly honorable be utterly praised~~

v May the one who is utterly honored, the deity, the ruler, God, place among you the consolation of our queenly advocate, the precious and honored time of sadness that she now shows to us, gives to us. The precious and honored time that we are in now swells and spreads sadly through the world everywhere. O beloved honored people, here you attend to the very pure one whose precious and honored sacred countenance greatly illuminates things everywhere in the world. From it comes out, from it flows, the meeting together in a sacred way, the loving of one another in a sacred way,[1] as our mother holy church commands us. Here she scatters them as if they were precious jades, jewels, gold and silver, their pendants shimmering greatly like precious water about to drip. But we, we just waste them and squander them, as if they were flowers that have withered, that have fled from before us, that are no longer necessary for us. So then, is it just flowers that we squander and waste? God's beloved mother places before us her sadness. Reverently, humbly she places before us her sadness, her weeping swoon. But as for us, we just waste her precious and honored tears, which here on earth lie flowing on account of our sins. And likewise here on earth [11v] the precious blood of our beloved honored savior, our lord Christ, has been wasted. Today he gives and shows to all of us sinners his precious and honored passion. And to whomever serves him lovingly, lives very purely here on earth, honors him very much, he will give eternal joyfulness, as you will see today. O beloved honored people, be patient for a little while.

(Wind instruments are played. Lorenzo enters, along with his wife and an angel who stands in the middle. They speak.)

---

1. See Lorenzo's speech, below.

Lureso y tla xihualmohuiCa notlançonāmictzinne tlaçonçihuapille yn axca huel nictequipachoz ȳ motlaçonyollotzin ȳtechcacopā ȳnic titonemitizque ȳn itlalticpactzinco ȳn ontechmochihuilli ȳ totechiuhcatzin y dios Ca ye Cuel yzquilhuitl ȳn otechmoçentililitzinno ȳ tt⁰ dios huel yc notequipachohua⁹ y niquilnamiqui y tle ticchihuazque yn axCa Cuix çan yehuatl y toaxCa y totlatqui y tictequinpanozque¹⁰ ȳ tictoCuitlahuizqᵉ ynic tlapihuiyaz ynic miyequi yaz maCamo yehuatl tictoCuitlahuica ma ça yehuātzin ȳ tt⁰ dios ytetzinco titopiloCa ynic techmomaquilliz y neyollaliliztli yn chicahualiztli ma momoztlaye tiCalaquiCa yn ichantzinco ma tictotlatlauhtiliCa y dios ytlaçonātzin Ca yehuatzin topanpa quimotlatlauhtiliz yn itlaçoconetzin Auh ȳ toaxCa y totlatqui ytlanel oyezquiȳa Cuix yehuatl tictlatlauhtizque Auh āC oquichiuh aqui OquiyoCox Cuix amo yehuatzin y dios yn iuhqui tehuatin ontechmochihuilli y niCa tlalticpac auh yn axCa yn tochan ·y tocallitic maCamo çeCa techteq̄pachoz Ca çan quezquilhuitzintli onCa tocotochiēlizque [12r] y dios yc tomotlatequipānilhuiz¹¹ ticmotlachpānililiz timotlaCuiCuilliz ynic oCa moquixtia ȳ çençenyohual çençemilhuitl techmomaquillia yn iteyollalilitzin ȳ dios maCamo ticmolcahuiliz yn ixquich onimitztenehuili ynic tictotequipanilhuizque y dios notlaçonnāmictzinne—

Çihuatl y notlaçonamictzin ynon ticmotenehuilia Ca çenCa mahuiztic ȳ motlatoltzin yc ninoyollalia y niCaqui ma yuhqui quimonequiltitzinno ȳ dios Ca mochi yc paCaçenlia¹² y quexquich ticmonequiltintzinnoz Ca mochi mochihuaz y motlatoltzin Ca nocochixtica—

Lureso y notlaçonamictzinne ÇeCa nictlaçocamati ȳ motlatoltzin y nicaqui y motemahuiztililiztlatoltzin ma mochipa yuhqui quimonequiltitzinno ȳ dios ynic techmomaquiltzinnoz¹³ yn iteyollalilitzin yn igrāçiatzin yⁿⁱc teOyotiCa netlaçotlaliztiCa titonemiltizque Auh yn axᶜᵃ ma Oc tictotlatlauhtillitin yn itlaçoñatzin dios ȳpampa yn otechmoCahuiltehuaque y tonātzin ȳ totatzin y capā quimotlalilia y dios Cuix Otiquimonitaque Cuix yuhqui ȳ telpilloa Caten tiquimonitatihui tiquitlapalotihui tiquimotlamaCatihui Ca nelli anyocmo tiquimitazque tiquinotzazque y tt⁰ dios¹⁴ ma Otiquimitani ma otechnotzani ma otechylhuiyani tle yc quimotlatzaCuiltilia y dios Cuix ytla quitehuiquilia y niCa tlalticpac ma ypapa Otiquixtlahuani y tlatquitli y teoCuitlatl yn iztac [?] ȳy coStic tlaçotli chalchihuitl Ca ça niCā tlami tlalticpac Auh yn iteycnoytanlitzin y dios y tlapaCayihiyohuiliztli y necnomachiliztli yn itlaçotlalloCa y tohuapohua Ca yehuatl tochimal yn ixpatzinco ȳ dios notlaçoñamictzinne ma oc tihuiya—[12v]

---

9. notequipachohua: standard *ninotequipachohua* as in the second version of the play.
10. tictequinpanozque: read *tictequipanozque*.
11. tomotlatequipānilhuiz: read *ticmotlatequipanilhuiz* as in the second version of this play.
12. yc paCaçenlia: read *nicpaccacelia* as in the second version of this play.
13. techmomaquiltzinnoz: read *techmomaquilitzinoz* as in the second version of this play.
14. tt⁰ dios: tt.⁰e d.e in the second version of this play.

LORENZO: Do come, O my beloved spouse, O beloved noblewoman! Now I shall greatly worry your precious heart in regard to how we will live on the earth of him who made us, our maker, God. Some days ago our lord God joined us together [in marriage]. It worries me greatly when I think about what we will do now. Will we just work for and occupy ourselves with our possessions, our goods, so that they will increase, so that they will become many? Let us not occupy ourselves with that. Let us rely on our lord God to give us consolation and health. Let us enter his home every day. Let us pray to God's beloved mother that for our sake she pray to her beloved child. And as for our possessions, our goods, if truly there should be any, are we to pray for them? And who made them, who created them? Was it not God, just as he made us here on earth? And now, in our home, in our house, let it not worry us very much, for it is just for a few days that we will await God there. [12r] You will work, you will sweep, you will tidy up, so that the consolation God gives us issues therefrom every night and every day. Do not forget all that I have declared to you, so that we will work for God, O my beloved spouse.

WOMAN: O my beloved spouse, those words of yours that you declare are very admirable. I am consoled by what I hear. May God wish it so. I receive it all joyfully, whatever you will want. Your words will all be carried out. I am awaiting them.

LORENZO: O my beloved spouse, I am very grateful for your words. I hear your respectful words. May God always wish it so, so that he will give us his consolation, his grace, so that with loving each other in a sacred way we will live. And now let us pray still to God's beloved mother on behalf of those who have left us behind, our mother, our father.[2] Where God places them, have we visited them? Is it as if they are in prison, [where] we are going to visit them, we are going to greet them, we are going to give them things? It is true that we will see them and call to them no longer. Our lord God,[3] if only we had seen them, if only they had called to us, if only they had told us why God punishes them. Do they owe something to someone here on earth? If only we had for their sake repaid the goods, the silver and gold, precious things, jades, for here on earth they come to an end. But the pity of God, patience, humility, loving of our neighbors, those are our shield before God. O my beloved spouse, let us go. [12v]

2. mother, father: in variant order, this common diphrase often means "parent."
3. In the second version of the play both terms are in the vocative: O our Lord, O God.

Cihuatl y Ma mochihua y motlanahuatiltzin ma tiCallaquiCa ȳn ichatzinco ȳ dios ma tictotlatlauhtilitin yⁿ ipā yn ānimaz y Capa quimoyeyamaquillitzinnohua y dios ma quimotlanextililitzinno ȳhua y tehuati ma techmomaquiliz yn itechiCahualitzin yhua yn ixquich totech monequiz y tiquazque yn tiquizque ynic ticchiCahuazque y totlallo y toçonquiyo ma tictintlanililitin[15] y dios notlançoñamictzin[16]— Auh nima yazque y teopa quimotlatlauhtilizque y dios tlapitzaloz[17] itlaçonatzin quiyaCatiaz y Agel auh ytla oÇique[18] teopaCalteco Calaquizque yn agel OnoCa moCahuaz teopaCalteco tlatoz—

1º Agel y dios ytlachihualtzintzinhuane ma huel ximochiCahuaca maCamo amexiCoz y mictla tzintzinmitli maCamo amechCotoⁿiliz yn ilhicac tlaçomeCatl ȳ çencam pēnpetlaCa y teOmatzantzaztli yniC oAnmechnomaylpillitzinno yn ātle quinenehuiliz y niCa tlalticpaᶜ yn iuhqui yc tlaçotli yniC amilpitinCate ylhcac hualehuatinCac maCamo Aquitlacozque ma huel xicmahuiztinliCa Ca yc amomaquixtizqᵉ yn ixpatzinCo y dios yhua ytetzinco ximopilloCa ximotzantzinliCa Ca yehuatzin amechmopalehuilliz yhua Ca niCa niCa Amotlatzinco ninemiz amo namechnoCahuiliz maCamo aquitlaCoz yn iuhqui Oanahuatiloque Ca ye niCa huitz yn amoyauh ȳ tlaCatecolotl yn amechyaochihuaquiuh Ca huel yehuatl ynic motlahuelpolohua amotechCacopa—

1º demº y y tiAgel yn ayc tinechCahuaz ytlan ipac tinemiz y tlalticpac tlaCa.ça tehuatl ticxixinia ȳ [13r] notzohuaz y notlatequipanoliz y notetlayecoltiCahua tinechyCuilhuillia Auh ye amo mitzylnamiqui Ayc mitzatzalia[19] Ayc mitztenehua ytla nehuatl yuhqui on ACa nechonpohua Auh tle niquimilhuizquia yn itla ninemizquia yn in ātle yc nechtlaçotla Cuix amo ça niquiCahuazquia Cuix notequihua[20] Amo tiquiCahua y tehuatl y tiAgel xinechiCahuilli y nōtetlayecoltiCahua—

1º Agel y y tehuatl y timictlatletzintzimitl ȳ timictlacohuatl yn ayc tlamiz y moztlac y motēquallac yn ipa ticnōnoquitinemi ytlamaquixtiltzintzinhua y notechiuhCatzin dios ynon tictenehua yn amo netzatzinlia yn amo nechylnamiqui Ca tehuatl tiquiCahualtia. yn āmo quilnāmiquin ȳn aqui ypāpa tlaOcoxtinemi ChoCatinemi ma xiquiCahua—

---

15. tictintlanililitin: read *tictotlanililitin*.
16. In the second version of this play it is (incorrectly) in the male vocative: notlaçonamictzinem.
17. tlapitzaloz: added later in the left margin in a different hand.
18. oÇique: read *acique*.
19. mitzatzalia: read *mitztzatzilia*.
20. notequihua: read *notequiuh*.

WOMAN: Let your command be carried out. Let us go into God's home. Let us pray for their souls, where[ver] God has placed them. May he illuminate them. And as for us, may he give us his health and all that is necessary for us, that which we will eat, that which we will drink, so that we will strengthen our earth, our clay.[4] Let us ask God for it, O my beloved spouse.[5]

(And then they go to the church. They pray to God's beloved mother. Wind instruments are played. The angel leads them. And when they reach the entrance of the church they go in. The angel remains there at the entrance of the church. He speaks.)

FIRST ANGEL: O creations of God, strengthen yourselves well! May the Tzitzimitl[6] of the place of the dead not deceive you! May he not cut the precious cord of heaven on you! Greatly does it shimmer, the sacred ring with which he tied your hands together. Nothing here on earth will equal in preciousness that with which you are tied together; it comes from heaven. Do not ruin it! Honor it well, for with it you will be rescued before God. And importune him, cry out to him, for he will help you. And I am here. I will live with you; I will not abandon you. Do not ruin it, as you were commanded. Here comes your enemy, the demon. He is coming to make war on you. He is lost in anger against you.

FIRST DEMON: You angel, you never will leave me. You will stay with the people of earth. You just tear down [13r] my snares, my work. You take my servants from me. But now they do not remember you, they never cry out to you, they never mention you. If it were me, would someone consider me like that? And what would I have said to them with whom I would have lived, who love me for nothing? Would I not just have abandoned them? Is it my business? You do not leave them, you angel. Leave me my servants!

FIRST ANGEL: You fire Tzitzimitl of the place of the dead, you serpent of the place of the dead, your drivel, your slaver[7] will never end. You go around spilling them all over those whom my maker, God, has saved. You declare that they do not cry out to me, that they do not remember me. It is you who makes them leave him. They do not remember the one who for their sake goes about sad, goes about weeping. Leave them!

---

4. earth, clay: here and below, a standard diphrase often found in testaments referring to the body.
5. In the second version of this play it is (incorrectly) in the male vocative.
6. In pre-Columbian religion, the Tzitzimime were monstrous female or androgynous numens of the western sky, the twilight, and world destruction. They came to be equated with devils.
7. drivel, slaver: this common diphrase means "lies, falsehoods."

1º demº v queni niquiCahuaz y tiAgel xihuanlauh xiCaqui y yehuati Ahuel nechoCahua achito Cahuitl. ȳtla ytlaquaya nechtzatzinlia ynic melçimazque ytla ycochia Amo quilnamiqui y Cruz yē nechtzatzinlia y manel y çan ~~qui~~ amo quitzatzinlia y dios. ça huel ye nehuatl ȳCamac niCa ytla mehuaz[21] ytla tlacuazque ytla no çen ȳconeuh oqui[13v]quallani yçiuhCa nechmaCatihuetzin ytla noço ontliCa moteCuinizque Amo quitzatzinlia y dios çannoC[22] achi motlahuelpollotihuiuh Auh y nehuatl.[23] oC achi yCa nināhuiltia yCa nihuehuentzCan yhua miyectlamantli ypā nicchihua y xolopinli yn amo mozCalilia queni niquiCahuaz ytla yehuatin amo nechoCahuazquina ȳ tiquintohua niquiCahuaz ytla yehuatin amo nechopolozquin—

1º Agel v Auh tla xinechylhui tlen iC otihualla y niCan tlateochihuallalpā yCaltepatzinco y Jerosalle Cuix ticmati mochi titlatlacohuanime y niCa ohualCalque[24] Ca quimopalehuilitzinnoz y dios y mohuiCacopan—

1º Dem̃oº v queni mopalehuizque y tiAgel huel xicmati ynic onihualla y niCa Onhuallaque ȳ çan ic millacatzotinemi yn itlahuel motlahuelpollotinemi tlahuelmictinemin momoztlaē y manel hualhui teopa Ca çan itech yetihuitz yn iqualla yn ihuetzquiz yn inepolliz[25] yn imatlamachilliz yn ihuēCapaniliz yn itepanahuiltoquiliz yn icnotlaCa yCa motopeuhtehua [14r] Amo quiyehuayta y manel tle ȳlhuillo ȳ niCa amo quiyehuaCaqui yn intemachtiCahua cānmo yehuatl i yn inemiliz y tlalticpac tlaCa—

1º Agel v Oyhitlahuelliltic ȳ tlalticpāc tlaCa ac tehuatl yn amo titlaOcoya tla ˣⁱᶜCaqui y monepohualiz yn ātle ypa tiq̄ta yn itlatoltzin y motechiuhCatzin dios yn āyc tichoCa yn āyc titlaOCoya onmoçentzontlahuelliltic ȳ çan tihuallanequixtia tihuallanepollo yCa ychātzin[26] y moteotzin y motlatoCātzi dios xiquitta xitlachia xitlaCaquin—
tlapitza[27] OCa hualquiztihuetzizque Çen Cihuatzintli quihualhuillatiaz yn iConeuh quihuiCaznequi y teopā ça quimictitehuaz yñ inatzin[28]

Çihuatzitli v xihualauh Cuix amo Onimitztitla ȳ teopa tiCaquitiuh ȳ Salue yhua ticpohuatiuh yñ itlacorosanriotzin[29] ȳ[14v]ȳ çihuapilli Santa maria Cuix onimitztitla ~~ti~~timaānhuiltiz y tixolopintli xinenemi niCa xitotoca—
quixtlatlatzinnitehuaz yn inātzī y piltotli yatehuaz—

piltotli v Xinechcahua diablo amo nimotequiuh ytla nimitztzonanaz diablo mitzhuicaz Cuix oc motequiuh ye otinechyzcazti[30] ye nihuey[31]

---

21. mehuaz: read *mehuazque*.
22. çannoC: read *çan oc*.
23. nehuatl: in the second version of this play y[e]huatl.
24. ohualCalque: read *ohualcalaque*.
25. inepolliz: read *inepohualiz* as in the second version of this play.
26. Yca ychātzin: read *nican ychantzinco* as in the second version of this play.
27. tlapitza: in a different hand.
28. Following this in the second version of this play: quixtlantlatzinintehuaz.
29. itlacorosanriotzin: read *itlaçorosariotzin*.
30. otinechyzcazti: read *otinechyzcalti*.
31. Added in superscript in the second version of this play: izca yn icolinechhuapauh.

FIRST DEMON: How am I to leave them? You angel, come here. Listen. It is they who are unable to leave me for a moment. If it is their time of eating they call out to me, so that they will choke. If it is their time of sleeping they do not remember the cross. They cry out to me, even though they do not cry out to God; it is really I who am in their mouths. If they are getting up, if they are eating, or if one of their children makes them angry, [13v] immediately they give it to me. Or if they stumble on the road they do not cry out to God. They just become still more lost in anger. And as for me, I make fun of them still more. I laugh heartily at them and I do many things to the fools, who do not catch on. How am I to leave them if they will not leave me?[8] You say that I am to leave them if they will not overcome me?[9]

FIRST ANGEL: But do tell me why you have come here to the blessed place, the entrance of Jerusalem. Do you know that all the sinners who have entered here God will help against you?

FIRST DEMON: How are they to help themselves? You angel, know well what I have come here for. They who have come here just go about wrapped up in their anger, they go about lost in anger, they go about dying of anger. Every day even though they come to church they just bring along their rage, their laughter, their pride, their presumption, their exaltation, their sense of superiority. The poor people just go off making fun of it [that is, what happens at church]. [14r] They do not esteem it, even though something is said to them. They do not pay attention to their teachers. This is not the [proper] life of the people of earth.

FIRST ANGEL: Oh how unfortunate are the people of earth! Who are you who are not saddened? Do hear your pride! You consider as nothing the words of your maker, God. You never weep, you never feel sad. Four hundred times[10] unfortunate are you! You just waste things, you just squander things here in the home of your deity, your ruler, God. See! Look! Listen!
(Wind instruments are played. Then a woman rushes there dragging her child whom she wants to take in the church. His mother just beats him up.)[11]

WOMAN: Come! Didn't I send you to the church? We are going to hear the Salve[12] and you are going to count the precious rosary of the [14v] noblewoman, Saint Mary. Did I send you to play, you fool? Move along here. Run along.
(His mother quickly slaps his face. Little Child goes forward.)

LITTLE CHILD: Leave me, devil! I am not your business. If I seize you by the hair the devil will take you. Is it still your business? You have already raised me. I am big now.[13]

---

8. The second version of this play reads: How am I to leave them if they do not want to leave me?
9. Tentative translation. The pragmatic thrust seems to be that the demon would leave only if they overcome him or drive him away. The second version of this play reads: You say that I will leave them if they do not want to overcome me?
10. Four hundred times: here and below, *four hundred* is a common idiom in the vigesimally based traditional counting system for "countless, innumerable."
11. The second version of this play adds: *She slaps his face.*
12. Salve Regina: Hail [Holy] Queen. A popular Catholic prayer.
13. Some text in superscript (*izca yn icolinechhuapauh*) follows in the second version of this play.

Çihuatẑtli y ma mitzmoyollali y dios y tinoconeuh maCamo moztla huiptla mopampa nechmotelchihuilitzinnoz y dios Ca ye yc ninoquixtia yn ixpatzinco Ca ye niyauh mopanpa nicnotlatlauhtilitiuh y dios—

Calaquiz y teopa ȳ çihuatzintli

1⁰ Demō⁰ y tla xiq̄ta y tiAg^el moyollo Opachiuh ^mixipā oquiz ȳ piltotli yn atle ypa quita ynātzin yxquich teto³² Auh ye huel atle ypa tlachia auh tiquitohua niquinCahuaz amo ytla ninemiz Cuix amo ticmati Ca huel ypiltia ȳ yehua yn amo nechCahuaznequi huel niq.pactia yn iquac amo nechtenehua amo pactiCate yñotlacoycnihua³³ [15r]

1⁰ agle y·Ca yCa yn itlatoCahuelitzin y ÇenmiCac moetztiCa yn Jesu x̄o ca timiquaniz y timictla miztli y titequani yn ayc tipachihui yn ayc tixhui ma xiCuitlaxitini Ca ypampa ontihuala monexiColiztiCa ynic tiquita quimotlaçotlayeColtilia ȳ dios yn amo quitlaCohua yn SaniCrameto yn onquimonahuatilitzino ~~yn tonatzin~~ Sancta ygleçia yniC amo quitlaCohua mochipahuaCanemitia yn ixpatzinCo y dios momoztlaye moCalaquiya y teonpa quimotlatlauhtilia y dios yntlaçonatzin quipohua yn itlaçomahuizroSanriotzin yn icpacxochitzi maCamo ytzala ynepatla xiCalaqui Ca quimoyollalili y Espirito Sanctu ma ximiquani—

Choloz hueCa moquetzaz y demoniō³⁴ yn iquac quimotenehuiliz y Jesu x⁰³⁵ yn Aḡle teonpaCalteCo moquetztiyez—

1⁰ demoni y y manel tinechtotoCa amo ninoxiCoz niCa nēmiz³⁶ ytla y manel oc quexquich Cahuitl quilCahuazque y dios ynic motlaçotla momahuiztilia mococolizque momictizque yñ adan onC achi huel chiCahuacque tlanpaltique oniquixiCo oniquihualquixti yn iparāySo yn iyecxochitlalpā· y dios yn oquinequia quimotlamachtiz quimoCuiltonozque auh ye yCa ononoCaCayauh auh yehuāti niquiCahuaz yn i manel huel chipahuaque: ynnoc³⁷ çequiti huel tlateomati y manel huel mimati ynic Calaqui y teonpa³⁸ amo quimatizque ȳ [15v] tleyn ipa nicchiuhtihuetzin niquimilnamictitihuetzin y manel ayemo tlami y miSsa y çermo ye Cuel oquilnamic y Capa yc nichuiCaz pampaquitihui motlamachtitihui ye Cuel oquinequixti onquinepolo oC achi qualli OquiCahuazquia amo onyazquiya y teopa onequiz onepoliuh yn itlatlauhtiliz yhua yn ixquich quimilhuiya quinōtza quimachtia ayocmo quiCaquiznequi auh y nehuatl ye huel quitlaçoyta³⁹ ynic niquiyaCana ynic niquipachohua y nōtlaçopilhua niCa niquichixtinemi amo niniquaniz y manel tinechtoCa Ca huel nechmotlaço.tilia—

---

32. teto: scribal error; the same appears in the second version of this play. Given the context we feel that *quito* "she said" or *tlato* "she spoke" was probably the original intention.
33. yñotlacoicnihua: read *yn notlaçoicnihuan*.
34. In the second version of the play: 1.⁰ demonio.
35. Jesu x⁰: only x⁰ appears in the second version of this play.
36. nemiz: read *ninemiz*.
37. ynnoc: read *yn oc*.
38. tiompa: read *teopan*.
39. quitlaçoyta: appears to be a scribal error; perhaps to be read *niquintlaçoitta*.

WOMAN: May God console you, my child. May God not scorn me tomorrow or the next day because of you. I have now fulfilled my obligations before him. Now I am going. I am going to pray to God for your sake.

(The woman enters the church.)

FIRST DEMON: Do look, you angel. You are satisfied with what has passed before you. The little child considers as nothing everything his mother said, and she has no consideration for him. But you say I am to leave them, I am not to live with them. Don't you know that it is right from their childhood that they do not want to leave me? I make them very happy. When they do not mention me, my beloved friends are not happy. [15r]

FIRST ANGEL: By the royal power of eternal Jesus Christ you will go away, you puma of the place of the dead,[14] you fierce beast who is never full, never sated. May your belly burst! You have come because of your envy, as you see that they serve God lovingly, they do not violate the sacraments ordered by ~~our mother~~ holy church, such that not breaking them they live purely before God. Every day they enter church, they pray to God's beloved mother, they count her precious and honored rosary, the chaplet. Do not enter among them, amid them.[15] The Holy Spirit has consoled them. Go away!

(The demon[16] flees, he stands far off, when the angel mentions Jesus Christ.[17] [The angel] stands at the church entrance.)

FIRST DEMON: Even though you chase me away, I will not be envious. I will live here among them however long a time it is until they forget God, so that those who love and honor one another will hate each other, will kill each other. They are stronger and more robust than Adam whom I deceived, whom I made leave paradise, God's good flowery land, which he wanted him to benefit from and enjoy. And I have already fooled him. And I am to leave them? Even though others are very pure, very devout, even though they are very prudent as they enter the church, they will not know [15v] what I will suddenly do to them, suddenly make them remember. Even before the mass and the sermon are finished, already they have remembered where I will take them, [where] they will go to be joyful, they will go to enjoy themselves. Already they have wasted and squandered it. It would have been better if they had neglected it, if they had not gone to the church. Their prayers have been wasted and squandered. And they no longer want to hear all that they say to them, that they announce to them, that they teach them. And as for me, now I look very lovingly at my beloved children, as I lead them, as I govern them. I go about here waiting for them. I will not go away, even though you chase me away, for they really love me.

---

14. mictlan: here and below translated as "the place of the dead" (locative senses such as "in" or "at" are already contained in the Nahuatl term), it was usually rendered by colonial translators as *infierno* (hell).

15. This may be a traditional idiom that in this context means "Do not be a troublemaker." See Molina 1977, 81r on the Spanish-Nahuatl side under "Malsin," and on 111r on the Nahuatl-Spanish various entries beginning with "Tetzalan." See also Carochi 1983, f. 20, under *"Nepantlâ."*

16. In the second version of this play: *First Demon*.

17. *Jesus Christ*: this is only *Christ* in the second version of the play.

y demoni⁰ moteCaz quauhtzintla Auh y teopa OCatCa hualquiçazque OCa qui^(nchi)xtiyez⁴⁰ y aḡle oc tlatoz⁴¹—

1⁰ aḡle v dios ytlaçohuane ma huel yxquich amotlanpal xicchihuaCa yniC amo amexiCoz yn tlaCateColotl Ca huel amechyahualotinemi amechtoCatinemi ynic amechmotlaCauhtiznequi ynic moxiCohua ynic amechita ynic anquimotlaçotilia yn dios

nima hualquiçazque quiya^(ca)tiyaz ^(tla)pitzalos⁴² Aḡle yazque yn incha motlalizq^(e 43)

lureso v auh yn axCa notlaçonamictzine huel yc tequipachohua⁴⁴ y mix y moyollotzin yn o[16r]quic ayemo tictomaÇehuia yn itelaçotlalitzī y dios y çetetl tlaxCaltzintli oC ach^(to)pa nimitznonahuatilia y moztla ypanpa tictotlatlauhtilizque y dios yn ānimaz y Capa oquimotlalilitzinno y tt⁰ dios Cuix qualCa Cuix nōçe amo huel tetlaoColti yn imomiyotzin yn intetepo yn opa cemātoc tepeuhtoc yn ichatzinCo y dios y teopan nōtlaçonanmictzine çihuapile—

Çihuantl v maCamo ximotequipachotzino Cuix amo ye ticmomachitia y çeçexihuitl. yc timachtilo yn iquac tiCui y nextli ynic techmomachtilia yn itlatequixtiCatzitzinhua y dios yn tlaçonteOnpixCatzitzinti yniC oCa titolnamiquizque⁴⁵ Ca titomiquilizque Ca tinexti Ca titlalti = ti=toCuepazque maCamo ximotequipachotzinno notlaçonamictzin ma tictomaçenhuiCa yn itelaçotlalitzin y dios ma ximoçehuitzinon— motlalizque⁴⁶ tlaquazque yn aḡle⁴⁷ OCa mo^(tla)pitzaloz⁴⁸ Etztiyez tlatoz

Aḡle 1⁰ v ma mochipa amotzala amonepatla moyetztiye yn iteyollalilintzin y dios Esp.ritu S.tu ynic aquimomahuiztililizque y dios ytlaçonatzin y çihuapili Sancta maria maCayc xiquilCahuaCa yn tla[16v]çoxochiCozCatzin⁴⁹ yn ilhuiCac tlatoCaçihuapilli Sancta maria ~~Ca yehuatzin~~ Ca y yehuatzin ayc tlami yn intepātlatolitzi yn intlatlauhtilitzin yn ixpatzinCo yn itlaçoConetzin yn oamechmochihuili yn anmotechiuhCatzin dios ma ytetzinCo ximoCahuaCa Ca huel moyolCoCohua yn amechyta y tlaCateColotl huel amechyahualotinemi y moxiCohuani Auh y nehuatl Ca nanhmechnopiyelitiCa⁵⁰ amo namechnoCahuilia amotlatzinCo ninemi

---

40. qui^(nchi)xtiyez: superscript material apparently added later in a different hand.
41. The stage directions are somewhat different in the second version of this play: [t]lapitzaloz ~~✦~~ hualquisasque. Lorenço. yhuan iCihuauh = yn itec teoCalli. ~~hualquizazque~~. Ocatca = auh yn. 1.⁰ angel. Oncan quichiztiez. Auh yn. 1.⁰ Dem.⁰ moteCaz. Cuauhtzintla. tlantoz. 1.⁰.
42. tlapitzalos: in a different hand.
43. The stage directions are somewhat different in the second version of this play: tlapitzalos =. yc hualquiÇa. yn teopa. Lurenço. Çihuatl yc yasque. yn incha motlalizque. Auh yn 1.⁰ angel quinyacantiyaz.
44. huel yc tequipachohua: read *huel nictequipachohua* as in the second version of this play.
45. titolnamiquizque : perhaps to be read either as *tictolnamiquiltizque* or *tiquilnamiquizque*.
46. motlalizque: in the second version of this play: ^(tla)pitzalos.
47. yn aḡle: in the second version of this play: 1.⁰ Angel.
48. Added in a different hand.
49. tlaçoxochicozcatzin: read *itlaçoxochicozcatzin*.
50. nanhmechnopiyeliti: standard *namechnopielitica*.

(*The demon lies down under a tree. And they who were in the church enter. There the angel waits for them. He still speaks.*[18])

FIRST ANGEL: O God's beloved ones, exert all your effort lest the demon deceive you! He goes about surrounding you and following you in order to enslave you, as he is envious when he sees how you love God.

(*Then they enter. The angel leads them. Wind instruments are played. They go to their home. They sit down.*)[19]

LORENZO: And now, O my beloved spouse, I must disturb your face, your heart,[20] [16r] since we still do not yet merit one little tortilla of God's charity. First of all I command you that tomorrow we will pray to God on behalf of the souls who are there where our lord God has placed them. Perhaps it is a good place, or perhaps it is not so consoling. Their bones, their tibias[21] lie all spread about, lie all scattered there, in the home of God, in the church, O my beloved spouse, O noblewoman.

WOMAN: Do not worry. Do you not yet know how we are taught each year, when we take the ashes, how God's spokespersons, the precious priests, teach us, so that we will then remember that we will die, that we will turn into ashes and earth? Do not worry, O my beloved spouse. May we merit God's love. Rest yourself.[22]

(*They sit down to eat. The angel is there. Wind instruments are played. He speaks.*)

FIRST ANGEL: May God the Holy Spirit's consolation always be among you, amid you, so that you will honor God's beloved mother, the noblewoman Saint Mary. Never forget the precious [16v] flowery necklace[23] of the heavenly royal noblewoman, Saint Mary. For never ending are her advocacy and her prayers before her beloved child, he who made you, your maker, God. Entrust yourselves to her. She feels very sick at heart; she sees that the demon goes about surrounding you, the envious one. And as for me, I am guarding you, I do not leave you, I live with you.

---

18. The second version of this play has somewhat different stage directions at this point: *Wind instruments are played. Lorenzo and his wife enter. Those who were in church enter. And First Angel awaits them there. And First Demon lies down under a tree.*

19. The second version of this play has somewhat different stage directions at this point: *Wind instruments are played. Thus Lorenzo and the woman enter from the church, thus they go to their home. They sit down. First Angel leads them.*

20. face, heart: The possessed metaphorical diphrase *-ix, -yollo* (face, heart) has many connotations. The first "by itself often has to do with presence, perception, wisdom" while the second "is associated with emotion and volition" (Karttunen and Lockhart 1987, 54). In combination they often refer to one's "spirit, spirits, mood, state of morale" (54), which is the sense present here. For a more extended discussion see Karttunen and Lockhart (1987, 54–55).

21. bones, tibias: here and below, a traditional metaphorical diphrase has been used whose precise pragmatic thrust is not entirely clear.

22. The second version of the play includes stage directions that are somewhat different than those immediately following, as well as a speech by Lorenzo that is entirely missing from the first version but that seems to refer to the end of the drama. Note that in this variant the person who speaks next is Lorenzo, not the First Angel.

   Wind instruments are played. They eat. And First Angel is there. He speaks.

LORENZO: May it so be done, O noblewoman. May it be that we merit it [that is, God's love]. O people of earth, now you have seen the exemplary model, and how our lord God judges people. And admonish your children. May it not happen to you as it happened to him [that is, the condemned youth, at the end of the play?].

23. This alludes to the rosary.

Auh y demonio çan opa yez y quauhtzitla quihualytztiyaz auh ytla atle tlatohua yn aḡle nima hualmeuhtehuaz tlatoz huel qualaniz yn quimitaz—

1º demoº v huel ninontlahuelpalahua⁵¹ y niquimita ȳ tlaCatotli yhua y çihuātotli huel ye nechçotlahua yn ichiCahualiz ye nechhuihuiyotza ynic tlapaltique ynic yoltepitztique Ca huel chiCahuac yn intlaneltoquiliz Ca huel yuh nicmati Ca ahuel niquinxiCoz ahuel niquihuiCaz nicnepolohua nicnequixtiya y nontlatequipanoliz Ca ye cuel yxquich Cahuitl yn intla ninemi niquinonepachihuitinemi Ca ahuel niquixiCohua onC achi huel motlapaltiliya yn imaḡlel auh yeçe onC achi huel nechyoltonehua nechchichinatza y missa ȳ çermō huel quihuelCaqui y tle ylhuilo nonotzalo: huel ytech quitlaliya yn iyollo oc çeCa yn ihuāpohua yn ōmique. yn opoliuhque yn opa tepeuhtoc yn imomiyon yn intetepo y teopa yn iquac: qui[17r]quimita⁵² huel quitlaoColtia ypampa: choCa: tlatlatlauhtia momoztlaye Calaqui y teopa huel OC achi yc nechtlahuelCuitia yc nipatzmiqui: auh niquitohua ytla yehuati momaquixtizque Cuix mochi quihuiCazque yn ixquichti tlaltipcac Onoque Cuix amo yehuati niquihuiCaz yn amo ça tlapohualti yn itla ninemi yn manel huel mamahuiztique⁵³: yn atle yntech maxitlani y moyecchichihua y momahuiçolani yn imixCo yn imicpac nemi yn icnontlaCa atle ypa quimita yn ihuapohua Ca nehuatl niquiCuitlahuiltia y niCa ytla ninemi amo niquiCahua achito Cahuitl Cuix nel ninoxiCoz tla Oc niquimochiya yn antlamatque yn atle ypa tlachiya yn atle ypa teyta auh yn axCa tla Oc niqualyahualotihuetzin ȳ çenmanahuantl tla ninotlalotihuetzin ye nihuecahua y niCa—

---

nima yaz y demoniº hualmotlaloz auh y lureSo moquetzazque yn itlaquaya huel quitlaçonCamatiz

lureso v auh yn axCa notlaçonamictzinne ma yehuatzin y ttº dios otechmotlaqualtilitzinno auh y moztla Cuix no yuhqui tictomaçehuizque yn itetlaçotlalitzin y dios Cuix noçe ytla topa oquihualmihuanliz yn itetlaçotlalitzi: ma [17v] ma⁵⁴ çā ytetzinCo titoCahuaCa Ca yehuatzin techmopalehuiliz y tocochiya y totlaquanya y tonenemiya ma techmopalehuili ȳ dios ytlaçonatzin Auh yn axCa ma Oc tihuia ticçetlaliti yn totlatlacol ynic otictoyollitlaCalhuique yn totechiuhCatzin dios Ca ye yma y titochipahuazque titoyollitizq̄.⁵⁵ ma moztla tihuiya yxpatzinco y dios yxiptlatzintzinhua y tlaçoteopixCatzintziti—

Çihuatl v notlaçonāmictzin ma yuhqui mochihua: Ca ye ima y totichipahuazque⁵⁶ ma yçiuhca tihuiya

tlapitzalos⁵⁷

Calanquizque nima hualquiçaz y demoniº—

---

51. ninontlahuelpalahua: perhaps to be read *ninontlahuelpolohua*.
52. quiquimita: read *quimitta*.
53. mamahuiztique: although it reads the same in the second version of this play, read *momahuiztique*.
54. ma ma: read *ma*.
55. titoyollitizq̄.: read *titoyolcuitizque*.
56. totichipahuazque: read *titochipahuazque*.
57. tlapitzalos: in a different hand.

(And the demon is just there under a tree. He goes on watching them. And if the angel says nothing[24] then he gets up, he speaks, he is very angry. He looks at them.)

FIRST DEMON: I really lose myself in anger when I see the miserable little man and woman. Their strength really makes me feel faint. They make me tremble, they are so robust and firm-hearted. Their belief is very strong. Thus I know well that I will not be able to deceive them, I will not be able to take them. I waste and squander my work. Already all the time that I have lived with them, I have gone about lying in wait for them in vain. I am unable to deceive them. Their angel strives harder. And moreover, what pains me and hurts me more is the mass and the sermon. They really approve of what is said to them and what they are admonished. They set their hearts on it. Especially when they see their neighbors who have died, who have perished, whose bones and tibias lie scattered there at the church, [17r] then they really make them grieve. They weep and pray for their sake. Every day they go into the church, by which they anger me much more, by which I am oppressed. But I say, if they will be saved, will they take along all who dwell on earth? Am I not to take those without number among whom I live? Even though they are highly honored, unapproachable, well dressed and want to be esteemed, they have no respect for the poor, they have no esteem for their neighbors. I induce them [to do bad things], I live here among them. I do not leave them for a moment. Am I, truly, to be envious? Let me yet wait for the presumptuous ones, the inconsiderate ones, the disrespectful ones. And now let me yet make a quick circle about the world. Let me quickly run off. I have now tarried here a long time.

(Then the demon goes. He runs. And Lorenzo [and his wife] arise from their meal. He gives thanks.)

LORENZO: And now, O my beloved spouse, it is our lord God who has fed us. And tomorrow, will we likewise merit God's charity? Or will he send something of his charity to us? Let us [17v] just entrust ourselves to him. He will help us in our sleeping, in our eating, in our going about. May God's beloved mother help us. And now, let us yet go and gather together our sins with which we have offended our maker, God. It is now time that we purify ourselves, that we confess. Tomorrow let us go before God's representatives, the precious priests.

WOMAN: O my beloved spouse, may it so be done. It is now time that we purify ourselves. Let us go quickly.

(Wind instruments are played. They go in. Then a demon enters.)

---

24. That is, when he stops speaking?

2 demō y̆ huel niçiyauhtihuitz yn onnicyahualoto ȳ. çenmanahuactli ypapa y niCa onihuala. huel miyequiti Omoçentlalique yn telpopochtototi yn ichpopochti ~~tiCa~~ axCa moyolCuitizque huel miyec quilCahuazque ymauhCaConpa ypīnahuiliztiCa amo quitozque yn intlatlacol yc teyxco teycpac oneque amo quiteCuepilizque y temahuizyo yhua yn itahua yn ināhua. y ^{qui}mixtlatzinniya amo quimoCuitizq̄.
ȳmixpa⁵⁸ yn iteyolCuitiCauh quitlatizque y momati aço ye yC opoliuh yn ixpa y dios tla Oc niquimochie
Motlatiz y demō. y Cani yez quauhtlatli⁵⁹ nima hualquiçazque yeyti telpopochti: ȳ.
[18r] tlapitzalos⁶⁰ quechtla quihualhuiCaz Rosanrio y çen yc momaquixtiz y Cruz yn iquac moteCaz yn oc çen amo moteonchihuaz yni moteCaz quauhtla Cochtiyezq^e.

1º telpochtli y̆ notlaçoycnihuane ma niCa toçehuiCa ȳ quauhtla Ca ye Otlayohuaz: Ca oc hueCa y taçizque yn itic altepetl Ca tel oC moztla: ȳ titoyolCuitizque—

2 telpochtli y̆ ma yuhqui mochihua ma niCa techmoçehuilitzinno y tt⁰ dios notlaçoycniuhtzitzihuane yn oquic ayemo huel tlaquauhtlayohiā⁶¹ ma ytla toconamicti niCa: Ca huel OhuiCa ȳ quauhtla—

3 telpochtli y̆ y nehuatl huel oniçiyauh ma yçiuhca titoçehuiCa Ca huel nicochiznequi nocninhuane—

Calaquizque quauhtla huel onhuiCa yez motlalizque mononotztiyezque

---

1º telpochtli y̆ nocniuhtzitzinhuane huel yuhqui queni mochihua y noyollo ȳ niquilnamiqui y queni yxpatzinCo nonaçiz y noteyolCuitiCatzi y moztla—
San hueCa hualtzatziz y Sn^{ta} ag̃le—iCa mitzmopalehuiliz y dios ytlaçonatzin xi^cmotlatlauhtilitzino—[18v]

2 telpochtli y̆ ça ño yuhqui niquitohua huel ne^{ch}tequipachohua y niquilnamiqui amo niteoçihui yn axCa ma techmopalehuilitzinno y tt⁰ dios—

2 ag̃le y̆ yn āquin quichoctiya quitlaOnColtia yn itlatlacol ca quimotlapopolhuililiya yn tt⁰ dios—

3 telpochtli y̆ y nehuatl tle nechmauhtiz y ninonomamauhtiz y niCa ~~huel~~ amo OnāmechhualiCazquiya Cuix huel melahuac y niCa mononotza yn amoneyolCuitiliz y nehuatl ma ninoyolCuiti maCamo Cuix tequitli Cuix aCa ye nechahuaz—

Opa quihualtzatziliz y demonī⁰ hueCa yez

2º demonī y̆ huel mahuiztic yn ōtiquilnamic amo ticmolCahuiliz ca oc titelpochtli—

1º telpochtli y̆ nōtlaçonycniuhtzinne cuix tiCamanalti cuix nocen monel⁶² y tiquitohua—

---

3 telpochtli y̆ huel ypaltzin⁶³ y dios Ca melahuac y niquitohuan—

---

58. ȳmixpa: read *yn imixpan*.
59. quauhtlatli: standard *quauhtla* (as below).
60. tlapitzalos: added in a different hand.
61. tlaquauhtlayohia: read *tlaquauhtlayohua*.
62. monel: probably the intent was *amo nel*.
63. ypaltzin: read *ypaltzinco*.

SECOND DEMON: I have come in a big hurry. I have gone around the world. I have come here because many youths and maidens have gathered together. They are to confess today. They will forget quite a lot through their fear, through their shame. They will not tell their sins, with which they offended people. They will not restore honor to people. And they will not confess before their confessor that they were slapping the faces of their fathers and their mothers. They will hide it. They think that perhaps now it is thereby pardoned before God. Let me yet wait for them.

(*The demon hides where there is a forest.*[25] *Then three youths enter.* [18r] *Wind instruments are played. One wears a rosary around his neck. He saves himself with the cross*[26] *when he lies down. The others do not bless themselves when they lie down. They sleep in the forest.*)

FIRST YOUTH: O my dear friends, let us rest here in the forest, for it is about to get dark. It is a long way till we will reach the city. So, we will confess tomorrow.

SECOND YOUTH: May it be done so. May our lord God give us rest here, O my dear friends. As long as it is not entirely dark yet, let us put something together here, for it is quite dangerous in the forest.

THIRD YOUTH: As for me, I am really tired. Let us rest right away. I really want to sleep, O my friends.

(*They enter the forest. It is very dangerous. They sit down addressing each other.*)

FIRST YOUTH: O my friends, my heart is troubled as I think about how I will arrive before my confessor tomorrow.

(*From a ways off the holy angel cries out:*) God's beloved mother will help you! Pray to her! [18v]

SECOND YOUTH: I say the same. It really worries me when I think about it. I am not hungry now. May our lord God help us.

SECOND ANGEL: Our lord God will pardon anyone whose sins make him weep, make him sad.[27]

THIRD YOUTH: As for me, what will frighten me? What will I be afraid of? I would not have woken you up here.[28] Is it really correct, what is being admonished here, your confessions? As for me, whether I confess or not: is it a requirement? Will someone scold me?

(*At that point the demon cries out; he is far away.*)

SECOND DEMON: What you have thought of is very splendid. You will not forget that you are still a youth.

FIRST YOUTH: O my dear friend, are you joking? Or do you not speak truly?

THIRD YOUTH: By God, what I say is correct.

---

25. The second version of this play adds a preceding stage direction: *Winds instruments are played.*
26. That is, he will make the sign of the cross.
27. Although the Nahuatl is gender-neutral, this translation specifies "him" because the statement is addressed to a male.
28. That is, he is complaining that his friends are keeping him awake with their pointless chatter [?].

1º telpochtli y Jesuz tle tiquitohua Cuix amo ticminmaCaxilia y motatzin yhua y monatzin—

3 telpochtli y tle niquimaCaxiliz ȳ notatzin y nonātzin Cuix mozCalia yquac niquimonana yquechtlan oquequetza⁶⁴ niquimixtlatlatzinnia amo tle nechilhuizque—

2 demoniº y ximiçihuiti oc çenqui xicmitalhui

[19r]

2 telpochtli y maCamo quimonequiltiz y dios yn iuhqui ticchihuazque y tehuati: Ca amo techmoCahuilia ytzinco⁶⁵ titlachiyazque y totatzi yn ōtechmozCaltili topapa moçiamiquititinemi techmotemolilia y tocochCa y toneyeuhCa yhua yzn iz cuellaCa⁶⁶ huel tinahuatilo ytic timaCaxilizque tictenamiqui yn imatzin yn iquac yxpatzinCo taçi maCamo quimonequilti y dios yn iuhqui ticchihuazque y ticmochihuilia—

1º telpochtli y ma techmoçenhuilitzinno y ttº dios ma titoCochitica xihualmohuica nocniuhtzīne ma niCa tomexti titoçenhuiCa xicmoCahuili ȳ tocniuhtzin Canel atle quimauhtiya y nica quauhtla—

moteCazque⁶⁷ quitlalcahuizque yn imicniuh achi tlanahuac yçenl⁶⁸ yez

1º telpochtli y ma techmoçenhuilitzinno yn iteyollalilitzin y dios espīritu S.tu—
2 telpochtli y ninōmachiyotia ȳCa y Crůz ma techmopalehuilitzinno.—
Ytla ye Cochticate nima mehuaz Ave mariztellā hualmoquixtiz yn totlaçonatzin ynhua agēles nahui quihualhuiCazque Cadela⁶⁹

Virgē y ā y tilhuiCatl y ticemanahuactli y tintlalticpactli yn tantl ȳ titepetl yn omitzmochihuili ȳn ōmitzmoyoColili ȳ [19v] notlaçoConetzin ȳ motech meya ȳ motech i quiça ynnin ixquich⁷⁰ yn onmitzmonemactili y nōtlaçoConetzin maçonelihui yn atle motlatlaCol Ca huel no titetlaoColti no timomauhtia no tihuihuiyoca t̶i̶m̶o̶m̶a̶u̶h̶t̶i̶a̶ y timolnamiqui⁷¹ yn iquac hualmohuicaz yn nōtlaçoConetzin yn ipa moquixtiquiuh yn ipanpa Omotlayȳyohuilti y tlachiya ȳ tlaCaqui auh ye amo momauhtiya amo huihuiyoCa auh ȳ tehuatl atle monācaz atle motlachiyeliz timomauhtiya tihuihuiyoCa y tiquilnamiqui yn ipā tihuetziz yn ipā tixitiniz Onyhçentzotlahueliltic ma huel tlachiyaCan ma huel tlaCaquiCa.. ma huel quitaCa ȳ notetlaçotlaliz huel ymixpa nictlalia nicnēxtia yn ipalehuiloCa y niCa yxtlahuaCa choCohuaya—

---

64. oquequetza: perhaps scribal error; maybe the intent was *niquinquequetza*.
65. ytzinco: read *ixtzinco* as in the second version of this play.
66. yn iz cuellaCa : the intent here is not clear; perhaps *yn iz cuel tlaca* is meant.
67. moteCazque: this is not in the second version of this play.
68. ycenl: read *ycel* as in the second version of this play.
69. Following this in the second version of this play: hualtlahuintiyazque.
70. ynnixquich: read *yn ixquich*.
71. timolnamiqui: perhaps to be read *ticmolnamiqui*.

FIRST YOUTH: Jesus! What are you saying? Don't you fear your father and your mother?

THIRD YOUTH: What shall I fear from my father and my mother? Do they wake up when I seize them by the neck? I beat them, I slap their faces. They will say nothing to me.
SECOND DEMON: Hurry up! Say more! [19r]

SECOND YOUTH: May it not be God's will that we do this, for our father, who raised us, does not allow us to gaze into his face. He goes about wearing himself out for our sake, searching for our dinner, our breakfast. And we are ordered to fear him.[29] We kiss his hand when we arrive before him. May it not be God's will that we act like you do.

FIRST YOUTH: May our lord God give us rest. Let us go to sleep. Come, O my friend. Let the two of us rest ourselves here. Leave our friend, for he is afraid of nothing here in the forest.
(They lie down. They leave their friend, who is by himself a little to the side.)

FIRST YOUTH: May the consolation of God the Holy Spirit give us rest.
SECOND YOUTH: I sign myself with the cross. + May it help us.
(When they sleep then the Ave Maris Stella is raised.[30] Our beloved mother enters along with four angels. They bring candles.)[31]

VIRGIN: You heaven, you world, you earth, you water, you hill, my beloved child made you, created you. [19v] From you flows, from you emerges all that my beloved child bestowed on you. Even though you have no sins, you also arouse compassion, you also are afraid, you also tremble. You think about when my beloved child will come, will come to appear to those for whose sake he suffered. They look, they listen. And yet they are not afraid, they do not tremble. But you, who have no ears, who have no vision, you are afraid, you tremble, you think on the time that you will fall and crumble. Oh four hundred times unfortunate are they! May they look well, may they listen well, may they see my love, which I place right before them. I show them what helps them here on the plain, in the place of weeping.[32]

29. We left "iz cuellaca" untranslated.
30. *Ave Maris Stella*: Hail, Star of the Sea. A very popular Catholic prayer and hymn to the Virgin Mary. It is used for all the Marian feasts in the reformed (Tridentine) breviary (see the *Breviarium romanum*, 1961, 1:1122–23, 1202, 2:748, 840–41, 878–79).
31. In the second version of the play is added: *They go along providing illumination.*
32. The phrasing here is reminiscent of Nahuatl renditions of the Salve Regina prayer's "vale of tears."

nima hualquiztehuaz y demonio y quauhtla motlatitiyez yxpatzinCo motlaquaquetzaz ça hueCa quihualhuiCaz yn imacpal yquimixtlatzinniya⁷² yn itahua ȳn ināhuan

_____[20r]

2 demō. v dios ynatzinne ma xinechymomaquili y niCa CoCochtiCate y telpochtototi Ca omitzmolCahuilique yCochiya ma huel xicmotili yn itlahueliloCayo Ca huel mitzmolCahuilia yn iquac pactiCate atle quitequipaChohua amo mitzmolnamiquiliya mitzmolCahuiliya⁷³ auh tlapanahuiya yn inpa timeȳehuitia çan iquac yn itla ypa hualauh netoliniliztli CoColiztli quin iquac y mitzmoteteuhtzatzinlilia tla xicmotili yn inemiliz amo mitzmomahuiztililia yhua yn itāhua yn ināhua quimictiya quimixtlatzinnia atle ypā quimita Ca niCa niqualhuiCa yn inmacpal yn quimixtlatzinnia yn itahua yn inahua y manel oc tlalticpac nemi pāctinemi Ca ye nichuiCa yn imacpal ȳ momati amo tlatlaColi yn quichihua yhua yn īteyolcuitiCahua quiCahualtia amo quineltoCa çannoC⁷⁴ achi tlahuelCui amo quintequipachohua ȳ tle ylhuilo auh yni ma çā xinechimomaquili y niCa CoCochtiCate Ca huel ye ypa mozCaltia yn atle ypa tlachiya—

_____[20v]

Virgē v xihualauh y huel timoxiCohuani yn ayc tlamiz yn ayc tzoquiçaz y monexiColiz Canel yehuatl yniC otihualtemoc yniC otihualaçaloc y monexiColiz y monepohualiz y matlamachiliz auh yn axCa ytech timotlahuelpolohua timotlahuelquixtiya yn itlamaquixtiltzintzinhua y notlaçoConetzin Ca y yezyyotiCatzinCo ytlapalotiCatzinCo onquiᵐᵒmaquixtili y tlatlacohuanime auh atle yxtlauhCa yCuepCa yn itlayhiyohuilitzin y notlaçoConetzin yn i.miquilitzin atle yc quixtlahua atle yc quiCuepCayotia auh ȳ notlaçonConetzin Ca quihualmonochilia qui.hualmotzatzinlilitiCa yn āmo tlacaqui yn āmo tlachiya Onyntlahueliltic y tlalticpac tlaCa yn amo quimaCaçi y miquiztli—

agel 1º v Çihuapile tonechixCaylitzinnen mixpatzinCō tixtlapachtlaçan timitztotlatlauhtilia ma xiquimopalehuili ma xiquimomaquixtili y tlatlaCo.[21r]huanime yn imacpa y tlacatecōtl⁷⁵ y quimitlaniya y niCa CoCochtiCate ma çan ipampa xicmochihuilitzinno y motlaçoRonSanriotzin y moxochiCoronatzin Ca yquechtla quihualhuica ma ça yehuatl ymaquixtiloCa mochihua y tlatlacohuanime—

.2 agel v y çenmiCac timotemiltitiCa yn ilhuiCatl ytic yhua y niCa tlalticpac y nohuiya çenmanahuac tetimani y moçihuapillatoCateycnelilitzin y motepalehuilitzin yn ixpatzinCo y motlaçoConetzin Ca yehuatl ypalehuiloCa mochihua yn iSanta Cru̇ztzin ma çemiCac quilnamiquiCa Ca ytech: Onquimomaquixtili y tlatlaCohuanime: maCayc quilCahuaCa yn iCochiya yn ineyehuaya Ca yehuatl yc momaquixtia y momoztlaye mitzmoyectenehuilia yn mitzmotzatzinlilia yn amo achito Cahuitl mitzmolCahuilia yhua y motlaçoConetzin—[21v]

72. yquimixtlatzinniya: perhaps to be read *yc quimixtlatziniya*.
73. amo mitzmolnamiquiliya mitzmolCahuiliya: this passage is not in the second version of this play.
74. çannoC: read *çan oc*.
75. tlacatecōtl: read *tlacatecolotl*.

(Then the demon quickly comes out from the forest where he is hiding. He kneels before her, just at a distance. He holds the hand of the one who slaps his fathers, his mothers, in the face.) [20r]

SECOND DEMON: O mother of God, give me the little youths who are sleeping here, for they have forgotten you in their sleep. Observe well their wickedness. They really forget you when they are having a good time. Nothing worries them. They do not remember you; they forget you. And you protect them extremely well.[33] Only when some affliction or sickness comes upon them, then do they cry out strongly to you. Do look at their lives. They do not honor you and they beat their mothers and their fathers, they slap their faces. They have no esteem for them. Here I come bringing by the hand one who slaps the faces of his fathers and his mothers, although he still lives and goes around happy on earth. I bring by the hand one who thinks that what he does is not a sin and he restrains his confessors [from correcting him?]. He does not believe them. He just becomes more irritated; what is said to him does not worry him. And so, just give me those who are sleeping here. They have no consideration now for the way they were raised. [20v]

VIRGIN: Come, you very envious one! Never will your envy be finished, never will it come to an end, for it is through your envy, your pride, your presumption that you went down, that you were cast out.[34] And now you vent your anger, you take out your anger, on those whom my beloved child has saved. With his blood, with his dye[35] he saved the sinners. But there is no payment, no return for my beloved child's suffering and death. They pay nothing for it, they return nothing for it. And my beloved child just calls to them, he is crying out to them; They do not listen, they do not look. Oh, how unfortunate are the people of earth, who do not fear death.

FIRST ANGEL: O noblewoman, O our hope, before you we humble ourselves, we pray to you. Help me! Save the sinners [21r] from the hands of the demon who is asking for those who are sleeping here. Do it just for the sake of your precious rosary, your flowery crown, which they are wearing around their necks. Let this just become the salvation of these sinners.

SECOND ANGEL: Forever you are filled up[36] [with grace], in heaven and here on earth. Your noblewomanly and royal favor, your help, spreads about filling everywhere in the world, in the presence of your beloved child. His holy cross + becomes what helps them.[37] May they always remember that it was on it that he saved the sinners. May they never forget, in their sleep and in their rising, that through it they are saved. Every day now they praise you, they cry out to you. Not for a moment do they forget you and your beloved child. [21v]

---

33. Due to the lack of several words in the second version of this play, the last two lines would read a little differently if based on that alternate text: They were not remembering you. And you protect them.

34. An allusion to the expulsion from heaven of Lucifer and his followers.

35. blood, dye: this can also be translated "blood, blood," which makes it boringly repetitive in English. Perhaps there is a double meaning here for this is a common diphrase, necessarily possessed, for "[someone's] offspring."

36. This Nahuatl verb often refers to the Virgin being filled "with grace" as in the Hail Mary prayer.

37. Alternate translation: becomes their salvation.

3 agel v y çenmiCac timitztoyectenehuilia y tineçetlamachtilitzi yn tihuiCactli mixpatziCo ninotlaquaquetza ma xiquimotlaonColili maçihui y tlachiya ȳ tlaCaqui Camo quita amo quiCaqui y motlatlatlauhtilitzin yn ixpatzinCo y motlaçoConetzin amo achito Cahuitl tiquimoCahuilia auh y yehuati Ca mitzmolCahuilia amo quimati ytla ypa timoquixtia y çençenmilhuitl y çeçenyohuali tiqui^{mo}maquilia yn ixquich y moteyectililizgraçiatzin

4 agle v çihuapile toneyollalililitzine Ca mixpatzinCo nicnoCuitia ynin tlatlaCohuani Ca yxquich yc nictzatzinlintinemi. ninōchoquilitinemi y nitlaOnCoxtinemi yCapa ninōtzatzintitinemi amo nechCaqui auh yn axCa amo nicmati y tley yc nicnicnomaquiliz⁷⁶ Cueta ȳ motlaçoConetzin auh yn axCa tle nel oc niquitoz Ca mochi mela[22r]huac neltiliztli y tlen ic motelhuia⁷⁷ y tlaCatecolotl⁷⁸ y mixpātzinco auh yn axCa Ca momactzinco niCahua y huel yollotepitztli yn amo tlaCaquini—

Virge v auh yn axCa xihualauh ma xichuiCa y tictlatlani Canel yehuati ^{quiti}telchihua yn iximachoCatzin y notlaçoConetzin yn amo quimotzatzinlilia yn iCochiya yn inenemiya Cuix amo quimati yn itech Omaquixtiloque y Sancta Crūz

tlatzotzonaloz moCalaquiz y totlaçonatzin quimohuiquiliz$\bar{q}$^{e} y agelez mochiti auh y demō. oquic tlatzotzonaloz quichichihua y queni quimamatiquiçaz—
3 telpochtli v nocniuhtzitzihuane ma xinechmopalehuiliquiCa Ca ye nechhuiCaznequi y te[22v]quani yn amo onicneltoCaya Ca huel ohuica y quauhtla

tlaCueponiz OCa polihuizque nima hualiçazque yn oc Ome monotzazque

1º telpochtli v ma yehuatzin tt^{o} dios Ontechmotlathuiltilitzinno notlaçoycnicniuhtzinne⁷⁹

2 telpochtli v ma ça no yuhqui y tehuatzi—

2 telpochtli v y tocniuhtzin Cuix oquimotlathuilti y dios—

1º telpochtli v Ca āyoCac onC achi quali Oquichiuh ytla OmoCuep̄ nincha⁸⁰ Ca huel tequallani yn itlatol—
2 telpochtli v nocniuhtzinne huel OnnechCanCayauh y Cochiztli Oniquitac Onhuala çen tequani huel temamauh^{ti} yuhqui ye techquaznequi—[23r]
1º telpochtli v notlaçoycniuhtzinne amo xicmoneltoquiti y Cochiztli yn techintitia Ca çan toCa moCaCayahuan Ca amo neltoquiztli ma ye yhciuhCa titotoCatihuentziCa ma^{ca}mo ypa tonançiti y neyolCuitiliztli—

---

76. nicnicnomaquiliz: read *nicnomaquiliz*.
77. y tlen ic motelhuia: perhaps to be read *yn tlein quimotalhuia*.
78. y tlaCatecolotl: not in the second version of this play.
79. notlaçoycnicniuhtzinne: read *notlaçoycniuhtzine*.
80. nincha: read *ichan*.

THIRD ANGEL: Forever we praise you, who are utter bliss, who are heaven. Before you I kneel. Have compassion for them. Even though they look and listen they do not see, they do not hear the prayers you make before your beloved child. We do not leave them for a moment. But as for them, they forget you. They do not know what you attempt for them. Every day and every night you give them all your restoring grace.

FOURTH ANGEL: O noblewoman, O our consolation, before you I acknowledge that this sinner does not hear me, for all that I go about crying out to him, I go about weeping, I go about sad, I go about crying out behind him. And now I do not know how I will give an accounting to your beloved child. And now what else am I to say? It is all correct, [22r] it is the truth, what the devil[38] says before you. And now I leave in your hands the very hard-hearted one who does not listen.

VIRGIN: And now come. Take what you ask for, since he scorns the knowing of my beloved child. He does not cry out to him in his sleeping, in his going about. Does he not know that they were saved on the holy cross?

(Instruments are played. Our beloved mother exits. All the angels accompany her. And the demon, while the instruments are playing, arranges how he will carry him off.)
THIRD YOUTH: O my friends! Come help me! A fierce beast is about to carry me off! [22v] I did not believe it was so dangerous in the forest!

(Things explode. They disappear. Then the other two wake up. They call to each other.)

FIRST YOUTH: May our lord God get us up, O my dear friend.

SECOND YOUTH: May it be the same for you.

SECOND YOUTH: As for our friend, has God gotten him up?

FIRST YOUTH: He is no longer there. He would have done better if he had returned home, for his words were really provocative.
SECOND YOUTH: O my friend, sleep has really deceived me. I saw a fierce beast come. It was very frightening. It was as if it was about to eat us. [23r]
FIRST YOUTH: O my dear friend, do not believe what sleep shows us. It just deceives us. It is not believable. Let us run quickly, lest we not get to confession on time.

---

38. the devil: not in the second version of this play.

2 telpochtli y Ca ye otonaçiCo Ca ye niCa yn Can y teonCali ma toCalaquiCa aço ye neyolCuitilo ma yçiuhCa tonaçiCa nocniuhtzine—

tlapitza[81] Calaquizque yn Cani yez teoCanli tlapitzaloz hualquiçazque yn loreso yhua yçihuauh yhua agel

---

Loreso y nonamictzinne[82] yn axCan Ca tel ye toyollo pachiuhtiCa yn itechpa yn toneyolCuitiliz auh ynnaxCan[83] Cuix nel nimitznotlatililiz huel chiCahuac yn nechCoCohua y nōma y nocxi y notzoteCon auh ma Oc tepitzin ninocenhui aço achitzi nechtlalCahuiz qui^moneltiz[84] yn dios—

Çihuantl y nontlaçonamictzin: tle ticmitalhuitzinnohuan maCamo ~~que~~ quimonequiltitzinno ȳ dios ytla mopatzinCo quihualmihuanliz Ca tinnoteyollaliCatzin ma ximoçehuitzino—

MoteCaz yn iCochiya auh yn āgel ȳtzotla yez tlapitzaloz ynhua yn içihuauh—

Çihuatl y notlaçonamictzin huel niquita y moCoColitzin ma ti[85] huel timotlanahuitia—[23v]

Loreso y Macamo nimitztequipacho y nehuatl ytla ninomiquiliz onC achi huel titetequipacho Ca tēCal^tepan timomiquilitiuh ayac mitzmoCuitlahuiz ayac mitzyntaz auh y nehuatl Ca nicnomaçenhuia y motetlaçontlalintzin amo ximotequipachontzinno aço quimonequiltitzinnoz y dios anchitzin niçehuiz—

---

tlapitzalos[86] hualquiÇaz y miquiztli quiminaz achtopa yn iÇihuauh Çatepa yn inamic

---

Miquiztli y huel onihualiçiuhta ypampa yçiuhCa namechtlatlaliz yeyCa huel oñquimotlaçotlayeColtilique onhuāquimohuelamachtilique yn amoteyoCoxCatzin y dios ypanpa amo atlayhiyohuizque ȳ niCa tlalticpāc huel yçiuhCa namechponponloCo namechtlatlantico quemach huel amehuati yn onamechchocti yñ oamechtlaOColti yn omitl yn opa tepeuhtoc ȳn opa chayauhtoc yñ ayocmo tlatohuā ȳn ayocmo molinia huetzCa motlalohua ayocmo tepampanahuitiquiça ayoctle yh in ichiCahua~~z~~liz ayoctle y yn intepozmaquauh yn imac ayoctle y çenCa mahuiztic yn itlaque OCatCan auh yn axCa onCa huetztoc onCa ponpoztectoc xaxamatoc auh yn oc yoltiCate ypan chocholohua ynpa moquequetza ayocmo qualani ayocmo [24r] tlatohua ayocmo moliniya ayocmo tlachiya auh yn iquac tlalticpac oneCan ayac huel yxpa onquiçaya ayac huel onquitlatolpanāhuiya yuhqui teotl ypa ^amomatia tla xinechhuallita Ca nehuatl y nicnechiCohua ȳn amochiCahualiz na^mech q̄xtilia xiquitaCa yñ amonemiliz ma āmechchocti amechtlaonColti Ca moztla huiptla amopa niquiztihuetzinquiuh Ca ye niyauh—

---

81. tlapitza: added in a different hand.
82. nonanmictzinne: in the second version of this play: notlaçonamictzine.
83. ynnaxCan: read *yn axcan*.
84. qui^moneltiz: read *quimonequiltiz*.
85. ma ti: either scribal error or a sentence was started but never completed.
86. tlapitzalos: added in a different hand.

SECOND YOUTH: We have already arrived. Here is the church. Let us go in. Perhaps people are already confessing. Let us arrive quickly, O my friend.
(Wind instruments are played. They go in where the church is. Wind instruments are played. Lorenzo and his wife and an angel enter.)

LORENZO: O my spouse, now we are satisfied regarding our confession. And now, can I truly hide from you that which very strongly hurts my hands, my feet, my head? But let me rest for a little longer. Perhaps in a little while God will want it to leave me.

WOMAN: O my beloved husband, what are you saying? May God not want to send something upon you. You are my consolation. Rest yourself.

(He lies down in his sleeping place. And the angel and his wife are at his head. Wind instruments are played.)

WOMAN: O my beloved spouse, I can see your sickness. You are gravely ill. [23v]

LORENZO: Let it not be I that cause you worry if I die. Better you worry that you are going to die in the street, that no one will take care of you, that no one will see you. But as for me, I benefit from your love. Do not worry. Perhaps God will want me to rest a little.

(Wind instruments are played. Death enters. He shoots arrows first at his wife and afterward at her spouse.)

DEATH: I have really come in a hurry so that I will quickly get you set up,[39] because you have very lovingly served and well pleased your creator, God. Therefore you will not suffer here on earth. Very quickly I have come to obliterate you, I have come to hide you. How fortunate are you whom the bones that lie scattered there, that lie dispersed there made weep, made sad. No longer do they speak, no longer do they move, laugh, run. No longer do they go passing people by. No longer do they have any strength, no longer do they have swords in their hands, no longer is what was their clothing very splendid. And now they lie fallen there, they lie broken up and shattered there. And those who are still alive jump around on them and stand on them. They no longer get angry, no longer [24r] speak, no longer move, no longer look. But when they lived on earth no one could pass before them, no one could surpass them in speech. They considered themselves to be like gods. Do look at me, for I am gathering up your health and taking it away from you. Look at your lives. Let them make you weep and make you sad for tomorrow or the next day I will suddenly come to find you. I am going now.

---

39. That is, prepare them for death.

tlapitzalos[87] Calaquiz y miquiztli tlapitzaloz

Çihuatl y notlaçoñamictzi huel nechCoColhuia y nōtzoteco y moCoColitzin ynic motlatzinCo nehuatiCa huel neçi ȳ Ca huel chiCahuac timococotzinnohua—

loreso y çihuapile nonāmictzinne huel quimati y noyollo Camo ninehuaz ytla oninomiq̄li çan ixquich nictlatlani yxpatzinCo y dios huel hueCatla tlali ytzintla tinechmaquiliz—

Çihuatl y maCamo ximotequipachotzinno Can mochihuaz y motlañahuatiltzin ytlaCamo hualtotoCaz yn itetlaçotlalitzin ȳ dios Ca huel quimati ȳ noyollo Ca ye onnōnipeuh Ca huel acmo huelti yn nōtlalo y noçoquiyo çannixquich[88] nechtequipachohua aqui techitaz aqui techaCoCuiz [24v] Otoçetzotlahuelliltic y titlatlacohuaniem[89]—

Loreso y noñamictzinne ma oC achitzin xinechmotlalCahuili maCamo OC achi ximoCoColizeuhtzinno—

Motecaz oc çecni y cihuantzitli auh yn agel OCa moetztiyez ȳtlan

---

1º aḡel y dios ytlachihualtzintzinhuane Ca ye yxquich Ca ye ontlamiCo yn amonemiliz Ca ye anmechhualmonochilia yn amotantzin dios yncenmactzinco xomocahuaca—

demoniº hualquicaz[90] motlaCachichihuaz hualaz ytla y CoCoxque quinotzaz—

2º demō y yxquich amotlapal notelpotztzine ynhua yni tehuatzin nochpotzinne maCamo ximoçotlahuaCa ytla xinetlamatiCa aço apantizque aCa xicnotzaCa amechpatiz amotolinia namechyoyollalico—

Loreso y aqui tehuatzin amo timitztiximachilia y titechmolhuilia tictemozque yn aqui techpatiz Ca ye oninonyollCuiti[91] yhua y nonamic ~~yea~~ ye teoyotiCa ontitopatique neyolCuitiliztiCa otictoçelilique y totechiuhCatzin dios Ca ça ticchixtiCate y queni [25r] quimonequiltiz Ca yehuatzin çeuhtzintli pātzintli[92]—

1º aḡēl y Yn timictlatlentexcali ma opa xihuetzin ȳ çenCa ohuiCa yn āyc tlamiz yn anyc tzoquiçaz ma ºpa xitleCoCotonCa monexicoliztiCa axCa ticmahuiçoz yn imicneliloCa xiquitlalCahui y timictlacuitlamiztitli—

quihuihuitequiz quichololtiz y demō

Loreso y nontlaçonāmictzinne nictlatlani y nontlapōpōlhuililoCa ynpanpatzinCo ȳ dios ma nimitznōnahuatequili—

---

87. tlapitzalos: added in a different hand.
88. çannixquich: read *çan ixquich*.
89. titlatlacohuaniem: read *titlatlacohuanime*.
90. hualquicaz: read *hualquiçaz*.
91. oninonyollCuiti: read as standard *oninoyolcuiti*.
92. Stage directions follow in the second version of this play: *quihuinhuitequiz. yn demonio—yn angel quichololtiz*. This anticipates (with relatively minor differences) the stage directions that immediately follow First Angel's lines.

(Wind instruments are played. Death exits. Wind instruments are played.)

WOMAN: O my beloved spouse, my head really hurts me. Your sickness, as I sit beside you, really appears very strong; you are ill.

LORENZO: O noblewoman, O my spouse, my heart knows well that I will not get up. When I have died, all I ask for before God is that you will bury me deeply under the ground.

WOMAN: Do not worry. Your command will be carried out, if I do not die right away myself.[40] My heart knows well that I have already begun [to die]. My earth, my clay is no longer strong. All that worries me is, who will see us, who will lift us up?[41] [24v] Oh, we are four hundred times unfortunate, we sinners!

LORENZO: O my spouse, leave me for a little longer. Do not become more sick.

(He lies down, and in another place the woman. And the angel is there with them.)

FIRST ANGEL: O creations of God, that is all, your lives have already come to an end. Your father, God, is calling you now. Leave yourselves entirely in his hands.

(The demon enters. He dresses himself as a human being. He comes close to the sick ones. He calls to them.)

SECOND DEMON: Give it all your effort, O my son, and you, O my daughter. Do not faint! If you are discontented, perhaps you will recover. Call someone who will cure you. You are afflicted. I have come to console you.

LORENZO: Who are you? I do not know you. You tell us that we are to seek someone who will cure us. I have already confessed, along with my spouse. Already through confession we have healed ourselves in a sacred way. We have received our maker, God.[42] We are just awaiting what [25r] he will want, for he is repose and medicine.

FIRST ANGEL: You, who are the fiery crag of the place of the dead, fall in the very dangerous place that will never be finished, never come to an end. Be broken up by the fire there, through your envy. Now you will behold how they are favored. Leave them, you puma of the place of the dead!

(He repeatedly beats and drives away the demon.)

LORENZO: O my beloved spouse, I ask that I be pardoned for the sake of God. Let me embrace you.

---

40. Literally, "if God's love does not come rushing." Death is often spoken of as "God's love" in Nahuatl wills.
41. That is, carry them for burial?
42. That is, we have also taken communion.

Çihuatl v notlaçonamictzi. ma ypanpa yn dios ytlaçonatzi ylh^c çihuapilli Sancta maria ma xinechmotlaponpolhuilili ma yctenamiq̄[93] y momatzin—
Ytla omotlaponpolhuique ȳ CoCoxque nima hualquiçazque ȳn añimaz huel miyequiti[94] hualyaCanaz~~que~~ on ome oquihualhuicazque ome Candela huallalatiyaz[95] ymac tlatlaz y momiquilizque yhua motlapoz yn ilhuiCaC huel pampaquizque yn agelz—quipalehuizque yn animaz ynic momiquilizque[96]—[25v]
1º añimaz v Ca otiquixtlahuaCo y motetlaçotlalitzin totlaçoycniuhtzinne—
2 añimaz v Ca oticCuepCayotiCo ynic topanpa OtimoChoquilitineCa—

3 animaz v Ca otimitztopalehuiliCo yn iuhqui Ontitechmopalehuili yn ixpatzinCo y dios—

---

4 animaz v Ca ontiquixtlahuaCo yniC omitztlaonColti yn tomiyotzin ȳ totetepontzin—
5º animaz v Ca otamechtanniliCo yteCopatzincon yn dios yciuhCa tiyazque—
6 anīmaz v yñayolliliztin ma yçiuhCa xictlalCahuica yn amotlalo yn amoçōquiyo Camechhualmonochilia[97] amechhualmotzatzinlilia y toyolilinçenCatzin dios ȳ tloctzinco amopaCançenhuizque—
\# huel çençenyaCa hualquiztiyazque yñ animaz ynic quitlatlauhtizque ȳ CoCoxque ymac momiquilizque ȳn ānimaz çan ye tlapochtiyez yn ilhuiCac—
agel v xihualmoquixti animā amo ximomauhti tle mitzmauhtiya y niCa Ca mopampa y pampacohua yn h^c[98] ytic [26r] y çenCa ohuaquimotlaçotlayecoltillique y tt^o[99] dios y niCa tlaticpa Ca niCa motlatzinCo ^{ninemini} amo nāmechnocahuilia—
Onpa y quitoz yn itlatol yn agel nima momiquilizque yçiuhCa quihuiCazque yn progatoriō yn imanima mochichihuazque ome huel tepītzitzin yn piltzintzi Cololhuitiyazque yñ animaz ni[100] hualquiçazque Ometi telponpochti ^{tlapitzaloz}[101]—
1º telpochtli v nocniuhtzinne mach ye oquimopolhui y dios y Loresotzi yhuan içihuauhtzin qui huel achitoCa yn onniquimitac yxquich tlaCatl ōpa hualquiquiça tla toyollo onpachihui aço ytla totlamatlanizque[102] yc motoCatzinozque—

2 telpochtli v ma dios quimotlanexmaquili ca huel mahuiztique tlaCa OCatCan ma onpa tonaçitihuetzinCa[103]—
1º telpochtli v ma dios amotlatzinco moyetztie nōtlaçoyCauhtzinne yhua y tehuatzin çihuapile—

---

93. iyctenamiq̄: probably to be read *nictennamiqui*.
94. huel miyequiti: in the second version of this play: 6.
95. huallalatiyaz: read *huallatlatiyaz*.
96. Additional text follows in the second version of this play: yn lorenço—yhua yn içihuauh.
97. Camechhualmonochilia: read *Ca amechhualmonochilia*.
98. h^c: read *ilhuicatl*.
99. tt^o: this superscript addition is not present in the second version of this play.
100. ni: read *niman* as in the second version of this play.
101. tlapitzaloz: added in a different hand. Another addition (not sure where it goes) is the following, in tentative transcription: motzaquaz yn [ih^c?].
102. totlamatlanizque: perhaps to be read *tontlamactlanizque*.
103. In the second version of this play stage directions follow: *niman ic yazque. yn icha. Lorenço.*

WOMAN: O my beloved spouse, for the sake of God's beloved mother, the heavenly noblewoman, Saint Mary, pardon me. Let me kiss your hand.

(When the sick ones have pardoned each other, then a lot[43] of souls enter. The two who lead the way come carrying two candles which are burning. They burn in the hands of those who will die and heaven opens.[44] The angels really rejoice. The souls help them[45] to die.)
[25v]
FIRST SOUL: We have come to repay your love, O our beloved friend.

SECOND SOUL: We have come to make return for the way you went about weeping for our sake.

THIRD SOUL: We have come to help you as you helped us before God.

FOURTH SOUL: We have come to repay the way our bones, our tibias made you sad.

FIFTH SOUL: We have come to take you, by order of God. We will go quickly.

SIXTH SOUL: You lives, quickly abandon your earth, your clay. The owner of our lives, God, is calling you, is crying out to you. With him you will rest happily.

(One by one the souls come passing by to address the sick ones. In the hands of the souls they die. Heaven remains open.)

ANGEL: Come out, soul, do not be afraid. What frightens you here? For your sake there is rejoicing in heaven. [26r] You have served our lord God very lovingly here on earth. I live here with you. I do not leave you.[46]

(At that point the angel makes his statement. Then they die. They quickly take their souls to purgatory. Two very small children are dressed up. The souls go surrounding them. Then two youths enter. Wind instruments are played.)

FIRST YOUTH: O my friend, they say that God has now destroyed Lorenzo and his wife. Barely a moment ago I saw all the people coming out of there. Do let us satisfy ourselves. Perhaps we will order that something be given so that they can be buried.[47]

SECOND YOUTH: May God give them light. They were highly esteemed people. Let us get there quickly.[48]

FIRST YOUTH: May God be with you, O my dear friend, and you, O noblewoman.

---

43. The second version of this play specifies the number of souls: *Six*.
44. We interpret the preceding to mean that the souls place the candles in the hands of Lorenzo and his wife who are probably lying on their backs, holding the lit candles on their chests.
45. The second version of this play clarifies this referent: *Lorenzo and his wife*.
46. The second version of this play reads: I will not leave you.
47. Tentative translation.
48. The second version of this play adds the following stage directions: *At that point they go to Lorenzo's house*.

2 telpochtli y auh Can oyaque yn ixquich tlaCatl y niCa ONCatca Ca huel tetzahuitl yn axCa tiquita yn oquimochili[104] dios ma yçiuhca titenotzāti ximohuiCa nocniuhtzine [26v] ma yçiuhCa hualhuilohua ȳnic motoCatzinnozque—
1º telpochtli y ma ninōtlalotihuetzin ynic ȳçiuhCa motoCatzinnozque—
Mochiti hualquiçazque tetoCazque mēhuaz rezponso ytla omotoCaque nima tlapitztzaloz motlapoz yn ȳīħ.Cac—tlapitzaloz[105]

Vrigē[106] y notlaçōconetzi: noyezyotzin nōtlapālotzin çenCa mitzmetiçihuitilia yn itlatlacol yn tlalticpac tlaCa ma nalquiça y moJustiçiatzin yn itechcacopa yn ōpa caten y motletenchipahuayatzinco[107] y progāturio Ca ye mixpatzinCo Onnictlali y nochoquiz y notlaOCol ma xiquimotlamachtili ȳ motloctzinCo y monahuactzin[108] yn ilhuiCatl ytic y motlachihualtzintzihua—
pōx[109] nonotlaçomahuiznatzinne Ca mochihuaz Ca tzoquiçaz y motlanequilitzin Ca yehuatl niquilnamiqui ynic oyetiçiuh y motlaçomatzin ynic otinechmonāpal[27r]tineCa yhua Ca anmo çan iyo y ñopampa oticmiyhiyohuilti nopampa Ontimochoq̄ˡlitinenCa yn iquac Onechtlayhiyohuiltique y noteCoColiCahuan auh amo quitlaçoCamati y tlalticpac tlaCa yn ixqᶜch[110] ypāpa ticmochihuilia auh ma quihualquixtiti y ñotlaçontzitzinhua y çenCa onechCuiltononque yCa y motlaçōmahuizroSanriotzin—
Vrige y ytecopatzinCo y nontlaçōconetzin xiquihualquixtiti yn opa Cate y progātorio yhua yn onnechylcauh yn inenemiya yhua yn iCochiya yn anmo Onquitlali yn ixquac y Crůz yn̄ opa quauhtla OquihuiCac y huey tequanni y çan[111] [?] niCa yn inaCayo yn oquihuiCaᶜ ma niCa yxpatzinCo neçi y notlaçoConetzin[112]—

tlapitza[113] # nima quihualquixtitihui y progatorio Caten auh ytla oquihualhuiCaque y Cani yez ylhuiCatl—nima quitzatziliz y diayablome .3. [27v] yn agel mochiti yazq̄ y agelz

---

1º agel y xihualmoquixtiCa y çenCa ohuāquimotlaçotlayecoltilique y dios ȳtlaçonnatzin—
y nima quitzatzinliz y demoñios yn agel ytla ohuaçico yxpatzincon y pōx̄o—
1º agel y xihualquiçan Ca y mictla amilpitoque xiqualqnixtiCa[114] yn oāquihuiCaque y tlatziuhqui[115]

---

104. oquimochili: read *oquimochihuili*.
105. tlapitzaloz: in a different hand.
106. Vrigē: here and below, read *virgen*.
107. motletenchipahuayatzinco: in the second version of this play: motetlechipahuayatzinco.
108. monahuactzin: read *monahuactzinco*.
109. pōx: here and below in various nonstandard variants, this usually appears in Nahuatl church texts as xp̄o.
110. ixqᶜch: read *ixquich*.
111. çan: something follows that is crossed out and illegible.
112. Following this is in the second version of the play: 2.º angel = ma nima ticchihuati yn motlatocatla[nahua]tiltzin toteyoCoxcatzine Diose xpo.e.
113. tlapitza: added in a different hand.
114. xiqualqnixtiCa: read *xichualquixtican*.
115. Immediately following, in superscript, is an additional item in the second version of this play: molcahuani. There are also what appear to be doodles, for the purpose of practicing writing.

SECOND YOUTH: But where did all the people go who were here? It is very ominous. Now we see what God has done. Let us quickly call people. Go, O my friend. [26v] Let people come quickly so that they may be buried.

FIRST YOUTH: Let me run off in a hurry so that they may be buried quickly.

(All enter. They perform the burial. The responsory is raised [in song]. When they have been buried, then wind instruments are played. Heaven opens. Wind instruments are played.)

VIRGIN: O my beloved child, my blood, my dye,[49] the sins of the people of earth weigh very heavily upon you. May your justice reach unto those who are there in your place of fiery purification of people, purgatory. I have already placed before you my weeping, my sadness. Make your creations happy next to you, beside you, in heaven.

CHRIST: O my beloved honored mother, what you desire will be done, will be carried out. I remember how your precious hands were heavily weighted as you carried me about in your arms, [27r] and it was not solely for my sake that you suffered, for my sake that you went about weeping when those who hated me tormented me. But the people of earth are not grateful for all that you do for them. And let them bring forth my beloved ones, who pleased me very much with your precious and honored rosary.

VIRGIN: By order of my beloved child, go bring out those who are there in purgatory, along with the one who forgot me, who in his going about and in his sleeping did not place the cross on his forehead, whom the great beast carried off there in the forest. Right here is his body, which it carried off. Let him appear here before my beloved child.[50]

(Wind instruments are played. Then they go to bring out those who are in purgatory. And when they have brought them out to where heaven is then the angel cries out to the three demons. [27v] All the angels go off [to purgatory].)

FIRST ANGEL: Come out, you who lovingly served God's beloved mother.

(Then the angel cries out to the demons who have come before Christ.)

FIRST ANGEL: Come out, you who lie tied up in the place of the dead. Bring out the one you carried off, the lazy one.[51]

---

49. blood, dye: see above footnote on the same diphrase. In this context not only is the pragmatic thrust "my offspring" but there are also connotations of noble birth.

50. The second version of this play has another speech following this one by the Virgin: SECOND ANGEL: Let us then carry out your royal command, O our creator, O God, O Christ.

51. The second version of this play adds in superscript: the forgetful one.

cētlapal[116] momanazq̄ qualti yhua yn agelz çentlapal yez y codenadon—

3O.[117] demō. y̲ Ca ye otiqualhuiCaque ȳ nantle[118] ypa tlachiya

---

p̄ōx y̲ xihualauh notlachihuale xinechnaquili tle yCa yn ōmitzychteqto y quauhtla y tlacatecolotl [28r] tlen ic omitzmoxicti Cuix amo onñamechhualCahuilitia yn āmomaq̄xtiloca yn tlalticpac +—

codenado y̲ Ca ytlatlacol ȳ notatzin[119] amo onechyximachti y motoCatzi yhua çan onechpaCayhiyohui yn oniquixtlatzinyaya yn ixCo ycpac onine ytla onechtla-Cahualtiyani aço ᵃmo yuhqui nopā omochihuazquiya onoçētzōtlahuellitic—

2 agel y̲ noteotzinne notlatoCatzinne tlen ec[120] niquitoz y mixpatzinco Ca anmo onnechCac yn i Capā OnotzatzintitineCa y niCa mixpatzinco quiteyxpahuiya—

---

3 demō y̲ y tehuāti Cuix amo ça çentetl yniC otitechhualmotelchihuili auh yni Cuix ça çenpa yn ixCo ycpac one yn itantzi yn inantzin yhua y motoCatzin ça oqui-tlapic[28v][121]tenehuaya ytla onxicmoCahuiliani y tlalticpac Ca amo ça tlapohualti yn oquimictizquiya yn ihuapohua yninC[122] omitzmopanahuilizquiya—

p̄xō y̲ xihualhuiya xichuiCan Ca onpa yn tletexCalCo xicpiloCa Opa xichuitequiCa xictzatzayaCa ypanpa Ca nehuatl yn ōnechyxtlatzini y nixCo nocpac one—

3 demōno y̲ Otitechmocnelili ma yçiuhCa ticchihuati y motlatocatlanahuatiltzin—

Vrige y̲ auh yn amehuantzitzin y huel ōhuamotlaçontlaque y tlalticpac ma huel pam-paqui yn ilhuicatl xihualmotlecahuiC—Cuicō[123]

---

codenado y̲ yn ātlacahuapahua yn atlaCazCaltia maCamo ça xixoxolopititiCa yuhqui yn amo amozCalia xictlapoCa yn amonaCaz xicCaquiCa ȳy çermo yhua y nex-Cuitilmachiyᵒtl amo ahuetzitiʰᵘⁱ y tletexCalco ȳ yn iuhqui axCa ye niauh—

---

116. Preceding these stage directions in the second version of this play: hualquiztehuazque. yn demonios.
117. 3O: in the second version of this play: 2.O.
118. yȳnantle: read *yn atle*.
119. In the second version of this play is added in superscript: i nonantzin.
120. ec: standard *ic*.
121. Something illegible immediately precedes these characters *tenehuaya*.
122. yninC: read *ynic*.
123. Cuicō: Cuicos in the second version of this play.

(On one side are spread about the good ones and the angels. On [the other] side is the condemned one.)[52]

THIRD DEMON:[53] We have brought the disrespectful one.

CHRIST: Come, O my creation. Answer me. Why did the demon steal you in the forest? [28r] Why did he disdain you? Did I not leave you your means of salvation on earth?

CONDEMNED ONE: It is my father's[54] fault. He did not make your name known to me, and he just patiently put up with me when I used to slap his face, when I offended him. If he had stopped me, perhaps it would not have happened to me like this. Oh, four hundred times unfortunate am I!

SECOND ANGEL: O my deity, O my ruler, what will I say before you? Wherever I went about crying out to him, whom they bring to justice here before you, he did not listen to me.

THIRD DEMON: As for us, was it not just one thing that you scorned us for?[55] And was it just one time that he offended his father and his mother? And he would just pronounce your name in vain. [28v] If you left him on earth innumerable are his fellows whom he would have killed, by which he would have surpassed you.[56]

CHRIST: Come. Take him there to the fiery crag. Hang him, beat him, rip him apart there, because it is I whom he slapped in the face, I whom he offended.

THIRD DEMON: Thank you. Let us quickly go to carry out your royal command.

VIRGIN: And you who have loved one another well on earth, rejoice much in heaven. Come on up.

(There is singing.)

CONDEMNED ONE: You who bring up children, you who raise children, do not be idiotic, as if you were not rational. Open your ears! Listen to the sermon and the exemplary model. You are not going to fall into the fiery crag like I am now about to do!

---

52. The second version of this play adds at the beginning of these stage directions: *The demons hurriedly enter.*
53. The second version of this play marks this character: SECOND DEMON.
54. The second version of this play adds in superscript: and my mother's.
55. That is, the devils were cast out of heaven for committing only one sin.
56. That is, disregarded you?

Present Location
Library of Congress
Washington, D.C.

[44r]

NeyxCuintilli yntechpa tlantohua yn pochtecatl Auh axcan NiquiCuilohua nehuatl notlatqui Notoca .d. Joseph gaspar y nica Nocha S. Juā bap.^ta Tolatzin.^co auh nictlalia yn tonali. ynhua y xihuitl Axcan sabado a 15 de nobienbre de 1687 años.

Tlahtolpepechtli

<u>v</u> Ma yehuatzin. Amotlantzico quimotlalili yn itetlamatcanemitiayatzin y dios espū sancto y nica Oanhualmohuicaque anquimoCuilico anquimocaquiltico yn ihiyotzin yn itlahtoltzin y tlacatl tlatohuani dios Ca nican amixpantzin.^co Tocōtlalizque Toconchihuazque Centlamātli neyxCuitilmachiyotl yn Cenca temamauhti yn queni OquimotlatzaCuiltili yn tt.^o dios yn Cen tlacatl moCuiltonohuani motlacamatini tetech tlayxpanani yhuan teaxca tetlatqui quixpachohuaya. auh macihui yn omoyolCuiti. yhuan OquimoCenlili yn itlaçomahuiznacayotzin yn itlaçomahuizezotzin yn totemaquixticatzin Jesu X͞p͞o. Ca amo yc otlaocoliloc Ca oc Cenca ye yc otelchihualoc ypanpa Amo oquiteCuepili. y. teaxca yn tetlatqui yc Cenca temamauhti. teCueCuechmicti. yn ipā omochiuh yn inacayo yhua yn ianima ma huel y^tech ximixCuintica yn tetech antlaxitlapanani¹ macamo yuhqui Amopā mochihuaz yn iJusticiatzin yn tt.^o dios yn āmochinti y nican Amonoltitoque ma yc ximomauhtican ynic amo ypa ahuetzizque y huey tlatlancolli y tetech tlayxtlapānaliztli y tetech tlamiyecaquixtiliztli auh ynī ma huel ypaltzin.^co yn dios yntech tictlalica yn toyollo ynin neyxcuitilmachiyotl. Auh ytla ytla toconitlacozque ma ça yehuantzin yn tlacatl tlantohuani dios atechmotlapopolhuililyzque²—

OnCan hualquiçaz yn poChteCatl—

Quitoz—[44v]

Pochtecatl <u>v</u> yn ipā yn ixquich y nohuelitiliz Ayac huel nechaçiz yn ipa yn ixquich noaxca notlatqui yn Coztic teoCuitlatl yn iztac teoCuitlatl yn chalchihuitl yn quetzalitztli ynnepyollotli³ auh yn ixquich y nepanpa tlaçotli y nopapāquiliz yn tlaçotilmātli yn tlaçotlaquemitl ayac huel nechaçiz aquin yacachtopa tenehualo hitolo yn iquac. teCohuanotzaloyā amo ça ye nehuatl auh yn iquac yn nenamictilo yn Cuico aqui yacatopa notzalo temolo: Amo çan ye nehuatl Ca huel nolhuil nomaCenhual Oc nocotimalotinemi yn tlalticpac auh Cenca nechpanpaquiltia yn icnotlaCantototi y nohuicpa ytztihui ynic niquintlatlaneuhtia auh yn iquac amo yciuhca quixtlahua auh oc cenca nichuecapanohua ynic nechtlaxtlahuilia yehica ynic amo polihuiz y noaxca notlatqui amo ye huitze tla oc niquimōchie. Oncan hualquiças huehuentzin ~~yhuā~~ ylamatzin⁴

---

1. antlaxitlapanani: read *antlaixtlapanani*.
2. atechmotlapopolhuililyzque: read *techmotlapopolhuililitzino*.
3. ynnepyollotli: read *yn epyollotli*.
4. Oncan hualquiças huehuentzin ~~yhuā~~ ylamatzin: added later in a different hand, with lines above and below.

The Merchant
Translated by Barry D. Sell, with assistance from Louise M. Burkhart

[44r]

Edifying example that speaks about a merchant. I am writing it today; it is my property. My name is Don Joseph Gaspar and I am a resident here in San Juan Bautista Tollantzinco. I am setting down the day and year: today is Saturday, 15 November, of the year 1687.

Prologue.

May God the Holy Spirit set down among you the peace of our lord.[1] You have come here to grasp and hear the fine words of God, lord and ruler. Here before you we will set down and perform a model edifying example, very frightening, [concerning] how our lord God punished a person who was happily rich. He was a moneylender and hid other people's goods and property. Even though he confessed and had received the precious honored body and precious honored blood of our savior, Jesus Christ, he was not therefore shown mercy but was especially despised because he had not returned to others their goods and property. Thus what happened to his body and his soul was very frightening and very terrifying. You who are moneylenders, really take an example from it, let not the same justice of our lord God happen to you. Be frightened by it, all of you who are assembled here, so that you will not fall into the great sin of moneylending and usury. Now then, for the sake of God[2] let us set our hearts on this model edifying example. But if [in spite of this moral instruction] we should err in something may God, lord and ruler, pardon us.

(At that point Merchant enters. He says:) [44v]

MERCHANT: No one can equal me in all my power, in all my goods and property, the gold and silver, the jades and emeralds, the precious pearls. No one can equal me in all the diverse precious things that are my pleasures, the expensive cloaks and expensive garments. When it is time for banquets: who is first mentioned and spoken of? Is it not I? When there are weddings and singing: who is the first summoned, who the first spoken to? Is it not I? I go about increasing my rewards and fortunes here on earth. The miserable little poor people give me great pleasure when they go looking to me to make them loans. And when they don't quickly pay them back I especially increase what they are to repay me so that my goods and property will not perish. Are they not coming now? Let me await them.

(At that point Old Man enters ~~with~~ Old Woman.)

---

1. Molina 1977, 42v: "Itetlamatcanemitiaya in dios. la paz de nuestro señor" (see also 74r, 108v). Abbreviations in the original Nahuatl and Spanish have been resolved here and in the other footnotes to this translation.

2. While these and similar constructions (with a few exceptions) have been translated here as "for the sake of," translators sometimes have used the phrasing "for the love of." For "ypaltzinco," consult Molina 1565, 7r: "ypaltzinco Dios" / "por amor de Dios"; see also Carochi 1983, 17r. For "ypampatzinco" see Molina 1984, 116r: "ypampatzinco totecuiyo Dios" / "por amor de nuestro señor dios." See also Arenas 1982, 35: "*hazlo por amor de Dios*—ma ipampatzinco yn toTecuiyo Dios xicchihua." For "icatzinco," see Siméon 1988, 53: "*icatzino in totecuiyo,* por el amor de nuestro Señor, o gracias a nuestro Señor."

huehuetzin v Nopiltzintzine tlacatle tlatohuanie mixpātzin^co ninopechteca Cenca nimitznotlatlauhtilia ypaltzinco yn tt.º. dios ma Xinechmotlaneuhtilitzinno matlactli pesos ynic niquixtiz nopiltzin ilpitica ynic amo tzauhcan quicahuazque Ca çan nimā yciuh[5] nimitznocuepililiz Axcan Caxtolilhuitl.

Pochtecatl. v Ye nicaqui y motlatol yn tehuatl. Auh Cuix çan amehuanti Amopanpa y nictemotinemi yn teoCuitlatl. ynic namechtlatlaneuhtiz Ca ahuelitiz nimitzmacaz XimohuiCatiuh Auh ytla ylpitiCa mopiltzin Cuix noteq̄uh ma ça quinamācacan ma tzauhcan quicahuacā Cuix namechyximati Cuix anezohuan Anotlapalohuan. Ximohuicatihuiya Amo namechmaCaz—[45r]

Ylamatzin ynamic v Noquichpiltzin NoteCuiyotzin ma çan ipanpatzin.^co yn tt.º d. ma ça Xitechmotlaneuhtili y motomintzin Auh ca toCotlapehuizque yn ipa y cen pesso Tehuatzin ticmomachiltia yn quexquich ypā toCotlalizque.

Pochtecatl. v Ca tel ye qualli Ca tel ye melahuac y tiquitohua y tehuatl. y tilamatlacatl. Ca namechmacaz y notomin Auh ca ye anquimati yn çe peso. nahui tomi ypan anquitlalizque Ca ye qualli ma namechmaca auh çan caxtolilhuitl. AquiCueppazque auh ytla quipanahuiz caxtolilhuitl ytla oc quezquilhuitl aquipiezque ca cenpohualli pessos anechmacazquē ytla yuh aquinequi Ca namechmacaz y notomī.

huehuentzin v. Ca tel ye qualli nopiltzintzine ma yuh mochihuaz ȳ motlanequilitzin yn iuh ticmonequiltitzinohua Ca nican cā y nonamic yhua y nehuatl ca nima yçiuhcan timitztoCuepililizq̄. Ca amo quipanahuiz y caxtolli tonatiuh ca nima yçiuhca timitztoCuepililizque Caxtolli peso ynic ocan tocotlalizque totlahuecahuaya maCuilli peso—

Pochtecatl. v. Ca yzcatqui ye namechmacan y matlactli pesos. auh ça caxtolilhuitl. annechCuepillizque yc āquiCuepazq̄ Caxtolli pesos—

ylamatzin v Ca çenca tocōtlaçocamati y motepalehuillitzin otlacauhqui y moyollotzin otitechmocnelili Ca ye tiyatihui—

huehuentzin v Ma mitzmochicahuili yn tt^o dios ma.oc timitztotlalcahuilican—

Pochtecatl v Ximochuicatihuia ma dios Amechmohuiquili—

Tlapitzaloz oca hualquiçaz ychpochtli motlatlanehuiz—[45v]

---

5. yciuh: read *yciuhca*.

OLD MAN: O my nobleman, O personage, O ruler, I humbly bow low before you. I greatly implore you: for the sake of our lord God lend me ten pesos so that I will free my child who is in custody, so that they will not deliver him to a textile manufacturing shop.[3] I will straightaway return it to you fifteen days [from] now.

MERCHANT: I hear your words but is it on your account I go about searching for gold and silver[4] to lend you? I will not be able to give it to you. Be going along. If your child is in custody, is it my responsibility? Let them sell him off, let them deliver him to a textile manufacturing shop. Do I know you? Are you my offspring? Be going along. I will not give it to you. [45r]

OLD WOMAN (his spouse): O my son, O my lord, let it just be for the sake of our lord God. Lend us your money. We will pay interest on each peso; you can decide how much interest we will pay.

MERCHANT: Very well, old woman, what you are saying is true. I will give you my money. But you already know that you will add four tomines for each peso you borrow. Very well, let me give it to you. You will return it within fifteen days. But if more than fifteen days pass, if you have it a few days more, you will give me twenty pesos. If that's the way you want it I will give you my money.

OLD MAN: O my nobleman, very well, may your will be done as you want it. Here are my spouse and I. We will straightaway restore it to you; it will not exceed fifteen days. We will extremely quickly repay you [a total of] fifteen pesos. We will put down five [additional] pesos in a second part [to pay] for our grace period.[5]

MERCHANT: Here are the ten pesos I am giving you but you will return it to me in just fifteen days. As [agreed] you will return fifteen pesos.

OLD WOMAN: Thank you very much for your help. We give you many thanks for the favor you have shown us.[6] We are going now.

OLD MAN: May our lord God give you health. Let us leave you now.

MERCHANT: Be going along. May God go with you.

(*Wind instruments are blown. At that point Young Woman enters to ask for a loan.*) [45v]

---

3. tzauhcan: while the neutral term "textile manufacturing shop" has been used here and below, modern pejorative "sweat shop" may more accurately capture the tone of this colonial institution. For the term itself, see Pérez 1713, 179: "obraxe" / "tzaccan."

4. gold and silver: here and below, Nahuatl *teocuitlatl* (literal meaning probably "divine/god excrement" but general thrust is "precious metal[s]") with the modifiers *coztic* (yellow) and *iztac* (white) that refer, respectively, to "gold" and "silver." Since the more specific meanings are given in the merchant's first speech, with all the following references being to generic *teocuitlatl*, I have interpreted the latter as meaning (in the context of this play) "gold and silver." Note, however, the following two entries in Arenas 1982, 141: "Coztic teocuitlatl—*Oro*," followed immediately by plain "teocuitlatl—*plata*" (that is, the unmodified form means "silver").

5. totlahuecahuaya / our grace period: see related terms in Molina 1977, 144r.

6. The fortuitous phrasing here and below can be found in Molina 1984, 118v: "¶ Notecuiyoe tlatohuanie, otlacauhquin moyollotzin otinechmocnelili" / "¶ Señor mio, hagoos muchas gracias, por los beneficios que me aueys hecho."

ychpochtli y Ma mitzmotlaçochicahuili y motlaçotatzin dios Noquichpiltzin note-Cuio mixpātzin.^co cenca ninopechteca ȳ nehuatl y nimocnomaÇenhualtzin ma ypaltzin^co yn tt.^o Jesu X p̄o. Ma xinechmopalehuilitzino Ca y nonātzin yhuan y notatzin Çencan motoliniticate huel huey cocoliztli ypā quimochihuilia ȳ tt.^o dios auh ynic tiquimopalehuiliz Ca yehuatl ynic nica Onihuanla mixpātzin^co Aço nitlacnopilhuiz tinechmotlaneuhtiliz Çenpohuali pesos Ca nima niCueppaz Cenpohualilhuitl. auh can icatqui[6] Prenda ticmopieliz y notlapac y notlapāchiuhcan yhua y nohuipilli.[7] Cencan nimitznotlatlauhtilia ypaltzin^co y. tlaçoychpochtli Sta m.^a—

Chocaz yn ichpochtli

Pochtecatl. y Tle ticnequi ychpochtle ynic nixpā tichoca auh macihui yn qualli mitzmomaquilia yn dios y moxayac Ca anmo yehuatl nictemohua. Ca çenca nicnequi ynic miyec yez motlapehuiz y noteoCuitl auh ȳtla ticnequi ynic nimitztlaneuhtiz noteoCuitl Ontlamātli ticchihuaz ynic Çentlamātli yn ipanpa Cenpohualli pesos nimitztlaneuhtia Ca Açiz cenpōhualomālactli ynic tinechcueppiliz auh ytla ticnequin ynic ontlamātli ticchihuaz ynic çan achintzin nictzinquixtiz ynic amo miec ypā tictlaliz Ca tinechtlacamatiz. Ca nican notlan ticoChiquiuh auh ytlacamo ticnequi ma xiyauh amo nimitzmacaz y notomin—

ychpochtli y Ca nimā Amo huelitiz yn tle ticmitalhuia Ca y nehuatl. Ca amo nelihuiztlancatl. Ca amo nicnānamaca y nonācayo yntlacamo ticmonequiltia ynic tinechmotlaneuhtiliz motomintzin macamo Ma nimitznotlalcahuili—.

Niman Calaquiz hualquiçazque Omenti Cocoxque Motlatlayehuizque. [46r]

1° Cocoxqui y Ma ycatzin^co y motlaçotatzin dios ma ytlatzin xitechmotlaocolili por amor de dios.

2 Cocoxqui. y Ma çan icatzin.^co yn ilhuicac tlatocaychpochtli Sta m.^a Ma ytlatzi. xitechmocnoytilli Ca ça no yuh mitzmotlaocoliliz y yehuantzin y motlaçotantzin dios.

Pochtecatl y Notlacahuanē Amo aquicaqui yn ōpa Calten^co tzatzatzitimani Cocoyo xiquintocacan[8] ma huiya yn ilihuiztlacan yxpopōyome Cuix yehuantin Niquitlatlayecoltia ynic niquimacaz y naxca notlatqui Xiquitocacan[9] Ma huian = ma quiçacan Auh xiquimamauhtican Amo nica hualazque.

Ocā quitoCazque[10] Y Cocoxque

Tetlānequi y Xihuian xiquiçancan Amo nican xitzatzintimāca Aquimotzoteconehuilia yn tlatohuani ytla oc çenpa nican Ahualazque huel nican Tamechquatzatzanyanazque.

1° Cocoxqui y Yyoyahue diose tlatohuanie melahuacantetlatzōte=quiliyanie ma huel xicmomelauhcaytili yn ineyolpololiz yn ixhuintiliz y motlachihualtzin Ma xicmotlachieltili = Macamo xicmotelchihuili.—

OnCan Calaquizque Yn Cocoxque hualq.çaz yyolloco toquichti—

---

6. auh can icatqui: read *auh ca izcatqui*.
7. nohuipilli: read *nohuipil*.
8. xiquintocacan: read *xiquintotocacan*.
9. Xiquitocacan: read *xiquintotocacan*.
10. quitoCazque: read *quintotocazque*.

YOUNG WOMAN: May your beloved Father, God, give you precious health. O my son, O my lord, I humbly bow very low before you. I am your humble subject. For the sake of our lord Jesus Christ, help me. My mother and my father are suffering greatly. Our lord God has worked a very great sickness upon them. The reason that I have come before you is so that you will help them. Perhaps I will be so fortunate that you will lend me twenty pesos. I will return it right away to you [in] twenty days. Here are the pledges you will keep: my clean clothes, my headdress and my blouse. I greatly implore [this] of you, for the sake of the precious maiden Saint Mary.
(Young Woman cries.)

MERCHANT: What do you want, O young woman, that before me you cry? Although God has given you a pretty face that is not what I am searching for. What I very much want is for my gold and silver to be greatly increased. You will do two things if you want me to lend you my gold and silver. The first thing is that on account of the twenty pesos I will lend you, the amount you will return to me will total thirty pesos. If you want, the second thing you will do so that I will knock a bit off the price, so the interest you pay is not so great is you will obey me [by] coming here to sleep with me. If you don't want to, go, I will not give you my money.

YOUNG WOMAN: What you say is absolutely impossible. I am not an improper person.[7] I am not selling my body. If you do not want to lend me your money, don't. Let me leave you.
(At that point she exits. Two sick people enter to beg for things.) [46r]

FIRST SICK PERSON: For the sake of your beloved Father, God, have mercy on us with a little something. For the love of God!

SECOND SICK PERSON: For the sake of the heavenly royal maiden, Saint Mary, have mercy on us with a little something. Your beloved Father, God, will likewise be merciful to you.

MERCHANT: O my servants, do you not hear the howling of the coyotes there outside the house? Run them off! Let them go, those who are the frivolous people, the blind! Do I serve them such that I will give them my goods and property? Run them off! Let them go, let them leave. Frighten them [so that] they will not come here.
(At that point they run off the sick people.)

LOWLY SERVANT: Go, leave! Do not howl here. You are giving the ruler a headache. If you come here again we will really crack open your heads!

FIRST SICK PERSON: Alas, O God, O ruler, O righteous judge, look very clearly and directly at the doubts and confusion of your creature. Make him see. Do not despise him.
(At that point the sick people exit. Mature Man enters.)

---

7. Ca amo nelihuiztlacatl: here and below, I am here following what I consider to be the general thrust of the entries regarding *ilihuiz* in Molina's *Vocabulario* of 1571 (see Molina 1977, 37v). Nonetheless, note the following entry in Arenas 1982, 48, repeated (in reverse) on p. 145: "*embustero*—ilihuiztlacatl" (that is, an "ilihuiz" person is a "liar" or "trickster").

yyolloco toqchti. y Nopiltzintzine tlahtohuanie Ma motlantzin^co Moetztie yn dios Çencan nimitznotlatlauhtilia Mixpantzinco Ninopechtecan Ac. nimitznomaChiltitzinohuan Can izcatqui notomin Ma oc mopaltzin^co Xinechmopielili. Ca amo niCa niez. Ca oc nipa niyauh Onpa onaçitiuh y quauhtenmālan niCanatiuh y nonāmic. auh ca ypanpa nimitznotilia. Ca timahuiztic tlancatl. tihuey X͞piano: ca nican catqui Ontzontli ypan matlacpohualli pesos—. [46v]

Pochtecatl y Tla yuhqui yn Ca tel ye qualli Ma huallauh yn tomines nimitzpieli:[11] auh yn iquac in tihualmoCueppaz yn iquac tinechytlaniliz. Ca nima yçiuhcan nimitzCueppilliz—ha ye onicÇenlli Ontzontli = ypan Matlactli[12] pesos y nimitzpieliz.

—hualquiçazque huenhuetzin yhua ylanmatzin Ynamic—yas yn iyolloco toquichtin[13]

ylamātzin y Notlaçonamictzin Noquichpiltzin Ca ye ticmotilia Ca oaçico y Caxtolilhuitl ynic tiCuepilizque yn itlatqui yn poch=tecatl. Ca yalhua oniCac tiyaquizco quilmach Ayamo huenCauh çe oquichtli yhua çen Çihuatl. tzauhcan Oquincahuato: Onpan OquinamaCato yn ipanpa yn itomin Macamo = no yuhqui topa moChihuaz auh ypanpa yn ma xocomotemoli y mAçican moChihuaz ca nica nicpiya chicomē pesos Auh yn ChiCuey pesos ma yçiuhca xocomotemoli: ynic noconaxiltizque[14] yn Caxtolli macamo ypan tihuetzizque yn iqualan Ca anmo tlancatl ca çenca huey tlahuelliloc—.

huehuentzin y Ca ye qualli Cihuapille ma nocotemotihuetzin Ma yçiuhca ticmacanca ca ye ohuaçico y caxtolli tonatiuh—.

Pochtecatl y Xihuallauh yn tinonecauh: Ca ye ticmatin: Ca ye otzonquiça.^co y caxtoli tonatiuh: yn ipa motlatlalilinque ynic quixtlahuazque notomines nima yCiuhca xiyauh xiquimitlānili ytlacamo nima yciuhca mitzmacazque Telpiloyan xiquitlalli. nima amo mitztlaocoltizque y manel mixpan chocazque tlaocoyazque Xiquita Amo tiquitlacoz ytla tiquintlaocoliz ca tehuatl nimitzChoctiz nimitztequipachoz— Yaz ytlan i huehuentzin quitlanitiu quito[15]

Tetlāneq. y Ca ye qualli tlatohuanie ma niquimita ma niyauh Ca nica Onihualla ca nica niquitlanico y caxtolli pesos ytlacamo ni=ma yciuhca xinechmacancan: namechtlaliz Teylpiloya [47r] anoço namechhuiquiliz yn amoaxca yn amotlatqui—

huehuetzin y Notlaçopiltze ca nican ca yn itlatquitzin y yehuatzin yn topiltzin y tlacatl tlantohuani macamo yc ximoteq̄pachotzino—

+ Onca hualquiçaz Teuctli—

Teuctli y Notlaçopiltzintzine Ma ximehuiltitie nican mixpantzin^co Onihualla nictenamiquico y momātzin y mocxitzin tinechmopalehuiliz: notech monequi matlactzontli pesos tinechmotlaneuhtiliz yn ipa. Çen metztli Ca nima nimitznoCueppililiz Ma xinechmotlacamachititzino ma çan ica y motocatzin—

---

11. nimitzpieli: probably to be read *nimitzpieliz* as below; in a different hand.
12. Matlactli: scribal error; read *matlacpohualli* (as above and below).
13. yas yn iyolloco toquichtin: in a different hand.
14. noconaxiltizque: read *toconaxiltizque*.
15. Yaz ytlan i huehuentzin quitlanitiu quito: added at the end of this dialogue; in a different hand.

MATURE MAN: O my nobleman, O ruler, may God be with you. I greatly implore you, I humbly bow low before you. I hold you in great esteem.[8] Here is my money. Guard it for me out of respect for who you are. I am going to be absent for I am going all the way to Guatemala to get my spouse. The reason I am seeing you is because you are an honorable person, a great Christian. Here are one thousand pesos. [46v]

MERCHANT: Very well, let it be so. Let the money come that I will guard for you. When you return then ask me for it and I will promptly return it to you. Ah, I have now received the one thousand pesos I will guard.

(Old Man and his spouse, Old Woman, enters. Mature Man exits.)

OLD WOMAN: O my dear spouse, O my son, you now see that the fifteen days when we will return the merchant's property have passed.[9] Yesterday I heard them say in the marketplace that not long ago they took a man and woman to a textile manufacturing shop. They sold them off there because of his [i.e., the merchant's] money [not being repaid on time]. Let the same not happen to us. Because of this [latest development] see that it is thoroughly taken care of. I have seven pesos here. Quickly go on to search for the [other] eight so that we can make it reach the fifteen. Let us not incur his wrath for he is inhuman and very wicked.

OLD MAN: Very well, O noblewoman, let me quickly search for it. Let us quickly give it to him for the fifteen days have already passed.

MERCHANT: Come, you who are my servant. You already know the fifteen days in which they obligated themselves to repay my money have come to an end. Go quickly then and ask them for it. Put them in jail if they do not give it to you straightaway. Do not let them inspire the slightest pity in you, even though they cry and grieve before you. See to it. Make no mistakes. If you have mercy on them I will make you weep, I will inflict pain and worry on you.

LOWLY SERVANT: Very well, O ruler, let me see them. Let me go.

(He goes to Old Man. He goes to ask him, saying:)

LOWLY SERVANT:[10] I have come here to ask for the fifteen pesos. If you do not quickly give them to me I will put you in jail [47r] or perhaps take your goods and property away from you.

OLD MAN: O my beloved child, here is the property of our child, the lord and ruler. Do not worry yourself over it.

(At that point Lord enters.)

LORD: O my beloved nobleman, do remain seated. I have come here before you, come to kiss your hands and your feet. You shall help me. I need four thousand pesos. You will lend it to me. I will return it to you in one month. Heed me just out of respect for your name.

---

8. See Molina 1977, 2v.
9. Literally, here and below, "arrived."
10. The last several lines had to be rearranged to make sense. Otherwise there is confusion between the statements of the Lowly Servant to the Merchant and the Old Man as well as in the stage directions.

Pochtecatl. v Oticmihiyohuiltitzino yn titlacatl onicac y mihiyotzin yn motlantoltzin auh yn ticmonequiltia ynic nimitznotlaneuhtiliz: yn notomines Ma yuhqui mochihua auh ca ye ticmomachitia. Ca yc ninotlayecoltia auh ytla nimitznotlaneuhtiliz Matlactzontli pesos: yn ipa Çen metztli Ca oncan hualmantiaz Centzontli pesos yn ipan Ce metztli.[16]

Teuctli v Ca tel ye qualli Ma yuhqui mochihua yn iuh ticmonequiltia—

+ Niman MacoS y tomines Conceliz Nima yas

Yyolloco toq̃ch v Nopiltzintzine tlacatle tlatohuanie que timoyetzinnotica = Cuix anchitzin omitzmomaquilli yn itechicahuallitzin y. motantzin dios Çeca nimitznotlatlauhtilia Ma Xinechmomaquili y nimitznopieltili Notomines ca ye oniqualhuicac y nonamic auh yc nocotlacocohuiz.

Pochtecatl. v Ca nipactica Ma mitzmochicahuili yn dios ca qualli ynic otihualmocuepp.auh[17] tle tomines yn tinechytlanilia amo nicmati yn tle tinechylhuia.

Yyolloco toq̃ch v Tlacatle tlantohuanie Acaçomo ticmolnāmiquilia Ma = huel xicmolnamiquilitzino Ca ye axca nahui metztli yn onimitznopieltilitzinno Ontzontli ypā Matlacpohualli pesos. Ma ça ypaltzin[co] yn dios Xinechmaquilli—[47v]

Pochtecatl. v Ye nimitzilhuia Amo tle nicmati Aço otitlahuan Anoçen tiyolloCocoxqui xinechcahuan xiyauh—

yyolloco toq̃chti v Ca nima Amo nitlahuanqui. Amo niyollopoliuhqui Ca huel melahuac Ca onimitznomaquili yn iuhqui ticmitalhuitzinohua Ma xicmoqueChili Crus Juramento xicmochihuili—

Pochtecatl. v Ca melahuac y nimitzilhuia ca huel neltiliztli nicchihua mixpan Juramēto niquentza Crus nictenamiqui ypaltzinco dios ca amo tle nicmati ca amo tle Otinechmacac y motomin Atle nimitzpielia.

Yyolloco toq̃chti v Ca tel ye qualli Axcan pachihui y noyollo ynic tinechyxpachilhuia y notomines. Ca tel moetztica yn dios nococacahua Ma yehuantzin Mitzmotilili y motetlayxpachilhuilliz amo nica axcan ninotlahuelquixtiz—

Pochtecatl. v Xiyauh xinechtlalcahui ytlacamo yçiuhca tinechtlalcahuiz Ca nican Cante y notlacanhuan huel nican mitzhuihuintequizque Xihualhuian Nonencahuane xiquixtican i.y loco yn tlahuaquin—

+ OnCan quitoCazque quihuihuitequizque: hualquiçaz Nātli yhuā Ypilhuan

nātli v Noquichpiltzin noteCuiyotzin Ma motlatzin[co] motztie yn igraciatzin dios Spū S.[to] timitztotlapalhuico y timocnomaÇenhual=tzintzinhuan y nehuatl yhua y nopilhuan Auh ma ycnoyohua y moyollotzin Ca huel ninotolinia yhua huel motolinia y nopilhuan Ma Xinechmomaquilitzinno yn inTestanmēto y nonāmictzin yhua yn ixquich yn imaxca yn itlatq̃. yn itlal yn imil yn iteoCuitl. yn ichalchiuh Ca ye ticmomaChitia ynic Amo nixpan Omomĩquili altepetl ypa onihuia ōniquintlayecoltito y nopilhua Ma ypaltzin[co] yn tt.[o] dios Ma xiquimocnoytili ȳ mocnotlancantzintzinhuan—[48r]

---

16. metztl: read *metztli*.
17. otihualmocuepp.auh: read *otihualmocuep auh*.

MERCHANT: Greetings, lord. I have heard your fine words. As to you wanting me to lend you my money: let it be done. You already know that that is how I earn my living. But if I lend you the four thousand pesos for one month you will pay interest of four hundred pesos.

LORD: Very well. Let it happen as you want.
(He is given the money right away. He accepts it. Then he exits.)
MATURE MAN: O my nobleman, O personage, O ruler. How are you? Has your Father, God, given you a bit of his health? I greatly implore you to give me the money I entrusted to you for now I have brought my spouse here. I want to buy her things with it.
MERCHANT: I am healthy. May God grant you health. It is good that you have returned but what money are you asking me for? I do not know what you are telling me.
MATURE MAN: O personage, O ruler, perhaps you do not recall. Remember well that it is now four months [since] I entrusted the one thousand pesos to you. For God's sake, give it to me! [47v]
MERCHANT: I am telling you now I know nothing of it. Perhaps you are drunk or a madman. Leave me; go.
MATURE MAN: I am absolutely not a drunk, not deranged. Truly indeed I gave it to you. The way you are talking: hold up a cross and make an oath on it.

MERCHANT: What I am saying to you is correct, it is the very truth. I make an oath before you [by] raising up the cross, kissing it [and affirming that] by the love and respect of God I know nothing. You gave me none of your money. I have nothing of yours.
MATURE MAN: Very well, now I am satisfied that you are hiding my money from me. But God exists [as does] my property. Let him see you are hiding people's things from them. It is not here and now for me to vent my anger.
MERCHANT: Go, leave me. If you do not quickly leave me I have servants right here who will severely beat you. Come, my servants, eject this crazy drunkard.

(At that point they pursue him, severely beating him. Mother enters along with her children.)
MOTHER: O my son, O my lord, may the grace of God the Holy Spirit be with you. My children and I, your humble subjects, have come to greet you. May your heart be compassionate. I am very poor and my children are very poor. Give me the testament of my spouse along with all his goods and property, his fields, his gold and silver, and his jades. You already know that he did not die in my presence [because] I went to work in the altepetl[11] to support my children. For the sake of our lord God have pity on your humble servants. [48r]

---

11. altepetl: Nahuatl term applied to various kinds of sovereign sociopolitical units; most of those existing in central Mexico at this time were of approximately city-state dimensions. During colonial times it was translated in many ways including *ciudad* (city) and *pueblo* (people, settlement).

Pochtecatl. v. Tle tiquitohua Cihuatzintle Acaçomo huel tiquilnanmiq̄. acaçomo nehuatl. aço çan timotlapololtia ca y nehuatl. amo tle nicpian testamento auh yno tlalli yn milli y tictenehuan Ca notlacohual ca ye huecauh yn onicohuilli ȳ monāmic auh y teoCuitlatl. y chalchihuitl amo tle nicmati yn tictenehuan aço tehuatl Oticpōpolo: anoçe amo Oquichiuh yn itestamēto anoço aca motlahuical: amonehua Onaquipōpoloque[18] yn tlatquitl. Ximohuicatiuh amo tle nicmati. y tle tiquitohuan yntla otitlahuan: xiyauh xicochi amo xinechtequipacho +

Nantli. v Ca nelli: melahuac y niquitohua ca amo nitlahuanqui: ca huel neltiliztli y nimitznolhuilia. ca tehuantzin ticmopielia Ma çan icatzin[co] yn dios ma xicmochihuili yn itetlaçotlalitzin Ma xiquimotlaocolili y nopilhuantzintzin—

Pochtecatl. v Ca ye nimitzilhuian ȳ tiÇihuatl amo nic[c]aqui y tle ti.quitohuan xiyah[19] amo xinechamāna tinetzonteconehua xiyauh xiquitemoli yn intech monequiz y mochtacanpilhuan amo notequiuh xiyauh ayocmo nica nimitzintaz—Xihuallauh y tinonencauh xinechnochili yn Escriuāno y notlaçoycniuh—

Tetlanenqui v. Ca ye qualli tlatohuanie Ma nicnonochili—

+ OnCan hualquiçaz Escriuano—

Escriuano v Ma mitzmochicahuili yn dios tlatohuanie. aço ytla motenahuatiltzin: Ca onihualla nicaquico—

Pochtecatl. v Nocniuhtzine tla nica timohuicatz nima yçiuhca Xocomochihuili Cen Amatl. Oncan ticmotlaliliz OniCouh y calli: yhua y tlalli Xochimilcopa ytzticac auh y milli huel huey tepeyaca[c]copan ytztimani auh onicouh. Ontzontli ypan Matlacpohualli Onnicten. auh huel yuh xictlali ypan yñamatl.[20] ca yei xihuitl y nicouh ypan [48v] ypan[21] 1627 años xiquita huel qualli ticchihuaz amo tiquitlacoz Ca ye ticmati ca tinotlaçoycniuhtzin auh ca çenca nimitztlaçotla yhua Ca nimitztlaxtlanhuiz—

Escriuano v Notlaçopiltzine macamo ximotequipachotzino Ca nicneltiliz y motlaçotlatoltzin Ca ye ticmomachitia Ca nimocnomaCenhualtzin auh ca çenca nimitznotlatlauhtilia Ma achintzin xinechmotlaocolili ȳ mocococantzin ynic niquitlacohuiz y nopilhuan—

Pochtecatl v ynon macamo mitztequipachon Ca nimitzmacaz: ça ye yçiuhca xiquiCuillo yn amatl.—

+ Hualquiçaz yn alCalde

---

18. Onaquipōpoloque: read *oanquipopoloque*.
19. xiyah: read *xiyauh*.
20. yñamatl: read *yn amatl*.
21. ypan ypan: read *ypan*.

MERCHANT: O woman, what are you saying? Perhaps you do not properly remember. Perhaps it was not I or you are just confused, for I have no testament. That land and the fields you mention are my purchases for I bought them from your spouse long ago. As for the gold and silver and the jades that you mention, I know nothing. Perhaps you squandered it or he did not make a testament or you and some companion of yours wasted the property. Be going along. I know nothing of what you are saying. If you are drunk, go, sleep it off. Do not bother me.

MOTHER: What I am saying is true and honest. I am not a drunkard. What I am saying to you is the very truth. You have it. Let it just be for the sake of God that you perform [an act] of his loving charity. Have mercy on my poor little children.

MERCHANT: What I am telling you, woman, is I do not understand what you are talking about. Go, do not disturb me. You are giving me headaches. Go, search for what your bastard children need. It is not my business. Go, I will no longer see you. Come, you who are my servant, summon my dear friend the notary.

LOWLY SERVANT: Very well, O ruler, let me summon him.

(At that point Notary enters.)

NOTARY: O ruler, may God give you health. Perhaps you have some order? I have come to hear it.

MERCHANT: O my friend, please be welcome here.[12] Make a document right away. There you will put down that I bought the house and lands facing Xochimilco and the very big fields lying toward Tepeyacac. I bought them for one thousand [pesos]. In the document you are to put precisely that I bought them three years ago in [48v] the year 1627. See to it that you do it well and do not make a mistake. You already know you are my dear friend and I greatly love and esteem you; in addition, I will make it worth your while.

NOTARY: O my beloved child, do not worry yourself for I will carry out your precious words. You already know I am your humble subject. I greatly implore you to favor me with a little of your property so that I [can] buy things for my children.

MERCHANT: Do not let that bother you for I will give it to you. Quickly write the document.

(Alcalde enters.)

---

12. tla nica timohuicatz: see Carochi 1983, 67v, 80r, and Sahagún 1997, 296. The command/optative particle *tla* can sometimes indicate a more pleading or, at least, less imperious request than its much more frequently seen counterpart *ma*; see Carochi 1983, 25r–v.

nantli y tlacatl tlatohuani Ca nica mixpantzin^co onihualla ma xicmomachiltitzino aço ye chiCuaçemetztli yn omomiquili noñamic ahuitech[22] oquicauh y yehuantzin Pochtecatl yn ipalehuilocan yn ianima. yhua yn ixquich yn axca yn itlatquin[23] yn totech Oquipouh y nehuatl yhua y nopilhuantzintzin auh yn axca ayocmo quimoCuitia y nocal y nomil ye mochi quimaxcatia quimotlatquitia auh yn axcan. y.panpa y Ca çencan mixpantzin^co ninopechtecan nimitznotlatlauhtilia ma quinotzacan ma mixpantzinco neçiquin ma mixpātzin^co quimoCuitiqui ma çan ipaltzin^co. yn tt.^o ma xinechmopalehuilli ca çenca ninotolinicantzintli amo tle ma ytla nicpia yc niquihuanpanhuaz y nican caten mocnomaçēhualtzintzinhuan Ma çan ipāpatzin^co yn tt.^o yhuan ypāpatzin^co y tlaçoçinhuapili xicmochihuillitzin[24] ca huel çenca nimitznotlatlatilia.[25] [49r]

Alcalde. y Ca tel ye qualli Çihuantzintle ca nimitzpalehuiz macamo ximotequipachon—Topile xiyauh xicnotza y yehuatl y pochtecatl yn oncan on tiyanquiztēco ychan—

Topile y Ca ye qualli tlantohuanie ma nicnochinli—

+ Niman yaz quinotzatiuh y pochtecatl.

Topile y Nopiltzintzine ȳ yehuatzin alcalde mitzmonochilia Onpā tomaxitiz centlamantli yc mitzmononochiliznequi yçiuhca timohuicaz amo huel nimitznocahuiliz—+ quihuicaz—

Pochtecatl y Onticmihiyohuiltitzinno tlacantle tlantohuanie tle ticmonequiltitzinnohua Ca nica nica Aço ytla yc nimitzōnotlayecoltiliz ca nicChihuaz—

alcalde. y Ontihualmohuicac Xicmatin Ca nican ca y çihuatzintli mitzteyxpāhuia ca motech oquicauhtia yn iaxca yn itlatquit[26] yn iquac omomiquili ynāmic auh yn axca Ayocmo ticmocuitia xicquetza Crus̄ nican teyxpan xictlali moma ma xiquitta y tle motech ȳtlacauhtica yn ixquich yn iaxca yn itlatqui yn ical yn imil Cuix oticcouh

Pochtecatl y Ca nictenamiqui Nican can Sta Crus̄ Auh ma quimonequilti. yn tt.^o dios Ma diablo nechhuican Ca amo neltiliztli y quitohuan y nican can Çihuantzintli auh ca nica moetztica yn escriuano = ca yxpantzin^co yn onicCohuili yn itlal yn imil yhuan yn ical auh ca amo tle nicpielia yni Cihuantl—

alcalde y Cuix ye nelli Melahuac yn quitohuan y nican ca topiltzin auh catli yn ezCrituran—

---

22. ahuitech: read *auh itech*.
23. yhua yn ixquich yn axca yn itlatquin: read *yhuan yn ixquich yn iaxca yn itlatqui*. Here as in many other places in the manuscript are abundant examples of intrusive and omitted characters, especially *n*; the orthographic loss of possessive prefixes like *i*-, however, is uncommon.
24. xicmochihuillitzin: read *xicmochihuilitzino*.
25. nimitznotlatlatilia: read *nimitznotlatlauhtilia*.
26. itlatquit: read *itlatqui*.

MOTHER: O lord and ruler, I have come here before you. Know that about six months ago my spouse died. He left the merchant what would be of help to his soul along with all his goods and property, which he assigned to me and my children. Now he no longer admits he made my house and my fields his own goods and property. Wherefore now I greatly and humbly bow low before you, imploring you to summon him to appear before you. Let him come to acknowledge it in your presence. Let it just be for the sake of our lord. Help me, for I am very poor. I have absolutely nothing with which to raise your humble little subjects here. Let it just be for the sake of our lord and for the sake of the high-born noblewoman [Saint Mary]. I very greatly implore you, do it! [49r]

ALCALDE: Very well, O woman, I will help you. Do not worry yourself. Constable, go summon the merchant. His residence is over there at the edge of the market.

CONSTABLE: Very well, O ruler, let me summon him.
(He goes right away to summon Merchant.)
CONSTABLE: O my nobleman, the alcalde summons you. You are to go. He wants to consult with you concerning something. You are to go quickly. I must accompany you.[13]
(He accompanies him.)
MERCHANT: Greetings, O lord, O ruler, what do you want? Here I am. Can I serve you in some way? For [if so,] I will do it.
ALCALDE: Welcome.[14] Know that the woman here makes an accusation about you before the law. When her spouse died he left his goods and property with you but now you no longer admit to it. Hold up the cross, set it down here in public with your [own] hands. Look: what do you wrongly hold[15] of all her goods and property, her house and fields? Did you buy them?
MERCHANT: I kiss the holy cross here. Let it be the will of our lord God that the devil take me [if I lie but] what the woman here is saying is not true. Here is the notary. I bought her land and her fields along with her house in his presence. I owe nothing to this woman.
ALCALDE: Is what our child[16] here saying true and honest? What has become of the document [in question]?

---

13. Literally, "I will not be able to leave you."
14. Literally, "you have come (rev.)" but the thrust seems to be "welcome."
15. tle motech ytlacauhtica: these and variants are tentative translations.
16. That is, Merchant.

EScriuano v Ca nica catqui yn Escritura Ca huel melanhuac ynic oquinamacac yn ical yn imil y nican ca çihuantzintli yn ināmic Ca nixpan yhua ymixpan y teStigos Ca oquimacac Ontzontli ypā Matlactzontli pesos Oquicenli y teoCuitlatl huel oquicuic nixpā [49v] nixpan[27] Oquihuicac auh ynteztamento Ca no nixpan y quichiuh Ca amo tle ma ytla Onquicauh ça quezquitzin yn oquicauh ynic motocaz yn inācayo auh ca melahuac ynic amixpantzinco mitohua Cuix ypanpan iztlancatiz y nican ca Pochtecatl—

Quinextiz Testamento =

alcalde v Cihuantzintle ye otiquittac Ca ye mixpan Onmopouh yn amatl: Ca āmo tle ytech ytlacahui y nican ca Pochtecatl. Ma ximohuicatiuh—

Hualquiçaz Teopixqui =

Teopixqui v Nopiltzine ma motlantzin^{co} moetztie yn dios Espū sancto macamo nimitzte=quipachoz Macamo nimitzamanaz auh yzcatqui Ca timahuiztic titlancatl. Ca dios tipiltzin auh ca omitzmomaquili yn tt.º dios yn axcantzin[28] yn itlatquitzin Ca ticalpixcatzin yn tt.º dios ypanpa y ma xicmocnelili ma xicmotlaocolili: y cihuantzintli yn otiCuili yn ical yn imil yn inamic Ca ye ticmomachitian Ca anchitzin miyec yn ipatiuh ȳ calli ma xicmopalehuili yhuan yn ipilhua Auh ȳ tle ticmo.maquiliz Ca mochi quimoÇenliliz yn dios Ma çan ipanpatzinco Xicmochihuilitzino notlaçopiltzine—

Pochtecatl v Tlaçoteopixque Ca ye onicac y mihiyotzin y motlatoltzin = Ca melanhuac y nimitznolhuilia Ca huel ninotolinia yn axca—Ca miec yn tetech ytlacauhtican notomin ayamo nechmaca. auh ytla ye oniCuixano ytech nicpōhuaz auh ynin ma tzanhuan ma yquitti aço quemanian niquilnāmiquiz auh yn axcan ma oc xinechmotlalcahuili: ca oca notequiuh—

Teopixqui. v Ma Xicmomachiti nopiltze ca yn ixquich y moaxcan y motlatqui Ca anmo tiquitquiz yn iquac timiquiz Ca çan çentzontzomantzintli ynic moquimiloz y motlallo y moçoquiyo [50r] auh y quenin atl. quiçenhuia yn tletl. Ça no yuhqui y tetlaocoliliztli quiçenhuia y tlatlancolli auh ynin ma xicpalehui y moyollia ȳ manima yc achitzin tepintzin mitzmopalehuilliz yn dios ma ximonom̄apalehui. ayac aquin mitzpalehuiz Ca ye nimitztlalcahuia—

Calaquiz yn Teopixqui

Pochtecatl. v ha. notlanecahuane Ca huel ninococohuan axcan çenyohual nimā amo achitzin onnicoch cenyohual huel nechcocohuan y notzontecō yuhquin acan quixtlanpanā Ma xinechnochilican Tiçitl—

Tetlanequi v Ca ye qualli Nopiltzintzine tlantohuanie ma niqualnonochili yn Tiçitl—.

Yaz quinotzatiuh yn ticitl Contzontzonaz yn <u>poertan</u>.

Tiçitl v Oticmihiyohuilti: Notelpotzine tle ticmonequiltitzinnohuan—

Tetlaneq̄. v Notlaçopiltzintzine mohuic^copatzin^{co} Onechhualmihuanli yn yehua=tzin Pochtecatl ynic ticmopalehuiliz mococotzinnohuan—

---

27. nixpā nixpan: read *nixpan*.
28. yn axcantzin: read *yn iaxcatzin*.

NOTARY: Here is the document. It is very true that the spouse of the woman here sold him his house and fields for he gave him one thousand pesos in my presence and in the presence of witnesses. He received the gold and silver, he really took it, in my presence he took it [off with him]. [49v] He also made his testament in my presence. He left not a thing, just a little something with which his body would be buried. What is said in your presence is true. Would the merchant here lie about it?

(He produces the testament.)

ALCALDE: O woman, you have already seen and heard read before you the document. The merchant here holds nothing wrongly. Be going along.

(Priest enters.)

PRIEST: O my child, may God the Holy Spirit be with you. Let me not bother or disturb you. Look, you are an honorable person, a child of God. Our lord God has given you his goods and property. You are the steward of our lord God. Because of that have pity and mercy on the poor woman from whose spouse you took her house and fields.[17] You already know the value of the house was a bit considerable; help her and her children. What you give to her will all be received [on behalf of] God. O my beloved child, just do it for his sake.

MERCHANT: O dear priest, I have heard your fine words. I am telling you the truth. I am very poor now for much of my money is wrongly in the hands of other people who have not yet given it to me. If I had it in my care I would assign it to her. But as for this one, let her spin and weave;[18] perhaps sometime I will remember her. Now leave me, for I have work [to do].

PRIEST: O my child, know that when you die you will not take any of your goods and property with you, just a little piece of worn-out clothing with which your earthly body will be enshrouded. [50r] As water snuffs out fire likewise compassion snuffs out sin. And as for this matter at hand, help your spirit and your soul and God will thus help you a bit. Help yourself [for] no one else will help you. I am leaving you now.

(Priest exits.)

MERCHANT: Ah, O my servants, I am very sick. Last night I did not sleep at all. All last night my head hurt me a lot as though someone were breaking it. Summon the doctor for me.

LOWLY SERVANT: Very well, O my nobleman, O ruler. Let me summon the doctor.

(He goes to summon the doctor. He knocks on the door.)

DOCTOR: Greetings, O my young man. What do you want?

LOWLY SERVANT: O my beloved nobleman, the merchant sent me to you so that you will help him. He is ill.

---

17. her house and fields: alternatively, this could easily be rendered "his house and fields."
18. The thrust of this reference to gender-typed tasks may be a thinly disguised idiom that means "let her attend to her female responsibilities." This remark also seems especially dismissive if seen from a Hispanic perspective (and this is, after all, a Church-inspired effort). Perhaps it carries the added implication that she should be too busy doing women's work to waste a man's time with her frivolous claims.

Tiçitl. v̄ Ca ye qualli Notelpotzine ma tihuian Ma nicnotili tle quimococolhuintzinnohua—

Quihuicaz: Ynhuan yn pilli—

Tiçitl. v̄ Notlaçopiltzintzine tlahtohuanie. Ma mitzmochicanhuili ȳ motlaçontatzin dios quen timomatzinnohua tle mitzmotequipachilhuian—

Cocoxqui. v̄ Otinechmocnelili Otlacauhqui yn moyollotzin Çenca ninoCocohuan Ca huel nohuian moCocohua y notlallo y noçoquiyon tlantohuanien—[50v]

Tiçitl. v̄ Notlaçopiltzintzine Ma Ximochicauhtzinno: Ma mitzmochicahuili yn motlaçotatzin dios Ma Ximohuican yn iChantzin^co dios ma XimoyolCuiti Ma XimoCencanhuan Ma Xicmoçenlili yn itlaçomahuiznācayotzin y motlaçotemaquixticatzin Jesu Xp̄o. ca yuhcan tonahuatil ynic yacachtopan MoyolCuitizque yn cocoxque ynic çatepa palehuillozque yn itlallo yçoquiyo—

Cocoxqui v̄. Xicahua ynon yn tiquitohua ma quitepan mochihuaz ma ça oque²⁹ yçiuhca xinechpalehui ca cenca huel nimiquizneque³⁰ yn axca—

Tiçitl. v̄ tlē ticmitalhuitzinohuan Nopiltzinne ca amo qualli y ticmolnanmiquilia Ma çan ye nima yciuhcan Mitzmohuiquilica yn ichantzin^co dios Ca yn tanimā ca ytech quiça yn cocoliztli—

pilli v̄ Notlaçopiltzintzine tlantohuanie Ca huel melanhuac y mitzmolhuilia y nica moetztica y ticitl ca cenca motetzin.^co neçi Ca çenCan totocaznequi ȳ Justiciatzin³¹ dios Ma nimā yciuhca ti:mitztohuiquilican Ca huel monequi yn achtopa titoyolCuitizque ma ximoyolCuititzino ma ximoçencauhtzinno ynnic çatepa palehuiloz yn tlalli çoquitl. ca huel yuh qui[?]monequiltia yn dios auh yni ma timitztohuiquilicā—

Cocoxqui v̄ Huel anechtzonteconehuan huel Antetzonteconeuhqe Ma ça tel niyauh Auh ye çen huel yuh oquinequia y noyollo yniquiçiuhcan³² nipantiloz auh yni ma tel niyauh—[51r]

+ oncan quihuicazque yn teopan: quicalaquizque = Auh yn oquic: quicalaquiya hualquiçazque 3 dem.º

1º dem.º v̄ Ha Omochiuh Ototlahueliltic Ca ye moyolCuitiznequi yn totetlayecolticauh yn tetech tlayxtlapananin—ytla mochi quimoCuitiz yn itlatlacol ca nima atle yez yn totlapalihuiz yn totiyacauhyan ca mochi nequi–çaz nepolihuiz yn ye hixquich cahuitl yn ye techtlayecoltia—

2 dem.º v̄ Ca niman Amo huelitiz y nequiçaz nepolihuiz yn totlateq̄.panoliz auh y tehuatin tle ypan techmati Cuix amo cenca tiChicahuaque titlapaltique: Ca nima Amo huel tic^canhuazquen ca y nehuatl ca nicmacaz y nemauhtiliztli yhuan y pinanhuiliztli ynic Amo huel quimoCuitiz ynic teca Omocancayuh³³ yhua ynic otetlayxpachilhui auh cuix yequiCa³⁴ Ocan comoCuintiz ye ixpan Justiçian amo quimoCuintia amo quimomaChitocan nimā yztlancanJurāmēto: Onquichiuh ynic Otlaneltili ynic Oquixpancho Teaxca Tetlatquin—

---

29. oque: read *oc ye*.
30. nimiquizneque: read *nimiquiznequi*.
31. ȳ Justiciatzin: read *yn iJusticiatzin*.
32. yniquiçiuhcan: read *ynic içiuhca in*.
33. teca omocancayuh: read *teca omocacayauh*.
34. yequiCa: scribal error; perhaps to be read *yequene* or even *ye ic nican*.

DOCTOR: O my young man, very well. Let us go. Let me see him. What is hurting him?

(He accompanies him along with Nobleman.)

DOCTOR: O my beloved nobleman, O ruler, may your beloved Father, God, give you health. How do you feel? What is bothering you?

SICK MAN: I give you many thanks for the favor you have shown me. I am very sick. O ruler, my earthly body hurts absolutely everywhere. [50v]

DOCTOR: O my beloved nobleman, take heart, may your beloved Father, God, give you health. Go to the home of God, confess, prepare yourself, receive the precious honored body of your beloved savior, Jesus Christ. Such is our [that is, doctors'] obligation that first the sick will confess so that afterward the earthly body will be helped.

SICK MAN: Leave it, let what you say be done later. Just quickly help me for I am very much and really about to die now.

DOCTOR: What are you saying? O my child, what you are thinking about is bad. Let them just take you straightaway to the home of God, for it is out of our souls that sickness comes.

NOBLEMAN: O my beloved nobleman, O ruler, what the doctor here is saying to you is very true. It is very apparent in you that the illness, the justice of God, is about to greatly worsen. Let us immediately take you for it is very necessary that we first confess. Confess, prepare yourself, so that afterward the earthly body will be aided for that is the very will of God. Now then, let us take you.

SICK MAN: You are giving me a big headache, you are really a pain, let me just go. I am very desirous that I be quickly restored to health. Now let me go. [51r]

(They take him to the church and put him inside. While they are putting him inside three demons enter.)

FIRST DEMON: Ah, woe is me! Our servant the moneylender is about to confess. If he confesses to all his sins our help and effort will be for naught. All the time he served us would be futile and uselessly spent.

SECOND DEMON: It is absolutely impossible that our work should be futile and uselessly spent. As for us: what does he think we are? Are we not very powerful and strong? We will absolutely not abandon him for I will give him fright and shame so that he cannot admit to deceiving people and to hiding their property from them. Will he confess there what he would not admit to and acknowledge before the officers of the law? Then it was a false oath he made when he verified that he had [not[19]] concealed other people's property and goods.

---

19. A necessary and logical addition missing from the original text.

3. dem.º v̲ Ma ça ye yçiuhca tihuian ylhuiz tohuecahuan ma ça nimā Onpan titlamelahuancan yn ōpan Oquihuicaque Ma ylhuiz OnmoyolCuitin Ma tonequiztin tlen aquimati Ma titoChicahuacan tocnihuanne—

+ Calaquizque Auh yn iquac ocalaq̄. hualquiçaz [51v] ȳ cocoxqui quihualhuicazquen: ȳ tlatlacatecolo yhua Angle: Sa quihualhuelcapahuitizq.ᵉ quitlalizque yn itlapechco =

Cocoxqui v̲ Ha Omochiuh Onotlahueliltic tlen onicchiuh tlen onax: Ca y noyollo Ca çenca tonehua: chichinanca nima amo achitzin Cenhui tlen onechoquixti tlen itechcopa Onoconittac yn tlalticpaccayotl tlen itech Onicnexti: ha onotlahueliltic—

ynamic v̲ Notlaçonamictzin tlen ic Cenca timomoçihuitzinnohuan tlen ic Cenca timotequipachotzinnohua Cuix ytla ticmonequiltia Cuix onquitla³⁵ ticmolnanmiquilia ytla mitzmotequipachilhuia Ma xicmitalhui: Canel yuh ca. yn itlalticpactzinco dios Ca tlaanlanhuan Ca tlapetzcahuin Ca anmo çan quexquich ynic ytzinco ycpactzinco tinemi y tlancatl tlanto=huani dios. Ma xinechmolhuilli—

Cocoxqui v̲ Otinechmocnelilitzinno Otlacauhqui y moyollotzin Ca melahuac yn ticmitalhuian—

oncan hualquicaz³⁶ teopixqui =

Teopixqui v̲ Ma moçenquizcanyectenehuan yn itlaçomahuiztocatzin Jesu X͞p͞o—que timoetztica Notlaçomahuizpiltzine—

Cocoxqui v̲ Notlaçomahuiztatzine Otlaçotic ȳ moyollotzin Otinechmocnelilitzino Ca çenca Onocuiltono³⁷ Oninotlamachtin ypaltzinco yn dios: ca ye polihuiznequi ynānimā³⁸ Ca cencan huel Oçoquiyac y tlalli yn çoquitl.—[52r]

Teopixqui. v̲ Notlaçomahuizpiltzine Ma ximochicahua ximotlapaltili yhuicopatzinᶜᵒ y moteºuh y motlantocatzin dios Ma xicmocnelilmachiti ynic mitzmocnelilia yn oc Achitzinca mitzmocahuilia Ca amo mitzmotelchihuilia Ca quimonequiltitzinohuan yn timomaquixtiz ynic mocnpil Momaçenhual mochihuaz yn itlantocanchantzinᶜᵒ Ca amo monemachpan. C̶a̶ a̶m̶o̶ Otimomicquiliyani auh yn axcan: Ca mitzmomacahuililia yn cahuitl. yn ipan ynic timomaquixtiz ynic timoyoloCuintiz Mochi tiquitoz = y motlatlacol maçonelihui ȳn otimoyolCuiti: Açoquitla³⁹ Oticpinahuizcauh Ma xiquito Ca ye timomicquiliznequi—

1º dem.º v̲ Macamo mitztequipancho Macamo yc xinetlamati: Camo cenca timococohuan Cuix amo ye quezquipan y timococonhuan ça nima yçiuhca tipanti yece mitzmochicahuilia yn dios: Ca çan o yuh mopā mo=chihuaz yn axcan Ca tipatiz—

---

35. onquitla: read *oc itla*.
36. hualquicaz: read *hualquiçaz*.
37. Onocuiltono: read *oninocuiltono*.
38. ynānimā: read *yn naniman*.
39. Açoquitla: read *aço oc itla*.

THIRD DEMON: Let us go quickly; we are uselessly wasting time. Let us go right there to where they took him. Let him especially not confess, let us not be in vain. Pay attention![20] O our friends, take heart!

(They exit. After they have exited Sick Man enters. [51v] Devils accompany him along with [Guardian] Angel. They just follow him from a distance. They will place him on his litter.)

SICK MAN: Ah, woe is me! What oh what have I done? For my heart suffers great burning pain. It is not a bit rested and cooled off. What did it avail me? What earthly thing did I get out of it? What did I gain from it? Ah, woe is me!

HIS SPOUSE: O my beloved spouse, what are you so greatly disturbed by? What are you so bothered about? Do you want something? Are you still thinking of something else? Something troubling you? Speak, for that is how it is on God's earth, it is slippery and slick[21] and we offend the lord and ruler, God, in countless things. Speak to me.

SICK MAN: I give you many thanks for the favor you have shown me. What you are saying is true.

(At that point Priest enters.)

PRIEST: Perfectly praise the beloved honored name of Jesus Christ. O my beloved honored child, how are you feeling?

SICK MAN: O my beloved honored father, I give you many thanks for the favor you have shown me. I have become rich and have enjoyed myself through the agency of God [but] my soul is about to perish and my earthly body is very mired down.[22] [52r]

PRIEST: O my beloved honored child, take heart and [seek] comfort in your deity and ruler, God. Be grateful that he shows you favor. What he gives to you in a short while [shows] that he does not despise you [but rather that] he wants you to save yourself so that you merit and attain his royal home, for you are likely to die when you least expect it. And now he concedes to you time to save yourself by confessing. You are to say all your sins. Even though you have [already] confessed perhaps you left out something because of shame. Say it, for you are about to die.

FIRST DEMON: Do not let it worry you, do not be discontented for you are not extremely ill. Have you not already been sick many [other] times and then quickly recovered? In any case God will grant you health. You are just going through bad times now; you will recover.

---

20. See the following related items in Molina 1977, 17r: "Cenca tle anquimati. mirad mucho en este negocio" and "Cenca tle ticmati. mira mucho y ten gran cuidado desto que te encomiendo. &c."

21. This is an obvious allusion to a well-known traditional Nahuatl metaphor. It appears on the idiom list included in book 6 of the *Florentine Codex*: "TLAALOA, TLAPETZCAVI IN JXPAN PETLATL, ICPALLI: AQUJNEUHIAN, AQUJXOAIAN: qujtoznequj: amo vel nemaqujxtiloian: aiac vel ixpan momaqujxtia in tlatoanj," which is translated by the editors as "IT IS SLICK, IT IS SLIPPERY BEFORE THE REED MAT, THE REED SEAT: IT IS THE PLACE OF NO DEPARTURE, THE PLACE OF NO EXIT It means, it cannot be a place of refuge; no one can escape the presence of the ruler" (Sahagún 1950–1982; 6:254). The accompanying Spanish gloss is also of interest: "Dize esta letra. Resbalan y deslizanse muchos en presencia del trono y del estrado y nadie se escapa. Por methaphora qujere dezir: el que caye en la yra del señor o reyno, [no] se puede escapar de sus manos."

22. Evidently a play on words. Literally, "the earth, the mud is very greatly stuck in the mud."

Angel tepixq̱. v̱ Dios ytlaneltocācatzinne Macamo xicneltocan y moyaouh yn tlacatecolotl Ca ça moca mocacayahuazne⁴⁰ Mitzponpololtiznequi ynic çan ipa timicquiz
y motlatlacol ynic Onpa mitzhuicaz yn mictlan Cuix amo tiquitta Ca tetlan-
pololtiyani teyxcueppani Motenepachinhuiyani Ca amo ça quexquichtin yn oquitlapololti yn inca Omocancanyuh⁴¹ ye mictlan tlanyhiyohuitoque yn opa Cemicac
chi=chinantzallo ma yçiuhca ximoyolCuiti Ca ayocmo tiçemilhuitiz Ma yehuatzin
Jesus mitzmopalehuiliz—

2 dem.º v̱ Yztlancati Amo axcan timiquiz Ca tipactica Cuix ye tihuehuen ca
titelpochtli: Oc ocan yn tinemi Ayamo axcan y timiquiz—

Teopixquin v̱ Ma huel xiquitztimotlali Ca y tlacantecolotl ca yxquich ytlapal quichi-
huan ynic mitztlapololtiznequin mitzyollomalacanchoznequi ynic amo melahuac
ticmoCuintiz Motlatlacol Macamo xic=neltocan Ma xiquito Ma xicmomachitoca
yntla ytla otic[52v]tipināhuizcauh⁴² Ca axcan qualcan Ca nemaquixtilizpan auh =
ytla ça ticmauhcancahuaz yn anoçe ticpināhuizcahuaz y motlatlacol ma yuh ye y
moyollo ca yn iquac timiquiz ca nima Onpa titlamelanhuaz yn mictlan Onpa çemicac titonehualoz tichinchinatzaloz yn intlan tlantlacatecolo yc motechpa ni=
noquixtia ypaltzinᶜᵒ yn dios—

Cocoxqui. v̱ Otinechmocnelili Notlaçotatzine Otlacauhqui y moyollotzin ma niquinto
y niquilnamiqui: Ca çan Onitechicoytohua teca Oninhuetzcac⁴³ Onitequalacanytac
Ca ça ye ixquich notlaçotatzine—

Teopixqui v̱ Notlaçopiltzen Ma mitztlapollolti Ma moca mocacanyuh⁴⁴ yn diablo yn
tlacatecolol⁴⁵—

Angel tepixq̱ v̱ Ma ximocnelli ximocnoytta Ca ye timiquiz ye tipolihuiz = xiquitta Ca
ytla otimic yn amo moch ticmoCuititiyaz yn motlatlancol yn amo mitzchoᶜtiz
mitztlaocoltiz Ca çemincac tipolihuiz Ma tt.º dios mitzmotlachieltili Ma mitzmotlanextilili—

Cocoxqui v̱ Ca niman Atle nicahuan Notlaçotatzine Ca mochi oniquinto yn notlatlancol—

Teopixqui v̱ Ca ye qualli tehuatl ticmati: ye ninoquixtian yn ixpantzinᶜᵒ ȳ dios Ma
yehuantzin mitzmotlaçopiel⁴⁶ Ca ye niyauh—

Cocoxqui v̱ Ca ye qualli ma tel ximohuica Ha huel namiqui ma xinechmomaquilican
achitzin Atzintli Ca huel çenca namiqui ye notehuahuanq̱—

Angel tepixqui. v̱ Yntla ça tepiton Cocoliztli: yc çenca titehuāhuanqui yn cenca
tamiqui queni huel tiquiyhiyohuiz: yn mictlan tletl. yhuan yn mictlan tehuanhuan-
quiliztli yn atle Oc centlanmātli = [53r] yc tipatiz ytlacamo tletepozchapōpoatl y
cencan tōtoquin: y cenca techichinatz yn cenca teyolCuitlantzaya mitzintizque—

Cocoxqui v̱ Cuix huelitiz yn nechmocneliliz yn dios yn axca—

---

40. mocacayahuazne: read *mocacayahuaznequi*.
41. yn inca Omocancanyuh: read *yn inca omocacayauh*.
42. otic[52v]tipināhuizcauh: read *oticpinahuizcauh*.
43. Oninhuetzcac: read *oninohuetzcac*.
44. Ma moca mocacanyuh: read *ma moca mocacayauh*.
45. tlacatecolol: read *tlacatecolotl*.
46. mitzmotlaçopiel: read *mitzmotlaçopieli*.

GUARDIAN ANGEL: O believer in God, do not believe your enemy the devil for he just wants to mock and confuse you so that you will die right in your sins and he will take you to hell. Do you not see he is a confounder of people, an ambusher of people? He has confused innumerable people, mocked them. Now they suffer in hell, are made to suffer eternal pain there. Quickly confess for you will no longer last an entire day. Let Jesus help you.

SECOND DEMON: He lies. You will not die today for you are healthy. Are you an old man? [No,] you are a young man. You will yet live there, you are not about to die.

PRIEST: Ponder well for the devil is exerting all his effort in order to confuse and pervert you so that you will not correctly confess your sins. Do not believe him. Speak, acknowledge if there is something you left out because it was shameful, [52v] for now is a good time to save oneself. If you leave out your sins just because of fear or shame be sure [that] when you die you will go straight there to hell. There you will be eternally tormented and made to suffer pain among the devils. For the sake of God I thus fulfill the obligation I have to you.

SICK MAN: O my beloved father, I thank you very much for the favor you have shown me. Let me say what I remember: I have just lied about others, I laughed at people, I looked angrily at others. O my beloved father, that is all.

PRIEST: O my beloved child, do not let the devil confuse and mock you.

GUARDIAN ANGEL: Do yourself a favor, have mercy on yourself for you will die and perish. Look, when you have died and you pass on without confessing all your sins and they have not made you weep and sad, then you will perish forever. May our lord God make you see, may he give you a revelation.[23]

SICK MAN: O my beloved father, I have left absolutely nothing out. I have said all my sins.

PRIEST: Very well, you already know I have fulfilled my obligations before God. May he dearly guard you for I am going.

SICK MAN: Very well, go. I am very thirsty. Give me a little something to drink for I am extremely thirsty and my lips are dried up.

GUARDIAN ANGEL: If your lips are so dry with just a little illness, if you are so thirsty, how can you suffer the fires of hell and the dried cracking of lips in hell, which have no other cure? [53r] They will make you drink molten lava, which is very hot, very painful, and very heartrending.

SICK MAN: Is it possible that God will show me favor now?

---

23. ma mitzmotlanextilili / may he give you a revelation: see related forms on the Spanish-Nahuatl side of Molina 1977, 104v, and on the Nahuatl-Spanish side, 128v.

Angel tepixqui v Ca quemacan Ma xicmotzatzinlili Ca nimitzmopalehuiliz[47]—
+ yas yn Angel
3. dem:º v̲ Macamo xicneltocan Ca çan iztlacati yn angel Ca ye titonemac: Ca ye omitzmocentelchihuili yn dios yehica yn amo otitlamaceuh =
Cocoxqui v̲ Ca ye nelli: Ca mictlā nipouhqui yehica Ca cenca miec y notlatlancol Ca nima ahuel mopohuaz ay ma monotzanca y pipiltin yn tlantoque ytech nicanhuaz yn ixquich: noaxca notlatqui =
+ Oncan hualquiçazque Omentin pipiltin =
1º pilli. v̲ Tle mitzmotequipachilhuian tlantohuanie. ynic titechmonochilia: ca otihuallaque Ma ximochicauhtzinno: Ma mitzmochiCanhuilli yn tlancatl tlantohuan[48] dios Xicmotzatzinlili Macamo Ximotlapololti: yçemactzin^co ximocauhtzinno = Ca tlatlancantzintli Ca moteycnoytiliyani Ca mitzmocneliliz: Ca mitzmotlaocoliliz yhua yehuatzin tlatocanychpōchtzintli Sancta M.ª ma mopā motlatolti yn ixpantzinco yn itlaçoconetzin ynic mitzmotlaocoliliz auh tle ticmonenquiltia Ca otihuallaque—
Cocoxqui v̲ Notlaçopiltzintzine Cenca ayocmo nichuelmati y noñacayo huel niçontlanhua ye huel nimiquiznequi. ayocmo huel nitlaCuiloz Ca yehuatl yn ixquich noaxca notlatqui amotetzin.^co nicahuan Amehuantzintzin: aquimochihuilizque y Noteztanmēto aquimoxexelhuizque amotetzinco nicauhtiuh: yn ixquich noaxcan notlatqui—[53v]
2 pilli v̲ Ca ye qualli Ca ticneltilizque y motlanequilitzin Ca timitztopalehuilizque yn tlen ic titechmonahuatilitiuh ma yxquich y motlapaltzin ma ximochicauhtzino Ma oc timitztotlalcanhuilican Ca cencan timitztomocihuilia—
+ Canlaquizque auh. y dem.º nimā quiquechmateloz
2 dem.º v̲ Ma xicquechmatelocan xicquechpachocan ma tichuicancan yhua y tlanhuelliloc y huey tlatlancohuani yn ianimā—
+ Onca quiquixtilizque yn ianima auh ytla omic nima hualquiçaz tliltic yn iamā miec Coetes ytech =
ynami. v̲ Onocentzotlahuelliltic Ca ye omomiquili y notlaçonamictzin Ca amo huel nicmati y tlen ipa Omochiuh y çan içiuhcan Miquiliztli ypan Oquihualmihuali yn iteuh yn itlantocatzin Ma yçiuhca ypa motlatoltican yn ixquichti nohuayolque ynic motocaz yn iñacayo Ma tzillinin y micantepoztli ma quinotzancan y Cuihcanimē yhua yn ixtlanmatque yn teopixquen ynic quimotoquilizque—
+ Onca hualquicazq̄.[49] y tetocanime mehuaz Rezponso yc calaquizq̄. Quitocazq̄. nima hualq̄.çazque. Angeles

---

47. nimitzmopalehuiliz: standard *nimitznopalehuiliz*.
48. tlantohuan: read *tlatohuani*.
49. hualquicazq̄: read *hualquiçazque*.

GUARDIAN ANGEL: Yes. Cry out to him. I will help you.

([Guardian] Angel exits.)

THIRD DEMON: Do not believe him for the angel just lies. You already belong to us for God has entirely despised you because you have not done penance.

SICK MAN: It is true that I belong to hell because I have a great many sins that are absolutely uncountable. Ah! Let the nobles and rulers be summoned. I will assign to them all my goods and property.

(At that point two noblemen enter.)

FIRST NOBLEMAN: O ruler, what is troubling you that you summon us? We have come. Take heart. May the lord and ruler, God, give you health. Cry out to him. Do not be confused. Leave yourself entirely in his hands, for he is humane and compassionate. He will befriend you and have mercy on you along with the royal maiden Saint Mary. May she intercede for you before her beloved son so that he will have mercy on you. What do you want? We have come.

SICK MAN: O my beloved noblemen, I no longer feel my body is healthy. I am very faint and I am really just about to die. I will no longer be able to write. I leave all my goods and property with you. You will make my testament. You will divide all my goods and property I am leaving you into discrete parts. [53v]

SECOND NOBLEMAN: Very well, we will carry out your will. We will help you in what you go ordering us [to do]. Be of good cheer, take heart. Let us leave you for we are greatly upsetting you.

(They exit. The demon then strangles him with his hands.)

SECOND DEMON: Strangle him with your hands, squeeze his neck. Let us take him along with the soul of the scoundrel and great sinner.

(At that point they take his soul out of him. After he has died his blackened soul emerges. Many rockets are attached to it.)

HIS SPOUSE: I am four hundred[24] [times] unfortunate! My beloved spouse has just died and I do not know what happened to him. His god and ruler just quickly sent death upon him. May all my relatives speak quickly on behalf of him so that his body will be buried. Let the bells[25] be rung, let them summon the cantors and the prudent ones, the priests, to bury him.

(At that point the gravediggers enter. A responsory for the dead is said.[26] They bury him. Then angels enter.)

---

24. This is an idiomatic usage that means "countless, innumerable."

25. *miccatepoztli* / bells: see Lockhart 1992, 221, where he points out that the term is an early circumlocution that literally means "'dead-person metal,' that is, the metal object sounded to announce someone's death." Chimalpahin also uses this circumlocution and the Spanish loanword, sometimes in tandem and sometimes each term by itself, in speaking of church bells (see Chimalpahin 1965, 2:39, 40, 44, 48, 50, 87, 100, 101, 104).

26. Literally, "raised," often used in expressions like "raised up in song."

Angel tepixqui y Ha yyoyahuen Omochiuh Onotlahuelliltic yn atle nolhuil yñ atle nomacenhual y nimotlachihualtzin quemachameque: yn oc cenquintin y notlaço-ycniuhtzintzinhuan Angeles y nican = yn itlapielhua y qualli yn ipan monemitia yn tlalticpac = auh y nehuatl Omochiuh Onotlahueliltic yn atle nolhuil: no:macenhual: Cuix amomoztlaye y tiquinnotzan yn tiquitzatzinlian yn tiquiyollotia y qualli yectli y tiquimilnanmictia auh y yenhuantin amo quimocacannenequi: ye ylhuicen quitlacamatin yn diablo yn tlacatecolotl: huel quinacātzatzantilia quinnontilia: quimixtlapachohua: ha yyoyahuen Ca quin onpa y mictlan: quimixtlapohuan quinaCaztlanpohua auh Cuix oc onca Ca nimā ayocmo Oncā Ca nica tlalticpac yn ocomixcahualtique yn Cencan tlaçotli yn inemac omochihuazquia—

GUARDIAN ANGEL: Ah, woe is me! I am a creature of yours, undeserving and without merit. How fortunate are the others, my beloved friends the angels, whose charges live in good[ness] on earth. But as for me, woe is me! I am undeserving and without merit. Do we not talk to them every day, cry out to them, inspire them to what is good, remind them of what is proper? But they do not want to hear it; [rather] they want to obey the devil much more. He makes them very deaf and mute and covers up their eyes. Ah, alas! Afterward, over there in hell, he opens their eyes and opens their ears. Do they still exist? In no way do they still exist for here on earth they lost by their faults and negligence what is very precious, what would have been bestowed on them.[27]

---

27. What this inheritance means could refer to so many things mentioned in the play, from God's mercy and loving charity to his royal home in heaven, that perhaps this is shorthand for all the specific points raised in this play.

Present Location
Graduate Theological Union Library
Academy of American Franciscan History Collection
Berkeley, California

[1]
Loa en nahuatl

De oastepec

[2] [blank] [3]

Prologo
Yn amixquichtin Yn nican oamechmocentlalili Yn tona.tzin Sta Yg.^a Yn oamechmoquanochili Ynic anhuallazque anConanazq.^z Yn ocuhtacatl, machiotl Yn nican, in Campa amixpan quimotlalilia Yn neixcuitil, machiotl Ynic amontlachiesque amicampa Yhuan anmotlâtlanizque SeseYâca, amoYollo ihtec ancontlazasque Yn amotlalnamiquiliz anquitlâtlanizque Yn amoYollo Cuix huel chipahualiztica Ynic annemi, Cuix huel anquimohuellamachtilihtinemi, in Dios, quallachihualiztica? Cuix nocê âmo? Yntlacamo itla qualli tlachihualiztli anquinextia amotechCopa ma xihualmotocahuican, itech niin¹ neixcuitilmachiotl Yn amechmotitilia Yn tonantzin Sta Yglecia Yn campa Ytechcopa tlatohua Se tlâtohuani Yn San Cemihcac omoxochipolotinenca Ytechcopa Yn itecâcayahualiz Yn tlalticpactli Yn aic, itla oquimocahuali[?]Co Yn Dios San mochipa oquitlacaq[ui?] Yn ixtlacat[i?]liz² San no Yuhqui Yn tlacatecolotl Yn tlein oquiti[o?]aya, ânoce oquilnamictiaya mochi oquichihuayâ ca niman aic omotlacahualti Ytechcopa Yn quexquich YYolihtlacolocatzin Yn tt.^o D.^s Auh Yn inamic San no Yuhqui mochipa oquipâpaquilti atliliztica tlaqualiztica Yhuan nechihchihualiztica nican tlalticpac oquipix Yn pâpaquiliztli, auh Yn ihquac oyac onestito Yxpantzinco, Yn momelahuacatetlatzontequililiani Juez Yn tt.^o JeSu xp̄o otlâtoltiloc Ytechcopa Yn iteotenahuatiltzin D.^s Yn manel san ce quallachihualiztli âtle oquichiuh, auh Yn ihuanpohuan aic oquintlazôtlac Yn motolinihcatzitzinti aic oquintlaocolili San no iuhqui Yn Cihuapilli Ynic onecia huel mahuiztic Yn inemiliz oyaya teopan oquittaya Missa oquiCaquia temachtilli, Auh Yn manel ocalaquia teopan San oncan ohualaya oteixelehuiaya, San ohualaya mononotzas Yn onca^n teiztlacohuaya,³ oquimpinahuiaya Yn icnotlaca Yn âmo quimopielia Yn tlein ic quimopachosque Yn intlalo, Ynsoquis⁴; Auh Ypampa on ocentelchihualoc Mictlan oya Yn ianiman Yn Campa anquitztimotlalizque Yn ihquac ancalaquizq.^z
[4] Yn ichantzinco Dios achtopa mochi anquitelchihuazque Yn ixquich âmo qualli

---

1. niin: read *inin*.
2. ixtlacat[i?]liz: perhaps to be read *iztlacatiliz*.
3. teiztlacohuaya: perhaps to be read *teiztlacahuiya*.
4. Ynsoquis: read *ynzoquio*.

The Life of Don Sebastián

Translated by Barry D. Sell, with assistance from Louise M. Burkhart

[1]
Praise Play in Nahuatl

From Huaxtepec

[2] [blank] [3]

Prologue[1]
Our mother holy church has gathered you all together here. She has invited you to come to grasp the measuring stick, the model,[2] here where she places before you the exemplary model so that you each will look behind you and examine yourselves, cast it into your hearts, examine your memories and your hearts. Do you live very purely? Do you really go about pleasing God with good deeds, or not? If you do not discover some good deeds concerning yourselves, follow this exemplary model that our mother holy church shows you, where it talks about a ruler who always went about indulging himself with delicacies, and about the deceptions of the earth. He never abstained from anything [prohibited by?] God. He always listened to the lies, likewise, of the demon. He used to do everything that [the demon] would say to him or make him think. He absolutely never restrained himself concerning whatever was an affront to our lord God. And likewise he always delighted his spouse with drink, with food, and with adornments; here on earth he had pleasures. But when he went to appear before the true sentencer of people and judge, our lord Jesus Christ, he was made to talk about the sacred commandments of God. He had not done even just one good deed. And as to his neighbors, he never loved them. As for the afflicted, he never had pity on them. Likewise the noblewoman appeared to have a very honorable life. She used to go to church to see mass[3] and hear the sermons,[4] but even though she used to enter church she just went there coveting people, she just came to chat. She used to deceive people there, she used to shame the poor people who had nothing with which to cover their earth, their clay.[5] And because of that his soul was completely despised; it went to the place of the dead. From that you are to contemplate, when you enter [4] the home of God, that you are, first, to despise all bad

---

1. Parts of this prologue are tentatively translated.
2. measuring stick, model: here and below, a common diphrase that means "[sound] moral advice" (as opposed to that given by the demons to don Sebastián later in the play).
3. see mass: an early colonial idiom whose pragmatic thrust is "hear mass."
4. temachtilli: here and below translated as "sermon(s)" as it almost invariably was in contemporary ecclesiastical Nahuatl texts, it has the more general meaning of "teaching(s), doctrine."
5. earth, clay: here and below, a standard diphrase (often found in testaments) that means "earthly body/ies."

tlalnamiquiliztli huel mochi iCa Yn amoYollo anquimotlanililizque Yn noma amechmihquanilili mochi Yn ipan amotlalnamiquiliz Yn quexquich Yn âmo yhuellamachtilocatzin ma San Yêhuatl Yn tlein ic motolinia Yn amoanima Yhuan Yn amonacayo ixpantzinco xictlalican Yehica ca in quenin amotechiuhcatzin Yhuan amoteyocoxcatzin amechmomaquilis mochi Yn tlein anquimihtlanililizque intla huel huey tlateomatiliztiCa, necnomatiliztica Yhuan nepechtequiliztica antlaihtlanizque No ihuan huel monequi anquineltilizque Yn iteotenahualtiltzin D.^{S} Cm̅c̅ amixpan, ihuan amotlalnamiquilisp^n anqualhuicatinemizque⁵ Ynic âmo amechtlapololtiz Yn tlacatecolotl; Auh yntla quemmanian, itla iC amechmoyeyecoltiz ma xiquilnamiquican Ca in Yehuatl âmo Ytla qualli Yn amechmacas Yn ompa Mictlan ca san Yehuatl Yn cemicac tlatlaliztli Yn campa, ic cemmayan tlayohuaYan Anyesque Yn niman ayc cepa anquimotililizque Yn itlasôxayacatzin Yn D.^{S} Ypampa Ynon ma huel ximimmatinemican macamo Ytla amopan mochihuas in tlein Ympan omochiuh Yn tlatlacohuanime Yn nican amechmotililia tonantzin Sta Yg.^{l} ipan, i ocuhtatcatl machiotl ca intla chipahualiztica annemizque Yntla anquimotlazôtilizq.^{z} Yn D.^{S} Yhuan in amohuanpohuan Ca ic anquimomâCehuizque Yn iteyecnemitiayatzin Yn tt.^{o} D.^{S} nican tl p̅c̅ Auh Yn iquac anmomiquilizque Ca amechmomaquiliz Yn cm̅c̅ netlamachtiliztli Gloria

Amen Jesus M.^{a} Y Joseph
Joaquin i + Anna

---

5. anqualhuicatinemizque: read *anquihualhuicatinemizque*.

thoughts with absolutely all of your heart. You are to ask God to take away from you everything that is in your thoughts that is not pleasing to him. Just set before him that which troubles your souls and your bodies. Because, as your Progenitor and your Creator, he will give you everything you ask for if you ask with very great devotion, humility, and reverence. And it is also necessary that you carry out the sacred commands of God that are always before you, and that you go about taking them in your memory so that the demon will not confuse you. But, if he tempts you with something sometime, remember that what he will give you there in the place of the dead will be something bad; it will just be eternal burning where, once and for all, you will be in darkness. Absolutely never again will you see the precious face of God. Because of that, live very prudently. Do not let something bad happen to you [as] happened to the sinners whom our mother holy church shows to you here in the measuring stick, the model. For if you live with purity, if you love God and your neighbors, you will earn here on earth our lord God's instrument of causing people to live properly.[6] And when you die he will give you eternal riches, glory.

Amen. Jesus, Mary and Joseph.
Joachim and Anne[7]

---

6. the instrument of causing people to live properly: this and similar Nahuatl terms are often paired with the Spanish loanword *gracia*, "grace."

7. That is, Mary's father and mother.

[5]

v̲ Neyxcuitilli Ytechpa tlatohua Ynemilis D.ⁿ Seb,ⁿ—hualquisas D.ⁿ Seb.ⁿ Yhuan D.ª Juana Yhuan 1º Dem.º Yhuan OMentin Pajes Yhuâ 1º Ang.l—

hualMoquixtis Yn Miquistli Motlatoltiz—

v̲ Tlalticpac tlacaye D,ˢ Ytlamaquixtiltzitzinhuane Yn nican anCenquistoq.ᶻ Yn teOyotica amechmotetlalilia AmechmoCohuanochilia Yn S.ᵗᵃ Yglesia ma xicmatican Yhuâ ma huel xiquilnamiquican Y niYo Y notlatol, Yn axcâ niCan amixp.ⁿ niCac, aquipa.¹ anechita: aquipa: anechmati. anoso tlen notoCa. Yn iuh âquimati. xinechilhuiCan xinechnâquiliCan xiquitocan Cuix nitlaltp.ᶜ nitlaCatl, Cuix nitlatohuani: ~~Cuix noso niRey anoso niRoq.ᶻ Cuix noso niConde: anoso niMarquez: Cuix noso niemperador: Cuix noso nehuatl ni[?] anoso Cuix niarsoBispo anoso:~~ Cuix noço ~~aca~~ niteopixCatlatohuani: Ye neltilistli: Y naMechilhuia: Ca niman amo Ca Yn nehuatl, Ca nitlachihualtzin Yn D,ˢ Nititlantzin nitopileCatzin: niJustiÇiatzin nitetlatzaCuilticatzin Yeyca Yn ixquichtin Oniquinteneuh: Ca mochintin: nomac cate. Yn iquac Nechmonahuatilya Yn D,ˢ Yn saso ac Yehuatl Y nictlatlatis nicpoctlatilis Yn iYolia, Ca iuhqui mochihuas Yuhqui nicneltilia Ca amo Yuh niCahua. Yn manel amo S.ⁿ queXquich Ytlatqui ō ca Yn manel: Amo Sⁿ tlapohuali Yn ialtepeuh âmo. Yc momaquixtis Yn aquin tlatlaCohuani Yno.ⁿ Yn axcan nican Onechmotitlani Yn tlatohuani D,ˢ Yn itechpa Yn tlatohuani Yn nican Yn moxochitlamachtitica moxochipolotica Yuhqui nicneltilia Yn itenahuatiltzin Yn iÇel teotl D,ˢ Ca ye yxquich otlami[6]co Yn iCahuiuh Yhuan huel oquimamanili huel itzinco Ycpactzinco one AYomo² quimopaCayohuiltzia³ Ca çeca Oquimotequipanilhui Yquip.ⁿpa⁴ Yn axcan nictlatlatis nicpopolos; Auh Ompa tlasalos: Ompa tlatzaCuiltilos, Yn ompa Sentlanin mictlan, Ypampa Yn ixquich Yn iaqualnemilis; Yn niCan Oquichiuhtinenca Yn niCan Ytlaltp.ᶜtzinco; Yn D,ˢ Ypampa Yn tlaltp.ᶜ tlaCae ma ytech ximixCuitican, Yn tlahuelilocatlatohuani Ca Yasq.ᶻ Yn Centlani mictlan, Yhuan Yn tlahuelilocaSihuatl ca ytencopantzinco Yn tt.º D,ˢ macamo San camanali Ypan xicmatican ma huel xiquilnamictinemican Yn iYotzin Yn itlatoltzin tlaltp.ᶜ tlacaYe

tlapitzalos moCalaquiz Yn miquistli—

v̲ hualquiCas⁵ Don Sebastian yhuan D.ª Juana yhuan 1º Demonio yhuan Omentin PaJes ~~Yhuan 1º agel Don Sebastian~~

D.ⁿ Seb,ⁿ Tla XihualMohuica notlasotatzine Yn axcan Ca oc tepitzin techmochicahuilia Yn D,ˢ Ca oc tlaltp.ᶜ Yn ticate Ca atle CoColistli totech ca ca Atle techcocohua Auh niquitohua Yn axcan ma tiquintonochilican Yn tocniuhtzitzinhuan ma titoSep.ⁿYolalican Yn manel quaresma ticate ma tonpapaquican Canel Oc tlaltp.ᶜ Yn ticate—

---

1. aquipa: here and below, read *ac ipan*.
2. AYomo: read either as *aocmo* or *ayamo*.
3. AYomo quimopaCahuiltzia: perhaps to be read *ayamo quimopaccaihiyohuiltitzinoa*.
4. Yquip.ⁿpa: read *yc ipampa*.
5. hualquiCas: read *hualquiçaz*.

[5]

Moral example which speaks about the life of don Sebastián.
(Don Sebastián enters along with doña Juaña and First Demon and two pages and First Angel.
Death enters. He speaks.)

[DEATH:] O people of the earth, O God's saved ones, you who are all here together, whom the holy church spiritually detains and invites, know and remember well my breath, my words.[1] Now I stand here before you. Who do you see me as? Who do you think I am? What is the name you know me by? Tell me, answer me, say it. Am I a person of the earth? Am I a ruler? ~~Or am I a king, or a rook, or a count, or a marquis, or an emperor, or a [?], or an archbishop?~~ Or am I someone who is a priestly ruler [that is, bishop or pope]? I tell you the truth, that is absolutely not me, for I am a creature of God, I am his messenger, I am his constable, I am his officer of justice, I am his castigator. Because all those whom I have mentioned are all in my hands. When God orders me, whoever it is, I will burn him, I will burn his spirit up like smoke. For such will be done, I will carry it out in that way, for I spare none even though he has great wealth, even though his realms are countless, for he[2] who is a sinner will not save himself with that. Now the ruler, God, has sent me here concerning the ruler here who enjoys delicacies, indulges himself with delicacies. Thus I carry out the commands of the sole deity, God. That is all. [6] His time has come to an end, and he really disturbed, he really offended him; he no longer has patience with him. He worked hard at [offending God], wherefore now I will burn him, I will destroy him. And he will be cast there, he will be punished there, there in the depths of the place of the dead,[3] because of all his bad living he went around doing here, here on God's earth. Wherefore, O people of the earth, take an example from the wicked ruler and the wicked woman who will go to the depths of the place of the dead, by order of our lord God. Do not regard it as a joke. Remember his breath, his words, O people of the earth!

(Wind instruments are played. Death exits.)
(Don Sebastián enters along with doña Juana and First Demon and two pages ~~and First Angel. Don Sebastián~~:)

DON SEBASTIÁN: Do come, O my beloved father. Today God is keeping us alive a bit longer, for we are still on earth, there is no sickness in us, nothing makes us ill. And I say now let us summon our friends, let us console one another. Even though we are in Lent, let us enjoy ourselves, since we are still on earth.

---

1. breath, word: a common diphrase that means "message" or "command," sometimes "fine and elegant speech."
2. Or she; list of titles suggests male frame of reference.
3. mictlan: here and below translated as "the place of the dead" (locative senses such as "in" or "at" are already contained in the Nahuatl term), it was usually rendered by colonial translators as *infierno* (hell).

1.º Dem.º v Auh Ynon Ca huel Oc quali Yn tiquilnamiqui Ca huel oc YmonecYan Yn timoyolalis cuix oc tipiltontli tiConetontli Ma Oc xipapaqui Cuix ye tihuehue Ma yquin Yquac Yntla Ye tihuehue titlamasehuas ma timomecahuitequis Cuix amo ye tiquimita Ynin Ca huel miequintin Yn telpopochtin quipactitinemi Yn telpochYotl ca quitotinemi quilnamictinemi Yn inpapa[7]quilis Ca S,^{n} quitohua Ma yquin YCuac Yn tihuehuetisq.^{z} titocahuasq.^{z} Yn titlateomatisq.^{z}—

D,^{n} Seb,^{n} v Notlasomahuistatzine Ca huel teYolali Yn motlatoltzin Auh yn tehuatzin Notlasonamictzine tleyn ticMitalhuia Canel oc tiuhq.^{z} Yn Canel oc tipipiltotontin ma oc ticpapaquiltican Yn tlaltp.^{c}CaYotl Yn necuYLtonolistli Yn papaquilistli ma Oc motelchihua Yn teop.^{n}nemilistli ma Oc motelchihua Yn neYolCuitilistli Ma Yquin quesquilhuitl Yn ticchihuasq.^{z} Yn qualnemilistli—

D^{na} Juana v Notlasonamictzin notelpotzin Ca Yn otzintic Yn ticmitalhuia Ca noma Amo niCualita Yntlacamo timoYolCuititzinosnequi Ca Yn nehuatl Ca niYauh in ichantzinco D,^{s}—

D^n Seb,^{n} v Ninomati tinechtlahuelnanquilia tle Yca Yn amo tinechtlacamati ^{in} tleYn nimitzilhuia Ca ticchihua Ca tinechtlacamatis Ca ticneltilis Yn notlatol—

1,º Dem.º v Tla xihualMohuica nochpochtzine macamo ximoqualanalti tla xicmo-Caquiltitzino Ca Yntla timohuicas Yn teop.^{n} manoso iquin Ycuac Yn timoCoCotzinos Auh Yn axcan ma xicmotlacamachilti Yn motlasonamictzin ca huelitis Yntla moqualanaltis Ca mitzmomictilis Auh Ynin tlasosihuapile ma no xinechmotlacamachilti Ca amo nipiltontli Ca ye niuhqui Ca Ye nihuehue tlacatl Yn nimotatzin—

D,^{na} Juana v Notlasotelpochtzin NoteCuyo ma xinechmotlapòpolhuilitzino Ca niman amo huel nicchias⁶ Yn nehuatl Yn tleyn ticMitalhuia Ca Yn axcan Ca quaresma Yn ticate Ca ticneltilisq.^{z} Yn itenahuatiltzin Yn D,^{s}—

   Yaz Yn D,^{na} Juana hualquisas 1º # Angel [8]

D^n Seb.^{n} v Notlasomahuistatzine macamo tlen xicmolhuiliz Yese mochihuas Yn tleYn ticmitalhuis Ca nicchihuas Auh Yese niquitohua Ca Yntla nechqualanis Ca niquichtacamictis Ca tinechmopalehuilis Yn tleyn nicchihuas—

1.º Dem.º v Notelpotze noxocoyohue macamo mitzmotequipachilhuis Ca nimitzpalehuis Amo ximomauhti—

1.º Ang.^{l} v Nopieltzine tleyn ticchihuasnequi Cuix ticochi ma axcan ma mitztequipacho Ym motlatlaCol Cuix amo ticmati Yn ca axcan tlamasehualisCahuip.^{n} Yn ticate ma ximoCuitihuetzi ma xitlachie—

D^n Seb,^{n} v Tla xihualhuian Yn amehuantin Yn tehuatl Yn ti[PaJe?] ma xonaci Yn ichantzinco Yn Do^n alberto~~tzin ma xicmonochili Auh Yn tehuatl Yn tiMig.^{l} ma xicmonochili Yn D^n Sebastiantzin~~ Ma nican hualmohuica Ca niCan niquinnochielitica Ca nican tôtoYolalisq.^{z} Ytlauctzinco Ynahuactzinco Yn mahuistlatlacatzintli Yn huehue tlacatzintli Canel ~~Domingo [?]~~ ⁷

2.º PaJe. v Ca Ye qualitzin tlacatle tlatohuanie ma tiquintonochilitin—

Mig^l v Ma ticneltilitin Yn miYotzin motlatoltzin—

   Callaquizque Yn PaJes

---

   6. nicchias: read *nicchihuaz*.
   7. There are words in super- and subscript: [?] yehuatzin ang^l hualmohuicas Yn nica[n?] [?].

FIRST DEMON: And that, what you are thinking, is very good, for it is a very opportune time for you to console yourself. Are you still a little kid, a baby? Enjoy yourself for now. Are you an old man already? Do penance and whip yourself when you are an old man. Do you not see the multitude of young men who go about enjoying the things of youth, who go about speaking of and thinking of their pleasures? [7] For they just say, "when we are old men we will stop, we will engage in spiritual activities."

DON SEBASTIÁN: O my beloved honored father, your words are very consoling. And you, O my beloved spouse, what do you say? Since we are still this way, since we are still little kids, let us for now enjoy the things of the earth, wealth and pleasures. Let hanging around at church be despised for now, let confession be despised for now. Let us work at the good life for a few days.

DOÑA JUANA: O my beloved spouse, O my son, as to what you have just finished saying, I myself do not approve if you do not want to confess. As for me, I am going to the home of God.

DON SEBASTIÁN: I think you are answering me in an angry way. Why do you not obey me? What I say to you, you are to do. You will obey me; you will carry out my words.

FIRST DEMON: Do come, O my daughter, do not be angry. Do listen. If you go to church perhaps then you will become ill. But now, obey your beloved spouse for it could be, if he gets angry, that he will kill you. And so, O precious noblewoman: obey me also for I am not a little kid. My nature is that I am an old person, I am your father.[4]

DOÑA JUANA: O my beloved young man, O my lord, pardon me for I absolutely cannot do what you are saying, for we are now in Lent and we will carry out God's orders.

(Doña Juana leaves. First Angel enters.) [8]

DON SEBASTIÁN: O my beloved honored father, do not say anything, yet what you say will be carried out. I will do it. And yet I say, if she makes me angry I will secretly kill her. You will help me do it.

FIRST DEMON: O my son, O my youngest, let it not trouble you for I will help you. Do not be afraid.

FIRST ANGEL: O my charge, what are you about to do? Are you sleeping? May your sins trouble you now. Do you not know that we are now in the time of penance? Come to your senses, see!

DON SEBASTIÁN: Do come. You, page, go to the home of don Alberto; ~~summon him. And you, Miguel, summon don Sebastián~~; may he come here. I await them here, for here we will console ourselves next to and alongside the honored humane person, the old man, since it is ~~Sunday [?]~~.

SECOND PAGE.: Very well, O lord, O ruler, let's go summon them.

MIGUEL: Let's go carry out your breath, your words.

(The pages exit.)

---

4. That is, he belongs to the same generation as her father and demands the same respect and obedience she would give him.

D.n Seb,n v Notlasomahuistatzine tla nimitznotlatlanili tleYn nicchihuas Yn itechcopa Yn nonamic q.z huel nicchihuaz Yn ipnpa Yn amo huel nechtlamati[8]—

1.º Dem.º v Notelpotze noxoCoYohue macamo mitztequipachoS ca nehuatl nicmati Ca nimitzpalehuis Ca nimitzilhuis Yn qn huel ticchihuas Ca nimitzilhuis Ca Yn Campa tiquitas Ca nimitzYecanas Yese Ca nimitzmacas Yn tleYn Yc ticmictis Yn mosihuauh ma notech ximochicahua macamo ximomauhti Ca nimitzpalehuis—[9]

D.n Seb,n v Ynontzin Ca Cenca ninoYolalia Yn nicCaqui Yn motlatoltzin Nopiltzintzine tlatohuanie ma Oc tepitzin titoSehuitin Yn oquic hualMohuica Yn tocniuhtzitzinhuan Ynic titoYolalisq.z timochintin—

Calaquisq.z hualquisas Dna Juana Yhuan 2º Ang.l
2.º Demo san huel quisas ~~Dem~~ nepantla quisasqz.

D,na Juana v Noteotzin notlatocatzin D,S campa nias Yn mohuitzin Yn nictocas Ynic nias Yn motheop.nChantzinco—

2º Ang.l v Cihuatzintle Campa Yn timohuiCasnequi ma xinechmolhuili—

D,a Juana v NotlasoConetzin Ca Ompa nonasisnequi Yn ichantzinco D,S—

2.º Ang.l v Tla nimitznotlatlanili tleyn timaYlis Cuix itla mitzmotequipachilhuia Ma xitechmolhuili—

D,na Juana v Tla xicmoCaquilti Ca Ynic nias Ca ninoYolCuitis Yn axcan Canel motenahuatilia Yn tonantzin S.ta Yglecia Ynic neSenCahualos Ynic nealtilos Yn ixp.n-tzinco D,S—

2º Ang.l v Ca senca mahuistic Yn ticmolnamiquilia Auh Yn nehuatl Ca nimitznonahuatilia macamo Ytla ticmopinahuiscahuilis Ynic timoYolCuititzinos ma huel mochi ticmoSenquixtili Yn motlatlaCol huel huey yn iteycnoytalistzin Yn tt.º Dios—

2º Demo v Macamo xicneltoca Yn itlatol Yn piltontli Yn tleyn mitzilhuia Ca San mitzitztlacahuia[9] amo xicneltoca—Yas mictlan

Dna Juana v Onomasehualtic Otinechmocnelilitzino Ca huel mahuistic Yn motlatoltzin Auh ma xinechMohuiquili Yn teop.n ma xinechmoYecanili Ynic quali nictocas Yn iYotzin yn tt.º D,S—

Yazq.z yn teop.n hualquisasq.z Lucifer Yhuâ omentin Demonios

Luçifer tla xihualhuian Yn annotetlaYeColtiCahuan tleyn amay tleYn anquichihua Cuix ancochi Ca Ye Ynma Ca Ye oncâ Yn ticate ma anquichihuasq.z Yn amotequiuh ma xicte[10]tecacan Yn amotzohua Yhuan Yn amomatl Yn anmochimal Yn amotlahuis Cuix amo Yn teopixcatotontin Ca huel monequi Yn techpanahuisq.z Yn ica Yn inNeYolCuitilis Yn tlaltp.c tlacatotontin ma yxquich Amotlapal xicchihuacan ca ye Anquimati Ca huel teoCruztica Yn Mictlan—

---

8. nechtlamati: read *nechtlacamati*.
9. mitzitztlacahuia: read *mitziztlacahuia*.

DON SEBASTIÁN: O my beloved honored father, let me ask you: What am I to do about my spouse? What can I do about the fact that she does not obey me?

FIRST DEMON: O my young man, O my youngest, let it not trouble you, for I know about it and I will help you. I will tell you what you can do, I will tell you where you will find her, I will lead you [there]. Moreover I will give you what you will kill your wife with. Rely on me. Do not be frightened, for I will help you. [9]

DON SEBASTIÁN: I am very content to hear your words, O my nobleman, O ruler. Let us rest a little more while our friends are coming so that we will all be consoled.[5]

(They exit. Doña Juana enters along with Second Angel.)
(Second Demon [likewise] enters. They enter in the middle.)[6]

DOÑA JUANA: O my deity, O my ruler, O God, where am I to go? I will follow your road so that I will go to your temple.

SECOND ANGEL: O woman, where do you want to go? Tell me.

DOÑA JUANA: O my beloved child, I want to reach the home of God.

SECOND ANGEL: Let me question you. What's the matter? Is something troubling you? Tell me.

DOÑA JUANA: Do listen. I am going to confess now since our mother holy church orders people to prepare themselves, to bathe themselves in the presence of God.

SECOND ANGEL: What you are thinking is very worthy of esteem. But I order you: do not omit something for shame. When you confess, gather together absolutely all your sins, for the mercy of our lord God is very great.

SECOND DEMON: Do not believe the words of the little kid, what he is saying to you, for he is just lying to you. Don't believe him!

(He goes to the place of the dead.)

DOÑA JUANA: I am fortunate. Thank you, for your words are very splendid. And accompany me to church, lead me so that I will properly follow the breath of our lord God.

(They go to the church. Lucifer and two demons enter.)

LUCIFER: Do come, you who are my servants. What's wrong with you? What's the matter with you? Are you sleeping? For it is the time, it is the moment[7] for us to be [up and about]. Do your job, lay [10] your snares and your nets, your shields, your insignia. Is it not the miserable little priests who find it very necessary to overcome us with the confessions of the miserable little people of the earth? Exert all your effort, for you already know that it is really through the sacred cross [that people avoid?] the place of the dead.[8]

---

   5. Tentative translation.
   6. The physical setting is not specified.
   7. Ca Ye Inma Ca Ye oncâ: translated here as "it is the time, it is the moment," its general thrust is "it is high time that something happen or be done." See Carochi 1983, 103v.
   8. This sentence tentatively translated.

1.º Demº y Tlacatle tlatohuanie macamo mitzmotequipachilhuis Ca Yn nehuatl Ca niman ayc nictlalcahuis¹⁰ Yn tlaltp.ᶜ tlacatotontin Ca momostlaYe Yn inp.ⁿ niquistinemi Yn niquintoCatinemi Auh tla xicmocaquiltitzino tlatohuanie ca se tlacatl tlatohuani nictlapololtitinemi huel momahuistiliani huel mos.totocatinemi. Yn teYxp.ⁿ Ynic nemi Auh amo San iCel Ca huel miequintin Ca oc Cequintin onCan cate Yn totetlaYecolticahua Yhuan Yn Cihua no miequintin Yn moSihuapilYtotinemi Yn atle Yp.ⁿ teYtztinemi Ca mochintin maxcatzitzinhua Yesq.ᶻ macamo ximotequipachotzino tlacatle tlatohuanie—

Luçifer y Axcan huel Senca nipapaqui Yn nicaqui Yn motlatol Ynic tinechnanamiqui huel Senca ninoYolalia ninotlamachtia Auh Ca ayemo tel quitequipaChohua Yn ineYolCuitilis Ca Yquin iquac Yn asisq.ᶻ Yn Semana S,ⁿᵗᵃ Yxtomahuasq.ᶻ Ca ymahuililp.ⁿ quimatisq.ᶻ Yp.ⁿpa On acmo mochi quitosq.ᶻ Yn intlatlaCol tla xiquitocan¹¹. Yn Ye ce xihuitl ca huel Miequintin Yn oquilcauhqᶻ Yn intlatlaCol nel cequintin Amo OmoYolCuitiqᶻ Auh Yn nehuatl Ca huel ic nipaqui ninotlamachtia Auh Ynin nopilhuane noCoscahuane ma huel Yxquich Amotlapal xicchihuacan macamo xiquincahuacan Yntla Calaquisq.ᶻ Yn teop.ⁿ ma xiquintzaCuilican Yn otlica ma ximotlacanextitinemican Ynic amo quicaquisq.ᶻ Yn temachtilli—[11]

2º Dem.º y Auh Yn nehuatl tlacatle tlatohuanie [?] [Yc?] tlaYhuali¹² nicnonahualtia Yn manel pipiltotontin Ca huel miequintin niquinmamauhtia Ynic amo quilnamiquisq.ᶻ Yn inneYolCuitilis Yhuan Yn tlatquihuaq.ᶻ huel Yⁿpapac Ynic huel quiⁿtequipachos Yn inⁿetlaYeColtilis Ynic amo Ysiuhca quiⁿtequipacho Yn inⁿeYolCuitilis Ye Oc Senca quiⁿtequipachohua Yn inⁿechichihual Ynic mochi tlacatl quiⁿmahuistilis Auh Yntla quitos Se achi Ytzotzomatzin Ytatapatzin Aucmo quimoucniuhtia Sᵃn ica huetzca Yca no topehua Auh Ynon Acmo quitlatlaColmati Oc Senca Yehuâtin¹³ Yn mochpoch tlapiquitinemi Ca mochintin maxcatzitzinhuâ Yesq.ᶻ maCamo ximotequipachotzino Ca yxquich totlapal ticchiuhtinemisq.ᶻ tlacatle tlatohuanie—

Lucifer y Notlasopilhuane Ca senca Yc nipapaqui Yn nicaqui Yn amotlatol Ca huel mahuistic ma huel ximochicahuacan macaYac techpanahui maCaYac techpinauhti tla xiquimitaCan ca yn teopixcatotontin Ca huel mochiCahua Ca huel techpanahuisnequi maCamo Yuhqui mochihuas Yn polihuis Yn totenyo in tomahuiso Ynic amo Aquin toCa huetzcas maSihui Yn asi Yn amotequiuh ma Oc tepitzin ninoSehui—

1.º Dem.º y Ma iuhqui mochihua ma oc ximoSehuitzino Yn motlatocaYecYantzinco—Calaquisqᶻ hualMoquixtis Yn xpº Yuhqui Ecce homotzin Yhuan home Angeles se quihualhuicas Cruz Yn oc cequih Qualhuicas¹⁴ lanza—

---

10. nictlalcahuis: read *niquintlalcahuiz*.
11. xiquitocan: probably scribal error for *xiquittacan*.
12. tlaYhuali: read *tlayohualli*.
13. Yehuâtin: read *yehuatzin*.
14. Qualhuicas: read *quihualhuicaz*.

FIRST DEMON: O lord, O ruler, let it not trouble you. I will absolutely never abandon the miserable little people of the earth, for I pass by them every day and follow them around. And do listen, O ruler, for there is a certain ruler whom I go about confusing who really glorifies himself, really goes about imagining he is a saint; that is how he lives in public. But it is not just him, for there are a great many other [men] who are our servants as well as many women who go about calling themselves noblewomen, who are of no account. They will all be your property. Do not be troubled, O master, O ruler.

LUCIFER: Now I am very happy to hear your words with which you help me. I am very consoled, I am enjoying myself greatly. And their confessions do not yet give them concern. When they reach Holy Week they will act stupid, they will regard it as a time of entertainment. Because of that they will no longer say all of their sins. Do see that now it has been a year. A great many have forgotten their sins. In truth, some did not confess [at all]. But as for me, I am very happy about it, I am enjoying myself greatly. So then, O my children, O my jewels, exert absolutely all your effort. Do not relinquish them. If they [try to] enter church, detain them on the road. Go around putting on a [good] act so that they will not hear the sermon. [11]

SECOND DEMON: And I, O lord, O ruler, [?⁹] I hide myself in dark places. Even if it is little kids, I frighten a great many so that they will not think about their confessions. And it is the pleasure of the wealthy that their making a living is what worries them, so their confessions do not soon distress them. What especially worries them is their adornment, so that everyone will honor them. But if he will say "[so-and-so] had [only] a bit of rags and worn-out clothing," he will no longer make friends with him. He just laughs at him, and also pushes him away. And they no longer regard that as sin, especially your daughter who goes about making things up. They will all be your property. Do not worry for we will go about exerting all our effort, O lord, O ruler.

LUCIFER: O my beloved children, I am very happy to hear your words for they are very splendid. Really exert yourselves. Let no one overcome us, let no one shame us. Look at the miserable little priests: they really exert themselves, they really want to overcome us. Let it not thus happen [that] our fame and our honor will perish, so that no one will laugh at us although your task is achieved.[10] Let me rest a bit.

FIRST DEMON: May it so be done. Rest for now in your royal quarters.

(They exit. Christ enters as the Ecce Homo along with two angels. One brings a cross and the other brings a lance.)

---

9. Text is mostly illegible in this section.
10. maSihui Yn asi Yn amotequiuh: literally, "although your task arrives." Tentative translation.

xp̄o v̄ Tla xihualmohuicacâ Yn annotitlantzitzinhuan ca huel Senca ninotequipachohua Yn inp.ⁿpa Yn tlaltp.ᶜ tlaca niman aOcmo nechtlaCamati Yn aOcmo YnYolotica [12] Ynic Calaqui Yn nochantzinco Yn aOcmo quitlasotla Y noteoyotzin amo quitlasocamati Ynic oniquinmaquixti Yn inp.ⁿpa Onicnonoqui Y notlasoYessotzin Auh Yn amehuantzitzin. Yn annotititlantzitzinhuan ma Yxquich Amotlapal xicmochihuiliCan ma ximohuiCaCâ Ynic anquinYaOchihuasq.ᶻ Yn notlatelchihualhuan Yn tlatlaCatecolo Ynca Yehuantin Yn tlaltp.ᶜ tlaca nechtelchihuasq.ᶻ Ca no nehuatl niquintelchihuas niquintlaSas Yn onpa sentlani mictlan Yn aOquic Oc Cepa niquimicnoYta—

          MOtlanquaq.ᶻtzaz Yn Ang.ˡ—

1.º Ang.ˡ v̄ Noteotzine notlatocatzine Ca huel melahuac Yn ticmotalhuitzinohua Auh Ca yxquich totlapal ticchiuhtinemi Yn inhuiCopa Yn tlaltp.ᶜ tlaca Oc Cenca Yehuantzitzin Yn motlatenquixticatzitzinhuan Yn teopixq.ᶻ Yn motemachticatzitzinhua Ca niman Aic quincahua Yn quintzatzilia Yn imixpa Yn quitlalia Yn motonehuilistzin Yn motlasohuilitzin Ynic onoquiuh Yn motlaSoesotzin Yhuan Yn quexquich moteYcnoYtalitzin Ynic senca titlatlaCatzintli Yn ticnohuaCatzintli Auh Ca san mixCoYan monomatelchihua Ca san Yehuatl quitlacamati Yn motlasentelchihualtzitzinhuan Yn tlatlaCatecolo—

xp̄o v̄ OYtlahueliltic Yn tlaltp.ᶜ tlaca niman acmo quilnamiquisnequi Yn q.ᶻnin Oquinmomaquixtili Yese niquitohua Ca Yn aquiq.ᶻ amo nechtemosnequi Yn amo nechilnamicquisnequi Ca in iCuac Yn niquinnotzas Yn nixp.ⁿ hualasq.ᶻ ca niquincemixnahuatis Ynic aOquic quitasq.ᶻ Yn notlasoxaYaCatzin Ca semicac Mictlâ tlalohuasqᶻ—motlanquaq.ᶻtzas

2.º Ang.ˡ v̄ Yo noteotzine notlatoCatzine canel otiquinmochihuilitzino Ca motlachihualtzitzinhuan Auh Ca motetlaYecolticatzitzinhuan OtiquinMomaquixtilitzino macamo ticmone[13]quiltitzino Ynic polihuisq.ᶻ Ca Ye ticmomachiltitzinohua Yn niCan Catqui Yn tepostlachichtli Ca Yehuatl Yc omotlapo Yn ilhuicatl Yn motlasoYomotlantzin Ynic otiquinmotlasotilitzino Auh macamo polihuis Yn imanima Ca huel nimitznotlatlauhtilitzinohua ttᵒᵉ Diose—

xpo v̄ Ca huel Senca nichuelcaqui Yn amotlatol Yn amehuantin innannotlachihualtzitzinhuan¹⁵ Yese Yehuantin Amo Yuh quimati—Tla xihualauh Yn tehuatl ma xiyauh ma xicnotza Yn ~~toPile~~ Ma nican nixp.ⁿ hualauh—

1.º Angˡ v̄ Ca Ye qualitzin noteotzine notlatocatzine ma niYauh ma nicnotza—

          # Yaz quinotzatiuh Yn Miquistli Ytopil quihualhuicasque—

1.º Angˡ v̄ Ma nican timohuicatz tlatohuanie Ca nican moetzinotica Yn Jesus Yn Dˢ Ypiltzin YsRael—

---

15. innannotlachihualtzitzinhuan: read *in annotlachihualtzitzinhuan*.

CHRIST: Do come, you who are my messengers, for I am very much troubled by the people of the earth. They absolutely no longer obey me, no longer willingly [12] enter my home, no longer love my sacraments, are not thankful that I saved them and spilled my precious blood for their sake. And you, who are my messengers, exert all your effort. Go to make war on those whom I despise, the demons, through whom the people of the earth will despise me. I will also despise them. I will cast them into the depths of the place of the dead. Never again will I have pity on them.

([First] Angel kneels down.)

FIRST ANGEL: O my deity, O my ruler, what you are saying is very true. We go about exerting all our effort towards the people of the earth, especially those who are your spokespersons, the priests, your teachers. For they absolutely never abandon them. They cry out to them, they set before them your torments and your suffering when your precious blood was spilled, and how much pity you have, how very humane and compassionate you are. But they just despise their very selves, they just obey those whom you have entirely cursed, the demons.

CHRIST: How unfortunate are the people of the earth! They absolutely do not want to think any longer about how he[11] saved them. But I say, as to those who do not search me out, who do not want to remember me, when I summon them, when they arrive before me, I will completely condemn them so that they will never again see my precious face, for they will flee to the place of the dead forever.

([Second Angel] kneels.)

SECOND ANGEL: Ah, O my deity, O my ruler, since you made them, they are your creations. And they are your servants; you saved them. May it not be your will [13] that they will perish. You already know that here is the nail[12] with which heaven, your precious side, was opened, [demonstrating] that you loved them. And may their souls not perish, I greatly implore you, O our lord, O God.

CHRIST: I listen very approvingly to your words, you who are my creations, but they do not see it that way. Do come, you. Go, summon the ~~constable~~, may he come here before me.

FIRST ANGEL: Very well, O my deity, O my ruler, let me go summon him.

(He goes to summon Death. They bring his staff.)

FIRST ANGEL: Please be welcome here,[13] O ruler, for here is Jesus, God, child of Israel.

---

11. That is, Christ. Evidently a scribal error since Christ is talking about himself and should say "I."
12. tepostlachichtli: see Bautista 1606, 114, where this is paired with a Spanish term: "ce clauo tepuztlaxichtli."
13. Ma nican timohuicatz: here and below in variants it has been translated as "Please be welcome here." See Carochi 1983, 67v, 80r, and Sahagún 1997, 296.

xp̄o y̱ Tla xihualmohuica notopileCatzine ma ximohuica Yn câpa moSentlalisq^z Yn tlatoq^z ma huel iCuac Yn pa[n?]t[i?]sq.^{z} Ca timoteYtilis Yhuan xichuica home tzonteComatl Oncâ Yxp.^{n} tictlalis Yn D^n Seb.^{n} tiquilhuis Ca niCan Ca Yn motatzin Yn monantzin Ca Yehuatl Yn intzonteco Cuix tiquimiXimati—

Miquistli y̱ Noteotzine notlatoCatzine ma niYauh ma nicchihua Yn moteotenahuatiltzin ma niquimita ma niquintzatzili Ma san tehuatzin Motencopatzinco Ynic moYolehuasq^z Ynic monemilisCuepasq.^{z} Ca miequintin Yn tlalp.^{c} tlaca Yn Cuac[16] nechita Ca niman Mitzmotzatzililia mitzmolnamiquilia momauhtia Ca niman monemiliscuepa Yn mixp^{n}tzinco—

xp̄o y̱ Auh Yn amehuantin ma xichuicaca Yn notopilecatzin sese tzontecon yn AnquihuiCasq^z Ce Yn tatli Se Yn nâtli ma xicmohuiCaCâ xicneltilitin Yn noteotenahuatiltzin—[14]

2° Ang.^{l} Ca Ye Cualitzin noteotzine notlatoCatzine ma ticneltilitin Yn moteotenahuatiltzin—

Mocalaquis Yn xp.^{o} Yhuan Miquistli Yhuā Ang.^{l} quiCas[17] D^n Seb.^{n} Yhuâ D^n Alberto D^n Fabian homêtin Pajes Yhua. 1° Dem,^{o}—

D,^{n} Seb.^{n} y̱ Ma nican anmohuicatze notlasoteachcauhtzitzinhuane AnmoSianmiquiltitzinohua Ma niCan tepitzin ximohuetzititzinoCan telpochtle ma xiCualmoquixtili ~~Yn huehuetl ma moYolalitzinocan tlein intetzinco monequis Yn~~ Yn mahuistiq.^{z} tlaca—

1.º PaJe y̱ Ca Ye qualitzin tlatohuanie ma niCan huitz Yn hue~~huetl yn yntetzinco monequis yn tlatoq.^{z}~~

Calaquisq^z quihualquixtisq^z YnMessatlaCuau[18] Yhuan Yn ~~huehuetl~~ vino

D,^{n} Fab,^{n} y̱ Otomasehualtic Yn motetlasotlalitzin Ca amo ticpia Ynic tiquixtlahuasq.^{z} Yn ixquich tetlasotlalistli tlacatle tlatohuanie—

D,^{n} Seb,^{n} y̱ Notlasotatzine ma xiquinmoYecanili Yn mopilhuantzitzinhuan ma ximohuetziltica—

D^n Alberdo y̱ Ma ximohuetziltican ma ximoSehuitzinoCan—

1° Dem^o y̱ Notlasopilhuane macamo namechnotequipachilhui Ma ximosehuitzinoCan—

Motlallisq^z Mochintin

D^n Alberdo y̱ Nopiltzintzine ma ximotlateochihuilitzino Canel YaCachtopa homitzmochihuilitzino Yn tt,^{o} D,^{s}—

1° Dem^o y̱ Notlasopilhuane Ca niman Amo nihuelitis Ca nica nichane Yhuan tla xicmoCaquiltiCan Ca Ye anquimomachiltia Yn Cuac titehua yn tihualquisa quiYahuac Cuix amo niman titoteoChihua Yhuan niman no Yquac Motlateochihuilia yn Dios mochi quimoteochihuiliaya Yn quechquich Yn quechquich[19] totech monequis Yn tiquisq^z Yn tiquasq.^{z} Auh Ynintzin ma ximotlaqualtican Nopilhuane—[15]

---

16. Yn Cuac: here and below, read *yn icuac*.
17. quiCas: read *quiçaz*.
18. YnMessatlaCuau: perhaps to be read *ynmesatlacahuan*.
19. Yn quechquich Yn quechquich: so written in the original text.

CHRIST: Do come, O my constable. Go where the rulers will gather. Right when you come upon them you are to show yourself.[14] And bring the two skulls. You are to place them there in front of don Sebastián. You are to say to him: "Here is your father, your mother. There are their heads. Do you recognize them?"

DEATH: O my deity, O my ruler, let me go, let me carry out your sacred commands. Let me see them, let me cry out to them. May they just be inspired by your orders to change their lives. For there are many people of the earth who, when they see me, cry out to you, remember you, and are afraid. Then they change their lives in your presence.

CHRIST: And you, bring my constable each skull. You are to bring them to him. One is the father, one is the mother. Bring them to him. Carry out my sacred command. [14]

SECOND ANGEL: Very well, O my deity, O my ruler, let us carry out your sacred command.

(Christ exits along with Death and [Second] Angel. Don Sebastián enters along with don Alberto, don Fabián, two pages, and First Demon.)

DON SEBASTIÁN: Please be welcome here, O my beloved older brothers. You are most welcome. Sit here for a bit. O young man, bring out ~~the drum~~ what ~~Let~~ the honored people ~~be consoled~~ need.[15]

FIRST PAGE: Very well, O ruler, let ~~the drum~~ what the lords need be brought here.

(They exit. Those serving at the table bring it along with ~~a drum~~ wine.)[16]

DON FABIÁN: We are so fortunate [as to be enjoying] your hospitality but we do not have anything with which to repay all the hospitality, O lord, O ruler.

DON SEBASTIÁN: O my beloved father, lead your children [to their seats], sit down.

DON ALBERTO: Sit down, rest yourselves.

FIRST DEMON: O my beloved children, let me not trouble you. Rest yourselves.

(All sit down.)

DON ALBERTO: O my nobleman, make the blessing, since our lord God made you first [for that purpose].[17]

FIRST DEMON: O my beloved children, I absolutely cannot for I am a resident here. And listen, for you already know that when we get up and come out of the door: are we not then blessing ourselves? And also at that time God blesses things. He blesses everything, whatever we need to drink and to eat. And now, eat, O my children. [15]

---

14. Tentatively translated.
15. To avoid confusion: the original read "O young man, bring out the drum. Let the honored people be consoled." The emended version reads "O young man, bring out what the honored people need."
16. Tentative translation.
17. That is, as the eldest in the party he should say grace before their meal. A demon, of course, must decline the privilege. His excuse is that he resides there and thus should defer to the guests, and anyway the blessing is not necessary.

D.ⁿ Seb.ⁿ v Notlasotiachcauhtzitzinhuane Ca melahuac Yn quimitalhuia Canel yxe naca²⁰ Cenca momachtiani Yn tlasopilli macamo Ximotequipachotzino ma Ximotlaqualtican Auh Yn nehuatl, Ma Oc namechnoYollaliliz—

~~OCa tlatzotzonalos tlapitza~~quasq.ᶻ—

D.ⁿ Fabiâ v Ma oquichquich²¹ Yn ~~tinotlatzotzo[ca]huan~~ tlein amechmolnamiquilia nocniuhtzine Ca amo axcan monequi ho Yn paquilistli Ca axcan monequi Yn tlamasehualistli Yn neyolCuitilistli Ca ye axcan Yn motenahuatilia Yn tonantzin S.ᵗᵃ Yglesia Ynic tiaAltisque²² titopapaCasq.ᶻ—

D.ⁿ Alberto v tleyn ticmitalhuia Cuix titemiqui Cuix tiCochi Yn tehua OnCan moyolalitzinosnequi Yn tlatoq.ᶻ Yn pipiltin ca tenepⁿtla timaquitinemi xitechcahua Oc titoYolalisq.ᶻ Cuix ticmati Yntla mostla Yntla huiptla titomiquilisq.ᶻ Ma xitechCahua—

1.º Dem.º v Telpochtle Yn tiquitohua XiquinmoCahuili ma Oc mopapaquiltican, Yn tlatoq.ᶻ Canel oc telpopochtin pipiltzitzintin ma Oc xicahua Yn teopⁿ huel ohicalistli

D.ⁿ Fab.ⁿ v Tla nimitznotlatlanili Auh Yn Yehuatzin tlasoCihuapilli Can omohuiCac tlaCatzintli nicnotilia—

D.ⁿ Seb.ⁿ v MaCamo xicmotenehuili teotzin tlatohuanie Ca Ye omomiquili Ca Ye nahui metztli Axcan Yn otictotlalaquiliqᶻ—

D.ⁿ Alberto v Nomati Amo titlaCaquisnequi Yn amo molnamiqui Auh Yn tehuatl Oncan tleyn ticteYlnamictia tla xitechcahua Yntla noso Diablo techhuicas Cuix motequiuh xitechcahua nose xitechtlalcahuis—

hualquisas Miquistli Yhuan Ang.ˡ moquetztehuas Yn Dem.º quitlasq.ᶻ
Messaquac Yn tzōtecontin—

1.º Ang.ˡ v D,ˢ Ytlamaquixtiltzitzinhuane maCamo Ximomauhtican Ca ytêcopatzinco Yn D,ˢ YniC ohualMohuicac Yn topiletzin—

1.º Dem.º Macamo xicneltocacan Ca Sⁿ amechmamauhtia Ca San Ypan asiz Yn temictli—

1º Ang.ˡ v tleYn tiquitohua tlatelchihualpol Ynin ca notlamamal Ca nop[iel?] [Ca amo?] huel tichuicas MoxiCohuanie—

1.º Dem.º Ca nichuicas Ca ye naxca Ca ye notlatqui—[16]

---

20. naca: read *nacace*.
21. oquichquich: here and below, read *oc ixquich*.
22. tiaAltisque: read *titaltizque*.

DON SEBASTIÁN: O my beloved older brothers, what he is saying is true since he has eyes and ears,[18] he is very learned, a high-born nobleman. Do not be troubled. Eat. And as for me, let me console you.

(~~At that point drums are beaten, wind instruments are played.~~)

DON FABIÁN: Let that be all, ~~my musicians~~. What are they making you think of? O my friend, those pleasures are not necessary now, for today penance and confession are necessary, for today our mother holy church commands that we bathe, that we wash ourselves.

DON ALBERTO: What are you saying? Are you dreaming? Are you sleeping? The rulers and noblemen want to console themselves along with others there, [and] you are interfering. Leave us, while we console ourselves. Do you know if we will die tomorrow, or the day after?[19] Leave us!

FIRST DEMON: O young man, what are you saying? Leave them alone. Let the rulers enjoy themselves since they are still young men, little children. Leave the church. [It is dangerous?].[20]

DON FABIÁN: Let me question you. And as to that high-born noblewoman, where did she go? I see her as a human being [alive?].

DON SEBASTIÁN: Do not mention the deity, O ruler, for she has already died. It has been four months now since we buried her.[21]

DON ALBERTO: I think you do not want to hear what is not being remembered. And you there, what are you reminding people of? Leave us. If the devil should take us, is it your business? Leave us or abandon us.

(*Death enters along with [First] Angel. [First] Demon protests. They cast the skulls on top of the table.*)

FIRST ANGEL: O God's saved ones, do not be frightened, for it is by God's orders that the constable has come.

FIRST DEMON: Do not believe him for he just frightens you. It just comes to him in dreams.

FIRST ANGEL: What are you saying, miserable despised one? This one is my burden [of responsibility], my charge. You can[not] take him, O envious one.[22]

FIRST DEMON: I will take him away for he is already my goods, he is already my property. [16]

---

18. to have eyes, to have ears: a common diphrase that means "to be acute, alert, sharp."
19. tomorrow, the day after: here and below, a common diphrase that often means "soon, in the near future."
20. huel ohicalistli: perhaps read *huel ohuicaliztli.* .
21. Perhaps the woman being discussed is don Sebastián's mother, whose skull Death is about to deliver. Why don Sebastián says "Do not mention the deity" is not clear.
22. Tentative translation.

Miquistli = Tla xihualauh Yn tiD.ⁿ Seb.ⁿ tlen tay tlen ticchihua Cuix ticochi ma xisa Cuix aYac tictemohua Cuix aYac ticpolohua Campa Yn otiquis Cuix itec quahuitl hanoso y tetl ma xinechnanquili tla xiquita Yn is ca Cuix tiquiximati Yhuan Yn nehuatl Cuix tinexiximati²³ Yhuan Yn is cate Cuix amo tiquimiximati aquiq.ᶻ Auh ac nehuatl Cuix amo tiquilnamiqui Ca nihualas Yn amop.ⁿ niquisaquiuh tla xiquita Yn nican ca Ca Yehuatl Yn motatzin catca Yn huel motlaCamatia Ca huel miec tlaca Yn quitequipanohuaya Auh Yn is ca Ca yehuatl Yn monantzin ocatca Auh Catli Yn iAxca Yn itlatqui hi catca Yn inechichihual Yn oquitlaliaya huel xiquimita Yntech ximixCuiti Ca mostla Ca huiptla Yuhqui timotas ma xicahua Yn tlaltp.ᶜCaYotl Yn papaquilistli ma xiquilnamiquica tipolihuis Ca titzonquisas xiquilnamiqui Ca Onca Yn gloria papaquilistli Yhuan Ca Onca Yn mictlan tla-Yohuilistli tla xiquilnamiqui Ca mop.ⁿpa Omotlacatili Yn D.ˢ Yhuan Camop.ⁿpa homotlaYohuilti ᶜAmop.ⁿpa Omomiquili amop.ⁿpa OtoCoc hoc cepa homozcali yn Omotlec[ahui?] Yn ilhuicac Omotlalitzinoto YmaYecCampatzinco Yn itlasotatzin D,ˢ Ca mitzhualmotztilitica ma xicmaquixti Yn manima ma mitztequipacho Yn motlatlaCol—

1º Dem.º v Notelpotze D,ⁿ Seb,ⁿ Macamo mitztequipachos notech xicahua Yn manima Ca nehuatl nimitzmaquixtis Ca mopapa nitlaMAcehuas—

Dⁿ Seb,ⁿ v Yo notehotzine notlatoCatzine Ca onimitznoYolitlacalhuitzino Ca mohuiCopatzinco ninoCuepa Ynic nicaqui Yn motlasotlatoltzin Ca yn aquin mohuiCopatzinco MoCuepaz Ca ticmotlaOcolilis ticmopopolhuililis Auh ma xinechmotlapopolhuililitzino ca huel onitlatlaCo—Chocas ho ca tehuatzin notlasotatzine Yhuâ in tehuatzin yn ᵗⁱnotlasonantzin Canel otinechmotlacatilili Auh Campa Yn oamechMoYeYanmaquili Yn tt.º D,ˢ Ca aYac huel quimati—

Miquistli v Yhuâ xicaqui xicmati tleYn mitztlapololtitica [17] Yn ticmictisnequi Yn monamic Cuix amo OmitzMomaquili yn tonantzin S.ᵗᵃ Yglesia Cuix amo Ypⁿ Ca yn iteotenahuatiltzin Ynic Sentetl ticmotlasotilis Yn D,ˢ Yn Contetl²⁴ tiquintlasotlas Yn mohuanpohuan Yn iuh timotlasotlas Auh Ynin ma xictlasotla Yn monamic xiquita Ca tiMiquis tipolihuis—

Dⁿ Fab,ⁿ v Ca Yn nehuatl ca huel nicnalquixtis Yn motlanahuatiltzin Canel Ytlatoltzin Yn tt.º D.ˢ—

D,ⁿ Alberto v NotlasoYcniuhtzitzinhuane nomati Anmomauhtia maCamo Ximomauhtican Ca san amechnenmamauhtia huel neli Ca sa amotonal Yn amechmamauhtia—

Calaquis yn miquistli Yhua Angˡ—

Dⁿ Sb,ⁿ v [?] onotlahueliltic tleyn nop.ⁿ mochihua D,ˢ Cuix nitemiqui Anoso niCochi Ca amo Onisatoc tleYn nicchihuas Ca huel ninotequipachohua = tla xoConita Aquin hualasi aquin quitzotzona Yn puerta—

2º Demº v Macamo ximomauhtitzinocâ Ca San namechnomamauhtilia Yn amotlalnamiquilistzin—

Yaz quitatiuh Yn PaJe Calitic monotzazque—

23. tinexiximati: read *tinechiximati*.
24. Yn Contetl: read *ynic ontetl*.

DEATH: Do come, don Sebastián. What is wrong with you? What is the matter with you? Are you sleeping? Wake up. Is there no one you are looking for? Is there no one you have lost? Where did you come from? From inside wood or stone? Answer me. Do look. The one who is here: do you know him? And I: do you know me? And those who are here: do you not know who they are? And who I am? Do you not remember? For I will come, I will come among you. Do see that the one who is here was your father, who was very rich; a great many people used to work for him. And she who is here was your mother. And what has come of her goods, her property, her adornments she used to put on? Look at them well, take an example from them, for tomorrow or the day after you will see yourself in this condition. Abandon the things of the earth, the pleasures. Remember that you will perish, you will come to an end. Remember that there in glory is happiness and there in the place of the dead is suffering. Do remember that for your sake God was born and for your sake he suffered, for your sake he died, for your sake he was buried [and then] he again revived, he rose to heaven, he went to sit down at the right hand of his beloved father, God. He is watching you. Save your soul; may your sins trouble you.

FIRST DEMON: O my young man, don Sebastián, don't let it trouble you. Leave your soul to me for I will save it for you. I will do penance on your behalf.

DON SEBASTIÁN: Ah, O my God, O my ruler, I have offended you. I turn to you to hear your precious words for you will have mercy on him who turns to you. You will pardon him. And pardon me for I have sinned greatly.

(He cries.)

O you, O my beloved father, and you are my beloved mother, who truly gave birth to me. And where has our lord God placed you? No one can know.

DEATH: And listen, know what is confusing you. [17] You want to kill your spouse. Did not our mother holy church give her to you? Is it not the first of his sacred commands that you will love God, the second that you will love your neighbors as you love yourself? Well then, love your spouse. See [to] it, for [otherwise] you will die, you will perish.

DON FABIÁN: I perfectly understand[23] your commands since it is the word of our lord God.

DON ALBERTO: O my beloved friends, I think you are afraid. Do not be afraid, for it just uselessly frightens you. Truly indeed it is just your fate[24] that frightens you.

(Death exits along with the angel.)

DON SEBASTIÁN: Unfortunate am I! God, what is happening to me? Am I dreaming or perhaps sleeping? I am not awake. What will I do, for I am very anxious and afflicted. Do go see who has come, who is knocking at the door.

SECOND DEMON: Do not be afraid, for I am just frightening your minds.

(He goes to see the page, who is inside the house. They talk to each other.)

---

23. nicnalquixtis/I perfectly understand: perhaps scribal error for *nicnalquizcamatiz*.
24. That is, death, as represented by the skulls.

2º Dem.º v̱ tla xihualmohuica telpochtle tla nimitznotlatlanili Cuix OnCan moetztica Se huehue tlacatl Ytocatzin Bercebo—

1º Paje v̱ Jesus tleyn ticmitalhuia Ca ynon ca tlacatecolotl Yn ticmotenehuilia Ca xpianome Yn niCan motlalia Ca ayac niCan ca tlacatecolotl—

2º Dem.º v̱ Macamo ximomauhti telpochtle Ca san YahuiltocatzinCuix aYc ticmoCaquiltia Yn ixquichtin tlaca tleY mach quimahuiltocaYotia ca San no Yuhqui Yn tehuantin—

1,º PaJe v̱ Auh Yn tehuatzin tley mahuiltocatzin YniquinYolo pachihuis[25]—

2º Demº v̱ Ma xicmomachilticâ Ca nican quimonochilia Satanas niCan nimitznochielia—

hualquisas Yn PaJe quinotzaz Yn 1º Demonios—

1.º PaJe v̱ Notlasotatzine Ca niCan mitzmotemolia ce tlacatl quimahuiltocaYotia Satanas mitzmonochilia quiYahuac—

Dⁿ Seb,ⁿ v̱ Tlein tiquitohua sequi [?] masehualic[26] tlanotzale Yn notlasotatzin. Yuhqui Onechmolhuilico—[18]

1º Demo v̱ Macamo ximomauhtitzinocan ca nahuiltoca Auh Yn techmotemolia YahuiltoCatzin bercebo Ca Oc tipipiltotontin Yn otechtoCayotiqᶻ ma Yca Yn amotlasohuelitzin ma oc noConnotili aso Ytla quimotequipachilhuia—

Dⁿ Seb,ⁿ v̱ Ca niman ahuel mochihuas Yn quiYahuac timoquixtis Cuix amo mochantzinco Yn timoetztica ma moCalaqui Yn aqui mitzmotemolia Nopiltzintzine—

1º Dem.º v̱ telpochtle ma xicmonochili ma hualmocalaqui—

2º PaJe v̱ Ca Ye Cualitzin ma nicnonochili = Ma nican timohuicatz tlatohuanie ma ximocalaqui—

2º Dem.º v̱ Ma ximehuiltitiecan tlatoq.ᶻYe ma namechonnotlapololtili Ac Yehuatzin Yn D,ⁿ Seb,ⁿ Ca yehuatzin Yn nicnotemolia Centlamantli nicnolhuilis—

D,ⁿ Fab,ⁿ v̱ Ca nican moetztica ma Oc ximononotzinocan Auh Yn tehuatzin ma Oc tamechtotlalCahuilican—

Yasq.ᶻ D.ⁿ Fab,ⁿ D,ⁿ Alberto mochintin PaJes mocahuas D,ⁿ Seb,ⁿ Yhuan Dem.ᵒˢ—

D,ⁿ Seb,ⁿ v̱ Tla nican timohuicas tlatohuanie tleyn ticmitalhuia ma niccaqui Yn motlatoltzin—

2.º Dem.º v̱ Notelpotze ma xicmoCaquiltiCan Ca Ya ticpolohua ano[?]so tictemohua Anoso ticmolnamiquilia—

Dⁿ Seb,ⁿ Ca qᶻmacatzin Ca niquinnotemolia Yn onechnochililiq.ᶻ Campa Yn oquinmoYeanmaquili Yn tt.ᵒ D,ˢ auh Yn oniquinnotili Ca Sa Omitzitzintin Yn intzonteContzin—

---

25. YniquinYolo pachihuis: read *ynic in noyollo pachihuiz*.
26. masehualic: read *macehualli ic*.

SECOND DEMON: Come, O young man, do let me question you. Is there an old man there named Beelzebub?

FIRST PAGE: Jesus, what are you saying? For that is a demon you are talking about. Those seated here are Christians; nobody here is a demon!

SECOND DEMON: Do not be afraid, O young man, for it is just his nickname. Have you never heard the [sorts of] names all the people give themselves? We do likewise.

FIRST PAGE: And you, what is your nickname? It is so I will be satisfied.

SECOND DEMON: Know that Satan here summons him [that is, Beelzebub]. I await you here.

([First] Page enters. He talks to First Demon.)

FIRST PAGE: O my beloved father, a person whose nickname is Satan is here looking for you. He summons you from the entrance.

DON SEBASTIÁN: What are you saying? It [must] be some vassal of my beloved father who is thus called [Satan] who has come to speak to me. [18]

FIRST DEMON: Do not be afraid; it is my nickname. And the nickname of the person looking for us is Beelzebub. We were still little kids when they named us. Let me have your precious permission to see him. Perhaps something is bothering him.

DON SEBASTIÁN: It certainly shall not happen [that] you should go out to the entrance. Are you not in your home? Let him who seeks you come in, O my nobleman.

FIRST DEMON: O young man, summon him. Let him enter here.

SECOND PAGE: Very well, let me summon him.

Please be welcome here, O ruler. Come in.

SECOND DEMON: Remain seated, O rulers, let me not distract you. Who is don Sebastián? For it is he whom I am seeking. I have something to say to him.

DON FABIÁN: Here he is. Talk to each other. And let us leave you.

(Don Fabián, don Alberto, and all the pages leave. Don Sebastián remains, along with the demons.)

DON SEBASTIÁN: Please be welcome here, O ruler. What do you have to say? Let me hear your words.

SECOND DEMON: O my young man, listen, for now you are losing what you are ~~perhaps~~ looking for or thinking of.

DON SEBASTIÁN: Yes, I am searching for those who called to me from where our lord God has placed them. And I have seen them; their heads are pitiful bones.

2º Dem.º y Nopiltzintzine macamo xicmolnamiquili hotzin aso san itla moCatzinco mocacaYahua Ca Ye tiuhq.ᶻ Yn titlaca ca San totonal Yn techmamauhtia tla Oc ticahuacati tla Ye Oc xicmoCaquilti Ca amo Yehuatl o YniC onihuala Ca Oc Sentlamantli Yn onimitznolhuilico Ca yp.ⁿpa Yn monamictzin Ca huel moca mocacaYahua ca huel paqui Yn moYolia Yn iCuac Calitic timetztica Auh Yn Yehuatl. ca san tlapic Yn mitzmolhuilia Ca ye niauh Yn teop.ⁿ auh amo Yauh çan otlica telpochtotontin quintocatinemi. Cahuiltitinemi ca huel moca mocacaYahua Ynic âhuel mitzpinauhtia timotolinia notelpotze Ca Yehuatl [19] YniC onihuala Yn nimitznolhuilico tleyn quitohua Yn moYolotzin—

Dⁿ Seb,ⁿ y Tleyn tinechmolhuilia notlasotatzine Ca mochi nicneltoca Yn motlatoltzin Ca Yn axcan nicChihuas Yn tleYn niquilnamiqui Auh Ca OniquitoAia ninonemilisCuepas ninoYolcuitis nitlamasehuas. Auh Yn axcâ Aucmo nicnequi ca huel axcan Ypⁿ Yn tonali Ca nicpopolos Yn noCihuauh Ca niman amo nictlapopolhuis Auh Ca namechnotlatlauhtilia ma annechmopalehuilisq.ᶻ Ynic amo temac nihuetzis canel Annotatzitzinhuan—

1º Demº y Macamo ximotequipachotzino telpochtle Ca nican ticate Ca amo tipipiltotontin Ca Ye ticmati Yn tleYn ticchihuasqᶻ Ca yn iuh titelpopochtin ticatca qᶻchquich²⁷ Oticchiuhq.ᶻ Cuix san tlapic Yn tleYn Otechahu[?]tiq.ᶻ Ca huel tiloCotin Oticatca Auh Ynin nimitzilhuia Amo niCan Ytec Yn altepetl Yn ticmictis Yn monamic cana hueca texcalco Yn tichuicas Ca ticnahualhuicas tel timitzYecanasq.ᶻ Yn Campa moChihuas Yn tlamahuisoli amo ximotequipacho ximoYolChicahua—

Dⁿ Seb,ⁿ y Ca Yehuatl on Yn Cenca Yc ninoYolalia ma yuhqui mochihuas ma namechnohuiquili Yese Yn tleYn anquimonequiltisq.ᶻ Ca nicchihuas Ca nicneltilis Ca namechnotlacamaChiltis ma tihuian ma nictemo Yn nosihuAuh—

2º Dem.º y Ca Ye Cuali ma tihuian tictemosq.ᶻ—Calaquisq.ᶻ Mict.ⁿ
  # quisas Yn Ang.ˡ quinotzaz Dⁿ Seb,ⁿ—

1.º Angˡ y Otimotlahueliltic Ca Ye mictlan tipouhqui Yese ca huel tinechtolinia Ynin Cuenta nicnomaquilis Yn tt.º D,ˢ in amo timonemiliscuepasnequi Ca huel senca tinechpinauhtia Yn ixp.ⁿtzinco Yn D,ˢ Onotlahueliltic—²⁸

  # Chocas Yaz hualquisas Miquistli Yhuâ home Ang,ˡ quihualhuicasq.ᶻ espada
    Mictlan hualquisas Lusifer Yhuan Omentin Demonios—

Miquistli y Tla xihualauh Yn timictlantlatelchihualpol tla xinechilhui tle Yca tle Yp.ⁿpa Yn huel timoxicohua Yn huel tiquinmoYahotia tlaltp.ᶜ tlaca tleyn huel mohueli xiquito xinechilhui—[20]

Lusifer y Tla xicᵃqui Omitl Ca Y nehuatl Ca onca nohueli Yn mictlâ ca no nitlatohuani YeYca Ca Yn tlaltp.ᶜ tlaca Ca momostlaye Yn intenco niCan Ytla mahuasq.ᶻ Semicac nechtenehua nechtzatzilia Auh Yn itech Yn D,ˢ Ca q.ᶻmanian Yn quinotza San iquac temoCoCohua Anoso YCuac Yn itla Ynnetequipachol [?] Ca—

---

27. qᶻchquich: read *quexquich*.
28. There are stage directions in the margin: Calaq.ᶻ D.ⁿ Seb.ᵃⁿ mocuepatiuh condenado.

SECOND DEMON: O my nobleman, do not think of that. Oh, perhaps they are just mocking you in something. For we people are like that. Our fate just frightens us. Do let us get away from them [the skulls]. Leave it. Do listen now, for that is not why I came, for there is something else I came to tell you concerning your spouse. She is really mocking you, she is really having fun. She is content when you are in the house. But she just tells you falsely, "I am going to the church." But she does not go but, rather, follows after young boys on the road, who go around giving her a good time. She really mocks you. You are in bad shape, as it does not cause you shame. O my young man, that is what [19] I have come to say to you. What is your heart saying?

DON SEBASTIÁN: What are you saying to me, O my beloved father? For I believe all your words. Today I will do what I was thinking. And I was saying I would change my life, I would confess, I would do penance. But now I no longer want [to do] it for right now, during this day, I will destroy my wife for I absolutely cannot pardon her. And I implore you, since you are my fathers, help me so that I will not get caught.

FIRST DEMON: Do not be troubled, O young man, for here we are. We are not little kids. You already know what we will do, for we did things in that way when we were youths. Is it just false what they [scolded?] us with? For we were really crazy! And I say this to you: you will not kill your spouse here in the altepetl [but rather] you will take her, secretly take her, somewhere far away to a crag. But we will lead you where the marvelous deed will be done. Do not be troubled. Be stronghearted.

DON SEBASTIÁN: I am very content with that. May it so be done. Let me accompany you. What[ever] you want me to do, I will carry out, for I will obey you. Let us go. Let me search for my wife.

SECOND DEMON: Very well, let us go search for her.

(They enter the place of the dead.

[First] Angel enters. He talks to don Sebastián.)

FIRST ANGEL: Unfortunate are you! You already belong to the place of the dead. Nevertheless you are really bothering me [with] this accounting I will give to our lord God that you do not want to change your life. You shame me very greatly before God. Unfortunate am I!

(Don Sebastián enters; he turns into the condemned one.[25]

He weeps. He leaves. Death enters along with two angels. They bring a sword from the place of the dead. Lucifer enters along with two demons.)

DEATH: Come, you despised one of the place of the dead. Do tell me, why and for what reason are you so envious? You make war on the people of the earth. By what authority? Say it, tell me! [20]

LUCIFER: Do listen, bones, for I have authority in the place of the dead. I am also a ruler. Because the people of the earth quarrel over things every day they always mention me, they cry out to me. But they only call to God sometimes, only when people are made ill or when they have some care.[26]

---

25. That is, he changes costume to appear as the condemned one. These stage directions are actually in the margin; see transcription.

26. This entire paragraph is tentatively translated.

1.º Ang.ˡ v̱ Tla xihualauh Yn tibersebo ma xiquito tleyn huel mohueli moxicohuanipole tle yca Yn huel titechpanahuisnequi tla xitechilhui—

2º Ang.ˡ v̱ Yn tehuatl Yn tiSatanas tle ica Yn tinechCuilis Yn nopiel Cuix amo nican nica tle yca Yn iuhqui ticchihua tlatelchihualpole—

2º Dem.º v̱ Tle yca Yn amo nimitzCuilis Ca tiquitos Ca nimitzCuilis Ca nicchihuas Yn notequiᵘh macamo mitztequipacho—

Miquistli²⁹ v̱ Nocniuhtzine tleyn a[?] [?] ma tiquintocacan Yn tisentelchihualtin—

quintocasq.ᶻ Mictlan Calaquisq.ᶻ mocahuas Yn Miquistli Yhuan Angeles—

Miquistli v̱ NotlasoYcniuhtzitzinhuane ma Oquixquich Amotlapaltzin xicmochihuilican maCamo xiquinmoxicCahuilican Y tlaltp.ᶜ tlaca Auh Yntlacamo amechmotlacamachiltiq.ᶻ Ca tel YmixcoYan motepexihuisq.ᶻ Atle amotlatlacoltzin Yez—

2º Ang.ˡ v̱ Cuix amo ticmomachilti Yn niman Aic tiquincahua Ca CmC Ynnahuac tinemi. Yn sesemilhuitl Yn seseYohual Auh Yn iCuac Amo Cuali quichihua Ca tiquintlacahualtia Auh amo techtlacamati Ca Oc achi quintlacamati Yn tlatlacatecolo—

1º Ang.ˡ v̱ Ma Oc Yxquich ma Oc Ynp.ⁿ tiquisatin Yn oc cequintin topielhuan nocniuhtzitzinhuane ma xoConmanilican Yn amocxitzin—

Calaquisq.ᶻ hualquisasq.ᶻ Dⁿ Fab,ⁿ Dⁿ Alberto—³⁰

Dⁿ Fab,ⁿ v̱ Quenin in qᶻn omochiuh Cuix oticmomachilti tlatohuanie Dⁿ Albertotzine Yn itechcopa Yn telpochtli Yn Dⁿ Seb,ⁿ tleyn Oquichiuh YniC oquichtacamictito Yn inamic Cuix Ye neli Yn huel hueca OquihuicaC Yn texCalco Yn atlauhco Yn oquimictito ho tt.ᵉ D,ᵉ tleYn oquichiuh tleYn Oquitlapololti Ca huel mahuistiq.ᶻ tlaca Oncatca Ca huel mochipa Ynahuactzinco OtitoYolaliaya Ca Ye ticmomachiltia ca OquitaYa netolinilis[21]tli Auh tleYn Yp.ⁿ Omochiuh Camo huel ticmati—

Dⁿ Alberto v̱ Tleyn nimitznolhuilis Ca huel melahuac Yn ticmitalhuia Yese Yn nehuatl niquitohua Ca huel Yehuatl Yn itlan onenca in huehuenton Ca huel oquitlatolmacaya Yn tleyn mach Oquilhuiaia OquiYolcocoltiaia Ynic ten Oquichiuh San onicac Yn iquac Oquimicti niman Ocholo Yn huehuenton Yhuan Yn oc se YhuehueYcniuh Oquicalquixtico Auh niquitohua Yn manel Ye huehuentoton san amo Cuali tlaca San ahuilhuehuetq.ᶻ mach ce tlaCatl Yahuiltoca bersebo Auh Yn oc se tlaCatl Yahuiltoca Satanas Ynin Cuix ticmoqualitilia Yn tleYn nimitznolhuilia tlatohuanie—

Dⁿ Fab,ⁿ v̱ Jesus tleyn ticmitalhuia Jesus Ca huel temauhti Ynon tlatoli aquin christiano quimotoCayotis Auh Yese niquitohua yn aquin Amo quimimaCaxilia Yn D,ˢ ca quimotoCaYotico Ca san no qui Yn iahuil Yp.ⁿ quimati Auh Yese Yn tlahueliloc Ca huel ic papaqui Ototlahueliltic Yn itlaltp.ᶜtzinco Yn tt.º D,ˢ Yhuan niquitohua Amo quali Yn aquin tochan tictlalisque ca San no Yehuatl techtlatlatos techcocolis Ca San no Yehuatl Yp.ⁿ mixehuas Yn tlacatecolotl Yehuatl quipehualtis Yn amo quali Yn amo Yectli—

---

29. This should probably be Lucifer talking. If so, scribal error.

30. There are additional stage directions that are difficult to read: Auh Yno mictla [?] in 2o ——— Ylhcac Yn Ang.ˡ

FIRST ANGEL: Do come, Beelzebub, say what is your real authority, O wretched envious one. Why do you want to completely overcome us? Do tell us.

SECOND ANGEL: You, Satan, why do you take my charge from me? Am I not here? Why do you do such, O wretched despised one?

SECOND DEMON: Why will I not take him from you? You will say that I am taking him from you. I will do my job. Don't let it bother you.

DEATH[27]: O my friend, what [?]. Let us who are completely accursed pursue them.

(They pursue them. They enter the place of the dead. Death remains along with the angels.)

DEATH: O my beloved friends, exert all your effort. Do not abandon the people of the earth. But if they will not obey you, well, they will cast their own selves down from the precipice.[28] It will not be your fault.

SECOND ANGEL: Do you not know we absolutely never abandon them? We always go about among them each day and each night. And when they do something that is not good, we restrain them. But they do not obey us; they obey the demons more.

FIRST ANGEL: Let that be all. Let us pass by our other charges. O my friends, make haste.

(They exit. Don Fabián and don Alberto enter.)

DON FABIÁN: How oh how did it happen? Do you know, O ruler, O don Alberto, about the young man, don Sebastián, what he did? He went to kill his spouse in secret! Is it true? He took her far away to a crag, a ravine. He went to kill her. Ah, O our lord, O God, what has he done? What confused him? For he was [one of] the very honored people with whom we always used to console ourselves. You already know he experienced troubles. [21] And what happened to him? We really do not know.

DON ALBERTO: What am I to say to you? For what you are saying is true, yet I say it was the little old man from his household who led him on, that whatever he used to say to him, he would make him angry at her so that he did something. I heard that after he killed her, the little old man ran away along with the other old man, his friend; he came to get him out of the house. And I say, even though they were little old men they were really bad people, just corrupt old men. They say the nickname of one person was Beelzebub, and the nickname of the other was Satan. Do you approve of what I am saying to you, O ruler?

DON FABIÁN: Jesus! What are you saying? Jesus! Those words are very frightening. What Christian would take [such] names? But nevertheless I say, he who does not fear God will come to name himself [such] for likewise he will regard [his name] as a plaything. But nevertheless a scoundrel takes great joy in it. Unfortunate are we on the earth of our lord God! And I say, it is not good that we would put someone [like that] in our home. Likewise he will harangue us, he will hate us; likewise he will be possessed by the demon, he will undertake bad and improper things.

---

27. This should probably be Lucifer talking. If so, scribal error.
28. to cast oneself from the precipice: common idiom meaning "place oneself in danger [through immoral acts]."

D^n Alberto y Ca huel melahuac Yn ticmitalhuia Yn iuhqui Oomochiuh yn axcan Auh cuix no Oticmomachilti Yn tleyn ip.^{n} Omochiuh Yn D^n Seb,^{n} cuix neli mach çan oquiCuatepachoq.^{z} amo OmoYolcuiti YniC omomiquili Yhuan amo nican Yp.^{n} Altepetl hueca hoYa Ca ocholotinenca ypanpa Yn inamic axcan Ye Otlapopoluis Yn axcan ho tt,^{e} D,^{se} Ca niman amo ticmatin Yn tlalp.^{c} San iuhqui tixpopoYome Ototlahueliltic—

D^n Fab,^{n} y Motolinia Yn nohuanpotzitzinhuâ Yn tley Yp^n Omochiuh campa Yn oquimoYeYanmaquilitzino Yn D,^{s} ma ympanpa tictoYectehuilican[31] aso quinmocnelilis aso quinmotlaOcolilis Yn inYolia Yn imanima ma oc tihuian Yn teop.^{n} aso Ye pehuas Yn temachtili ma ticaquitin—

D^n Alberto y Ca Ye Cualitzin ma tihuian nopiltzintzine—

Calaquisq.^{z} niman motlapos ilhuicatl Auh cosamalotl Yp.^{n} mehuiltitiez xp.^{o} Yhuan Sta M.ª Yhua Ome [22] Angles xp̄o Yecancopatzinco xochitl YopochCopatzinco espada—

xp̄o y Ma nican xihualauh nican xinesi topilletzine Ca nimitzonnotza = # Tlatzintla hualquisas Yn Miquistli—

Miquistli y Ca Ye onihuala noteotzine notlatoCatzine tleyn ticmonequiltitzinohua—

xp̄o y Yn axcan ma ximohuica Yn onpa mictlan tiquinmanilitiuh Yn omentin tlaca Ynon Ymac Omic Yn inamic Yhuan Yehua Yn San oquittaq.^{z} YniC omic Auh Ca Ompa Ylpiticate Yn mictlan ma xiquinnotza Yhuan Yhuan[32] yn tlatlacatecolo ma nican nixp.^{n} nesiqui Ca niquinnotza—

Miquistli y Ca Ye Cualitzin ma nicchihua Yn motlanahuatiltzin—

Yaz Yn mictlan Caltenco quixopehuas

Miquistli y tlatelchihualtine ma nican xihualquisacan ca amechmonochilia Yn melahuac motetlatzontequililiani Jues—

hualquistihuetzq^z 2° Demonio—

2° Dem.^{o} y Tleyn ticmonequiltia Yn titechmotzatzililia Ca Oncan tiquintlatzaCuiltia Yn Yolpoliuhque Yn tlatlacohuanime—

Miquistli y Ma xiquinnotza Yn motlacatecoloYcnihuan Ca amechmonochilia melahuac Yn motetlatzontequililiani—

Ontzatzis yn Demonio—

2.º Dem.^{o} y Ma xihualquisacan nocnihuane ma tictotilitin Yn huey tlatohuani D,^{s} Ca techmonochilia—

quisas Lucifer Yhuan 2° Dem.^{o}—

Lucifer y Ma tihuian tocnihuane ma tictotilitin tleyn quimonequiltitzinohua—

Yasq.^{z} Yxp.^{n}tzinco xp̄o—

Miquistli y Noteotzine notlatocatzine Ca Ye oniquinhualhuiCac—

Motlanquaq^{z}tzazque

xp̄o y Xihualhuian xicaquican Yn amehuantin Yn annotlasentelchihualhuan namechnahuatia ma niCan xiquinhualhuicaca Yn onpa Anquinpie Çe Sihuatl Se tlatohuani ma nican nixp.^{n} nesican—[23]

---

31. tictoYectehuilican: read *tictoyectenehuilican*.
32. Yhuan Yhuan: so written in the text.

DON ALBERTO: What you are saying is very true. That is how it happened now. But did you also know what happened to don Sebastián? Did they really break his head with rocks? He did not confess when he died and it was not here in the altepetl. He went far away, he was going about fleeing because of his spouse. Now he will be obliterated. Now, ah, O our lord, O God, we do not know at all [how things are faring] on earth, for it is just as though we are blind people. Unfortunate are we!

DON FABIÁN: What has happened to my suffering neighbors? Where has God placed them? Let us praise him for their sakes. Perhaps he will favor them; perhaps he will have mercy on their spirits, their souls. Let us go to church. Perhaps the sermon will begin soon. Let us go hear it.

DON ALBERTO: Very well, let us go, O my nobleman.

(*They exit. Then heaven opens. And Christ sits on a rainbow along with Saint Mary and two* [22] *angels. To the right of Christ a flower and to his left a sword.*)

CHRIST: Come here, show yourself here, O constable, for I summon you.

(*At the bottom Death enters.*)

DEATH: I have now come, O my deity, O my ruler. What do you want?

CHRIST: Go now there to the place of the dead. You will go to seize the two people. That one whose spouse died at his hands and those who just saw how she died. And they are tied up there in the place of the dead. Summon them along with the demons. Let them come to appear here before me. I summon them.

DEATH: Very well, let me carry out your command.

(*He goes to the house at the edge of the place of the dead. He gives it a disdainful kick with his foot.*)

DEATH: O despised ones, come out here for the true sentencer and judge summons you.

(*Second Demon quickly enters.*)

SECOND DEMON: What do you want, you who cry out to us? For there we punish the confused, the sinners.

DEATH: Summon your demonic friends, for the true judge summons you [all].

(*The demon cries out.*)

SECOND DEMON: Come out, O my friends. Let us go see the great ruler, God, for he summons us.

(*Lucifer enters along with Second*[29] *Demon.*)

LUCIFER: Let us go, O my friends, let us go see what he wants.

(*They go before Christ.*)

DEATH: O my deity, O my ruler, I have brought them now.

(*They kneel down.*)

CHRIST: Come, listen, my accursed ones. I command you: bring here those whom you have over there, a woman and a ruler. Let them appear here before me. [23]

---

29. This is evidently a scribal error for *"First"* since Second Demon is already onstage.

Lucifer v̱ Ca Ye qualitzin tt.ᵒᵉ Diose ma ticneltilican Yn motlatoltzin ma tiquimanati—

xp̄o v̱ Yhuan tehuatl xiyauh topille—

Miquistli v̱ Ca Ye Cualitzin ttᵒᵉ Diose = # Yasq.ᶻ quimanatihue Omentin animas tliltiq.ᶻ Yesque—

Miquistli v̱ Ca Ye Otiquimanato Ca ye nican cate ttᵒᵉ Diose—

xp̄o v̱ tla xihualauh Yn tehuatl Yn ti~~Dⁿ Sebⁿ~~³³ ma xinechilhui xinechnanquili tleyn motlachihual ma nicCaqui tleyn Oticchiuh Yn tlaltpᶜ tleYn motetlasotlalis Oticchiuh Yn tehuatl Yn ti~~D,ᵃ Juana~~ Cihuapilli Catli Yn moCualachihualis huel otimoCualitohuaya titlateomattinenca Axcan xiquitocan xitlananquilican xihualauh ~~topille~~ in tinotitlan xiquintlatlani Yn notenahuatiltzin Cuix oquichiuhque Cuix oquineltiliq.ᶻ Yn tlaltp.ᶜ ma nicaqui—

Miquistli v̱ Ma nicchihua Yn moteotenahuatiltzin ttᵒᵉ Diose tla xihualauh Cuix Oanquichiuhq.ᶻ Yn iteotenahuatiltzin Yn iCel teOtl, D,ˢ Ynic Centetl Cuix Oanquimotlasotiliq.ᶻ Yca mochi moYolo—

Motlanquaqᶻtzas Yn Demᵒ quimolhuilis Yn xp̄o,

1ᵒ Dem.ᵒ v̱ Ca niman amo Omitzmotlasotiliq.ᶻ Yn ⁱca mochi Yn inYolo—

Miquistli v̱ Auh YniC ontetl Cuix Oanquitlapicteneuhq.ᶻ Yn itocatzin Yn D,ˢ YeYca OanmoYolCuitiqᶻ Cuix mochi Oanquitoq.ᶻ Yn amotlatlaCol—

2.ᵒ Dem.ᵒ v̱ Ynontzin Ca huel itequiuh Ocatca Yn tlaltp.ᶜ Yn San tlapic ConanaYa Juramento—

Miquistli v̱ Auh Ynic Yetetl Yn Domingo Yhuan Ylhuitl ip.ⁿ Cuix Oantlateomatiqᶻ—

Lucifer v̱ Ca niman A³⁴ Otlateomatq.ᶻ ca San quixcahuiaya Yn ahuilnemilistli Yhuan tlahuanalistli—

Miquistli Auh Ynic nauhtetl Cuix Oanquimahuistiliq.ᶻ Yn amotahuan Yn amonahuan—

1.ᵒ Dem.ᵒ v̱ Ca amo Oquichiuhq.ᶻ amo Oquinmahuistiliq.ᶻ San imixco Ymicpac Onenq.ᶻ Yn intahuan Yn innahuan—

Miquistli v̱ Auh Ynic macuiltetl Cuix aca Amomac Omic—[24]

2.ᵒ Dem.ᵒ Ca Oquimicti Yn inamic Yn nican ca Auh Yn nican ca Cihuatl Ca yp.ⁿpa Otemictiloc—

Miquistli Ynic ChiCuasentetl Cuix oamahuilnenq.ᶻ—

1.ᵒ Dem.ᵒ v̱ Ca Semicac hoahuilnenq.ᶻ Yn Yehuâ Yn iquac tlalp.ᶜ Onenca—

Miquistli v̱ Auh Ynic chiContetl Cuix Oamichteq.ᶻ—

Lucifer Ca Ynin Ca Yc³⁵ Oquichiuhq.ᶻ—

Miquistli v̱ Auh Ynic chiCuetetl Cuix Oantetentlapiquiq.ᶻ Cuix tetech Oanquitlamiq.ᶻ Yn tlatlaColli—

Lucifer v̱ Ca Ynin cihuatl Ca huel itequiuh Ocatca Yhuan Yn nican catqui ca no Yuhqui Ocatca—

---

33. Something written over this, perhaps *tlatohuani*.
34. A: read *amo* or *aic*.
35. Yc: perhaps *ye* was meant.

LUCIFER: Very well, O our lord, O God. Let us carry out your words, let us go seize them.

CHRIST: And you, go, constable.

DEATH: Very well, O our lord, O God.

(They go to seize them. The two souls are black.)

DEATH: We have now gone to seize them. Here they are, O our lord, O God.

CHRIST: Do come, you, ~~you who are don Sebastián~~. Tell me, answer me: what are your deeds? Let me hear what you did on earth, what [works of] charity you performed. You, ~~you who are doña Juana~~, noblewoman, what are your good deeds? You praised yourself a great deal while you went about engaging in spiritual exercises. Now say it, answer. Come, ~~constable~~, my messenger, examine them concerning my commandments. Have they done them? Have they carried them out on earth? Let me hear it.

DEATH: Let me carry out your sacred commands, O our lord, O God. Do come. Have you carried out the sacred commands of the only deity, God? The first: have you loved him with all your heart?

(The demon kneels down. He speaks to Christ.)

FIRST DEMON: They absolutely did not love you with all their heart.

DEATH: And the second: did you take the name of God in vain because of your confession? Did you declare all your sins?

SECOND DEMON: That was his very task on earth, that he took false oaths.

DEATH: And the third: did you engage in spiritual exercises on Sundays and feast days?

LUCIFER: They absolutely did not engage in spiritual exercises but occupied themselves exclusively in lustful living and drunkenness.

DEATH: And the fourth: did you honor your fathers and your mothers?

FIRST DEMON: They did not do it. They did not honor them. They just offended their fathers and their mothers.

DEATH: And the fifth: did someone die at your hands? [24]

SECOND DEMON: The one here killed his spouse. And someone was killed on account of the woman here.

DEATH: The sixth: did you go about living lustfully?

FIRST DEMON: They always lived lustfully earlier, when they lived on earth.

DEATH: And the seventh: did you steal?

LUCIFER: That they did.

DEATH: And the eighth: did you give false testimony about others? Did you falsely impute sin to others?

LUCIFER: It was the very occupation of this woman and the [other] one here was the same.

Miquistli y Auh Ynic chiucnauhtetl Cuix otiquinteCuili Yn tecihuauh Yn tehuatl Cuix otiq.^{z}lehui Yn tenamic—

2.º Dem.º y Ynontzin Ca huel itequiuh OCatca Yn tlatohuani auh Yn Sihuapilli ca San tlapiC Yn oYaYa Yn teop.^{n} Auh San nopa[36] teyxilehuitica[37]—

Miquistli y Auh Ynic matlactetl Cuix Oanq^{z}lehuiq.^{z} Yn teaxca Yn tetlatqui—

Lucifer y Ca Ynontzin Ca semicac hoq.^{z}lehuiaya Yn tetlatqui Yn teaxca yhuan huel Miec Miccatlatquitl Oq.^{z}lehuiq^z Oquixpoloq^z—

Miquistli y Ynic matlactetl teotenahuatilli Yn anquimotlasotilisq.^{z} Yn iÇel teotl D,^{s} Yhuan Yn amohuanpohuan Cuix Oanquichiuhque—

Lucifer y Ca niman atle Oquichiuhq.^{z} Yn tlaltp.^{c} Yn motenahuatiltzin Ca mochi Oquitlacoq.^{z} Auh Yn iCuac moteop.^{n}chantzinco Ocalaquiya Ca amo YnYolotica Yn oquitaYa Missa ca San nopo[38] Omonono[?]catca Auh San no yuhqui Yn ihuanpohuan Ca amo quintlasotlasnequi ma xitechmoCahuililitzino tt^{o}e D,^{se}—

Miquistli y Ca ye onicneltili Yn motenahuatiltzin noteotzine notlatoCatzine Catle Cuali YniC omitzmotequipanilhuiq.^{z} Auh ca amo Oquineltiliq.^{z} Yn moteotenahuatiltzin tleYn nel tiquitosq.^{z} ca tehuatzin ticmomachiltitzinohua [25]

xp̄o y OAnmotlahueliltieq.^{z} Ca niman atle qualli Oanquichiuhq^z Auh Yn amehuantin Yn antlasentelchihualtin Ca huel namechtlaquauhnahuatia ma huel Ompa Yn ixico Yn mictlantli XiquinmaYahuiCan XiquintlaSatin huel xiquintlatzaCuiltican Yn aYc tlamis Yn aYc polihuis tzonquisas Yn notlatoltzin—

Sta M.^{a} y Yn tinotlasomahuizConetzin Ca senca huel miec tlamantli Ynic mitzinco mocpactzinco nemi Yn tlaltp.^{c} tlaca Auh ca nican mixp.^{n}tzinco ninixtlapachtlasa nonopechteca ma huel xicmonep.^{n}tlaYtilitzino moJusticiatzin Ca Ye ticmomachiltitzinohua Cemicac mixp.^{n}tzinco nocontlalia Yn nochoquis Yn nixayo Ymp.^{n}pa Yn tlatlacohuanime Canel motlachihualtzitzinhuan macamo nenpolihuis macamo nenquisas Yn motlasoYessotzin Yn inp.^{n}pa Oticmononoquilitzino notlasoconetzin nochalchiuhtzin nomaCuetzin Ca Senca tonehua Yn noYolo Yn iCuac se tlacatl tlaltp.^{c} tlacatl ticmotelchihuilitzinohua—

xp̄o y Notlasonantzine Ca melahuac Yn ticmitalhuitzinohua Ca Senca miec Yn moChoquilistzin Yn miXayotzin Yn inp.^{n}pa ticmonoquilia Yn tlaltp.^{c} tlaca Auh Yn Yehuantin [?] yuh quimati Oytlahueliltic Auh in nican cate Yn tlatlaCohuanime Ca huel oquipanahuiq.^{z} Yn noteotenahuatiltzin Yn iuhqui Oticmitalhuitzino Yn niman atle manel centetl Oquichiuhq.^{z} Auh Yntla tehuatzin mitzmotlatlauhtilisquia mitzmotequipanilhuisquia Yn tlaltp.^{c} Ca mop.^{n}patzinco nicchihuasquia Canel tinotlasonantzin Auh Yn ip.^{n} Yn tetlaOcolilistli Yn oRra de MiSeriCordia[39] Yn nop.^{n}pa Oquichihuasquia Ca amo Oquichiuhq.^{z} Ca miecpa Yn caltenpa ninoq^{z}tzaYa ninotlaYtlaYtlaniaya ca niman aic OnechtlaOcoliq.^{z} Ca san OnechhualtotoCaYa ca San niquintlayeltiYaYa Auh ca san [26] Yehuantin Yn intlatocaYcnihuan Yn quinCohuanotzaYa Auh Ca nican ca yn angel ma Yehuatl quito motlaneltili Yntla Ytla quali Oquichiuhque—

---

36. nopa: read *onpa*.
37. teyxilehuitica: read *teixelehuitica*.
38. nopo: read *onpa*.
39. oRra de MiSeriCordia: read *obras de misericordia*.

DEATH: And the ninth: did you take others' wives from them? You, [woman,] did you desire the spouses of others?

SECOND DEMON: That was the very job of the ruler. And the noblewoman just went to church on false pretenses; she just coveted people there.

DEATH: And the tenth: did you desire the goods and property of others?

LUCIFER: That is it. They always desired other people's goods and property along with desiring and wasting a great deal of the property of the dead.

DEATH: The tenth sacred commandment: you are to love the only deity, God, and your neighbors. Did you do it?

LUCIFER: They carried out absolutely none of your commandments on earth for they broke them all. And when they used to enter church they did not willingly see mass for there they just talked to each other. And likewise they did not want to love their neighbors. Leave them to us, O our lord, O God.

DEATH: I have carried out your commands, O my deity, O my ruler. What is the good that they labored at for you? They did not carry out your sacred commands. What will we truly say [in their defense] for you know [the truth]? [25]

CHRIST: Unfortunate are you! For you did absolutely nothing good. And you, who are completely accursed, I very firmly order you: hurl them and cast them right there in the navel of the place of the dead, really punish them. My words [that is, sentence?] will never finish, never perish, never come to an end.

SAINT MARY: You, my beloved honored child, the people of the earth offend you in a great many things. And here before you I cast myself face down, I humbly bow low. Show your justice among them for you already know I always set down my weeping and my tears before you for the sake of the sinners. Since they are your creatures, let the precious blood you spilled for their sakes not be uselessly wasted, not be in vain. O my beloved child, O my jade, O my bracelet, my heart is very hurt when you despise a person of the earth.

CHRIST: O my beloved mother, what you are saying is true. Very abundant are the weeping and tears you spill on behalf of the people of the earth. And they know it is so. They are unfortunate! And here are the sinners who have violated my sacred commandments. As you said, they carried out none of them at all. But if they had prayed to you and served you on earth, I would do it [that is, save them] for your sake, since you are my beloved mother. But they did not do the acts of compassion, the works of mercy, that they could have done for my sake. For I stood begging outside their houses many a time. They absolutely never had pity on me; they just ran me off for I disgusted them.[30] And [on the contrary] [26] they just invited their royal friends to eat. And here is the angel. Let him say it, and verify if they did something good.

---

30. The fourteen works of mercy *(obras de misericordia)* were part of the standard Catholic catechism; as here, they were called *tetlaocoliliztli*, "having compassion for others," in Nahuatl. They include feeding, clothing, and sheltering the needy.

1.º Ang.¹ v Noteotzine notlatocatzine tleyn niquitos tleyn nimitznolhuilitzinos ca Yn tehuatzin Ca nohuian timotztilitica Yn tetl Yn quahuitl Ytic Ca niman maYac tleyn mitzmolhuilitzinos Yese Ca Ye ticmomachiltitzinohua Ca Ye Yxquich notlapal Onicchiuh Canel amo Onechtlacamatq.ᶻ Auh Yn axcan Ca tehuatzin ticmomachiltitzinohua ma mochihua Yn motlasotlanequilistzin—

chocas Yn Angel—

2º Demº v Ma mochihua Yn moteotenahuatiltzin—

xp̄o v Ma xihuian ma xiquinhuicacan Canel amotech pouhque Yn atle Ymilhuil Yn atle Ynmasehual Canel YmixCoYan Omotelchiuhq.ᶻ Ca ye yxquich ca Ye oniquinmaCauh—

Lucifer v hotitechmocnelilitzino melahuac motetlatzontequililiani Diose ma ticneltilican Yn motlatocatlanahuatiltzin—

Motzacuas Ylhuicatl—

1.º Dem.º Ma tihuian ma tiquinhuicacan ca Ye tomalhuan Ca Ye totech pouhque Canel totetlaYecolticahuan OCatca—

Condenado v Ay otoSentzontlahueliltiq.ᶻ tleYn Oc ticchihuasqᶻ Yn tlaltp.ᶜ ttºe Diose Catli in papaquilistli catli Yn neYolalilistli ma nechpalehuiqui Omochiuh Onotlahueliltic—

2.º Dem.º v Aucmo xitlato ximocahua AOcmo honca axcâ ompa tiquitas Yn tochan Yn mopapaquilis Ompa timitzmacasq.ᶻ xinenemi ma tihuian—[27]

Condenado v OnoSentzontlahueliltic Yn nehuatl Yn nitechouhti Yn nitetlaOcolti nehuatl ma notech ximixcotican⁴⁰ Yn annohuanpohuan maCaYac Moqualitas macaYac MoYequitos yn tlaltp.ᶜ Ca huel nicnoCoytia Yn tleYn Onicchihuaya Yntla ninonemilisCuepani asocamo Ymac nimiquisquia Yn nonamic aso OninoYolCuitisquia YniC onimiquisquia Ay OnoSentzontlahueliltic ma sentelchihualo Yn Cahuitl Yn ip.ⁿ OninemiYa—

Lucifer v Ma Yxquich Yn tleYn mach tiquitohua ma ysiuhca ma tihuian ma tiquinhuicacan ma xiquinnenemiltican—

1.º Demº v Xitotocacan xinenemican ximotlalocan Yn amochan Yn mictlan—

Calaquisq.ᶻ Mictlan tzatzitiasq.ᶻ Cueponis bonbas Yc tlamis nexcuitilli finis Laus Dᵉº Amen Axcan hotla Ynin nexcuitilli A 1 de Abril del Ano de 169i2 Anos [simple rubric]

---

40. ximixcotican: read *ximixcuitican*.

FIRST ANGEL: O my deity, O my ruler, what will I say? What am I to say to you? For you see everywhere, into stone and wood. Absolutely no one can say something to you for you already know about it. I have exerted all my effort but they did not obey me. And now you know. May your precious will be done.

([First] Angel cries.)
SECOND DEMON: May your sacred commands be done.
CHRIST: Go, take them for they belong to you. They are undeserving and without merit since they condemned themselves. That is all, for I have given them permission.
LUCIFER: Thank you, true judge, O God. Let us carry out your royal command.

(Heaven closes.)
FIRST DEMON: Let us go, let us take them for they are already our captives, they already belong to us since they were our servants.
CONDEMNED MAN: Oh, we are four hundred [times][31] unfortunate. What will we do on earth? O our lord, O God. What has come of joy? What has come of contentment? May they come to help me! O, unfortunate am I!
SECOND DEMON: Speak no more. Be quiet. They no longer exist. Now there you will see our home, there we will give you your joy. Get walking! Let's go! [27]
CONDEMNED MAN: I am four hundred [times] unfortunate! I provoke weeping, I provoke sadness. May you who are my neighbors take an example from me. Let no one be pleased with himself, let no one praise himself on earth. I finally confess what I used to do. If I had changed my life perhaps I would not have died at the hands of my spouse, perhaps I would have confessed when I died. Ah! I am four hundred [times] unfortunate! Let the time in which I lived be despised.
LUCIFER: Let that be all of whatever it is you're saying. Let it be quick, let us go, let us take them, let us get them walking along.
FIRST DEMON: Hurry, get walking, run along to your home in the place of the dead.
(They enter the place of the dead. They cry out. Bombs explode.) Thus comes to an end the moral example. Finis. Laus Deo.[32] Amen.
This moral example was finished today, the first of April of the year one thousand, six hundred, ninety and two.[33]

---

31. Four hundred [times]: here and below, *four hundred* is a common idiom in the vigesimally based traditional counting system for "countless, innumerable."
32. *Finis. Laus Deo*: The end. Praise God.
33. A simple rubric follows.

[27]

D.ⁿ Seb.ᵃⁿ Condenado = YYô Omochiuh, otocentzontlahueliltic Yn niman aic otitosCalizq.ᶻ Yn tlp̄c̄ Ca nelli melahuac atle ipan pouhqui Yn tlp̄c̄ pâpaquiliztli têhuatl motlatlacol, Yn titlahuelilocaCihuatl: Yntla oxinechtlacahualtiani YtechCopa, Yn nâqualnemiliz asocamo Ymmac onihuetzquiaya Yn nican cate Yn Mictlan tequanime Yn cenca temâmauhtique Ynic tlachie Yhuan Yn amêhuantin Yn antlatlacatecolo q.ᶻnin oannechcâcaYauhque, Ca oannechilhuiaya annechpalehuizque Yn YtechCopa nonemaquixtiliz q.ᶻnin cenca nitlaihYohuia Yn axcan, Ynic nitlatla Yn âmo YhYohuiliz, Yn âehualiztli Yn Mictlan tletl Ca huel neci Ca nica Yn amo tenêecoltiliztli: Yn oan¹ [28] Yn oannechcacayauhq.ᶻ Ai Omochiuh oninotlahueliltic Ym manel nimauhcatzatzi san niman ayc acmo ic ninomaquixtiz. Auh Yn axcan cenca tlatla Yn noYollo in iquac niquilnamiqui Yn acmo nicnotiliz Yn Dios! Ay, ay, oc achi qualli oyezquia Yn macamo onitlacatini. Yn tlp̄c̄ manoso san onechcochpachohuani Yn nonantzin, Yn ihCuac ocuh nitetepiton; tlein onax Yn tlp̄c̄, Yn Dios Oquimonequilti Ynic monahuac Onechmixnamictili, inic tonehuantin, otictotequipanilhuizquia: Auh Ye san no têhuatl, ica in moteixCuepalliz otimonômaCauh Ynmac Yn nican Cate Yn nexiColizti Ca tel axcan tonehuan Ye techhuica Yn aquique anq.ⁿtlacamatque; Yn Dios miecpa Yn otechmixnamicnamictiliaya, inic tiquallachihuasque Auh Yn nican Cate Yn nexiColizti YCa, in intecanecâcaYahualiz otechmonêecoltiliq.ᶻ ic achpa² Yn âquallachihualiztli. O! [?] ticholiloni titetlaocolihque Yn san quinempoloq.ᶻ Yn Cahuitl, in ipan otineq.ᶻ tlp̄c̄ = Auh Yn[in?] Mochintin Yn ocuh annemi tlp̄c̄ macamo xicnempolocan Yn Cahuitl Yn ipan annemi ma xiquilnamiquican ca San Sen [?]ixcueyonalizt[?] Yn ontlantihuetziz in amonemiliz: Yn manel huel anhuehuetizq.ᶻ Yntlacamo anquallachihuazque Ca san niman aic anquimotililizque Yn itlazomahuizxayacatzin Yn tt.º Jesu xp̂o. ma totech ximixCuitican Yn tehuantin Yn aic otiquallachiuhque Yn san c̄m̄c̄ otictoYolîtlacalhuilitinenca Yn D.ˢ Ca Ye techhuica Yn ompa centlani Mictlan Yn campa aoquic ceppa tictotilizque Yn D.ˢ Yhuan, in campa acmo tihuelitisque, tiquallachizq.ᶻ³ Yn amêhuantin. Ca huelitiz Yn antlacnopilhuizque Yntla oanquimoYolihtlacalhuihq.ᶻ Yn D.ˢ ammomaquixtizq.ᶻ Cualla[29]Chihualiztica, tlamâcehualiztica Ynic anYaque Anquimotilitihui Yn D.ˢ huelitiz Auh Yntlacamo, ca in quename axCan antechita Ca san no Yuhqui amopan mochihuaz Yn ihquac anmiquizque Ca amechmoCentelchihuiliz Yn D.ˢ Yn ompa Mictlan.

Fin del [?]

---

1. Yn oan: repeated on the following page.
2. achpa: perhaps to be read *achtopa*.
3. quallachizq.ᶻ: read *quallachihuazque*.

[27]

DON SEBASTIÁN, CONDEMNED MAN:[1] Oh, four hundred [times] unfortunate are we who never educated ourselves on earth! For truly and honestly the pleasures of the earth are of no account. It is your fault, you wicked woman. If you had restrained me concerning my evil life, perhaps I would not have fallen into the hands of the fierce beasts that are here in the place of the dead, who look so very frightening. And you, who are demons: how did you deceive me? For you used to tell me you would help me concerning my salvation. How greatly I suffer now. I am burning with the breathless and unbearable fire of the place of the dead. It is clear that there is no temptation here; [28] you deceived me. Ah, unfortunate am I! Even though I cry out in a frightened way I will absolutely never save myself with it. And now my heart greatly burns when I remember I will never again see God! Ah, ah, it would have been better not to have been born on earth, or if my mother had just smothered me to death in my sleep when I was still little. What did I do on earth? It was God's will to match me with you so that we would work for him together. And likewise you, with your deceptions, left yourself in the hands of the envious ones here. But today those whom you obeyed are taking us away together. Many times God provoked us so that we would do good things. But here are the envious ones who, through their deceptions, tempted us from the first with bad deeds. Oh! We inspire weeping and sadness, who just wasted time while we lived on earth. And all of you who still live on earth, do not waste the time in which you live. Remember that in just one blink of an eye your lives will quickly come to an end. Even though you grow very old, if you did not do good deeds, you will absolutely never see the precious and honored face of our lord Jesus Christ. Take an example from us who never did good deeds but rather always went about offending God. Now they are taking us away to the depths of the place of the dead, where we will never again see God. And there we will no longer be able to do good deeds. It will be possible for you to obtain favor if you have offended God; it will be possible for you to save yourselves with good deeds, [29] with penance, so that you can go to see God. But if not, the way you see us now is the same that will happen to you when you die, for God will completely condemn you to the place of the dead.

End of the [?]

---

1. Some of what follows is tentatively translated.

Appendixes

Appendix 1

SPANISH AND LATIN SPOKEN LOANS IN SEVEN NAHUATL PLAYS IN MODERN ORTHOGRAPHY AND IN ALPHABETICAL ORDER

1. 1627 años "the year 1627"
2. Abrahán "Abraham"
3. alcalde "city council member/judge"
4. amén "amen"
5. ángel "angel"
6. ángeles "angels"
7. ánima "soul"
8. ánimas "souls"
9. arzobispo "archbishop"
10. Ave Maria "Hail Mary"
11. Balaán "Balaam"
12. Belcebú "Beelzebub"
13. Belén "Bethlehem"
14. bula "[papal] bull"
15. capítulo "chapter [of a book]"
16. chicharrones "pork rinds"
17. conde "count"
18. corona "crown"
19. cristiana "[female] Christian"
20. cristiano "[male] Christian"
21. Cristo "Christ"
22. cruz "cross"
23. cuaresma "Lent"
24. cuenta "accounting"
25. David "David"
26. diablo "devil"
27. Dios "God"
28. domingo "Sunday [unit of time]"
29. Egipto "Egypt"
30. emperador "emperor"
31. escribano "notary"
32. escritura "document"
33. Espíritu Santo "Holy Spirit"
34. gloria "glory [religious]"
35. gracia "grace [religious]"
36. Herodes "Herod"
37. hora "hour [unit of time]"
38. incienso "incense"
39. Isaac "Isaac"
40. Isaías "Isaiah"
41. Israel "Israel"
42. Jacob "Jacob"
43. Jerusalén "Jerusalem"
44. Jesucristo "Jesus Christ"
45. Jesús "Jesus"
46. Jesús, María y José "Jesus, Mary and Joseph"
47. Joseph "Joseph"
48. Judea "Judea"
49. judiazos "lousy/rotten Jews"
50. judios "Jews"
51. juez "judge"
52. Juicio Final "Final Judgment"

53. juramento "oath"
54. justicia "justice"
55. loco "crazy person [male]"
56. Lorenzo "Lorenzo"
57. Lucifer "Lucifer"
58. luto "mourning clothes"
59. maitines "matins"
60. marqués "marquis"
61. mesa "table"
62. Mesías "Messiah"
63. mirra "myrrh"
64. misa "mass"
65. misericordia "mercy"
66. Moab "Moab"
67. Moria "Moria [mountain]"
68. obra de misericordia "work of mercy"
69. paje "page [low status servant]"
70. paraíso "paradise"
71. pasión "passion [religious]"
72. Pater Noster "Our Father"
73. patriarcas "patriarchs"
74. Persia "Persia"
75. peso "peso [unit of money]"
76. pesos "pesos [units of money]"
77. por amor de Dios "for the love of God; for nothing"
78. prenda "pledge; security"
79. profetas "prophets"
80. puerta "[Spanish-style] door"
81. purgatorio "purgatory"
82. responso "responsory"
83. rey "king"
84. reyes "kings"
85. Roma emperador, César de Agusto "Cæsar Augustus, Emperor of Rome"
86. roque "rook"
87. rosario "rosary"
88. sacerdote "priest"
89. sacramento "sacrament"
90. Salve "Hail [Holy Queen]"
91. San Miguel "Saint Michael"
92. San Miguel arcángel "Saint Michael the Archangel"
93. santa bula "holy [papal] bull"
94. santa cruz "holy cross"
95. santa iglesia "holy church"
96. Santa María "Saint Mary"
97. santas "[female] saints"
98. Santísima Trinidad "Most Holy Trinity"
99. Santo Joseph "Saint Joseph"
100. santos "[male] saints"
101. santo sacramento "holy sacrament"
102. Satanás "Satan"
103. semana santa "Holy Week"
104. sermón "sermon"
105. Set "Sheth"
106. surgite mortui venite a judicium "Arise, O dead, and come to judgment"
107. testamento "testament [last will]"
108. testigos "witnesses"
109. tomín "unit of money"
110. tomines "units of money"
111. vino "[Spanish-style] wine"

Appendix 2

SPANISH AND LATIN SPOKEN LOANS IN SEVEN NAHUATL PLAYS, IN DESCENDING ORDER OF FREQUENCY AND DATE OF FIRST APPEARANCE

Loans	Frequency	First Appearance
Dios	317	1548
ánima	35	1550
misa	22	1550
Jesucristo	19	1545
Lucifer	19	1552
ánimas	17	c1607–1629
Herodes	17	c1607–1629
pesos [money]	17	1548
santa iglesia	14	1553
tomín	13	1545
cruz	12	1560–1570
purgatorio	11	1552
ángel	10	1552
diablo	10	c1562–1569
Jesús	9	1552
Santa María	9	1552
cuenta [accounting]	8	c1607–1629
Isaac	8	
Jerusalén	8	1631
juez	8	1548
cristiano	7	1560
Espíritu Santo	7	1566
Abrahán	6	1631
judíos	6	1552
rosario	6	1552

Loans	Frequency	First Appearance
tomines	6	1547
domingo [unit of time]	5	1553
gracia	5	1586
juramento	5	1547
justicia	5	1548
testamento	5	1552
Belcebú	4	
Belén	4	1631
Cristo	4	c1607–1629
gloria	4	c1607–1629
Israel	4	1637
peso [money]	4	1548
responso	4	1570
reyes	4	c1607–1629
Satanás	4	
sermón	4	1611
cuaresma	3	1550
David	3	1631
Joseph	3	1605
Judea	3	c1607–1629
luto	3	1574
misericordia	3	
santa cruz	3	c1607–1629
santo sacramento	3	1550
vino	3	1553
amén	2	1550
capítulo [chapter of a book]	2	c1607–1629
chicharrones	2	
escribano	2	1547
escritura	2	1553
judiazos	2	
patriarcas	2	c1607–1629
profetas	2	c1607–1629
sacramento	2	1549
San Miguel arcángel	2	c1607–1629
1627 años	1	
alcalde	1	1547
angeles	1	1548
arzobispo	1	c1562–1569
Ave Maria	1	1570
Balaán	1	c1607–1629
bula	1	1570
conde	1	c1607–1629
corona	1	c1607–1629

Loans	Frequency	First Appearance
cristiana	1	1658
Egipto	1	c1607–1629
emperador	1	1550
hora [unit of time]	1	c1607–1629
incienso	1	c1607–1629
Isaías	1	
Jacob	1	1631
Jesús, María y José	1	1695
Juicio Final	1	
loco	1	c1607–1629
Lorenzo	1	1550
maitines	1	1552
marqués	1	c1540
mesa	1	1550
Mesías	1	
mirra	1	c1607–1629
Moab	1	
Moría [mountain]	1	
obra de misericordia		
paje	1	c1607–1629
paraíso	1	
pasión [religious]	1	1614
Pater Noster	1	
Persia	1	c1607–1629
por amor de Dios	1	1608
prenda	1	1654
puerta	1	1581
rey	1	1550
Roma emperador, César de Agusto	1	
roque	1	
sacerdote	1	1552
Salve	1	
San Miguel	1	1549
santa bula	1	
santas	1	
Santísima Trinidad	1	1588
Santo Joseph	1	c1607–1629
santos	1	c1607–1629
semana santa	1	1570
Set	1	
surgite mortui venite a judicium	1	
testigos	1	1548
TOTAL	784	

Legend:
  Loans = all 111 spoken Spanish and Latin loans in the seven translated plays.
  Frequency = total number of occurrences in all seven translated plays.
  First Appearance = first appearance in a Nahua-generated text. (See Sell 1993, 312–15, 328–40; Karttunen and Lockhart 1976, 53–84; Chimalpahin 1965, 37–146; Chimalpahin 1997, 2:130–83; Solís et al. 139–229; and Anderson et al. 1976.)

Appendix 3

SPANISH AND LATIN SPOKEN LOANS IN SEVEN NAHUATL PLAYS, IN DESCENDING ORDER OF FREQUENCY WITH OCCURRENCE IN OTHER ECCLESIASTICAL NAHUATL AND DATE OF FIRST APPEARANCE

Loans	Saha	Moli	Anun	Baut	León	Mija	First Appearance
Dios	X	X	X	X	X	X	1548
ánima	X	X	X	X	X	X	1550
misa	X	X	X	X	X	X	1550
Jesucristo	X	X	X	X	X	X	1545
Lucifer	X	X	X	X	X	X	1552
ánimas	X	X	X	X		X	c1607–1629
Herodes	X	X	X	X		X	c1607–1629
pesos [money]		X		X	X		1548
santa iglesia	X	X	X	X	X	X	1553
tomín	X	X	X	X	X	X	1545
cruz	X	X	X	X	X	X	1560–1570
purgatorio	X	X	X	X	X		1552
ángel	X	X	X	X	X	X	1552
diablo	X	X	X	X	X	X	c1562–1569
Jesús	X	X	X	X	X	X	1552
Santa María	X	X	X	X		X	1552
cuenta [accounting]				X			c1607–1629
Isaac	X			X	X	X	
Jerusalén	X		X	X	X	X	1631
juez	X		X	X	X	X	1548
cristiano	X		X	X	X	X	1560
Espíritu Santo	X	X	X	X	X		1566
Abrahán	X		X	X	X	X	1631
judíos	X	X	X		X	X	1552

314—APPENDIXES

Loans	Saha	Moli	Anun	Baut	León	Mija	First Appearance
rosario	X		X				1552
tomines	X	X	X	X	X	X	1547
domingo [unit of time]	X	X	X	X	X	X	1553
gracia	X	X	X	X	X	X	1586
juramento		X	X	X	X	X	1547
justicia	X	X	X	X	X	X	1548
testamento		X		X	X	X	1552
Belén	X		X	X		X	1631
Belcebú						X	
Cristo	X		X	X	X		c1607–1629
gloria		X	X	X	X	X	c1607–1629
Israel	X	X	X	X	X	X	1637
peso [money]		X		X	X		1548
responso					X		1570
reyes	X	X	X	X		X	c1607–1629
Satanás	X			X			
sermón		X		X			1611
cuaresma	X	X	X	X	X		1550
David	X	X	X	X		X	1631
Joseph	X	X		X		X	1605
Judea	X		X			X	c1607–1629
luto							1574
misericordia							
santa cruz	X	X	X	X	X		c1607–1629
santo sacramento	X	X	X	X	X		1550
vino	X	X	X	X	X	X	1553
amén		X		X	X		1550
capítulo [chapter of a book]	X	X	X	X		X	c1607-29
chicharrones							
escribano		X			X		1547
escritura							1553
judiazos							
patriarcas	X	X	X	X		X	c1607–1629
profetas	X	X	X	X	X	X	c1607–1629
sacramento	X		X	X	X	X	1549
San Miguel arcángel		X	X	X			c1607–1629
1627 años							
alcalde		X	X	X			1547
angeles	X		X		X		1548
arzobispo			X	X	X		c1562–1569
Ave Maria	X	X	X	X		X	1570
Balaán	X			X		X	c1607–1629

Loans	Saha	Moli	Anun	Baut	León	Mija	First Appearance
bula				X	X		1570
conde							c1607–1629
corona	X	X	X	X		X	c1607–1629
cristiana			X				1658
Egipto	X	X	X	X		X	c1607–1629
emperador	X	X	X	X		X	1550
hora [unit of time]		X		X		X	c1607–1629
incienso	X			X			c1607–1629
Isaías	X			X	X	X	
Jacob	X		X	X	X	X	1631
Jesús, María y José							1695
Juicio Final							
loco							c1607–1629
Lorenzo	X		X				1550
maitines	X			X			1552
marqués							c1540
mesa			X	X		X	1550
Mesías				X			
mirra	X		X				c1607–1629
Moab				X		X	
Moría [mountain]							
obra de misericordia							
paje							c1607–1629
paraíso	X	X	X	X	X		
pasión [religious]	X	X		X		X	1614
Pater Noster	X	X	X	X			
Persia	X		X				c1607–1629
por amor de Dios							1608
prenda							1654
puerta	X			X	X		1581
rey	X	X	X	X		X	1550
Roma emperador, César de Agusto							
roque							
sacerdote	X	X	X	X		X	1552
Salve							
San Miguel	X		X				1549
santa bula			X		X		
santas							
Santísima Trinidad		X	X	X	X		1588
Santo Joseph	X			X			c1607–1629
santos	X	X		X	X	X	c1607–1629
semana santa							1570

Loans	Saha	Moli	Anun	Baut	León	Mija	First Appearance
Set							
surgite mortui							
venite a judicium							
testigos		X		X		X	1548

Legend:
    Saha = Sahagún 1548 (in Sell 1993) and Sahagún 1583.
    Moli = Molina 1984 and Molina 1578.
    Anun = Anunciación 1575 and Anunciación 1577.
    Baut = Bautista 1599, Bautista 1600b, Bautista 1605, and Bautista 1606.
    León = León 1611.
    Mija = Mijangos 1607 and Mijangos 1624.
    First Appearance = first appearance in a Nahua-generated text. Taken from Sell 1993, 312–15, 328–40; Karttunen and Lockhart 1976, 53–84; and Chimalpahin 1965, 37–146.

Appendix 4

SPANISH AND LATIN SPOKEN LOANS IN SEVEN NAHUATL PLAYS, IN DESCENDING ORDER OF FREQUENCY WITH FREQUENCY OF OCCURRENCE IN EACH OF THE SEVEN TRANSLATED PLAYS

Loans	3Kings	Isaac	Souls	Final	How to	Merchant	Don Sebastián
Dios	21	24	39	36	83	50	64
ánima	7	3	3	8	2	6	6
misa			18		2		2
Jesucristo			5	7	1	4	2
Lucifer			1	2			16
ánimas			15		2		
Herodes	17						
pesos [money]			1			16	
santa iglesia	1		4		2		7
tomín			3			10	
cruz	3		1	1	3	3	1
purgatorio			9		2		
ángel			1	1	6	1	1
diablo	2			1	3	3	1
Jesús			1	2	1	1	4
Santa María			1	1	4	3	
cuenta [accounting]				6	1		1
Isaac		8					
Jerusalén	7				1		
juez			4	2			2
cristiano			2	2		1	2
Espíritu Santo				1	3	3	
Abrahán	1	5					
judíos	6						

Loans	3Kings	Isaac	Souls	Final	How to	Merchant	Don Sebastián
rosario			2		4		
tomines						6	
domingo [unit of time]			3				2
gracia	1			1	2	1	
juramento			1			3	1
justicia						3	2
testamento						5	
Belén	4						
Belcebú							4
Cristo			4				
gloria			2	2			
Israel	3						1
peso [money]						4	
responso			4				
reyes	4						
Satanás							4
sermón			1		3		
cuaresma			1				2
David	3						
Joseph	3						
Judea	3						
luto			3				
misericordia			3				
santa cruz					2	1	
santo sacramento				3			
vino			3				
amén	2						
capítulo [chapter of a book]	2						
chicharrones	2						
escribano						2	
escritura						2	
judiazos	2						
patriarcas	2						
profetas	2						
sacramento				2			
San Miguel arcángel			1	1			
1627 años						1	
alcalde						1	
angeles						1	
arzobispo							1
Ave Maria			1				
Balaán	1						

Loans	3Kings	Isaac	Souls	Final	How to	Merchant	Don Sebastián
bula			1				
conde							1
corona					1		
cristiana				1			
Egipto	1						
emperador							1
hora [unit of time]				1			
incienso	1						
Isaías	1						
Jacob	1						
Jesús, María y José	1						
Juicio Final				1			
loco						1	
Lorenzo					1		
maitines	1						
marqués							1
mesa		1					
Mesías	1						
mirra	1						
Moab	1						
Moría [mountain]		1					
obra de misericordia							
paje							1
paraíso					1		
pasión [religious]					1		
Pater Noster			1				
Persia	1						
por amor de Dios						1	
prenda						1	
puerta							1
rey							1
Roma emperador, César de Agusto	1						
roque							1
sacerdote	1						
Salve					1		
San Miguel				1			
santa bula			1				
santas				1			
Santísima Trinidad		1					
Santo Joseph	1						
santos				1			
semana santa							1

320—APPENDIXES

Loans	3Kings	Isaac	Souls	Final	How to	Merchant	Don Sebastián
Set	1						
surgite mortui venite a judicium				1			
testigos						1	
	37	7	32	25	24	28	30
TOTAL	113	43	140	86	132	135	135

Legend:

Loans = all 111 spoken Spanish and Latin loans in the seven translated plays.

3Kings = the frequency of occurrence of a particular loan in the play "The Three Kings."

Isaac = the frequency of occurrence of a particular loan in the play "The Sacrifice of Isaac."

Souls = the frequency of occurrence of a particular loan in the play "Souls and Testamentary Executors."

Final = the frequency of occurrence of a particular loan in the play "Final Judgment."

How to = the frequency of occurrence of a particular loan in the play "How to Live on Earth."

Merchant = the frequency of occurrence of a particular loan in the play "The Merchant."

Don Sebastián = the frequency of occurrence of a particular loan in the play "The Life of Don Sebastián."

Total = top number in plain font is total entries for that play and bottom number is total occurrences for that play.

REFERENCES

Adorno, Rolena. 1990. "Iconos de persuasión: La predicación y la política en el Perú colonial." In *Iconografía política del Nuevo Mundo*, ed. Mercedes López-Baralt, 27–49. Puerto Rico: EDUPR.
Anderson, Arthur J. O., Frances Berdan, and James Lockhart, eds. and trans. 1976. *Beyond the Codices: The Nahua View of Colonial Mexico*. Berkeley and Los Angeles: University of California Press.
Andrews, J. Richard. 1975. *Introduction to Classical Nahuatl*. Austin: University of Texas Press.
Anunciación, fray Domingo de la. 1565. *Doctrina christiana breve y compendiosa por vía de diálogo entre un maestro y un discípulo*. Mexico: Pedro Ocharte.
Anunciación, fray Juan de la. 1575. *Doctrina christiana muy complida*. Mexico: Pedro Balli.
———. 1577. *Sermonario en lengua mexicana*. Mexico: Antonio Ricardo.
Arenas, Pedro de. 1982. *Vocabulario manual en las lenguas castellana y mexicana*. Photoreproduction of the 1611 edition, with an introduction by Ascensión H. de León-Portilla. Mexico: Universidad Nacional Autónoma de México.
Arróniz, Othón. 1979. *Teatro de evangelización en Nueva España*. Mexico: Universidad Nacional Autónoma de México.
Augustine, Saint. 1950. *The City of God*. Translated by Marcus Dods, D.D. New York: Modern Library.
Bataillon, Marcel. 1966. *Erasmo y España*. Translated by Antonio Alatorre. Mexico: Fondo de Cultura Económica.
Baudot, Georges. 1976. *Utopie et histoire au Mexique: Les premiers chroniqueurs de la civilisation mexicaine (1520–1569)*. Toulouse: Privat.
Bautista, fray Juan. 1599. *Confesionario en lengua mexicana y castellana*. Mexico: Melchor Ocharte.
———. 1600a. *Advertencias para los confesores de los naturales*. Mexico: Melchor Ocharte.
———. 1600b. *Huehuehtlahtolli: Pláticas morales de los indios para doctrina de sus hijos, en mexicano*. Mexico: [Melchor Ocharte?].
———. 1604. *Libro de la miseria y brevedad de la vida del hombre y de sus cuatro postrimerías, en lengua mexicana*. Mexico: Diego López Dávalos.
———. 1605. *Vida y milagros del bienaventurado San Antonio de Padua*. Mexico: Diego López Dávalos.
———. 1606. *Sermonario . . . en lengua mexicana*. Mexico: Diego López Dávalos.

Bazarte Martínez, Alicia. 1989. *Las cofradías de españoles en la Ciudad de México (1526–1860)*. Azcapotzalco: Universidad Autónoma Metropolitana.

Berceo, Gonzalo de. 1980. *Signos que aparecerán antes del Juicio Final*. Edited by Arturo M. Ramoneda. Madrid: Castalia.

Bevington, David. 1975. *Medieval Drama*. Boston: Houghton Mifflin.

Bhabha, Homi K. 1994. *The Location of Culture*. London: Routledge.

Bierhost, John. 1985. *Cantares Mexicanos: Songs of the Aztecs*. Stanford: Stanford University Press.

Braswell, Mary F. 1983. *The Medieval Sinner: Characterization and Confession in the Literature of the English Middle Ages*. Rutherford, N.J.: Fairleigh Dickinson University Press.

Breviarium romanum ex decreto SS. Concilii Tridentini. 1961. 2 vols. New York: Benziger Brothers.

Buber, Martin. 1968. *On the Bible*. New York: Schocken Books.

Burkhart, Louise M. 1989. *The Slippery Earth: Nahua-Christian Moral Dialogue in Sixteenth-Century Mexico*. Tucson: University of Arizona Press.

———. 1993. "The Cult of the Virgin of Guadalupe in Mexico." In *South and Meso-American Native Spirituality: From the Cult of the Feathered Serpent to the Theology of Liberation*, ed. Gary H. Gossen, 198–226. New York: Crossroad.

———. 1996. *Holy Wednesday: A Nahua Drama from Early Colonial Mexico*. Philadelphia: University of Pennsylvania Press.

———. 1999. "'Here Is Another Marvel': Marian Miracle Narratives in a Nahuatl Manuscript." In *Spiritual Encounters: Interactions between Christianity and Native Religions in Colonial America*, ed. Nicholas Griffiths and Fernando Cervantes, 91–115. Birmingham, England: University of Birmingham Press.

———. 2001. *Before Guadalupe: The Virgin Mary in Early Colonial Nahuatl Literature*. Albany: Institute for Mesoamerican Studies, State University of New York at Albany.

Carochi, Horacio. 1983. *Arte de la lengua mexicana*. Photoreproduction of the 1645 edition, with an introduction by Miguel León-Portilla. Mexico: Instituto de Investigaciones Filológicas, Instituto de Investigaciones Históricas, Universidad Nacional Autónoma de México.

Carrasco, David. 1990. *Religions of Mesoamerica: Cosmovision and Ceremonial Centers*. New York: HarperCollins.

Carrasco, Pedro. 1997. "Indian-Spanish Marriages in the First Century of the Colony." In *Indian Women of Early Mexico*, ed. Susan Schroeder, Stephanie Wood, and Robert Haskett, 87–103. Norman: University of Oklahoma Press.

Cartas de Indias. 1980. 3 vols. Mexico: M. A. Porrúa.

Chimalpahin Quauhtlehuanitzin, Don Domingo de San Antón Muñon. 1965. *Die Relationen Chimalpahin's zur Geschichte México's*. Edited by Günter Zimmermann. 2 vols. Hamburg: Cram, De Guyter.

———. 1997. *Codex Chimalpahin*. Volumes 1 and 2. Edited and translated by Arthur J. O. Anderson and Susan Schroeder. Norman: University of Oklahoma Press.

———. 1998. *Las ocho relaciones y el memorial de Colhuacan*. Edited and translated by Rafael Tena. 2 vols. Mexico: Consejo Nacional para las Culturas y las Artes.

Cilveti, Angel. 1977. *El demonio en el teatro de Calderón*. Valencia: Albatros.

———. 1989. "Teología dramatizada y teología dramática en los autos de Calderón," *Boletín Bibliográfico Menéndez y Pelayo* 45:139–77.

Clendinnen, Inga. 1991. *Aztecs: An Interpretation*. Cambridge, England: Cambridge University Press.

Cline, S. L., and Miguel León-Portilla, eds. and trans. 1984. *The Testaments of Culhuacan*. UCLA Nahuatl Studies Series No. 1. Los Angeles: UCLA Latin American Center Publications.

Cline, Sarah. 1986. *Colonial Culhuacan, 1580–1600: A Social History of an Aztec Town*. Albuquerque: University of New Mexico Press.

———. 1993. *The Book of Tributes: Early Sixteenth-Century Nahuatl Censuses from Morelos*. Nahuatl Studies Series No. 4. Los Angeles: UCLA Latin American Center Publications.

———. 1998. "Fray Alonso de Molina's Model Testament and Antecedents to Indigenous Wills in Spanish America." In Kellogg and Restall, 13–33.

———. 2000. "The Spiritual Conquest Reexamined: Baptism and Christian Marriage in Early Sixteenth-Century Mexico." In *The Church in Colonial Latin America*, ed. John F. Schwaller, 73–101. Wilmington, Del.: Scholarly Resources.

Códice franciscano, siglo XVI: Informe de la provincia del Santo Evangelio al visitador Lic. Juan de Ovando. 1941. Mexico: Salvador Chávez Hayhoe.

Córdoba, fray Pedro de. 1988. *Doctrina cristiana y cartas.* Santo Domingo: La Fundación Corripio.

Cornyn, John H., and Byron McAfee. 1944. "Tlacahuapahualiztli (Bringing Up Children)." *Tlalocan* 1:314–51.

Cortés y Zedeño, Jerónimo de Tomàs de Aquino. 1967. *Arte, vocabulario y confesionario en el idioma mexicano.* Photoreproduction of the 1765 edition. Guadalajara, Jalisco: Edmundo Aviña Levy.

Cotarelo y Mori, Emilio. 1904. *Bibliografía de las controversias sobre la licitud del teatro en España.* Madrid: Revista de Archivos, Bibliotecas y Museos.

Cuevas, Mariano. 1928. *Historia de la iglesia en México.* 3 vols. El Paso, Texas: Editorial "Revista Católica."

Cuevas García, Cristóbal. 1982. "Introducción." In fray Luis de León, *De los nombres de Cristo,* 13–129. Madrid: Cátedra.

Daniélou, Jean. 1964. *The Theology of Jewish Christianity.* Vol. 1. Translated by John A. Baker. Chicago: Henry Regnery.

Dávila Padilla, fray Agustín. 1955. *Historia de la fundación y discurso de la provincia de Santiago de Mexico, de la orden de predicadores.* Photoreproduction of the 1595 edition. Mexico: Editorial Academia Literaria.

Díaz Balsera, Viviana. 2001. "A Judeo-Christian Tlaloc or a Nahua Yahweh? Domination, Hybridity, and Continuity in the Nahua Evangelization Theater." *Colonial Latin American Review* 10:209–27.

Doctrina, evangelios y epístolas en nahuatl. N.d. Manuscript in the John Carter Brown Library, Brown University, Codex Indianorum 7.

Doctrina cristiana en lengua española y mexicana, por los religiosos de la orden de Santo Domingo. 1944. Photoreproduction of the 1548 edition. Madrid: Ediciones Cultura Hispánica.

Doctrina cristiana en lengua mexicana. 1548. Mexico: Juan Pablos.

Durán, fray Diego de. 1971. *Book of the Gods and the Ancient Calendar.* Edited and translated by Fernando Horcasitas and Doris Heyden. Foreword by Miguel León-Portilla. Norman: University of Oklahoma Press.

Duverger, Christian. 1978. *L'esprit du jeu chez les Aztèques.* Paris: Mouton Editeur.

Eire, Carlos M. N. 1995. *From Madrid to Purgatory: The Art and Craft of Dying in Sixteenth-Century Spain.* Cambridge, England: Cambridge University Press.

Enders, Jody. 1999. *The Medieval Theater of Cruelty: Rhetoric, Memory, Violence.* Ithaca: Cornell University Press.

Escalona, fray Alonso de. N.d. *Sermones en mexicano.* Manuscript in the Biblioteca Nacional de México, Fondo Reservado, no. 1482.

Farmer, David Hugh. 1992. *The Oxford Dictionary of Saints.* Oxford: Oxford University Press.

Feijóo, fray Benito Jerónimo. 1958. *Teatro crítico universal.* Vol. 6. Madrid: Espasa-Calpe, S.A.

Fernández del Castillo, Francisco, ed. 1982. *Libros y libreros en el siglo XVI.* Reedition. Mexico: Fondo de Cultura Económica. Originally published 1914 in Mexico by the Archivo General de la Nación.

Fernández de Oviedo y Valdés, Gonzalo. 1959. *Historia general y natural de las Indias y Tierra Firme.* Edited by Juan Pérez de Tudela. Madrid: Atlas/B.A.E.

Flowers Broswell, Mary. 1983. *The Medieval Sinner: Characterization and Confession in the Literature of the English Middle Ages.* Rutherford, N.J.: Fairleigh Dickinson University Press.

Flynn, Maureen. 1994. "The Spectacle of Suffering in Spanish Streets." In *City and Spectacle in Medieval Europe*, ed. Barbara A. Hanawalt and Kathryn L. Reyerson, 153–68. Minneapolis: University of Minnesota Press.

Furst, Jill Leslie McKeever. 1995. *The Natural History of the Soul in Ancient Mexico*. New Haven: Yale University Press.

Gante, fray Pedro de. 1981. *Doctrina cristiana en lengua mexicana*. Photoreproduction of the 1553 edition. Edited by Ernesto de la Torre Villar. Mexico: Centro de Estudios Históricos Fray Bernardino de Sahagún and Editorial Jus.

García Icazbalceta, Joaquín. 1877. "Representaciones religiosas en México en el siglo XVI." In Fernán González de Eslava, *Coloquios espirituales y sacramentales*. Mexico.

———. 1954. *Bibliografía mexicana del siglo XVI*. Mexico: Fondo de Cultura Económica.

———. 1968. "Representaciones religiosas de México en el siglo XVI." In *Obras de D. J. García Icazbalceta*, vol. 2. New York: Burt Franklin.

Garibay K., Angel María. 1953–1954. *Historia de la literatura náhuatl*. 2 vols. Mexico: Editorial Porrúa.

Gibson, Charles. 1964. *The Aztecs under Spanish Rule*. Stanford: Stanford University Press.

Graef, Hilda. 1963–1965. *Mary: A History of Doctrine and Devotion*. 2 vols. New York: Sheed and Ward.

Grijalva, fray Juan de. 1624. *Crónica de la orden de N. P. S. Augustin en las provincias de la Nueva España*. Mexico: Juan Ruiz.

———. 1985. *Crónica de la Orden de N.P.S. Agustín en las provincias de la Nueva España*. Original edition 1624. Mexico: Porrúa.

Gruzinski, Serge. 1988. *La colonisation de l'imaginaire: Sociétés indigènes et occidentalisation dans le Mexique espagnol, 16e–18e siècle*. Paris: Editions Gallimard.

Gurevich, Aron. 1993. *Medieval Popular Culture: Problems of Belief and Perception*. Translated by Paul A. Hollingsworth. Cambridge, England: Cambridge University Press.

Harris, John Wesley. 1992. *Medieval Theatre in Context: An Introduction*. London and New York: Routledge.

Hill, Jane H., and Kenneth C. Hill. 1986. *Speaking Mexicano: Dynamics of Syncretic Language in Central Mexico*. Tucson: University of Arizona Press.

Homza, Lu Ann. 1999. "The European Link to Mexican Penance." In Sell and Schwaller, 33–48.

Horcasitas Pimentel, Fernando. 1948. "Piezas teatrales en lengua náhuatl." *Boletín Bibliográfico de Antropología Americana* 11:154–64.

———. 1962. "Textos de Xaltepoxtla, Puebla." *Estudios de Cultura Náhuatl* 2:83–91.

———. 1967. "Los xoxocoteros: Una farsa indígena." *Estudios de Cultura Náhuatl* 7:225–32.

———. 1968. *De Porfirio Díaz a Zapata: Memoria náhuatl de Milpa Alta*. Foreword by Miguel León-Portilla. Mexico: Universidad Nacional Autónoma de México.

———. 1972a. "El entremés del Señor de Yencuictlalpan, una farsa en náhuatl." *Anales de Antropología* 9:125–41.

———. 1972b. *Life and Death in Milpa Alta: A Nahuatl Chronicle of Díaz and Zapata*. Norman: University of Oklahoma Press.

———. 1974. *El teatro náhuatl: Épocas novohispana y moderna*. Mexico: Universidad Nacional Autónoma de México.

———. 1977. "Para la historia de Tlalocan." *Tlalocan* 7:11–19.

———. 1980. "La danza de los tecuanes." *Estudios de Cultura Náhuatl* 14:239–86.

Horcasitas Pimentel, Fernando, and Bente Bittmann Simons. 1974. "Anales jeroglíficos e históricos de Tepeaca." *Anales de Antropología* 11:225–94.

Horcasitas Pimentel, Fernando, and Wanda Tommasi de Magrelli. 1975. "El Códice de Tzictepec, una nueva fuente pictórica indígena." *Anales de Antropología* 12:243–72.

Horcasitas Pimentel, Fernando, and Sara O. de Ford. 1979. *Los cuentos en náhuatl de doña Luz Jiménez*. Mexico: Universidad Nacional Autónoma de México.

Horn, Rebecca. 1997a. "Gender and Social Identity." In *Indian Women of Early Mexico*, ed. Susan Schroeder, Stephanie Wood, and Robert Haskett, 105–22. Norman: University of Oklahoma Press.

———. 1997b. *Postconquest Coyoacan: Nahua-Spanish Relations in Central Mexico, 1519–1650*. Stanford: Stanford University Press.

———. 1998. "Testaments and Trade: Interethnic Ties among Petty Traders in Central Mexico (Coyoacan, 1550–1620)." In Kellogg and Restall, 59–83.

Hunter, William H. 1960. *The Calderonian Auto Sacramental El Gran Teatro del Mundo: An Edition and Translation of a Nahuatl Version*. In Middle American Research Institute Publication 27, 105–202. New Orleans: Tulane University.

The Interpreter's Bible. 1952. Edited by Nolan B. Harmon. 12 vols. New York: Abingdon.

Israel, Jonathan I. 1975. *Race, Class, and Politics in Colonial Mexico*. Oxford, England: Oxford University Press.

Karttunen, Frances. 1982. "Nahuatl Literacy." In *The Inca and Aztec States, 1400–1800: Anthropology and History*, ed. George A. Collier, Renato I. Rosaldo, and John D. Wirth, 395–417. New York: Academic Press.

———. 1983. *An Analytical Dictionary of Nahuatl*. Austin: University of Texas Press.

———. 1985. *Nahuatl and Maya in Contact with Spanish*. Texas Linguistic Forum 26. Austin: Department of Linguistics, University of Texas.

———. 1992. *An Analytical Dictionary of Nahuatl*. Norman: University of Oklahoma Press.

Karttunen, Frances, and James Lockhart. 1976. *Nahuatl in the Middle Years: Language Contact Phenomena in Texts of the Colonial Period*. University of California Publications in Linguistics 85. Berkeley and Los Angeles: University of California Press.

———, eds. 1987. *The Art of Nahuatl Speech: The Bancroft Dialogues*. Nahuatl Studies Series No. 2. Los Angeles: UCLA Latin American Center Publications.

Kellogg, Susan. 1998. "Indigenous Testaments of Early-Colonial Mexico City: Testifying to Gender Differences." In Kellogg and Restall, 37–58.

Kellogg, Susan, and Matthew Restall, eds. 1998. *Dead Giveaways: Indigenous Testaments of Colonial Mesoamerica and the Andes*. Salt Lake City: University of Utah Press.

Klor de Alva, Jorge. 1982. "Spiritual Conflict and Accommodation in New Spain: Toward a Typology of Aztec Responses to Christianity." In *The Inca and Aztec States, 1400–1800: Anthropology and History*, ed. George A Collier, Renato I. Rosaldo, and John D. Wirth, 345–65. New York: Academic Press.

———. 1993. "Aztec Spirituality and Nahuatized Christianity." In *South and Meso-American Native Spirituality: From the Cult of the Feathered Serpent to the Theology of Liberation*, ed. Gary H. Gossen, 173–97. New York: Crossroad.

Krickeberg, Walter. 1961. *Las antiguas culturas mexicanas*. Translated by Sita Garst and Jasmín Reuter. Mexico: Fondo de Cultura Económica.

Kuschel, Karl-Josef. 1995. *Abraham*. Translated by John Bowden. New York: Continuum.

Lachowski, Joseph Michael. 1967. "Guilt (in the Bible)." In *New Catholic Encyclopedia* 6:850–52. New York: McGraw.

Las Casas, fray Bartolomé de. 1967. *Apologética historia sumaria*. 2 vols. Edited by Edmundo O'Gorman. Mexico: Universidad Nacional Autónoma de México, Instituto de Investigaciones Históricas.

———. 1995. *Historia de las Indias*. 3 vols. Edited by Agustín Millares Carlo. Mexico: Fondo de Cultura Económica.

Launey, Michel. 1979. *Introduction à la langue et à la littérature aztèques*. Paris: L'Harmattan.

León, fray Martín de. 1611. *Camino del cielo en lengua mexicana*. Mexico: Diego López Dávalos.

———. 1614a. *Manual breve y forma de administrar los Santos Sacramentos a los indios universalmente*. Mexico: Imprenta de María de Espinosa.

———. 1614b. *Primera parte del Sermonario del tiempo de todo el año, duplicado, en lengua mexicana.* Mexico: Imprenta de la Viuda de Diego López Dávalos, por C. Adriano César.

León-Portilla, Ascensión H. de. 1988. *Tepuztlahcuilolli / Impresos en náhuatl / Historia y bibliografía.* 2 vols. Mexico: Instituto de Investigaciones Históricas, Instituto de Investigaciones Filológicas, Universidad Nacional Autónoma de México.

León-Portilla, Miguel. 1974. "Testimonios nahuas sobre la conquista espiritual." *Estudios de Cultura Náhuatl* 11:11–36.

———. 1982. "Fernando Horcasitas Pimentel en la historia de Tlalocan." *Tlalocan* 9:11–40.

Leyva, Juan. 2001. *La pasión de Ozumba: El teatro religioso tradicional en el siglo XVIII novohispano.* Mexico: Universidad Nacional Autónoma de México.

"The Life of Don Sebastián." 1 April 1692. Nahuatl manuscript held by the Academy of American Franciscan History. 29 pages. Berkeley, California.

Llaguno, José A. 1962. *La personalidad jurídica del indio y el III Concilio Provincial Mexicano (1585): Ensayo historico-jurídico de los documentos originales.* Mexico: Editorial Porrúa.

———. 1983. *La personalidad jurídica del indio y el III Concilio Provincial Mexicano (1585): Ensayo histórico-jurídico de los documentos originales.* Mexico: Editorial Porrúa.

Lockhart, James. 1991. *Nahuas and Spaniards: Postconquest Central Mexican History and Philology.* Stanford: Stanford University Press.

———. 1992. *The Nahuas after the Conquest: A Social and Cultural History of the Indians of Central Mexico, Sixteenth Through Eighteenth Centuries.* Stanford: Stanford University Press.

———. 1999. *Of Things of the Indies: Essays Old and New in Early Latin American History.* Stanford: Stanford University Press.

Lockhart, James, Frances Berdan, and Arthur J. O. Anderson. 1986. *The Tlaxcalan Actas: A Compendium of the Records of the Cabildo of Tlaxcala (1545–1627).* Salt Lake City: University of Utah Press.

Lopétegui, León y Félix Zubillaga. 1965. *Historia de la Iglesia en la América Española.* Madrid: Biblioteca de Autores Cristianos.

López Austin, Alfredo. 1977. *Tamoanchan, Tlalocan.* Translated by Bernard R. Ortiz de Montellano and Thelma Ortiz de Montellano. Niwot: University Press of Colorado.

———. 1984. *Cuerpo humano e ideología.* 2 vols. Mexico: Universidad Nacional Autónoma de México.

———. 1988. *The Human Body and Ideology.* Translated by Thelma Ortiz de Montellano and Bernardo Ortiz de Montellano. Salt Lake City: University of Utah Press.

Lorra Baquío, Francisco de. 1634. *Manual mexicano de la administración de los santos sacramentos conforme al manual toledano.* Mexico: Diego Gutiérrez.

Mansfield, Mary C. 1994. *The Humiliation of Sinners: Public Penance in Thirteenth-Century France.* Ithaca, N.Y.: Cornell University Press.

Matos Moctezuma, Eduardo. 1984. "The Templo Mayor of Tenochtitlan: Economics and Ideology." In *Ritual Human Sacrifice in Mesoamerica,* ed. Elizabeth Hill Boone, 133–64. Washington, D.C.: Dumbarton Oaks.

McAfee, Byron, and Robert H. Barlow. 1947. "Un cuaderno de Marqueses." *El México Antiguo* 6:392–404.

McGinn, Bernard. 1994. *Antichrist: Two Thousand Years of the Human Fascination with Evil.* San Francisco: Harper.

McMillen Villar, Susan. 1993. *Drama and the Theater in the Millenarian Project of the Franciscans in New Spain.* Ph.D. diss.: University of Minnesota.

McNeill, John T., and Helena M. Gamer. 1990. *Medieval Handbooks of Penance.* New York: Columbia University Press.

Mendieta, fray Gerónimo de. 1980. *Historia eclesiástica indiana.* Edited by Joaquín García Icazbalceta. Third edition. Mexico: Editorial Porrúa.

———. 1988. "Informe biográfico y linguístico del P. Jerónimo de Mendieta, OFM, sobre los 238 franciscanos pertenecientes a la provincia del Santo Evangelio de Méjico." *Archivo Ibero-Americano*, segunda época, 48:557–68.

Mijangos, fray Juan de. 1607. *Espejo divino en lengua mexicana*. Mexico: Diego López Dávalos.

———. 1624. *Sermonario*. Mexico: Juan de Alcázar.

Miller, Mary, and Karl Taube. 1993. *The Gods and Symbols of Ancient Mexico and the Maya: An Illustrated Dictionary of Mesoamerican Religion*. London: Thames and Hudson.

Molina, fray Alonso de. 1552. *Ordenanzaz para aprovechar los cofradias que han de servir en estos hospitales*. Manuscript no. M-M 455 in the Bancroft Library of the University of California, Berkeley. Included in full transcription and translation in Sell, Barry D., ed. and trans. 2002. *Nahua Confraternities in Early Colonial Mexico: The 1552 Nahuatl Ordinances of fray Alonso de Molina, OFM*. Academy of American Franciscan History, pp. 82–141.

———. 1555. *Vocabulario en la lengua castellana y mexicana*. Mexico: Juan Pablos.

———. 1565. *Confesionario breve*. Mexico: Antonio de Espinosa.

———. 1578. *Doctrina cristiana en lengua mexicana*. Mexico: Pedro Ocharte.

———. 1977. *Vocabulario en la lengua castellana y mexicana y mexicana y castellana*. Reedition of the 1571 edition. With a preliminary study by Miguel León-Portilla. 2nd edition. Mexico: Editorial Porrúa.

———. 1984. *Confessionario mayor, en lengua Mexicana*. Photoreproduction of the 1569 edition. Mexico: Universidad Nacional Autónoma de México.

Most, W. G. "Grace (in the Bible)." 1967. In *New Catholic Encyclopedia* 6:672–74. New York: McGraw.

Motolinia, fray Toribio de Benavente. 1951. *History of the Indians of New Spain*. Translated by Francis Borgia Steck. Washington: Academy of American Franciscan History.

———. 1979. *Historia de los indios de la Nueva España*. Edited by Edmundo O'Gorman. Mexico: Editorial Porrúa.

———. 1985. *Historia de los indios de la Nueva España*. Edited by Georges Baudot. Madrid. Castalia.

———. 1996. *Memoriales*. Edited by Nancy Joe Dyer. Mexico: El Colegio de México.

Muñoz Camargo, Diego. 1981. *Descripción de la ciudad y provincia de Tlaxcala de las Indias y del mar océano para el buen gobierno y ennoblecimiento dellas*. Edited by René Acuña. Mexico: University Nacional Autónoma de México.

———. 1986. *Historia de Tlaxcala*. Edited by Germán Vázquez. Madrid: Historia 16.

Nacar Fuster, D. Eloino, and Alberto Colunga, O. P. 1961. *Misal ritual latino-español y devocionario*. Barcelona: Vallés.

Nalle, Sara T. 1999. "Printing and Reading Popular Religious Texts in Sixteenth-Century Spain." In *Culture and the State in Spain: 1550–1850*, ed. Tom Lewis and Francisco J. Sánchez, 126–56. New York: Garland.

The New International Dictionary of New Testament Theology. 1975. 3 vols. Edited by Colin Brown. Grand Rapids, Mich.: Zondervan.

Nicholson, Henry B. 1971. "Religion in Pre-Hispanic Central Mexico." In *Handbook of Middle American Indians* 10:395–446. Austin: University of Texas Press.

Nietzsche, Friedrich. 1956. *The Genealogy of Morals*. New York: Doubleday Anchor.

Offutt, Leslie S. 1992. "Levels of Acculturation in Northeastern New Spain: San Esteban Testaments of the Seventeenth and Eighteenth Centuries." *Estudios de Cultura Náhuatl* 22:409–43.

Ortiz de Montellano, Bernard R. 1990. *Aztec Medicine, Health, and Nutrition*. New Brunswick: Rutgers University Press.

Paso y Troncoso, Francisco del. 1890. *Invención de la Santa Cruz por Santa Elena*. Mexico: Museo Nacional.

———. 1899. *El sacrificio de Isaac*. In *Biblioteca Náhuatl I*. Florencia: Tipografía de Salvador Landi.

———. 1900a. "Comedies en langue nahuatl: Une petite vieille et le gamin, son petit fils." Congres International des Americanistes (Paris), 309–16.

———. 1900b. *La adoración de los Reyes*. In *Biblioteca Náhuatl II*. Florencia: Tipografía de Salvador Landi.

———. 1902. *La comedia de los Reyes*. In *Biblioteca Náhuatl VI*, cuaderno 3. Florencia: Tipografía de Salvador Landi.

———. 1907. *La destrucción de Jerusalén*. In *Biblioteca Náuatl* I, cuaderno 4. Florence: Tipografía de Salvador Landi.

Potter, Robert. 1986. "Abraham and Human Sacrifice: The Exfoliation of Medieval Drama in Aztec Mexico." *New Theater Quarterly* 2:306–12.

Procesos de indios idólatras y hechiceros. 1912. Directed by Luis González Obregón. Mexico: Publicaciones del Archivo General de la Nación.

Ramoneda, Arturo M., ed. 1980. "Introducción." In *Signos que aparecerán antes del Juicio Final*. Madrid: Clásicos Castalia.

Ravicz, Marilyn Ekdahl. 1970. *Early Colonial Religious Drama in Mexico: From Tzompantli to Golgotha*. Washington, D.C.: Catholic University of America Press.

Read, Kay Almere. 1998. *Time and Sacrifice in the Aztec Cosmos*. Bloomington and Indianapolis: Indiana University Press.

"Las representaciones teatrales de la Pasión." 1934. In *Bolétin del Archivo General de la Nación*, 332–56. Mexico: Talleres Gráficos de la Nación.

Reyes García, Luis, Eustaquio Celestino Solís, Armando Valencia Ríos, Constantino Medina Lima, and Gregorio Guerrero Díaz, eds. and trans. 1996. *Documentos nahuas de la ciudad de México del siglo XVI*. Mexico: Centro de Investigaciones y Estudios Superiores en Antropología Social and Archivo General de la Nación.

Ricard, Robert. 1966. *The Spiritual Conquest of Mexico: An Essay on the Apostolate and the Evangelizing Methods of the Mendicant Orders in New Spain: 1523–1572*. Translated by Lesley Byrd Simpson. Berkeley and Los Angeles: University of California Press.

———. 1991. *La conquista espiritual de México*. Translated by Ángel M. Garibay. Mexico: Fondo de Cultura Económica.

Rojas Garcidueñas, José J. 1935. *El teatro de Nueva España en el siglo XVI*. Mexico: Published by the author.

Román Bellereza, Juan Alberto. 1987. "Offering 48 of the Templo Mayor: A Case of Child Sacrifice." In *The Aztec Templo Mayor*, ed. Elizabeth Hill Boone, 131–43. Washington, D.C.: Dumbarton Oaks.

Rouanet, Léo, ed. 1979. *Colección de autos, farsas y coloquios del siglo XVI*. 4 vols. Hildersheim, N.Y.: George Olms.

Rubial García, Antonio. 1997. "Los santos milagreros y malogrados de la Nueva España." In *Manifestaciones religiosas en el mundo americano*, ed. Manuel Ramos Medina and Clara García Ayluardo, 51–87. Mexico: Universidad Iberoamericana.

Sahagún, fray Bernardino de. 1563. *Sermonario de dominicas y de sanctos en lengua mexicana*. Manuscript no. 1485, Ayer Collection, Newberry Library, Chicago.

———. 1583. *Psalmodia cristiana*. Mexico: Pedro Ocharte.

———. 1950–1982. *Florentine Codex, General History of the Things of New Spain*. Edited and translated by Arthur J. O. Anderson and Charles E. Dibble. Santa Fe, N.M.: School of American Research and University of Utah.

———. 1986. *Coloquios y doctrina cristiana*. Edited and translated by Miguel León-Portilla. Mexico: Universidad Nacional Autónoma de México.

———. 1989. *Historia general de las cosas de la Nueva España*. 2 vols. Edited by Alfredo López Austin and Josefina García Quintana. Mexico: Alianza Editorial Mexicana.

———. 1990. *Historia general de las cosas de la Nueva España*. 2 vols. Edited by Juan Carlos Temprano. Madrid: Historia 16.

———. 1993a. *Adiciones, apéndice a la postilla, y ejercicio cotidiano*. Edited by Arthur J. O. Anderson. Mexico: Universidad Nacional Autónoma de México.

———. 1993b. *Psalmodia Christiana (Christian Psalmody)*. Edited and translated by Arthur J. O. Anderson. Salt Lake City: University of Utah Press.

———. 1997. *Primeros memoriales: Paleography of Nahuatl Text and English Translation*. Completed and revised, with additions, by H. B. Nicholson, Arthur J. O. Anderson, Charles E. Dibble, Eloise Quiñones Keber, and Wayner Ruwet. Norman: University of Oklahoma Press.

Schroeder, Susan. 2000. "Jesuits, Nahuas, and the Good Death Society in Mexico City, 1710–1767." *Hispanic American Historical Review* 80:43–76.

Schwaller, John Frederick. 1989. "Constitution of the Cofradía del Santissimo Sacramento of Tula, Hidalgo, 1570." *Estudios de Cultura Náhuatl* 19:217–44.

———. 1991. "Nahuatl Manuscripts in the John Carter Brown Library (Providence, Rhode Island)." *Estudios de Cultura Náhuatl* 21:311–24.

———. 1999. "Don Bartolomé de Alva, Nahuatl Scholar of the Seventeenth Century." In Sell and Schwaller, 3–15.

Sell, Barry D. 1988. "Linguistics as a Tool of Historical Analysis: Loanwords in Colonial Nahuatl Religious Plays." Unpublished paper.

———. 1993. *Friars, Nahuas, and Books: Language and Expression in Colonial Nahuatl Publications*. Ph.D. diss.: University of California at Los Angeles.

———. 1999. "The Classical Age of Nahuatl Publications and Don Bartolomé de Alva's Confessionario of 1634." In Sell and Schwaller, 17–32.

———. 2000. "Our Lady of Solitude of San Miguel Coyotlan, 1619: A Rare Set of Cofradía Rules in Nahuatl." *Estudios de Cultural Náhuatl* 31:331–58.

Sell, Barry D., and Susan Kellogg. 1997. "We Want to Give Them Laws: Royal Ordinances in a Mid-Sixteenth Century Nahuatl Text." *Estudios de Cultural Náhuatl* 27:325–67.

Sell, Barry D., and John Frederick Schwaller, with Lu Ann Homza, eds. and trans. 1999. Don Bartolomé de Alva, *Guide to Confession Large and Small in the Mexican Language*. Critical edition of the 1634 edition. Norman: University of Oklahoma Press.

Sermones y santoral en mexicano. N.d. Manuscript no. 464 in the Bancroft Library, University of California at Berkeley.

Siker, Jeffrey S. 1991. *Disinheriting the Jew*. Louisville: Westminster/John Knox Press.

Siméon, Rémi. 1977. *Diccionario de la lengua nahuatl o mexicana*. Translated by Josefina Oliva de Coll. Mexico: Siglo Ventiuno.

———. 1988. *Diccionario de la lengua nahuatl o mexicana*. Mexico: Siglo Ventiuno.

Solís, Eustaquio Celestino, Armando Valencia R., and Constantino Medina Lima, eds. and trans. 1985. *Actas de cabildo de Tlaxcala, 1547–1567*. Mexico: Archivo General de la Nación, Instituto Tlaxcalteca de la Cultura, and Centro de Investigaciones y Estudios Superiores de Antropología Social.

Sousa, Lisa, Stafford Poole, C.M., and James Lockhart, eds. and trans. 1998. *The Story of Guadalupe: Luis Laso de la Vega's Huei Tlamahuiçoltica of 1649*. Stanford: Stanford University Press.

Soustelle, Jacques. 1955. *La vie quotidienne des aztèques à la veille de la conquète espagnole*. Paris: Hachette.

Sten, María. 1982. *Vida y muerte del teatro náhuatl*. Xalapa, Mexico: Biblioteca Universidad Veracruzana.

Sten, María, Oscar Armando García, and Alejandro Ortiz Bullé-Goyri, eds. 2000. *El teatro franciscano en la Nueva España: Fuentes y ensayos para el estudio del teatro de evangelización en el siglo XVI*. Mexico: Universidad Nacional Autónoma de México and Consejo Nacional para la Cultura y las Artes.

Stern, Charlotte. 1996. *The Medieval Theatre in Castille.* Binghamton, N.Y.: Center for Medieval and Renaissance Studies, SUNY.

Sullivan, Thelma D. 1987. *Documentos tlaxcaltecas del siglo XVI en lengua náhuatl.* Mexico: Universidad Nacional Autónoma de México.

Sumario de las Indulgencias concedidas a los cofrades del sanctissimo sacramento. 1584. Mexico: Pedro Balli.

Taix, Hieronimo. 1576. *Institucion, modo de rezar, y milagros e indulgencias del rosario de la Virgen Maria, nuestro Señora.* Edited by Domingo de Salazar. Mexico.

Taylor, William. 1996. *Magistrates of the Sacred.* Stanford: Stanford University Press.

Tentler, Thomas N. 1977. *Sin and Confession on the Eve of the Reformation.* New Jersey: Princeton University Press.

"Three Indian Dramas." Manuscript owned by the Clements Library, University of Michigan. 52 folios. Contains three plays: "The Three Kings," "The Sacrifice of Isaac," and "Souls and Testamentary Executors." The last concludes with the date 1 February 1760. Ann Arbor, Michigan.

"Three Plays." Manuscript owned by the Library of Congress. 53 folios. Contains three plays: "Final Judgment," "How to Live on Earth" [two copies], and "The Merchant." The last begins with the date 15 November 1687. Washington, D.C.

Torquemada, fray Juan de. 1986. *Monarquía indiana.* 3 vols. Introduction by Miguel León-Portilla. Mexico: Porrúa.

Vetancurt, fray Agustín de. 1982. *Teatro mexicano, Crónica de la provincia del Santo Evangelio de México, Menologio franciscano.* Photoreproduction of the 1698 edition. Mexico: Editorial Porrúa.

Vollert, C. 1967. "Transubstantiation." In *New Catholic Encyclopedia* 14:259–61. New York: McGraw-Hill.

Weckmann, Luis. 1984. *La herencia medieval de México.* 2 vols. Mexico: El Colegio de México.

Williams, Jerry. 1992. *El teatro del México colonial: Época misionera.* New York: Peter Lang.

Wood, Stephanie. 1991. "Adopted Saints: Christian Images in Nahua Testaments of Late Colonial Toluca." *The Americas* 47:259–294.

———. 1998. "Testaments and Títulos: Conflict and Coincidence of Cacique and Community Interests in Central Mexico." In Kellogg and Restall, 85–111.

Zumthor, Paul. 1972. *Essai de poétique médiévale.* Paris: Éditions du Seuil.

INDEX

Abraham, 12, 16, 86–88, 90–101, 103–108, 108n3, 109n8, 109n10, 110n19, 110n20, 136–37, 146–61
Academy of American Franciscan History, 4, 26n11, 268
Accounting (made at judgment), 13, 46, 52; in plays, 63, 164–65, 192–93, 198–99, 202–203
Actopan, 34, 39
Adam, 33, 81n18, 83n33, 219
"Adoración de los reyes." *See* "Three Kings, The"
Adorno, Rolena, 78
Advent, 42, 71, 97, 109n15
Afterlife: Nahua concepts of, 30, 32, 71; Spanish/Christian concepts of, 30
Akedah, 85–111
Alcalde, 5, 21; character in "The Merchant," 21, 66, 254–57
Alcohol. *See* Drunkenness
Alfonso X, King, 59
Altepetl, 5, 16–18, 25n4, 28n41; in plays, 118–33, 137n44, 141n56, 154–55, 224–25, 250–51, 290–91, 294–95
Alva [Ixtlilxochitl], don Bartolomé de, confession manual of, 18, 21, 22, 33, 48
Andrew, Saint, 97
Angels, 31, 63; as characters in "Final Judgment, 200–203; as characters in "How to Live on Earth," 210–41; as characters in "The Life of Don Sebastián," 274–87, 290–93, 300–301; as characters in "The Merchant," 262–65; as characters in "The Sacrifice of Isaac," 12, 92, 93, 148–49, 160–63; as characters in "Souls and Testamentary Executors," 172–75; guardian angel, 45, 174–75, 202–203, 262–65
Antichrist, 72; as character in "Final Judgment," 75, 198–203; *Play of Antichrist*, 72
Anunciación, fray Domingo de la, 50
Anunciación, fray Juan de la, 32, 33, 36, 37, 38, 41–42, 48
Aranda, Council of, 59
Arróniz, Othón, 74, 83n36
Ars moriendi, 48–49
Articles of Faith, 39
Ash Wednesday, 33, 220–21
Augustine, Saint, 88, 92, 97, 98, 104, 110n18, 111n26
Augustinians, 50, 71
Augustus, Caesar, 126–27

Balaam, 124–25
Balak, 125n18
Balthasar, 12, 119n2, 132–33, 142–43
Bancroft Dialogues, 14, 119n6, 137n42
Baptism, 37–38, 48

Baudot, Georges, 79n6
Bautista (Viseo), fray Juan, 13, 15, 26n13, 96–97, 115; "Book of the Misery and Brevity of the Life of Man" of, 38, 43; confession manual of, 22, 24; *contemptus mundi* of, 38; "Life of Saint Anthony of Padua" of, 13; *Sermonario* of, 15, 18, 27n36, 42–43, 96–101, 110n21, 137n48
Bells, rung for dead, 47, 50, 176–81, 184–85, 264–65
Berceo, Gonzalo de, 73
Bevington, David, 66, 78, 81n21
Bhabha, Homi, 108
Bloodletting, 68, 69
Body: Nahua concepts of, 31, 44; Spanish/Christian concepts of, 33
Bones, 30, 31, 200–201, 220–23, 232–33, 236–37, 282–89
Braswell, Mary F., 81n19
Burials, 36, 43–47, 50, 238–39, 264–65

Cabildo (town council), 5, 14, 17, 24
Calpan, San Andrés, 12, 23, 39, 201n18
Calpolli, 16
Cantares mexicanos, 135n40
Carochi, Horacio, 14, 27n33, 165n1, 199n15
Casper, 12, 118–19, 130–31, 136–39
Cauli, Giovanni da, 106
Chalco, 60, 61
Charles V, King, 61
Chichimecs, 62
Chimalpahin Quauhtlehuaniztin, Don Domingo de San Antón Muñon, 13, 79n2
Christ: in Calpan sculpture, 12; as character in plays, 76, 180–81, 186–87, 200–207, 238–41, 278–83, 295–301; as judge, 39–43, 52, 64; Passion of, 34–35, 60, 103–105, 106, 111n26, 228–29; as redeemer, 101–102
Cipactonal, 102
Clements Library, 4, 26n11, 118, 146, 164
Clendinnen, Inga, 92
Cline, Sarah, 47–48
Commandments of the Church, 32, 66, 82n26, 184–87
Communion, in the plays, 172–73, 184–89, 234–35, 258–59
Confession, 32, 36, 48, 50, 53n6, 63, 64, 69, 73, 81n19; in the plays, 51, 65, 196–99, 222–25, 32–35, 258–63, 274–79, 284–85, 296–97; preconquest rite of, 64, 69

Confession manuals, 4, 18, 21, 22, 24, 28n44, 57. *See also* Alva, Bautista, Molina
Confraternities, 49–51, 53n17, 60–61; confraternity of the rosary, 49–50; confraternity of souls in purgatory, 50, 61
"Conquest of Jerusalem, The," 74
Córdoba, fray Pedro de, 90
Cornyn, John H., 4, 81n16, 109n6
Cortés, Hernando, 61, 62, 81n18
Cortés y Zedeño, Jerónimo Tomás de Aquino, 25
Council of 1642, 58
Culhuacan, 22, 23, 24, 32, 45, 48

Dances, 59
David, King, 128–29, 136–37
Dead, as characters in "Final Judgment," 200–203; service to, 51–52, 63, 68–69, 164–89
Death: as character in "Final Judgment," 75, 82n29, 194–95; as character in "How to Live on Earth," 232–33; as character in "The Life of Don Sebastián," 31, 82n29, 272–73, 280–83, 286–87, 290–99; as character in plays, 30, 52; friars' teachings on, 32–39; Nahua views of, 29; Nahuas' visions of, 32; Nahuatl guidebooks for, 48–49; Spanish/Christian views of, 29, 30, 33–39
Demons and devils, 29, 32, 34, 70, 75, 77, 262–63, 268–69; as characters in "Final Judgment," 32, 63, 76–77, 202–207; as characters in "The Sacrifice of Isaac," 148–51; as characters in "Souls and Testamentary Executors," 166–77, 180–81, 186–89; as characters in "How to Live on Earth," 214–29, 234–35, 240–41, 258–65, 274–79, 282–301; as characters in plays, 51, 70. *See also* Lucifer, Satan, Tzitzimitl
Disease. *See* Epidemics, Sickness
Dominicans, 26; *Doctrina cristiana* of, 9, 35, 36, 39, 81n18
Drunkenness, 22, 51, 176–79, 182–83, 268–69, 296–97
Duverger, Christian, 68

Eden, 76
Eire, Carlos, 29
Enders, Jody, 64
Epidemics, 18, 29, 62, 73, 101
Escalona, fray Alonso de, 32, 33
Eschatology, 61, 70, 71–72, 83n33

Eve, 33, 81n18, 83n33, 83n34
Extreme unction (last rites), 47–48, 53n14

Farmer, David Hugh, 119n2
Fasting, 69, 186–89, 192–93
Feijóo, fray Benito Jerónimo, 80n11
Fernández de Oviedo, Gonzalo, 74
Final Judgment, 12, 64, 71, 73, 77, 78, 190–209; in Indo-Christian art, 39; in Nahuatl doctrinal literature, 39–43
"Final Judgment," 39–43, 71–78, 82n28, 83n32, 83n36, 190–209; angels as characters in, 200–203; Antichrist as character in, 72, 198–203; authorship and date, 6, 10, 15; calque in, 13; characters in, 73, 74–76, 82n22, 82n30; Christ as character in, 200–207; confession in, 196–99; the dead as characters, 200–203; Death as a character in, 31, 194–95; demons as characters in, 202–207; eternal punishment given in, 51; fasting in, 192–93; fireworks in, 75, 198–203, 206–209; loanwords in, 12, 13; Lucifer/Satan as a character in, 32, 204–209; manuscripts and transcriptions of, 4, 7–8, 9; marriage as sacrament in, 192–95, 198–99, 204–209; orthography of, 26n14; Penance as character in, 190–91; priests as characters in, 18, 75, 196–99, 208–209; restitution in, 206–209; resurrection of dead in, 31; Saint Michael as a character in, 73, 74, 76, 190–191, 200–203; Sweeping as character in, 192–93; Tlatelolco performance of, 60, 74, 79n2, 83n36; violence in, 22, 76
Fiore, Joachim de, 73
Fireworks: used in plays, 31, 67, 69, 75, 180–81, 198–203, 206–209, 230–31, 264–65, 300–301
Fiscales, 47
Flynn, Maureen, 82n27
Francis, Saint, 18
Franciscans, 5, 9, 14, 50, 66, 71, 73, 74, 78, 93; first twelve missionaries in Mexico, 61, 62, 91, 108n5
Fuente, Agustín de la, 13, 18, 24, 26n13, 27n36, 38, 96, 115
Funerals. *See* Burials
Furst, Jill, 30

Gante, fray Pedro de, *Doctrina christiana* of, 39, 48–49

Gaona, Juan de, 110n23
García Icazbalceta, Joaquín, 81n18, 83n36
Garibay Kintana, Ángel María, 83n36, 89, 96
Gaspar, Don Joseph, 5–6, 242–43
Genesis, Book of, 33, 86, 93, 98
Gerona, Council of, 59
Gilberti, fray Maturino, 80n10
Good Death Society, 50–51
Gregory, Saint, 32
Gregory of Nisa, 104
Guilt, 65, 67, 82n27, 111n27
Gurevich, Aron, 56–57, 60, 80n7

Hagar, 12, 90, 108n3, 150–155
Hail Mary prayer, 35, 176–77, 208–209, 229n36
Hebrews, Book of, 88, 92
Hell, 35, 36, 43, 53n9, 71, 72, 76, 186–87. *See also* Mictlan
Herod, 12, 13, 27, 118–31, 144–45
Holy Sacrament, confraternity of, 61
"Holy Wednesday," Nahuatl play, 89
Horcasitas, Fernando, 4, 6–8, 72, 79n2, 81n16, 81n18, 81n20, 82n28, 83n36, 83n39, 90, 93
Horn, Rebecca, 19
"How to Live on Earth," 62–64, 210–41; angels as characters in, 210–41; authorship and date, 6, 9, 10, 15; bones in, 31, 220–23, 232–33, 236–37; calque in, 13; characters in, 33, 62–64; Christ as character in, 238–41; Death as a character in, 31, 232–33; deaths in, 51; demons as characters in, 214–29, 234–35, 240–41; fireworks in, 67, 230–31; loanwords in, 12; manuscripts of, 4; Mary as advocate in, 35, 62, 210–13, 220–21, 224–25, 236–37; Mary as character in, 226–31; orthography of, 26n14; service to dead in, 36; souls as characters in, 236–37; violence in, 22, 64
Huaxtepec, 5, 6, 268–69
Huehuetlatolli, 14, 21, 27n36, 101, 110n23
Huitzilopochtli, 76
Human sacrifice, 86, 90, 91–92, 93, 95, 96, 103, 105, 107, 108, 109n5

Idolatry, 28n40, 37–38
Ihiyotl, 53n1
Indulgences, 35, 49–50, 53n17; plenary, 38
Inquisition, 50, 60, 70
Ipalnemoani (deity title), 124, 132, 136, 138, 142

Isaac, 12, 87, 88, 90–94, 97–101, 103–104, 106–107, 109n9, 146–63
Isaiah, 128–29
Ishmael, 12, 90, 108n3, 148–55

Jacob, 124–25
James, Epistle of, 87, 93
Jerome, Saint, 73
Jesse, 129n29
Jesuits, 50–51
Jesus. *See* Christ
Joel, Book of, 53n7
John, Gospel of, 87
John Carter Brown Library, 38
Joseph, Saint, 135n38, 144–45
Judaism, 87–88, 91, 104
Judgment Day. *See* Final Judgment
Judgment, of souls after death, 33, 34–35, 38–39, 45, 46, 65, 164–65, 180–89, 202–203, 238–41, 296–303
"Juicio Final." *See* "Final Judgment"

Karttunen, Frances, 10, 14

Land titles, 67
Las Casas, Bartolomé de, 64–65, 79n2, 81n18
Laso de la Vega, Luis, 57
Last Supper, 60
Lent, 33, 60, 272–73
Leo the Great, 104
León, fray Luis de, 110n23
León, fray Martín de, 43, 44, 48, 49, 105–106
León-Portilla, Ascensión H. de, 96
León-Portilla, Miguel, 71, 85
Library of Congress, 4, 26n9, n11, 190, 210, 242
"Life of Don Sebastián, The," 268–303; angels as characters in, 274–87, 290–93, 300–301; authorship and date, 5, 6, 9–10, 15; calque in, 13; Christ as character in, 278–83, 295–301; dead reproaching living in, 42; Death as character in, 31, 82n29, 272–73, 280–83, 286–87, 290–99; deaths in, 51; demons as characters in, 32, 274–79, 282–301; fireworks in, 300–301; hell represented in, 35; loanwords in, 12, 27n38; Lucifer as character in, 32, 82n29, 276–79, 290–91, 294–301; manuscript of, 4; Mary as character in, 298–99; orthography of, 26n21; violence in, 22; works of mercy in, 298–99

Limbo, 35, 38
Loanwords, 6, 10–15, 27nn27–29, 27n38, 307–20
Lockhart, James, 6, 8, 10, 14, 16, 18, 28n41, 56, 57, 80n7, 89, 102
López Austin, Alfredo, 68
Lucifer, 11, 32, 53n2, 68, 77, 82n29; in plays, 166–67, 180–87, 204–207, 276–79, 290–91, 294–301
Luke, Gospel of, 42, 72

Mansfield, Mary C., 82n27
Marriage, sacrament of, 73, 192–95, 198–99, 204–209
Mary, Virgin, 106, 143n61, 246–47; as character in plays, 35, 62, 178–81, 226–31, 298–99; as sinners' advocate, 35, 45, 48, 62, 178–79, 208–209, 210–13, 220–21, 224–25, 236–37, 264–65, 298–99
Mary Magdalene, 106
Mass, 102, 103, 105, 166–67, 184–85, 222–23, 268–69; for dead, 36, 38, 46–47, 49, 50, 51, 52, 82n28, 111n24, 164–65, 168–75, 178–79, 184–85
Matthew, Gospel of, 53n8, 72, 87, 97, 119n2, 127nn21–22, 131n30, 131nn33–34, 133n37, 143n62, 145n65
Mayas, 3
McAfee, Byron, 4, 81n16, 83n36
McGinn, Bernard, 72
Melchior, 12, 119n2, 124–25, 132–35, 138–41
Mendieta, fray Jerónimo de, 14, 133n36
"Merchant, The," 66–67, 242–67; angels as characters in, 262–65; authorship and date, 6, 10, 15; characters in, 17, 66–67; confession and penance in, 67, 70, 258–63; demons as characters in, 258–65; fireworks in, 264–65; loanwords in, 11, 12, 27n38; manuscript of, 4; moneylending in, 19–21, 66, 242–51; priests as characters in, 18, 256–57, 260–63; realistic setting of, 16–25; similarity to medieval dramas, 65; swearing of oaths in, 250–51, 254–55, 258–59; testaments in, 20, 43, 250–53, 256–57, 264–65; violence in, 21–22, 66
Mexico City, dramas enacted in, 79n2, 83n36
Michael, Saint: as character in "Final Judgment," 73, 74, 76, 190–91, 200–203; as character in "Souls and Testamentary Executors," 82n29, 180–89

Mictlan (Nahua underworld), 30, 33, 34, 35, 38, 42, 52, 53n2, 67, 73, 75, 76; mentioned in plays, 154–55, 174–75, 180–81, 186–91, 194–95, 198–201, 204–207, 214–15, 218–19, 234–35, 238–39, 262–73, 276–77, 286–87, 290–95, 300–303. *See also* Hell
Mictlantecuhtli, 53n2
Mijangos, fray Juan de, 101–105, 110n22, 110n23, 111n24, 111n25
Mixtecs, 3
Moab, 124–25
Molina, fray Alonso de, 14, 44, 50, 80n10, 83n41, 143n59; confession manual of, 21, 38, 43
Moneylending and borrowing, 23–25, 51; in "The Merchant," 19–20, 66, 242–51; in "Souls and Testamentary Executors," 166–67
Morality plays: medieval, 65, 66; as Nahuatl genre, 30
Motolinia (fray Toribio de Benavente), 64, 69, 71, 79n2, 81n18, 90, 91
Muñoz Camargo, Diego, 71, 72, 77, 82n31

Nahuatl: literacy in, 3; stages of linguistic change, 10–11, 13, 14
Neixcuitilli, neixcuitilmachiotl (Nahuatl terms for plays): used in plays, 118, 162, 190, 240, 242, 268, 272, 300
New Fire ceremony, 76
Nietzsche, Friedrich, 67

Oaths, swearing of, 18; God's oath to Abraham, 93, 98; in "The Merchant," 21, 66, 250–51, 254–55, 258–59; in "Souls and Testamentary Executors," 182–83
Oaxtepec, Morelos, 26n8
Obraje (textile manufacturing shop), 19, 22–23, 244–45, 248–49
Ocharte, Pedro, 50
Olmos, Andrés de, 27n36, 83n36, 97
Origen, 104, 119n2
Orthography, 7–10
Ortiz de Montellano, Bernard, 68
Otomis, 19
Our Father prayer, 176–77
Oxomoco, 102
Ozumba, 60, 80n13

Paredes, Father Ignacio de, 27n30
Paso y Troncoso, Francisco del, 4, 7

Passion plays, 60, 79n2, 80n13
Paul, Saint, 87, 91, 104, 110n20
Pedraza, fray Bermúdez, 110n23
Penance, 33, 35, 65, 68, 69, 81n19; as character in "Final Judgment," 190–91; in plays, 63, 150–1, 170–71, 184–85, 188–89, 192–93, 274–75, 284–85
"Penitential of Silos," 81n19
Pérez, fray Manuel, 25
Philo of Alexandria, 87, 93
Polygamy, 90, 108n3
Potter, Robert, 93, 109n8
Priests: attendance at death, 47–48; as characters in plays, 18, 75, 174–77, 196–99, 208–209, 256–57, 260–63
Provincial Council (Mexican): First, 58; Third, 53n15, 59
Purgatory, 33–34, 35–38, 51, 76; in plays, 30, 62, 68, 82n28, 164–65, 168–81, 184–87, 238–39

Ravicz, Marilyn Ekdahl, 81n16, 82n30, 109n7
Responses, prayers for dead, 46–47, 50, 164–65, 168–89, 174–75, 178–79, 184–85, 238–39, 264–65
Restitution, 64, 66, 69, 70, 206–209
Ricard, Robert, 79n6, 110n23
Romans, Book of, 99
Rosary, 13, 178–79, 184–85, 216–21, 228–29, 238–39; confraternity of, 49–50

"Sacrifice of Isaac, The," 82n30, 85–96, 146–63; angel as character in, 12, 93, 94, 148–49, 160–63; authorship and date, 5, 6, 10, 15, 90; demon as character in, 148–51; God as character in, 156–57; *huehuetlatolli* in, 14; loanwords in, 11, 27n38; manuscript of, 4, 9; orthography of, 26n16; penance in, 150–51; personal names in, 12; violence in, 22, 91, 93, 94; works of mercy in, 150–51
Sahagún, fray Bernardino de, 15, 26n17, 26n20, 70, 80n10, 81n15, 83n40; *Adiciones* of, 109n12; *Apéndiz* of, 97; *Arte adivinatoria* of, 89; *Florentine Codex* of, 14–15, 137n42, 137nn45–46, 139n53, 140nn36–37, 141nn57–58, 261n21; *Historia General* of, 69, 75, 76; *Psalmodia christiana* of, 26n20, 33, 135n40; sermons of, 33, 34, 42
Salamanca, Council at, 58
Sarah, 146–49, 152–55

Satan: as character in "Final Judgment," 204–209; as character in "The Life of Don Sebastián, 288–89, 292–93. *See also* Demons, Lucifer

Sermons, 4, 18, 56. *See also* Bautista, León, Mijangos, Sahagún

Sexual transgressions, 20, 51, 178–79, 184–89, 190–91, 198–99, 204–205, 246–47, 290–91, 296–97

Sheth, 124–25

Sickness, 36, 44, 48, 68, 232–35, 246–47, 256–65. *See also* Epidemics

Siete partidas, 59

Siker, Jeffrey, 88

Sin, 32, 64, 81n19, 102–103, 111n27; in plays, 62, 63, 70, 172–73, 182–83, 186–87, 190–209, 260–65; original, 63, 104

Souls: at death, 48; as characters in plays, 31, 51, 52, 63, 172–73, 176–81, 236–37; Nahua concepts of, 30–32; in purgatory, 33, 164–89; Spanish/Christian concepts of, 30–31; treatment in testaments, 43–47

"Souls and Testamentary Executors," 67–70, 82n28, 164–89; angels as characters in, 172–75; authorship and date, 5, 6, 10, 15; characters in, 18, 51–52, 68, 69, 82n30; Christ as character in, 180–81, 186–87; commandments in, 182–87; communion in, 172–73, 184–89; deaths in, 51; demons as characters in, 32, 166–77, 180–81, 186–89; fireworks in, 180–81; fasting in, 186–89; judgment in, 180–89; loanwords in, 12; Lucifer as character in, 166–67, 180–87; manuscript of, 4, 9; Mary as character in, 178–81; mass in, 174–75, 184–85; moneylending in, 166–67; orthography of, 26n16; penance in, 170–71, 184–85, 188–89; priests as characters in, 174–77; punishment of negligent executors in, 49, 180–89; purgatory in, 168–81, 184–87; realism in, 17–18; responses chanted in, 46; service to dead in, 36, 70; souls as characters in, 172–73, 176–81; testaments in, 43, 164–67; tolling of bells in, 47, 176–81, 184–85; violence in, 22, 69

Sousa, Lisa, 57

Sten, María, 79n2

Stern, Charlotte, 59–60

Sweathouse (temazcalli), 76, 83n41, 188–89, 204–205

Sweeping, 212–13; as character in "Final Judgment," 192–93

Taix, Hierónimo, 50

Tarascans, 3

Taylor, William, 108

Tecalco, 70

Tecamachalco, 50

Ten Commandments, 22, 23, 24, 32; in plays, 18, 21, 66, 68, 82nn28–29, 109n10, 182–85, 202–205, 268–71, 296–99

Tepeyacac, 5, 252–53

Testaments, 4, 19, 28n43, 43–47, 51, 67, 164–67; Culhuacan collection of, 22, 23, 24, 45, 48; dispute over, in "The Merchant," 20, 250–53, 256–57, 264–65

Tezcatlipoca, 76, 93, 94, 95, 108

Thirst, 68, 262–63

"Three Kings, The," 118–45; authorship and date, 15; *huehuetlatolli* in, 14; loanwords in, 11, 13, 16; manuscript of, 4; orthography of, 26n16; relationship to *Florentine Codex* and *Bancroft Dialogues*, 14, 137n42, 137n45, 139n53, 141nn57–58; *tlatoque* equated with *reyes* in, 16, 17, 27–28n39; use of personal names in, 12; violence in, 22

Tlacatecolotl. *See* Demons

Tlalmanalco, 60

Tlaloc, 91, 92, 94, 95, 108

Tlalocan, 76

Tlatelolco, performance of Final Judgment play in, 60, 74, 79n2, 83n36 79n2

Tlatoani, 14, 16, 17, 27n39, 92; equated with *rey*, 16, 17, 27–28n39

Tlaxcala, 21, 44, 77, 81n18, 90; town council *Actas*, 23, 28n42, 28nn48–49

Tlaxilacalli, 16, 17, 28n47

Tlazolteotl, 69

Tloque nahuaque (deity title), 122, 124, 132, 136, 138, 140, 142

Toledo, Council of, 58, 59

Tollantzinco, San Juan Bautista, 5, 18–19, 24, 25n7, 242–243

Tonalli, 31, 53n1

Torquemada, fray Juan de, 81n18

Trent, Council of, 58, 111n24

Tula, 49, 50

Tuxpan, 61

Tzitzimitl, 62, 70, 76, 77, 214–15. *See also* Demons

Ucelo, Martin, 70, 84n42
Urban VIII, Pope, 58, 59
Usury. *See* Moneylending

Valadés, fray Diego, 36
Valencia, fray Martín de, 61
Valeriano, don Antonio, 137n48
Vázquez, Bernabé, 5, 162–63
Veracruz, Alonso de la, 110n23
Vetancurt, fray Agustín de, 18, 38
Villar, Susan McMillen, 83n36
Violence, 23, 106; in medieval drama, 64; in the plays, 21–22, 64, 66, 69, 91, 93, 94; in preconquest ritual, 94
Virgin of Guadalupe, 57

Weckmann, Luis, 79n5
Williams, Jerry, 83n36, 109n7
Wills. *See* Testaments
Works of mercy, 36, 41–42, 150–51, 298–99

Xochimilco, 5, 26n20, 60, 252–53
Xochiquetzal, 83n34

-Yolia (spirit), 30, 33, 44, 52, 52n1

Zapotecs, 3
Zárate, fray Jerónimo de, 13
Zumárraga, fray Juan de, 108n5
Zumthor, Paul, 77, 84n43

www.ingramcontent.com/pod-product-compliance
Lightning Source LLC
Chambersburg PA
CBHW081157230426
43666CB00016B/2842